Fifth Edition

Essentials of Public Speaking

Cheryl Hamilton
Tarrant County College—NE Campus

WADSWORTH
CENGAGE Learning

Australia • Brazil • Japan • Korea • Mexico • Singapore • Spain • United Kingdom • United States

WADSWORTH
CENGAGE Learning

Essentials of Public Speaking, Fifth Edition
Cheryl Hamilton

Executive Editor: Monica Eckman

Assistant Editor: Rebekah Matthews

Editorial Assistant: Colin Solan

Media Editor: Jessica Badiner

Marketing Manager: Amy Whitaker

Marketing Coordinator: Gurpreet Saran

Marketing Communications Manager:
Caitlin Green

Senior Content Project Manager:
Michael Lepera

Art Director: Linda Helcher

Print Buyer: Justin Palmeiro

Rights Acquisition Specialist, Image:
Mandy Groszko

Rights Acquisition Specialist, Text:
Shalice Shah-Caldwell

Production Service: Integra-Chicago

Text Designer: Lou Ann Thesing

Cover Image: Gene Lower/Contributor/
Getty Images/©Getty Images; Jermal
Countess/WireImage/©Getty Images;
©JGL/Tom Grill/Blend Images/Corbis

Compositor: Integra-India

For product information and technology assistance, contact us at
Cengage Learning Customer & Sales Support, 1-800-354-9706

For permission to use material from this text or product,
submit all requests online at **www.cengage.com/permissions**.
Further permissions questions can be emailed to
permissionrequest@cengage.com.

Library of Congress Control Number: 2011920244

ISBN-13: 978-0-495-90113-6

ISBN-10: 0-495-90113-X

Wadsworth
20 Channel Center Street
Boston, MA 02210
USA

Cengage Learning is a leading provider of customized learning solutions with office locations around the globe, including Singapore, the United Kingdom, Australia, Mexico, Brazil, and Japan. Locate your local office at:
international.cengage.com/region

Cengage Learning products are represented in Canada by
Nelson Education, Ltd.

For your course and learning solutions, visit **www.cengage.com**.

Purchase any of our products at your local college store or at our preferred online store **www.cengagebrain.com**.

Instructors: Please visit **login.cengage.com** and log in to access instructor-specific resources.

Printed in the United States of America
1 2 3 4 5 6 7 15 14 13 12 11

Essentials of Public Speaking, Fifth Edition,
is dedicated to Doris S. Redd
(I'm so lucky to have her for my mother—and she's a great copyeditor
as well! Thanks, Mom.)

Brief Contents

Contents

TWO • Preparing Your Speech   71

Chapter 4 • Analyzing Your Audience   72

Chapter 12 • Persuasive Speaking: Individual or Team 277

Preface

Do you want to improve your relationships, your ability to land and excel at jobs, your self-esteem, and even your health and happiness? Improving your communication and speaking skills in a course like this one can help with all these areas of your life. However, if you are like the typical person today, you are so busy that you only have time for the basics.

Essentials of Public Speaking was created with you—the busy person—in mind. This text outlines the essentials of making a successful speech that really communicates with your audience without burdening you with unnecessary filler. For example, some of the practical and essential topics covered in this book include:

How and why to analyze your audience.

Selecting a powerful topic.

Researching important facts and interesting supporting materials without wasting time.

Ways to incorporate current technology.

Managing your anxiety.

Delivering your speech with enthusiasm and power.

Designing and using professional visual aids.

Although *Essentials* is based on contemporary research as well as classical rhetorical theory, the approach is very practical and reader-friendly. Concepts and skills aren't just explained—they are illustrated with interesting and relevant examples, real student speeches, and excerpts from professional speakers. One student reviewer said she found the text so interesting and enjoyable that she read far more than requested!

Features of the New Edition

Updated to include the most current information and examples, the Fourth Edition of *Essentials* continues to focus on the absolute essentials of public speaking.

New Features

- *Flash Forward:* Each chapter includes a new Flash Forward feature that relates the Flash Back advice from ancient Roman and Greek orators to today's world and asks a critical thinking question to stimulate discussion on the chapter content.

- *Chapter Objectives:* The "Key Questions" that began each chapter in the fourth edition have been turned into chapter objectives in the current edition. These chapter objectives serve as a guide to what is in the chapter and what the reader should know when they finish reading it.

- *Active Critical Thinking Questions:* Each major heading is followed by one or two Active Critical Thinking questions to stimulate student thinking.

Students can complete these questions on their own or they can be assigned (especially helpful for online student activities).

- *Personal Skill Building:* The activities at the end of each chapter are divided into two parts. The Personal Skill Building activities are one of them. These activities provide practice and critical thinking questions for the individual student.

- *Collaborative Skill Building:* The second type of activities provided at the end of each chapter is the Collaborative Skill Building activities which provide practice and critical thinking for small groups or the class as a whole.

- *Speaking to Make a Difference:* The "Speakers Who Made a Difference" feature from the last edition was changed to "Speaking to Make a Difference" so some contemporary speakers could be added to the historical speakers who used their speaking skills to inspire, persuade, or enlighten on a broad scale. Still included are the contextual information about each speaker and the speaking occasion, an excerpt from the speech, a brief analysis of the speech, and questions for discussion. Most of the speeches are available in video and/or audio format online, and links are provided. New speakers added include musician David Carroll (Chapter 4), financial expert Harry Markopolos (Chapter 5), and President Barack Obama (Chapter 14), Speakers carried over from the previous edition include Bill Gates, Arnold Schwarzenegger, Barbara Jordan, Christopher Reeve, Ann Richards, Martin Luther King, Jr., Abraham Lincoln, Steve Jobs, Barbara Bush, John F. Kennedy, and Mary Fisher.

- *Special Occasion Speaking:* A new chapter on special occasion speaking was added as Chapter 14—the original chapter 8 was omitted with content moved to various other chapters, which keeps our chapter count at 14.

- *New student speeches:* New student speeches were added to this edition as well as speech analysis added in the margins of four speeches to provide plenty of models and explanation for students at all stages of the speech preparation process. New speeches include "Endometriosis" by Rebecca DeCamp; "Bacterial Meningitis" by Emily Wilson; and "Together, We Can Stop Cyber-Bullying" by Adam Parrish; and "My Grandfather, John Flanagan Sr" by Tara Flanagan.

Updated Features

- *Quick Start Guide:* Don't overlook the revised Quick Start Guide which is a handy guide for students that helps them give quality speeches at the beginning of the course without having to jump ahead in their book for needed information. This guide is not intended to take the place of the detailed information presented throughout the textbook, but rather to help students get up to speed for their first speeches and then serve as a handy reference guide for later speeches.

- The Speech Communication CourseMate brings concepts to life with online interactive learning, study, and exam preparation tools. The CourseMate for *Essentials of Public Speaking* contains dynamic tools to maximize students' experiences by enabling them to read, watch, listen to, critique, and analyze the sample speeches provided. It also includes numerous student and instructor resources, including Web links, interactive version of the Personal Report of Communication Apprehension (PRCA-24), PowerPoint tutorials, an appendix of sample speeches, a digital glossary, speech preparation forms and evaluation checklists, and chapter-by-chapter practice quizzes. ➔ See the Student Resources section for more about the CourseMate for *Essentials of Public Speaking*.

- *Continued emphasis on critical thinking:* Critical thinking is emphasized throughout the book in several ways. "Test Your Knowledge" questionnaires at the beginning of each unit stimulate and direct student thinking toward the material presented in the unit. The "Flash Back" feature boxes that begin each chapter present advice given by famous Greek and Roman rhetoricians and the new "Flash Forward" feature encourages students to compare classical rhetoric to contemporary public speaking. The new "Active Critical Thinking" questions at the end of each major heading in each chapter stimulate student thinking. Also, the "Personal Skill Building" activities and the "Collaborative Skill Building" activities at the end of each chapter includes questions, activities, and prompts to InfoTrac College Edition articles designed to promote critical thinking. Finally, specific chapters, such as Chapter 3, "Listening: What Speakers and Listeners Should Know;" Chapter 4, "Analyzing Your Audience;" Chapter 11, "Informative Speeches: Demonstrational and Informational;" and Chapter 13, "Persuasive Methods and Theories," relate directly to the importance and use of critical thinking in public speaking.

- *Sample student speeches, speech excerpts, and speech topics:* Nine sample student speeches are featured throughout the text with one informative speech, "Our Solar System and the Three Dwarves," and one persuasive speech, "Drinking and Driving," used as running examples throughout the text. Four new speeches were added in this edition for a total of nine sample speeches.

- *Major reorganization in four chapters, revised material in all chapters:* Many chapters have received major reorganization especially chapters 7, 10, 11, and 13 and one chapter was removed entirely to cut out redundancy. New photos were added throughout. Revised materials include:

  - Chapter 2. Update on "Other Methods for Managing Anxiety"

  - Chapter 3. Title changed to indicated that listening now includes (1) what speakers need to know about listeners, and (2) what listening skills listeners need to develop. Chapter also includes new "Stages of listening."

  - Chapter 5. Updated information on using the Internet.

  - Chapter 6. New information on supporting materials and new, updated examples of each support.

  - Chapter 7. New Patterns of organization added.

  - Chapter 8. Examples changed or updated.

  - Chapter 9. New persuasive speech on Endometriosis.

  - Chapter 10. Benefits of using visuals reorganized and updated; entire Chapter reorganized; new visuals.

- Chapter 11. Demonstration and Informational speeches now have evaluation included in margins; one new speech on endometriosis.

- Chapter 12. New information on persuasion, effective arguments, and persuasive appeals.

- Chapter 12 & 13: both have been reorganized for clarity and ease of student reading. Also, more relevant photos.

- Chapter 13. Persuasive theory updated along with more practical application of theory. New persuasive speech on cyber-bullying.

- Chapter 14. New chapter on Special Occasion Speaking; Eulogy by President Obama and a sample speech of tribute.

Public Speaking Essentials

Essentials of Active Learning Students are invited to take an active role in the learning process by evaluating sample student and professional speeches, taking the "Test Your Knowledge" and online practice quizzes, and making decisions about his or her own speeches. Speech evaluation forms and sample formats for preparing informative and persuasive speeches are included for student use. Each chapter begins with a "Flashback" that makes classical rhetorical theory interesting and relevant and a "Flash Forward" that encourages application to today's world. "Remember" boxes provide opportunities to stop and review. Special tidbits and advice that will help students prepare and deliver quality speeches are integrated throughout the text. To encourage students to reflect on and expand on what they have read, "Active Critical Thinking" questions are included at the end of each major chapter section and "Personal Skill Building" and "Collaborative Skill Building" activities are included at the end of each chapter. In addition, at appropriate places in each chapter, the margins include InfoTrac College Edition exercises and "Express Connect" prompts to Speech Builder Express, an online speech organization and outlining tool.

Essentials of Confidence Building Speaker anxiety often keeps students from achieving success. Unfortunately, no amount of lecture, encouragement, or practice will make students confident, professional speakers as long as deep down inside they believe themselves to be "poor" speakers. For this reason, *Essentials of Public Speaking* approaches anxiety head-on in Chapter 2, "Building Speaker Confidence," so students can have improvements well under way by the time their first major speech is due. Although a variety of confidence-building techniques are discussed, Chapter 2 concentrates on positive imagery. This technique requires only minor instructor guidance and does not need special out-of-class sessions to be successful. In fact, interested students can use positive imagery with success simply by following the suggestions in the text.

Essentials of a Quick Start Instructors want students to begin speaking early in the semester, but they know that to give good speeches, students need information not available until later chapters. *Essentials of Public Speaking* opens with a Quick Start Guide so that students can begin giving quality speeches immediately without having to jump ahead for needed information. This guide highlights the essential characteristics of a successful public speaker and provides an overview of the basic speaking process. Beginning speeches, such as the speech of introduction, the humorous incident speech, the artifact speech, the pet-peeve speech, or the one-point speech, can be given with success in the first or second week of class.

Technology Essentials *Essentials of Public Speaking* includes up-to-date coverage of the use of technology in the speechmaking process. Chapter 5, "Selecting and Researching Your Topic," includes a detailed section on using the Internet and computer databases, such as InfoTrac College Edition, EBSCOhost, and CQ Researcher, to research speech topics. Also included in this chapter are valuable suggestions on what to do if a search produces too many or too few hits, how to use Boolean operators, how to evaluate Internet sources, and how to find quality websites.

Chapter 10, "Preparing Effective Visual Aids," includes complete information about designing and using visual aids of all types. The chapter covers topics such as selecting proper fonts, point sizes, and colors for a variety of media and audiences, and includes a full-color insert of professional looking visual aids created by students with PowerPoint presentation software. The Essentials website includes a PowerPoint User's Guide to creating quality computer visuals.

Technology tips are integrated into each chapter when appropriate, such as "Plagiarism and Technology" in Chapter 1, "Listening Filters: Technology" in Chapter 3, and "Make PowerPoint Your Ally" in Chapter 10, and "Speaking to Make a Difference" in Chapter 4 deals with the role of social networking in persuasion.

Chapter Organization Essentials Following a traditional pattern of organization, *Essentials of Public Speaking* divides the chapters into four units: "Foundations," "Preparing Your Speech," "Presenting Your Speech," and "Types of Speeches." Chapters 1 through 3 comprise the foundations of the course—the importance of public speaking and ethics, building speaker confidence, and listening from the speaker's and listener's perspective.

Chapters 4 through 7 are devoted to speech preparation for all types of speeches and include information on audience analysis; topic selection, outlining, and research; supporting materials; and speech organization for successful speaking.

Chapters 8 through 10 give guidelines for presenting a speech—delivering the message, perfecting language style, and preparing effective visual aids. These chapters are designed so they can be used at any point during the semester.

Chapters 11 through 14 present specific information for various types of public speaking: demonstration, informative, persuasive (including persuasive theory), team speaking, and special occasion speaking.

Essential Sample Speeches Each chapter is illustrated with one or more speech outlines, manuscripts, or excerpts from students or professionals. The text includes nine complete student speeches—four of them are new—some of which also include visual aids, outlines, and speaking notes. Additional student and professional speeches are located on the Essentials of Public Speaking website.

Essential Student Resources

The **CourseMate for *Essentials to Public Speaking*** brings course concepts to life with interactive learning, study, and exam preparation tools that support the printed textbook. Watch your comprehension soar as your class works with the printed textbook and the textbook-specific website. The CourseMate for *Essentials to Public Speaking* goes beyond the book to deliver what you need, and includes:

- Videotaped versions of many of the speeches featured in the text maximize students' experience by enabling them to read, watch, and listen to the models provided. Students can also read and analyze the text of several other sample student and professional speeches provided in the section "Additional Speeches for Analysis."

- Chapter-by-chapter resources include maintained Web links, InfoTrac College Edition activities, a digital glossary, the "Test Your Knowledge" quizzes featured throughout the book, "Active Critical Thinking" exercises, the end-of-chapter "Personal Skill Building" and "Collaborative Skill Building" activities, and chapter-by-chapter practice quizzes.

- An interactive version of the Personal Report of Communication Apprehension (PRCA-24) is featured, as is a PowerPoint tutorial.

InfoTrac® College Edition Four months of free "anywhere, anytime" access to InfoTrac College Edition, the online library, can be bundled on request with this new book. InfoTrac College Edition puts cutting-edge research and the latest headlines at your students' fingertips, giving them access to an entire online library for the cost of one book. This fully searchable database offers more than 20 years' worth of full-text articles (more than 10 million) from almost 4,000 diverse sources such as academic journals, newsletters, and up-to-the-minute periodicals, including *Time, Newsweek, Science, Forbes,* and *USA Today*—a great tool for topic selection and speech research. Exercises for using InfoTrac College Edition are included in marginal boxes throughout the text.

Speech Builder Express 3.0 Available 24 hours a day, seven days a week, Speech Builder Express coaches students through every step of the speech organization and outlining process. This program is not simply a template that does the outlining for students. Instead, it is comprised of a series of interactive activities that actually coach them through the various stages of building a speech. Students can even click a "Video" icon wherever it appears, to see an example of a student or professional speech that illustrates the concepts students apply to craft their speech outline.

Speech Builder Express activities cover such fundamentals as speech goals and specific purposes, thesis statements, organizational patterns, main points, supporting material, transitions, internal previews, summaries and signposts, speech introductions and conclusions, and bibliographies.

Practice and present with **Speech Studio™**. With Speech Studio, you can upload video files of practice speeches or final performances, comment on your peer's speeches, and review your grades and instructor feedback. Speech Studio's flexibility lends itself to use in traditional, hybrid, and online courses. It allows instructors to: save valuable in-class time by conducting practice sessions and peer review work virtually; combine the ease of a course management tool with a convenient way to capture, grade, and review videos of live, in-class performances; simulate an in-class experience for online courses.

The Art and Strategy of Service Learning Presentations *by Rick Isaacson and Jeff Saperstein, both at San Francisco State University.* This handbook can be bundled with the text and is an invaluable resource for students in the basic course that integrates (or is planning to integrate) a service learning component. The handbook provides guidelines for connecting service learning work with classroom concepts and advice for working effectively with agencies and organizations. The handbook also provides model forms and speeches for students to use throughout the course.

A Guide to the Basic Course for ESL Students *by Esther Yook, University of Mary Washington.* Available bundled with the text, this guide assists the non-native English speaker. It features FAQs, helpful URLs, and strategies for accent management and overcoming speech apprehension.

Essential Instructional Resources

Instructor's Resource Manual This guide is designed for beginning as well as seasoned instructors. It includes suggested course syllabi and schedules, teaching ideas, chapter outlines, ready-to-use evaluation forms, classroom exercises including online exercises, ideas for using the practice suggestions in each chapter of the text, and test questions for each chapter.

InfoTrac College Edition Student Activities Workbooks (Public Speaking and Public Speaking 2.0) These unique workbooks can be bundled with this text. Each workbook features extensive individual and group activities, focusing on specific course topics that make use of InfoTrac College Edition. Also included are guidelines for instructors and students that describe how to maximize the use of this resource.

Videotape Library Also available to instructors adopting this book is a wealth of video resources. Video policy is based on adoption size; contact your Wadsworth Cengage representative for more information.

- *Student Speeches for Critique and Analysis Video:* Five volumes feature introductory, impromptu, informative, and persuasive speeches. These videos are great tools for helping students learn to analyze and provide effective feedback on both imperfect and award-winning speeches. Select speeches feature non-native English speakers and the use of visual aids. A table of contents, packaged with each cassette, includes the running time of each speech. All speeches have been videotaped within the past three years.

- *Wadsworth Communication Video Library:* A comprehensive library of videos covering key communication topics, including "Great Speeches: The Video Series;" "Great Speeches: Today's Women;" "Dynamic Business Presentations: Effective Communication in Teams;" "Media Power;" and more.

- *Videos for Speech Communication 2010: Public Speaking, Human Communication, and Interpersonal Communication.* This DVD provides footage of news stories from BBC and CBS that relate to current topics in communication, such as teamwork and how to interview for jobs, as well as news clips about speaking anxiety and speeches from contemporary public speakers, such as Michelle Obama and Senator Hillary Clinton.

- *ABC News DVD: Speeches by Barack Obama.* This DVD includes nine famous speeches by President Barack Obama, from 2004 to present day, including his speech at the 2004 Democratic National Convention; his 2008 speech on race, "A More Perfect Union"; and his 2009 inaugural address. Speeches are divided into short video segments for easy, time-efficient viewing. This instructor supplement also features critical thinking questions and answers for each speech, designed to spark class discussion.

PowerLecture for *Essentials of Public Speaking* This dynamic presentation tool offers the perfect software to help you present outstanding lectures. It includes book-specific Microsoft PowerPoint slides, which feature text, art, and video clips, plus the ability to import information from previously created lectures. Video clips included on the Essentials of Public Speaking website, in addition to select professional speeches, are included in this tool. Additionally, an electronic copy of the Instructor's Resource Manual and ExamView Computerized and Online Testing are available with PowerLecture. Create, deliver, and customize tests and study guides (both in print and online) in minutes with this easy-to-use assessment and tutorial system. ExamView offers both a "Quick Test Wizard" and an "Online Test Wizard" that guide you step by step through the process of creating tests—you can even see the test you are creating on the screen exactly as it will print or display online. You can build tests of up to 250 questions, using up to 12 question types. Using ExamView's complete word-processing capabilities, you can enter an unlimited number of new questions or edit existing questions.

Instructor Workbooks: *Public Speaking: An Online Approach, Public Speaking: A Problem Based Learning Approach,* **and** *Public Speaking: A Service-Learning Approach for Instructors.* Written by Deanna Sellnow, University of Kentucky, these instructor workbooks include a course-syllabus and icebreakers; public speaking basics such as coping with anxiety, learning cycle and learning styles; outlining; ethics; and informative, persuasive, and ceremonial (special occasion) speeches.

Guide to Teaching Public Speaking Online. Written by Todd Brand of Meridian Community College, this helpful online guide provides instructors who teach public speaking online with tips for establishing "classroom" norms with students, utilizing course management software and other eResources, managing logistics such as delivering and submitting speeches and making up work, discussing how peer feedback is different online, strategies for assessment, and tools such as sample syllabi and critique and evaluation forms tailored to the online course.

Acknowledgments

Many people helped in the creation of this edition of *Essentials of Public Speaking*. For example, Erin Hamilton, who wrote many of the valuable "Speaking to Make a Difference" boxes and updated the online activities; Doris M. Redd, who gave excellent suggestions and final copyediting advice; Debi Blankenship, who wrote the Quick Start Guide and whose students produced several of the new speeches; Lisa Benedetti, who helped locate the student speeches; and Alycia Ehlert at Volunteer State Community College, who revised the Instructor's Manual.

I also want to thank the creative professionals at Wadsworth Cengage: Monica Eckman, executive editor; Greer Lleuad, senior development editor; Rebekah Matthews, assistant editor; Michael Lepera, content project manager; Amy Whitaker, marketing manager; Colin Solan, editorial assistant; Jessica Badiner, media editor; Justin Palmeiro, print buyer; Eric Arima at Integra Software Services, Inc; Jayavardhan Sampath, photo researcher; and Amanda Groszko, rights specialist. It was a joy to work with all of these people.

Special thanks go to the educators who have shared their pedagogical and academic expertise in this and past editions. Reviewers for this edition were: Jacob Arndt, Kalamazoo Valley Community College; Alycia Ehlert, Volunteer State Community College; Eric Harlan, Mississippi University for Women; Jason Makowsky, Colorado Christian University; Marjorie Nadler, Miami University; Miri Pardo, St. John Fisher College; Fran Pelham, Holy Family University; and Gary Rybold, Irvine Valley College. Reviewers from past editions were: Alycia Ehlert, Darton College; Marty Ennes, West Hills College; Evene Estwick, Wilkes University; Russell B. Gordon, Pacific Baptist College; Jennifer Graber-Peters, Reedley College; Richard Harmon, Seminole Community College; Elayne Hayes-Anthony, Belhaven College; Adna Howell, Delta College; Paulette Jacques, Northwestern Connecticut Community College; Scott Johnson, Bethel College; William Martello, St. Edward's University; Anna Martinez, Reedley College; Stephanie Poole Martinez, St. Edward's University; and Ron Shope, Grace University. Reviewers for past editions (including their colleges at the time of their reviews) were Nicholas Burnett, California State University at Sacramento; Ginger Carney, Milwaukee Area Technical College at Mequon; Russell Church, Middle Tennessee State University; Robert Cocetti, University of Nebraska at Kearney; Bonnie Creel, Tarrant County College; Michael Eidenmuller, Northwestern State University; David Gaer, Southeast Community College; Kathy German, Miami University of Ohio; Cindy Greenburg, Kingsbourough Community College, CUNY; Amanda Grunrud, University of North Carolina at Chapel Hill; Martha Haun, University of Houston; Paul Hemenway, Miami Dade College; Mark Hickson III, University of Alabama at Birmingham; Ralph Hillman, Middle Tennessee State University; Heather Howley, Rend Lake College; Larry Hugenberg, Youngstown State University; Susan Huxman, Wichita State University; Harold Kinzer, Utah State University; Lois Leubitz, Cedar Valley College; JoAnn Lowlor, West Valley College; Ben Martin, Santa Monica College; Phil Martin, North Central State College; Allison Mintz, Arizona State University West; Mark Nelson, The University of Alabama; Neil Patten, Ferris State University; Jane Patton, Mission College; Douglas Rosentrater, Buck County Community College; Cami Sanderson, Ferris State University; Roy Schwartzman, University of South Carolina; Terri Sparks, Mesa Community College; Deborah Stollery, Xavier University; Mark Stoner, California State University at Sacramento; Loretta Walker, Salt Lake Community College; and Marianne Worthington, Cumberland College.

Finally, to the many students who not only tried out the materials in class but also allowed their speeches, visual aids, and outlines to be used as samples in the text and on the Essentials website, I give a special THANKS; you are all wonderful!

Cheryl Hamilton, Ph.D.
Fort Worth, Texas

Quick Start Guide to Public Speaking

Worried about how to prepare a quality speech that listeners will enjoy? Use this handy guide to help you prepare your first speeches and as a quick reminder for later speeches as well. Although, it is not intended to take the place of the detailed information that is presented in the textbook, it is a great place to begin.

STEP 1

ANALYZE YOUR AUDIENCE

Have you ever been bored to death by a speaker whose presentation was extremely dull, overly technical, or too-simplified? Here are some ways you can avoid being such a speaker:

A. First, get to know your audience by conducting a poll to determine audience knowledge of your topic, audience beliefs and values, cultural makeup, gender, and age.

➔ *For more on analyzing your audience, see Chapter 4.*

B. Determine what type of listeners they are likely to be, and plan ways to help them listen better and remember more. For example:

- Listeners want to know "What's in this for me?" (WIFM), so you must establish common ground and show how the speech will personally benefit the audience.

- Never begin by introducing your topic. Start with a strong attention-getter that pulls the audience into your presentation.

- Use a dynamic style of delivery, including unexpected volume changes and plenty of movement and gestures.

- Use well-designed visual aids.

- Include interesting and pertinent personal experiences.

➔ *For more on understanding listeners, see Chapter 3.*

C. Review Maslow's hierarchy of needs (p. 331) to determine which needs most closely relate to your audience. An audience is more likely to stay involved in (or be persuaded by) a speech that relates to their basic human needs.

STEP 2

DETERMINE TOPIC, EXACT PURPOSE, AND MAIN POINTS

A. Select a topic that:

- *Highlights your knowledge, experience, and abilities.* You will feel much more confident discussing something you already know about.

- *Reflects your interests.* If you choose a topic you are passionate about, you'll speak with energy and enthusiasm, which will energize the audience.

- *Stimulates and motives your audience.* Listeners don't have to be interested in your topic before you begin speaking, but they should find interest and value in the topic by the time you are finished.

- *Allows you to be creative.* Think outside the box. Think current. Think interesting.

- *Fits the requirements of the assignment.* This should include speech type (informative, persuasive, or special occasion) and time limit.

→ *If you have been assigned a topic that holds little interest for you, check out some of the suggestions in Chapter 6 for supporting material that will spice up your speech.*

Beginning Speeches

Your first speech will probably be a brief special occasion, informative, or persuasive speech. The most common types are listed below:

Artifact speech: Share an item or group of items that, if found years from now by an archaeologist excavating your home, would accurately highlight your life. (In the sample speech in Chapter 1, Monica discusses how her collection of T-shirts reflects important events in her life.)

Cultural ritual speech*: Select a ritual from your culture—explain it and tell what it means to you and/or how it helps explain who you are.

How-to speech: Explain or demonstrate how to do or to make something.

Humorous incident speech: Share a funny incident from your life.

Introductory speech: Introduce yourself or a classmate by highlighting several interesting facts.

One-point speech: State a personal opinion, and clarify the reasons for your opinion.

Personal opinion speech: State a personal opinion, and either clarify your position or persuade the audience to your way of thinking.

Pet-peeve speech: Select something that irritates you (such as drivers who tailgate), and explain why it bothers you so much.

For more on special occasion speeches, see Chapter 14.

*Adapted from Virgil R. Miller (2004). *Communication Teacher, 18*(1), 17–19.

B. Next, decide on the exact purpose for your speech. This will help you narrow your topic and keep on track. An *exact purpose* is a clear, simple sentence that specifies exactly what you want your audience to gain (know, perceive, understand) from the speech.

Begin with, "After hearing my speech, the audience will . . . ." For example, "After hearing my speech, the audience will be able to insert a movie clip into a PowerPoint slide show."

As you begin to organize the speech, if your points do not relate to the exact purpose, they are unnecessary and can be eliminated.

C. Determine your main points. This can be an overwhelming task. If you're unsure of the main points you'd like to include, try a brief brainstorming session. Set aside five minutes and make a list of every possible content idea that comes to mind. Consider each one, combine ideas, remove ideas, and determine the three to five main points that suit your presentation. In her "Closet Artifacts" speech, Monica introduces herself by taking a brief look at four aspects of her life: college, career, marriage, and family (see Chapter 1, p. 20).

→ *For more on topic selection, exact purpose, and main points, see Chapter 5.*

STEP 3

PREPARE A ROUGH-DRAFT OUTLINE OF MAIN POINTS (SHOWING NEEDED INFORMATION)

Although the word *outline* strikes fear in the heart of many beginning speakers, it is necessary for good organization. By writing a rough-draft outline, you can see the organizational pattern of your main points and tell which points have too much supporting material and which don't have enough.

For a rough-draft outline:

Use Roman numerals for your main points.

Use capital letters for your subpoints.

Use Arabic numerals for second-level supporting materials.

→ *For more on rough-draft outlines, see Chapters 5, 11 and 12.*

Sample Rough-Draft Outline

"Fundamentals of CPR"

I. Time is extremely critical to CPR
   A. For every minute that CPR is not started, the survival rate drops 7–10% (*paramedic textbook*)
      1. Determine Patient responsiveness
      2. Check breathing
      3. Open airway (*talk with campus nurse*)

(Continued)

B. Begin CPR (*steps from American Heart Association website—update*)
1. Do two breaths, once every five seconds
2. Check pulse
3. Begin chest compressions

II. Proper hand placement on the patient, even half an inch, can make a big difference (*find quote and source*)
A. Ribs
B. Three finger rule (*demonstrate and use source from textbook*)

III. Begin compression (*use personal experience*)
A. Pressure
1. Amount of pressure (*find source*)
2. 30 compressions, two ventilations, repeat (*American Heart Association*)
3. Personal example? (*search databases*)

Step 4

Research Topic for Material to Support Main Points

Beginning speakers often skimp on research because they believe personal knowledge will be sufficient. Although using personal knowledge is fine (as long as it is firsthand experience and relates directly to your topic), you should have a minimum of two additional sources.

Researching your topic and having strong, reliable sources shows the audience that you are objective, have credibility, and have done some research on your topic.

A. Don't rely too heavily on the Internet for your research. Too much information on the Web is biased and out of date. Start with *printed material* in your college or local library, and include some of the following:

- Brochures and pamphlets.
- Magazines and newspapers.
- Specialized dictionaries and encyclopedias.
- Quotation books.

- Other resources, such as yearbooks of statistics, films, or government documents.
- Personal interview with an expert.

B. Use databases (like Communication and Mass Media Complete, EBSCOhost, and InfoTrac College Edition) that include referred journal articles.

C. Take careful notes while doing your research, and include names of authors and page numbers in case you need to gain further information from the source.

In researching, you are primarily looking for three types of supporting material:

- Material to *clarify*.
- Material to *prove*.
- Material to *add interest*.

→ *For more on researching your topic, see Chapter 5.*

Step 5

Select Quality Supporting Materials

Beginning speakers often overuse explanations and statistics, making their presentations too technical or too dry to appeal to an audience.

Supporting Materials

There are several options for supporting materials that can *clarify, prove,* or *add interest* to your speech:

Explanations. Use explanations to *clarify* relationships between items, or give additional information about a topic. Be sure to use them sparingly.

Statistics. When used correctly, statistics can be very powerful supporting materials to *prove*. Round off numbers to make them easily understood. Find a way to relate your statistics to your listeners' frames of reference to add interest. Always orally cite the source of the statistic, and if possible, present statistics in a graph or chart.

Instances (Examples, & Illustrations). A specific case that *clarifies, adds interest,* and sometimes *proves a point* is an *instance*. An instance can be *brief* (called an example), *detailed* (called an illustration), *factual* (actually happened), or *hypothetical* (hasn't happened, but could possibly occur).

(Continued)

Comparisons. These are used to compare or contrast items and *add interest* to a presentation. They can be *literal* (items of the same class like two types of art) or *figurative* (items of different classes like an individual and a snowflake).

Expert opinions. Presenting and giving credit for the ideas of others who are considered experts on your topic adds *proof* and *clarification* to your topic. You can give an expert opinion in a quotation, or you can paraphrase the experts by putting their thoughts into your own words. Experts should be credible and, if not well known, their qualifications should be included when orally citing this type of source.

Fables, sayings, poems, and rhymes. This is a creative and interesting way to incorporate supporting material. Rather than relying on dry statistical information, why not spice up your speech with a clever poem, a familiar saying, or an interesting fable? Although none of these can provide proof, they will generate audience interest in your presentation.

Demonstrations. These are invaluable supporting materials that can also serve as visual aids. The audience can see your point in action, which boosts retention of your presentation. Unless you are giving a demonstration speech, keep any demonstration to no more than 30 seconds, and make sure it *clarifies* something in your speech.

→ *For more on supporting materials, see Chapter 6.*

STEP 6

DETERMINE HOW TO BEST ORGANIZE YOUR MAIN POINTS

A. There are basically nine patterns for organizing your main points. Some are designed for informative topics and others work best for persuasive topics. However, some type of organizational pattern is *imperative* for preparing a professional speech. Writing a speech without an organization pattern is like planning a road trip without a map. If poor organization causes you to ramble, the audience will tune you out.

Organizational Patterns

Causal pattern. Arrange your main points so they have a cause–effect or effect–cause relationship. You can't just assert that a relationship exists; you must use evidence and reasoning to prove it. The causal pattern works in both *informative* and *persuasive* speeches. An informative speech on the AIDS crisis in Africa could have two main points: (1) Lack of health care and education has created an AIDS crisis in Africa (cause); (2) The number of homeless orphans is rising every year (effect).

Chronological pattern. Normally used in *informative* or *demonstration* speeches, this pattern is arranged by date or in a step-by-step order. For instance, a speech on how to make lasagna could use the chronological pattern to show a progression of actions.

Claim or reason pattern. Used in *persuasive* speaking, the claim pattern is similar to the topical pattern (discussed below). For instance, a persuasive speech stating a claim against the legalization of drugs would include the main points (reasons) why drugs should not be legalized.

Comparative advantages pattern. This pattern is useful when the audience is already in agreement with you on the problem but doesn't agree on a solution. It focuses on the advantages of one course of action over another. For instance, a speech about foreign aid could briefly touch on the problem, but offer more effective solutions than the current programs. This organizational pattern is used in *persuasion*.

Criteria satisfaction pattern. In this pattern—used in *persuasion,* especially when the audience disagrees with your position—criteria (guidelines or rules) are established, followed by explanations of how your plan meets or exceeds the criteria. For instance, a speech on health care reform would work well in the criteria satisfaction pattern by defining criteria for health care reform and demonstrating how your plan is better than the current plan.

Problem–solution or problem-cause-solution pattern. The problem-solution pattern presents a problem and then suggests a solution to the problem. It is normally used in *persuasion* and can be presented as problem–solution–benefits or problem–solution–action. For instance, a speech on the homelessness problem in America would be easily organized in the problem–solution

(Continued)

pattern by showing the problems homeless people have and then offering solutions to the problems. Another version of this persuasive pattern is the problem-cause-solution pattern where you discuss the causes of the problem after introducing a serious problem and before presenting a solution to the problem.

Spatial or geographic pattern. The main points are arranged by location. This pattern is used in *informative* speeches and would include comparisons of different parts of the country or speaking about something from top to bottom or front to back. For instance, if your presentation deals with a trip to Hawaii, you could use the spatial or geographic pattern to organize the trip by island locations.

Topical pattern. A common organizational pattern for *informative* speeches, in the topical pattern no time, spatial, or causal relationship exists between the main points, although all the main points are related. When using this pattern, you might put the most important point first, the least compelling points in the middle, and an important point last. For instance, a speech about fly fishing could cover gear, techniques, and rivers. All of these points relate to fly fishing, but do not fit the criteria for other organizational patterns.

Motivated sequence pattern. Used in *persuasive* speaking, the motivated sequence pattern has the following five steps: attention, need, satisfaction, visualization, and action. When using emotional appeals, this pattern can be particularly effective in a speech to actuate.

→ *See Chapters 7, 11, and 12 for organization specific.*

B. Effective organization also includes *highlighting* your main points. When you write a paper for English class, you know there must be some type of transition between thoughts. This is also true when preparing and delivering a speech. The audience is better able to listen and stay on track when things move in a logical progression. The following are some ideas for highlighting your main points and keeping the audience on target:

- *Signposts* (which indicate where the speaker is going) are road signs for listeners. Signposts include words and phrases such as

  "First, I will show you ..."
  "The second step in the process is ..."
  "Third ..."
  "Finally ..."

- *Internal summaries* aid audience retention by giving periodic reviews of the material you've covered. When the audience is reminded of the main points, they are more likely to remember what you've talked about so far and be aware of how your points are interrelated. For example:

  "I've told you about the gear needed for fly fishing. This leads me to my second point, which is a specific technique that will ensure your success."

  After your second point is complete, you could use another internal summary by saying:

  "I've told you about the gear and one of the techniques used in fly fishing. This brings me to my final point, in which I'll share with you some of the better fly fishing locations in our area."

- *Transitions* provide bridges from one point to another and make it easier for the listeners to follow the speech. The following are some examples of transitions:

  "For example ..."
  "In addition ..."
  "If you don't remember anything else from this speech, be sure to remember this ..."

- The audience seems to have better retention when points are repeated or restated. Repetition is used when you want exact words or figures to be remembered. Restatement uses different words to make an idea stand out for the audience.

When you begin to use these main point highlighters, you may feel peculiar or stilted, but now is the perfect time to learn to use new speaking techniques. Tools like these improve your skills and will give you an advantage when delivering a speech, regardless of the setting.

→ *For more on organizing your main points, see Chapter 7.*

Step 7

Plan Introduction and Conclusion

Organizing Your Introduction An introduction grabs audience interest and clarifies the direction of the speech. Several things are necessary in a speech introduction.

A. Begin with an Attention–Getter.

Speakers, whether they are beginners or experienced, too often step up to the podium and begin their presentations with, "Today, I'd like to talk to you about . . . ." These words often inspire a stifled, collective yawn from the audience and a sudden interest in thinking about something other than the presentation.

Because we are all subjected on a daily basis to noise overload, it is your responsibility as a speaker to grab your audience and pull them into your speech. You cannot do this by merely announcing your topic; you must engage your audience and entice them to listen.

Attention-Getters

Here are some successful attention-getters:

A **detailed instance** is a true or hypothetical story of a personal, family, famous, business, or humorous experience that relates to the speech. It is vivid and told in a narrative style.

A **brief instance** or illustration is much the same but is less detailed and shorter.

Humor is a popular way to begin a speech, but keep in mind that everyone does not have the same sense of humor. What might be funny to you might be offensive to some members of the audience. Not every speech lends itself to humor as an attention-getter, and not everyone is good at telling a joke or humorous story, so make sure this is one of your strong suits before attempting to use humor as an attention-getter.

A **quotation** or paraphrase can also grab the interest of the audience—if it is delivered with enthusiasm and energy. Nothing can make a speech fall flat more quickly than a long quotation read from a paper, with no vocal inflection or no eye contact.

Revealing one or two **startling facts** in your introduction can effectively grab listeners' attention. People will sit up and listen when they hear something shocking. When using a startling fact, cite the source of the fact to increase your credibility and the power of the statement.

Asking a **question** of the audience will also involve them in the speech. A *rhetorical question* is designed to make the audience think and has no real answer. You can also pose an actual question and ask for a show of hands.

Referring to a **specific occasion** or event is essential if you have been invited to speak on a special occasion. This method is difficult to use in classroom settings.

Opening with a brief **fable, saying, poem,** or **rhyme** can be a good way to stimulate listener attention. These are often catchy or clever and will immediately involve the audience with your speech.

A brief **demonstration** of a procedure or skill can be an impressive way to get the attention of the audience. Remember to keep your demonstration very brief, as you don't want the demo to become the speech.

Additional ways to gain audience attention include pictures, sound clips, brief video clips (30 seconds maximum), or visual aids.

→ *For more examples of visual aids, see Chapter 10.*

B. Motivate Your Audience to Listen.

Even though you have gained the interest of the audience with your attention–getter, they may not continue to listen. The audience must feel that there is something in your speech that will benefit them. This is where your audience analysis from Step 1 is used again. Determine what audience needs you are going to appeal to, and tell the audience how listening to your presentation will directly benefit them.

C. Establish Credibility and Rapport.

A credible person is one who can be believed and trusted. You can establish credibility with the audience by stating your expertise on the topic you have chosen. It is important to state your credibility in the introduction of your presentation so that the audience feels you know what you are talking about. If you don't feel that you are an expert, cite an expert in your introduction. This shows that you have interest and have done research on the topic.

D. Present Your Thesis Statement. A good thesis statement includes your purpose followed by a preview of your main points.

- *Your specific topic or purpose*, which is built from the exact purpose that you developed in Step 2, will let the audience know the topic of your speech. If the audience has to work too hard to figure out your topic, they will tune you out. Unless you want to build suspense or the audience is hostile, you will want to state your purpose (informative presentations) or position (persuasive presentations) in your introduction.

- Your *preview of main points* is simply a summary of the points to come. Listing your main points on a visual aid makes it easier to remember your exact points.

There is an old speech adage that says, "Tell them what you're going to tell them; tell them, and then tell them what you told them." The more the audience hears the purpose of the speech, the more likely they are to remember your presentation. To follow the steps of this old adage, you should preview your main points in the introduction. If you are using visual aids, this would be a great time to include a slide that previews your main points.

Organizing Your Conclusion A conclusion provides closure to the audience and ties up any loose ends. Several things are necessary in a speech conclusion.

A. Summarize Your Main Ideas.
Referring back to the old speech adage, this is the time in your speech to "tell them what you told them" or review your main points. Don't give the entire speech again and don't introduce a new point, but touch briefly on the main points that were presented. Referring again to the fly fishing speech, you could review points by saying, "Tonight we discussed the necessary gear, a successful technique, and local rivers where you can fly fish." A review of points reminds the audience, one more time, of what you've told them.

B. Refocus Audience Attention. Try to make your final thought so memorable that the audience leaves the room thinking about what you've said. You can tie the conclusion back to the introduction by using one of the previously mentioned attention-getters. Never

end your speech by saying, "That's all I have" or "That's it." A speech without a strong conclusion is like a house without a roof.

→ *For more on organizing your introduction and conclusion, see Chapter 7.*

Step 8

Make a Preparation Outline, Apply Critical Thinking, and Plan Speaking Notes

A. When preparing your final outline:

- Outline the body of your speech using the number system discussed in Step 3.

- Write out transitions between main points in sentence form.

- Include a list of references at the end of the outline.

- Identify types of supporting materials in brackets so that you can tell if you are using a good variety of supporting materials for each main point.

- Identify the locations of visual aids in your speech with boldface type and brackets.

- Write your introduction and conclusion in complete sentences, partial sentences, or phrases.

- Write your introduction and conclusion last. It's hard to grab the attention of the audience and leave them feeling glad they listened if you are not sure of the shape the speech will be taking.

B. Before leaving your outline, subject it and everything in it to the *critical thinking* **questions** in Figure 11.6 (p. 269), making sure that your speech has clarity, accuracy, depth, and significance.

C. Now that you have completed your outline and thought critically about it, it's time to *develop your speaking notes.* Don't try to speak from an outline, because notes hamper successful eye contact and it is easy to lose your place. Instead, prepare speaking notes on index cards, and include only key words or phrases to jog your memory. Use color and underlining to make important words stand out.

→ *For more information on the preparation of outlines and speaking notes, see Chapters 11 and 12.*

STEP 9

PREPARE VISUAL AIDS

Using high-quality visual aids in your presentation will increase audience retention, quicken comprehension, and add interest. There are several types of visual aids that you can use:

- Computer generated slides.
- Flip charts and posters.
- Markerboards and chalkboards.
- Objects, models, and handouts.
- Audiovisual aids.

Here are some things to remember:

- Don't write your entire speech out on your visual aid. Your audience should be able to grasp the content of each visual in six seconds or less. Use key words or phrases—avoid sentences.
- Make your visuals pleasing to the eye.
- Make your visuals easy for audience members to see without straining their eyes.

→ *For more on preparing quality visual aids, see Chapter 10.*

STEP 10

PRACTICE YOUR SPEECH

A. Effective speakers don't read their speeches. Nothing is guaranteed to put an audience in a coma more quickly than reading your speech. Speakers who read usually have little or no eye contact or facial expressions and speak in a monotone. This type of speaker appears unprepared and even untrustworthy. On the other hand, when a speaker makes good eye contact, appears calm, and smiles, the audience feels they're listening to a trustworthy, experienced presenter. Make your gestures natural and feel free to move about during transitions.

B. Effective speech delivery is *natural, conversational,* **and** *believable—let your personality shine through.* The *only* way to make sure your presentation is polished and within specified time limits is to *practice out loud,* with a timer; edit if necessary; and practice again, and *again,* and AGAIN. Practicing several times will lessen your anxiety and polish your verbal, visual, and vocal delivery into a high-quality speech.

C. Effective speakers cite sources during their presentations. When you use information from a source other than yourself, you need to let the audience know where this information came from. You could cite your sources by saying something like this: "Dr. Cheryl Hamilton tells us in her book *Essentials of Public Speaking* that it is quite common to feel anxious in a new communication situation." You can cite a website in the same way and tell the audience when you last accessed the site. This will let them know that the information you're presenting is valid, current, and important.

Citing your sources will not only add to your credibility, but it will also make you more professional and should help in calming your nerves.

D. If you're still feeling anxious about giving a presentation, here are some tips on calming speaker anxiety:

- *Avoid thinking negatively.* Speakers often become anxious because they picture the worst possible scenario. If you've had a negative speaking experience in the past, forget about it, as the chances of this happening again are very slim. Practicing the speech out loud can help you avoid stumbling and forgetting what you plan to say.

- *Use positive statements.* Instead of focusing on negative aspects of speaking, begin to look at your speech as an adventure. List several things about speaking that worry you. Write these things down and then change them into positive statements. Here's an example of how to do this:

  "I'm afraid my hands will shake." (Negative)

  "I'm worried that I'll forget what I'm going to say." (Negative)

Make these statements positive by changing them to:

> "My hands gesture effectively in a calm manner when I give presentations." (Positive)

> "I am a dynamic speaker and keep the audience engaged and interested in my speech. The practice I have done keeps me on track, and I easily remember what I planned to say." (Positive)

Once you've created your positive statements, say them to yourself at least once each day for three to four weeks. At the same time, see yourself speaking successfully and feeling confident. This technique has been used successfully by professional golfer David Duval, swimmer

Michael Phelps and Olympic champions Jackie Joyner-Kersee and Sarah Hughes.

→ *For more on practicing your speech, see Chapter 8.*

Remember, the audience wants you to succeed—they are on your side. When you begin to see the audience as friendly rather than negative or dangerous, your nerves will be much calmer, and you will begin to enjoy giving speeches.

If you've followed the steps in this Quick Start Guide, you should be prepared to deliver a professional, well-developed, and well-prepared presentation. Best wishes and good luck!

Prepared by Debi Blankenship and
Cheryl Hamilton

Foundations

Can you identify the myths about public speaking?

Some of the following statements are sound public-speaking principles based on research discussed throughout this book; other statements are misconceptions often thought to be true by beginning speakers.

Directions: If you think the statement is generally accurate, mark it T; if you think the statement is a myth, mark it F. Then compare your answers with the explanations at the end of Chapter 1. You can also take this quiz online through your Online Resources for *Essentials of Public Speaking*, and, if requested, e-mail your responses to your instructor.

_____ **1.** In persuasive speeches, your most important tools are logic and evidence.

_____ **2.** Good speakers rarely get nervous.

_____ **3.** Visual aids are nice but are not essential to a good speech.

_____ **4.** Speakers should be experts in the field on which they are speaking.

_____ **5.** Red is an excellent color for highlighting graphs and for emphasizing key data.

_____ **6.** Audiences consider male speakers to be more credible than female speakers.

_____ **7.** Passing around handouts during the speech helps to keep the audience's attention.

_____ **8.** In a small conference room when the audience is seated around a table, the speaker should stand.

_____ **9.** Wearing bright, colorful clothing and accessories adds to your power and credibility as a speaker.

_____ **10.** Only accomplished public speakers can deliver effective presentations.

1

Public Speaking, Ethics, and You

FLASH BACK

From the beginning of recorded time, educated people have been skilled public speakers. For example, educated Greeks and Romans studied **rhetoric**—the art of persuasive public speaking. The first known handbook of speaking was Aristotle's *Rhetoric*. In it he divided speaking into the following three categories: **forensic** (speaking in court), **deliberative** (political or legislative speaking), and **epideictic** (ceremonial speaking).

FLASH FORWARD

Can you imagine a Greek or Roman speaker loading a speech outline or manuscript onto an iPhone, sending a copy by Internet to a friend for a critique, posting a speech on YouTube, or talking about their speech success on a social-networking site like Facebook? Although skilled public speaking is just as important for citizens today, Aristotle's categories don't accurately describe what we do now. *What label would you add to Aristotle's speaking categories to describe today's speaking environment?*

CourseMate

Learning Objectives
As you read Chapter 1,

- Explain several personal and civic benefits of taking a public speaking course or seminar.
- List the three different types of presentations and a sample topic for each.
- Identify the main elements of the basic communication model and explain why understanding this transactional process can lead to speaking success.
- Explain why being ethical is a public speaker's obligation, and compare professions that are viewed by the American public as the most ethical with professions that are considered the least ethical.

DO YOU FEEL MORE COMFORTABLE TALKING ON YOUR iPHONE OR ON FACEBOOK THAN MAKING A SPEECH IN FRONT OF OTHERS? If your answer is yes, you are not alone. In fact, you may be thinking that with your job and personal life you won't really need to be skilled in public speaking. If so, you will probably view with skepticism my telling you that there are several extremely important reasons for taking a course in public speaking. By the time you finish reading this chapter, I think you will begin to see several personal benefits for learning to give speeches in public. By the time you complete this course, you will be able to say firsthand how learning to give speeches and communicating publicly has benefited you. So let's begin by looking at the potential roles of public speaking in your life, as well as the elements and ethics of the communication process.

> ### Personal Assessment
> Before reading further, **complete McCroskey's Personal Report of Communication Apprehension (PRCA-24) questionnaire,** accessible through your Online Resources for *Essentials of Public Speaking*. At the end of the course, you will retake the PRCA-24 and compare scores to see specific areas of improvement. There are additional surveys, like the PRPSA, on our website, that your instructor may request you take as well.

Public Speaking: Benefits in Your Life

Although you may be thinking that speaking won't be necessary in your life, actually as you become successful in your career, get involved in your community, and pursue various activities and causes, you will be surprised at how many opportunities you will have to give speeches. These opportunities can enhance your personal development, influence society, and advance your career.

Enhancing Your Personal Satisfaction and Development

One of the greatest benefits of learning to give a good speech is the personal satisfaction it brings. It's a wonderful feeling to be able to stand in front of a group of people and present a well-organized, dynamic speech that your listeners obviously appreciate. Also, once you learn to give effective speeches, you can stop dreading the possibility that someone will ask you to speak. For example, on the first day of class, a student, Karen (not her real name), told me that she had dropped the course five times before and would probably drop it again because she simply couldn't give a speech. But when she looked at the confidence-building techniques covered in the course, she was intrigued enough to give it a try—and for the first time was able to keep her fears under control and give a successful speech. → *See Chapter 2 for more on confidence building and more on Karen.*

Being able to speak in public will also give you more control over your life. That is, knowing how to research, conceptualize, organize, and present your own arguments helps you get your ideas across to others. Learning to analyze audiences and to adapt your ideas and arguments to them makes you a more flexible communicator and a better critical thinker (Allen et al., 1999). Moreover, knowing how to evaluate the persuasive arguments of others keeps you from feeling manipulated. In short, although you may find it difficult to believe right now, learning to speak in public really can be beneficial to you personally. Although Rachel (a less nervous student than Karen) also did everything she could to get out of taking a public speaking course, once it was finished, she had these comments:

> Sweaty hands in my pockets, flipping my hair, and the words "uh" and "um" only begin the list of mistakes I made while giving my introductory presentation. I even forgot to mention my husband of ten years! Standing in front of the class that day was the most nervous I have been in a very long time. My self-esteem was very low—to the point that I was telling myself that I could

Despite being born without any arms or legs, Australian Nick Vujicic uses his public speaking skills to make a positive impact on the world.

not give a speech. However, during this semester I have realized that I am capable of giving wonderful presentations and capable of capturing the attention of others. I am so glad that I took this course. Not only have I learned how to prepare and deliver a speech and use visual aids, but I have realized my capabilities.

Influencing Your World

Learning to give speeches can also be beneficial to society. Because our form of government depends on citizen participation, opportunities to speak are almost limitless. Start with your own neighborhood. Many neighborhoods hold regular meetings to discuss and solve community problems, such as setting up a crime watch program. Similarly, citizens can address key issues at city council and school board meetings. The same goes for campus issues, such as the student council's stance on a faculty member's dismissal, the English club's position on political correctness, or a campaign to keep the library open for longer hours—all are situations requiring public speaking. Even college courses often require you to share information with the class or make an oral presentation. It's hard to find a situation that wouldn't benefit from public speaking.

Here are some examples of people who are influencing their worlds through public speaking:

- Jill Esplin, a motivational speaker in her 20s, uses her degree in communications from Chapman University to inspire and motivate teen audiences (See her blog at **jesplin.blogspot.com**).

- Nick Vujicic, also in his 20s, was born in Melbourne, Australia, with no arms or legs. After many personal and physical hurdles, Nick is now an inspirational and motivational speaker for religious and corporate audiences around the world. His speaking supports many international charities. (Learn more about Nick at **lifewithoutlimbs.org**.)

- Mae Jemison, the first black female astronaut in space, is also a physician and public speaker. Although space and science served as her original platform, she now spends most of her time speaking on the inequities of today's health care.

- Arnold Schwarzenegger, bodybuilder, actor, and politician, is a "charismatic, persuasive, and inspirational" speaker (Gallo, 2006), but he had to work hard to achieve his current level of success. He honed his skill by giving frequent speeches at charity events and by visualizing himself as a successful speaker. His speaking skills came in handy while Governor of California. ➤ *See Chapter 2 for more on confidence building through visualization/positive imagery.*

- Bill Gates, founder of Microsoft, is this chapter's "Speaking to Make a Difference" speaker (see page 5). Gates has influenced the world with his software, his Bill and Melinda Gates Foundation, and his public speaking. He is currently working with his wife and Warren Buffett to challenge billionaires to "pledge to give at least half their net worth to charity, in their lifetime or at death" (Loomis, 2010, p. 83).

Speaking to Make a Difference

On June 7, 2007, some thirty years after his own class had graduated without him, Bill Gates walked to the podium to address Harvard's current graduating class and accept an honorary doctoral degree from the university. Gates, Harvard's "most successful dropout," gave a moving speech imploring the 2007 graduates to do more with their talents and degrees than just line their pockets. Here is a short excerpt from that address; you can find the full text and video of the speech on the Bill and Melinda Gates Foundation website at **www.gatesfoundation.org/default.htm**. Search for "Harvard University Commencement."

I've been waiting more than 30 years to say this: "Dad, I always told you I'd come back and get my degree"....

I applaud the graduates today for taking a much more direct route to your degrees. For my part, I'm just happy that the *Crimson* has called me "Harvard's most successful dropout." I guess that makes me valedictorian of my own special class...I did the best of everyone who failed.

* * *

I left campus knowing little about the millions of young people cheated out of educational opportunities here in this country. And I knew nothing about the millions of people living in unspeakable poverty and disease in developing countries. It took me decades to find out.

You graduates came to Harvard at a different time. You know more about the world's inequities than the classes that came before. In your years here, I hope you've had a chance to think about how—in this age of accelerating technology—we can finally take on these inequities, and we can solve them.

Imagine, just for the sake of discussion, that you had a few hours a week and a few dollars a month to donate to a cause—and you wanted to spend that time and money where it would have the greatest impact in saving and improving lives. Where would you spend it?

For Melinda and for me, the challenge is the same: How could we do the most good for the greatest number with the resources we have?

During our discussions on this question, Melinda and I read an article about the millions of children who were dying every year in poor countries from diseases that we had long ago made harmless in this country: measles, malaria, pneumonia, hepatitis B, yellow fever. One disease I had never even heard of, rotavirus, was killing half a million kids each year—none of them in the United States.

We were shocked. We had assumed that if millions of children were dying and they could be saved, the world would make it a priority to discover and deliver the medicines to save them. But it did not. For under a dollar, there were interventions that could save lives that just weren't being delivered.

If you believe that every life has equal value, it's revolting to learn that some lives are seen as worth saving and others are not. We said to ourselves, "This can't be true. But if it is true, it deserves to be the priority of our giving."

So we began our work in the same way anyone here would begin it. We asked, "How could the world let these children die?"

The answer is simple, and harsh: The market did not reward saving the lives of these children, and governments did not subsidize it. So the children died because their mothers and their fathers had no power in the market and no voice in the system.

But you and I have both.

* * *

I remember going to Davos some years back and sitting on a global health panel that was discussing ways to save millions of lives. Millions! Think of the thrill of saving just one person's life—then multiply that by millions. Yet this was the most boring panel I've ever been on—ever. So boring even I couldn't bear it.

What made that experience especially striking was that I had just come from an event where we were introducing Version 13 of some piece of software, and we had people jumping and shouting with excitement. I love getting people excited about software—but why can't we generate even more excitement for saving lives?

You can't get people excited unless you can help them see and feel the impact.

Being invited to speak at the 2007 Harvard graduation gave Bill Gates a great opportunity to influence the younger generation using the power of speech. Let's examine just what makes Gates' speech so effective:

- *Existing influence.* Bill Gates is known worldwide as the software mogul that directed Microsoft to its success. This in and of itself most likely gives him enough credibility to get his audience's attention. Those who know of the Bill and Melinda Gates Foundation and its work toward better education, better health care, and ending poverty will have an even better chance of receiving the message Gates wants to convey.

- *Humor.* "I've been waiting more than 30 years to say this: 'Dad, I always told you I'd come back and get my degree.' [Laughter and applause]...I applaud the graduates today for taking a much more direct route to your degrees. [More laughter] For my part, I'm just happy that the *Crimson* has called me 'Harvard's most successful dropout.' I guess that makes me valedictorian of my own special class...I did the best of everyone who failed." Gates' opening remarks set a lighthearted tone for a somewhat serious and daunting message. Opening with humor is a good way to establish rapport with your audience and get their attention.

continued

• *Personal anecdotes.* At various points in the speech, Gates stays connected with his listeners by relating personal experiences. "I remember going to Davos some years back and sitting on a global health panel that was discussing ways to save millions of lives. Millions! Think of the thrill of saving just one person's life—then multiply that by millions. Yet this was the most boring panel I've ever been on—ever. So boring even I couldn't bear it." To further establish his credibility, Gates' stories help show that even when in a business setting, his thoughts are constantly on the humanitarian issues.

In an appeal to the ethics and morality of his audience, he says, "I love getting people excited about software—but why can't we generate even more excitement for saving lives?" Gates' focus here on worldwide socioeconomic issues tugs at their conscience. Humor and anecdotes are good ways to get the audience to pay attention, but Gates wants to make sure his message is heard in the correct mood. By bringing attention to the fact that today's information technology gives modern graduates plenty of knowledge about world problems, Gates hopes to influence the graduates to act. "We asked, 'How could the world let these children die?' The answer is simple, and harsh: The market did not reward saving the lives of these children, and governments did not subsidize it. So the children died because their mothers and their fathers had no power in the market and no voice in the system. But you and I have both."

Ultimately, the Harvard graduates had to decide for themselves whether to act on his words, but there can be no question that Gates used the right combination of speaking techniques to create a moving speech with a poignant message.

Questions: In addition to influencing graduates to change the world, what ways can commencement speeches be used? Did Gates use the right speech for the occasion, or was there another, more suitable topic for a commencement address?

Advancing Your Career

Not only is learning to speak in public personally satisfying and beneficial to society, but it can also advance your career. The National Association of Colleges and Employers conducts a survey of employers each year about the qualities/skills employers look for in new graduates. The latest NACE survey (Job Outlook 2010), which rates the most sought-after skills in new hires, reports that **communication skills** (speaking and writing) topped the list again, as it does year after year (see Table 1.1 for the top 21 skills). In addition, this same NACE survey found that almost 50 percent of employers listed communication skills as the quality "most lacking" in new college graduates (Figure 36, p. 24).

Although most of us assume that executives in large corporations such as Microsoft and General Electric are expected to give speeches, we overlook the fact that smaller businesses also need employees who are skilled in public speaking. For example, salespeople and accountants must present their products to customers. Even some assembly-line workers participate in decision making and formally present group ideas to management. The fact is, no matter what job you choose, you will need the speaking skills discussed throughout this book. As Jennifer, a public speaking student, said:

> When asked the first day of class why I took this class, my answer was because my company required it. Now I can honestly say that I am really glad I took it. I learned so much—I have more confidence, I am more comfortable speaking in front of an audience, and I think these new skills will be a great advantage at work.

Speakers Bureaus Many organizations have their own speakers bureau, which they use as a public-relations tool or as a way to spread their message. A **speakers bureau** is made up of employees who have expertise in some aspect of the company and are willing to share it with interested groups. For example, the National Oceanic and Atmospheric Administration posted this comment about their speakers bureau on their website **externalaffairs.noaa.gov/speakers.html**:

Table 1.1   Employers Rate Importance of Specific Qualities/Skills

Qualities	Rating (on 5-point scale)
Communication skills	4.7
Strong work ethic	4.6
Initiative	4.5
Interpersonal skills	4.5
Motivation/Initiative	4.5
Problem-solving skills	4.5
Teamwork skills	4.5
Analytical skills	4.4
Flexibility/Adaptability	4.3
Computer skills	4.2
Detail-oriented	4.1
Leadership skills	4.1
Technical skills	4.1
Organizational skills	4.0
Self-confidence	3.9
Tactfulness	3.8
Friendly/Outgoing personality	3.7
Creativity	3.6
Strategic planning skills	3.3
Entrepreneurial skills/Risk-taker	3.2
Sense of humor	3.0

Source: From Figure 34: Employers rate the importance of candidate skills/qualities (November 2009, p. 23). *Job Outlook 2010 NACE Research.* National Association of Colleges & Employers, **jobweb.com**.

The NOAA Speakers Bureau is composed of many of our top scientists, engineers, policy specialists and others who represent the agency at external events around the country. Each year, we provide speakers and make presentations to thousands of organizations (About, 2010).

Lockheed Martin, Dow Chemical, NASA, the United States military, and most colleges and universities are a few of the organizations that communicate with the public through speakers bureaus. Unless you remain in an entry-level job your entire career, your chances of needing to speak increase each time you are promoted—so you might as well get ready. Take, for example, a comment make by Mike Mullane in his book, *Riding Rockets: The Outrageous Tales of a Space Shuttle Astronaut* (2007):

With the astronaut title came two duties few of us had ever performed in our past careers: giving public speeches and press interviews. While NASA didn't force astronauts onto the speaking circuit, they did expect everybody to voluntarily take about a dozen trips a year to represent the agency at the head tables of America. The astronaut office received hundreds of requests a month for speakers, so there were plenty of events to pick from (p. 80).

Oral Communication Skills If you still aren't convinced that public speaking will be important in your particular career, consult Google, InfoTrac College

Edition, or one of the periodical guides or databases in your college library and look for articles written by people in your profession about oral communication skills. For example, a brief search for engineering articles found the following information:

- A survey of electrical engineers conducted by Vest et al. (1996) found that most engineers spend more than half of each day communicating. Discussing this study, Tenoper & King (2004) noted that 1/3 of the engineers surveyed reported taking a public speaking course while in college.

- These results match a more recent survey which found that over 50 percent of the engineers listed public speaking as the most important oral communication skill for success—more important than meetings, interpersonal communication, training, or selling (Darling & Dannels, 2003).

- An engineering task-force study ranked oral communication skills second in importance after problem-recognition/solution skills and more important than technical skills (Evans et al., 1993).

- The Accreditation Board for Engineering and Technology (**abet.org**) includes communication skills (including speaking) as a standard for evaluating college engineering programs in the United States (*2010–2011 Criteria, 2009*, p. 2). Graduates must be able to "plan, organize, prepare, and deliver effective technical reports in written, oral, and other formats appropriate to the discipline and goals of the program" (p. 2).

- Herb Flink, an engineer with 40 years of experience and author of *Tell It Like It Is: Essential Communication Skills for Engineers* (2007) made this observation:

    . . . communicating technical information is certainly a professional requirement of any engineer's job. In the end, the engineer's ability to communicate successfully can make or break his or her career and have a significant impact on the company's culture as well as its reputation and sales (p. 48).

Learning to speak was certainly a benefit for one engineer who enrolled in a six-week public speaking seminar I taught through the training department at Bell Helicopter Textron. Although reluctant at first, less than two months later she was promoted to senior engineer because, as her boss stated, her presentations were "so professional."

Although you may not yet feel comfortable giving formal speeches, you most likely already speak informally fairly often—in the classroom, in clubs or organizations, and at work. So, you already have many of the skills necessary for successful public speaking—you just need to polish them.

Active Critical Thinking

To think further about the importance of oral communication, complete the following:

- Check current job ads for engineering and at least two other careers that interest you personally. How often do you see the requirement "excellent written and oral communication skills"?

- Summarize a past opportunity that you missed due to lack of oral communication skills, and discuss one specific way that public speaking skills will likely benefit your future life.

The Right Speech for the Occasion

Now that you have an idea of some of the benefits of a course in public speaking, let's take a look at the types of speeches you may be asked to give—whether in class, at work, or in your community. There are three basic categories of presentations: informative, persuasive, and special occasion.

Informative Versus Persuasive Speeches

If your intent is simply to make listeners aware of a subject or to present some new ideas or information, your presentation is an informative one. In other words, **informative speeches** promote understanding of an idea or convey a body of related facts. They can also demonstrate how to do or make something. Examples of topics for informative speeches include the following:

- Performing the Heimlich maneuver.
- The effects of stress on your body
- The growth of YouTube and Twitter.
- New ways to prevent and handle oil spills in deep-ocean drilling.
- The vanishing honeybees.

By contrast, **persuasive speeches** seek to influence beliefs, choices, or opinions. Topics for persuasive speeches may include the following examples:

- It should be illegal to sell K2, synthetic marijuana, in hookah bars.
- City and county libraries are the surest avenue for maintaining our democracy.
- On-campus parking lots should be expanded.
- Daily exercise is necessary for health.

You need to determine whether your speech is informative or persuasive before you begin preparing it, because the two types require different approaches. Nevertheless, only a thin line separates informative and persuasive presentations. Persuasive presentations must inform as well as persuade. How can speakers persuade listeners unless they are informed of the facts? In the same way, many informative presentations indirectly persuade listeners to take action. For example, an informative speech may be so interesting or enlightening that listeners decide to follow up on the information or make some change in their lives, even though the speaker only intended to inform. → *See Chapters 12 and 13 for more on informative and persuasive speaking.*

Special Occasion Speeches

Special occasion speeches give a sense of distinction to important events in our lives. We normally think of special occasion speeches as those given at weddings, company award ceremonies, and funerals. For example, Sandra Bullock's acceptance speech for Best Actress (*The Blind Side*) during the 2010 Academy Awards, President Reagan's eulogy for the victims of the *Challenger* explosion, and Mayor Giuliani's speech to New Yorkers after the September 11 terrorist attacks are all examples of special occasion speeches. If you are called on to introduce a new student to the class, toast your softball team's victory, or pay tribute to a retiring professor, these are also special occasion speeches. → *See Chapter 14 to learn more about the special occasion speeches you are most likely to give.*

To think further about the three types of presentations, complete the following:

- List two topics that would make good informative speeches, two topics that would make good persuasive speeches, and two topics that would be good for special occasion speeches.
- Exchange your lists of topics with another person. Read the other's topics, putting a check by each that is labeled correctly or writing the correct type by any that seem incorrect.

The Communication Process and the Public Speaker

There is more to giving a speech than selecting a topic and planning content—you have to communicate with your audience. Therefore, the best speakers are those who understand the communication process. Although you may have studied communication in another course—English, perhaps—you probably have not viewed communication from a public speaking perspective. By understanding the communication process, you will be able to better communicate with your listeners.

The *Oxford English Dictionary* lists the Latin root of *communicate* as *communicare,* which means "to make common to many, share." According to this definition, when people communicate, they express their ideas and feelings in a way that is understandable (common) to other people. Therefore, **communication** is a process in which people share thoughts, ideas, and feelings in understandable ways. The model in Figure 1.1 shows the basic elements of the communication process: speaker/listeners, stimulus and motivation, message, encoding and decoding, codes, feedback, environment, and noise. Let's look at each of these elements to see how they relate to your speaking success.

Speaker/Listeners

Keep in mind that even though the **speaker** is generally considered to be the sender of the message and the **listener** to be the receiver, both are simultaneously sending and receiving throughout the speech. As audience members listen, they are

Figure 1.1

Basic Model of Communication

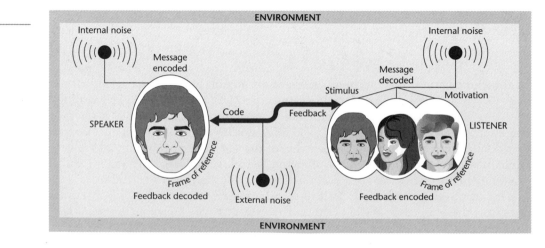

sending messages through laughter, frowns, bored looks, or sometimes questions. Similarly, while you are speaking, you are also receiving audience responses and adjusting your speech as needed. Adjustments might include speaking louder, giving a more detailed explanation, showing a visual aid you had originally planned to omit, or adding another example. → *Being able to interpret your audience's nonverbal cues is so important to speaking success that additional discussions are included in Chapters 3 and 8.*

Stimulus and Motivation

If you expect your audience to pay attention, they must be sufficiently stimulated and motivated. A **stimulus** triggers and directs attention to your topic; **motivation** provides a personal benefit that ensures continued audience attention. To illustrate, think about how many times an instructor has asked a question in class, and even though you thought you knew the answer—that is, you were stimulated—you did not respond. Perhaps you were not sufficiently motivated—that is, you saw no personal benefit in answering. Or perhaps you saw a greater benefit in not answering—you were afraid of being criticized by the professor or looking foolish by risking a wrong answer. Of course, if you knew that the professor graded on class participation, your motivation to answer would probably be greater.

Similarly, an audience must be stimulated and then motivated to listen. Just because audience members are looking at you doesn't mean they are paying attention. They may be preoccupied with problems at home or work (internal stimulus) or be distracted by a person or object (external stimulus), such as the good-looking person sitting nearby. As a speaker, you must provide the stimulus that grabs your audience's attention and focuses it on your topic. At the same time, you need to motivate audience members to continue listening by showing them how your presentation will be of value to them. Will your speech be entertaining? Will it help listeners save money, look and feel healthier, or enjoy life more? → *See Chapter 3 for more specific information about stimulus and motivation.*

Message Encoding and Decoding

The process of putting your message into a form that your specific audience will understand is called **encoding.** It includes organization of content, language choice, volume, tone of voice, facial expressions, and gestures, to name a few. Careful analysis of your audience is important for effective encoding. When your listeners pick up your message, they try to determine exactly what you mean. This process of interpreting meaning is called **decoding.**

Encoding and decoding are responsible for many of the misunderstandings that occur between speakers and listeners. As a speaker, you use your own **frame of reference**—your experiences and background—to encode messages. Your listeners, however, use their own frames of reference to decode those messages. Because our frames of reference include our educational background, race, gender, cultural background, hometown, parents, attitudes, personality, and past experiences, no two of us have exactly the same frame of reference.

AP Photo

If this American coach were visiting Australia or Germany, the audience would view his A-OK gesture as obscene.

Speakers and audience members have particular difficulty interpreting each other's messages when there are cultural differences, as illustrated in the following examples:

- The A-OK gesture that speakers in the United States make by forming a circle with thumb and forefinger has different meanings in other countries. In France it means zero or worthless; in Australia, Brazil, and Germany, it is an obscene gesture (Axtell, 1998, p. 47).

- Getting right to the point, which is generally seen as being honest and efficient in the United States, may be seen as being pushy by people from Asian countries, such as China, Korea, and Japan, as well as many Arab countries. In these countries, slowly working up to the point is preferred (Munter, 1993, p. 74).

- When audience members nod their heads in Bulgaria, they mean no, not yes (Munter, p. 76).

International marketing can be especially difficult across cultures:

- Allstate Insurance's commercial "You're in good hands with Allstate" shows two hands held out. However, in Germany and several other countries, instead of conveying a sense of security, the hands signify begging (Leaper, 1999, pp. 33–36).

- A toothpaste commercial that promises white teeth may be unsuitable for parts of Southeast Asia, where black teeth, caused by chewing betel nuts, is a sign of higher social status (Lamb et al., 2004, p. 120).

- Car commercials have had more than their share of problems (Javed, 1993): the Chevette by Chevrolet (*chevette* means horse in France); the Nova by General Motors (*no va* means no go in Spanish-speaking countries); and the Silver Mist by Rolls-Royce (*mist* is the colloquial expression for manure in Germany).

Different cultures obviously have frame-of-reference differences. Consider the differing values of citizens from the United States, Japan, and Arab countries reported in Figure 1.2. Compare these value differences with the individualistic/ collectivistic and low context/high context cultures discussed in Chapter 3.

To minimize encoding/decoding problems, keep the audience's frames of reference in mind. Try to anticipate possible misunderstandings and, by carefully choosing your words and examples, avoid many potential problems.

Figure 1.2

The Top 10 Cultural Values of Citizens from the United States, Japan, and Arab Countries

Differences in Cultural Values

Citizens from the United States	Citizens from Japan	Citizens from Arab countries
1. Freedom	1. Belonging	1. Family security
2. Independence	2. Group harmony	2. Family harmony
3. Self-reliance	3. Collectiveness	3. Parental guidance
4. Equality	4. Age/Seniority	4. Age
5. Individualism	5. Group consensus	5. Authority
6. Competition	6. Cooperation	6. Compromise
7. Efficiency	7. Quality	7. Devotion
8. Time	8. Patience	8. Patience
9. Directness	9. Indirectness	9. Indirectness
10. Openness	10. Go-between	10. Hospitality

Verbal, Visual, and Vocal Codes

The messages conveyed to your audience consist of symbols carried by light waves and sound waves. Each time you speak to an audience in person, three communication codes carry your messages: (1) the **verbal code,** which includes spoken and written words; (2) the **visual code,** which includes personal appearance, facial expression, eye contact, and visual aids; and (3) the **vocal code,** which includes tone of voice, volume, pitch, rate, emphasis, and vocal quality. Face-to-face and televised communications use all three codes, messages sent by telephone and radio use only two codes (the visual code is missing), and written messages (such as brochures and e-mail) contain only the verbal code. To take the place of vocal and visual codes, e-mail, blog, and chat-room users have developed a type of shorthand or abbreviations as well as **emoticons**—keyboard symbols that resemble facial expressions—such as LOL for laughing out loud or ;-) for a wink.

The difference between the verbal, visual, and vocal codes can be illustrated in the following example. Suppose you have purchased a new outfit for a special occasion. As the occasion draws nearer, however, you begin to wonder if the outfit is appropriate, and you ask a friend for advice. When the friend responds, "It looks great on you!" do you breathe a sigh of relief at the words? Or do you look closely at your friend's facial expression and listen carefully to the tone of voice for any indication that your friend may be insincere? For example, a slight raise of the eyebrows and a brief pause after the word *great* could reverse the meaning of the comment. Studies have found that when adults attempt to determine the meaning of a statement, they rely more on vocal and visual cues than they do on the actual words spoken (Archer & Akert, 1977; Burgoon & Hoobler, 2002; Thompson et al., 1998). Unfortunately, too many speakers think that the only important code is the verbal one and tend to overlook the other two. Effective speakers make sure they send the same powerful message by all three codes. → *See Chapter 3, page 61, for more specific information about codes.*

Feedback

When you evaluate your own speaking behavior, when you ask a friend to give an opinion about a practice speech, or when audience members respond to your presentation, you are experiencing feedback. **Feedback** is verbal, visual, and vocal responses to messages. Not only is feedback helpful for *self-monitoring* (evaluating and modifying your behavior until it meets your expectations), but it is the only way you can know whether listeners have interpreted your message the way you intended it to be interpreted. Usually feedback from an audience is visual (such as facial expressions or posture) or vocal (such as a collective sigh, laughter, or groans). Occasionally a listener will make a verbal comment or ask a question. Without feedback, you don't know whether your message has been interpreted correctly. Therefore, as a speaker, you want to pay close attention to the feedback from your audience.

Design Pics Inc/PhotoLibrary

What does the feedback from this audience tell you about the speaker?

Environment/Context

In public speaking situations, the context in which the presentation occurs usually refers to the **environment**—the time, place, and physical and social surroundings (Holm, 1981). A speech during dinnertime (when people wish they were eating) or right after lunch (when they might be feeling groggy) will probably be less successful than one given earlier in the morning or later in the evening. The size of the room, the brightness of the lights, the room temperature, and the comfort and arrangement of chairs can also affect the success of a speech. For example, 40 people crowded into a small conference room gives the impression that the speaker must be really good to attract such a crowd, but the same 40 people scattered in an auditorium gives the impression that the speaker must not be very compelling. An effective speaker plans and controls the environment as much as possible.

→ *Adapting visual aids to various speaking environments is discussed in Chapter 10.*

Noise

Anything that interferes with communication by distorting or blocking the message is called noise. **External noise** includes distractions in the environment, such as people talking, lighting that is too bright or too dim, and even improper grammar or poor delivery by the speaker. **Internal noise** refers to distractions within the listener, such as headaches, preoccupation with problems, or lack of knowledge about the topic. Internal noise can also affect you as a speaker. If you are tired from studying too late the night before or if you are worried about your speech, you are experiencing internal noise. When possible, select speaking environments that are relatively free of external noises, and provide stimulus and motivation to divert your audience's attention from their internal noises.

As you can see, successful communication involves more than just talking and listening—it's hard work and requires careful preparation. However, the reward for all the work and preparation is an enthusiastic, powerful speech. Successful speakers:

- Stimulate and motivate their listeners.
- Encode their presentations for each audience by being aware of frame-of-reference and cultural differences.
- Try to make their visual and vocal codes reinforce their verbal messages.
- Pay careful attention to audience feedback.
- Control the speaking environment and noise factors as much as possible.

Active Critical Thinking

To think further about the communication process, select one of the basic elements included in Figure 1.1 on page 10 that gives you the most difficulty (e.g., frame-of-reference differences), and complete the following):

- Discuss why the element causes you problems, and give a personal example to illustrate it.
- Suggest at least one solution that might solve your problem and how you plan to use it.

In addition to preparing a speech that communicates with your audience, you also have the obligation of being an ethical speaker.

Ethics: The Public Speaker's Obligation

Because speakers can influence other people, they must be **ethical speakers**—that is, they must research information carefully, present only truthful information, and give credit for all ideas and words that come from someone else. This is a serious obligation that is not always met. In fact, a May 2010 Gallup poll found that 76 percent of Americans say "moral values in the United States are getting worse" (Jones, 2010). More specifically, the American public is fairly skeptical about the honesty and ethics of politicians and many other professional people (Saad, 2009). For example, since 1976, Gallup pollsters have asked this question: "How would you rate the honesty and ethical standards of people in these different fields—very high, high, average, low, or very low?" Based on the most recent (December 2010) data available at the time this edition went to press (see Table 1.2), nurses were again at the top with 81 percent; next, scoring in the 70 or 60 percent range, were druggists, pharmacists, and medical doctors; while police officers and clergy scored in the 50 percent range. Notice that bankers, lawyers, and business executives scored quite low in the 2010 poll; their ethical standards were judged to be only slightly higher than those rated at the very bottom—congresspeople, advertising practitioners, and car salespeople. Apparently the American public has little faith in the honesty or ethics of its professionals. Where does your chosen profession stand (see poll results in Table 1.2)?

Table 1.2 Percentages of Respondents Rating Each Profession as Having "High" or "Very High" Ethical Standards

Profession	Rating (percentage)							
	2003	2004	2005	2006	2007	2008	2009	2010
Nurses	83	79	82	84	79	84	83	81
Druggists, pharmacists	67	72	67	73	67	70	66	71
Medical doctors	68	67	65	69	63	64	65	66
Police officers	59	60	61	54	53	56	63	57
Engineers	59	—	—	61	—	—	62	—
Dentists	61	—	—	62	—	—	57	—
College professors	59	—	64	58	—	—	54	—
Clergy	56	56	54	58	53	56	50	53
Bankers	35	36	41	37	35	23	19	23
Accountants	—	—	39	—	35	38	—	—
Journalists	25	—	28	26	26	25	23	—
Real estate agents	—	—	20	—	19	17	—	—
Lawyers	16	18	18	18	15	18	13	17
Business executives	18	20	16	18	14	12	12	15
Stockbrokers	15	—	16	17	12	12	9	—
Senators	20	—	16	15	—	—	11	—
Congresspeople	17	20	14	14	9	12	9	9
Insurance salespeople	12	—	—	13	—	—	10	—
Advertising practitioners	12	10	11	11	9	10	11	11
Car salespeople	7	9	8	7	5	7	6	7

Source: Adapted from Lydia Saad (Dec. 5, 2006), "Nurses Top List of Most Honest and Ethical Professions," Jeffrey M. Jones (Dec. 4, 2007), "Effects of Year's Scandals Evident in Honesty and Ethics Ratings," Lydia Saad (Dec. 9, 2009), "Honesty and Ethics Poll Finds Congress' Image Tarnished," and Jeffery M. Jones (Dec. 3, 2010), "Nurses Top Honesty and Ethics List for the 11th Year," *The Gallup Poll Tuesday Briefing Online*, **galluppoll.com**. NOTE: the poll comes out in December of each year.

Examples and Costs of Unethical Behavior

Unfortunately, we don't have to look too far to find cases that may have led to this loss of public confidence. The news is full of unethical and scandalous behavior of politicians, corporate personnel, researchers, journalists, media stars, educators, students, and even clergy. Let's look at a few recent cases:

Case 1: In 2006, an investigation committee appointed by the dean of the Engineering School at Ohio University reported that "37 former graduate students in engineering had plagiarized portions of their theses or dissertations" and that the plagiarism, which occurred over a span of 20 years, was both "rampant" and "flagrant" (Wasley, 2006). The committee recommended the following measures (Wasley, 2006; Bartlett, 2006):

- Dismissal of the chair of the Mechanical Engineering Department.

- Dismissal of a professor "who had approved 11 plagiarized theses."

- Two years probation for a third professor involved with five plagiarized theses.

- Removal of all "plagiarized documents" from the library.

- Punishment of the authors of the plagiarized documents—they would be required to re-defend their work. (The dean announced that any of these past students who did not respond in writing within nine months would have their degrees revoked.)

Case 2: In April 2007, an anonymous tip was received by the Massachusetts Institute of Technology that its admissions dean, Marilee Jones, had lied on her resume way back in 1979 (Winstein & Golden, 2007). Jones, a board member of the National Association for College Admission Counseling, coauthor of *Less Stress, More Success: A New Approach to Guiding Your Teen Through College Admissions and Beyond,* and a well-respected educator, would often sign her admission letters to students with "your mom away from mom" (p. B1). Jones's resume states that she has a bachelor's and a master's degree from Rensselaer Polytechnic Institute as well as a degree from Albany Medical College. In fact, she has no degrees and attended college part-time for only one year. According to MIT Chancellor Phillip Clay: "We take integrity very seriously, and it was on that basis that as soon as we determined that these facts [on her resume] were not true we dismissed her even though she has done a great job" (p. B2).

Dean of Admissions at Massachusetts Institute of Technology, Marilee Jones, was dismissed in April 2007 when it was discovered that she had lied on her resume when first hired in 1979 in a junior position.

AP Photo/Chitose Suzuki

Case 3: Also in 2007, CBS and Katie Couric, anchor for the CBS Evening News, found themselves in an unpleasant ethical situation. Each broadcast includes a brief segment called "Katie Couric's Notebook," where she gives a personal look at a problem of interest to her listeners (the Notebook is also available in video format on the CBS website and on Couric's blog). On April 4, her Notebook comments began with "Hi, everyone. I still remember when I got my first library card" (Roberts,

2007). Although that may be true, this comment and many others matched closely or were verbatim from a piece in the *Wall Street Journal* by Jeffrey Zaslow. Once this was brought to CBS's attention, they apologized to Zaslow, removed the entry from their website and blog, fired the Notebook's producer, and posted this message: "Much of the material in the 'Notebook' came from Mr. Zaslow, and we should have acknowledged that at the top of our piece. We offer our sincere apologies for the omission" (Baram, 2007). Although the *Wall Street Journal* said they were "happy with the way this was resolved" (Roberts, 2007), blogs like The Hairy Beast on **wordpress.com** were not so kind to Couric, questioning why she "presented an essay on her blog as her own, yet written by another?" and saying that "These anchor blogs are a fraud and so is Katie" (hairybeast, 2007, April 11).

Not only has each of these cases further eroded public confidence in politicians, professionals, and the media and deprived the country of possible role models, but the people involved have seen an end to their dreams or seen their dreams greatly diminished.

Exaggeration, Distortion, and Plagiarism

As these examples illustrate, to be an ethical speaker you must be careful to tell only the truth, without exaggeration or distortion. Listeners expect the truth from public speakers. Unfortunately, when speakers feel pressured or insecure, they may abandon ethical standards and exaggerate or distort the facts. **Exaggeration** is overstating or presenting facts as more important than they are; **distortion** is misrepresenting or twisting facts or stating that they are true when they are only partially true. Both exaggeration and distortion are forms of lying and as such are unethical. As a public speaker, you must keep in mind that exaggeration and distortion are only half a step away from overt lying.

In addition to doing careful research and reporting only the truth, you must be careful not to plagiarize. **Plagiarism** is using the ideas of others (whether paraphrased or word for word) without giving them credit. If you read an article or see a TV program and then use the information from it in your speech without citing the source, you are plagiarizing—even if you paraphrase the content. Using materials obtained from the Internet without giving credit is also plagiarism. A senior pastor of a church in Keene, New Hampshire, took parts of sermons and some entire sermons from the Internet without giving credit (Pastor Resigns, 2004). As a result, his congregation lost trust in him and he resigned. A North Carolina school board chairman used a large part of a speech he found on the Internet in his 2004 commencement address, thinking that since the speech was not attributed to anyone, it was fine to use it. However, the speech was given by Donna Shalala in 1998 when she was U.S. Secretary of Health and Human Services (Manzo, 2004). The board chair resigned his position. Plagiarism is also serious for students, as indicated in the case of the Ohio University engineering students discussed earlier. A college student who plagiarizes any part of a speech will receive a failing grade for the speech and maybe for the course, and may even be expelled from school.

Plagiarism and Technology

The Internet can be a wonderful place to find valuable help and information for your speeches. For example, a brief search of "speech writing" using Google found over 5.3 million hits. Among these hits were sites giving advice on finding topics, making speeches, finding quotes, and overcoming anxiety, as well as sites (such as

Great American Speeches and the History Channel) that include text, audio, and video of speeches by famous people.

Unfortunately, when it comes to preparing a speech, the Internet has also created some serious problems. First, because it is so easy to copy/paste information directly from articles into a speech or paper, some students either unintentionally or deliberately use information without citing its source. A study of approximately 700 undergraduates from nine colleges found that 8 percent reported that they often or very frequently copy/paste information from the Internet without citing sources; however, these same students estimated that 50.4 percent of their peers fail to cite sources (Scanlon & Neumann, 2002). ➜ *Chapter 5 discusses how to conduct your research to avoid accidental plagiarism.*

The second problem posed by the Internet relates to the many websites willing to sell both canned and custom speeches for the classroom (as well as for weddings, birthdays, graduations, campaigns, after dinner, and business meetings). As your professor knows, beginning speakers are often tempted to go online and buy their speeches from one of these sites. Unless you plan to purchase a speech as a model only, you are on dangerous ethical ground—plagiarism is a serious offense. It is better to use the many sample speeches in this text and its website to give you ideas. If your professor has a doubt about your speech, there are several online sites he or she can use to check your work for plagiarism. For example, **turnitin.com** reports plagiarism from both print and Internet sources. Therefore, if you are tempted to buy your speeches from online speech writers (or even fraternity/sorority files or friends), don't! You already know the reasons:

- It's unethical to pass off someone else's work as your own.

- The consequences of plagiarism can be severe and may haunt you later in life as well.

- You won't learn the necessary skills for successful speech preparation—although the chances are better than 90 percent that you will need these skills in the future. In fact, your educational and business success may depend on your knowledge of these skills.

- Delivering a speech you didn't write is very difficult—especially if you are already nervous. Your professor is no fool! In fact, your professor has already heard many of these speeches and will recognize them for what they are.

- You will be wasting money and taking a great risk—when the skills necessary to write your own quality speeches are in your text, in your professor's lectures, and in your own mind and experience.

- Don't fall into the plagiarism trap: Prepare your own speeches!

Classroom Ethics

In one of my public speaking classes, I asked students to come up with a code of ethics acceptable to everyone in the class. One student didn't see why everyone was so hung up on ethics when using facts and statistics. After all, he said, speaking is entertainment. Why shouldn't he make up information if it made the speech more entertaining? Another student said that in a previous speech class, she had fabricated a detailed account of her grandmother dying from cancer as an attention-getter. The illustration had touched her audience; several people even had tears in their eyes. The student felt that if she had used a hypothetical example, the

Use a database like InfoTrac College Edition, CQ Researcher, or EBSCOhost to further investigate the costs of unethical acts. Do a keyword search on *plagiarism, cheating,* or *lies* and look for at least three relevant articles. Also, do a keyword search using *ethical communicators* to find an article in *Communication World* by Dilenschneider & Salak. Prepare a brief review of these articles to share with your class. NOTE: If a Pass Code to InfoTrac College Edition came bundled with your text, you can access InfoTrac through your Online Resources for *Essentials of Public Speaking.*

Table 1.3 Code of Ethics for Public Speaking Class (Partial List)

Speaker	Audience
1. Always show up when scheduled to speak.	1. Support speaker—no homework or daydreaming.
2. Show respect by being prepared.	2. Be on time; take job as audience evaluator seriously.
3. Respect audience opinions.	3. Respect speaker's opinions.
4. Be honest—no plagiarism, exaggeration, or distortion of facts or visuals. Cite sources.	4. Be open-minded; don't take offense during speeches or class discussions.
5. Limit use of Internet sources.	5. Don't distract speaker in any way.
6. Carefully research all sides of topic.	6. Give honest, tactful critiques, including strengths and weaknesses.

speech would not have been as moving or effective. She admitted, however, that her audience was upset and felt manipulated when they realized she had lied about her grandmother. As you can imagine, a lively discussion followed. The discussion ended with the class agreeing that although there is an entertaining element to speaking and that the desire to touch an audience is strong, the end does not justify the means. Several of the students also said that they would have trouble trusting or respecting a classmate who fabricated or plagiarized information in a speech. See Table 1.3 for a partial code-of-ethics list that the class approved. What would you add to the list?

Keep in mind that ethical behavior in the classroom is no different than ethical behavior in the office. What you practice now is what you will feel comfortable doing in the real world. I urge you to think seriously about developing your own personal **code of ethics** during this course. Don't wait until an ethical problem arises—you may not be prepared to handle the situation. The following advice is offered by Dennis A. Gioia (1992), a bureaucrat involved in Ford's decision not to recall the Pinto even though they knew its gas tank could burst into flames in rear-end collisions at speeds as low as 25 miles per hour:

> . . . develop your ethical base now! Too many people do not give serious attention to assessing and articulating their own values. People simply do not know what they stand for because they haven't thought about it seriously . . . be prepared to face critical responsibility at a relatively young age, as I did. You need to know what your values are . . . so that you can know how to make a good decision. Before you do that, you need to articulate and affirm your values now, before you enter the fray. I wasn't really ready. Are you? (Trevino & Nelson, 2004, pp. 131–132)

Active Critical Thinking

To think further about communication and ethics, complete the following:

- Find a magazine or billboard ad campaign. Visually, what is the ad campaign communicating? Does the ad violate any standards of ethics? If so, how? Share your findings with others.

- If you were to write out a personal code of ethics, what two things would definitely be in it? Why do you consider them to be so important?

Sample Student Speech: "Closet Artifacts" by Monica E. Wolfe

In the following sample speech, student Monica Wolfe discusses how her collection of T-shirts reflects important events in her life. Her assignment specified a two- to three-minute speech on one or more artifacts that, if found by an archaeologist in the future, would reveal the most about her. This speech, which was the first speech Monica gave to her public speaking class, was transcribed from the videotape filmed in class. Chapters 4, 8, 11, 12, 13, and 14 of this text also feature sample student speeches. ➔ *See the Quick Start Guide for a discussion of the artifact speech and other types of introductory speeches.*

Sample Introductory Speech

CLOSET ARTIFACTS

by Monica E. Wolfe

In this box are the archaeological ruins of my closet. As my very southern mother says, "You can tell a lot about a lady by her closet." Although I don't think this is what she had in mind, I'm going to let the T-shirts in my closet tell you about me. My T-shirts will show how my life has changed from my first try at college to world travel as a flight attendant to settled married life and another go at college.

I was born and raised in Austin, Texas. I had never been anywhere but Austin, so of course I went to the University of Texas. I joined a sorority [*T-shirt*] and went for two years until they hounded me to say what my major was going to be, but I had no idea.

So I left and became a flight attendant for Continental Airlines [*T-shirt*]. While I was a flight attendant, I had a lot of great experiences. I went to Australia [*T-shirt*], which I loved—got to hug a koala bear. I went to Mexico [*T-shirt*] and all around the United States.

One of the best things about being a flight attendant was that on a trip I met this T-shirt [*T-shirt*]. His name is John, and he is from Newport Beach, California. This is pretty ragged [*T-shirt*] because it's his favorite T-shirt. John is a pilot—at the time for Continental

Sample Introductory Speech *(continued)*

Airlines as well, so we had the chance to work together and travel together.

On one of our trips we went to Hawaii [*T-shirt*], and while we were in Hawaii, we decided to combine our closet space and got married.

A few months after we got married, he decided to get a new job with American Airlines [*T-shirt*], and this is how we ended up in the Fort Worth/Dallas area [*Cowboy T-shirt*].

After we were here for about one year, we took another vacation to Ruidoso, New Mexico [*T-shirt*], and I taught him to ski, which was very interesting. We had a really good time.

When we got back from Ruidoso, I had to wear this shirt [*maternity T-shirt*]. I know it looks plain, but after nine months, I had this shirt [*T-shirt turned around to show baby T-shirt pinned on it*]. She is now two years old and the joy of our lives.

As you can see, the T-shirts found in the archaeological ruins of my closet tell a lot about my life. But this last shirt is the shirt that we all wear [*imaginary T-shirt held up*], because we are unsure of what it says or where we are going, but we hope that it will be as well worn as all of these [*imaginary T-shirt added to stack of other shirts*].

Summary

Throughout life you will have many opportunities to give speeches that can benefit your career, your self-esteem, and even society. There are three basic types of speeches:

- Informative speeches, which promote understanding of an idea, convey a body of related facts, or demonstrate how to do or make something.

- Persuasive speeches, which influence opinions or choices.

- Special occasion speeches, which are given at such events as weddings and award presentations.

To minimize misunderstandings between you and your audience, you need to pay particular attention to your and their frames of reference (background and experiences). Different frames of reference increase the probability that speakers and audience members will have difficulty interpreting one another's messages.

Consider the three types of communication codes—verbal, visual, vocal—as inseparable. Communication is greatly improved when speakers use all three codes effectively. Studies have found that when people attempt to determine the meaning of a statement, they rely more heavily on vocal and visual cues than on verbal cues. Be especially careful to avoid exaggeration, distortion, and plagiarism; all are unethical and may cause others to consider you untrustworthy.

Essentials of Public Speaking Online CourseMate

Use your Online Resources for *Essentials of Public Speaking* for quick access to the electronic study resources that accompany this chapter. The Online Resources feature the Test Your Knowledge Quiz on page 1, the PRCA–24 (Personal Report of Communication Apprehension) questionnaire described on page 3, access to InfoTrac College Edition, the Active Critical Thinking activities, the Personal Skill Building Activities, Collaborative Skill Building activities, a digital glossary, sample speeches, and review quizzes.

Key Terms

code of ethics 19	ethical speakers 15	persuasive speeches 9
communication 10	exaggeration 17	plagiarism 17
communication skills 6	external noise 14	rhetoric 2
decoding 11	feedback 13	speaker 10
deliberative speaking 2	forensic speaking 2	speakers bureau 6
distortion 17	frame of reference 11	special occasion
emoticons 13	informative speeches 9	speeches 9
encoding 11	internal noise 14	stimulus 11
environment 14	listener 10	verbal, visual, and
epideictic speaking 2	motivation 11	vocal codes 13

Personal Skill Building

CourseMate

1. If you haven't completed the PRCA–24 (Personal Report of Communication Apprehension) questionnaire accessed through your Online Resources for *Essentials of Public Speaking*, do so now and turn in your scores to your instructor. You will retake the questionnaire during the last week of class, compare your "before" and "after" scores, and analyze your progress. Scores will be kept confidential.

2. Make a list of the opportunities to give speeches that came your way in the past year (whether or not you accepted) through your community, your campus, your classes, your job, clubs or organizations (including religious ones), and volunteer work. If you spoke in any of these settings, what was the outcome? If you have declined speaking in public, why did you refuse? What do you feel are the three main reasons you have declined speaking opportunities? Be prepared to share your list and reasons in class.

Source: Personal Report of Communication Apprehension (PRCA-24), accessible through your Online Resources for Essentials of Public Speaking.

3. Select someone in your class whom you don't know personally. For 15 minutes or less, interview each other to find out all the normal information people usually share (for example, major and minor field of study, home state, marital status, and hobbies). In addition, find out something unusual or unique about each other. This could be something that is true today or something that happened years ago (for example, one of you is from a family of 10, fought in Iraq, or reads five books each week). When your interview time is up, use the information you have gathered to introduce one another to the class.

4. Select one of the types of beginning speeches described in the Quick Start Guide at the beginning of this text and prepare a 2- to 3-minute speech. Your instructor may wish you to prepare a brief outline to hand in the day you speak. Practice giving your talk several times, but do not memorize or read it—just speak as you would if talking to good friends.

5. Begin a list of speech topics to use during the course. Carry a notepad or a few note cards in your purse or wallet. When you think of, read about, or hear about a topic that interests you, write it down (along with the source when relevant). With this habit, you will be ready when topics are needed.

6. Check out the following websites. Use your Online Resources for *Essentials of Public Speaking* to access these sites.

   • Go to **ted.com/talks.** Click on the Global Issues tag on the left to narrow your search and watch videos of people using speech as a tool to make a difference.

- For the complete text of Reagan's Challenger eulogy, check out **reaganlibrary.com**'s "The Great Communicator" page.

- See if you agree with the six tips for enhancing your ethical obligation as a public speaker presented by **sideroad.com**. Click "Public Speaking" then "Ethics in Public Speaking,"

- Go to **www.schoolforchampions.com/speaking/character.htm**, and compare the suggestions on why a speaker should maintain character as a public speaker with the suggestions in this chapter.

- The ethics in various professions found in Table 1.3 are updated every year or two around December or February by the Gallup Organization at Princeton. To check for new ethics polls or video reports (as well as many other interesting polls), go to **galluppoll.com** and type "Honesty and Ethics Poll" in the site search box. Scroll until you locate a new ethics poll or video that is open to the public.

- Codes of ethics are very important. Here are two: First, check out the "NCA Credo for Ethical Communication" published by the National Communication Association, whose members exceed 7,500 from more than 20 countries. Go to their website at **natcom.org** and search for "NCA Credo." Second, look at the "Code of Professional Ethics" produced by the National Speakers Association, whose members include hundreds of professionals who give 20 or more paid speeches a year. Go to **nsaspeaker.org/ABOUTNSA/Education.aspx** and scroll down to Ethics.

Collaborative Skill Building

1. In groups of four or five, decide on a code of ethics for your class (see Table 1.3 for examples). If you are using InfoTrac College Edition, use it prior to the class discussion to locate at least two articles that focus on codes of ethics in current use. If a keyword search using "code of ethics" doesn't locate what you need, check for additional keywords by entering "ethics" as a subject guide search. All groups should present their codes of ethics to the class, making a complete list on the board. After combining and eliminating items through discussion, agree on a final list that will serve as a model for the class/group.

2. In small groups, create your own model of communication—be creative and draw your model out on flip-chart paper. Present your model to the class or other groups, mentioning any elements that were omitted (see page 10 for a summary of model elements) and any that you have added and why. Make sure that each person in the group has a chance to speak. If time allows, vote to select the best/most creative model.

3. In small groups, get to know each other by sharing answers to as many of the following questions as time allows:

   a. What is your major field of study and a career goal you have for the future?

   b. Where were you born and what is one really good memory you have about the town in which you were raised?

   c. What specific things about the course excite(s) you or worries you the most?

    d. What speeches have you given in the last year? Where would you rate yourself as a speaker using a scale of 1 (inexperienced) to 5 (experienced)?

    e. As a speaker, which is your brightest star: content, organization, visual aids, or delivery? Why?

    f. Other than making an "A" in the class, what two main goals do you hope to achieve by the end of the course?

Quiz Answers

Answers to Unit One Quiz on page 1: Test Your Knowledge About Public Speaking.

1. *False.* Although logic and supporting evidence are important in persuading others, research has indicated that these alone are not enough to sway most listeners. In fact, one study found that most audience members couldn't distinguish the logical arguments in a presentation from the illogical ones (Bettinghaus & Cody, 1997). For example, if the speaker used words and phrases that implied a logical progression of thought (such as "It is obvious that," "Therefore," and "As a result"), people judged the speech to be logical even if it was not. Moreover, when listeners favored the speaker's proposal and/or considered the speaker to be credible, they were likely to judge the speech as convincing. No matter how strong your logic and evidence may be, your most persuasive tool is to relate your arguments to the personal and organizational needs of your listeners. ➜ *Chapter 13 has more on methods of persuasion.*

2. *False.* Although good speakers may feel more positive about speaking than do inexperienced ones, every new situation causes a certain amount of "butterflies" for all speakers. Good speakers view this feeling as a sign that their body is gathering the additional energy needed for a dynamic speech; poor speakers see it as a sign that they are falling apart and are going to do a lousy job. Good speakers also know they will feel more confident if they are well prepared. Success is more likely when you have researched your audience, have carefully supported your main ideas for this particular audience, have prepared professional-looking visual aids, and have anticipated possible questions and objections. In general, the more you prepare and practice, the more confident you will be. ➜ *Chapter 2 offers more information on coping with speech anxiety.*

3. *False.* The role of visual aids may be one of the biggest misconceptions of all. Although you can give a speech without visual aids, research has indicated that we learn and remember more when we can "see" the speaker's ideas at the same time as we hear them. This is especially true for technical speeches—those that cover complicated information, such as "How a 747 Gets off the Ground" or "Three Football Plays Everyone Should Know." Visuals are so powerful that audience members are more likely to remember what they have seen than what they have heard. Make sure your visual aids are accurate and directly related to what you want the audience to remember. Use of visual aids is the rule, not the exception. ➜ *Chapter 10 focuses on how to develop and use visual aids.*

4. *False.* You don't have to be an expert to give an excellent talk on a subject. In fact, sometimes experts are so immersed in the subject matter that they have difficulty communicating to a general audience. In some cases you might arrange to have an expert available to answer technical questions, or you could refer technical questions to the appropriate person for a later response.

5. *False.* Although red is an attention-getting color, using it on visual aids has one big problem—some members of your audience may be color blind to reds and greens. Blue is a safer color for emphasizing points.

6. *True.* Although gender stereotypes are definitely waning, audiences unfortunately still generally consider male speakers more knowledgeable and credible than female speakers. A poll conducted by AdweekMedia and Harris Poll (Dolliver, 2010) found that 28 versus 7 percent of those polled said that a male voiceover would more likely sell them a car; 23 versus 7 percent said that a male voiceover would more likely sell them a computer.

7. *False.* Distributing handouts during a speech almost always ensures audience inattention. The distractions that are created as papers are passed around make it almost impossible to pay attention to the speaker, and audience members may begin reading and tune out the speaker. Unless listeners need the handout while you are talking, pass it out at the end of the speech.

8. *True.* Normally, the only time the speaker should sit down is if he or she is blocking the audience's view of visual aids. Standing gives speakers a better view of audience reactions and adds to their authority. If a speaker is seated, everyone appears to have equal status, and listeners may interact with one another rather than listen to the speaker. If they are argumentative, they are also more likely to argue with one another as well as with the speaker.

9. *False.* Colorful clothing and accessories are appropriate in some situations (for example, in the fashion industry), but many businesses prefer conservative colors and minimal accessories. Dress consultants advise the following: (1) Jackets and suits broadcast professionalism, and (2) darker jackets or suits convey more authority (Egodigwe, 2003; Greenleaf, 1998; Maysonave, 1999; Molloy, 1996). If your organization is more casual or you wish to downplay your authority, choose a lighter color or remove your jacket before or during the presentation. ➤ *Chapter 8 contains more information on delivery and appearance.*

10. *False.* Accomplished public speakers have learned the do's and don'ts of effective speaking through trial and error. There is nothing mysterious about this knowledge. Even someone who has never made a speech before can give an effective presentation simply by following the guidelines presented in this book.

2

Building Speaker Confidence

FLASH**BACK**

Isocrates, a Greek contemporary of Plato and Aristotle, is one of the prestigious ten Attic orators. However, he suffered from speaker anxiety and had a voice that wouldn't project. Even so, he founded the first permanent and financially successful school of rhetoric. For over 50 years his graduates became prominent citizens. Most scholars agree that his program of study and his philosophy of educating "the good man skilled in speaking" have greatly influenced education even to the present time (Conley, 1990, p. 20).

FLASH**FORWARD**

Today's speakers have something that Greek and Roman speakers did not—technology like computers, television, Internet, microphones, and PowerPoint software for making visual aids. Isocrates would certainly have found it easier to project his voice with today's technology. But the question is, for today's "good man skilled in speaking," *does technology make public speaking easier or more difficult, and does technology decrease or increase speaker anxiety?*

Learning Objectives

As you read Chapter 2,

- *Define* the terms *situational anxiety* and *trait anxiety,* and decide which type or types describes you best.
- *List* several specific tips for managing situational anxiety, and select a tip to try the next time you feel speaker anxiety.
- *Define* the term *positive imagery* (visualization), and *explain* why and how it helps manage trait anxiety.
- *List* and *describe* several other methods of managing anxiety that public speakers find helpful.

A 2001 GALLUP POLL FOUND THAT FEAR OF PUBLIC SPEAKING IS THE NUMBER TWO FEAR of Americans—only the fear of snakes is greater (Brewer, 2001). In fact, it's estimated that up to 95 percent of speakers in the U.S. experience some degree of anxiety (Richmond & McCroskey, 1998) and that 20 percent of students may experience severe public speaking anxiety (Robinson, 1997). If your goal is to become a confident speaker, Chapter 2 may be one of the most important chapters in this course for you.

Understanding Communicator Anxiety

Not all cultures experience the same level of communicator anxiety. For example, the Chinese in Taiwan and on the mainland experience more anxiety than do Americans (Hsu, 2004; Zhang et al., 1996), but Puerto Ricans are much less apprehensive than Americans as long as they are not asked to speak in English (McCroskey et al., 1985). In most cultures, including our own, if you experience a high level of anxiety in communication situations, you are at a great disadvantage compared to more confident people. People who feel comfortable expressing themselves are perceived as more competent, make a better impression during job interviews, and are more likely to be promoted to supervisory positions than are anxious people (Richmond & McCroskey, 1998).

The reason that speaker confidence makes a positive impression (whereas an anxious person causes a negative one) is because, when we speak, we are communicating in three ways—verbally, visually, and vocally. Our verbal message may be clear and well organized, but if we are nervous, listeners are more likely to focus on our negative vocal and visual cues (such as lack of eye contact, poor posture, hesitant delivery, and strained vocal quality). But when we are confident and our verbal, visual, and vocal signals are in harmony, we are more believable. According to Bert Decker, author of *You've Got to Be Believed to Be Heard*:

> Believability is an emotional quality.... If you don't believe in someone on an emotional level, little if any of what they have to say will get through. It will be screened out by your distrust, your anxiety, your irritation, or your indifference. Even if the facts and content are great by themselves, they are forever locked out because the person delivering them lacks believability (Decker & Denney, 1993, pp. 35–36).

Therefore, if we want people to believe us when we speak and we want to make positive impressions, we need to manage our anxieties. First, however, we need to know which type of anxiety we have.

There are two basic types of anxiety: situational and trait. You may have either one or both of these types of anxiety. **Situational anxiety**—often referred to as *state anxiety* (Booth-Butterfield & Booth-Butterfield, 1992; Motley, 1995)—is anxiety caused by factors in a specific situation (for example, speaking before a new audience or in front of the boss or being graded while speaking). **Trait anxiety** (Beatty et al., 1989; Daly & Friedrich, 1981) refers to the internal anxieties an individual brings to the speaking situation (for example, feelings of inadequacy in a group or fear of looking like a fool in front of others). In other words, situational anxiety is caused by a new or different situation, whereas trait anxiety is caused by internal feelings of the speaker that exist regardless of the situation. Your own anxiety may be situational, trait, or a combination of the two.

Situational Anxiety

Feeling nervous in a new communication situation is normal. Firing a troublesome employee, interviewing for a position, and presenting a controversial idea to your classmates are all situations that can trigger butterflies in the stomach. Any time you become anxious, afraid, or excited, your body gets ready for action by giving you a big shot of adrenaline; your heart rate is accelerated; extra oxygen is sent to the central nervous system, muscles, and heart; your eyes are dilated; blood-sugar levels increase; and perspiration is triggered.

As alarming as all that may sound, we should be glad for this extra boost of energy. Our bodies are preparing to deal with the extra demands of the new situation. The extra oxygen and sugar sent through the blood by the rapidly beating heart provide the energy necessary for clear thinking, quick reaction, and intense physical exertion; dilated pupils produce sharper vision; and perspiration flushes out excess wastes and cools the body (Bostrom, 1988, p. 57). Can you imagine athletes with absolutely no anxiety before a big game? Their performance would no doubt fall far short of expectations. Neither age nor experience seems to alleviate speaker anxiety. Well-known speakers who have acknowledged feeling nervous before new speaking situations include journalist Mike Wallace, former CEO Lee Iacocca, evangelist Billy Graham, and talk-show host Susan Powter. You can determine your level of situational anxiety from your score on the PRCA-24 (McCroskey, 1982) discussed in Chapter 1. A total score between 65 and 79 or a subscore between 18 and 23 indicates that you have situational anxiety.

Personal Assessment #2

If you have not yet taken **McCroskey's PRCA-24** (Personal Report of Communication Apprehension), *please stop reading and take it now.* You can access this survey through your Online Resources for *Essentials of Public Speaking*. This online survey will score automatically, and you can have the results e-mailed to you and your instructor.

CourseMate

Note that although the speakers mentioned above experienced situational anxiety, they still achieved speaking success. One key to their success may be that they learned to view the symptoms of situational anxiety as normal excitement necessary for dynamic communication. With this positive attitude, anxiety not only becomes manageable but usually disappears as the speech progresses. Poor communicators allow symptoms of situational anxiety to increase their fear. They view the symptoms as further indication that indeed they are poor speakers. As a result, their anxiety gets worse as they continue speaking.

Trait Anxiety

Whereas practically everyone experiences some degree of situational anxiety, fewer people experience trait anxiety, often referred to as *communication anxiety* or *apprehension*. Trait anxiety is a more personal, internal feeling about communication. You can determine your level of trait anxiety from your scores on the PRCA-24. A total score of 80 or above or any subscore of 24 or above indicates some trait anxiety.

The current view of trait anxiety is that it is both inborn and learned. If you have extremely high trait anxiety and it seems that nothing you have tried so far has helped, you may have inborn—or genetically caused—anxiety that some researchers refer to as **communibiology** (Beatty & McCroskey, 1998; McCroskey & Beatty, 2000; Littlejohn & Foss, 2008). Before you say, "I knew it! That's just the way I am—I can't do anything about it," realize that there are also studies that have documented a decline in the stress felt by high-anxiety speakers (Witt, et. al., 2006); so it does seem that anxiety reduction is possible. Therefore, although biology may play an important role in anxiety, it is likely not the only factor (Conditt, 2000). In fact, biopsychologists view behavior as the interaction of three factors: (1) our genetic makeup, (2) our experiences, and (3) how we see our current situation (Kimball, 1989; Pinel, 2006, p. 23). Each of these three factors interacts with and influences the others.

For many of us, trait anxiety is a learned behavior. If your anxiety about speaking is learned, you will likely experience two or more of these characteristics: (1) feel that you are different from other speakers ("I'm more nervous and less effective than other speakers"); (2) have a history of negative speaking experiences ("I know I will do poorly, because I have always been a poor speaker since 7th grade"); and (3) consider yourself inferior to others ("My audience is sure to know more about my topic than I do") (Beatty, 1988; Beatty et al., 1989). If your anxiety is learned, it is possible to unlearn it. For example, you may assume that you are different from everyone else just because no one else *seems* to be nervous. Although some people do show outward signs of nervousness, most nervousness is internal and is only minimally obvious to an audience. The best way to prove this to yourself is to videotape yourself giving a speech. Most people are amazed at how much less visible their inner turmoil is than they expected. ➜ *Additional ways to unlearn anxiety are covered in the section below on managing trait anxiety.*

Once you have identified which type of anxiety is causing your lack of confidence, you can do something to correct or manage it. Although situational anxiety is easier to manage than trait anxiety, both can be controlled with effort.

Active Critical Thinking

To think further about communicator anxiety, complete the following:

- Which types of anxiety do you have—situational, trait, or both? Give a personal example of each type of anxiety you have experienced.
- How serious would you say your anxiety is on a scale of 1 (low) to 10 (high)? Does your assessment of your anxiety match the results of the PRCA-24? Why or why not?

Managing Situational Anxiety

Accept the fact that every speaking situation will cause butterflies. According to the legendary journalist Edward R. Murrow, "The only difference between the pros and the novices is that the pros have trained their butterflies to fly in formation" (Bostrom, 1988, p. 57). The following suggestions will help you control your butterflies (Hamilton, 2011, pp. 150–152).

Prepare and Practice

Nothing will make you more nervous than knowing you are not adequately prepared. After all, isn't your nervousness really fear that you will look foolish in the eyes of your coworkers, classmates, or friends (Bippus & Daly, 1999)? Preparation makes such a possibility less likely. Lilly Walters (1993), speech consultant and author of *Secrets of Successful Speakers,* estimates that careful preparation can reduce anxiety by as much as 75 percent! Researchers have also found that taping yourself, speaking in front of a mirror, and practicing before an audience make you a better speaker (Smith & Frymier, 2006). In fact, students who practiced before an audience (four or more people worked best) got better grades than did students who practiced alone. Unfortunately, perhaps because they feel overwhelmed, anxious people prepare less rather than more thoroughly (Daly, Vangelisti, & Weber, 1995).

To prepare properly, first analyze your audience and plan your presentation and visual aids for this particular group. Next, prepare easy-to-follow notes. Using these notes, rehearse your presentation three or more times from beginning to end—*always speaking out loud*. Mentally thinking through your speech is not the same as practicing aloud. Your practice environment should be as close as possible to the actual speaking environment. For example, if you will be standing during your presentation, stand while practicing; if you will be using visual aids, practice using them. As you rehearse, time yourself to see if you need to shorten or lengthen the presentation. Practice allows you to eliminate the unexpected from the speaking situation (Buss, 1980). In fact, La Velle Goodwin (2007)—a speaking consultant for 20 years—recommends that you plan ahead how you will "recover" from errors if they happen and actually "practice your recovery plans ahead of time." Finally, anticipate possible questions, and prepare and practice answers for them. Knowing that you are well prepared will help ease much of your anxiety (Behnke & Sawyer, 1999; Daly et al., 1989; Daly et al., 1995). ➜ *See the Quick Start Guide at the beginning of the text for a brief overview of how to prepare a speech. Chapters 11 and 12 discuss in detail how to prepare for informative and persuasive speeches.*

Warm Up First

Just as singers warm up their voices and athletes warm up their muscles before a performance, you'll want to warm up your voice and muscles before giving your presentation. A variety of techniques can help you do this. For example, sing up and down the scale the way singers do before a concert. Read aloud a page from a book, varying your volume, pitch, emphasis, and rate. Do stretching exercises such as touching your toes and rolling your head from side to side. Practice various gestures such as pointing, pounding your fist, and shrugging your shoulders. These warm-up exercises will help you relax and ensure that you are ready to perform at your best (Richmond & McCroskey, 1998).

Use Deep Breathing

One quick way to calm your nervousness is deep breathing. Take a deep breath through your nose, hold it while you count to five, and then slowly exhale through your mouth. As you exhale, imagine that the stress and tension are slowly draining down your arms and out your fingertips, down your body and legs and out your toes. Repeat the process a second or third time if needed. Deep breathing slows the heartbeat and lowers tension, making us feel more in control (Pletcher, 2000). One researcher (Hamilton, 2000) found that using deep breathing can lower our feelings of anxiety by up to 15%. A good time to use deep breathing is right before you go out in front of the audience to begin your presentation. ➜ *A more detailed explanation of deep breathing is given in the section "Practicing Positive Imagery," Exercise 1, later in the chapter.*

Plan an Introduction to Relax You and Your Listeners

Most speakers find that once they get a favorable audience reaction, they relax. This is one reason that many speakers start with humor—it relaxes them as well as their listeners (Detz, 2000). If a humorous introduction is inappropriate or you are not comfortable with humor, relate a personal experience. One engineering speaker advises that since "stories travel further and faster than facts," a story makes a great introduction (Anderson, 1999, p. 88). Whatever your preference, make your

Digital Vision/Alamy

Putting your audience at ease right from the start will help you to relax and set the tone for the rest of the speech.

introduction work to put you and your audience at ease. ➔ *See Chapter 7 for a detailed discussion of attention-getting introductions.*

Concentrate on Meaning

Instead of worrying about how you look or sound and whether you are impressing your audience, center your energy on getting your meaning across. Make sure your listeners are following the organization of your speech and understanding your points. Pay close attention to their nonverbal reactions. If they look confused, explain the idea in different words or add another example. A speaker who is concentrating on the listeners soon forgets about being nervous. ➔ *Chapter 3 contains a detailed discussion of listeners and how to "read" their nonverbal reactions.*

Use Visual Aids

Researchers have found that anxious speakers feel more confident when they use visual aids (Ayres, 1991). For one thing, *visual aids give you something to do with your hands,* such as clicking between slides, holding an object, or pointing to information on a screen or chart. Of course, to appear really confident, you will need to practice smoothly shifting from one visual to the next while talking and maintaining eye contact with your audience.

    Visual aids also shift audience attention away from you—at least for a few seconds. To illustrate this point, have a classmate or your instructor put up an interesting transparency or computer visual while continuing to talk about something unrelated to the visual. Try to look only at the speaker, not at the visual. The urge to look at the visual is overwhelming, isn't it? Although the shift in audience attention to the visual is brief, it gives you time to relax and regroup.

    Finally, *visual aids make it almost impossible to forget what you want to say.* If you suddenly forget your next point, all you have to do is put up the next visual and you will instantly remember what you planned to say. Also, you don't need to worry about remembering specific facts or statistics if that information is included on a text or graphic visual. However, this does not mean that you should write every word you want to say on your visuals! Effective visuals include only phrases and keywords, as you will see in Chapter 10. If you feel you need a few notes in addition to your visuals, use caution. A few words written lightly in pencil on a flip chart or underneath printed thumbnails of PowerPoint slides may be an option. Don't forget to practice using your visuals until you feel confident with them.

Use Positive Imagery

Researchers have found that positive imagery (discussed in the next section) is not only beneficial for managing trait anxiety, but helps control situational anxiety as well (Ayres et al., 1998).

Active Critical Thinking

To think further about situational anxiety, complete the following:

- Make a list of several situations that make you nervous (e.g., speaking before large audiences or with family members present or at a job interview).
- Which of the suggested methods for managing situational anxiety do you think will work the best for you and why? Give an example to illustrate your answer.
- Suggest an additional method for managing situation anxiety that you or someone you know have used in the past. Be prepared to share your method with classmates.

Managing Trait Anxiety: Positive Imagery

Although there are several techniques for managing trait anxiety, most of them require the help of trained professionals. Positive imagery (also called visualization or mental imagery) simply requires the use of your imagination and is a successful technique that you can do on your own. Researchers have found positive imagery to be easy to use and to have a long-term effect (Ayres, 1988; Ayres & Ayres, 2003; Ayres & Hopf, 1989, 1990; Ayres, Hopf, & Ayres, 1997; Bourhis & Allen, 1992). What is **positive imagery?** It is creating a positive, vivid, and detailed mental image of yourself giving a successful and confident speech. When you imagine yourself speaking confidently, you become more confident, just as you would if you had actually given a successful speech.

When I ask students and seminar participants to say out loud together, "I am an excellent speaker," most of them say they feel like phonies, and some of them can't even say the words. How about you? Try saying, "I am an excellent speaker," and make it sound as though you mean it. If we can't even say it, how can we expect to do it? Once you begin to *see* yourself as a good speaker, you will find that it is easier to *be* a good speaker.

Although positive imagery has only recently been applied to speaker confidence (Beatty, 1984), it has been used successfully in sports for years. One of the first studies of positive imagery investigated its effects on basketball players. Students were divided into three groups. Group 1 was told to practice shooting baskets 20 minutes a day. Group 2 was told not to touch a basketball but to spend 20 minutes a day imagining themselves shooting baskets; if they imagined a "miss," they were to correct it and continue practicing. Group 3 had no physical or mental practice of any kind. After three weeks, the students in the three groups were tested. The students who had practiced neither physically nor mentally had not improved at all. But the students who had practiced mentally had improved by the same amount as those who had practiced physically—about 24 percent (Richardson, 1952, p. 56).

In 1989, sports psychologist Jim Loehr reported that 80 to 85 percent of top athletes used positive imagery as part of their training. That percentage appears to have increased over the years. For example, basketball great Michael Jordan, golfer David Duval, figure skaters Sarah Hughes and Kristi Yamaguchi, swimmer Michael Phelps, and gymnast Mary Lou Retton are just a few of the athletes who make regular use of positive imagery.

One of my former students is a good example of a speaker with high trait anxiety successfully using positive imagery. Karen (introduced in Chapter 1) told me at the end of the first day of class that she would probably drop the class when we got

Use a database like InfoTrac College Edition, CQ Researcher, or EBSCOhost to learn more about managing anxiety. Locate several articles on communication anxiety by using the keywords *positive imagery, visualization, visualizing,* or *mental imaging.*

to the first individual speech—she had already dropped the class five times—because there was just no way she could ever give a speech on her own. I encouraged her to read the chapter on building speaker confidence and to begin using positive imagery. With great hesitation, she agreed. Karen gave the first speech (a great accomplishment), although she was obviously nervous. With each speech she improved, and by the final persuasive speech she was like a different person. Not only was she selected by the class as the *most improved* speaker, she was also voted as the *best* persuasive speaker. As Karen accepted the award, she proudly told the class that she had given a report in her psychology class as well. The applause was thunderous.

Why Positive Imagery Works

According to Gail Dusa, past president of the National Council for Self-Esteem, "Visualization, in many ways, is nothing more complicated than involving your imagination in goal setting. It's not hocus-pocus or magic. When you use your imagination to enhance goal setting you get fired up, excited. This enthusiasm equips you with more mental energy to put into the task" (McGarvey, 1990, p. 35).

This mental energy has many of the same effects as physical action. Researchers have known for some time that "vividly experienced imagery, imagery that is both seen and felt, can substantially affect brain waves, blood flow, heart rate, skin temperature, gastric secretions, and immune response" (Houston, 1997, p. 11). Using brain-imaging technology, neuroscientists demonstrated why visualization works for athletes. In this study, athletes who imagined a movement activated the same areas in the brain as did athletes who performed the actual movement (Kosslyn et al., 1999; Stephan et al., 1995). Another study found similar results in the language sphere—both imagined and spoken words activated the same prefrontal and pre-motor areas of the brain (Wise et al., 1991). Of course, visualization alone doesn't turn athletes into winners; they must practice long and hard as well. In the same way, using positive imagery is unlikely to turn you into a confident, polished speaker unless you also prepare and practice your speech carefully.

Another way that positive imagery works is more difficult to explain. Psychologists tell us that the role of our subconscious mind is to keep us true to our "picture" of ourselves (Maltz, 1960). Every time we react to something we have done or respond to a compliment or criticism, we are sending messages to our subconscious about how we see ourselves. Our present thoughts and words determine our picture of ourselves, which in turn shapes our future reactions. In other words, *we act as the person we "see" ourselves to be.* If you say to yourself, "I don't see myself as a confident speaker," then you likely won't be one.

According to the authors of *The Mental Athlete,* "If you 'visualize' yourself as a mediocre athlete, if you go into a workout or competition 'seeing' yourself performing on an average level or slower or less perfectly than those around you, this is the way you will perform in reality" (Porter & Foster, 1986, p. 71; Porter, 2003). For example, when runner Mary Decker Slaney—who fell during the 3,000-meter race in the 1984 Olympics—was asked if she had visualized the race, "She said she had dreamed about it and visualized it for weeks, even months. She paused, and then said, 'But I never saw myself finishing the race'" (Porter & Foster, pp. 22, 24).

On the other hand, Alpine skier Jean-Claude Killy (winner of gold medals in three Olympic events) reports that one of his best performances occurred after an accident prevented him from practicing on the snow and his only practice was to ski the course mentally (Sheikh, 1983). Arnold Schwarzenegger, actor and politician, and Barbara Corcoran, New York entrepreneur, are both excellent speakers who used positive imagery to build their confidence and speaking abilities

(Gallo, 2006). According to Gallo, Schwarzenegger "enjoyed extraordinary success in every aspect of his life—bodybuilding, movies, and politics—because he always visualized his performance first. He had such a clear vision of his path that he never questioned it. In his mind, his dreams had already come true" (¶7). To help his dreams along, he practiced and perfected his speaking at numerous charity events. Schwarzenegger, highlighted in the Speaking to Make a Difference feature on page 36, talks about the importance of visualization. Corcoran became a successful speaker because, as she said: "I pictured myself in great detail, including the clothes I'd wear to address an audience of thousands of people eager to hear my expert advice" (¶10). She perfected her speaking ability by teaching classes at New York University.

Mastering Positive Imagery

So far we have defined *positive imagery* and discussed why it works. This section will show you how to use positive imagery to manage your own trait anxiety and begin to see yourself as a confident speaker. The method discussed here is used across the nation in many athletic programs, business seminars, and coaching sessions (Porter, 2003; Porter & Foster, 1986; Tice, 1980; Tice & Quick, 1997; Tice & Steinberg, 1989).

AP Photo/Mark J. Terrill

Athletes such as swimmer Michael Phelps commonly use positive imagery to enhance performance. Positive imagery helped Phelps win eight gold medals in the Beijing Olympics.

Step 1: Develop the Habit of Positive Self-Talk Self-talk includes the way you think and talk about yourself. Is your self-talk negative? When you make a mistake, what do you say to yourself? "There I go again. It's just like me to mess up like this!"? When someone compliments you on a speech, do you reject the compliment by saying, "Oh, it was just dumb luck" or "Well, I did mess up on my visual aids"? Dr. Kay Porter (Porter & Foster, 1986; see also Porter, 2003), who teaches mental training techniques to athletes, says that an athlete's self-talk between points and between games can make the difference between winning and losing. She uses herself as an example of what not to do:

> In the years between age 10 and 22, I played tennis. While I never quite mastered my tennis game, I mastered the negative game totally, doing everything that I have spent the last few years teaching people not to do. I choked, blew my concentration, cursed myself, mentally abused myself, and considered myself a total loser when it came to tennis. I was a master of self-defeat (Porter & Foster, p. 225).

Instead, use only positive self-talk. If you are in the middle of a speech and suddenly realize that you have forgotten to use your visual aid for the first main point, use positive self-talk: "That's not like me. The next time I'll practice using my visuals." And when you are complimented for your speech, accept the compliment without dwelling on whatever faults you think your speech had. Say, "Thank you. I worked hard on that speech," even if you feel it was not perfect.

Speaking to Make a Difference

When Arnold Schwarzenegger was young, he already knew how to "visualize" what he wanted in his bodybuilding career. During his first Mr. Universe competition, he could see himself winning and felt like he "owned" the competition (Webster, 2006). Below is an excerpt from Schwarzenegger's speech "The Education of an American" (**schwarzenegger.com**, 2001), given at a Perspectives 2001 Conference in Sacramento before 3,000 people. In this speech he talks about the importance of visualization in developing self-confidence and achieving your goals. To see the rest of the speech, go to his website (**www.schwarzenegger.com**), click on "Schwarzenegger.com Archive Web Site," and search for "Perspectives 2001 Conference."

AP Photo/Matt Sayles

The bottom line is: if you feel passionate about your goal—and it's what you really want—then you'll do whatever it takes to achieve it. No matter *how* much sweat, pain, and sacrifice—no matter how many obstacles you have to break through—just don't ever say no!

And I was dead right about this one, too: just don't listen to "no"!

Now when you've got your goal, you have to not only visualize it, live it, and breathe it. You also have to telegraph it to everybody around you.

"I'm going to be the strongest man in the world!"

"I'm going to make it in America!"

"I'm going to be a Hollywood star!"

It's a way to *commit* yourself to it.

Of course, when you announce these ambitious goals to people, what do you think they'll do? Well, some people will laugh. Some will roll their eyes. And a lot of them will just tell you, "You'll never make it, kid!"

I've experienced *all* of those.

Plenty of people laughed at me. My own mother actually went to the family doctor: "Doctor, my son is losing his mind! He's got pictures plastered all over his walls. Of men! Men with oiled bodies, with little posing trunks! He says he wants to look like them! Help, Doctor ... Where did we go wrong?"

The doctor heard my story and calmed down my parents.

Then, when I got to Hollywood, people really laughed their heads off. The agents said: "No one's ever made it with that big a body—or that bad an accent—or that long and foreign a name. You in movies? Stop it! You're killing me!"

You know, even Maria's parents didn't think I could make it. I told the Shrivers that I was going to be a number-one box office star some day, like Clint Eastwood. They said that was very, very lovely, but didn't I think I should have a fallback—like a nice master's degree in nutrition? They were worried about their daughter's security.

Of course, as soon as the first movie started taking off, they said: "Way to go!" And they've been behind me 100 percent ever since!

The bottom line? Listen to yourself as you follow your dreams. And surround yourself with people who bring out the best in you and believe in you. And just *don't* listen to people who don't.

Reading the text of his speech, it's hard to realize that Schwarzenegger's speaking skills had to be learned. According to speaking coach Carmine Gallo (2006), "The comfort he enjoys on stage did not come easily. He had to apply the same discipline that catapulted him to the top of the bodybuilding world to improve his skills as a speaker." Visualization helped him to perfect his speaking skills, which in turn led him to great success.

As you can tell by the advice he gave in the Sacramento speech, Schwarzenegger always visualizes his performance first (Gallo, 2006). His current success in speaking has a direct correlation to the positive imagery and visualization that helped him win bodybuilding competitions so many years ago. With a lack of experience and a heavy Austrian accent to contend with, it would have been all too easy for Schwarzenegger to listen to the naysayers and let in the negativity—a sure path to failure. According to Schwarzenegger, "There's no room for fear in the picture." Instead of adopting a fearful, can't-do attitude, he got involved in volunteer work and participated in every speaking event his staff could find for him (Gallo). It must have worked, because the audience at Sacramento gave him two standing ovations.

As a direct result of his dedication to becoming an excellent speaker—and his use of positive visualization—Schwarzenegger has been able to give numerous notable speeches. For example, in 2004 he was the keynote speaker for the Republican National Convention; in 2005 the governor went with several California business representatives to China to participate in trade talks (**gov.ca.gov**, 2005); in 2010, he presented the commencement keynote address at Emory University; and, of course, public speaking was a regular part of his job as governor of California.

In the inspirational speech at Sacramento, Schwarzenegger gives the best advice possible to a new public speaker: "The bottom line? Listen to yourself as you follow your dreams. And surround yourself with people who bring out the best in you and believe in you. And just *don't* listen to people who don't." You too can become a more confident speaker by creating a vivid positive mental image of your success before giving a speech.

Questions: Why do you think that Schwarzenegger was so successful in using positive imagery as a tool for improving his public speaking? What does his success have to offer the beginning speaker?

With positive self-talk, you also avoid using the words *have to, ought to,* or *need to.* Such thinking only makes you feel obligated to do certain things, and your subconscious tries hard to get you out of it. Think about what happens when you say to yourself, "I have to get up early to prepare tomorrow's report." How many times have you been so sleepy that you couldn't drag yourself out of bed? The trick is to substitute positive trigger words such as *want to, like to, enjoy,* or *choose to* in place of negative words. For example, instead of saying, "I've got to work on my speech," say, "I want to prepare my speech" or "I'm looking forward to finishing my speech" or simply "I've decided to work on my speech." It's amazing how using positive words instead of negative ones can change your attitude. Instead of spending your time resisting the task, you can now complete it and go on to enjoy something else without feeling guilty.

Step 2: Refocus Negative Mental Pictures into Positive Ones To begin the refocusing process, picture yourself as the speaker you would like to be. What specific speaking characteristics would you like to possess? To help you see the "ideal you," imagine that you are giving a speech to a class or club three months from now. How do you look, sound, and feel? What are you wearing? How is the audience responding? Are you confident, organized, and dynamic?

Get a complete picture of the "ideal you" in your mind. As a guide, focus on achieving a few of the following speaking characteristics and accomplishments:

- Look audience members in the eye.
- Feel relaxed and confident.
- Sound dynamic.
- Keep a loud volume and a steady voice.
- Use visual aids smoothly and professionally.
- Concentrate on audience rather than self.
- Give speeches that are organized and easy to follow.
- Remain confident during Q&A (questions and answers).

When you have completed your list of desired characteristics, use them as the basis for writing five to ten positive statements that describe you as though the future has arrived and the changes you want have already occurred. Avoid "I want/I will/I hope...." Instead, use the present tense, action verbs, and words that will trigger positive feelings.

> **Stop reading at this point and make a list of the speaking characteristics you wish to develop.**

See how the desired speaking characteristics from the above list can be turned into sample positive statements:

1. I find it easy to look directly at individual audience members while speaking.
2. I feel as relaxed and confident giving a formal speech as I do entertaining good friends in my own living room.
3. My delivery is as dynamic and enthusiastic as it is when I talk about an exciting football game.
4. When presenting speeches, my voice is strong and steady and loud enough to be easily heard.

5. I handle visual aids confidently and smoothly.

6. While speaking, I do not worry about pleasing everyone; rather, I please myself with what I have to say.

7. I give speeches that are clear, understandable, and well organized.

8. I find question-and-answer sessions stimulating and enjoyable.

As you write your positive statements, be sure to get rid of negative wording. For example, instead of "I will try to make eye contact with audience members when I speak," say, "I make direct eye contact with audience members when I speak." Instead of "I won't let large audiences scare me," use a positive image and say, "I feel confident giving speeches regardless of the size of the audience."

Once you have completed your positive statements, begin visualizing them. Every morning and evening for about a month, *read* the statements out loud. After reading each one, take a few seconds to close your eyes and mentally *picture* yourself being the person the statement describes. Make this mental picture as detailed and vivid as possible (Ayres, et al., 1994; Marks, 1999). At the same time, *feel* relaxed, confident, and competent. For example, for the statement "I find it easy to look directly at individual audience members while speaking," see yourself standing confidently in front of the room, looking directly at various audience members as you give a clear, well-organized, and entertaining talk. For the statement "I handle visual aids confidently and smoothly," see yourself standing confidently beside a flip chart or computer, calmly flipping pages or using the computer remote or space bar. Feel a sense of satisfaction in your performance.

For positive imagery to work—to refocus the negative pictures you have of yourself into positive ones—you must do more than merely read your statements. For change to occur, you need to *say them* (concrete words), *see them* (vivid mental pictures), and *feel them* (Zagacki et al., 1992). To put it another way, words + vivid mental pictures + feelings = confidence. If you have trouble with the "feeling" part of some of your positive statements, build feeling cues into them. For example, if you can't "feel" confident while looking listeners in the eye, think of a situation in which you do feel confident making eye contact and add it to your statement: "It's as easy for me to make direct eye contact with my audience as it is when I _____."

One student commented that she viewed her past speaking history like a videotape. Although she couldn't erase any of her past failures, she could tape over them with both real and imagined speaking experiences. Once she had taped over all the negative experiences, she started to see herself as a good speaker and actually began to enjoy speaking.

Step 3: Don't Compare Yourself to Others No matter who you are or how long you have been speaking, there will always be people who are better speakers than you. At the same time, you will always be better than some people. It's not a contest between you and the other students in your class. If someone gives a really outstanding speech right before yours is scheduled, resist the temptation to say, "There's no way I can follow such a good speech. I can never be that good." Your goal isn't to be better than other speakers. Your goal is to be the best speaker you can be—you are competing only with yourself.

© Ann Dowie

To increase speaker confidence, mentally picture yourself on the day of your presentation, looking good, feeling confident, and giving a great presentation.

On the other hand, it's perfectly all right to borrow techniques from other speakers (students as well as professionals). For example, if the colors Jack used on his visuals made them come alive, you might try using the same colors. Or if Alounsa's gestures seemed especially sincere and expressive, you might try using similar gestures. You may even wish to ask Alounsa if she uses any special techniques or has any pointers for you. Borrowing public speaking ideas and practices from a person is not the same as wanting to be that person. It is simply another tool for becoming the best speaker you can be.

If you use positive imagery as outlined here, in about four weeks you will begin to feel comfortable with the "new" you (Tice & Quick, 1997). By "taping" over your past negative experiences and fears, you will begin to think of yourself as a good speaker who actually enjoys giving speeches.

Remember

To create positive mental images . . .

- Look two or three months into the future.
- Picture yourself as the "ideal" speaker you would like to be.
- Write five to ten positive statements that describe this "ideal" you.
- Twice a day for four weeks, read, visualize, and feel yourself successfully performing each statement.

Practicing Positive Imagery

In addition to visualizing your positive statements, tape yourself reading the following positive-imagery exercises. For best results, play this tape at least once a week and the night before each scheduled speech. As you listen, see and feel yourself giving a successful speech. Studies have found that speakers who used similar visualization exercises even once had less communication anxiety than did speakers who did not use them or who used some other anxiety-reduction method (Ayres & Hopf, 1985, 1989; see also Bourhis & Allen, 1992). Exercise 1 is based on Ayres & Hopf (1989).

Exercise 1

It's important to get in the mood to visualize. Close your eyes and get as comfortable as you can in your chair. For the next 10 minutes or so, try to keep an open body posture, with your feet flat on the floor and your arms resting comfortably but not touching. Now, take in a deep breath . . . hold it as you count slowly to three . . . and exhale slowly. As you exhale, feel the tension in your neck and shoulders draining down your arms and out your fingers; feel the tension in your back and hips draining down your legs and out your toes. Take another deep breath . . . hold it . . . and slowly release it through your mouth. Feel the tension leaving your body. Now, one more time, breathe deeply . . . hold it . . . slowly exhale, and begin normal breathing.

Imagine yourself at the sink in your bathroom. You lean toward the mirror to get a better look at your face. Do you see your face? The mirror suddenly clouds over. When it clears again, you are looking through the mirror into the future. You can see yourself getting up on a day when you are going to give a particularly important speech. You jump out of bed, full of energy, full of confidence, and looking forward to the day. You are putting on one of your favorite outfits, which makes you feel professional and confident. See how good you look and feel? Imagine yourself arriving relaxed at the speaking site. When you arrive, people comment on your appearance and how relaxed you look. You feel thoroughly prepared for this presentation. You have researched carefully, have professional visual aids, and have practiced several times. Now see yourself standing or sitting in the room where you will make your speech, talking very comfortably and confidently with others in the room. Everyone seems friendly and supportive. You feel absolutely sure of your material and of your ability to present the information in a forceful, convincing, positive manner. It's time for the speech. See yourself walk confidently to the front and smile at the audience. They smile back. You set up your visual aids and begin your presentation.

Now see yourself speaking. Your introduction goes the way you had planned. You are dynamic, forceful, and interesting. Your speaking rate is just right, your pauses and emphasis couldn't be better, your gestures and body movements are powerful. As you flow from one main point to the next, the audience smiles and nods. They are really paying attention and seem impressed by your visual and verbal supporting material. As you wrap up your main points, you have the feeling that it could not have gone better. The audience applauds with enthusiasm. Do you hear the applause? Now see yourself answering questions with the same confidence and energy you displayed in the actual speech. The speech is over. People come up and shake your hand and congratulate you. You accept their thanks in a relaxed and pleased manner. You are filled with energy, purpose, and a sense of well-being. Congratulate yourself on a job well done!

The future fades, and the mirror again shows your reflection—but the confident smile remains on your face. Now take a deep breath … hold it … and slowly let it out. Do this several more times and slowly return your attention to the room.

If you can't "see" yourself while doing this exercise, don't be concerned. Positive imagery is easier for some people than for others (Isaac & Marks, 1994). If you have difficulty seeing any images at all, "think of what it might be like if you could see the pictures you're thinking about" (Carr-Ruffino, 1985) and concentrate on the "feeling" part of the exercise.

The next exercise was adapted from a seminar participant who highlighted specific speaking qualities that she wanted to develop (Hamilton, 2011, p. 155). You may want to write your own positive-imagery exercise and tailor it to your specific goals. Begin with the relaxation and deep breathing described in Exercise 1. When you feel relaxed, play your taped version of this next exercise and imagine yourself as the person being described.

Exercise 2

I am looking at myself sitting in my usual seat in speech class on the day of my first speech. It is my turn to speak. As I rise from my seat, I direct the butterflies of excitement in my stomach into positive energy. I can do this because I have practiced carefully and know I am well prepared. As I turn to face my fellow classmates, I draw in a deep breath, stand up straight, and begin to speak. An aura of confidence radiates from within as I speak. My body is relaxed. My breathing is paced. My motions are fluid, and my gestures are graceful. My shoulders stay relaxed and down. My voice is steady and strong. It is pitched low and is well modulated and easy for everyone to hear. My eyes scan from student to student, drawing their complete attention. My mind is rested and calm, allowing my words to flow evenly and to be clear and concise.

As I speak, I easily remember each point of my speech. I can see the out-line of my speech clearly in my mind and refer to my notes only briefly. I make use of dramatic pauses to stress important points within the speech. It is obvious that the class understands what I am saying and that they are enjoy-ing my speech. My words continue to flow smoothly, and my transitions are especially good. Each idea is spoken clearly and confidently. There are no mistakes. As the speech winds down, my words are chosen carefully and powerfully. The audience is paying complete attention. I end with a bang! I know from the enthusiastic applause and positive comments that my speech has been a total success. I pause and then ask if there are any questions. As I rephrase each question, I continue to feel relaxed and confident. My answers are brief and to the point. I can tell the audience is impressed with the visual aid I used to answer a question. When the Q&A is over, I pause for effect and then present my final wrap-up. Again the audience applauds with enthusiasm. I feel proud and confident as I walk back to my seat.

Active Critical Thinking

To think further about trait anxiety, complete the following:

- Write out five to ten positive statements that represent the speaking characteristics you wish to develop or polish. Make sure that each statement is written as if it were true right now even though you know it isn't yet. Avoid using *want, will,* or *hope* in your statements. Ask a classmate to check the wording of your statements. If necessary, make minor changes.

- To see a change in confidence, visualize yourself confidently doing each of your positive statements twice a day for four weeks. Read each statement, see yourself doing each statement, and work to feel confident doing each statement. For example, (correct) "My voice is strong, steady, and enthusiastic when I speak"; (incorrect) " I hope my voice is strong" or "My voice does not shake when I speak."

Other Methods for Managing Anxiety

Positive imagery isn't the only method for reducing anxiety, although it works for both situational and trait anxiety and you can use it successfully without the help of a trained professional. Several other methods that public speakers have found successful in managing anxiety are discussed below—you may want to try one or more of them. According to researchers, "the widest possible combination of methods" is often the most effective in reducing communication apprehension (Allen et al., 1989, p. 63; see also Kelly & Keaten, 2000).

Relaxation with deep breathing Deep breathing (inhaling through the nose and slowly exhaling through the mouth) was mentioned earlier as a way to manage situ-ational anxiety. Relaxation with deep breathing involves (1) learning to relax using deep muscle relaxation and breathing—tense and relax each muscle group from your head to your toes, and (2) visualizing yourself giving a successful presentation while

Eri Morita/Getty Images

Easing tension through deep breathing and relaxation helps get control of those butterflies and lowers anxiety.

remaining relaxed. If just the thought of giving a speech breaks your relaxation, try learning to remain relaxed while visualizing a series of communication situations progressing from low anxiety to high anxiety (Richmond and McCroskey, 1998). Anytime you feel a surge of panic or out-of-control butterflies, taking a deep breath, holding it, and then slowly exhaling will help get you back in control.

Cognitive restructuring of self-talk
It may not be the speaking situation that is causing you anxiety; it may be the way you are viewing the situation and your self-talk about it. If your self-talk is defeating, it is probably also irrational according to psychologist Albert Ellis (2004). For example, imagine the stress created by this irrational belief: "If I make any mistakes during my speech, I am a worthless person." Fortunately, we can change our irrational beliefs and replace them with rational statements. Cognitive restructuring involves (1) identifying irrational self-talk that produces speaker anxiety, (2) developing alternative coping statements, and (3) practicing the coping statements in stressful situations (Meichenbaum, 1985).

Skills Training Skills training involves (1) identifying reasonable speaking goals, (2) determining behavior or skills needed to achieve each goal, and (3) developing procedures for judging the success of each goal (Phillips, 1991). Taking this course is a form of skills training, so you are already working to build your speaker confidence. Try selecting at least one new skill from each chapter you read and working to apply it in your next presentation. Communication researchers found that taking a communication course teaching public speaking can reduce speaker anxiety as effectively as other anxiety-reduction methods (Duff et al., 2007).

Technology One of the main fears expressed by speakers with anxiety is that they will forget what they want to say—so they write out the speech in manuscript form and try to memorize it. Not a good idea! What this does is actually increase stress and anxiety and make you sound even more nervous. If you are looking for a way to assist your memory and give a boost to your confidence, try electronic visual aids like PowerPoint. Of course, you have to use them correctly to avoid "PowerPoint Poisoning" as described in the Dilbert cartoon (see Chapter 10 for PowerPoint pointers). Impressive, state-of-the-art visual aids add to your credibility and make you feel more confident. David, a former student, had this to say after his informative speech:

> My PowerPoint slides that I used in my speech on Jack Russell Terriers were well received, and the audience seemed to enjoy and appreciate the anecdotes I was able to relay. My PowerPoint also helped keep my main ideas organized and easy to follow. With a "main idea" slide followed by supporting slides, it was easier to relax and keep my thoughts in order and my speech on track.

Although electronic visuals may seem complicated at first, you will soon find that they are easy to prepare, easy to revise, and easy to use as long as you focus on your audience. For electronic presentations using Microsoft PowerPoint, follow the suggestions in Chapter 10. With just a little practice, you will be able to offer professional-looking presentations with a confidence you didn't think was possible.

As you work to decrease speaker anxiety, keep in mind that because a part of apprehension is likely influenced by genetics, *learning to handle your anxiety won't happen overnight.* Awareness of your anxiety and its effect on you and others around you is a definite beginning. Anxious people do not have to take a back seat to more-confident people. Taking control of nervousness and anxiety is much easier once you identify it and take steps to manage it.

Active Critical Thinking

To think further about managing anxiety, complete the following:

- Brainstorm 10 reasons why you experience anxiety or communication apprehension when speaking in public. Next, rank these reasons from most serious to least serious.
- Take the top 3–5 reasons and list any negative or irrational statements you say to yourself. Write out a positive statement for each irrational belief.
- Finally, taking the top 3–5 reasons, picture or visualize how you would change as a public speaker if each "reason" were no longer part of you. Continue moving down your list, visualizing how you would act and feel as a public speaker if each reason no longer existed.

When finished, write a reaction paper listing the original anxiety reasons, irrational beliefs, and rewritten positive statements and your success in visualizing change.

Summary

"I am relaxed and in control while giving speeches" is a good positive statement to sum up this chapter. Gaining confidence while speaking may not be easy, but it can be done with practice and effort. The first step for controlling anxiety is to identify whether it is situational, trait, or both.

Situational anxiety is something almost everyone experiences in new situations. We can manage this type of anxiety by preparing and practicing, warming up, concentrating on our message, planning introductions that relax us as well as our audience, using visual aids effectively, and using positive imagery.

Trait anxiety is the personal fear that we bring to a speaking situation. Trait anxiety is both learned and inborn (genetic). Although it is more difficult to control than situational anxiety, trait anxiety can be effectively managed—one way is through positive imagery. Positive imagery—which requires the use of your imagination to create a positive, vivid, and detailed image of yourself giving a successful speech—can be used without professional help and is long lasting. Successful use of positive imagery includes three basic steps: (1) concentrate on positive self-talk, (2) refocus negative mental pictures into positive ones, and (3) don't compare yourself with others—just be the best speaker you can be.

Trait anxiety can also be reduced through cognitive restructuring and skills training. Both of these methods requires some help from trained professionals. Using a combination of methods may produce better results. With time and effort, your situational or trait anxiety can be managed so that you can give confident, successful speeches.

Essentials of Public Speaking Online ⚡CourseMate

Use your Online Resources for *Essentials of Public Speaking,* which features the PRCA-24 (Personal Report of Communication Apprehension) question-naire described on page 29, the Speech Template and PowerPoint Speaker's Guide described in Chapter 10 on pages 240–241, access to InfoTrac College Edition, Personal Skill Building Activities and Collaborative Skill Building Activities, a digital glossary, sample speeches, and review quizzes.

Key Terms

cognitive restructuring 42	positive imagery 33	skills training 42
communibiology 29	relaxation with deep breathing 41	technology 42
McCroskey's PRCA-24 29	self-talk 35	trait anxiety 28
	situational anxiety 28	

Personal Skill Building

1. Have you given one of the speeches of introduction described in the Quick Start Guide yet? If so, did you have more or less anxiety than you expected? If not, were you asked to introduce yourself or a classmate the first day of class? In both of these situations, did you experience any situational or trait anxiety? Write out your plans for managing your anxiety, and keep a brief weekly journal of your efforts and successes.

2. Use a database like InfoTrac College Edition, CQ Researcher, or EBSCOhost, or ProQuest to fi nd articles with suggestions for overcoming speaking anxiety. Run keyword searches using the keywords *stage fright* and *public speaking anxiety.*

3. Find three inspirational/motivational quotes that can be used as a mantra for positive self-talk to share with your classmates. Use Google or InfoTrac College Edition to find great quotes.

4. Blow up, or imagine blowing up, a balloon. With each breath needed to inflate the balloon, visualize your speech anxieties flowing into the balloon. After you feel that you have filled the balloon with some or all speech anxieties, tie it up. Take a moment to experience how it feels to have fewer anxieties. Now visualize popping the balloon and bringing an end to those anxieties. Take in a deep breath, hold it, and slowly exhale.

5. Check out the following websites. You can access these sites through your Online Resources for *Essentials of Public Speaking*

    •   Watch the video called "Positive Self Talk" on **YouTube.com** (search for Ryan Caudle and Positive Self Talk). Here you will find some suggestions to help with confidence building.

⚡CourseMate

- Read the five major reasons we feel anxious in public speaking situations. Go to **ehow.com**, and search for "reasons for fear of public speaking."

- For helpful hints and tips on how to better prepare for a public speaking event and reduce your speaker anxiety, go to **ezinearticles.com**, scroll to the "Search Ezine Articles" search box, and type in "6 Tips to Reduce Public Speaking Anxiety."

- For another helpful ezine article on breaking down public speaking misconceptions, follow the instructions above and search for "5 Myths About Public Speaking."

- Some people's public speaking anxiety may be attributed to Social Anxiety Disorder. For information on treatment, visit **webmd.com** and search for "Social anxiety disorder."

- A good place to practice speaking in a nonthreatening environment is a local Toastmasters International club. There may be a club on your local college campus. Visit the **toastmasters.org** website to find a club near you. While at their site, search for "10 Tips for Successful Public Speaking."

Collaborative Skill Building

1. One way people indicate confidence is by using a falling pitch (called downspeak)—especially when introducing themselves. If you follow your name with a rising pitch (called upspeak), it sounds as if you're asking a question; a falling pitch sounds as if you're making a statement and sounds more confident. In small groups, complete the following:

   - Have all members practice saying their names until everyone can do so with both a rising pitch and a falling pitch and can easily hear the difference.

   - Then, each member should walk confidently to the front of the room and say, "Hello, my name is _____ _____" (with a falling pitch), pause, read a positive statement that also ends with a falling pitch (e.g., "When speaking, I make eye contact with all members of my audience"), and walk confidently back to a seat and sit down. Be careful not to roll your eyes or do anything else that indicates anxiety.

   - Most of us have a habit of ending sentences with upspeak, as this assignment indicates. Discuss how you felt during this activity. Did sounding more confident help you feel more confident? What role did practice play in your level of confidence?

2. In small groups (or as a class) watch a scene from the 1998 movie *Elizabeth*, where Queen Elizabeth I played by Cate Blanchett is nervously rehearsing a speech she must give to a hostile audience of rival clergy. Then watch her successful presentation. A clip of the movie is available at **AmericanRhetoric.com**

under Movie Speeches (http://www.americanrhetoric.com/MovieSpeeches/ moviespeechelizabeth.html). In small groups discuss the following questions:

- Which type of anxiety do you think bothered Queen Elizabeth the most? How do you know?

- What role do you think her preparation and practice played in her success at persuading her audience to vote for a Unified Church of England?

- What other methods of handling anxiety discussed in this chapter could have helped?

3. In small groups of three to five, work on speaker confidence by completing at least one of the following:

- As a group, watch a short speech and identify where and how the speaker showed nervousness (such as: didn't make direct eye contact during introduction, tapped pen on the desk, or showed nervous foot movement). Select one of the student speeches available in the Online Resources for *Essentials of Public Speaking* or on **YouTube.com**.

- If you taped your previous speeches in this class, view one for each group member looking for when and how anxiety was shown. Identify at least two tips for each member to help them appear more confident.

- Have each group member practice confident speaking by presenting the introduction of a speech (from one given in the past, or one they will present in the future). If a flip camera is available, tape each speaker for later viewing. Group members should comment on any anxiety noted and make helpful suggestions on how to appear more confident.

- Each group member should write out three impromptu topics that can be answered without prior research—personal opinion topics are usually the best. Put the topics in an envelop and stir them up. Each group member should draw a topic from the envelop and give a one-minute answer that can be either serious, humorous, truthful, or inventive. Be sure to include one personal example. At the end of each impromptu presentation, group members should comment on how confident the speaker was and any areas that showed nervousness. If time allows, have each member draw and speak on a second topic working to appear confident and enthusiastic.

3

Listening: What Speakers and Listeners Should Know

One way listeners may avoid being persuaded is by convincing themselves that the speaker's credibility is questionable and therefore not to be trusted. Aristotle, trained as a Greek field biologist to rationally investigate subjects, writes about the importance of creating credibility (ethos) during a presentation through arguments that are sound, truthful, and show the audience that you have their interests at heart. Even so, Aristotle came to realize that a speaker's credibility depends less on logical proof and more on the listener's perception of the speaker.

In Aristotle's time, speakers and audience members were face-to-face. Today's technology may completely separate a speaker from the audience, which makes audience perception of the speaker's credibility more difficult and Internet fraud relatively easy. Researchers have found that when persuasive messages are posted on the Internet and the speaker uses emotional appeals that relate to the listeners' value systems, the listeners are likely to view the speaker as honest and give little attention to the substance of the message. *Who has the most responsibility for speaker credibility—the listener or the speaker? How has it changed from Aristotle's time to today?*

FLASH *FORWARD*

Learning Objectives

As you read Chapter 3,

- *Identify* the stages of the listening process.
- *Define* what is meant by listening filters, and *discuss* how the three filters of culture, gender, and technology affect the listening process.
- *List* and *discuss* several strategies that speakers can use to encourage effective listening from their audience members.

WHAT DO THESE TWO SITUATIONS HAVE IN COMMON?

Situation 1: You are excited about doing business with a Japanese firm and are looking forward to presenting your proposal to the firm's team. You are especially pleased that with the help of a translator, your visuals are in Japanese. After the introductions, you and your interpreter get right to business presenting an excellent presentation. Gauging from the reactions of the team members, who one after the other are nodding in agreement, you feel confident that your proposal has been well received. They promise to look over the proposal and get back in touch. But they never do. When you call, they politely give yet another reason for not being able to meet with you "at this time" (Hamilton, 2008, p. 152, Checkpoint 5.4).

Situation 2: You are the last speaker of the day. The previous speakers each took more than their allotted time. Even though there are only 20 minutes remaining before the program is scheduled to end, the director assures you that you can have your full time. As you speak, you are impressed by the fact that the audience seems to be listening intently—most of them are looking directly at you and sitting very still. By omitting the less important items, you manage to end on time and conclude with a startling bit of information. However, you are surprised that no one acknowledges your unexpected information as they file out of the room.

Use a database like InfoTrac College Edition, CQ Researcher, or EBSCOhost to do a keyword search for articles on listening. For InfoTrac, use the ★ wildcard (*listen*★) to search for all forms of the word (*listen, listening, listener,* and so on). A subject guide search on *listening* will list additional categories of interest. Find at least one listening tip that is not covered in your text. What value does this tip have for speakers?

Can you tell what each of these speakers failed to do? Both apparently prepared their presentations carefully and took their specific audiences into consideration. The first speaker even prepared visuals in Japanese. The second speaker ended the presentation with a startling statement designed to reestablish audience interest. So what did they do wrong? Here's a hint: Neither speaker understood audience members as listeners. To help you identify what went wrong in the above scenarios, this chapter will discuss: (1) what successful speakers need to know about listening and listeners; (2) how listening filters such as culture and gender affect listening; and (3) specific techniques you can use to counteract listening problems that often occur in various stages of the listening process. When you finish reading this chapter, you will be ready to try out two or three of these listening techniques during your next speech.

We will begin our chapter on listening by discussing the stages that we all go through in the listening process.

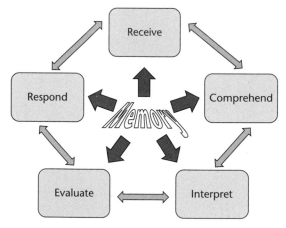

Figure 3.1

Stages of Listening

Source: Adapted from "The Integrative Listening Model: An Approach to Teaching and Learning Listening" by Kathleen Thompson, Pamela Leintz, Barbara Nevers, and Susan Witkowski, 2010. In A. D. Wolvin (Ed.), Listening and Human Communication in the 21st Century (pp. 266–186). Malden, MA: Wiley-Blackwell.

Stages of Listening

Identifying the stages involved in the listening process allows us to identify our listening strengths and weaknesses—we are all listeners. In fact, the best speakers are likely the best listeners. One sure way to improve your speaking ability is to first improve your listening ability. Then you will understand your audience well enough to prepare successful messages. According to listening specialist Judi Brownell, "Speaking is viewed as the *outcome* of listening" (2010, p. 144). As shown in Figure 3.1, the process of listening has five primary stages: *receive, comprehend, interpret, evaluate,* and *respond,* plus *memory,* which works with every stage of the listening process (adapted from the ILM Listening Process Model by Thompson et al., 2010).

The Receive Stage

In the **receive stage,** listeners attend to (or ignore) one or more stimuli from the multitude of stimuli that bombards us continually. It's impossible to notice every sound, sight, and smell or to acknowledge every event or feeling. We learn to become highly selective; we pay attention to things that are of interest to us and tune out everything else. In his book *Listen for Success,* Arthur K. Robertson (1994) cites an example:

> Eugene Raudsepp of Princeton Creative Research tells the story of a zoologist walking down a busy city street with a friend amid honking horns and screeching tires. He says to his friend, "Listen to that cricket!" The friend looks at him with astonishment. "You hear a cricket in the middle of all this noise?" The zoologist takes out a coin and flips it into the air. As it clinks to the sidewalk a dozen heads turn in response. The zoologist says quietly, "We hear what we listen for" (p. 45).

Multiple stimuli are competing for the attention of these listeners

In addition to needs and interests, our gender, age, cultural background, biases, and emotions, as well as environmental distractions, affect what we sense. *As a speaker, your goal* is to get listeners to focus their attention on the message at hand without daydreaming or getting distracted by the environment or personal problems. → *Suggestions for how to do this are discussed beginning on page 57.*

The Comprehend Stage

Just because we receive a message doesn't mean that we actually comprehend or understand it. I may become aware of a couple arguing in an unknown language. Even though I hear their words, I can't comprehend what they are saying other than making guesses based on their tones of voice and facial expressions. Even when we speak the same language, we have different frames of reference, assumptions, vocabulary, attitudes about the speaker and subject, and listening differences due to culture, gender, and technology—to name just a few that serve as filters to what we hear and observe. The goal in the **comprehend stage** is to understand, not interpret or evaluate. Listeners who know how to ask questions, clarify through paraphrasing, and take careful notes to organize ideas are often the most successful at comprehending what the speaker means. *As a speaker,* your goal is to help audience members from diverse backgrounds and experiences understand your message. → *Suggestions for how to do this by focusing on listening filters are discussed beginning on page 59.*

The Interpret Stage

Some of the most serious listening problems occur in the **interpret stage,** where listeners supply meaning to the messages they have sensed in the first stage. In other words, they try to figure out what the speaker really means. The problem is that words can have different meanings. For example, suppose your boss says in a staff meeting that raises are "likely" this year. What's the chance that the audience's and the boss's interpretation of the word *likely* will be the same? Or when your boss gives you a "rush" assignment, how much time do you have to complete the task? One printing company had so many misunderstandings over the word *rush* that it posted the following definitions:

As soon as possible: Do within two or three days.

Rush: Do by the end of today.

Hot: Don't drop what you're doing, but do it next.

Now: Drop everything.

The same factors that cause faulty sensing can also cause faulty interpretation. Listeners often assume that they understand and don't bother to ask questions or **paraphrase** (summarize the speaker's ideas in their own words). Sometimes they are so sure they understand that they stop listening.

Many of the problems in the interpreting stage are clarified by **attribution theory,** which describes how people process information and use it to explain the behavior of others and themselves (Griffin, 1994; Heider, 1958; Littlejohn & Foss, 2008). Sometimes these problems occur because listeners jump to conclusions, experience fatigue or information overload, or have the mistaken belief that 100 percent understanding happens with ease. *The goal of the speaker* is to anticipate problems in the interpreting stage in order to maximize listener understanding.

➔ *Suggestions for how to do this are discussed beginning on page 61.*

Attribution Theory

- **Original Theorist:** Fritz Heider, *The Psychology of Interpersonal Relations,* 1958.

- **Definition:** The process of drawing inferences, or how people process information and use it to explain the behavior of others and self.

- **Involves the Three-Step Process:** (1) Perceive an action, (2) judge intent of action, and (3) attribute reason for action.

- **Fundamental Attribution Error** (Ross, 1977): Our tendency to overestimate the role of the person's character and underestimate the role that the situation has in behavior (i.e., we usually assume that the things that happen to people are a result of something they did).

The Evaluate Stage

In the **evaluate stage** listeners "think about the message, make more extensive inferences, evaluate and judge the speaker and the message" (Goss, 1982). In assigning a value judgment to what they have sensed and understood, listeners decide whether the speaker seems qualified, the information and evidence appear accurate, and the comments are relevant and worthwhile.

Listeners' evaluations are often affected by their attitude toward the speaker. Imagine yourself speaking before audience members who think you are too young or have biases about your gender or ethnic group. Listeners' evaluations are also affected by their previous experiences, their expectations, and their beliefs and emotional states. As a result, listeners sometimes make evaluations based on assumptions without waiting to make

What value judgment do you think the listeners in this picture are making?

Eric Audras/PhotoAlto Agency RF/Jupiter Images

sure they have all the facts. Here is an example from a rescue-squad member about a call for help from a police officer:

> A 38-year-old man had pulled off the road and hit an obstruction. [After calling the rescue squad, the] patrolman had called back: "Cancel the call. The man is not really injured. He's just complaining of chest pains and probably bumped into the steering wheel." The squad went out anyway. When they arrived, they could see immediately that the man was having a heart attack. "What happened," he told them between gasps, "was that I had this chest pain and went off the road." And with that he passed out. We got to work on him right away and got him to a hospital, but it was too late. Now he had told the patrolman the same thing he had told us—"I had this chest pain and went off the road." The patrolman heard him, perhaps understood him, but despite his knowledge and experience, did not evaluate what he heard, and in this case not evaluating correctly was fatal. I never forgot that (Steil et al., 1984, pp. 27–28).

Listener interpretations, evaluations, and attitudes toward you and your message often depend on verbal, visual, and vocal impressions. Your words (verbal code); your appearance, gestures, and visual aids (visual code); and your speaking voice (vocal code) are as important to your listeners as are your ideas. Listener evaluations are even more important when your topic is a persuasive one, because listeners (especially those who disagree with you) will attempt to avoid being persuaded. Therefore, *the goal of the speaker* is to anticipate possible listener resistance to new ideas and persuasion and counteract them when possible. ➡ *Suggestions for how to do this are discussed beginning on page 61.*

The Respond Stage

Once listeners have sensed, interpreted, and evaluated you and your ideas, they respond (give feedback). The **respond stage** is very important, because without feedback, speakers can only assume that they have communicated. Listeners won't always agree with what the speaker is saying, but their responses show whether they were listening and whether they understood.

Listener response can take many forms. Listeners communicate agreement, disagreement, or confusion through obvious nonverbal expressions (such as frowning or nodding). If the situation allows, they might make comments and ask questions during or after the speech or during a question-and-answer period. All these responses are invaluable in judging the success of your presentation.

Sometimes listeners don't make such obvious responses. In this case you must try to interpret their unintentional responses to see if they understand or are even listening. Just because everyone is staring at you doesn't mean they are listening attentively. Speakers make a big mistake when they assume that attentive posture and intent eyes equal listening. People who are actually listening tend to shift around in their seats, doodle on their papers, cough, and glance at the clock and the floor. *The goal of the speaker* is to accurately interpret listener feedback—especially the nonverbal, which is more difficult to "read." ➡ *Specific suggestions on how to do this are discussed beginning on page 63.*

The Memory Stage

Memory storage is accomplished in the **memory stage,** where listeners decide what parts, if any, of the speaker's comments to retain and then attempt to store those in memory. Memory is needed in all five of the primary listening stages.

Unfortunately, no matter how brilliant your speech, most audience members will remember only about 10 to 25 percent of your presentation (Nichols, 1996; Wolff et al., 1983). The parts they don't recall may have contributed to their favorable evaluation of your talk, but they didn't store the specific facts in their memories. From the listener's viewpoint, forgetting facts is not necessarily a bad thing—if they no longer need to know something, forgetting it is a way of clearing the clutter. As a speaker, however, you want your audience to remember the important facts from your presentation. In other words, you want listeners to transfer this specific information from their short-term memories into their long-term memories (Hauser & Hughes, 1988; Schab & Crowder, 1989). *The goal of the speaker* is to help listeners decide what information is important and to aid them in transferring this information from short-term to long-term storage. ➔ *Suggestions for how to aid listener memory are discussed beginning on page 65.*

Remember

In the stages of listening, listeners...

- Receive—they hear what is important to them.
- Comprehend—they listen to understand.
- Interpret—they assign meaning to what they see, hear, and feel.
- Evaluate—they determine speaker credibility and message importance.
- Respond—they react to the speech, usually through nonverbal cues.
- Remember—they retain parts of the message from each stage in memory.

Active Critical Thinking

To think further about the stages of listening, complete the following:
Recall some listening successes and failures. Which listening stage is the easiest part of the process for you? Which stage is the hardest part of the process for you? Discuss your thinking by giving examples to illustrate your answers.

Knowing the stages of effective listening is not enough. As a listener and a speaker, you must also be aware of listening filters that may cause you problems or cause some members of your audience to "hear" your message differently.

Listening Filters

It is important to realize that not all people in all situations listen in the same way or react to the listening stages in exactly the same manner. As speakers and listeners, we need to be aware that audience members filter (decode) what they hear speakers say through their own frames of reference. Although numerous **listening filters** exist, ranging from personal to situational, three main filters require the most adjustment: culture, gender, and technology. In this section, we will concentrate on how these filters affect audience members and what you, as a speaker, can do to minimize problems. As you read, see if any of these filters cause you personal problems when listening.

Culture

When you have a diversity of cultures in your audience or your audience's cultural background differs from your own, there are likely to be listening differences and even misunderstandings. Culture serves as a frame of reference through which audience members filter what they hear. It would be impossible to discuss every culture's listening preferences, but we can identify several similarities and differences by looking at three cultural dimensions: individualistic versus collectivistic, low context versus high context, and monochromic versus polychromic. → *See Chapter 4 on audience analysis for additional information on cultural differences.*

Individualistic / Collectivistic Cultures

Countries like the United States, Australia, Canada, and Great Britain tend to be **individualistic,** because the individual and individual rights are valued more highly than group identity or group rights. Countries like Japan, Mexico, Vietnam, South Korea, and Venezuela tend to be **collectivistic,** because they put more value on group membership, group obligations, and group goals than on the individual (see Table 3.1). Individualistic cultures are problem oriented; collectivistic cultures are more relationship oriented. Individualistic cultures value autonomy, assertiveness, and competition (Triandis, 1995), while collectivistic cultures value empathy, listening, and group friendships and consider saving face for themselves and others to be extremely important (Ting-Toomey & Chung, 2004).

Table 3.1   Individualistic Scores of Various Countries (ranging on a continuum from 100–0)

High scores are individualistic; low scores are collectivistic.

Country	Score	Country	Score
United States	91	India	48
Australia	90	Argentina	46
Great Britain	89	Japan	46
Canada	80	Iran	41
Netherlands	80	Russia	39
New Zealand	79	Arab Countries	38
Italy	76	Greece	35
Denmark	74	Philippines	32
Sweden	71	Mexico	30
France	71	Hong Kong	25
Ireland	70	Chile	23
Switzerland	68	China	20
Germany	67	Thailand	20
South Africa	65	Vietnam	20
Finland	63	W. African Countries	20
Poland	60	South Korea	18
Austria	55	Taiwan	17
Israel	54	Pakistan	14
Spain	51	Venezuela	12

Source: By permission of Geert Hofstede and Gert Jan Hofstede, "Cultures and Organizations: Software of the Mind." Revised and expanded 2nd edition. New York: McGraw-Hill USA, 2005, ISBN 0-07-143959-5, pp. 78–79.

Low Context / High Context Cultures

The second dimension that helps explain listening differences deals with **high and low context** (Hall, 1976; Hall & Hall, 1990). *Context* does not refer to the words in a message; it is defined as "the information that surrounds an event" (Hall & Hall, 1990, p. 6). People who communicate with low-context messages tend to come from individualistic cultures; people whose messages are high context tend to come from collectivistic cultures (Ting-Toomey, 2000). *Low-context/individualistic* cultures expect messages to be clearly spelled out—directly and explicitly. They feel that it is the speaker's responsibility to make sure the meaning is provided by the words and that the message is well organized and structured. Words are all-important—context (including gestures, facial expressions, and status) is of minimal importance. On the other hand, *high-context/collectivistic* cultures expect messages to be brief, indirect, and implicit. As receivers, they take the responsibility for determining a speaker's meaning. Words are of minimum importance—context is most important (context includes setting; facial expressions; gestures; the speaker's friends, family background, age, status, silence, and so on). High-context cultures are homogeneous (tightly bound by experiences, family, and tradition), so they don't need as many words for clear understanding (Hofstede, 2001; Samovar & Porter, 2004). They also expect words to be used very carefully—words can hurt and cause loss of face (Cohen, 1991).

Monochromic / Polychromic Cultures

The third dimension explains how listeners in different cultures view time. **Monochromic** (M-time) cultures, which are more individualistic/low context, view time as a "scarce resource which must be rationed and controlled through the use of schedules and appointments" (Smith & Bond, 1994, p. 149). "Saving" time is good; "wasting" time is not. On the other hand, **polychromic** (P-time) cultures, which are more collectivistic/high context, consider "the maintenance of harmonious relationships as the important thing, so that the use of time needs to be flexible in order that we do right by the various people to whom we have obligations" (Smith & Bond, p. 149). Relationships are important; "saving" time is an alien concept.

So, what do these three dimensions tell speakers about listeners and listening? Basically:

- *Individualistic/low-context/M-time listeners* prefer speeches that are on time and get right to the point; content that is direct, explicit, and well organized; conclusions that are clearly stated; and speakers that use effective words and take responsibility for meaning.

- *Collectivistic/high-context/P-time listeners* prefer speeches that build on audience history and take a cautious, back-door approach to points; content that is indirect, implicit, and filled with personal stories and analogies; conclusions that are obvious without being stated; and speakers who are aware of social face-saving and allow listeners to determine meaning.

Keep in mind that none of these dimensions are "either-or" categories; instead, it is better to think of them as a continuum ranging from one extreme to the other, with many cultures at various spots along the continuum. As Table 3.1 indicates, countries can range all the way from the most collectivistic (0) to the most individualistic (100). Also, keep in mind that even people within cultures vary on each of these dimensions. Therefore, speakers analyze listeners not to stereotype them but to communicate effectively with them. One culture's listening patterns and expectations are not better than any other culture's—just different.

People from different cultures listen differently. Some of these differences are discussed by Kiewitz, Weaver, Brosius, and Weimann in an article called "Cultural Differences in Listening Style Preferences." To locate the article in the *International Journal of Public Opinion Research,* use a database like InfoTrac College Edition, CQ Researcher, or EBSCOhost to conduct an advanced search for the lead author. For additional articles, search for *culture and listen*.* ➡ *Use of the asterisk allows you to find all forms of the word that precedes it (see Chapter 5 for more information).*

Gender

In addition to culture, gender plays a role in the way audience members listen. Researchers claim that women typically view communication as a cooperative tool, are better at decoding nonverbal cues in messages, and work harder at listening by initiating topics, asking questions, and giving supportive responses (verbal and nonverbal). Men, on the other hand, view communication as a competitive tool, tend to interrupt more often, are less likely to ask questions, and give minimal responses cues during conversations (Guerrero et al., 2006; Wood, 2011). Both men and women (especially in power positions) tend to use tag questions (such as "isn't it?") at the end of comments to make others feel less intimidated; they actually talk about the same amount (Wood, 2011; Dance, 2007). In addition, Richardson (1999) found that women are more likely than men to perceive the emotional aspects of your message; Borisoff and Merrill (1991) found that men are more likely than women to recall the factual aspects of your message; and both sexes tend to listen more carefully when the speaker is a man (Emmert et al., 1993).

What do you think? Are differences in the way men and women listen due to real biological differences between the sexes, are they learned behaviors that correspond to social stereotypes, or are they perhaps both? Of course, the general stereotype about men and women is that men are more assertive, rational, self confident, and willing to lead, while women are more submissive, emotional, nurturing, and less willing to take responsibility (Putnam & Heinen, 1976). In other words, men are seen as more task oriented while women are seen as more supportive. Studies using the Listening Styles Profile (Watson et al., 1995; Barker & Watson, 2000) have found that of the four **listening orientations** or styles—people, action, content, and time—women show a preference for the people orientation while men show a preference for the content orientation. These studies tend to lend support for biological listening differences. On the other hand, when specific listening situations were used in a study with the Listening Styles Profile, both genders preferred the content listening style in instructional situations and the people listening style in situations involving friends (Imhof, 1998).

Perhaps the communicator of the future will be more **androgynous.** The term *androgynous* comes from the Greek for *male* and *female* and denotes the integration of both masculine and feminine characteristics—each used when appropriate to the situation (Bem, 1981b; Wood, 2011). For example, union members judged the androgynous manager (whether male or female) as the most effective and satisfying manager. Geddes (1992) and Heath (1991) found that androgynous people are generally more successful at work and at home. A study of college students (House & Dallinger, 1998) using Bem's Sex-Role Inventory (Bem, 1981a) found unexpectedly high androgynous scores, indicating that American society may be moving toward a more androgynous style.

To ensure effectiveness with both genders, an androgynous approach, while keeping the following advice in mind, is recommended for public speakers:

- Analyze your audience carefully. ➝ *See Chapter 4 for specifics.*
- Don't talk down to either gender.
- In your introduction, be sure to relate the importance of your topic to both men and women.
- Use a variety of examples to keep the attention of all audience members.
- Make sure your vocabulary is nonsexist. ➝ *See Chapter 9 for specifics.*
- Use general terms rather than gender-linked ones. For example, "*low blow, on target,* and *playing hardball,* all elicit images of masculinity" (Brownell, 2006, p. 381).

Technology

Technology can both hamper and aid listening. In today's global markets, not all your listeners will be sitting across from you—e-mail, instant messaging (IM), and text messages also have "listeners." One often-overlooked communication aspect of these newer technologies is the importance of adapting messages to receivers. E-mail is the corporate message of choice, with the average employee receiving up to 171 e-mail messages per day (Bateman & Snell, 2009). E-mail is used to share information, solve problems, and manage conflicts. Researchers tell us two important things about e-mail: (1) receivers often interpret words as more negative than the sender intended, thereby creating conflicts or escalating disagreements; and (2) receivers are more likely to react positively to our messages if we use adjectives, verbs, and adverbs that mirror their preferred communication channel.

If you have ever received an e-mail that made you mad the minute you read it, you have experienced the first important point about e-mail. Researchers Raymond Friedman and Steven Currall (2003) warn that because e-mail messages have no vocal or nonverbal cues to aid meaning and because people look for meaning by reading a message more than once, even noncritical messages "can be easily misinterpreted as being more aggressive than intended" (p. 1342). In their theory of conflict escalation called **DEME** (the dispute-exacerbating model of e-mail), Friedman and Currall offer the following advice:

- Be careful about the tone of your e-mail—read it several times from the receiver's viewpoint, thinking how they might interpret it. This is especially important if your message is meant to be critical. Be friendly and cooperative even if the other person's e-mail sounds aggressive—they likely didn't intend it to sound so negative.

- Keep your sentences, paragraphs, and number of arguments relatively short; and make them easy to read by using bullets and clear headings. At the same time, be sure to include enough supporting information to clarify your position.

- If you have a social tie with the other person or know someone they know, be sure to mention it—we are more likely to give people we know "the benefit of the doubt."

- If a misunderstanding occurs, apologize even if you don't think it is your fault—apology goes a long way toward diffusing anger.

The second important research point about e-mail deals with using adjectives, verbs, and adverbs that mirror the receiver's preferred sensory channel when communicating—visual, auditory, or kinesthetic (Crook & Booth, 1997). For example, people who prefer the **visual channel** are more likely to use words such as *looked, looks like, visualize, see,* and *clear*. People who prefer the *verbal* or **auditory channel** are more likely to use words such as *talked, sounded, heard,* and *said*. And people who prefer the **kinesthetic** (or touch) **channel** are more likely to use the words *touch, grasp, feel,* and *run*. Which one of the following three wordings would generate the most positive response from you?

"The project *looks* like a winner."

"The project *sounds* like a winner."

"The project *feels* like a winner."

Although some people have no marked preference, most of us prefer one sensory channel over the others. If a count of sensory words reveals that one channel makes up 50 percent of the total, this indicates a preference (Coe and Scharcoff, 1985). When sending messages to someone whose sensory preference differs from your own, you can increase rapport by accommodating their preferred channel. Although the research given here doesn't include IM or text messages, it can be assumed that you should consider sensory preferences with these technologies as well.

Active Critical Thinking

To think further about listening filters complete the following:
- Do you think that culture, gender, or technology is the most likely to cause audience members to "hear" your message differently than you intended? Give a specific example to clarify your answer.
- Look at several of the e-mail that you have sent recently. Based on the words you use, do you prefer the visual, auditory, or kinesthetic channel? Give an example.

So far, we have covered the stages of listening, the listening problems that can occur in each stage, as well as the major listening filters that affect how audience members listen. The remainder of the chapter will cover specific things you as a speaker can do to ensure effective listening in each of the listening stages.

Receiving Stage: Stimulating and Motivating Your Audience to Listen

Stimulate and Motivate Your Audience

When customers come into a department store, there is no guarantee they will buy anything. Similarly, just because people show up at a meeting or walk into a classroom doesn't mean that they are going to listen to the speaker. In the receive stage, audience members must be stimulated and then motivated if careful listening is to occur.

Grab Audience Attention: Stimulate Them

Your audience isn't waiting passively for you to begin your speech; they are thinking of other things—some of these topics may be so interesting or worrisome that they may not even be aware when the speech actually begins. It is up to you to counteract these **internal stimuli** (thoughts generated by listeners that trigger additional thoughts or actions) with **external stimuli** of your own. Once you begin your speech, you have only a few seconds to grab the attention of your listeners and get them involved in your topic. For example, effective speakers often attempt to overshadow the listeners' internal stimuli with a powerful attention-getter, such as a startling statement, two or three brief examples, a personal experience, a short demonstration, a question, or a humorous anecdote directly related to the speech topic. Beginning your presentation with a statement of purpose is much less effective, because it works only for those few listeners who are already excited about the topic. ➔ *Additional methods of stimulating audience attention are discussed in detail in Chapter 7.*

Speaking to Make a Difference

Barbara Jordan was a politician, educator, and acclaimed professional speaker. She served as a United States Representative from 1973 to 1979 and was considered for Jimmy Carter's running mate in the 1976 presidential election. Jordan was the first African American woman to give the keynote address at a Democratic National Convention, which she did in 1976 at Madison Square Garden in New York City. She returned to Madison Square Garden as the keynote speaker at the 1992 Democratic National Convention. Here is a short excerpt from that speech; you can find the full text and video on the American Rhetoric website (**www.americanrhetoric.com**) by searching for "Barbara Jordan 1992 Democratic National Convention."

Terry Ashe/Time Life Pictures/Getty Images

It was at this time. It was at this place. It was at this event 16 years ago I presented a keynote address to the Democratic National Convention. With modesty, I remind you that that year, 1976, we won the presidency. Why not repeat that performance in 1992? We can do it. We can do it. We can do it.

What we need to do, Democrats, is believe that it is possible to win. It is possible. We can do it. Now, you have heard a lot about change tonight. Every speaker here has said something about change. And I want you to talk with me for a few minutes about change. But I want you to listen to the way I have entitled my remarks—"Change: From What to What?" From what to what? This change—this is very rhetorically oriented—this change acquires substance when each of us contemplates the public mind. What about the public mind?

There appears to be a general apprehension in the country about the future. That apprehension undermines our faith in each other and our faith in ourselves—undermines that confidence. The idea that America today will be better tomorrow has become destabilized. It has become destabilized because of the recession and the sluggishness of the economy. Jobs lost have become permanent unemployment rather than cyclical unemployment. The public mind. Public policy makers are held in low regard. Mistrust abounds. In this kind of environment, it is understandable that change would become the watchword of this time.

What is the catalyst which will bring about the change we're all talking about? I say that catalyst is the Democratic Party and our nominee for president.

We are not strangers to change. Twenty years ago, we changed the whole tone of the nation at the Watergate abuses. We did that twenty years ago. We know how to change. We have been the instrument of change in the past. We know what needs to be done. We know how to do it. We know that we can impact policies which affect education.

* * *

We need to change the decaying inner cities from decay [in]to places where hope lives. As we undergo that change, we must be prepared to answer Rodney King's haunting question, "Can we all get along?" "Can we all get along?" I say, I say we answer that question with a resounding *yes*! Yes. Yes.

We must change that deleterious environment of the '80s, that environment which was characterized by greed and hatred and selfishness and mega-mergers and debt overhang. Change it to what? Change that environment of the '80s to an environment which is characterized by a devotion to the public interest, public service, tolerance, and love. Love. Love. Love.

We are one, we Americans.

From the time she was winning national speaking competitions in high school (Crawford, 2003), winning debates in college (Lind, 1996), and winning cases as an attorney, Jordan's presentation style kept getting better. Ann Richards, when Governor of Texas, said of Jordan: "Listening to Barbara Jordan speak is like listening to God" (Minnich, 2006). Although Jordan's booming, well-articulated delivery may have captivated the crowd, there are many other reasons why her speech was such a success—let's focus on those that relate specifically to listening:

- First, Jordan's real success related to the way she evoked active listening in her audience—by connecting her audience "intimately to a specific physical place" (Carbaugh, 1999). In this case, Jordan made sure to remind her listeners that the last time she gave a speech at the Democratic National Convention in Madison Square Garden, the party won the election: "It was at this time. It was at this place. It was at this event 16 years ago I presented a keynote address to the Democratic National Convention. With modesty, I remind you that that year, 1976, we won the presidency."

- Jordan encouraged the audience to continue listening by suggesting that her comments would be different and worth listening to, and she proved it by tapping into audience values. She warned, "Every speaker here has said something about change. And I want you to talk with me for a few minutes about change. But I want you to listen to the way I have entitled my remarks—'Change: From What to What?' From what to what?" She then carried through her powerful theme of "change" by relating it to the "public mind" and important values held by her audience as Democrats and Americans.

- Jordan gave her audience another reason to listen by creating a collective identity that helped the audience feel personally vested in the message by using "we" and "our" language. For example, Jordan said, "our faith in each other," "our nominee for President," "We are not strangers to change," "We know what needs to be done," and "We are one, we Americans."

continued

- Finally, audience members were enticed to listen by actively participating either mentally, physically, or verbally. Jordan's use of repetition encouraged her listeners to chant and wave their banners or mentally join her when she said, "We can do it. We can do it. We can do it," "Yes! Yes. Yes," and "Love. Love. Love."

Questions: What are some possible barriers that can occur within individuals to hamper listening even at an event like this? Although Jordan used several methods to keep the attention of her listeners, what other suggestions would you have?

Table 3.2 Needs That Motivate Listeners (Can You Think of Any Others?)

Reduce stress and anxiety.
Earn more money.
Gain personal satisfaction.
Impress others and gain esteem.
Develop self-confidence.
Try something new and exciting.
Solve a pressing problem.
Achieve desired goals with less effort.
Increase prestige or power.
Advance rank/position with a new skill.
Gain a feeling of pride in a job.
Reach more customers.
Insure job stability and security.
Look more attractive.
Become healthier.
Improve parenting skills.
Help others.
Make a difference in the world.

Keep Audience Attention: Motivate Them

Robert Smith (2004), author of *The Elements of Great Speechmaking,* warns that "To be successful in the information age, professionals must be dramatic, interesting, and intellectually adventuresome communicators" (p. ix). However, no matter how effective your attention-getting external stimuli may be, it isn't enough for continued audience attention; sufficient motivation is also necessary—or, as Smith says, you have to know your audience well enough to "hook" them. To motivate an audience to give you their time, you must convince them that your presentation will in some way benefit them or people they care about. If they perceive that your topic has no personal value, their attention will soon drift to a more pressing topic. Table 3.2 lists possible audience motivators; add as many others as you can, and refer to this list each time you plan a speech.

Comprehend Stage: Maximize Listeners' Understanding

Maximize Listeners' Understanding

In the comprehend stage you want your listeners to understand what you are saying as close as possible to what you intended. Try the following suggestions:

- *Do your homework and carefully analyze your audience.* Try to encode your presentation in terms of the listeners' abilities, culture, and frames of reference. Make sure your vocabulary fits your audience, and watch out about using jargon or technical terminology that may be confusing. → *For more on audience analysis, see Chapter 4.*

- *Personalize your speeches with narratives.* One of the surest ways to guarantee that an audience will listen to you is to share something about yourself in narrative or story form (Ballard, 2003; Robinson, 2000). In *The Elements of Great Speechmaking,* Robert Smith (2004) says that "stories represent powerful tools and materials for connecting with audiences" (p. 21). We all enjoy hearing a speaker talk about real-life experiences—it makes us feel as if we know the speaker personally, and it adds to the speaker's credibility. For example, in discussing the importance of encouragement, Robert L. Veninga (2006) related this personal experience in a commencement address for graduate students at the University of Sioux Falls:

> The importance of encouragement cannot be overemphasized. Recently I had a midcareer student in one of my classes. She took notes religiously, which any professor will tell you is the mark of a highly educated person! Then she would frequently stay after class to discuss class content.
>
> One day, however, I saw sadness written all over her face. I asked her what was wrong. "Just before coming to class my supervisor handed me my performance review," she said. "Would you read it?" I read it and was quite impressed with all her accomplishments. And frankly I was puzzled as to why the student was upset until the student asked me to reread the appraisal. Upon rereading it I understood: There was not a word of thanks. There were no statements of appreciation. It was just a listing of facts related to her job. The student looked at me and said plaintively: "All I wanted was a simple thank you" (pp. 544–545).

If you can't think of a personal example related to the point you wish to make, tell about an experience that happened to someone you know or someone you have read about. Make sure your examples relate to both genders. The key is to give enough details to paint a clear and interesting picture, thus promoting listener attention and memory. Try the following suggestions:

- *Increase your speaking rate.* Another way to stimulate audience listening is by speaking a little faster than you normally do. Most speakers talk at a rate of about 100 to 175 words per minute. Listeners, however, can think at a rate of 400 to 800 words per minute (Lundeen, 1993; Wolff et al., 1983). In other words, listeners can easily follow every word you speak and still have some time to think about other things. Although attentive listeners use most of that time to think about your ideas, check your evidence, and even memorize important facts, less-dedicated listeners tend to use the "extra" time daydreaming. They may even become so engrossed in their own thoughts that they forget to tune back in. By delivering more than 100 to 175 words per minute, you give your listeners less time to daydream. According to researchers, "the optimal speaking rate for comprehension appears to be between 275 and 300 words per minute" (Wolvin & Coakley, 1996, p. 233).

- *Remember that the only message that counts is the one actually received.* It doesn't matter what you really said, what you thought you said, or what you meant to say; what's important is what your listeners think you said.

- *Remember that what you say to an audience and how you say it may mean less to them than what they see.* Therefore, make sure that what your audience sees adds to your intended message. Obviously, visual aids can be a very powerful tool here. ➔ *See Chapter 10 for specifics on using visual aids.*

- *Prepare for possible misunderstanding.* By anticipating potential sources of misunderstanding, you can prevent many communication breakdowns.

Interpret Stage: Don't Get Caught by the 100 Percent Communication Myth

Many speakers believe that if they give a good speech and their listeners are paying attention, 100 percent communication is possible. This is unlikely, however, because of *frame-of-reference* differences between the speaker and listeners. Think of your frame of reference as an imaginary window. Everything you see, touch, taste, smell, and hear is filtered through your own window. With so many different life experiences, it is highly unlikely that any two people will have an identical frame of reference on any topic.

Another reason 100 percent communication is unlikely relates to *code*. Many speakers assume that the only important code is the verbal (language) code. Analyzing results from 23 studies, J. S. Philpott (1983) found that verbal code accounted for only 31 percent of the variance in meanings, whereas vocal and visual codes accounted for the remaining 69 percent (see also Burgoon & Hoobler, 2002). In other words, as Figure 3.2 shows, audiences may pay more attention to your visual and vocal codes when interpreting meaning than to your verbal code unless your message is clearly factual and straightforward.

Another hurdle to 100 percent communication is that a speaker often sends *conflicting messages.* Take, for example, a company presenter speaking to a group of hostile customers who incorrectly think the company has been overcharging them. Although the presentation is well organized and clearly justifies the company's prices, the presenter acts nervous, speaks hesitantly in a fairly high pitch, and fails to make direct eye contact with listeners. If you were a customer, would you believe the verbal code, which says that all is well; the vocal code, which indicates nervousness; or the visual code, which suggests that the presenter may be lying? Combining verbal and vocal communication, one researcher found that "with initially equated signals the nonverbal messages outweighed the verbal ones at least five to one, and where they were in conflict the verbal messages were virtually disregarded" (Argyle, 1973, p. 78; see also Burgoon & Hoobler, 2002). As a speaker, work to avoid sending conflicting messages.

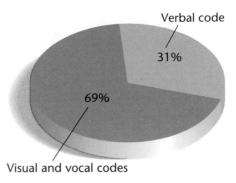

Verbal code
31%
69%
Visual and vocal codes

Figure 3.2

Meaning Carried by All Codes
Percent of meaning contained in visual and vocal codes, based on Philpott's research.

Evaluate Stage: Counteract Listeners' Resistance to Persuasion

When you speak on a controversial topic, audience attitudes toward your position may range from enthusiastic agreement to absolute opposition. Listeners who disagree strongly are the most difficult to persuade. In fact, even those who disagree mildly will likely do their best to avoid being persuaded. People are not willing to change without a struggle. As a result, during the evaluating stage, listeners may use a variety of methods to avoid being persuaded—or even informed. Let's examine some tactics you can use to foil the most frequently encountered listener-avoidance methods. → *See Chapters 12 and 13 for a detailed examination of persuasive speaking.*

Strengthen Your Personal Credibility

A credible person is someone whom people find believable—someone who inspires their confidence. Research has found that the greater a speaker's **credibility,** the more persuasive he or she is (O'Keefe, 1990). Therefore, one of the easiest ploys used by listeners to avoid being persuaded is to discount the speaker's credibility. For example, suppose Julianne is making a good, forceful argument that women are paid less than men for equal work, but John doesn't want to believe it. Her data makes him feel **cognitive dissonance** (discomfort when evidence is presented that is contrary to what we believe). But then he realizes that Julianne is at least 10 years younger than anyone in the room. Obviously, she is too young to really know how to collect firsthand information. John begins to relax. The dissonance is gone; he has avoided being persuaded.

To keep listeners from using this ploy, make sure that you are perceived as trustworthy and qualified to speak on the topic by giving a well-organized presentation that includes examples from personal experience as well as evidence from known experts. Use good-quality visuals and deliver your speech in a confident, dynamic manner. If you feel that your credibility might be in question, do one or more of the following:

- *Have a highly credible expert on the topic introduce you* as a competent and trustworthy speaker.

- *Identify your views with those of known experts* who are valued by the audience.

- *Indicate beliefs, affiliations, or problems* that you share with your listeners.

- Don't forget that if you want people to see you as confident, you must *look and sound confident.*

Highlight the Credibility of Your Sources

If the listener who is trying to avoid persuasion can't successfully devalue your credibility, the next ploy will be to criticize your sources. Most people seek information that supports their personal beliefs. If they are conservative, they read conservative newspapers; if they are liberal, they read liberal newspapers. Therefore, although listeners may know the sources on their side of an issue, they may know only hearsay about the speaker's side of the issue. Unsupported hearsay (such as "I read somewhere that the mayor is only marginally qualified to run this city") may keep your listeners from being persuaded. Therefore, to establish the credibility of your sources, do the following:

- Clearly describe the qualifications of your sources.

- Refute any expected criticism of your sources.

- Show some important quality that your sources and your listeners share.

Keep Listeners from Evading Your Message

Another listener ploy is to mentally evade persuasive messages that cause cognitive dissonance and instead hear what they want to hear (Larson, 2006; Littlejohn & Foss, 2008). To evade messages that might require them to change, listeners (1) deliberately misunderstand the message, (2) ignore the more discomforting parts of it, or (3) change its focus so that it doesn't personally apply. For example, if an audience were shown cartoons about prejudiced people, younger listeners might decide that the cartoons were about the prejudices of "older" people, or female listeners might tell themselves that the cartoons were about the prejudices of men and therefore exclude themselves from any need to change. ➜ *See Chapter 13 for a discussion of social judgment theory.*

To keep listeners from misinterpreting your persuasive message, first make sure that your ideas are clear and well organized. In addition, you might use one of the following tactics to make a change of opinion less threatening to listeners:

- *Make it clear that you view the "problem" as fairly common*—it isn't the fault or responsibility of only a few people or only your listeners.

- *Show that your solution won't be a strain on anyone* if everyone helps a little.

- *Show that your view is only a small distance from the listeners' current views*—a small change in opinion that has the potential to benefit all.

Keep the Listeners' Attention on the Speech

Another listener ploy is to tune out when they hear complicated information, react emotionally to an argument (claim) of the speaker, or experience an internal distraction. Sometimes listeners stop listening because it's easier to think of something else than listen to arguments that create internal discomfort or anger. In other words, these audience members aren't taking any chances of being persuaded. The following suggestions should make it more difficult for these listeners to avoid paying attention to you:

- Use a dynamic style of delivery—including unexpected volume changes and plenty of movement and gestures. → *See Chapter 8.*

- Include powerful stories and personal experiences. → *See Chapter 6.*

- Add humor to the presentation. → *See Chapter 7.*

- Use colorful, entertaining visuals. → *See Chapter 10.*

Remember

Listener-avoidance ploys include the following...

- Discounting the speaker's credibility.
- Criticizing the speaker's sources.
- Deliberately misunderstanding the speaker's message.
- Ignoring the more uncomfortable parts of the message.
- Deciding the message doesn't apply to them.
- Tuning out.

Respond Stage: Read Listeners' Feedback Cues

Because audience members do not always give obvious verbal, visual, or vocal feedback cues in the responding stage, you must learn to "read" listeners' responses. Certain feedback behaviors can be clues that your audience is drifting off. Before we discuss these behaviors, however, we need to caution that it is easy to misinterpret visual cues. For example, a student was giving a speech in class on the mysterious stone monoliths of Easter Island. In the middle of comparing the faulty theories of the past with today's more accurate assessment, he abruptly said, "Well, if that's how you're going to act, I quit!" and sat down. His classmates looked at one another in stunned silence. The speaker had observed several classmates with their foreheads wrinkled in thought and decided that these "frowns" meant they were rejecting his speech. When the class finally convinced him that he had misinterpreted their visual responses, he agreed to finish his presentation.

Put Feedback Cues in Context

Before you assume that you know what a feedback behavior means, consider the specific situation, environment, and time of day, as well as the cultural background and frames of reference of the listener(s). For example, several listeners with their arms locked across their chests would usually be a visual cue indicating disapproval, but the gesture takes on a different meaning in a room where the air conditioner is set much too low. A puzzling lack of audience participation during a question-and-answer period might be less confusing if you see that the company president has entered the room. Nodding heads may have different meanings depending on the culture of the listeners. American listeners tend to nod when they are in agreement, whereas Japanese listeners nod to indicate only that they have received the message, not that they agree. In England, audience members at formal presentations avoid nodding and instead blink their eyes—an indication of polite attention (Hall, 1992, p. 143).

Don't Generalize from Single Listener Response

Basing audience evaluation on a single verbal, visual, or vocal feedback behavior rather than on several simultaneous responses can result in misinterpretation. For example, someone who glances at his watch during your speech might be bored with your talk, but he might also have other reasons for this gesture. He might be consulting his watch for the date in reference to something you said, or he might habitually look at his watch at this time of day because this is when school gets out. Of course, if he glances at his watch continually, looks aimlessly around the room, and shifts uncomfortably in his seat (three related behaviors), you can feel more certain that he is probably tuning you out.

Look for Subtle Signs of Inattention or Low-Level Listening

Although it's risky to assign meanings to single behaviors, combinations of feedback behaviors can indicate whether a typical U.S. audience is listening. The following lists of visual behaviors (which often occur simultaneously) should give you an idea of when listeners are probably not listening or at least not listening effectively.

Signs of Inattention:

- Practically no movement, faces devoid of expression, unwavering eye contact or dropping eyelids, slouched posture.

- Restless movement, aimless looks around the room, drumming fingers or tapping pencils, repeated glancing at watches.

- Frowns, narrowed eyes or skeptical looks, arms locked across chest, raised eyebrows or rolling eyes.

Might Be Signs of Listening:

- Normal movement, smiles (or interested looks), occasional direct eye contact, erect or forward-leaning posture.

Which people in this audience are showing visual signs of inattention?

Doug Menuez/Iconica/Getty Images

- Occasional movement (maybe even some doodling), occasional glancing at watches—usually near the end of the presentation.

- Open posture, changing facial expressions depending on speech content, occasional nods of head.

In short, audience members rarely sit perfectly still unless they are daydreaming. Listening is not passive—it's active and requires conscious effort. On the other hand, too much movement is an indication of boredom and low-level listening.

Effective speakers constantly monitor the verbal, visual, and vocal feedback cues from their listeners. On the basis of the feedback they receive, they fine-tune their speeches as they go. If several audience members are showing similar inattentive behaviors, it's time to take a break, switch to a more interesting point, or show a catchy visual. If your speech is almost finished, you can recapture audience attention with a statement such as "I have one last point to make before concluding my speech" or "In conclusion…" The audience will visibly relax and give you a few more minutes of attention.

Memory Stage: Make Your Message Easier to Remember

It is up to you to make your presentations interesting and valuable enough for listeners to sense, interpret, evaluate, respond to, and remember. However, because so little of your entire presentation will be committed to audience memory, it is crucial for you to try to control what is remembered. Being organized, using good delivery, repeating important ideas, and relating the presentation to listeners' frames of reference are all important tools for improving audience memory and are discussed in detail in various later chapters. Some additional suggestions to promote better audience listening and retention are discussed next.

Incorporate Cues to Aid Memory

Unless your presentation is only for entertainment, you will want to assist your listeners in identifying and remembering important facts and concepts. To help listeners identify important facts, use spoken organizational cues such as "Now I will present a definition of…" or "Now we will turn to…" (Titsworth, 2001) or "The most important concept is…"

Not only do you want your listeners to accurately identify *what* to remember, you want them to actually remember it. Short-term memory can hold from five to nine bits or chunks of information—for most of us it is closer to four (Cowan, 2001). However, unless the information is transferred into long-term memory (through such things as repetition, visual depiction, and importance to self) and integrated into what you already know, it will be forgotten within 30 seconds or less (Kosslyn & Rosenberg, 2006). To help listeners move the important facts from short-term to long-term memory, try one or more of the following (Denman, 2005; Kosslyn & Rosenberg, 2006):

- Begin with an attention-getter such as a question that will be answered during the speech (attention improves encoding of information).

- Use acronyms and other mnemonic devices as memory aids for important concepts (acronyms aid memory).

- Periodically review previous points—PowerPoint and bulleted lists work well here (repeated information is easier to remember).

- Present a hypothetical situation or problem and then reflect with the audience on possible solutions (reflection improves memory).

- Visually present a short quiz, asking audience members to write or mentally think of the correct answers (participation improves memory).

- Include an emotional example to illustrate an important point when appropriate (emotional information is easier to remember).

- Relate new or novel information to commonly held beliefs or myths (new information is easier to remember when it relates to things already known).

- Show information in visual form when possible, such as a diagram or chart (organized, hierarchical data is easier to remember).

- Challenge audience members to share important facts from your speech with family and friends once they return home (repetition, practice, and reflection improve memory).

- Know your audience well enough so you can relate important ideas to audience experiences (familiar things are easier to remember).

Don't State Key Ideas in the First or Second Sentence

When a speech begins, most audience members are getting settled in their seats, yet many speakers expect them to immediately begin listening attentively. Because most listeners aren't ready to listen, they miss the first sentence or two of the speaker's introduction. Therefore, stating your central idea in your first couple of sentences is sure to catch many listeners off guard. And when listeners can't figure out the main idea fairly rapidly, they usually blame the speaker and feel justified in switching their attention to something more "important." Therefore, at the very beginning of your talk, your purpose is to capture and focus the audience's attention. This gives the typical listener time to tune in.

Use Visuals to Enhance Listening and Remembering

Have you ever seen a speaker set up a visual aid such as a poster before it was time to mention it or click on a new PowerPoint slide while still discussing the previous one? Was the audience listening to the speaker or reading the poster or slide?

Well-designed visuals encourage listening.

Li-Hua Lan/Syracuse Newspapers/The Image Works

Reading—of course. For some reason, when audience members see a message in print, they immediately begin reading it. Because audience members can't read and listen at the same time, they ignore the speaker for as long as it takes to read the visual. If the visual is too long and confusing, they give up and go into a text-induced coma that the Dilbert comic in Chapter 10 calls "PowerPoint Poisoning." This is the fault of the speaker, not the audience. Sandberg (2006) estimates that "bad PowerPoint presentations cost companies $252 million a day in wasted time" (B1). However, because "written cues are more powerful than spoken ones" (Nevid, 2006), properly prepared PowerPoint slides are a definite aid to listener memory (Hamilton, 1999; Vogel et al., 1986), especially if they include pictures that illustrate important concepts. Because pictures are coded both verbally and visually, humans have almost perfect recognition of them (Kosslyn & Rosenberg, 2006). Concepts associated with pictures and images are also easier to recall. → *See Chapter 10 for more details.*

Effective visuals are ones that allow listeners to absorb the content in one glance (around three to six seconds) and then refocus their attention on the speaker. This means you will have to limit the number of words, lines, and colors to only what is absolutely needed. You can have considerably more impact, hold the attention of your audience, and improve their retention if you use properly designed visuals, display them only when ready to speak about them, and remove them from audience view after you've referred to them. The power of visual aids cannot be overstated. → *See the color insert in Chapter 10 for a sample of both good and poor visuals. Chapter 10 also includes more on the benefits of using visual aids.*

Active Critical Thinking

To think further about helping your audience become better listeners, complete the following:

- Which two listening stages do you think give audience members the most problems? Explain why with at least one example.
- Select three suggestions for improving audience listening that you plan to include in your next presentation and explain how you plan to use them. Be specific.

Summary

Think back to the two communication situations presented at the beginning of the chapter. Have you determined what listener characteristic each speaker overlooked? The first situation involved a proposal to a Japanese firm. The speaker felt sure that the Japanese executives were going to accept the proposal because they were nodding in agreement. However, the speaker misinterpreted the visual-feedback clues; in Japan, nodding does not mean agreement, but merely that the message has been received. In the second situation the speaker believed that the audience was listening well because they were sitting totally still and making eye contact. The speaker was unaware that such feedback usually means that the audience members are not listening and are someplace else mentally.

Attentive listeners progress through these stages: receive, comprehend, interpret, evaluate, and respond. At each stage listeners may tune out or add memory. Effective speakers use various methods for each of these stages to help listeners stay on track. For example, using stimulation and motivation to grab audience attention will definitely help your listeners get started, and careful analysis of your audience's frame of reference can decrease the possibility of decoding problems. Knowing the ways in which listeners may attempt to avoid being persuaded (such as criticizing your credibility) can help you develop tactics to counteract them. Similarly, knowing the subtle signs of listening and inattention will help you adjust your presentation. In addition, you can make remembering easier for your audience by adding personal references, increasing your speaking speed, and using visual aids. Effective speakers are also aware of major listening filters (such as culture, gender, and technology) and plan ahead how to counteract the problems filters can create.

Essentials of Public Speaking Online CourseMate

Use your Online Resources for *Essentials of Public Speaking* for quick access to the electronic study resources that accompany this chapter. Your Online Resources include access to InfoTrac College Edition, Personal Skill Building Activities and Collaborative Skill Building Activities, a digital glossary, sample speeches, and review quizzes.

Key Terms

androgynous 55	external stimuli 57	memory stage 51
attribution theory 50	high context 54	monochromic 54
auditory channel 56	individualistic 53	paraphrase 50
cognitive dissonance 62	internal stimuli 57	polychromic 54
collectivistic 53	interpret stage 49	receive stage 48
comprehend stage 49	kinesthetic channel 56	respond stage 51
credibility 61	listening filters 52	visual channel 56
DEME 56	listening orientations 55	
evaluate stage 50	low context 54	

Personal Skill Building

1. We do our best listening and studying during our peak listening hours because we retain more then. Do you know what your peak listening hours are? For one week keep an active listening journal, recording each time you are listening to information. If you catch yourself using any of the listener–avoidance ploys included in this chapter, mention them in your journal. When listening to an instructor or a speaker on TV, online, or through your Online Resources for *Essentials of Public Speaking,* try this exercise: After listening for 15 minutes or so, stop and test your retention by writing down the speaker's main points. Are you listening by identifying keywords, writing down the keywords, and continually summarizing these words in your mind? If not, try using these techniques during the next 15 minutes of speech. Mention your success or lack of success in your journal. Finally, at the end of the week, assess the information contained in your journal to determine your peak listening times and your worst listening times.

2. Here's another listening-journal idea: During the next week, watch for times when you are "tuning out" a speaker (at a meeting, lecture class, church, and so on). Record what you were thinking about when you realized that you had tuned out. At what stage of the listening process did the difficulty occur?

3. Use InfoTrac College Edition to run a keyword search using *public speaking and listen*★ to narrow listening articles to those about speakers. Look for specific advice you can use to improve the listening of your audience. Share what you find with a classmate.

4. Check out the following websites. (You can access these sites using your Online Resources for *Essentials of Public Speaking*, Chapter 3.)

    • Search **YouTube.com** for a humorous video called "I Hate Public Speaking" by Spoken Impact.

    • Assess your listening skills by taking the Listening Quiz from the Consulting Team and CEO Marilyn Manning. Go to **theconsultingteam.com** and click on "Free" and then "Listening" (under Online Assessments). When you have answered all 20 questions, click on "Get Score" to receive your total score and its interpretation. Write a short paragraph saying whether you agree or disagree with your score and two reasons why you feel this way.

    • To obtain some interesting listening facts, go to the International Listening Association's home page at **listen.org**. Click on "Resources" and then on "Listening Facts." How do these "facts" compare with this chapter?

    • Check out Stephen Boyd's article "Effective Presentations: Getting the Audience to Listen," where he discusses how grabbing your audiences' attention early increases their listening potential. Go to **presentationmagazine.com/effective_presentation.htm**.

Collaborative Skill Building

1. In small groups, select a person on campus or in your community who is recognized as a good speaker. Attend one or more of this person's presentations. Look for the answers to some of the following questions and prepare a report to share with your classmates:

    a. How did the speaker focus the attention and interest of the audience on the topic and away from distractions? Did the speaker win audience attention immediately? How did this affect audience listening?

    b. Was there any point where the speaker's meaning was not clear? How did this affect audience listening?

    c. Was the audience convinced that the speaker was qualified to speak on the subject and did they believe what the speaker presented? How did this belief or lack of belief affect audience listening?

    d. What feedback did audience members give the speaker during and after the presentation? How did the speaker respond to their reactions?

    e. What techniques did the speaker use to help listeners remember the main points? Can your group list three important ideas that were presented? Were these ideas from memory or from notes?

    f. What is your overall evaluation of the presentation on a scale of 1(low) to 10 (high)? What two things could the speaker have done to improve the evaluation given by your group? Why?

2. In small groups of four or five, search **YouTube.com** or **ted.com/talks** for a speech that interests the group. Listen to the speech and identify and evaluate the following:

   a. How skillfully do you think the speaker adapted to his or her audience—be specific.

   b. What specific techniques covered in this chapter did the speaker use to relate to the audience? How well did these techniques work?

   c. Did the speaker use other techniques not covered in this chapter that helped keep audience attention? Discuss them briefly.

   d. Prepare to share your observations with another group or the class.

3. In groups of two to three members, prepare the following:

   a. Locate a speech from *Vital Speeches* or from one of the sample student speeches found in the online resources accompanying your text.

   b. Select two three-minute cuttings (sections) from the speech that can be read to an audience to test their listening skills.

   c. Create a five-question quiz to give the audience after hearing each speech cutting.

   d. Practice reading the cuttings for effective vocal delivery.

   e. Either before the entire class or with another small group, read your cuttings and test the listeners by having them complete the prepared quizzes.

   f. What did you discover about the listening abilities of you and your classmates?

Preparing Your Speech

Test Your Knowledge

What do you know about speech preparation?

The Quick Start Guide gave an overview of speech preparation. The following quiz will help you discover what more you have to learn about the process.

Directions: If you think a statement is generally accurate, mark it T; if you think the statement is a myth, mark it F. Then compare your answers with the explanations at the end of Chapter 4. You can also take this quiz through your Online Resources for *Essentials of Public Speaking*, and if requested, e mail your responses to your instructor.

_____ **1.** Although explanations are necessary to clarify and define, when a speaker overuses this type of supporting material, the result is a dull and boring speech.

_____ **2.** Because first impressions are the most important, you should normally develop your introduction before developing the body of your speech.

_____ **3.** If you are speaking to an uninterested audience, it's best to use a dynamic, theatrical tone of voice.

_____ **4.** It's a good idea to rough out your thoughts in outline form before beginning to research your topic.

_____ **5.** Statistics should be used as often as possible in informative speeches because listeners are impressed when you can back up your arguments with statistics.

_____ **6.** **Wikipedia.org** is a good place to find research for your speeches.

_____ **7.** If you're nervous, it's a good idea to tell the audience so that they will make allowances for you; also you will feel more relaxed.

_____ **8.** The best speaking notes are written out in complete sentences so you won't forget what you want to say.

_____ **9.** Although plagiarism should be a concern when speaking in public, it's only a minor concern to you as a classroom speaker because no one will know.

_____ **10.** Plan your speech so that the body takes approximately 50 percent of your total speech time.

4

Analyzing Your Audience

In his *Rhetoric,* Aristotle suggests that speakers may be more effective when they relate their proposals to things that "create or enhance" listener happiness—a type of audience analysis. His list of things that made Greeks happy included prominent birth, many children, good friends, health, beauty, athletic ability, wealth, honor, power, and virtue.

In the 21st century, speakers continue to be more effective when they relate their proposals to the frames of reference of their audience members. When an audience sees how your proposal or topic relates to them, they are more likely to be motivated to pay attention and even be persuaded to take a particular action. *Which of the items in Aristotle's list no longer motivate audiences today? Which three items would you add to Aristotle's list that are motivators for today's audience?*

Learning Objectives

As you read Chapter 4,

- *Define* the term audience analysis and *explain* why it should be the first step in preparing a speech.
- *Discuss* the four main ways to analyze an audience: situational, demographic, psychological, and audience receptivity.
- *Identify* several strategies for collecting audience information.

CHRISTOPHER COLUMBUS CERTAINLY KNEW THE IMPORTANCE OF AUDIENCE ANALYSIS:

Before Columbus met the King and Queen of Spain, navigational experts in both Portugal and Spain had already recommended against backing his rather unusual proposal to reach the Far East by sailing in the opposite direction—westward.

But Columbus understood the art of persuasion, of tailoring the message to the audience, and he knew how to put together an effective presentation. He knew, for example, that the Queen had a fervent desire to win more converts to her religion. So he made frequent references to the teeming masses of the Orient, just waiting to be converted.

Columbus learned that the Queen loved falcons and exotic birds, so he searched carefully through the accounts of Marco Polo's travels to the Orient and marked in the margin all references to those kingdoms where there were falcons and exotic birds.

He knew the King wanted to expand Spain's commercial power, so he made frequent references to gold, spices, and other fabulous riches of the East.

All these points were worked into his presentation, which won the backing that [he desired] (Brash, 1992, pp. 83–84).

When you analyze an audience as Columbus did, you aren't trying to trick, manipulate, or coerce them; you are simply making sure that your message fits their frames of reference so that they will give you a fair hearing. As simple as this sounds, lack of careful audience analysis is *the number one reason that speeches fail to meet their goals* (St. John, 1995). By the time you finish this chapter, you will be ready to use audience analysis in your next speech and will have completed Step 1 in the "Basic Steps for Preparing a Speech," covered in the Quick Start Guide to Public Speaking located at the beginning of this text.

Although there are many ways to analyze your expected audience, we recommend that as soon as the event is scheduled, you begin looking for the situational, demographic, and psychological information you will need to know about your audience in order to plan a speech that will hold their interest and satisfy their needs.

Analyzing Your Audience: Situational Information

A good place to begin when analyzing an audience is to learn as much as you can about what the speaking situation is most likely to be. The **situational information** includes the size and nature of the audience, their knowledge of the topic, and their opinion of you and your announced presentation. It is also important to know the nature of other speeches they will hear before or after yours. Here are some questions to keep in mind as you gather the situational information:

- *Are audience members attending voluntarily?* Do they have a particular interest in hearing you and your topic, or are they attending because they are required to do so? Voluntary audiences tend to be **homogeneous**—that is, members have a fair amount in common. Because your classroom audience is an involuntary or "captive" audience, it is probably fairly **heterogeneous**—that is, members differ in various ways, including interests, major and minor fields of study, work experience, and age.

- *How many people will be attending?* The size of your audience is a crucial factor for several reasons, including the type of visual aids you will use. For example, a flip chart works well for small audiences but is ineffective for audiences of 30 or more. Similarly, gestures must be larger and the volume must be louder for large audiences.

- *How much does your audience know (or think they know) about your topic?* If the topic is discussed frequently in the mass media, your audience will likely be somewhat familiar with it. If so, you won't have to give much background information. However, if your topic is fairly new or is not covered much in the mass media, you will need to present more background information and dispel any general misconceptions about the topic. In addition, the less the audience knows about your topic, the more important it is that you begin with a dynamic introduction that catches their interest. → *Chapter 7 gives detailed information on attention-getters.*

- *What does your audience know about you, and what general opinion does it have of you?* If members have heard you give other speeches or know of you through other activities, they probably have already formed an opinion of you. If their opinions are positive, they are more likely to feel positive about your speech topic. But if they don't know you or have a negative opinion of your expertise, establish your credibility by these methods: (1) Cite statistics and sources that your audience considers highly credible; (2) prepare professional visuals; and (3) use a forceful, controlled delivery. → *Chapter 13 gives additional information on establishing your credibility.*

- *What type of presentation is your audience expecting?* If your audience is expecting a multimedia presentation with color and sound but you give an intimate speech with only black-and-white computer visuals, members will be disappointed no matter how excellent your speech. Likewise, if the audience is expecting a serious, scholarly speech but you present a humorous, after-dinner-type talk, members will not feel satisfied either. Knowing your audience's expectations helps you choose appropriate topics, visual aids, delivery style, and appearance.

- *Will anyone be speaking before you?* If so, on what topic? At political rallies, at conventions, and in college classrooms, several speeches may be given in a row. The atmosphere created by each speech (whether positive or negative) lingers into the next speech. For example, as you step up to the lectern, you may see that the audience is still amused by the previous humorous speech.

Here is the attention-getter from an introduction to a speech given at the West 2010 conference of the Armed Forces Communications and Electronics Association, U.S. Naval Institute in San Diego, California, by Ralph W. Shrader (2010), Chairman and CEO of Booz Allen Hamilton Inc. Do you think his words would grab audience attention and direct it away from the mood set by a previous speaker?

> To begin this morning, I'd like to ask you to imagine it's a year from now, February 4, 2011, and some frightening things have happened in the past 12 months. It's your job to go back in time to today, and make things turn out differently. It's up to you to set things right, to save the future. It could be the future of our country, your organization, an individual colleague, or even your own future.
>
> The sci-fi mavens here in the audience can probably name dozens of movies, books, and TV shows built around this plot, including the current hit *Avatar.* Personally, I'm more of a casual fan who enjoys the escapism of Star Trek, and I find it striking how many heroes—from Captains Kirk and Piccard, to Denzel Washington and Nicolas Cage in more recent thrillers—find it in their job description to "fix the future" (p. 156).

When you follow another speaker, your introduction is even more important than usual. If the previous speech relates to yours, mention how. If it doesn't, mention how your speech will differ, or make a startling statement to shock the audience into another mood.

Remember

Situational information includes . . .

- Voluntary or required attendance.
- The number of people expected to attend.
- Audience knowledge of the topic.
- Audience knowledge of you (the speaker).
- The type of presentation the audience is expecting.
- Other speakers and their topics.

Use a database like Info-Trac College Edition, EBSCOhost, or CQ Researcher to locate polling *data* on specific target audiences. The following search terms also will find you interesting information: *American demographics, working women, baby boomers.* For additional information, do another search using *audience analysis.* Compare the information you find with the material in this chapter.

Active Critical Thinking

To think further about situational information, complete the following:

- For your next speech (probably an informative one), list two topics that you are considering using.
- For each topic, conduct a situational analysis of your audience by answering the six situational questions listed in the Remember Box above.

Analyzing Your Audience: Demographic Information

Your next task as you are planning your speech is to analyze the demographic makeup of your audience. **Demographic information** includes general audience characteristics such as age, gender, marital status, education, economic status, occupation (or current job), major field of study, political beliefs, religion, cultural background, and group identification. If you are familiar with the audience (your classmates, for example), you can observe many of these characteristics yourself. If you are unfamiliar with the audience, ask for input from the person who invited you to speak, as well as from two or three members of the prospective audience.

Identifying Specific Demographic Characteristics

Although audiences are made up of individuals, members often share similar attributes or demographic characteristics. To give you an idea of what demographic information could be helpful in planning your speech, let's take a brief look at the major demographic characteristics:

- **Age.** Because age is related to interests, knowledge of audience members' ages can guide you in selecting a topic and picking appropriate supporting materials to interest and persuade them. For example, what age group would you expect to prefer listening to Neil Diamond, Tony Bennett, and Peter, Paul, and Mary? What age group listens to Lloyd, Red Hot Chili Peppers, and Christina Aguilera? Would they be older or younger than the age group that prefers Linkin Park, Blink 182, Rihanna, Katy Perry, and B.o.B? Although knowing the general age of audience members can be helpful, it may also be misleading unless you explore other demographic factors as well. For example, some high school and college students enjoy listening to "golden oldies" from the sixties (such as the Beatles and the Beach Boys) as much as their parents do.

How might the interests of this audience differ from those of an audience of college sophomores?

Bob Daemmrich/The Image Works

- **Ethnic and Cultural Background.** Your classroom audience may be more diverse than the population of your hometown. If so, be aware that members of culturally diverse groups may have different interests and expectations of what makes a good speech. Take eye contact, for example. Some Asian cultures—such as Chinese, Thai, and Indian—generally prefer that speakers not make direct eye contact or even focus on individual faces in the audience (Hall, 1992). Similarly, animated facial expressions and spontaneous gestures, which are the norm in the United States, may appear brash and egotistical to some Japanese listeners. Visual aids may also cause cultural problems. For example, people from some cultures might be offended at the informality of writing on a flip chart during a presentation, viewing it as a lack of preparation (Dulek et al., 1991). Finally, the way you organize your main points could be interpreted differently depending on the culture. Individualistic/low-context audiences (like those in the United States) expect main ideas up front and respond negatively to speakers who take forever to get to the point. However, collectivistic/high-context audiences (like those in Japan and Latin American countries) expect ideas to be presented more slowly and respond negatively to "brash" speakers that are inappropriately direct (Guffey, 2010).

- **Gender.** Another demographic characteristic that can give you clues to possible audience interests is gender. Be careful to avoid gender stereotyping. To assume that all men enjoy sports and women do not or that all women are interested in cooking and men are not would likely lead to some negative audience reactions. If you have both men and women in your audience, you need to relate your topic to both genders; if you can't, select a different topic (Wood, 2011). Also, when speaking to a mixed audience, be sure that your word choices show gender sensitivity. It's best to avoid masculine or feminine terms and expressions and to substitute more gender-sensitive words. For example, instead of "policeman" or "policewoman," say "police officer;" instead of "stewardess," say "flight attendant." ➔ *A more detailed discussion of gender-sensitive words and phrases is included in Chapter 9; check Chapter 3 for additional gender information.*

- **Group Affiliation.** Most people are very proud of the groups to which they belong—whether it is the Campus Crusade for Christ, the marching band, the drama club, or a sorority. Knowing that your audience members belong to a particular social, religious, or political group (even if your topic isn't about their group) can help you identify what is important to them and what questions they are likely to ask. Referring to this group during your speech lets members know that you are aware of them and are speaking to them personally.

- **Marital Status, Children, and Elderly Parents.** Knowing whether your listeners are predominantly single, married, divorced, or cohabiting and whether they have children can help you select examples that will relate to rather than offend them. If you wish to give a speech on a subject related to marriage, divorce, children, or elderly parents, don't forget your classmates who are not married or don't plan on ever marrying, those who have no children or don't plan on having any, or those who are not caring for elderly parents. If you can't relate your speech to them personally, you may be able to do so indirectly. For instance, they likely have relatives, close friends, and even neighbors who have children or elderly parents, so your topic can still have relevance for them.

- **Occupation, Education, College Major, and Economic Status.** Focusing on one or more of these demographic characteristics could provide you with valuable information on audience members and their interests. Do you think an audience of well-paid professionals would have different interests than an audience of blue-collar workers? If you knew that your audience members had college degrees, would your choice of topic, vocabulary, and examples be different than if your audience members were still in high school? For your college speech class, knowing your classmates' majors and minors could be helpful. For example, if the majority of your classmates are majoring in the same subject as you, you can go much more in depth into your subject.

All the demographic characteristics discussed here can help you understand the frames of reference of your audience members and identify ways to communicate more effectively with them.

Use a database like Info-Trac College Edition, EBSCOhost, or CQ Researcher to find more audience-analysis information. Conduct a keyword search for *gender and nonverbal, gender and attitudes, sex roles, culture and values,* or *Rokeach and values.* Also, using Advanced Search, find one of these journals: *Sex Roles. A Journal of Research* or *American Demographics;* read two or more interesting articles. If using InfoTrac, be sure to type in *j=* before typing the journal name.

Using Technology to Search for Cultural Demographic Information

The Internet makes collecting audience information amazingly easy. For example, if you know that several of your audience members are from a group demographically different from your own, you can use the Internet to research the customs and beliefs of that group. Search engines such as Yahoo! and Google are good places to begin. For Yahoo!, click on "Categories" and "Regional;" for Google, go to "More," "Groups," and "Browse all group categories," and then select a category under "Region." For specific demographic information, check the following sites:

- Religion: ipl2—Information You Can Trust (**www.ipl2.org**). Click on "Arts & Humanities," "Religion."

- African Americans: African American Web Connection (**www.aawc .com/zaawc0.html**).

- Asian Americans: UCLA Asian American Studies Center (**www.aasc .ucla.edu/default.asp**).

- Native Americans: American Indians (**www.hanksville.org/ NAresources**).

- Hispanic Americans: The Library of Congress Hispanic Reading Room (**www.loc.gov/rr/hispanic**).

- Gender Issues: University of Texas "Statistics and Demographics" (**www .lib.utexas.edu/refsites/statistics.html**). Scroll down for valuable links.

Also, the organization or group that has asked you to speak may have its own website, which may contain additional information about the goals, beliefs, and values of its members. To locate the site, ask the person who originally contacted you or use a search engine.

Remember

Demographic information includes . . .

- Age.
- Ethnic and cultural background.
- Gender.
- Group affiliations.
- Marital status, children, and elderly parents.
- Occupation, education, college major, and economic status.

Choosing Which Demographic Characteristics to Use

Your topic determines which demographic characteristics are relevant for a particular speech. Suppose you want to give a speech on the importance of regular exercise. Political beliefs, religion, and cultural background would probably not be important considerations, but the age and gender of your audience members could be. For example, if your audience consisted of traditional college-age students, you might stress the value of regular exercise for maintaining a healthy, attractive body; identify the local physical-fitness club as a place to socialize; and suggest that exercise breaks make long hours of study less tedious. On the other hand, an audience consisting mainly of 30- to 40-year-olds is likely to be raising children and/or establishing careers, so they have probably slacked off on exercising. For such an audience, you might want to mention how valuable exercise is in reducing the stress associated with children and careers; how athletic clubs cater to parents by offering child-care facilities; how foldaway treadmills and exercise bikes make exercise at home convenient; and how exercising with a colleague during lunch or after work makes exercise more fun. Obviously, if you were speaking to an audience of senior citizens, your focus would shift again. You might stress that walking and using weight machines add years of mobility and enjoyment to people's lives even if they rarely exercised when they were younger.

For all three of these audiences, the basic topic is the same, but the focus of the speech changes to relate to their interests and needs. Of course, as with all of your speeches, no matter what approach you take, you will need to cite sources and give examples to convince listeners that you know what you are talking about.

→ *Chapter 6 discusses supporting your ideas in detail.*

Active Critical Thinking

To think further about demographic information, complete the following:

- Using the two speech topics you selected in the previous activity, list at least four demographic characteristics that you think will be the most important for each topic.

- Select one of the topics and conduct a demographic analysis of your audience through observation and by asking questions. If your audience will be the class, validate your collected data by comparing it with the data gathered by other class members.

Analyzing Your Audience: Psychological Information

Determining psychological information about your audience—their attitudes, beliefs, values, and needs—is also important in preparing a speech (especially a persuasive speech) that relates specifically to listeners' frames of reference. See Figure 4.1 for a pictorial view of how these characteristics relate to one another.

Values

Deep-seated principles that serve as personal guidelines for behavior are **values** (Rokeach, 2000). They are usually learned from social institutions, such as family, church, and school. Values provide the underlying support for beliefs and attitudes. Researcher Milton Rokeach identified two types of values: terminal and instrumental. **Terminal values** are life goals or ideal states of being—in other words, "ends." **Instrumental values** are guides for conduct that help us fulfill our terminal values—in other words, "means." Although we possess only a few terminal values, we possess a great many instrumental values (Warnick & Inch, 1994). For example, most of us seek an education (instrumental value) with the goal of a rewarding career (terminal value). People who work hard (instrumental value) usually have the goal of a comfortable life (terminal value) (Warnick & Inch, p. 213).

For three decades Rokeach researched how Americans ranked 18 key terminal values, and he found their rankings to be highly stable across time, with only minor changes in 30 years (Warnick & Inch, p. 215):

1. world peace
2. family security
3. freedom
4. a comfortable life

5. happiness
6. self respect
7. a sense of accomplishment
8. wisdom

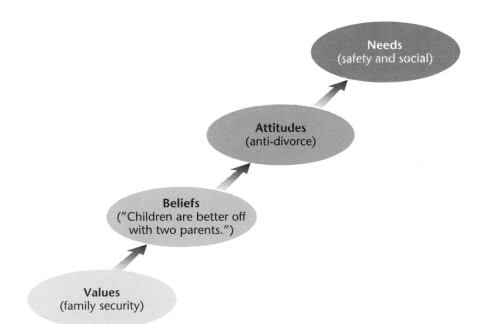

Figure 4.1

Psychological Factors Used in Audience Analysis

Values, beliefs, attitudes, and needs build on one another; the successful speaker relates these factors to listeners' frames of reference.

9.	equality	14.	mature love
10.	national security	15.	a world of beauty
11.	true friendship	16.	social recognition
12.	salvation	17.	pleasure
13.	inner harmony	18.	an exciting life

Not only do values appear to be stable across time, but Rokeach found only minor differences between the rankings by men and women and between those by blacks and whites. However, as you might expect, there were sizable differences between the rankings of Americans and people from other cultures (for example, Australians, Canadians, and Israelis). Thus, when you are speaking to multicultural audiences, don't automatically assume that your high-ranked values are necessarily the same as those of your listeners. For example, refer back to Chapter 1 to the comparison of the top 10 cultural values of citizens from the United States, Japan, and Arab countries (Figure 1.2). This list of values is similar to but different from Rokeach's list. Note that the top three American values (freedom, independence, and self-reliance) don't even appear in the top 10 lists of the Japanese or Arabs. In the same way, the top three Japanese values (belonging, group harmony, and collectiveness) as well as the top three Arab values (family security, family harmony, and parental guidance) do not appear in the top 10 list of American values.

Because values are so stable, they are more difficult to change than beliefs or attitudes. When giving a persuasive speech, you should generally try to highlight (or reinforce) one or more audience values and show how your ideas or proposals fit into those values. Also, knowing your audience's values will help you determine what evidence and emotional appeals will be needed to convince them that a particular belief or attitude conflicts with their basic values. ➡ *For more on how values and persuasion work, see "Social Judgment Theory" in Chapter 13.*

Beliefs

In your psychological analysis, discovering your listeners' basic values is an important step to learning their beliefs. A **belief** is the mental acceptance that something is true even if we can't prove that it is. For example, even though they may not be able to cite any definitive sources, some people believe that college is important, that women are discriminated against, that lateness shows disrespect, and that big government is bad. Although listeners may not realize it, these beliefs are a result of their terminal and instrumental values. If you discover that a belief is based on false information or that the audience thinks they know more than they actually do, you will have a better idea of what information and arguments to present in your speech.

Attitudes

An **attitude** is a feeling of approval or disapproval of a person, group, idea, or event. For example, you might approve of gay rights, disapprove of women in the military, or approve of recycling programs. A poll on the American family found single-earner couples to have the most rational attitudes, single parents to have the most modern attitudes, and dual-earner couples to have more-modern attitudes than do single-earner couples but to have traditional attitudes about divorce and one-parent families (McGuire, 1985).

Attitudes are based on beliefs (Jowett & O'Donnell, 2006). For example, someone may hold a pro-college attitude based on the belief that education is important, or someone may have a favorable attitude toward equal-rights legislation based on the belief that women are discriminated against. Attitudes may differ according to audience demographics including age, gender, and culture.

Attitudes can influence behaviors—the stronger the attitude, the more likely the action (Perloff, 2010). Therefore, your search for psychological information about your audience should begin with your audience's attitudes. Will they approve or disapprove of your topic? Will they favor or oppose your proposal? According to the **theory of reasoned action** (Fishbein & Ajzen, 1975; Hall et al., 2002), "people rationally calculate the costs and benefits of engaging in a particular action and think carefully about how others will view the behavior under consideration" (Perloff, p. 95). Effective speakers help in this thought process.

Needs

A **need** is a state in which an unsatisfied condition exists. *Needs are a result of values, beliefs, and attitudes.* We all have needs and wants that motivate us. If you can show in your introduction or supporting materials how listener needs will be completely or partially satisfied by information in your speech, the listener will pay close attention. Likewise, if you can show how taking a particular action will partially or completely satisfy a need, the listener will more likely take the action. In some cases you may have to show an audience that a need exists before you can use it to motivate behavior. For example, you won't be very successful selling a new type of lock to audience members who feel safe at home. But when you show them the police statistics on how many homes have been broken into in their community during the past six months and demonstrate how easy it is to pick the typical lock on a front door, they will have second thoughts about their feelings of security. And if you can anchor an unsatisfied need to audience beliefs or values (such as "It is the responsibility of parents to provide a safe home environment for their children"), your audience is even more likely to listen and be persuaded.

Maslow's Hierarchy of Needs In the mid-1900s, psychologist Abraham Maslow (1954, 1973) researched and published his theory of human motivation. Maslow believed that all people have the same basic needs, which he divided into five categories: physiological, safety, social, esteem, and self-actualization (see Figure 4.2). These needs are illustrated as levels in a pyramid with lower-level needs at the bottom. Although people may be motivated by several levels at a time, usually the needs at the bottom of the pyramid must be satisfied before higher-level needs become important. Maslow's hierarchy of needs is a useful guide for adapting your speech to your audience's needs and wants.

Self-actualization needs

Esteem needs

Social needs

Safety needs

Physiological needs

Figure 4.2

Maslow's Basic Hierarchy of Human Needs

Here are examples of needs at each level of Maslow's hierarchy (Lefton et al., 1991):

1. *Physiological needs*—food, shelter, clothing, air, water, and sleep.
2. *Safety needs*—a job and financial security; law and order; protection from injury, poor health, harm, or death; and freedom from fear.
3. *Social needs*—love, companionship, friendship, and a feeling of belonging to one or more groups.
4. *Esteem needs*—pride, recognition from others, status and prestige, and self-recognition.
5. *Self-actualization needs*—becoming the best person one can, developing to one's fullest capabilities, and achieving worthwhile goals.

Applying Needs Analysis Because audience members have different frames of reference, it's unlikely that they will all be concerned and motivated by the same needs. As illustrated in Figure 4.1, needs grow out of values, beliefs, and attitudes. If you have determined these, the audience's basic needs should be fairly obvious.

Remember that before your listeners can focus on the higher needs in Maslow's model, their lower-level needs must be mostly satisfied. For example, if your audience is concerned about safety issues (perhaps a series of drive-by shootings has made everyone very nervous), appealing to the high-level ideals of self-actualization and esteem is unlikely to interest or persuade. On the other hand, a need that has already been met (the gang members were caught and the community feels safe again) is no longer a motivator. Select two or three of the lowest levels that represent your audience's needs and use them as motivators in your speech. Fitting your message to audience needs is called **framing**. You might also keep in mind that listeners are often "more motivated by the thought of losing something than by the thought of gaining something" (Dillard & Pfau, 2002, p. 520). Therefore, framing your messages to stress potential losses that could occur if a certain action is not taken enhances persuasion. *Loss framing* is especially effective in situations where risk and uncertainty are prevalent (De Dreu & McCusker, 1997; Tversky & Kahneman, 1981). ➜ *A more detailed discussion of using audience needs to persuade appears in Chapter 13.*

Hazards of Incomplete Psychological Analysis

One recent example that illustrates what happens when analysis of an audience's attitudes, beliefs, values, and needs is used correctly is located in the "Speaking to Make a Difference" section on page 84. For a famous example of what happens when analysis is incomplete, consider the following incident. On August 31, 1997, Diana, Princess of Wales, died in a car accident in France. At the time of Diana's death, Queen Elizabeth and family were on holiday at Balmoral Castle in Scotland. It was the Queen's feeling that grief is a private affair and that Prince William and Prince Harry would be better off to remain where they were at Balmoral Castle until the funeral; other than confirmation of the death, she planned to make no statements to the press (Benoit & Brinson, 1999). Unfortunately, the Queen and her advisors seriously misread the effect her silence would have on the British people—in other words, their psychological analysis of the British audience was incomplete. Shock and grief at Diana's death turned to anger as people read the Queen's silence and failure to return to London (as well as her failure to fly the Royal Standard over Buckingham Palace at half-mast) as a sign that she was uncaring about the tragedy and unfeeling toward her subjects' grief. The extent of public anger was displayed by London newspaper headlines such as, "Your People Are Suffering. Speak to Us Ma'am," "Where is Our Queen? Where is Her Flag?" and "Show Us You Care" (Benoit & Brinson, p. 146). Due to the outcry of public indignation, the Queen was forced to make some unplanned adjustments. She and the Royal Family returned to London and were seen inspecting the "flowers, cards, candles, and other remembrances" (p. 145) that inundated the grounds of Buckingham Palace, Kensington Palace, and Westminster Abbey. Even though the Royal Standard only flies when the monarch is in residence and never flies at half-mast even upon the death of a monarch, the "Queen ordered the Royal Standard to fly at half-mast during Diana's funeral" (p. 146). She also scheduled an unprecedented speech the evening before Diana's funeral, where she told Britons, "So what I say to you now, as your Queen and as a grandmother, I say from my heart." (To listen to the Queen's speech, type in "Diana Princess of Wales Tribute" on **youtube.com**.) More than a million people lined the streets in London along the funeral procession, and an estimated 2.5 billion people worldwide watched on television and the Internet (Balz, 1997).

The Queen and Royal Family's incomplete audience analysis (overlooking the psychological factor) led to problems with unexpected public reactions. As mentioned at the beginning of the chapter, if Christopher Columbus had ignored the psychological factor in his analysis of the king and queen of Spain, it's unlikely that they would have agreed to finance his expedition. Audience analysis includes more than just situational and demographic characteristics; it also includes psychological characteristics in the form of *values, beliefs, attitudes,* and *needs* of your listeners. The result of incomplete audience analysis could be nothing more than bored listeners, but it could also be angry, disbelieving listeners who are motivated to work against your position. Although inadequate audience analysis is unlikely to cause such a dramatically negative reaction in a classroom audience, treat your classroom as a laboratory setting and try to find out as much about your classmates as possible. Use them to sharpen your audience-analysis skills.

Remember

Psychological information includes . . .

- Audience attitudes.
- Audience beliefs.
- Audience values.
- Audience needs.

Active Critical Thinking

To think further about psychological information, complete the following:

- Using the speech topic you gathered demographic information for in the previous activity, list any major *values, beliefs,* and *attitudes* your audience members seem to have that will impact their interest and attention toward your speech.

- What *unsatisfied need* exists in some of your audience members that you can use as a motivator in your speech? Will it work best as an attention-getter or as an element in the body of your speech? Why?

Speaking to Make a Difference

Technology has given customers powerful ways to retaliate if they are ignored or mistreated. For example, when United Airlines luggage handlers broke the guitar of Canadian musician and songwriter Dave Carroll on his way to a performance in March of 2008, Caroll took matters into his own hands. After nine months of getting the runaround by officials at United, Caroll recorded three entertaining musical videos called "United Breaks Guitars, Songs 1, 2, & 3," which he posted on YouTube. As of July 29, 2010, Song 1 had been viewed 9.7 million times on YouTube. To view all three songs, go to **youtube.com** or Carroll's website at **www.davecarrollmusic .com**. The lyrics for *United Breaks Guitars: Song 1* included below, shows his frustrations in dealing with United Airline employees:

AP Photo/The Canadian Press/ Andrew Vaughan

I flew United Airlines on my way to Nebraska
The plane departed Halifax connecting in Chicago's O'Hare
While on the ground a passenger said from the seat behind me
"My God, they're throwing guitars out there"

The band and I exchanged a look, best described as terror
At the action on the tarmac and knowing whose projectiles these would be
So before I left Chicago, I alerted three employees
Who showed complete indifference towards me

Chorus:
United, United
You broke my Taylor guitar
United, United
Some big help you are
You broke it, you should fix it
You're liable, just admit it
I should have flown with someone else or gone by car
'Cause United Breaks Guitars

When we landed in Nebraska, I confirmed what I'd suspected
My Taylor'd been the victim of a vicious act of malice at O'Hare
So began a yearlong saga of pass the buck, don't ask me,
And I'm sorry, Sir, your claim can go nowhere

So to all the airlines people, from New York to New Delhi
Including kind Ms. Irlweg who says the final word from them is "No"
I've heard all of your excuses and I've chased your wild gooses
And this attitude of yours I say must go

Chorus

Well, I won't say that I'll never fly with you again 'cause maybe
To save the world I probably would, but that won't likely happen
And if it did, I wouldn't bring my luggage 'cause you'd just go and break it
Into a thousand pieces just like you broke my heart when United Breaks Guitars

Chorus

Yeah, United Breaks Guitars
Yeah, United Breaks Guitars

Lyrics transcribed from the video; © 2009 Dave Carroll (SOCAN).

The facts of the story, according to Carroll (2009), include:

- Prior to deplaning in Chicago for the last leg of a trip to Omaha from Halifax, a passenger sitting behind Carroll noticed that baggage handlers were throwing guitars that belonged to Carroll and his band.

- He tried to complain to three different United flight attendants before leaving Chicago, with no success. When they arrived in Omaha at 12:30 a.m., there were no employees available at all.

- Early the next morning, after being picked up by the tour manager, Carroll discovered that his $3,500 Taylor guitar was broken into two pieces.

- Trying to file a claim and contact the "correct" person to discuss reimbursement for his guitar was even more frustrating. At various times he was told to talk to all of the following: The ground crew in Omaha, the airport where the trip began (Halifax), the airport where the damage occurred (Chicago), United's 1-800 number in India, and Central Baggage in New York. Carroll notes, "The system is designed to frustrate affected customers into giving up their claims and United is

very good at it." The last person he spoke with, Ms. Irlweg, told him nothing could be done even after he offered to settle for payment of $1,200 in flight vouchers to reimburse having the guitar repaired.

- He gave up after telling her he would write three songs about his experiences with United in video form, offer them as a free download online, and ask viewers to vote on their favorite song. His goal, he told her, was "to get one million hits in one year" —a modest goal, as it turned out.

"United Breaks Guitars" was posted on Monday, July 6, 2009, and by Thursday it had 400,000 hits. According to Benet Wilson in her July 9, 2009, blog post titled "United Airlines Sees Power of Viral PR Up Close and Personal," Carroll's video already had over 100 news stories and 2,000 blogs written about it, including multiple television-network reports. United Airlines even explained its actions and made apologies on Twitter. On July 10th, United posted on Twitter that, following Dave's request, they had donated $3,000 to the Thelonius Monk Institute of Jazz. A spokeswoman for United told the *Chicago Sun Times* that they were interested in using the video "for training purposes to ensure that all customers receive better service from us" (Jackson, 2009).

continued

By Sunday, just six day after the video was posted, more than 2.4 million viewers had watched it—one year later, almost 10 million viewers have seen it. Carroll and his band, Sons of Maxwell, are in constant demand—they are booked for tours over a year in advance; Carroll gives motivational speeches about his experience and the importance of customer service; and with Song 3 posted on YouTube in July 2010, United is still feeling the pressure.

When United ignored Carroll's request for reimbursement, he was forced to find a different avenue through which to communicate. So let's summarize what made "United Breaks Guitars: Song 1" so successful—more successful than Carroll had even dreamed:

- *Social Media.* As United Airlines found out, social media such as YouTube, blogs, Facebook, and Twitter can be quite persuasive. In her blog, Benet Wilson (2009) noted: "The lesson here is we now live in a world where anyone can use free social media tools to get situations resolved when companies won't listen."

- *Audience analysis* Carroll's audience was more than United Airlines—his message resonated with the many travelers who have experienced similar problems with airline customer service. His use of language painted a vivid picture that related to their own problems regardless of their ages or countries of origin.

- *Quality video/quality music.* In addition to making a point and getting the attention of United, Dave Carroll and his band were a hit! The song was clever, the video funny, and the music really enjoyable. Carroll's more than 20 years of experience singing and writing songs is obvious. Carroll ended his background explanation of the incident, after posting his first song, with this statement:

"I should thank United. They've given me a creative outlet that has brought people together from around the world ... So, thanks, United! If my guitar had to be smashed due to extreme negligence, I'm glad it was you that did it. Now sit back and enjoy the show" (Carroll, 2009).

Question: What other speech elements do you think helped make this video so successful? Did you enjoy it? If so, why?

Analyzing Audience Receptivity

Once you have analyzed your audience according to situational, demographic, and psychological characteristics, you need to factor in how generally receptive they will be to you. To do this, you need to determine your **audience type** which determines their receptivity:

- **Friendly audience**—This audience has heard you speak before, has heard positive things about you, or is simply sold on your topic. These listeners are looking forward to your speech and are expecting to enjoy themselves.

- **Neutral** or **impartial audience**—These audience members consider themselves objective, rational, and open to new information (even though many of them have already made up their minds). They are looking for logic and facts (not emotion) and will be more receptive if you signal credibility and authority.

- **Uninterested** or **indifferent audience**—These listeners have a short attention span and often wish they were someplace else; therefore, they're a real challenge. They will probably be polite, but will also plan to take a "mental holiday" during your presentation. A bit of razzle-dazzle may be needed to keep their interest.

- **Hostile audience**—Although you need to be careful not to stereotype any audience, this audience may be the greatest challenge of all, because they are predisposed to dislike you, your topic, or both. Don't be intimidated or defensive. Stay in charge by presenting a calm, controlled appearance while citing expert data.

Table 4.1 summarizes strategies for dealing with each type of audience. ➜ *For additional information, see also Chapter 6 on supporting materials; Chapter 7 on organization; and Chapter 8 on delivery.*

Table 4.1   Strategies for Dealing with Four Types of Audiences

Audience Type	Strategies		
	Organization	Delivery	Supporting Material
Friendly (predisposed to like you and your topic)	Any pattern. Try something new; ask for audience participation.	Warm, friendly, open. Make lots of eye contact, smile, gesture, and use vocal variety.	Humor, examples, personal experiences, quotations, statistics, comparisons, pictures, and Clip Art.
Neutral (consider themselves calm and rational; have minds already made up but stories, think they are objective)	Pro/con or problem–solution patterns. Present both sides of the issue. Save time for audience questions. Use logic.	Controlled, even; nothing "showy." Use confident, small gestures; adopt look of authority and credibility.	Facts, statistics, expert opinion, comparison and contrast. Avoid humor, personal flashy visuals.
Uninterested (short attention span, present against their wills, plan to tune out)	Brief—no more than three points. Avoid topical and pro–con patterns that seem long to the audience.	Dynamic and entertaining. Move around; use large gestures.	Humor, cartoons, colorful visuals, powerful quotations, startling statistics, and anecdotes.
	Do not: Darken the room, stand motionless behind the podium, pass out handouts, use boring view-graphs, or expect audience to participate.		
Hostile (looking for chances to take charge or ridicule speaker; attitude, due to bad past experiences)	Noncontroversial pattern such as topical, chronological, or geographical.	Calm and controlled. Speak slowly and evenly. Stay in charge.	Objective data and expert opinion. Avoid anecdotes and jokes.
	Avoid: Question-and-answer period if possible. Otherwise, use a moderator or accept only written questions.		

Source: Adapted from Janet E. Elsea, "Strategies for Effective Presentations," *Personnel Journal* 64 (September 1985), 31–33.

Active Critical Thinking

To think further about audience receptivity, complete the following:

- Using the speech topic from the previous activity, determine how receptive your audience is likely to be toward your speech by deciding their audience type—friendly, neutral, uninterested, or hostile.
- Which strategies does the text suggest you use when dealing with this type audience? Which one do you think will be the most successful? Why?

Sample Informative Speech: "Our Solar System and the Three Dwarves" by Kara Hoekstra

The following informative speech, "Our Solar System and the Three Dwarves," was given by Kara Hoekstra to her speech class and was transcribed after the speech was completed. Kara's class was an online course, but all speeches were given on campus with a classroom audience of 20 students. The assignment specified a 5- to 7-minute informational speech using PowerPoint slides followed by a 2- to 3-minute question-and-answer period and a 1-minute (or less) final wrap-up. Kara's speech will be referred to throughout the text to illustrate how she went through the process of preparing her speech (see Kara's audience-analysis procedures on pages 93–95. As you read this speech, think about changes you would make if you were speaking on the same topic.

Sample Informative Speech

OUR SOLAR SYSTEM AND THE THREE DWARVES

by Kara Hoekstra

Introduction

My very excellent mother just served us nine pizzas [*Visual 1*].
My very elegant mother just sat upon nine porcupines.
My very easy method just set up nine planets.

Now, the phrases I just stated are memory aids that help us remember the order of the planets by applying the first letter of each word to the first letter of each planet: Mercury, Venus, Earth, Mars, Jupiter, Saturn, Uranus, Neptune, and Pluto. But, what if I told you there were no more pizzas, no more porcupines, and no more planets? Now, as children we grew up knowing that there were nine planets in our solar system. However, experts have recently demoted Pluto to a dwarf planet. Now, speaking of experts, I don't happen to claim to be an expert in astronomy or anything—it just happens to have been an interest of mine since childhood. What is really interesting about this subject is that what we have known as children has recently changed. And even though Pluto has been reclassified, it is not alone. You are about to discover the changes in our solar system, including the new definitions for a planet and a dwarf planet, the reason Pluto didn't make the cut for a planet, and the two other objects in our solar system now considered dwarf planets as well.

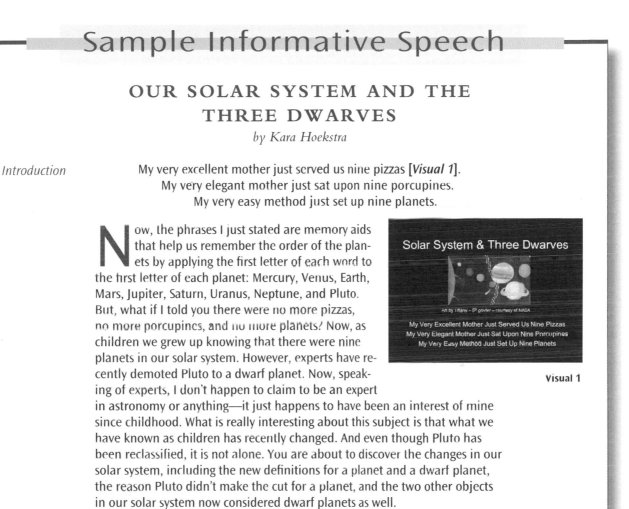

Visual 1

Body
1st Main
Point

The new definitions for a planet and a dwarf planet were voted on by the International Astronomical Union in August of 2006. Due to some new discoveries, the IAU felt it was important to redefine the term *planet* as well as establish the new term *dwarf planet*. NASA's website gives us the definition for both [*Visual 2*]. For an object to meet the definition "planet," it must meet three pieces of criteria: it must orbit the sun, be nearly spherical in shape, and have cleared the neighborhood around its orbit.

Visual 2

Sample Informative Speech *(continued)*

For an object to be considered a "dwarf planet," it must meet four pieces of criteria: it must orbit the sun, be nearly spherical in shape, not be a moon or satellite of another object, and has not cleared the neighborhood around its orbit [*Visual 3*].

2nd Main Point   Now that we know the definitions of a planet and dwarf planet, what does it exactly mean when a planet has not cleared the area around its orbit? Well, an online article in *Today's Science* tells us that the major difference between Pluto and the other eight planets is that Pluto "flunks" when it comes to clearing the neighborhood around its orbit. To explain this, picture the Earth [*Visual 4*]. Here it is making its way around the sun. It doesn't have to travel through asteroids or other bits of space rock. It's as if the Earth had taken a broom a long time ago and swept out its orbit along its path, leaving a nice, clean path to travel through.

Pluto, on the other hand [*Visual 5*], is in the Kuiper Belt region, and what the IAU decision really came down to was this: Pluto dwells in a cluttered home. Now the Kuiper Belt is a region of icy debris and asteroids, and Pluto's orbit is roughly in the middle of the Kuiper Belt, causing it to have to travel through all of this icy debris and space rock. So Pluto dwells in a cluttered home, and that is basically the difference between a planet and dwarf planet.

So to recap, they do have a few things in common: Both planets and dwarf planets must orbit the sun and be spherical in shape. In addition, a dwarf planet cannot be a satellite or moon of another object. The *major* difference here is that a planet has swept out its orbit while a dwarf planet dwells in a cluttered home. And now that we know the definition of a dwarf planet, there are two other dwarf planets in our solar system as well. Their names are Eris and Ceres.

3rd Main Point   An article in *Newsweek* tells us that astronomer Mike Brown confirmed the discovery of an object in the Kuiper Belt region in April of 2006. Brown named this object Eris and determined that its orbit is just outside the orbit of Pluto—also in the Kuiper belt [*Visual 6*]. Now Eris orbits the sun,

Visual 3

Visual 4

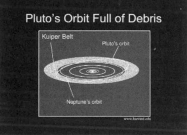

Visual 5

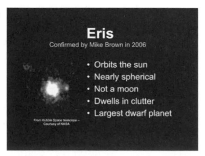

Visual 6

Sample Informative Speech *(continued)*

is nearly spherical in shape, is not a moon but is in the Kuiper Belt, so it meets all four requirements to be considered a dwarf planet. Eris is now considered to be the largest dwarf in our solar system.

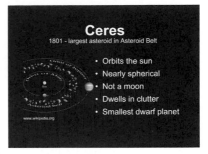

Visual 7

Online source Wikipedia tells us that Ceres, originally discovered in 1801, is the largest asteroid in the Asteroid Belt [*Visual 7*]. Now if you will remember back, the Asteroid Belt is located in between the orbits of Mars and Jupiter, and the Asteroid Belt is composed of many irregular-shaped asteroids in orbit around the sun. Not only does Ceres stand out because it is the largest, but it is also the only one that is round. So Ceres orbits the sun, is round, it is not a moon, and it dwells in the cluttered Asteroid Belt similar to the Kuiper Belt. So it is now considered the smallest dwarf planet in our solar system.

Initial Conclusion

Because of the new definitions set forth by astronomers, we now know the criteria involved in classifying planets. The main factor that sets Pluto apart from the other eight planets is that Pluto lives in a cluttered home, and is forced to orbit among lots of space debris in the Kuiper Belt. And because Eris and Ceres meet the dwarf planet criteria as well, they have been classified in the new group also.

Questions and Answers

Are there any questions?

Question: Can the definitions of a planet and dwarf planet be applied to other objects in the universe?

Answer: Yes. When the IAU decided to create these new terms, they did so planning that they would be applied to other celestial bodies in the universe.

Question: Kara, is this the first time an object in our solar system has had its status as a planet taken away?

Answer: No. As a matter of fact, Ceres was originally declared a planet when it was discovered in 1801. Shortly after its discovery, astronomers were finding other objects within the same orbit as Ceres and were calling them planets as well. What astronomers didn't know at the time is that they were actually discovering various asteroids in the asteroid belt. In the 1860s Ceres had its status as a planet stripped—ironically, astronomers at that time questioned why a planet would share an orbit with other objects. This is actually why astronomers reclassified Pluto to a dwarf planet in 2006—because of the logic astronomers used in the nineteenth century.

Question: Have astronomers discovered other objects in the Kuiper Belt as well?

Answer: Yes. Astronomers have cataloged other items in the Kuiper Belt region that do not appear to be asteroids or other icy debris. At this point, these scientists are not able to determine the shapes and sizes of these objects . . . but I can assure you they are keeping a close eye on these items of interest.

Sample Informative Speech *(continued)*

*Final
Conclusion*

Thank you for your questions. There are no longer nine planets in our solar system [*Visual 8*]. We now have eight classical planets and three dwarf planets. So how do we go about remembering the order of the planets and dwarf planets now? *Many Very Educated Men Just Shook Up Nonsense* and *Committees Prove Everything*. The IAU debate, of what I'm assuming consisted mostly of men, changed things as we know it—and as always, committees prove everything.

Visual 8

So now that we know Pluto, Eris, and Ceres are officially the three dwarves, what does this mean for the future of our solar system? As new discoveries are made in the Kuiper Belt region, it's possible that other objects may be classified as dwarf planets as well. Perhaps you will be interested in keeping your eyes and ears out for new discoveries, and who knows—pretty soon we may be calling our home the Solar System and the *Seven* Dwarves.

References:

Adler, J., Carmichael, M., Morris, N., Christian, J. A. (2006, September 4). Of cosmic proportions. Newsweek, 148(10), 44–50.

Ceres (dwarf planet). (2007). *Wikipedia*. Accessed March 27, 2007, from **en.wikipedia .org/wiki/ceres_%28dwarf_planet%29**.

Dwarf planets: What defines a planet? (2006). *NASA*. Accessed March 22, 2007, from **solarsystem.nasa.gov/planets/profile.cfm?object=dwarf&display=overview**.

Kuiper Belt: Overview. (2006, October 11). *NASA*. Accessed March 22, 2007, from **solarsystem.nasa.gov/planets/profile.cfm?object=kbos**.

Than, K. (2006, September). Pluto: A (dwarf) planet by any other name . . . *Today's Science On File*. Retrieved March 26, 2007, *from Today's Science* at **facts.com** database.

Collecting and Using Audience Information

Remember that your purpose for analyzing your audience is to make your communication as effective as possible. Therefore, collect situational, demographic, and psychological information—as well as information on potential audience type—before your speeches so that you can adapt to audience frames of reference. After your speech, collect information on audience reactions in order to evaluate the success of your presentation and make any needed changes in future speeches. Let's look in more detail at the collection of audience information both before and after your speeches.

Before the Speech

To gather all four types of information (situational, demographic, psychological, and receptivity) about your classroom audience, begin by observing and listening. Many demographic and situational traits become obvious through simple observation. Listening to your classmates' comments and opinions should give you a good idea of many of their beliefs and values. You might also interview a few classmates for additional information or give everyone a short questionnaire to complete at least one week before your speech. When speaking outside the classroom, a telephone interview of the person who originally asked you to speak will usually work.

Use a questionnaire including *situational questions* (the name of the organization or class and the seating arrangement), *demographic questions* (ages of audience members and identification of any important group affiliations), *psychological questions* (basic beliefs and needs of the group), and *receptivity questions* (for example, "How would you classify your response to my topic: friendly, neutral, uninterested, or hostile?"). As the person answers your questions, jot down the responses. If you feel that you still need more information, ask for the names of two people to contact who are familiar with the expected audience.

There is one more way to obtain audience information before presenting the speech: Arrive at the site early. After checking to make sure that the lectern and equipment for visual aids are in place, greet the first few audience members as they arrive. Introduce yourself and politely ask about their interest in your speech and their motivation for attending. Not only will you have some friends in the audience, but your conversation may help you verify areas that you have in common with them. If you discover new information, you might make last-minute adjustments in your introduction. The more things you and your audience have in common, the more believable you will be.

Watch political candidates to see how they adapt their clothing and hairstyle, manner of delivery, and use of examples to fit the taste of the voters to whom they are speaking. Most candidates dress differently for different audiences, with good reason. For example, a study conducted during the 2004 presidential campaign (Bedard, 2004) found that Republican areas preferred "khaki casual,[LT26]" while Democratic areas preferred "dressy grays and blacks" (p. 6). During his presidential campaign in 2008, Senator John McCain wore more casual clothing when holding a campaign rally at The Long John Center on the campus of the University of the Scranton, but wore a dark suit in 2009 when addressing the Heritage Foundation in Washington, DC, to speak about the war in Afghanistan.

Senator John McCain wore more casual clothing when holding a presidential campaign rally at The Long John Center on the campus of the University of Scranton.

Senator McCain wore a dark suit when addressing the Heritage Foundation in Washington, DC.

After the Speech

Many speakers fail to recognize the importance of soliciting feedback after a speech. Assessing listener reactions is the only way you can tell if your analysis before the speech was adequate; if it wasn't, you'll want to make changes before your next speech. Of course, the most immediate feedback you will receive after a speech is the applause. If your speech ended with emotion or was particularly profound or startling, there may be a moment of silence before the applause while the audience absorbs your conclusion. You can tell the difference between an enthusiastic response and a lukewarm one.

Make yourself available after the speech so that audience members can offer their comments. Except in the classroom (where another speech begins almost immediately), audience members will tend to come up and thank the speaker, ask questions, and offer valuable feedback. If you are off in the corner talking with officials or busy putting away equipment, most people will leave without speaking to you—a missed opportunity.

A brief questionnaire similar to the one shown in Figure 4.3 is another way to get feedback after your speech. You can place the questionnaire on a table by the door for audience members to complete as they leave, or you can send a thank-you letter and copies of your questionnaire to your contact person, with a request to have three or four people from the audience fill them out. Or you may simply ask specific questions of one or two people you know who attended the speech.

Once your speech is over, it's difficult to remember exactly what you said or what gestures you used, so a good way to get significant feedback is to have someone videotape your talk. If your contact person doesn't have a video camera, bring your own or rent one. Ask a friend to come along with you to tape

Directions: For each item, put a check mark in the blank that best describes your evaluation of my speech.

	1	2	3	4	5	6	7	
Dull	—	—	—	—	—	—	—	Exciting
Disorganized	—	—	—	—	—	—	—	Organized
Weakly supported	—	—	—	—	—	—	—	Well supported
Sources questionable	—	—	—	—	—	—	—	Sources believable
Poor delivery	—	—	—	—	—	—	—	Dynamic delivery
Unpleasant voice	—	—	—	—	—	—	—	Pleasant voice
Limited eye contact	—	—	—	—	—	—	—	Direct eye contact
Confusing visuals	—	—	—	—	—	—	—	Helpful visuals
Too soft	—	—	—	—	—	—	—	Easily heard
Poor overall	—	—	—	—	—	—	—	Excellent overall

Figure 4.3

Sample Speech Evaluation Questionnaire

both your speech and some audience reactions, if possible. As you watch later, analyze the speech for strengths and weaknesses.

Using Audience Analysis

After reading this chapter, you can see why speech preparation begins with audience analysis. Regardless of the type of speech you will be giving, before you finalize your topic selection and begin researching for information, review the situational, demographic, and psychological characteristics of your audience. For a classroom speech, you might ask yourself the following questions (Kara's answers to these questions in relation to her speech "Our Solar System and the Three Dwarves" are in italics):

Taking time to talk to audience members after your speech is a good way to get valuable feedback.

- At this point in the course, will my classmates' current opinions of me add to my credibility or take away from it? What can I do to improve my credibility?

  Kara: I didn't do as well as I had hoped on my introductory speech. Even though I had practiced a few times, I was extremely nervous and even skipped over an entire area. I actually revealed to the audience the fact that I suffer from anxiety. Because my classmates were aware of my goofs and anxious nature, I knew I had to redeem myself on the informative speech. Whatever topic I selected, I knew I needed to gain credibility with the audience. In order to do this, I decided I needed to select a topic I either knew a lot about or was willing to research as something I was greatly interested in. Also, I knew that I would have to practice much more than I did on the first speech.

- How much do my classmates know about the general topics I am considering? (If you don't have any specific topics in mind yet, come back to this question when you do.)

  Kara: As soon as my introductory speech was over, I was already debating on what topic I should pick for my informative speech. I started considering what the audience might be interested in. Should it be practical information that everyone could use, or something exciting that you don't get to explore very often? After the suggestion of a friend, I first thought about choosing a topic in my field of work (family-violence protective orders). Many people have heard of restraining orders, and protective orders are somewhat similar. Since this topic is my livelihood for forty hours a week, I knew credibility would be certain and the delivery would be natural and calm. I decided to narrow the topic down to the criteria involved for qualifying for a protective order. I also figured this selection was the easy way out, since it wouldn't require much additional research.

  However, after more thinking, I decided that a speech about my daily work would be boring to me and probably wouldn't be very interesting to the audience either. I began thinking about other interests, such as art, rock music, architecture, and astronomy. Then I remembered what I had heard in the news a while back about how Pluto is no longer considered a planet. At the time, I wasn't aware of why or how that decision was made, but I figured it would be fun to research since I like astronomy. I then considered my audience and what they would think about this topic. It's pretty safe to say that the entire audience was raised with the knowledge of nine planets in our solar system. Would they be more interested in the speech if they discovered that what they've known their entire lives is no longer true? This question is what helped me select the Pluto topic over the other. It was important for me to capture the audience's attention.

- What types of visual aids will be more likely to impress my audience? What types of attention-getters will interest them the most (for example, personal instance, startling statement, or quote)?

Kara: Developing the computer visuals through PowerPoint was crucial for this speech. Since planets are objects very few people have seen with their own eyes, visual aids were important for keeping the audience interested and on track with the level of information. I was able to find many wonderful pictures on the Internet, especially NASA's website. In order to create an outer-space feel to the speech, I decided to make the PP slides black with white letters and use colorful pictures.

To grab the audience's attention, I started by stating some of the mnemonics (memory aids) used to cite the order of the nine planets that I had learned as a child. To emphasize our childhood education on this subject, the visual aid used while stating the mnemonics was a child's coloring of the sun and nine planets in their proper order.

- On the basis of the demographic characteristics of my class (for example, age, marital status, children, major, group memberships, hobbies), how can I make my potential topics interesting and beneficial to them? (If you can't think of a way, you probably need to select a different topic.)

Kara: Although this was an online class, all students had posted a brief bio on the discussion board, and I met many of my classmates during the introductory speeches. My class's demographics varied widely: Ages ranged from 18 to 35; half were married; several had small children; women outnumbered men; almost everyone worked—most full time.

When considering the speech about protective orders, I figured most people knew something about domestic violence and have probably experienced it in some way— either personally or through observing others. Domestic violence occurs at all age levels and between married and unmarried people, and it tends to be more common in highly populated areas like this one. By discussing the criteria involved for qualifying for a protective order, the audience would likely learn valuable information for themselves or friends.

An informative speech about why Pluto is no longer a planet might appeal to all members of the audience as well. Until 2006, Pluto was considered the ninth planet, as taught by grade-school textbooks. This topic would affect college students of all ages. Astronomy is probably not a popular major among college students, but this campus has an astronomy club. By discussing why Pluto is no longer considered a planet, the audience would learn something contradictory to the preexisting knowledge about space, and perhaps develop an interest in astronomy and get involved with a campus club.

- What attitudes, beliefs, or values that are relevant to my topic already exist in the minds of my classmates? How can I use these psychological factors to communicate my ideas better?

Kara: As stated previously, I felt sure that the entire audience was raised with the knowledge that our solar system consisted of nine planets. Believing in the number of planets is the same as believing that each of them rotates around the sun. Discovering the truth about Pluto could be compared to learning that John Hancock wasn't the first to sign the Declaration of Independence—it challenges what we've been taught since childhood. For this speech, I knew it was important to focus on why Pluto was demoted as well as its similarities with other objects in our solar system. It was also important to appropriately convey what exactly makes a dwarf planet a dwarf planet. In my research I discovered that there were many harsh feelings among the general public, as well as astronomers, in regards to Pluto's demotion, and some declared that science should make an exception and that Pluto should remain the ninth planet. In case any members of the audience felt this way, I decided the final main point should reinforce the fact that Pluto is not alone and shares its dwarf planet status with other objects in our solar system.

- What basic needs (physiological, safety, social, esteem, and self-actualization) do most of my classmates have that will make the need for my topic obvious?

Kara: This was a hard question that took some thinking since my topic was not persuasive. I decided that both esteem and self-actualization needs could be used to convince the audience why listening to my informative topic could benefit them. Once they heard the new information about Pluto, my audience could feel proud that they were up to date and, by sharing these facts, could get recognition from others. Learning the most up-to-date information about the solar system could also fulfill the self-actualization needs of curiosity and desire to be challenged.

Most likely your classroom audience will be a friendly audience, like Kara's. These listeners will know what you are going through and be rooting for your success. Personal examples and humor will be especially effective, as will any extra effort you put into your visual aids (such as pictures or color). You can also add to class enjoyment if you refer to a speech given by an earlier speaker or cite the behavior or statements of a student from the class as an example to support your own ideas. If, by chance, your class does not fall into the friendly-audience category, review the section on types of audiences and adjust your speech accordingly.

Active Critical Thinking

To think further about collecting audience information, complete the following:

- To finalize your audience analysis for your next speech, compare it with the answers given by Kara (sample speech beginning on page 87), make any needed changes, and have the final analysis ready to give to your instructor if asked.
- What specific things do you plan to do to collect information after your next speech?

Summary

Speech preparation involves several basic steps that will be discussed more fully in the following chapters. This chapter covered the first step in speech preparation—analyzing your audience. You can collect four types of information to use in analyzing your audience: situational, demographic, psychological, and audience receptivity. *Situational information* (such as audience size and expectations and the possible presence of other speakers) helps you plan your speech to fit the specific situation. *Demographic information* (such as age; ethnic and cultural background; gender; group affiliation; marital status, children, and elderly parents; occupation; education; college major; and economic status) helps you know as much as possible about your audience and aids in selecting your topic and supporting materials. *Psychological information* (such as values, beliefs, attitudes, and needs) is especially important in relating to the frames of reference of your listeners. To interest audience members in your topic or persuade them to take some action, you must identify their attitudes, beliefs, values, and needs in order to decide what information or appeals will be most effective. Once you have gathered situational, demographic, and psychological information about your audience, you are ready to determine *audience receptivity*—how receptive they will be toward your speech. Audiences can be friendly, neutral, uninterested, or hostile. Each type of audience requires different verbal, visual, and vocal approaches.

All four types of audience information are gathered before your speech to allow you to adapt your presentation to listeners' frames of reference. Without this information, your chances of communicating successfully with your audience are diminished; with it, you can feel confident that your presentation will succeed. Similar information is collected after the speech to enable you to evaluate your effectiveness and make any needed changes in future speeches.

Essentials of Public Speaking Online ⬧ CourseMate

Use your Online Resources for *Essentials of Public Speaking* for quick access to the electronic study resources that accompany this chapter. Your Online Resources include access to InfoTrac College Edition, Personal Skill Building Activities and Collaborative Skill Building Activities, a digital glossary, sample speeches, and review quizzes.

Key Terms

attitude 80	homogeneous 73	terminal values 79
audience type 85	hostile audience 85	theory of reasoned
belief 80	instrumental values 79	action 81
demographic	need 81	uninterested or indif-
information 75	neutral or impartial	ferent audience 85
framing 82	audience 85	values 79
friendly audience 85	situational	
heterogeneous 73	information 73	

Personal Skill Building

1. Try to locate organizations in your community that have a speakers bureau. Call one of the speakers and ask how he or she analyzes the audience before a speech. Compare the answer with the suggestions made in this chapter.

2. First impressions are important. When you analyze your audience, anticipate their first reaction to your topic. Will it be interest, surprise, annoyance, or perhaps boredom? That first reaction can affect whether they really listen and whether they make the changes or decisions that you ask for. Once you've identified your audience's likely first reaction, rethink your introduction. What techniques should you use to get their attention before they learn of your topic? What can you say or do that will keep them listening once they know your topic? Take another look at Chapter 3—it includes many suggestions for "hooking" and keeping audience interest in each stage of listening. Select two specific techniques and incorporate them into your next speech. Your instructor may ask for a written report.

3. Evaluate audience analysis in regards to advertising and marketing. What top three products are you most likely to buy? Once you have answered this, find evidence of the products' advertising. Does the advertising address you as the consumer? Why has the advertising worked or not worked? What has the company selling the product decided about the audience's needs and wants?

4. Using a database like InfoTrac College Edition, EBSCOhost, or CQ Researcher, complete a keyword search for *attitude change* and select one of the many articles that discuss this. Share any new information on beliefs, attitudes, and values with your classmates. What message does the article hold for speakers?

5. Are you still visualizing your positive statements once or twice a day? If not, spend the next 10 minutes going over them. Remember to read, visualize, and feel confident performing each of your statements. If you can't seem to find time to work on all of your statements, select the one that you most hope to achieve, and concentrate on it for the next week. Every chance you get, visualize yourself successfully completing your statement for the week. Don't forget to feel confident and pleased while you are visualizing. When the week is over, select another positive statement, and spend the next week working on it.

6. Check out the following websites. (You can access these sites using your Online Resources for *Essentials of Public Speaking*, Chapter 4).

   • For an excellent discussion and evaluation of Maslow and his theory of needs, visit the personality-theories site prepared by Shippensburg University's Dr. C. George Boeree. Go to **personalityresearch.org**, click on "Personality Theories" on the right side of the page, and then click on "Abraham Maslow."

   • Check out Lenny Laskowski's mnemonic aid for audience analysis at his website **ljlseminars.com**. Click on "Public Speaking Tips," then "A.U.D.I.E.N.C.E. Analysis—It's Your Key to Success."

   • For a PBS special series on the American family and the generation gap, go to **pbs.org/americanfamily/gap**, and take the interactive poll—you may be surprised by the answers.

CourseMate

Collaborative Skill Building

1. In small groups, prepare a questionnaire to analyze the demographic characteristics of your speech class. Representatives from each group can meet to compare the questionnaires and select the best questions from each. Distribute the final questionnaire to all class members and tabulate the results for future use.

2. If you have difficulty anticipating audience reactions, try a devil's advocate discussion. Divide into groups of four or five, or plan to post to a discussion board or blog site. For informative topics, each person should post or present a thesis statement and explain why the topic is a good one. Group members then play devil's advocate and present or post all possible audience reactions and areas of possible confusion or disagreement. The speaker should respond with questions and comments, and a brief debate may occur. For persuasive topics, each person in your group should post or present a specific position on an issue, along with the facts and details that support that position. Group members then play devil's advocate, responding to the position by suggesting counterpositions and counterarguments. Speakers respond and clarify, and a brief debate may occur. Watch your time so that everyone in the group has a chance to post or share a topic. Speakers take notes or print off the discussion—you now have some valuable audience analysis to use in final preparation for your speech. Your instructor may ask you to write a report that includes what you learned and how this information fits into the four categories of audience analysis discussed in this chapter.

3. Learn more about audience analysis by completing the Cereal Box Activity (adapted from Jill Gibson, 2006). Divide into groups of five, and make a list of all the different types of dry breakfast cereals available—including those that members personally eat (such as Cheerios, Coco Puffs, Grape-Nuts, or Special K). Try to find five different cereals that would appeal to five different target groups, and assign one to each member. On an appointed day, each group member should bring an empty cereal box of the kind assigned to them and come prepared with ideas on what target audience the cereal is designed for (use situational, demographic, and psychological data in the analysis).

Quiz Answers

Test Your Knowledge

Answers to Unit Two Quiz on page 71: Test Your Knowledge About Speech Preparation.

1. *True.* The one thing most responsible for creating deadly dull speeches is the overuse of explanation. Instead of presenting statistics to illustrate the seriousness of a problem, speakers will "explain" how serious it is; instead of giving a real-life instance to show how rude drivers are today, speakers will "explain" that drivers are rude. Which of the following speeches do you think would be more interesting? ➡ *See Chapter 6 for a discussion of overuse of explanation.*

Speech 1	Speech 2

I. First main point

   A. Explanation

   B. Explanation

   C. Explanation

II. Second main point

   A. Statistics

   B. Explanation

   C. Explanation

III. Etc.

I. First main point

   A. Personal instance

   B. Figurative comparison

   C. Statistics

II. Second main point

   A. Explanation

   B. Quotation

   C. Humorous instance

III. Etc.

2. *False.* An introduction that grabs the attention of your audience is very important. However, preparing the introduction before developing your main points is usually a waste of time. Speakers normally add and remove main points several times before they are satisfied. Each time you change the body of your speech, you will probably have to change the introduction as well. → *Chapter 7 covers introductions.*

3. *True.* A warm, conversational tone of voice is not likely to grab the attention of audience members. A more dynamic and entertaining approach is needed, along with humor, colorful visuals, moving quotations, and startling statistics. → *See Chapter 8 for more on effective delivery.*

4. *True.* Roughing out an outline saves time because it limits and directs the amount of research needed. However, if you know nothing about your topic, you will need to do some research before making an outline. → *If you follow the advice for topic selection in Chapter 5, you will know enough about your topic to rough out an outline; Chapter 5 also contains outlining pointers.*

5. *False.* Although statistics lend clarity and support to your ideas, they can confuse, bore, and overload listeners if used incorrectly. You need to relate statistics to your listeners' frames of reference. For example, telling an audience that smoke-related diseases kill half a million people a year may leave them yawning unless you also tell them that this is 50 people an hour, 1,200 a day, and 8,400 a week—every week for a year—until half a million people die (Bristow, 1994). That would be like eliminating a city the size of Fort Worth, Texas, every year! → *Chapter 6 discusses other guidelines for using statistics effectively.*

6. *False.* **Wikipedia.org** is a "free encyclopedia that anyone can edit," which means that you can't be sure that the information in Wikipedia is accurate. In fact, the site warns you that there may be errors in its information. Therefore, always be sure to verify facts you find on Wikipedia with one or more reliable sources. Check your library for print sources or electronic databases (usually accessible from your dorm or home)—they are much more dependable. → *See Chapter 5 for a discussion of reliable print and electronic databases.*

7. *False.* It's never good to tell your audience that you are nervous or unprepared. You may momentarily feel better by confessing, but listeners may feel anxious and uncomfortable. Your credibility in the eyes of your audience sinks as well. Also, don't forget that your feelings of anxiety rarely show—unless you confess. → *See Chapter 2 for suggestions for overcoming speaker anxiety.*

8. *False.* Although beginning speakers think notes written in complete sentences will make them feel more secure, the opposite is more often true. When you glance down at complete sentences, the words run together and you are forced to either read the notes word for word or "wing it" without using the notes at all. Keyword notes are much more helpful. Only quotations should be written word for word. If you use visual aids, you probably won't need notes at all.
   → *See Chapter 11 for a discussion of speaking notes.*

9. *False.* An ethical speaker is always careful not to plagiarize—it doesn't matter how unlikely it is that anyone would ever know. Using other people's material without giving them credit is always unethical. → *See Chapter 6 for pointers on how to use supporting materials and avoid unintentional plagiarism.*

10. *False.* Although introductions and conclusions are important, the body of an effective speech usually takes about 70 to 80 percent of your total speech time. Therefore, in a 5-minute speech, the body should last approximately 3 1/2 to 4 minutes; in a 7-minute speech, 5 to 5 1/2 minutes; and in a 10-minute speech, 7 to 8 minutes. → *See Chapter 7 for suggestions on speech organization.*

Selecting, Outlining, and Researching Your Topic

Learning Objectives

As you read Chapter 5,

- *Identify* the guidelines for finding a good speech topic and *discuss* the importance of narrowing your topic while writing an exact purpose that is clear and strong.
- *Explain* the role of outlining in researching your topic.
- *Identify* specific ways to conduct quality research while avoiding plagiarism.

THE BEST SPEAKERS SELECT QUALITY TOPICS, ORGANIZE THEIR MAIN POINTS CAREFULLY, AND RESEARCH THOROUGHLY. As the Greek and Roman rhetoricians realized, the more you know about your topic, the better. Picking a topic that you already know quite a lot about, identifying main points you wish to include, and then updating, organizing, and supporting that topic with research are done after audience analysis. By the time you finish reading this chapter, you will have completed Steps 2, 3, and 4 of the "Basic Steps for Preparing a Speech," covered in the Quick Start Guide at the beginning of this text, and be on your way to giving an outstanding presentation.

Use a database like InfoTrac College Edition, EBSCOhost, or CQ Researcher to conduct a keyword search for *brainstorming*. See what advice you can find that will help you determine possible speech topics.

Selecting Your Topic, Purpose, and Main Points

Once you have analyzed your audience, you are ready to pick a specific topic. Although sometimes you may be given a topic by the organization asking you to speak, by the manager requesting a report, or by your instructor, most of the time the selection of a topic is up to you.

Determine Your Topic

One way to make sure you always have plenty of good speech topics on hand is to carry a notepad in your purse or wallet and use it to record possible speech topics as they occur to you. Then all you have to do is decide which one(s) to use. Finding good topics isn't difficult—the following four guidelines should help. They apply regardless of the type of speech you are asked to give—demonstration, informational, persuasive, or special occasion.

Select a Topic That Fits the Requirements of the Assignment As you think of possible topics, *make sure the topic you select is appropriate for the assignment.* Many topics that would make ideal informative speeches would not work as demonstration or persuasive speeches. For example, "Preparing an Effective Resume" would make a good informative speech but would be difficult to make persuasive and almost impossible to demonstrate. "Lowering Your Cholesterol" could be informative or persuasive but could not be demonstrated. "Using PowerPoint to Prepare Visual Aids" would make an excellent demonstration or informative speech but would hardly be an effective after-dinner speech. "Lowering the Incidence of Child Abuse" would lend itself more to persuasion than to any other type of speech. Persuasive topics need to be controversial—that is, have at least two conflicting views. Although everyone agrees that child abuse is a serious problem (no controversy), we may not agree about what can be done to solve it.

Also, *make sure your speech fits the allotted time.* Keep your main points to a minimum; three points is the norm, and five points is usually the maximum. The only way you can be certain of your length is to practice the speech and time it. Thinking it through in your mind doesn't work, as one student found out the hard way. Layla was presenting a demonstration speech entitled "How to Wrap Attractive Gifts." She started by showing a hilarious example of how her parents wrapped her Christmas gifts when she was a child. The box looked as if it had fallen down the stairs and been "rescued" by a pet. Then she showed the audience a beautifully wrapped gift and suggested that listeners could wrap eye-catching gifts themselves in three easy steps. Unfortunately, by this point in her speech, she had used up more than half of the allotted time and was forced to end without covering all the steps. Had she practiced her speech aloud, she would have realized that the introduction was too long and that she needed more time for explaining the three steps while she demonstrated them.

Select a Topic That Showcases Your Experiences and Knowledge You will feel more relaxed and confident giving your speech if you select a topic that is familiar—from personal experience, personal knowledge, or previous research. Try using the following suggestions to generate ideas for possible topics:

- *Step 1:* On a sheet of paper write the following topic categories down the center of the page leaving space above, below, and on each side to brainstorm additional speech topics for each category: Jobs—current or past, College, Family, Hobbies, Activities that you spend most of your time doing, Skills/Accomplishments of which you are especially proud, Research Papers that you've written, and Miscellaneous (for additional topics). Now, brainstorm three or more speech topics for each category—spontaneous listing of ideas is called **brainstorming**. Draw a line from the main category to each of your brainstormed speech ideas. For effective brainstorming, jot down anything that comes to mind, no matter how crazy it seems. "Crazy" ideas often lead to really good speech topics. To make your list more visual, use a variety of colors—such as black for the major categories and blue or green for the brainstormed speech topics.

Stop reading at this point and brainstorm your list of possible topics.

- *Step 2:* When you have completed your list, look at the sample topics in Figure 5.1. If they stimulate you to think of additional topics, add them to your list under the appropriate category.

- *Step 3:* Now circle in red the topics that would be appropriate for the speech assignment you are currently working on (such as an informative speech). For example, under the category of Jobs, you may have listed "Restaurant Waitstaff" as one of your jobs and circled it as appropriate for an informative speech.

- *Step 4:* Finally, take each topic circled in red and further break it down to even more-specific speech topics. For example, you might write the informative topics of "Appropriate Tipping" and "Dealing with Problem

Business
Why buy a hybrid?
Working in virtual teams
Hiring baby boomers

College/Education
Social networking tips
Credit-card debt
Internships

Family
Harry Potter mania
Dealing with Alzheimer's
Changes in adoption laws

Food/Beverages
HGC—safe diet?
Fat content of fast foods
Making great coffee

Health/Exercise
Dancing and weight loss
Cancer and cell phones
Government healthcare

Hobbies
Taking great pictures
Collecting baseball cards
The need for volunteers

Holiday/Gift/Home
Holiday safety tips
Remodeling suggestions
Make your own gifts

Magic/Games/Music
Do your own magic tricks
Relaxing benefit of music
World of Warcraft

Multicultural/Global
Diversity in the workplace
Illegal immigrants
Rearming of Japan

Miscellaneous
Topic related to job or major
Topic from research paper
Dream interpretation

National/Political
Debates on CNN/YouTube
Military and PTSD
Preventing terrorism

Pets/Animals
One-bite rule for dogs
Pets on airplanes
Pythons in the Everglades

Personal
Dressing professionally on a budget
Preparing resumes
Making a will

Social
Illegal immigrants
Breakdown of the family
Finance and ethics

Sports
Ethics problems in sports
Tennis tips
Violence at sports events

Figure 5.1

Sample Speech Topics

Customers" next to the circled "Restaurant Waitstaff." The next time you use this list of speech topics, you may be looking for ideas for a persuasive speech, a demonstration speech, or even a special occasion speech and can repeat the process to help you select the perfect topic. ➜ *More detailed lists of demonstration, informational and persuasive speech topics can be found in Chapters 11 and 12.*

After Kara (whose sample speech appeared in Chapter 4) had brainstormed possible topics and circled the appropriate ones, she was left with five topics that fit her assignment:

1. *Family-violence protective orders (she worked in a family-violence office and decided to narrow the topic down to the criteria involved for qualifying for a protective order).*

2. *Art (she had always been interested in art and was thinking of speaking on using art for home decorations).*

3. *Rock music (she was in a rock band in high school and was thinking about types of rock music or discussing a major rock star).*

4. *Architecture (at one point, Kara had considered majoring in architecture but wasn't sure what part of that topic would be interesting to her classmates).*

5. *Astronomy (she had shown a real interest in astronomy since childhood and thought she might focus on recent information about how Pluto is no longer considered a planet—it would require some research but would be very interesting to her personally).*

Select a Topic That Interests You Use personal interests to narrow your list of possible speech topics. Cross out topics that you know a lot about but that do not interest you. It's difficult to interest your audience in a topic that you don't care about yourself. Select a topic that you are enthusiastic and even passionate about, and your enthusiasm will carry over to your audience.

By eliminating the topics that least interested her, Kara narrowed her possible speech topics to two: criteria involved in qualifying for a family-violence protective order and Pluto's standing in our solar system. She had personal experience with the first topic and had done some research on the second due to her interest in astronomy.

Select a Topic That You Can Make Interesting and Valuable to Your Audience Audience members don't have to be interested in your topic before you begin speaking, but they should be by the time you finish. Your audience analysis prior to selecting a specific topic will help you interest and benefit your listeners in important ways. Ask yourself: Will my speech make my listeners healthier, happier, or more aware? Will it show them how to save money? Save lives? Communicate better with dates or parents? Study more productively for exams? Learn something new? Will it dispel a myth or add more excitement to their lives? In other words, a good speech topic should not only interest both you and your audience but also benefit your listeners in some way.

Although both family-violence protective orders and Pluto's place in our solar system interested Kara, she realized that few of her classmates would need the services of a family-violence protective order. However, because everyone in her class had grown up learning in school about the nine planets, they would likely be interested in learning that Pluto was no longer classified as a planet and why. Responses to a quick post on her online class's discussion board asking classmates to identify the number and names of the planets let her know that the class could benefit from a speech about Pluto. She was now ready to determine her exact purpose and possible main points.

In spite of all these suggestions, don't worry too much about finding the "perfect" topic. Just find a topic you and your audience will enjoy, that you are knowledgeable on, and that fits the criteria for your assignment—but don't spend time looking for the perfect topic. It probably doesn't exist anyway.

Speaking to Make a Difference

On February 4, 2009, Harry Markopolos, a veteran in the investment community, testified before the House Financial Services Committee. The hearing was titled "Assessing the Madoff Ponzi Scheme and Regulatory Failures," and Markopolos was there to present his view of the failures of the SEC (Securities and Exchange Commission) in "its 'disastrous' handling of the Madoff investigation" (Hovell & Barrett, 2009). Although he had been compiling research on Madoff since 1999 and had tried five times to get the SEC to investigate Madoff, he still spent over 100 hours preparing for this hearing (Markopolos, 2010). Below is an excerpt from Markopolos's opening remarks, transcribed from World News Network (2009). His remarks were essentially a summary of the detailed printed version sent to the committee members the evening before the hearing. To learn more about the complete hearing, search for "Harry Markopolos" on YouTube, or go to http://wn.com/SEC_Hearing_Harry_Markopolos_Testifies.

Thank you, Mr. Chairman. Good morning.

Thank you for inviting me here to testify before your committee today regarding my 9-year-long investigation into the "Madoff Ponzi Scheme." I would also like to recognize my congressman, Steven Lynch, who is a member of the committee. I look forward to explaining to Congress today, and the SEC's Inspector General tomorrow, what I saw, when I saw it, and what my dealings with the SEC were that led me to this case being repeatedly ignored over an 8 1/2-year period between May 2000 and December 2008.

First, I would like to extend my deepest sympathy to the victims of this scheme. We know that many of the victims lost retirement savings and are too old to start over. We also know that others have lost medical services, community services, and scholarships provided by charities that were wiped out by the Madoff fraud. This pains me greatly, and I will do my best to inform you, the victims, about my repeated and detailed warnings to the SEC. You above all others deserve to know the truth about this agency's failings, and I will do my best to explain them to you today.

You will hear me talk a great deal about over-lawyering at the SEC very soon. Let me say I have nothing against lawyers. In fact, I have brought two of my own here today. As today's testimony will reveal, my team and I tried our best to get the SEC to investigate and shut down the Madoff Ponzi scheme with repeated,

incredible warnings to the SEC that started in May 2000, when the Madoff Ponzi scheme was only a 3- to 7- billion-dollar fraud. We knew then that we had provided enough red flags and mathematical proof to the SEC for them that they should have been able to shut him down right then and there at under 7 billion dollars. But, unfortunately, the SEC staff lacks the financial expertise and is incapable of understanding the complex financial instrument being traded in the 21st century. In October 2001 when Madoff was still in the 12- to 20- billion-dollar range, again we felt confident that we had provided even more evidence to the SEC, such that he should have been stopped at well under 20 billion dollars. And again in November 2005, when Mr. Madoff was at 30 billion dollars, 29 red flags were handed to the SEC, and yet again they failed to properly investigate and shut down Mr. Madoff's operation. Unfortunately, as they didn't respond to my written submissions in 2000, 2001, 2005, 2007, and 2008, here we are today. A fraud that should have been stopped at under 7 billion dollars in 2000 has now grown to over 50 billion dollars. I know that you want to know why there were over 40 billion dollars in additional damages, and I hope to be able to provide some of those answers to you today.

* * *

But what I find the most disturbing about the Madoff case is that no one from the SEC has stepped forward to admit personal responsibility. Instead, all we've heard is one senior official after another saying that they cannot comment about the Madoff investigation because it is ongoing. We've also heard senior SEC officials bemoan the lack of both staff and resources while telling us that they receive thousands of tips each year. And that they have to conduct triage and can only respond to the highest-priority matters. I gift wrapped and delivered the largest Ponzi scheme in history to them, and somehow they couldn't be bothered to conduct a thorough and proper investigation because they were too busy on matters of higher priority. If a 50-billion Ponzi scheme doesn't make the SEC's priority list, then I want to know who sets their priorities.

Markopolos first became aware of Bernie Madoff in 1999, when the management of his firm asked him to recreate and duplicate Madoff's investment practices. He found it was impossible, which indicated possible fraud. After additional research, taking the information to several colleagues for their expert advice, and running numerous mathematical models, Markopolos was convinced of Madoff's fraud and was ready in 2000 to present his findings to the SEC in a 19-page memo called "The World's Largest Hedge Fund is a Fraud." They weren't interested. As the years progressed, Markopolos and a team of three colleagues continued to investigate Madoff, collecting more and more data. The original memo was expanded with new data

continued

and presented again in 2001, 2005, 2007, and 2008 (American Program Bureau, 2009). The first two times they received the memo, the SEC ignored Markopolos outright; and when they finally did take his information to heart, the investigation led nowhere. In 2007, Madoff was cleared of charges—a verdict largely due to the lackluster investigation of the SEC. In spite of this, "the investigation evidently convinced investigators that Madoff had 'misled' SEC examiners during the 2005 inspection," and additional investigations were considered (Kiel, 2008). However, less than a year later and before any action could be taken against him, Madoff turned himself in, admitted fraud, and was sentenced to 150 years in prison.

According to Markopolos in his book, *No One Would Listen* (2010), without careful SEC investigation of Madoff, his scheme could have doubled to 100 billion as long as the economy remained strong, allowing new money to continually flow into his operation. Likely his downfall was "caused by a worldwide recession that resulted in stock markets collapsing and led to investors desperately trying to pull their money from hedge funds to meet other demands. The moment a Ponzi scheme has to pay out more money than it is taking in, it's done" (p. 115).

Although, Markopolos wasn't able to save investors from Madoff's fraud, he tried. In his presentation to the House Financial Services Committee, he was speaking to make a difference. Let's summarize some of the things that made his presentation a success:

- *Topic selection.* Obviously, Markopolos selected a topic on which he was very well informed; it was a topic of great interest to him; and it was a topic of great interest to the committee members as well as to American investors and investors abroad. Since Madoff's arrest, Markopolos experienced some degree of fame and planned to use it to his advantage: "… suddenly, I was famous. Fame, or maybe recognition, is a fascinating tool, as I was discovering. People were intrigued by Madoff, and they wanted to hear what I had to say about his scheme" (p. 222).

- *Research and preparation.* As this chapter indicates, research and preparation are essential to successful presentations. Markopolos' presentation was based on almost nine years of data from research and investigations. Even so, he continued to prepare for the hearing so he could "focus attention on the SEC" and "celebrate the importance of whistleblowers to expose corruption in our system" (Markopolos, 2010, p. 222). According to Markopolos, "I spent more than 100 hours preparing for my two- or three-hour testimony. As I found out, it takes a lot of preparation and rehearsal to appear spontaneous" (p. 223).

- *Audience analysis.* As Markopolos prepared his oral presentation for the committee, he had four audiences in mind: (1) the people victimized by Madoff; (2) investors both domestic and international because "I wanted them to know that no one was protecting them" (p. 226); (3) American citizens; and (4) the government—both the SEC and the committee members.

Questions: Do you think Markopolos' opening remarks spoke to the four audiences he had identified? Why or why not? Was his purpose clear? Why or why not?

Define Your Exact Purpose

After you have analyzed your audience and decided on a general topic, you are ready to narrow your topic so that it will fit the time limit and the specific needs and interests of your audience. It is better to cover fewer points and thoroughly illustrate and support them than it is to skim over a larger number of points in an attempt to "say it all." Audiences tend to daydream when the speaker tries to cover too much material. Narrowing your topic to an exact purpose is one of the most difficult tasks a speaker faces, no matter how experienced he or she may be. An **exact purpose** is a clear, simple sentence that specifies exactly what you want your audience to gain (know, perceive, understand) from the speech. An exact purpose begins with "After hearing my speech, the audience will be able to …"

To illustrate the importance of narrowing your topic, let's assume that you are a fan of professional football and have selected football as your general speech topic. You have five minutes in which to present your informative speech. You start by making a list of possible speeches about football, writing each in the form of an exact purpose. Which of the following purposes are too broad for a 5-minute speech? How will you narrow the topic?

Exact purpose: After hearing my speech, the audience will be able to . . .

1. Explain the divisions and conferences that make up the NFL.

2. Understand the steps required for a team to make it to the Super Bowl.

3. Understand the role of the Competition Committee in making game rules.

4. Realize why the instant-replay rule has caused so much controversy.

5. Contrast and compare the roles of referee, umpire, and linesman.

6. Explain the job of coaching.

7. Realize how much power the commissioner of the NFL has.

8. Identify the qualities needed in a winning quarterback.

9. Understand the size, speed, and psychological requirements of each football position.

10. Perceive football as a moneymaker.

11. Understand the need for change in helmet design to prevent concussions and dementia.

12. Explain the argument over artificial versus natural turf.

13. Describe the personality of football fans in several cities.

14. Understand three facts that viewers need to know to watch football intelligently.

15. Perceive football cheerleaders as goodwill ambassadors.

16. Know the history of LaDainian Tomlinson (or some other well-known player).

17. Demonstrate how the football is held when thrown versus when it is caught.

18. Understand the history of the National Football League.

Although several of these purposes could be narrowed down if the speaker so desired, purposes 6, 9, and 18 are definitely too broad. For example, with regard to purpose 6, there are several types of football coaches, so the exact purpose for a 5-minute speech should focus on one type of coach (such as the head coach or the offensive coordinator). To narrow purpose 9, two positions (such as tight end and wide receiver) could be compared and contrasted. Purpose 18 could be narrowed to "Understand how the NFL got started" or "Have an understanding of the early years of the NFL." Of course, exactly how you narrow down your topic will depend on your own interests and the interests of your audience.

Once Kara decided to speak about Pluto and its place in our solar system, she knew that she definitely would need to narrow her topic. After listing several exact purposes, she decided on the following: "After hearing my speech, the audience will have a better understanding of what a planet is and where Pluto now fits into our solar system."

Determine Your Main Points

Once you have selected a topic that meets the guidelines discussed above, it is time to decide on your main points. You'll be able to complete your research

EXPRESS/CONNECT

You can use Speech Builder Express, a Web-based speech outlining and development tool, to help you create your exact purpose. To work on your exact purpose in Speech Builder Express, select "Speech Goal" from the left-hand menu and follow the instructions. For short reminders from this chapter about exact purposes, click on the "Tutor" button.

much faster once you're focused. Of course, during your research you may uncover additional information that you will wish to include in the speech, or you may discover that one or several of your points should be discarded. In fact, the main problem with beginning speakers is that they tend to include too many main points or so much information that each main point could be an entire speech on its own. All these changes will likely require a refinement of your purpose statement.

If you are assigned a topic that you know little about, you'll need to do some initial research just to discover what main points will work best. You might also try the brainstorming method suggested earlier. In five minutes or less, make a list of every possible content idea that comes to mind. Then consider each one, combining and eliminating until you settle on the three to five main points that will be most beneficial to your audience. ➡ *Refer to the Quick Start Guide for more on the selection of main points.*

Although Kara's purpose statement had identified her topic, when she began to list all the main points and subpoints that she really wanted to cover, her instructor suggested that she had enough for at least a 15- to 20-minute speech. Some of her initial points included the history of the word planet; *criteria for a planet; criteria for a dwarf planet; why Pluto is no longer a planet; the astrological catalyst that led to the new definitions of* planet *and* dwarf planet; *discoveries in 1801, 2003, and 2006; asteroids versus planets Ceres and Pluto; and Eris versus Pluto. Kara finally narrowed these possible points to three: (1) new IAU (International Astronomical Union) definitions for a planet and a dwarf planet, (2) why Pluto was demoted to a dwarf planet, and (3) why two other objects in our solar system are now classified as dwarf planets as well. She was now ready to rough out an outline of her main points and possible supporting materials to help her determine what research needed updating and what supporting materials were lacking.*

Preparing a Rough-Draft Outline

There are two basic types of outlines that will help you give a quality speech: the **rough-draft outline**, used to aid research, and the more detailed, polished **preparation outline**, used to aid final planning and organization. Business and other professional speakers always use outlines for four important reasons:

- First, *an outline serves as a map of the presentation.* Without the map, you can't be sure how the speech will flow and may not realize that problems exist. Writing out your speech word for word isn't nearly as effective. Looking for problem areas in a speech in manuscript form is like trying to do research in a book without a table of contents or section headings in the chapters. Without an overview to show what it contains and how the contents are organized, you would have to read every page of the book. With an outline of your speech, you can easily see the big picture and determine what changes are needed.

- Second, *an outline makes getting suggestions from others much easier.* If you have ever tried to get suggestions from a friend or classmate by showing them your speech written in paragraphs, you have experienced the problem. They probably said, "Looks good to me." It would be an unusual friend who carefully read the entire speech. However, if you hand them an outline, they can read it without too much effort and will be more likely to make some valuable suggestions.

Preparing a rough-draft outline before you begin your research will save you valuable research time.

- Third, *an outline makes it easy to tell where extra research and supporting materials are needed.* Making a rough outline of the main points and supporting information that you think you might use, before beginning your research, is an excellent way to help you streamline your content and tell which information you already know or have and whether additional research is needed. With a rough outline as a guide, you can avoid researching areas that won't be included in your speech and shorten your total research time.

After you analyze your audience and determine your topic and exact purpose, you are ready to rough out an outline (or list) of main points and possible supporting information. Take a look at Kara's rough-draft outline in Figure 5.2—she used this outline to prepare her speech in Chapter 4, "Our Solar System and the Three Dwarves." Compare her speech to the following suggested **guidelines for rough-draft outlines**:

- *Keep in mind that a rough-draft outline does not have to be perfect—it is rough.* Although exact rules for outlining aren't as important as they are for detailed preparation outlines, it is a good idea to use Roman numerals for your main points, capital letters for your subpoints, and Arabic numerals for second-level supporting materials. You may want to make this outline by hand so it can include erasures, mark-outs, and additions as you think of them.

- *Concentrate on main points and subpoints, indicating what supports are needed.* If you have ideas about where to get the supports (i.e., personal example, textbook, or newspaper article), indicate them in brackets—maybe using red for sources you don't have and green for those you already have or know where to locate. Of course, not all these ideas and supports will end

Figure 5.2

Kara's Rough-Draft
Outline

*Notice how it indicates where
research is needed.*

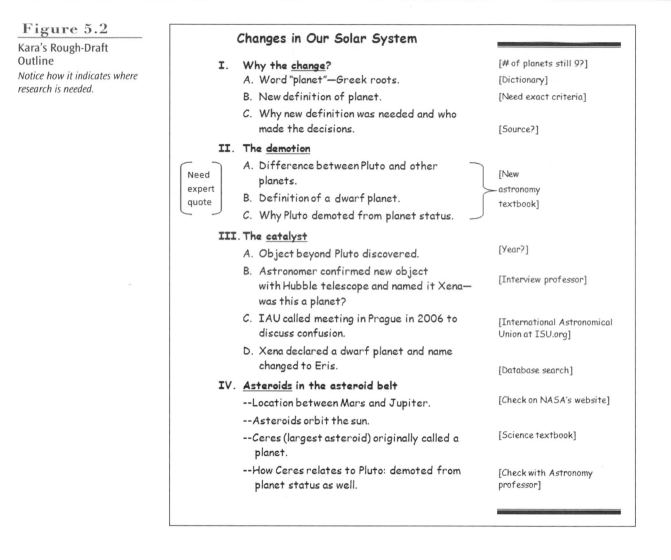

Changes in Our Solar System

I. **Why the change?**   [# of planets still 9?]
    A. Word "planet"—Greek roots.   [Dictionary]
    B. New definition of planet.   [Need exact criteria]
    C. Why new definition was needed and who
        made the decisions.   [Source?]

II. **The demotion**
    A. Difference between Pluto and other   [New
        planets.   astronomy
    B. Definition of a dwarf planet.   textbook]
    C. Why Pluto demoted from planet status.

(Need expert quote)

III. **The catalyst**
    A. Object beyond Pluto discovered.   [Year?]
    B. Astronomer confirmed new object
        with Hubble telescope and named it Xena—   [Interview professor]
        was this a planet?
    C. IAU called meeting in Prague in 2006 to   [International Astronomical
        discuss confusion.   Union at ISU.org]
    D. Xena declared a dwarf planet and name
        changed to Eris.   [Database search]

IV. **Asteroids in the asteroid belt**
    --Location between Mars and Jupiter.   [Check on NASA's website]
    --Asteroids orbit the sun.
    --Ceres (largest asteroid) originally called a [Science textbook]
      planet.
    --How Ceres relates to Pluto: demoted from   [Check with Astronomy
      planet status as well.   professor]

up in your actual speech, but the purpose is to focus and narrow your research. If you aren't sure where to find a needed example, fact, or statistic, ask your librarian or try google.com or ask.com as a start. ➤ *Refer later in this chapter for valuable research sources.*

- *This is not the time to worry about introductions or conclusions—so leave them out of the rough draft.* It is amazing how much time can be wasted trying to write an introduction before you are sure exactly what content will be in the final speech.

- *Update your outline as you research.* If you find that one of your main points will be impossible to support, omit it and add another one. Indicate the sources for ideas or quotes used for main points by noting author, date, page, etc.

- *As each support is located, put a check mark by it,* and write in the missing information noting the source or indicate where the information is located (author, date, title, etc.). It is no fun to find a perfect example or statistic and then forget where you found it.

As you can see, the rough-draft outline is a working outline that you take with you as you do your research; it is a valuable tool for narrowing your points and locating needed information. You will add to it or change prior entries depending on what you find. Notice how different Kara's rough draft is from her speech in Chapter 4 and her preparation outline in Chapter 7. This rough-draft outline not only helped her pinpoint information needing research, but also helped her clarify and narrow her topic into a quality presentation. Once your research is completed, you are ready to turn your rough-draft outline into a more detailed and polished preparation outline. ➡ *Preparation outlines are discussed more completely in Chapter 7.*

Active Critical Thinking

To think further about your rough-draft outline, complete the following:

- After you have selected and narrowed a topic for your next speech, prepare a rough-draft outline.
- Make sure your outline includes main points, subpoints, and notations of where to find information and needed research material. Share your outline with a classmate to see if they have any suggestions for other places to look for research material.

Researching Your Topic

Analyzing your audience, selecting an interesting and beneficial topic, and roughing out an outline are preliminary steps in speech preparation. However, without the information from the next step—researching your topic for verbal and visual supporting materials—your speech won't make much of an impression. Although it's a good idea to keep your eyes open for usable visual material such as pictures, maps, and graphs, most of your research will concentrate on verbal information that you can use to clarify and prove the main ideas in your speech. Ideally, some of your supporting materials should come from your own experiences, but it's also important to gather **supporting materials** (such as explanations, illustrations, statistics, quotations, and examples) from books, magazines, encyclopedias, journal articles, and the Internet. Using information from respected sources adds to your credibility as a speaker. The remainder of this chapter will cover where and how to research for information. ➡ *Chapter 6 will provide more specific suggestions for selecting all types of supporting materials from your research information.*

This speaker is validating information he found on the Internet by comparing it to authoritative print sources available at his local college library.

Avoid Research Mistakes

In researching their topics, beginning speakers often make one of two mistakes:
(1) they do too little research because they plan to rely primarily or completely on their personal experience, or (2) they use only the Internet to do their research.

First, even if you are speaking as an expert on your topic, you need to present additional sources as well. Using information from other respected sources shows that you are an objective and informed speaker and adds to your credibility.

Second, although the Internet can be a wonderful research tool, it is important to supplement and verify Internet information with facts obtained from more-traditional sources such as printed materials, electronic databases, and personal interviews. Therefore, your college library is still an important part of any quality research; librarians can help you find print materials, give you access to electronic databases, and direct you to reliable websites.

Begin with Printed Materials

If you are relatively unfamiliar with your topic (which may occur if you are assigned a speech topic), it's a good idea to begin your search for information with an overview from one or two current books on the topic. Then check your library for other printed materials.

- *Books.* To save time, check the Library of Congress Subject Headings for terms under which your topic is likely to be indexed before checking your college's online catalog of books. Also, don't forget to look in your college bookstore for textbooks on your topic—not only are they current, but additional sources are listed in footnotes and/or references. You can also search for current books by author, title, or topic on **amazon.com** and **ebooks.com**.

- *Brochures and pamphlets.* These can give you a useful thumbnail sketch of your topic. Check your library's Vertical File Index for pamphlets on your topic. You might also want to contact local or national organizations (like the American Cancer Society)—you can usually find contact information in the phone book or on the organization's website.

- *Magazines/journals.* An easy way to search for magazines and refereed journal articles is through the many electronic databases available at your library. Also, check out the reference section of the library for magazine indexes such as the Business Periodicals Index, Cumulative Index to Nursing and Allied Health, Education Index, or Index to Journals in Communication Studies. Expect to search using more than one word—it may take several tries before you find the exact term to locate the information you want. ➞ *See the following section on using electronic databases.*

- *Newspapers.* Although newspaper articles may not tell the complete story, they are more current than books and contain personal details and quotations that can serve as good supporting materials. Check your library for national, large-city, and local newspapers. Many libraries also have electronic indexes that include complete newspaper articles, such as EBSCOhost, LexisNexis, or the National Newspaper Index.

- *Specialized dictionaries and encyclopedias.* If you are new to your topic, begin your research with a specialized dictionary such as the *Dictionary of American History* or an encyclopedia such as *Encyclopedia of Sociology, Encyclopedia of Science and Technology,* or the *Physician's Desk Reference.* These reference books contain overviews of basic information in various fields—for example, the *Physician's Desk Reference* contains pictures and explanations on the Heimlich maneuver. Be careful about using **wikipedia.org** ("a free encyclopedia that anyone can edit"); always verify information obtained from Wikipedia from one or more reliable sources. Also, remember that anything taken from Wikipedia must be referenced to avoid plagiarism.

- *Other library resources.* Libraries also contain books of quotations such as *Bartlett's Familiar Quotations* and the *Speaker's and Toastmaster's Handbook,* as well as yearbooks loaded with facts such as *The Book of Lists, Facts on File Yearbook,* and the *Statistical Abstract of the United States.* Check with your librarian for government documents, special collections, and films or videotapes that are relevant to your topic. Also, you may be able to obtain additional materials through interlibrary-loan services.

Use Licensed Electronic Databases When Possible

Libraries are continually purchasing new and expanded electronic databases that contain books, magazines, journal articles, and government documents. These databases have been screened to include only reliable information from business, education, government, and international sources and contain complete text of most articles. Some databases that might be helpful for researching your speeches are Communication and Mass Media Complete, CQ Researcher, EBSCOhost, Education Index, Ethnic NewsWatch, First Search, InfoTrac College Edition, InfoTrac, LexisNexis Academic, Opposing Viewpoints Resource Center, and ProQuest. To maximize your database searches, always look at each database's "Help" icon for tips.

Use the Internet with Care

Most people don't realize what a recent creation the Internet is—it has only been in common use since 1992. Yet the growth of websites is staggering: 19,000 in 1995, 5 million in 2000, 47 million in February 2004, 92.5 million in August 2006, 231.5 million in April 2009, and a drop to 205.7 million in July 2010 (April, 2009; August, 2006; February, 2004; July, 2010; Saunders, 2000).

Although the Internet offers access to seemingly limitless information, you need to keep three facts in mind:

1. *Not all information on the Web is authoritative.* Some of it is outdated, fallacious, biased, and basically worthless. You will need to evaluate carefully what you find. → *See page 117 for "Evaluate Internet Sources Carefully."*

2. Unless you know where to look, *it is possible to spend hours on the Internet without finding the information you need.* Surfing the Web and researching the Web are not the same. → *See page 115 for "Using One Search Engine Isn't Enough."*

3. *Many valuable sources are not available on the Web* (or are not available for free). This material is often referred to as the "invisible Web" because it cannot be accessed by search engines due to the fact that search engines cannot type a login or password. A **search engine** is a tool, like Google, that searches the Internet and retrieves requested information. Google does have agreements with some academic libraries—thus Google Scholar—but this still just scratches the surface of available materials. It is only through licensed databases found though your college library that this "invisible" information can be found. Thus, quality research still requires a trip to the library.

Don't Go Online Until You Have Prepared How many times have you been frustrated because it took so much time to find what you needed online? Considering the three facts above, and to save the time and frustration of an inadequate search, do your homework before going online. First, *take a look at your rough-draft outline* at the main points and supporting information to see what information you still need (such as a fact, statistic, quote, or example).

Commercial databases like InfoTrac College Edition are especially helpful in researching magazines, journals, and newspapers. More than 35.5 million full-text articles from over 6,000 sources are available for your use on InfoTrac.

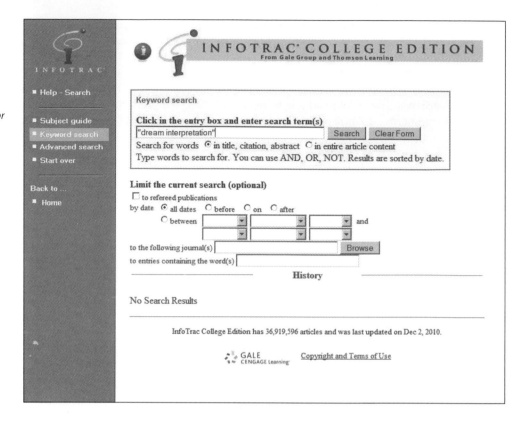

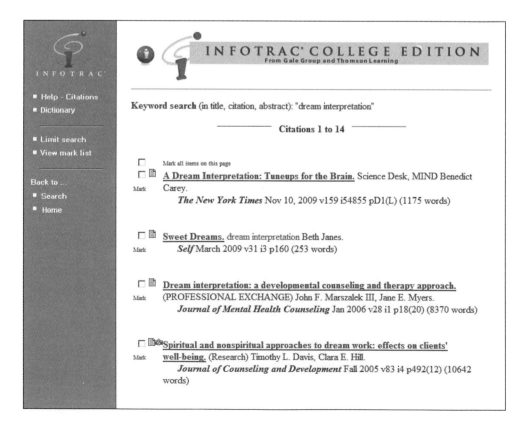

Second, when you visit the library looking for print materials and electronic databases, *make a list of keywords and phrases* to use when searching the Internet. The information you want may be on the Internet, but if you don't have the right keywords, you may never find it. For example, some important documents on positive imagery and speaking can be found only under the keyword *visualization;* other documents appear only with a search for *mental imaging.* To narrow a search of "positive imagery" to speaking situations, would you use the keyword *speech, presentation,* or *public speaking?* Consulting print materials on the subject first will help you identify appropriate keywords.

Third, *search one or more licensed electronic databases* (such as InfoTrac College Edition, EBSCOhost, or CQ Researcher). Because you know this information is reliable, you can use it to verify the credibility of sources you find on the Internet.

Now you are ready to effectively search the Internet looking for additional information to supplement your print and electronic database searches.

Using One Search Engine Isn't Enough Technology can be wonderful, but to find quality websites, you must use multiple search engines. As mentioned earlier, in 2010 a Web Server Survey by Netcraft (July, 2010)—an Internet services company based in Bath, England—found 205.7 million sites on the World Wide Web. Obviously, no single search engine can access all available sites. In 2000, Saunders reported that search engines covered less than 16 percent of the billions of pages of information available on the Web—it can only be worse now. When selecting search engines, the following guidelines are recommended (Barker, 2006; Berkman, 2000):

- *For broad or complex subjects,* pick a search engine that uses a **hierarchical index**—a subject directory organized into categories. This way, you are more likely to find relevant items. The most popular hierarchical search engine is Yahoo!.

- *For specific subjects,* use either a **standard search engine** or an alternative search engine. With a standard search engine, more of the Web is searched. This is because computer "robots" search the Web, index the pages found, and determine the relevance of the pages by mathematical calculation. Popular standard search engines include AltaVista, Excite, HotBot, and Yahoo! (both a hierarchical directory and standard search engine). **Alternative search engines** have different ways of sorting or ranking the pages located in the search. Popular examples include AskJeeves (which lets you input sentences instead of keywords), Google (which ranks hits by how many links to other pages each has), and ASK (which identifies the most authoritative sites on the Web). **Vertical search engines** search less of the Web, but a more specific part of the Web (Mossberg, 2005). For example, Indeed searches job openings from thousands of websites, and Ziggs searches for professional people (with specific characteristics, and who live in specific locations).

- *To search as many sites as possible,* use a **metasearch engine**—a search engine that searches other search engines. Popular metasearch engines include Dogpile, Surfwax, and Search (which searches 1,000 search engines at a time). Keep in mind that only 10 to 15 percent of each website is actually searched by metasearch engines; each time you use an engine, different hits will appear; and they focus on "smaller and/or free search engines and miscellaneous free directories" and are "highly commercial" (Barker, 2006).

Remember that quality searches require the use of multiple search engines.

Research Blogs Carefully Blogs, or weblogs, are personal journals located on the Internet that contain a variety of opinions on various diverse issues (Mazer et al., 2007). If you are unclear on current public views (especially on a persuasive topic), blog research could be a definite addition to your knowledge base. In fact, many blogs contain facts and cite sources. According to technorati.com in their State of the Blogosphere 2009, 75 percent of bloggers surveyed "blog to share their expertise" (McLean, 2009) and are well educated and fairly affluent (Sussman, 2009). Even businesses are beginning to realize the benefits of company weblogs (Stibbe, 2007), and many blog on Twitter (Lipsman, 2009). *Online magazines* like **forbes.com** also include blog sites of interest. You can use Google, Yahoo!, and **technorati.com** to search weblog[CE13] sites, or you can go directly to **social networking/social media** sites such as Facebook, MySpace, Blogspot, or Twitter.

When using blogs and social networking sites, be sure to critically assess them and the accuracy of their information, or you could destroy your credibility as a speaker (Painter, 2007). Presenting opinions from a blog as though they are fact will quickly make your speech questionable in the eyes of most audiences and certainly your instructor. Before using blog opinions, look for the blogger's frame of reference (such as gender, political affiliation, education level, religious affiliation, current job, etc.), goal or purpose (inform, persuade, or entertain), the credibility of the blog site (do they have restrictions such as real name required?), and the date of the blog.

Use Boolean Operators to Improve Search Effectiveness Whether you are using an electronic database or a search engine, **keyword searches** (an Internet search that matches a specific word or phrase) on some search engines will be more effective if you know how to link your search terms with **Boolean operators** such as *or, and,* and *not* (see Figure 5.3).

Although the number of hits a search produces is important, the *quality of hits* is much more important. Usually, if the first two pages of hits don't contain what you want, the wrong term or wrong search engine was used.

To narrow the number of hits, try the following suggestions:

* *Avoid the Boolean operator OR.* For example, in July 2010, a search for *motorcycle OR racing* resulted in 576,000,000 hits on Google!

  * *Use phrases* (enclose titles, common phrases, or specific diseases or procedures with quotation marks). For example, a search for *motorcycle racing* on Google returned 36,600,000 hits, whereas "motorcycle racing" returned fewer—2,130,000 hits. Specify *additional words using* + *or AND.* For example, "motorcycle racing" + women returned 280,000 hits on Google while "motorcycle racing women" found only 22,600 hits.

  * *Exclude words or phrases by using* - *(hyphen) or NOT.* For example, "motorcycle racing" NOT "dirt bike racing" returned 58,700 hits on Google; "motorcycle racing - dirt bike racing" found 54,100 hits.

To increase the number of hits, try these suggestions:

* Check that spelling and keywords are correct.

* Use the **wildcard** ★ to search for all forms of a word. For example, *legisl★* will search for *legislature, legislation, legislator,* and so on. This type of truncation will not work on Google, but you can search for synonyms by using the tilde (˜) before search words.

Even online searches for simple topics like motorcycle racing require knowledge of Boolean operators if you want a fast and effective search.

Marcel Jancovic.2010/Used under license from Shutterstock.com

Figure 5.3

Boolean Operators*
(such as AND, OR, NOT,
+, −, " ")

Basic Boolean Operators and Their Uses

Boolean Operator	Most Databases and Search Engines	Google
• OR (Searches documents with either word & both words = maximum number of hits.)	• *motorcycle* or *racing* • OR = all caps or lowercase.	• *motorcycle* OR *racing* • Searches documents with either word but not both words. • OR, − must be in all caps.
• AND (Searches only documents containing both words.)	• *motorcycle* AND *racing* • AND = all caps or lowercase.	• *motorcycle racing* • Google default puts AND between all words unless quotes are used.
• + [plus sign] (Searches documents with either word but not both words.)	• *motorcycle* + *racing* • Add space before but not after + sign.	• "*Star Wars Episode +1*" • Google omits words like *in, the, when, how,* and numbers unless a + sign (with space before but not after) is used to force inclusion of these words.
• "[phrase]" (Searches for content inside quotes as a single word or exact phrase.)	• "*motorcycle racing*" • If no quotes, searches each word separately.	• "*motorcycle racing*" skills • If no quotes, puts AND between words.
• NOT or − [minus sign] (Search excludes documents using word or phrase following -, NOT, AND NOT.)	• *motorcycle* NOT "*dirt bike*" • *motorcycle* and not "*dirt bike*" • *motorcycle* − "*dirt bike*" • Use all caps or lowercase.	• *motorcycle* − "*dirt bike*" • *motorcycle* NOT "*dirt bike*" • NOT must be in all caps. • Add space before the minus but not after.
• *[asterisk] (Searches for truncated endings of the search term.)	• *Listen** • Searches *listen, listening, listens, listeners,* etc.	• *listen + listeners + listening* • Google does not truncate but will find synonyms if a tilde (~) is placed immediately in front of a term; *~food* will find food, recipes, cooking, nutrition, etc.

*For more information on Google searches, go to google.com/help or Google to find *Googling to the Max* by
UC Berkeley.

- Use fewer search words.
- Connect similar search words with OR.
- Use alternative keywords—for example, *automobile* instead of *car.*
- Change full name to initials or initials to full name.
- Avoid using *-s, -ing,* or *-ed* on search words.

Evaluate Internet Sources Carefully The Internet is a blend of many interests: educational (such websites are identified with the suffix .edu or .cc), commercial (identified by .com), governmental (.gov), organizational (.org), military
(.mil), and personal. You can't assume that all the information you find on the

Internet is authoritative. Internet searches are as likely to include outdated, inaccurate, and biased information as they are to turn up valuable information. It's up to you to evaluate the credibility of your information by asking the following questions (Drake, 2005):

- *Is the author a qualified expert in the field?* Along with the author's name should be an indication of his or her occupation, position, education, experience, and organizational affiliations. If no author is given, is the website clearly attributed to a reliable source, such as a university or agency?

- *Is the information objective?* Are conclusions based on facts? Are sources cited? Are opinions and personal bias clearly stated? Is the purpose of the publication clear—to inform, persuade, sell? Is the author affiliated with an organization or group that might indicate a bias? For example, an article on animal testing of cosmetics on **majorcosmeticscompany.com** or **savetheanimals.org** might indicate the possibility of bias.

- *Is the information accurate?* Websites with grammatical and typographical errors should usually be avoided—content may be faulty as well. Can you verify the facts and conclusions in this publication with other sources you have read?

- *Is the information current?* When was the information written? Has it been updated? Some websites will include the date of last revision. If not, Netscape allows you to check the date—go to the File menu, select "Document Info," and select "Last Modified." Are the sources used by the author up to date? If no date is given, the information may be completely outdated.

As a speaker, you will be expected to use current, accurate, objective information that is attributed to a qualified expert. Always verify the credibility of documents obtained on the Internet by comparing the documents to information you find in the library's print materials and electronic databases.

It is amazing how little time it takes to locate materials through online library catalogs, electronic indexes and databases, and the Internet. Of course, reading and analyzing the information will take time, but because you will have picked a topic that you like, this part of your speech preparation should be enjoyable.

Conduct Personal Interviews

It is possible that not even your personal knowledge and library and Internet research will provide all the information you want. When this occurs, you may want to find more information by conducting some interviews. In many ways, conducting an interview is similar to presenting a speech. After you decide on likely candidates for your interviews, you should plan your questions and conduct the interview following these steps.

1. *Introduction:* Thank the interviewee for his or her time, and establish rapport by talking about your assignment or the reason you especially wanted to

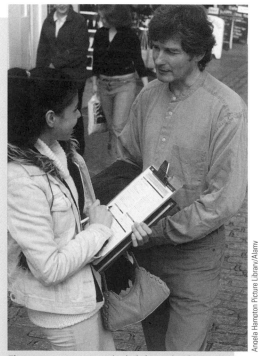

There are many ways to obtain information for a speech. This student is conducting a personal interview.

Angela Hampton Picture Library/Alamy

speak with him or her. Be relaxed and friendly, and make good eye contact. Next, state why you are there (unless already mentioned), how long you expect the interview to take, exactly what information you are looking for (if there are several points, list them), and how the responses will be used.

2. *Body:* Here is where you ask your questions, which you have already planned. Be sure to write out your questions and bring them with you. Most people will be more open and relaxed if you do not record the interview. Just listen carefully and take an occasional note to record an important fact, figure, or idea. Try to use mainly open-ended questions—you will get more information that way. An open-ended request (such as "Tell me about the accident") allows for any response. Specific questions (such as "Was he speeding?" or "How fast was he driving?") should be kept to a minimum. Use probing comments such as "Tell me more" or "What happened next?" to keep the interviewee talking. To make sure you haven't missed valuable information, end your questioning with "Is there anything else you think I should know?"

3. *Conclusion:* Use this step to verify information and give closure to the interview. Briefly summarize the main areas you covered in the interview (this allows both you and the interviewee to see if anything important was omitted). If you are planning to quote the interviewee directly, now is the time to review the quotation for accuracy and ask for permission to use it in your speech. End by thanking the interviewee, shaking hands, and making a timely exit.

4. *Follow-up:* As soon as you can, send the interviewee a thank-you note expressing the value of the information to you and your speech.

Use the results of the interview carefully. Expand your notes as soon as you get back so that you won't forget or misrepresent the interviewee's information. In deciding what part of the interview, if any, to use in your speech, be sure to keep all matters confidential that you agreed not to reveal.

Record Research Information Carefully to Avoid Plagiarism

Although some instructors may prefer that you write your research notes on 4-by-6-inch note cards, any organized method will work. Instead of taking notes, some students prefer to photocopy information and articles and keep everything in a special folder. If you use this method, circle or highlight important information, and use Post-it notes for summaries, messages, and ideas. What's important is to find a procedure that works for you. Of course, note cards have some definite advantages. For one thing, they are all the same size, so they are easy to handle and store. Also, because each card contains only one idea, it is easy to move a card from one main point to another until you have decided where it belongs (if at all) in your speech. On the other hand, a disadvantage of note cards is the length of time it takes to handwrite quotations and summaries of the ideas you might want to use. Another disadvantage is that you may later decide to use more information from the source and have to locate it again; or the summary that seemed so clear when you wrote it may be confusing when you get ready to prepare your speech.

No matter how you decide to record your research information, make sure to avoid unintentional plagiarism by using a method that does the following:

- *Provides ready access to researched information.*

- *Makes clear which passages you have paraphrased and which ones you quoted.* Paraphrasing is putting another person's ideas into your own words. If you use cards or Post-its, always put quotation marks around any material that is taken word for word from the source.

- *Includes complete source citations* (such as complete name of author, source, date, publisher, and page numbers). For books from your college library, you may want to add a call number.

- *Includes a bibliography.* Many experienced speakers prefer to have a separate note card for each source because the cards are so easy to manage, but you can also use a sheet of paper. When your bibliography record (card or page) includes the complete source information for each reference, each individual note card need include only the last name of the author, title of source, and page number.

Now that you know where to find research materials, you are ready to begin researching for valuable information that will clarify, prove, and add interest to your ideas.

Active Critical Thinking

To think further about researching your topic, complete the following:

- Begin researching for your next speech by finding a print source, a database source, and an Internet site that relate to your topic. Also, locate a knowledgeable person on your topic to interview.

- Select a main point to research, and locate information on that point from each of the above sources. Compare your findings. Which seem to be the most helpful? Which seem to be the most accurate? Why?

Summary

This chapter covered Steps 2, 3, and 4 of the Basic Steps for Preparing a Speech—determine a topic, prepare a rough-draft outline, and research for desired information. The best topics are those that fit the requirements of the assignment, showcase your experiences and knowledge, are interesting to you, and are interesting and beneficial to your audience. You will find that your research is more meaningful and will take less time if you prepare a rough-draft outline before starting your research. When researching your speech topic, you should look for information from several types of sources: (1) printed materials (such as books, magazines, newspapers, specialized dictionaries and encyclopedias, books of quotations, and yearbooks), (2) licensed electronic databases, (3) the Internet, and (4) personal interviews. The best types of information that will clarify your ideas, prove your points, and add interest to your speech will be covered in the following chapter.

Essentials of Public Speaking Online CourseMate

Use your Online Resources for *Essentials of Public Speaking* for quick access to the electronic study resources that accompany this chapter, which feature the links found in the discussion about finding quality websites on pages 113–118, access to InfoTrac College Edition, Personal Skill Building Activities and Collaborative Skill Building Activities, a digital glossary, sample speeches, and review quizzes.

Key Terms

alternative search
   engines 115
blogs 116
Boolean operators 116
brainstorming 103
exact purpose 106
guidelines for rough
   draft outline 109

hierarchical index 115
keyword searches 116
metasearch engine 115
preparation outline 108
rough-draft outline 108
search engine 113
social networking/
   social media 116

standard search engine
   115
supporting materials
   111
vertical search engine
   115

Personal Skill Building

1. Using your college library's online catalog, find a book that appears to contain helpful information on your next speech topic. List the title, call number, and campus location of this book. (If no books are listed under the term you chose, check the Library of Congress Subject Headings to see if your topic is listed under a different term.)

2. In the reference section of the library, locate a specialized dictionary or encyclopedia that relates to the subject area of your topic (such as *Encyclopedia of Sociology, Encyclopedia of Science and Technology, Dictionary of American History,* and *Physician's Desk Reference*). Photocopy at least one page from this source.

3. Using an Internet search engine, conduct a search on your speech topic. Find a webpage that meets this chapter's guidelines for quality websites and one that does not. Share your results with the class.

4. Using an electronic database (such as InfoTrac College Edition, EBSCOhost, or CQ Researcher), locate an article related to your topic. Print out the abstract (summary) of this article (or the complete article if you wish), including the title, author, magazine, volume number, issue date, and page numbers.

5. Check out the following websites. (You can access these sites using your Online Resources for *Essentials of Public Speaking,* Chapter 5.)

   - If you need some topic ideas, take a look at a subject-based search engine like **yahoo.com**, the Internet Public Library/Librarians' Internet Index (**www.ipl.org**), an online news magazine like the *Washington Times* (**washingtontimes.com**), or an Idea Generator like the one produced by Old Dominion University (**www.lib.odu.edu/researachassistance/ ideagenerator/**). In addition, take a look at Jim Peterson's "Speech Topics Help, Advice & Ideas" at **speech-topics-help.com**.

   - Try several of the following websites for printed materials:

     - For links to Web-accessible libraries worldwide, try **worldcat.org** and the University of California's LibWeb at **library.ucsb.edu**—click on "Research Sources," then click on "Online Reference Sources."

     - For newspapers, try **newspapers.com** or **newslink.org** (if you don't mind pop-up ads).

CourseMate

CourseMate

- For quotations, see *Bartlett's Familiar Quotations* at **bartleby.com**. Use the Search drop-down menu and type in a topic. For other links to quotations, see The Quotations Page at **quotationspage.com**.

- For statistics, go to: the U.S. Census Bureau at **census.gov** and scroll down to the Statistical Abstract or FedStats, gateways to statistics from over 100 U.S. federal agencies; **robertniles.com**, a guide to hundreds of data links; or the National Center for Education Statistics at **nces.ed.gov**.

- Listen to speeches about September 11. How do you think the speakers handled the tragedy as they prepared their speech? Go to **americanrhetoric.com** and click on "Rhetoric of 9-11."

- The following excellent websites discuss how to evaluate the credibility of print and Internet sources:

  - The Anti-Plagiarism website at the University of Maine at Farmington is very helpful. Go to **plagiarism.umf.maine.edu**.

  - "Evaluating Web Pages" by the UC Berkeley Library staff at **lib.berkeley.edu**. Under the "Help" tab, click on "Tutorials," "General Guides," and "Evaluating Web Pages."

  - "Evaluation Criteria" by Susan E. Beck at **lib.nmsu.edu/instruction/evalcrit.html**.

Collaborative Skill Building

1. In small groups, go to EBSCOhost, click on the Military and Government Collection, and select a speech that the group likes from a recent *Vital Speeches*. Have each group member read the speech, looking for the speaker's exact purpose, main points, and a list of the research sources used in the speech. Compare your results and critique the effectiveness of the speech. What changes would your group recommend to make the speech even better?

2. In small groups, generate a list of possible speech topics by following the four-step process discussed on pages 102–103. From this list of speech topics, select a topic that everyone likes and complete the following:

   - First, have each group member research for information on the topic using two of the types of research discussed in this chapter. When finished, share your research results and discuss which types of research uncovered the best information and why.

   - Based on your research, decide on three to five main points for your speech topic and one research fact for each point. Be prepared to share your list of main points and research facts with other groups or the class.

6

Supporting Your Ideas

FLASH **BACK**

The ancient Greek writer Aesop is credited with writing numerous fables (a type of supporting material)—such as "The Hare and the Tortoise" and "The Shepherd Boy and the Wolf." A fable is a short story that usually involves animal characters that are used to teach a moral lesson. Greek and Roman orators used stories and fables to make a moral point without offending the listener—this worked because the characters were usually entertaining, enjoyable animals.

FLASH **FORWARD**

Today, we also know that stories and fables are cultural tools that speakers can use to talk about conflict in a nonthreatening, indirect manner. This is especially good for collectivistic cultures that view conflict as both rude and harmful. Therefore, instead of saying, "This is how I think we should handle the problem" or "This is why you are wrong," the speaker can put the situation or desired result into a story that makes the point while allowing listeners to "save face." *Which conflict situations in today's world might the two Aesop's fables mentioned above be used to diffuse?*

Learning Objectives

As you read Chapter 6,

- *List* the seven types of verbal supporting materials, *identify* which are used only for clarification and which are used for both clarification and proof, and *discuss* several tips for using supports effectively.

- *Identify* several do's and don'ts for the supports that are often overused by speakers: explanations and statistics.

- *Identify* several do's and don'ts for the supports that are often underused by speakers: examples, comparisons, expert opinions, fables/sayings/poems/rhymes, and brief demonstrations.

DON WAS ASSIGNED TO GIVE A 7-MINUTE INFORMATIVE SPEECH. AFTER MUCH DEBATE, he decided to give his speech on global warming—a subject that really interested him. A search of the Internet found the following three sources and supporting materials that he decided to put in his speech:

1. A definition of global warming, a chart of global temperatures, and a list of several ways in which man has contributed to global warming, all from **www.wikipedia.org**.

2. Examples as proof of global warming: massive floods in China and Pakistan as well as an extreme heat wave and fires in Russia, as reported by **www. telegraph.co.uk**.

3. An explanation of coming water shortages and the amount of energy used by power plants from **www.environment.change.org**.

Based on the previous chapter on research, you should be able to help Don assess the quality of his sources. What do you think? Does Don have *enough sources* to support a speech on global warming? Are Don's sources *quality sources*? Are they *credible sources*? Does he have an appropriate *variety of sources*? (See Question 1 in "Suggestions for Practice and Critical Thinking" at the end of the chapter.)

One reason why the quality, credibility, and variety of Don's sources are so important is that they affect the quality, credibility, and variety of the supporting materials that come from them. **Supporting materials** are the verbal and nonverbal information that speakers use to clarify, prove, and add interest to their ideas. If you want to give excellent speeches instead of just average or good ones, it is your supporting materials that will make the difference. By the time you finish reading this chapter, you will feel confident in selecting and using effective supporting materials for your next speech. For a summary of the information in this chapter (which is Step 5 of the Basic Steps for Preparing a Speech), go to the Quick Start Guide at the beginning of this text.

Supporting Materials: Overview

Think of your main points and outline as the bones or skeleton of the speech—they give the speech structure and hold it together. However, without the supporting materials that add substance and flesh to your outline, your speech won't be very appealing to your audience.

Types of Supports

There are two types of supporting materials: visual and verbal.

- *Visual supports*—used to clarify and add interest to your speech ideas—include computer-generated graphs and clip art, charts, posters, pictures, objects, and models, sometimes accompanied by sounds or music.
  → *Visual supports are covered in detail in Chapter 10.*

- *Verbal supports*—used to clarify, prove, and add interest to your speech ideas—include (1) explanations; (2) statistics; (3) brief or detailed examples; (4) comparisons; (5) expert opinions; (6) fables, sayings, poems, and rhymes; and (7) simple demonstrations. Note, however, that explanations and statistics tend to be used too often, whereas the remaining types are not used often enough. Each of these verbal supporting materials is covered in detail later in this chapter.

Clarification Only	Clarification & Proof
• Explanations	• Statistics
• Hypothetical illustrations (detailed instances)	• Factual examples (brief instances)
• Figurative comparisons	• Factual illustrations (detailed instances)
• Fables, sayings, poems, & rhymes	• Expert opinions
• Demonstrations	• Literal comparisons (very weak proof)

Figure 6.1

Supporting Materials
Used for clarification only or clarification and proof?

Reasons for Using Supports

We have established that strong supporting materials are crucial to an excellent speech, but the fact is that not all supports have the same value. Some supports are used only to clarify and add interest; they do not add any believability or proof to your ideas. Other supports accomplish all three objectives: they clarify concepts and terms, they add evidence and proof to your points, and they keep your audience listening by capturing their interest. As a speaker, it's important to know what different supporting materials can do. Selecting supports to keep the listeners interested is easy—select ones that relate to your audience, and use a variety of them. However, knowing which supports only clarify and which both clarify and prove is more complicated. See Figure 6.1 for a handy chart that categorizes the types of supporting materials that we will discuss in this chapter:

Tips for Using Supports Effectively

In order for the supports you select to produce the greatest effect in your speeches, keep the following tips in mind:

- *Use a variety of supports*—this is one of the best ways to keep your audience listening. For example, some listeners may find statistics and expert opinion interesting. Others may tune out statistics but listen carefully to personal or humorous anecdotes. It's unlikely that all of your listeners will respond to the same type of support. Therefore, using a variety of supports helps ensure that you are relating to all of your listeners.

- *Use a minimum of two types of supporting material per point*—this not only helps create listener interest, but it also ensures clarity of your ideas and helps build effective proof. More than two types of proof are usually recommended for main points in persuasive speeches. Although statistics might begin the proof process, they likely won't work by themselves. For example, your proof would be much stronger if you also presented a detailed narrative of a real person's experience and a quote from a well-known expert.

- *Look for supporting materials that clarify.* Just because an idea is clear to you doesn't mean it will be equally clear to your audience—their frames of reference may differ. Therefore, it is important for speakers to clarify concepts and terms with both visual supports (such as graphs, charts, and pictures) and verbal supports (such as explanations, specific instances, and comparisons).

- *Look for supporting materials that prove.* Rarely will listeners accept your statements without some kind of proof. Verbal supporting materials (such as quotations from experts, statistics, or personal instances) serve as evidence for the ideas presented in a speech. Although supporting materials that prove your points are essential in persuasive speeches, they are also important in informative speeches.

- *Don't use too much explanation*—this is a sure way to bore your listeners, plus there is no proof in an explanation. To make sure that you are not overusing explanation, look at your outline and label the type of supports you are using under each main point. For example, of the two outlines below, obviously B would be the most interesting and include the most clarity and proof.

Outline A	**Outline B**
I. First main point	I. First main point
a. Explanation	a. Explanation
b. Explanation	b. Quotation
c. Explanation	c. Statistics
d. Explanation	d. Comparison
II. Second main point	II. Second main point

If you can't identify which type of support you are using, it is most likely an *explanation*. Your speeches will be much better if you can find some other type of support to replace most of your explanations; in other words, instead of explaining how serious the problem is, find an expert that you can quote or some statistics that cover the same information you were including in the explanation.

Types of verbal support will be described and illustrated in the sections that follow. Remember that explanations and statistics tend to be used too often, whereas the remaining types are not used often enough. As you read, note the types of support that you feel would be most appropriate for your topic.

Active Critical Thinking

To think further about supporting materials, complete the following:

- Based on your past presentations, English papers, and even e-mail messages, which types of supporting materials do you typically use? Which ones do you generally not use? Does this surprise you?

- What effect does your use (or lack of use) of these supports have on your spoken and written messages? Give an example.

Overused Supports—Use Them with Care!

Speakers, especially beginning speakers, tend to overuse explanations and statistics. Too many of these types of supports can make a speech terribly dull, but when used correctly they can add to listener understanding and enjoyment.

Explanations

An **explanation** defines or gives more information about a term or topic, gives instructions on how to do something, or describes how something works or the relationship between certain items.

Refer to Kara's sample speech in Chapter 4. In her first main point, she gives the new IAU definitions for a planet and a dwarf planet:

> *For an object to meet the definition "planet," it must meet three pieces of criteria: it must orbit the sun, be nearly spherical in shape, and have cleared the neighborhood around its orbit. For an object to be considered a "dwarf planet," it must meet four pieces of criteria: it must orbit the sun, be nearly spherical in shape, not be a moon or satellite of another object, and has not cleared the neighborhood around its orbit.*

George Ellard (2007), co-head of the white-collar and corporate-compliance section of Baach Robinson & Lewis Law Firm, defined business ethics in his speech "I Know It When I See It: Moral Judgments and Business Ethics":

> It is an honor to speak with you tonight about business ethics. It is also a very difficult task because the notion "business ethics" rests on the distinction between right and wrong. Most civilizations before the modern epoch accepted the existence of right and wrong, but by the time people reach college age in our society many, if not most, have absorbed the belief dominant in our culture that moral judgments are simply personal preferences (p.193).

Although explanations and definitions are important to successful speeches, nothing is more deadly than too much explanation. Think of a really boring lecture you've heard lately. Chances are this lecture included no comparisons, quotations, short or detailed instances, visual aids, or statistics—just explanations.

Remember

Explanations...

- Should be used sparingly because they tend to be dull.
- When used, they should be brief but specific.
- Are more effective when followed by one or two "for instances"—discussed further on page 132.
- Are used for clarification, not proof.
- Can be replaced by other types of supports, such as quotations, that clarify the same ideas as the explanations you planned to use.

Statistics

Another often-overused support is **statistics**, or numbers used to show relationships between items. When used correctly, statistics (which both clarify and prove your ideas) can have a powerful impact on listeners (Allen & Preiss, 1997). Too many statistics, however, create a confusing and boring speech. To make sure your statistics are a positive addition to your speeches, follow these simple rules (adapted from Hamilton, 2011):

Rule 1: *Make your statistics meaningful by relating them to your listeners' frames of reference.* Even audience members who don't like statistics will listen if you know how to use this rule. Audiences remember more when speech content is connected to familiar experiences. Consider the following examples:

- A student who was giving a speech on the meteorite crater in Arizona couldn't understand why the audience seemed unimpressed when she said, "This meteorite crater is two miles wide." During the Q&A after her speech, she discovered that very few in the audience could picture a two-mile-wide hole. In exasperation, she said, "Well, this meteorite crater is large enough to hold our entire college campus, with room left over for at least one football field!" Finally, the audience was impressed.

- An advertisement by Allstate that appeared in the *Wall Street Journal* (2007, May 22, A16) compared the 6,000 teens that die in car crashes each year (which is impressive enough by itself) to "12 fully loaded jumbo jets crashing every year" (the statistic now seems almost unbelievable). Or what about comparing the number of teens that die in car crashes each year to the total number of military and civilian casualties in Iraq since the war began: 3,086 as of September 14, 2007 (**www.defense.gov**)?

- In a speech called "Sticky Ideas" given in August 2007, Professor Richard Weaver made the word "billion" more meaningful:

  > ... Did you realize that a billion seconds ago it was 1959? A billion minutes ago, Jesus was alive; a billion hours ago, our ancestors were living in the Stone Age; a billion days ago, no one walked on the earth on two feet ... (p. 355).

Rule 2: *Eliminate any statistics that are not absolutely necessary.* Even people who generally relate well to statistics can experience overload when too many statistics are presented. Chris Christie (2010), Governor of New Jersey, gave a persuasive speech to the Legislature of New Jersey that required the use of statistics to make his point. If you had been in the audience, how would you have reacted to the following statistics?

> If government is left unchecked, with no changes in current law, spending by the state of New Jersey is projected to be $38.4 billion in the coming fiscal year. This is outrageous. 20 years ago, when Governor Florio took office, spending was only $12 billion. If we did nothing, spending will have increased 322 percent in 20 years over 16 percent a year, every year. That's right, state government spending would have gone up at 4 times the rate of inflation over the last 20 years. Today, we say, stop (p. 224).

Figure 6.2

Graph of Statistics

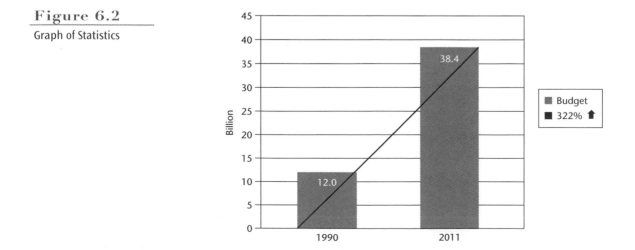

When you cannot avoid using several statistics, present some of them in graphic form (see Rule 3).

Rule 3: *Whenever possible, present your statistics in graphic form*—your audience will comprehend them faster and remember them longer. For example, Figure 6.2 is a graphic visual of some of the statistics on the projected New Jersey budget increase that Chris Christie could have used in his speech, "A New Course, Long Overdue" (see Rule 2 above). ➡ *For more on graphic visuals, see Chapter 10.*

Rule 4: *Round off the numbers to make them easy for your listeners to recall.* The audience is less likely to remember 8,211 than they are to remember 8,200 or, better yet, 8,000. Unless the audience expects it or your topic demands it, exact numbers are normally used only in handout materials and occasionally on graphic visuals. However, when you *discuss* the data on a graphic visual (even exact-number data), round off the numbers. Allan Freeth (2010), CEO of TelstraClear, used these rounded statistics to describe his company:

> But, in the past five years, our profit has grown—from $2 million to $18 million. Last year's profit increase from $7.5 million to $18 million was the single biggest increase in the company's history—in one of the toughest markets we have ever seen (p. 291).

Rule 5: *Demonstrate the credibility of your statistics* by citing the source, the reason the source is considered expert (if the audience doesn't already know), and the size of the population from which the statistics were compiled. Because sophisticated audiences know how easy it is to distort or falsify statistics, you want your listeners to feel confident that the statistics you are presenting are accurate. For example, "Four out of five dentists recommend Gleam-On toothpaste" sounds good until we realize that only five dentists had to be interviewed to make that claim. However, if we knew that 300,000 dentists were surveyed and four out of five of them (240,000) recommend Gleam-On, we could feel more confidence in the results. In a speech about Detroit and global competition, Richard E. Dauch (2004), Chairman of the National Association of Manufacturers, demonstrated the credibility of his statistics as follows:

> ... as a part of my role as chairman of the National Association of Manufacturers (NAM) ... [I] addressed the NAM's recent study entitled "How Structural Costs Imposed on U.S. Manufacturers Harm Workers and Threaten Competitiveness." ... The study concludes that external overhead costs, costs out of the control of manufacturers, conservatively add 22.4 percent to the price of production for U.S. manufacturers relative to our foreign competition. These overhead costs include:

> - Corporate tax rate and tax code (5.6 percent).

> - Employee benefits including health care and pension costs (5.2 percent).

> - Rising energy prices (3.8 percent).

> - Tort litigation ($1 per hour of expense).

> - Excessive government regulations (the equivalent of a 12 percent excise tax) (p. 539).

Remember

Statistics . . .

- Are numbers used to show relationships between items.
- Are more effective when related to listeners' frames of reference.
- Should be used sparingly.
- Should be rounded off.
- Are more credible when the source and the source's qualifications are given.
- Are easier to understand and remember when shown in graphic form.

Active Critical Thinking

To think further about overused supports, complete the following:

- For your next speech, research to find two explanations/definitions and two statistical supports.
- Which explanation and which statistical support are of the best quality? List several specifics to explain why.

Underused Supports—Use Them More Often

Among the effective types of underused supports are factual and hypothetical instances; literal and figurative comparisons; expert opinions; and even fables, sayings, poems, and rhymes. All of these supports can clarify ideas and add interest; in addition, some of them (factual instances, literal comparisons, and expert opinions) also add proof to your arguments. Let's take a more detailed look at these useful types of supports.

Instances (Examples and Illustrations)

An **instance** is a specific case (usually called an example or illustration) that is used to clarify, add interest, and (in some cases) prove a point. After we make a point, we usually say, "For instance . . ." and give one or more examples or illustrations. One of the surest ways to grab the attention of your audience and keep them listening is to use a variety of instances. Instances also increase the probability that attitudinal change will occur during persuasive speeches (Park et al., 2007).

Types of Instances An instance can be any of the following:
- Factual (actually happened).
- Hypothetical (made up but could happen).
- Brief (basic facts only)—usually called an **example**.
- Detailed (vivid picture or narrative)—usually called an **illustration**.

Often, effective instances are illustrations that are both factual and detailed (describing things, people, or events that actually happened, with enough detail that your listeners can picture events accurately). For example, if you were describing an accident, you would set the stage by telling what the weather was like on that day and what emotions the participant(s) were feeling prior to the accident. Kenneth A. Haseley (2004) included the following factual illustration in a speech on "Dealing with Public Anger":

> Some years ago, the plant manager of a chemical plant asked me to observe a public meeting for residents who lived near his facility. At one point, a woman stood up and angrily stated that she had three miscarriages, and was certain that they were caused by the plant's chemical emissions. The plant manager responded by citing a Johns Hopkins University study that showed no connection between the emissions and any ill human health effects. Think of how much better it would have been if he had first said to the woman, "I'm sorry to hear that. I have two children of my own, so I know how precious a life is." Then he could have mentioned the research study (p. 243).

Detailed **hypothetical illustrations** can also work well. Because the speaker creates the hypothetical instance, it's very important to cue the audience to the fact that it is not "real." Begin hypothetical instances with such words as "Suppose . . . ," "Imagine . . . ," or "What would you do if . . . ?" For example, Joseph N. Hankin (2003), President of Westchester Community College, used this hypothetical illustration in a presentation:

> Picture this: The scene is a seaside hotel breakfast room. Enter a resident. He summons the headwaiter and, to that gentleman's growing consternation, says, "I want two boiled eggs, one of them so undercooked it's runny, and the other so overcooked it's about as easy to eat as rubber; grilled bacon that has been left on the plate to get cold; burnt toast that crumbles away as soon as you touch it with a knife; butter straight from the deep freeze so that it is impossible to spread; and a pot of very weak coffee, lukewarm." The headwaiter rallied slightly and said, "That's a complicated order, sir. It might be a bit difficult." "Oh?" said the guest. "You didn't find it difficult yesterday" (p. 126).

One of the advantages of using hypothetical illustrations is that audience members can relate the instance to their own experiences and become more involved in your speech. For example, a speech on class attendance might include the following hypothetical illustration:

> Imagine that it's a school day and your alarm has just gone off. You reach over and after several tries finally get that awful noise to quit. You pull the cover from your head, force your eyes open, yawn, and roll over. You're thinking, "Should I get up and go to class, or should I skip the class and sleep in a bit longer? After all, the weather is bad today and I do have a cold . . . ."

You'll probably see some sheepish looks on your listeners' faces, because they've done a similar thing more than once—maybe even this morning.

Another type of instance is the example. **Examples**, which are always brief and usually factual, are more effective when used in groups of two or more because one by itself is easy to overlook. Sometimes examples are presented with just a few facts; other times they are presented as lists, as used by Indra Nooyi (2010), chairman and CEO of PepsiCo, in a speech to the Economic Club of Chicago:

> We have a large portfolio of products. Eighty per cent of our portfolio is made up of products we call Fun For You or Better For You products such as Pepsi, Diet Pepsi, Mt Dew, SoBe Life Water, Propel, Lays, Doritos, Fritos, Sun Chips, Cheetos and Tostitos—the world's most loved brands. The other twenty per cent is made up of products that we describe as Good For You—healthy products such as Tropicana, Quaker Oats, Naked Juice and Gatorade for athletes (p. 248).

In these instances, adding details about each product would take away from the effectiveness of the speech. At the same time, using only one example for each product line would not have the same impact, would it?

Instances are also used by speakers to add clarification after an explanation. Speaking to the V.A. Veterans Service, Michael P. Sullivan (2004) used an explanation followed by several examples to make his point that health care will need to make some changes to meet baby-boomer expectations:

> Boomers have never lost the need to be in control. They are less likely to accept the word of authority than their parents. [For example] Tell them they have to do things your way because those are the rules of the institution and they will choose another institution. "Take a number and wait" means they don't have control. In fact, most health care processes that devalue the patient's time and individualism run smack up against the Boomer need for control (p. 444).

Using Instances to Prove Although you can't prove an idea by using only instances, factual instances (whether examples or illustrations) can add some proof to your arguments. Suppose you are trying to prove that the lakes in your state are polluted. You describe in detail the pollution that you and other people who live near a local lake have experienced. You tell about the broken glass on the beach and the bottles and cans on the bottom of the lake, the soap scum and trash floating on the surface, the awful smell in the summer, the sign the city posted on the beach last summer that warned parents not to let their children come into contact with the water, and the disbelief of the community when two teenage boys died after diving into the polluted water. Would describing this one lake be enough to convince your audience that the state's other lakes were polluted? Of course not.

But imagine that you presented two detailed factual illustrations of polluted lakes—one in your community and another one elsewhere in the state. Then you showed a visual aid listing 10 other lakes and their pollution indexes and said, "Each lake on this list is as polluted or more polluted than the two I have described to you." Now your audience would likely be convinced. Presenting one or two detailed instances (illustrations) followed by several brief instances (examples) is a very powerful proof package. Add some statistics and a quotation from a water-pollution expert, and your proof would be complete.

Proof is more likely when two or more types of supporting material are used (such as an explanation, a factual illustration, and several examples). Even statistics, when used alone, are unlikely to prove a point.

Using Varied Topics for Your Instances As indicated previously, the greater the variety of instances, the better. Although there is no limit to the topics you can choose for your instances, using personal and/or family, famous, business, and humorous topic areas are very effective in speeches. Let's look at each of these topic areas in more detail.

Personal and/or family topics (experiences or events that you observed first-hand, often involving family life) are of special interest to your listeners because through them, they get to know you better. Personalizing your speeches is an effective way to aid audience listening and memory. Everyone listens to personal and family instances—even the daydreamer—and as a result is more likely to recall the point the instance is supporting. → *See Chapter 3 for more on the importance of personalizing speeches.*

In an informative speech on drunk drivers, Ken gave the following detailed personal instance of DWI to his speech classmates:

> On July 4th last year I was 18 years old. I got out of work early. A friend of mine bought a case of beer. We went to his house and drank three six-packs in an hour. Then we got this stupid idea to go to the beach. I had to go to my house, about three miles away, to change clothes. There are only three things I remember about that time. I remember turning the key; I remember putting in a hard-rock tape; and I remember hitting a tree, head-on. Apparently the police were following me. I was told that I was driving through parking lots screaming, with my beer out the window. I don't remember anything about it.

Deborah Gandy (2007), Senior Vice President of U.S. Trust, delivered a commencement speech called "The Secret to Becoming Very Wealthy: Knowing the Difference Between Wants and Needs." She connected with the audience by sharing important life lessons, using her mother as an example:

> My mother always taught us that it was important to give back. She always told us to care for those who are less fortunate.
>
> She despised credit card debt and knew how to stretch a dollar. There was a time that she went to the grocery store with $6 in her purse to feed a family of four. She made friends with everyone in the store, and she asked the butcher for chicken backs, which the butcher typically didn't even put out in the case. So, he would give her the backs. But for Sunday dinner, we would get chicken breasts. She lived within her means and taught us to be frugal too.
>
> My mom always believed in getting a good value and taught us to value what we had. And that meant we got one pair of shoes a year. But she always emphasized the importance of a good pair of shoes and was willing to pay a bit more for a pair that would last. At Christmas, we got one gift — always something that was special to us. She didn't spend money foolishly, but she tried to give you something you would appreciate.
>
> She taught us to know the difference between needs and wants. My mother knew that it doesn't matter how much you make—it's what you keep. I have multi-millionaire clients who haven't learned that yet! (p. 118)

Take a few minutes to think of personal or family experiences related to your speech topic. Remember: You are looking for examples that clarify, add interest, or provide proof for your main points. Ask family members and close friends if they can remember an instance involving you or your family that you may have forgotten. Make notes on these topics.

Famous topics (involving famous or well-known people) can also capture audience attention and add support for your ideas. A commencement speech called "Make a Contribution," by PBS television talk-show host Tavis Smiley (2007), concentrated on the importance of not giving up. In his speech, Smiley included a brief example of never giving up:

So much conversation over the last month or so around this campus, on this campus, around the nation and indeed, around the world, so much of that conversation centered on those remarks uttered by Mr. Imus, Don Imus. And while I don't want to belabor this point, I do want to use that controversy to just make one illustrative point, and it is simply this—you do not become a radio icon for 40 years in America, working to become an icon, you don't make the cover of *Newsweek* and get profiled on *60 Minutes* and have the whole country engaged in a conversation about you because you are an icon, you don't become an icon by giving up. You don't become an icon by giving up. Don Imus refers to his childhood as a horrific adolescence—his words, not mine—a horrific adolescence. Don Imus had a father who was an alcoholic. Don Imus went on to battle drug addiction and depression in his own life. Don Imus got fired any number of times. You do not overcome all those obstacles and find yourself the recipient of a $40 million contract and being elected to the National Broadcasting Hall of Fame and becoming an icon if along the way you kept quitting. You don't become an icon by giving up . . . (p. 307).

Business topics (including business experiences and advice of your own and from others) are also used to clarify, add interest to, and help prove your main points. In a speech on "Change Can Be Good," Jack Ma (2009), CEO of Alibaba Group, used the following personal illustration:

One of the beliefs I have is that if Jack Ma can be successful, then 80 percent of the people in this world can be successful. I don't have a financial background. I don't have a rich father. I do not have relationships with any government officials. I failed three attempts to enter university. Nobody has ever said to me, "Jack, you are smart. You are clever. You are a genius." It was only after November 6, 2007, when Alibaba.com launched its IPO, that people suddenly started to say, "Jack, you are smart."

A humorous instance is an excellent way to add interest and enjoyment to your speech.

Davis Barber/PhotoEdit

The reason why I think Alibaba survived is because we have long held onto the belief that customers are number one, employees are number two and shareholders are number three ... Most importantly, at Alibaba, we still have the dream in our hearts. We want to change the future (p. 257).

Humorous topics can also include personal, family, famous, or business topics that are humorous. Of course, before selecting a humorous instance, analyze your audience carefully, because what is humorous to some people may be offensive to others. James Whitworth (2003) used the following humorous and famous instance in a speech to the Miami Township Fire and Emergency Medical Services:

Of course, this is the same Winston Churchill that, during a visit with the Astor family at his cousin's palace, and after arguing most of the day with Lady Nancy Astor, had the following exchange. Lady Astor said, "Winston, if I were your wife I'd put poison in your coffee." To which Winston Churchill replied, "Nancy, if I were your husband, I'd drink it" (p. 26).

Joan Detz (2007), author of *It's Not What You Say, It's How You Say It,* gave a speech to the National Conference of State Legislators in Boston on the subject of speaking. One of her 12 speaking tips included advice on using humor in a speech. According to Detz, one of the most effective ways to use humor is to poke it at yourself, as long as you don't overdo it; but be very careful about poking fun at others. The following is an example to support her position:

Since we're here in Boston today, I should use at least one John F. Kennedy example. After JFK won his first Senate race in 1952, he faced wide criticism for "buying" the victory with his father's deep pockets. So at a Gridiron dinner, Kennedy addressed these rumors head-on ... with humor. He brought down the house by reading a telegram supposedly from his father: "Dear Jack: Don't buy a single vote more than necessary. I'll be damned if I'll pay for a landslide" (p. 541).

Remember

Instances . . .

- Are factual, hypothetical, brief, or detailed examples or illustrations used to clarify ideas, add interest, or prove points.
- When brief, are more effective when two or more are used at a time.
- When detailed, should paint a vivid picture for listeners.
- Can be of personal or family, famous, business, or humorous events.
- Will add spice to a speech and help ensure continued audience attention.

Comparisons: Literal and Figurative

Another type of underused supporting material effective in adding interest and clarifying points for your listeners is the **comparison**. You use this by comparing (or contrasting) something your listeners know a lot about with something they know little about, in order to make the unfamiliar clear.

There are two types of comparisons: literal and figurative. A **literal comparison** shows similarities or differences between two or more items in the same class or category. Literal comparisons include two species of saltwater fish, three well-known diets, or the way the people of two countries view the importance of product packaging. For example, Elaine L. Chao (2007), U.S. Secretary of Labor, in a speech titled "Remarks" at the Asian American Government Executives Network, used the following literal comparison:

> And Asian Pacific Americans need to be aware of the cultural differences that may impact the way in which they practice leadership in society. Let me give you an example. This goes back to classroom days.... In traditional Asian American communities, children are discouraged from speaking unless they have something to say. But in American culture, expressing one's opinion is encouraged and rewarded. And this makes sense in this society.... Leaders advance and defend the interests of their organization and their colleagues. So executives need to be articulate, both in written and in oral presentations.... You can see these trends in little children.... But most Asians are taught that it is rude to speak out of turn or to interrupt others. It is proper to defer to others. America, however, is a place where everybody speaks their mind.... I had to overcome my cultural reticence about speaking up (10–13).

In an address on "Customer Satisfaction Is the Most Important Thing," Ivan Seidenberg (2009), chairman and CEO of Verizon, used statistics and comparisons in explaining wireless sales:

> According to the latest Nielsen reports, the average American spends a little over 5 hours a day watching television and another hour a day surfing the Internet. On the other hand, U.S. wireless customers in 2008 use their phones an average of 26 minutes a day.
>
> Less than half an hour on the wireless side ... more than six hours on the TV and Internet side.
>
> If we can get even a modest amount of that usage to migrate to mobile, we have lots of headroom to grow.

Whereas a literal comparison is used for two or more items that are basically alike, a **figurative comparison** is used for two or more items from different classes or categories. Examples include comparing individual differences to snowflakes, which are never alike, or the mayor of a city to the skipper of a boat. Figurative comparisons cannot be used for proof, but they do add interest and clarify ideas. For example, in a speech delivered in Barcelona, Spain, speaker Robert E. Brown, communications professor at Salem State College (2010), used a figurative comparison when he stated, "The White House, Moscow, Beijing, Barcelona are well acquainted with ambiguity. Like Toyota and Tiger Woods, we seek to address our issues strategically lest they spread like an oil slick into a crisis (p. 298).

Figurative comparisons work very well in speech introductions. For example, Jessica, a student in a public speaking class, used a figurative comparison between butterflies and skin diseases:

> Imagine a butterfly, flying through your field of vision. You see it softly fluttering and landing on a flower. Such a soft and delicate creature. So delicate that you dare not even pick it up, because you know that if you are the slightest bit too rough, it will die. Imagine having skin that delicate. So delicate that the slightest touch would cause it to fall off. Such a disorder really exists, and one name that those afflicted go by is the "Butterfly People." Jonny Kennedy had such a disorder. He was afflicted with the genetic disease known as epidermolysis bullosa, or EB. The TLC special called "The Boy

Whose Skin Fell Off" chronicles the story of Jonny and his 36-year battle with this horrible disease. Dr. Rob Danoff from **tlc.com**, on September 14, 2005, gave an apt description of Jonny's condition. "Remember the pain you felt when that hot stove caught your fingertip by surprise? And what about the lingering hurt from the paper cut you received while opening up that envelope? Combine both that pain and lingering hurt, and imagine that suffering being inflicted 24 hours a day, 365 days a year."

If you aren't sure that a concept or main point will be clear to your audience, consider using a literal or figurative comparison. If no literal comparison comes to mind, creating a figurative comparison is as simple as saying, "This concept is just like ..." For example, in a speech about overcoming speaker anxiety, you might use this figurative comparison:

> The fear of giving a speech is similar to the fear you had as a child when you first learned to ride a bike. Remember how nervous you were, waiting for your dad to put you on the bike? But as soon as you began to ride, your fear was replaced by excitement, and by the time the lesson was over, the excitement had turned to a feeling of accomplishment and of being in control. And you wondered why you had been so nervous at all. Well, speaking is much the same. Once you start speaking, nervousness turns into excitement and then into a feeling of accomplishment. You will wonder why you bothered being nervous at all.

Remember

Comparisons...

- Compare or contrast an unfamiliar idea with one that is familiar to the audience.
- Are especially good for clarifying the unfamiliar.
- Are an excellent way to add interest and variety to your speech.
- Can be either literal (comparing items of the same type or category) or figurative (comparing items of different types or categories).

Expert Opinions

When you refer to the ideas of an expert on your topic, you are using a type of support known as **expert opinion.** This is an excellent way to clarify an idea or prove a point, whether you paraphrase the expert or quote him or her directly. When using expert opinion as proof, be sure to (1) state the name of the expert, (2) briefly describe his or her qualifications (unless you are sure that your audience is familiar with the person), and (3) briefly cite when and where the expert reported the information (such as in the latest issue of *U.S. News and World Report* or in a personal interview you conducted last week).

When paraphrasing the expert's ideas, make sure you don't misrepresent them as your own. Here is an example of a paraphrase:

> In his new book [*Re-Imagine! Business Excellence in a Disruptive Age*] Tom Peters quantifies that American women constitute—are you ready?—the largest economy in the world; followed by the entire nation of Japan, and then American men (Nelson, 2004, p. 339).

Next is an example of a paraphrase followed by a personal opinion:

> David Lawrence, the retiring CEO of Kaiser Permanente, noted that in the $1.5 trillion that Americans spend on health care, close to $300 billion of that in his estimation is due to medical mistakes and errors in medicine, and we [the California Endowment for Unequal Healthcare Treatment] think that some significant percentage of that $300 billion is due to mistakes as a result of language services and inappropriate interpretation and medical translation in the clinical setting (Ross, 2003, p. 53).

Lastly, here is an example of a direct quotation:

> Tim Brown, CEO and President of the design firm IDEO, said it well in a recent Harvard Business Review essay: "Edison's genius," Brown wrote, "lay in his ability to conceive a fully developed marketplace, not simply a discrete device. Edison understood that the light bulb was little more than a parlor-trick without a system of electric power generation and transmission to make it truly useful. So, he created that too" (Rodin, 2009, p. 262).

When you read direct quotations aloud, make sure that your delivery is lively and convincing—avoid a dull or monotone presentation.

When your audience is unfamiliar with your experts, you will need to introduce them thoroughly, as student and oratory winner Jenny Clanton (1989) did in a speech entitled "Plutonium 238: NASA's Fuel of Choice." In her attempt to inform the audience of the danger of Plutonium 238, she used the following paraphrase:

> Last July, *Common Cause* magazine contacted Dr. Gofman at Berkeley and asked him to place Plutonium 238 in perspective. Before I share Dr. Gofman's assessment, please understand he's no poster-carrying "anti-nuke." Dr. Gofman was co-discoverer of Uranium 233, and he isolated the isotope first used in nuclear bombs. Dr. Gofman told Karl Grossman, author of the article "Red Tape and Radioactivity," that Plutonium 238 is 300 times more radioactive than Plutonium 239, which is the isotope used in atomic bombs (p. 375).

If an expert is well known to your audience, it is not necessary to cite his or her qualifications. For example, when speaking at the Nebraska YWCA Women of Distinction Annual Dinner, Janice Thayer (2001), president of Excel Corporation, used the following quotation needing no detailed introduction:

> Barbara Bush must have been heartened, when in his acceptance speech her son said, "I believe in grace, because I have seen it. ... In peace, because I have felt it. ... In forgiveness, because I have needed it" (p. 408).

Whether you are paraphrasing or using a direct quotation, try to make sure that your audience understands what the expert is saying. If you feel that there is any chance of confusion, follow the paraphrase or quotation with a comment such as: "In this quotation, _____ is making the same argument I made earlier"; or "What is _____ saying? He or she is telling us ..."; or "I cited _____ because ..." Christopher Reeve, in his speech before the 1996 Democratic National Convention, followed a quote he used by FDR with these clarifying words: "President Roosevelt showed us that a man who could barely lift himself out of a wheelchair could still lift this nation out of despair." ➜ *Read about Reeve and his touching speech on page 140 in "Speaking to Make a Difference."*

Remember

Expert opinions . . .

- May be paraphrased or quoted directly.
- Should be kept brief to maintain listener interest.
- Can be used for both clarification and proof.
- Should be quoted as though the expert were actually speaking—not read in a dull or monotone voice.
- Should usually include the name and qualifications of the expert and the source and date of the information.
- In many cases, should be followed by a brief summary or explanation.

Fables, Sayings, Poems, and Rhymes

Fables (fictitious stories, usually with animal characters, meant to teach moral lessons), *sayings* (pithy expressions of truth or wisdom), *poems* (words written in meter or free verse that express ideas, experiences, and emotions in an imaginative style), and *rhymes* (verses that regularly repeat sounds) deserve to be used more often. Although these supporting materials are usually used in the introduction and conclusion, they can be effective at any point in your speech where clarification and variety are needed. They do not, however, provide proof. The impact of these supports depends on your delivery (enthusiasm and vocal variety are important) and on whether the audience can relate to them. Fables, sayings, poems, and rhymes that are well known to your audience are most effective.

Fables Jane Goodall (2003), naturalist and U.N. Messenger of Peace, used the following fable in a speech entitled "Dangers to the Environment: The Challenge Lies in All of Us" to show the importance of working together:

> It makes me think of a fable my mother used to read to me and my sister when we were little, about the birds coming together to have a competition: who could fly the highest? The mighty eagle is sure he will win, and majestically with those great, strong wings he flies higher and higher, and gradually the other birds get tired and start drifting back to the ground. Finally, even the eagle can go no higher, but that's all right, because he looks down and sees all the other birds below him. That's what he thinks, but hiding in the feathers on his back is a little wren and she takes off and flies highest of all.
>
> The reason I love this story is because . . . if we think of our life as an effort to fly always just a little bit higher and reach a goal that's just a little bit beyond our reach, how high can any of us go by ourselves? We all need our eagle . . . (p. 71).

Sayings Farah M. Walters (1993), president and CEO of University Hospitals of Cleveland, clarified the federal government's attitude toward health care reform with these words: "It's like that old saying: 'Success has many parents, but failure is an orphan'" (p. 687).

Speaking to Make a Difference

Peggy Noonan (1998), speech writer for Ronald Reagan and George Bush, writes, "The best speech at the Democratic National Convention in 1996 was not Bill Clinton's or Al Gore's but that of the actor Christopher Reeve." Reeve's entire speech can be found at www.americanrhetoric.com by searching for "Christopher Reeve and DNC."

AP Photo/Ron Edmonds

[Over] the last few years we have heard a lot about something called "family values." And like many of you, I have struggled to figure out what that means. And since my accident, I've found a definition that seems to make sense. I think it means that we're all family. And that we all have value.

Now, if that's true, if America really is a family, then we have to recognize that many members of our family are hurting. And just to take one aspect of it, one in five of us has some kind of disability. You may have an aunt with Parkinson's disease, a neighbor with a spinal cord injury, or a brother with AIDS, and if we're really committed to this idea of family, we've got to do something about it.

* * *

Right now, for example, about a quarter million Americans have a spinal cord injury, and our government spends about $8.7 billion a year just maintaining these members of our family. But we only spend $40 million a year on research that would actually improve the quality of their lives, and get them off public assistance, or even cure them. We have got to be smarter and do better.

The money we invest in research today is going to determine the quality of life of members of our family tomorrow.

Now, during my rehabilitation, I met a young man named Gregory Patterson. He was innocently driving through Newark, New Jersey, and a stray bullet, from a gang shooting, went through a car window, right into his neck and severed his spinal cord. Five years ago, he might have died. Today, because of research, he's alive.

But merely being alive—merely being alive is not enough. We have a moral and an economic responsibility to ease his suffering and to prevent others from experiencing such pain.

And to do that, we don't need to raise taxes. We just need to raise our expectations.

* * *

So many of our dreams—so many dreams at first seem impossible. And then they seem improbable. And then when we summon the will, they soon become inevitable.

So if we can conquer outer space, we should be able to conquer inner space, too.

And that's the frontier of the brain, the central nervous system, and all the afflictions of the body that destroy so many lives, and rob our country of so much potential.

Research can provide hope for people who suffer from Alzheimer's. We've already discovered the gene that causes it. Research can provide hope for people like Muhammad Ali and the Reverend Billy Graham, who suffer from Parkinson's. Research can provide hope for the millions of Americans like Kirk Douglas, who suffer from stroke. We can ease the pain of people like Barbara Jordan, who battled multiple sclerosis. We can find treatments for people like Elizabeth Glaser, whom we lost to AIDS. And now that we know that nerves in the spinal cord can regenerate, we are on the way to getting millions of people around the world, millions of people around the world like me, up and out of these wheelchairs.

Now, 56 years ago, FDR dedicated new buildings for the National Institutes of Health. He said that (quote), "The defense this nation seeks involves a great deal more than building airplanes, ships, guns, and bombs. We cannot be a strong nation unless we are a healthy nation."

He could have said that today.

President Roosevelt showed us that a man who could barely lift himself out of a wheelchair could still lift this nation out of despair.

In his keynote address, Reeve was able to communicate his sincerity and passion for spinal cord research through his use of various effective supporting materials. As discussed in this chapter, the term *supporting material* refers to information a speaker provides that will clarify, emphasize, prove, and add interest to points made in the speech. Without supporting materials, an oral presentation is little more than a string of assertions. In his address, Reeve's supporting materials (including such items as definition, quotation, explanation, statistics, and instances) were simple and conversational, yet vivid and poignant (Noonan, p. 56). Let's look at several of these in more detail:

- Reeve begins his presentation with a very personal *definition* of family values: "…And since my accident, I've found a definition that seems to make sense. I think it means that we're all family. And that we all

have value." He then *clarifies his definition* by citing statistics, which he makes personal with several brief examples:

> Now, if that's true, if America really is a family, then we have to recognize that many members of our family are hurting. And just to take one aspect of it, one in five of us has some kind of disability. You may have an aunt with Parkinson's disease, a neighbor with a spinal cord injury, or a brother with AIDS, and if we're really committed to this idea of family, we've got to do something about it.

- In addition to the "one in five" statistic, Reeve again uses *statistics* to show the disparity between the amount of money spent on spinal cord injuries and the amount spent on research. His statistics are effective because he rounds them off ("a quarter million Americans"), keeps them to a minimum, and combines them with a *comparison* to really make the disparity clear:

Right now, for example, about a quarter million Americans have a spinal cord injury, and our government spends about $8.7 billion a year just maintaining these members of our family. But we only spend $40 million a year on research that would actually improve the quality of their lives, and get them off public assistance, or even cure them.

- *Quotations* can be a very effective support to add proof to an argument, and Reeve selects a quote from a famous Democratic president who served the nation while in a wheelchair—Franklin Delano Roosevelt. "The defense this nation seeks involves a great deal more than building airplanes, ships, guns, and bombs. We cannot be a strong nation unless we are a healthy nation." Adding to the persuasiveness of the quote, Reeve follows with this simple statement: "President Roosevelt showed us that a man who could barely lift himself out of a wheelchair could still lift this nation out of despair."

- To add interest and poignancy to his request for money, Reeve uses both brief and detailed factual *instances*. He uses many brief examples, including Reverend Billy Graham with Parkinson's and Barbara Jordan with multiple sclerosis.

It is hard to imagine how difficult it was to be paralyzed and speak while exhaling through a breathing tube—but that didn't stop Reeve. Although he continued speaking, acting, directing, and writing after the accident, his most passionate goal was to raise awareness and money for spinal cord injuries. In fact, "Reeve ultimately raised $55 million in research grants and more than $7 million for nonprofit organizations that still help improve the quality of life for people living with disabilities" (Younis, 2006). This keynote address, aired before millions, helped with his quest.

Questions: What type of supporting materials do you think were the most effective in Reeve's speech and why? What else could he have added?

When inserting sayings into your speech, be sure to accurately represent the saying and connect it to the topic of your speech. "Accidents will happen" is a saying that, inserted in a speech about finding *accidental love*, could enhance the meaning of the message. Remember: Use sayings to add perspective, not to confuse.

Poems In a speech on "Make a Difference, Have No Regrets," Joseph N. Hankin (2002) read a poem that a student had written as an assignment during the Vietnam War. The poem was called "Things You Didn't Do."

Remember the day I borrowed your brand new car and scratched it—I thought you'd "kill" me, but you didn't.

And the time I nagged you to take me to the beach and you said it would rain and it did. I thought you'd say, "I told you so," but you didn't.

And the time I flirted with all the guys to make you jealous—and you were. I thought you'd leave me, but you didn't.

And the time I spilled pie all over your brand new strawberry rug. I thought you'd yell at me, but you didn't.

And the time I forgot to tell you that the dance was formal and you showed up in jeans. I thought you'd drop me, but you didn't.

There were lots of things you didn't do. You put up with me and you loved me and you protected me. There were lots of things I wanted to make up to you when you returned from Vietnam.

But you didn't (p. 507).

A graduate student teaching undergraduate students in the field of communication used the following poem in her speech on gender communication:

For every woman who is tired of acting weak when she knows she is strong, there is a man who is tired of appearing strong when he feels vulnerable.

For every woman who is tired of being called "an emotional female," there is a man who is denied the right to weep and to be gentle.

For every woman who is called unfeminine when she competes, there is a man for whom competition is the only way to prove his masculinity (Smith, 1994, p. 1).

Rhymes The following children's rhyme was used in the introduction of a speech on sexist fairy tales, to clarify the speaker's position that children are introduced to male and female stereotypes while they are very young:

> What are little boys made of, made of?
> What are little boys made of?
> Frogs and snails and puppy-dogs' tails,
> That's what little boys are made of.
> What are little girls made of, made of?
> What are little girls made of?
> Sugar and spice and all things nice,
> That's what little girls are made of. (dePaola, 1985)

Contemporary rhymes inserted into the speech provide direction and emotion for your topic. Consider quoting one or writing your own to add interest and engage your listeners.

Use a database like InfoTrac College Edition, EBSCOhost, or CQ Researcher to find examples of quotations, comparisons, fables, sayings, poems, rhymes, and humorous instances. Take each of these words and conduct subject guide and keyword searches for them. Compare results with similar searches using a search engine like Ixquick.

Remember

Fables, sayings, poems, and rhymes...

- Add interest and clarify meanings.
- Should be read with enthusiasm and good vocal variety.
- Are especially effective when they are familiar to your audience.

Demonstrations

The saying "A picture is worth a thousand words" expresses the importance of visual demonstrations. A **demonstration** uses objects or people to explain or clarify an idea. Telling about the efficiency of a vacuum cleaner may impress a client, but the client seeing the vacuum suck up a pile of pebbles, nails, and coins makes the sale. One of the reasons that TV infomercials are so successful is that we see demonstrations of the products. We see a lady with ordinary hair use the amazing hair dryer with a curling attachment to create a stunning hairstyle; we see a knife whack through a frozen block of ice and two soft-drink cans and still shave thin slices off a tomato.

Whether your demonstration involves objects or people or both, you should follow these guidelines:

- If your objects are not large enough to be seen by the entire audience, *show pictures of the objects* on computer visuals or posters.

- *Practice the demonstration* until you can perform it smoothly. One student meant to demonstrate that common drain cleaners are highly caustic, but she didn't practice. She filled a clear bowl with water, placed it in a large shallow pan of water, and then placed a Styrofoam cup full of water in the bowl. She planned to show how drain cleaner would eat a hole through the cup. But instead of carefully measuring the drain-cleaner crystals, she dumped in too much. When the drain cleaner hit the water in the Styrofoam cup, it began to bubble and fizz, devouring the cup and forming a mushroom cloud that reached the ceiling. At the same time, foam bubbled up and over the edge of the bowl of water, over the side of the desk, and onto the carpet. The fumes were so potent that the room had to be cleared.

Digital Vision/Jupiter Images

To keep your listeners from displaying the skepticism you see here, make sure you use supporting materials that prove as well as clarify your points.

- Unless you are giving a demonstration speech, *keep the demonstration extremely brief*—30 seconds or less. Showing the correct way to hold a racquet or swing a golf club adds clarity and interest to a speech, while taking only a few seconds. Be sure to clear all demonstrations with your instructor ahead of time. ➔ *See Chapter 11 for more on demonstration speeches.*

- While doing the demonstration, *maintain direct eye contact with your audience* and continue speaking as you demonstrate.

Active Critical Thinking

To think further about underused supports, complete the following:

- For your next speech, research to find four different supports that are underused by speakers in general and you in specific. Print out the supports and label each one.
- Critique the value of each support—strengths and weaknesses. Take one of the supports and briefly discuss how the support could be revised to give it more clarity, proof, and/or interest.

Summary

Supporting materials can clarify ideas, prove points, and add interest. The overview of supports covers the types of supporting materials, reasons for using them in a speech, and specific tips for using them effectively. Although explanations and statistics can be effective, they are often overused. The following types of supports are also effective and need to be used more often: instances (brief ones, called examples; detailed ones, called illustrations; factual; and hypothetical); literal and figurative comparisons; expert opinions (either paraphrased or direct quotes); and fables, sayings, poems, and rhymes. Demonstrations can also be used to clarify information. While your speech outline gives the speech structure, it is your supporting materials that add substance and flesh to that structure. Without effective supports, your speech will never be the success it could be with them.

Essentials of Public Speaking Online ⌐CourseMate

Use your Online Resources for *Essentials of Public Speaking* for quick access to the electronic study resources that accompany this chapter. Your Online Resources include access to InfoTrac College Edition, Personal Skill Building Activities and Collaborative Skill Building Activities, a digital glossary, sample speeches, and review quizzes.

Key Terms

comparisons 135	fables, sayings, poems, & rhymes 139	illustrations 130
demonstration 142	figurative comparison 136	instance 130
examples 130		literal comparison 135
expert opinion 137	hypothetical illustrations 131	statistics 127
explanation 127		supporting materials 124

Personal Skill Building

1. To see how difficult it is to listen to a speech containing nothing but explanations, select a paragraph from a speech that is nothing but explanation. Check for speeches by looking in your library for a magazine called *Vital Speeches,* or search in the Military and Government Collection, often available through the EBSCOhost electronic database. Read your paragraph aloud to the class, trying to make the explanation sound as interesting as possible. When the reading is completed, discuss whether your selection held the audience's attention or whether they kept drifting off. How could the original speaker have made this information more interesting?

2. Select one detailed family instance/example and prepare to present it to the class. Begin your presentation with a simple sentence of explanation, present the instance, and end with a moral or brief comment on the instance. Each presentation should take no longer than one minute. If time permits, ask listeners for suggestions on how to make the instance/example even better.

   If you and your instructor prefer, have a "family-instance talk down" where two students simultaneously present their family instance, each trying to capture and hold the audience's attention. This activity could include all members of the class or just volunteers. Not only is this activity a lot of fun, but it will demonstrate which types of instances tend to be the most effective.

   Let the student on the left be speaker A and the student on the right be speaker B. At the end of one minute, ask each audience member to hold up either the letter A or the letter B to indicate which speaker held their attention more of the time. Have an assistant quickly count and record the votes.

3. Select the topic for your next speech. Now find at least three examples of each type of supporting material that relates to your speech topic. Share these with some of your classmates, and have them evaluate which are the stronger and which are the weaker supports.

4. Audience analysis is essential for a good speech. Take a survey of your classmates to see which supporting materials they enjoy listening to the most and which ones they enjoy the least. For example, some people really like speakers to use statistics; others tend to daydream when statistics are presented. How will these results impact your next presentation?

5. Check out the following websites. You can access these sites using your Online Resources for *Essentials of Public Speaking,* Chapter 6.

   • A website by the University of Mary Washington has guidelines on how you can best use supporting material in your speech to maintain effectiveness: Go to **www.umw.edu/cas/speaking**, and click on "Resources," "Handouts," and "Preparing Supporting Materials."

   • This website offers tips and suggestions on how to use your supporting materials to help you achieve a great speech: **www.cfug-md.org/speakertips/783.html**.

   • For advice on using anecdotes, quotations, and excerpts, see the Power Tips on the left-hand side of **idea-bank.com/Tip.php**.

Collaborative Skill Building

1. Revisit the opening scenario about Don and his speech on page 124. In groups of four or five, discuss the answers to these questions: First, does Don have enough sources to support a speech? Are Don's sources quality sources? Are they credible sources? Does he have an appropriate variety of sources? Why or why not? Second, how would you evaluate his supporting materials as to quality and quantity? What else would you recommend Don add to his speech?

2. In small groups, find a speech that your group members like from InfoTrac College Edition or a recent issue of *Vital Speeches,* located in most libraries. *Vital Speeches* is also available in the Military and Government Collection that is part of the EBSCOhost electronic database. Each group member should read the speech, making a list of any supporting materials found and the page numbers.

   • As a group, compile all the types of support your group members found.

   • Select three of the best supports and discuss what made them so effective.

   • Next, discuss which support was the weakest and what the speaker could have done to make it more successful.

   • Be prepared to share your results with other groups or the class.

7

Organizing a Successful Speech

FLASH BACK

Ancient Greek and Roman rhetoricians knew the importance of organization and generally divided speech-making into five parts, or canons:
- *Invention*—researching the topic and the audience.
- *Disposition*—organizing materials in an orderly fashion.
- *Elocution*—choosing effective language and style.
- *Memory*—remembering the ideas to be presented.
- *Delivery*—presenting the speech (verbal, vocal, and visual aspects).

FLASH FORWARD

It is interesting to note that today's speakers generally study all the ancient canons except memory. Although Roman orators didn't have PowerPoint, they could have used note cards to aid their memories—but they didn't. Instead, they used a technique that is still taught in memory courses today: They mentally associated each point they wanted to make with a physical item at the speaking location (or in a room familiar to them). For example, the door on the left of the room might represent point one; the chairs at the front, point two; the statue on the right, point three; the window at the back, point four; and so on. *Do you think speakers today might be less nervous if they spent some time practicing this memory aid?*

Learning Objectives

As you read Chapter 7,
- *Explain* the role that organizing plays in a successful speech.
- *Identify* several informative patterns as well as several persuasive patterns for organizing the body of your speech, and *discuss* when each works best.
- *List* the main steps included in a speech introduction and those included in a speech conclusion and *discuss* what makes each successful.
- *Discuss* ways to add polish to your speech, including use of a preparation outline and clear transitions and connectors.

HEISH REINFELD (2007), A WRITER FOR THE *LAS VEGAS BUSINESS PRESS,* WAS ASKED to give a "light" 30-minute speech for a Rotary meeting. Trying to fit his needs as a humorous speaker into the expectations of the Rotarians while still keeping within the allotted time and the proper speech structure (introduction, body, and conclusion) was more complex than he had expected. In fact, he had to reject several interesting topic ideas because he felt organizing them would be too complicated.

As your speeches get longer, you too will find that organization becomes more complex. Think of your planned speech as a puzzle with jumbled pieces that include message needs, audience needs, and speaker needs; you must fit all these pieces together in order to effectively convey your message. You, like Reinfeld, will realize that if each piece of information doesn't fit into the puzzle, the result for your listeners will be confusion instead of clarity.

But by the time you finish this chapter, you will understand why structure is so important to the outcome of your speech, understand how to prepare a structured preparation outline, and be able to use several different structural patterns for both informative and persuasive speeches. The information in this chapter covers Steps 6 (organize your main points) and 7 (plan your introduction and conclusion) of the Basic Steps for Preparing a Speech. For a summary of this information, go to the Quick Start Guide at the beginning of this text.

Organization: How Important Is It?

From our discussion of listening in Chapter 3, you already know that organized, hierarchical data is easier for listeners to remember (Kosslyn & Rosenberg, 2009). We also mentioned that not all cultures expect the same type of organization. A summary of the cultural information from Chapter 3 that relates specifically to organization is included in Table 7.1.

There are four key reasons why organization is important in a speech:

- *Organized information is easier for speakers to remember.* As stated above, it is easier for your audience to recall information if you present it in a logical order; but likewise, when your speech is well organized, it is easier for you, the speaker, to remember what you want to say (and that means you will need fewer speaking notes).

- *Organized information gives the speaker confidence.* You can relax and speak with more assurance when you are not worried that you might forget an important point.

- *Organized information improves the speaker's credibility in the eyes of the audience.* Studies have long indicated that when you are organized and present information in a confident manner, your listeners judge you as more trustworthy and competent (Sharp, Jr. & McClung, 1966).

- *Organized information is easier for listeners to comprehend, easier to take notes from, and more likely to keep audience attention* (Holschuh & Nist, 2007, p. 125; Kosslyn & Rosenberg, 2009; Titsworth, 2004). As we know from Chapter 3, if content is confusing or difficult to comprehend, your listeners are likely to stop listening and think of personal interests or problems. Delivering organized content makes it easier for you to hold the attention of your audience.

As we discussed in Chapter 5, the only way to be sure you are getting these four organizational advantages for yourself and your audience is to follow a map—your

Table 7.1   Organization and Cultural Expectations of Listeners

Individualistic/Low-Context/M-Time Listeners	Collectivistic/High-Context/P-Time Listeners
Expect speeches to begin and end on time	Have no exact time expectations; time is flexible
Expect messages to be direct and explicit	Expect messages to be implicit and indirect
Expect clear organization to clarify points	Expect storytelling and analogies to clarify points
Expect speakers to get right to the point	Expect speakers to build on group's history and relationships
Expect conclusion/s to be stated (even in intro)	Expect conclusion/s to be obvious without being stated

outline. Putting your speech into manuscript form does not give you these advantages; preparing an outline does. In fact, as you know, successful speakers prepare a rough-draft outline before they begin seriously researching their speech topics. Not only does this rough-draft map send them in the correct direction toward locating needed information, it also saves them valuable time. The final preparation outline, to be discussed at the end of this chapter, is a more polished outline that allows you to fine-tune your presentation, easily locating any remaining problem areas. The preparation outline includes your introduction, body, conclusion, transitions, and references used in the speech. Let's look at how to organize each of these important parts of a successful speech, beginning with the body of your speech.

Active Critical Thinking

To think further about organization, complete the following:

- Consider the four main reasons why organization is important in a speech, and select the two that you think will be the most important in your own speaking situations to come.
- Explain why you made the choices you did, and give an example for each.

Organizing the Body of Your Speech

The body of your speech includes your main ideas and the material to support them. Professional speakers will tell you that they plan the body of their speech before the introduction and conclusion. They do this because each change to the body (changing, adding, or removing a main point) requires changes to the introduction and conclusion as well. By waiting until the body of the speech is complete to plan the introduction and conclusion, you save valuable time.

Whether the speech is a demonstration, informative, persuasive, or special occasion speech, it can be organized in a variety of patterns. Some patterns work best for informative speeches, some for persuasive speeches, and some can be used for any type of speech. Instead of settling on the first pattern you think of, try out several to see which one will make your speech the most interesting.

The body of your speech should take approximately 70 to 80 percent of your total speech time—3 1/2 to 4 minutes in a 5-minute speech, 5 to 5 1/2 minutes in a 7-minute speech.

Also, keep this tip in mind: The supporting materials for each of your main points may be organized in different patterns, but *the main points themselves can be organized in only one pattern.* For example, in a speech about racquetball, John organized his three main points—equipment, court, and history—in a *topical pattern.* However, the supporting points for each main point were organized in a variety of patterns—topical, spatial, and chronological:

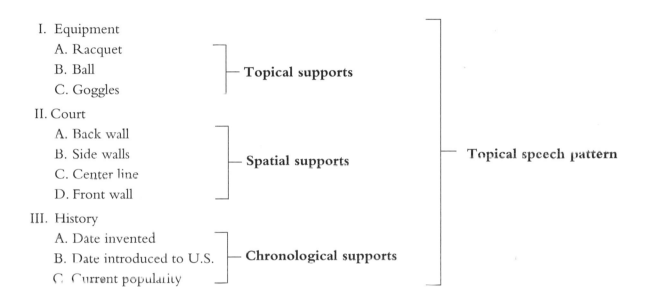

Selecting an Informative Pattern of Organization

There are four basic organizational patterns for informative speeches: (1) topical, (2) chronological, (3) spatial/geographic, and (4) causal (see Figure 7.1). Let's look briefly at each one.

Topical Pattern The **topical pattern** is often used for informative speeches when each main point is one of several categories, types, or elements of the basic topic. The best arrangement is the following:

* Your most important or interesting point first.
* Your least compelling points in the middle.
* An important or interesting point last.

It's important that the beginning and end of your speech have an impact. Listeners tend to remember better the information covered at the beginning and at the end of a speech. However, if you are speaking to a business or professional audience, you could organize your main points from the most to the least important, because some members of the audience may have to leave before the speech is finished.

Basic INFORMATIVE Speech Patterns*

Topical Pattern

   I. Point 1

   II. Point 2

   III. Point 3

Chronological Pattern

I. First		I. Past
II. Second	or	II. Present
III. Final		III. Future

Spatial or Geographic Pattern

I. North		I. Bottom
II. East	or	II. Middle
III. South		III. Top
IV. West		

Causal Pattern

I. Cause		I. Effect
II. Effect	or	II. Cause

* also used for special occasion and demonstration speeches

Figure 7.1

Organizational Patterns for Informative Speeches

When he was a senator, President Barack Obama used a chronological pattern to organize his speech that announced his candidacy for president.

AP Photo/Seth Wenig

Maria Kiehnle (2007, February 10), in her speech on sweat, structured her informative speech in a topical pattern. She previewed her main points as:

   I.   Why we sweat

   II. How we sweat

   III. How to control sweat

→ *To watch Maria's speech, go to* **www.youtube.com** *and search for "Informative Speech by Maria Kiehnle."*

Chronological Pattern When you arrange your main points in a step-by-step order or by dates, you are using a **chronological pattern** of organization. For example, a talk about what to do in case of a fire could be presented from the first step to the last. Or you could discuss the history of your favorite sport from the time it first became popular to the present. The chronological pattern is also used in demonstration and special occasion speeches. In a speech announcing his candidacy for president of the United States, Barack Obama (2007, February 10) used a chronological pattern to present a timeline of his life:

   I.   Moved to Illinois more than two decades ago, right out of college.

   II.   Got a job as a community organizer for $13,000 a year.

   III. Went to law school and became a civil rights lawyer/taught constitutional law.

   IV. Became a state senator supporting the rights of liberty and equality.

   V.   Next step: president of the United States.

   → *To read the full text or watch the video of Obama's speech, go to his website,* **barackobama.com**, *click on "Learn," "Speeches," and "Full Text of Senator Barack Obama's Announcement for President," or listen to Obama's speech at American Rhetoric.com at* **http://www.americanrhetoric.com/speeches/ barackobamacandidacyforpresident.htm**.

Spatial (or Geographic) Pattern When you arrange your main points according to location in space, such as front to back, left to right, first floor to third floor, or north to south, you are using a **spatial (or geographic) pattern**.

For example, when explaining the basic offense set to her high school players, basketball coach Tonya Ivie (2007) used the spatial pattern in structuring her informative team talk:

   I.   The point guard (P1) is positioned at the top of the key.

   II.   The first guard (P2) is located to the right of P1.

   III. The second guard (P3) is to the left of P1.

   IV. The first forward (P4) sets up at the top of the free throw line.

   V.   The second forward (P5) sets up on the box at the bottom of the free throw lane.

Causal Pattern When your main points have a cause-effect or effect-cause relationship, you are using the **causal pattern** of arrangement. If you decide to use a causal pattern, you must do more than simply assert that a causal relationship exists. You will still need to cite evidence and use a variety of supporting materials. An informative speech can be either cause–effect or effect-cause (although cause-effect is used more often). In a cause-effect speech, you discuss a problem or condition and then follow with the result or effects of the condition.

Figure 7.2

For example, an informative cause-effect speech about the negative effects of spanking might be organized as follows (Brannon, 2010):

I. Many parents use spanking to discipline their children.

   A. Over 54.4 percent of parents discipline by spanking.

   B. Spanking takes many forms.

II. Spanking can have negative consequences for the child.

   A. Spanking lowers a child's self-esteem.

   B. Spanking teaches that violence is acceptable.

   C. Spanking increases aggression by age 5.

The same speech arranged in effect-cause pattern would be organized as follows:

I. Spanking can have negative consequences for the child.

   A. Spanking lowers a child's self-esteem.

   B. Spanking teaches that violence is acceptable.

   C. Spanking increases aggression by age 5.

II. Even so, many parents use spanking to discipline their children.

   A. Over 54.4 percent of all parents discipline by spanking.

   B. Spanking takes many forms.

Notice that the speaker is not trying to persuade the audience to stop spanking children. The speaker is merely informing the audience about the causal relationship between spanking and certain characteristics of children.

Selecting a Persuasive Pattern of Organization

There are five basic organizational patterns for persuasive speeches: (1) claim or reason, (2) problem-solution or problem-cause-solution, (3) criteria satisfaction, (4) comparative advantages, and (5) the motivated sequence (See Figure 7.3).

Claim or Reason Pattern Some persuasive speeches use a variation of the topical pattern called the **claim or reason pattern**. In this variation, the main points are the claims (or reasons) for believing a particular fact, holding a particular value, or advocating a particular plan. Although the claim pattern is similar to the topical pattern, the language is definitely persuasive.

Figure 7.3

Organizational Patterns for Persuasive Speeches

Basic PERSUASIVE Speech Patterns

Claim or Reasons Pattern

I. Claim/Reason 1

II. Claim/Reason 2

III. Claim/Reason 3

Problem-Solution or Problem-Cause-Solution Pattern

I. Problem		I. Problem		I. Problem
II. Solution	or	II. Solution	or	II. Cause
III. Benefits		III. Action		III. Solution

Criteria Satisfaction Pattern

I. Any plan must meet the following necessary criteria

II. Solution X does (or does not) meet the criteria

Comparative Advantages Pattern

I. Plan X is ineffective

II. Plan Y is superior

or

I. Plan X is average

II. Plan Y is far better

Motivated Sequence

I. Attention   IV. Visualization

II. Need   V. Action

III. Satisfaction

In a motivational speech to college graduates, Rob Pocock (2010), associate vice president of Communications for Priority Health, used the claim pattern in his speech "The Power of Compound Interest."

    I. Be a good steward of the material things you gain in life. [**Claim #1**]

       A. Invest immediately.

       B. Invest wisely.

       C. Invest for the long term.

    II. Be an exceptional steward of the things in life that really matter by promising yourself that you will: [**Claim #2**]

       A. Identify ways to earn compound interest **intellectually**.

       B. Live a lifestyle that seeks compound interest **physically**.

       C. Earn compound interest **socially**.

       D. Earn compound interest **spiritually**.

The claim pattern can be ordered inductively or deductively. In **inductive reasoning**, the supporting evidence is presented first and leads up to the conclusion; in **deductive reasoning**, the conclusion is presented first and then the supporting evidence is provided. → *See Chapter 13 for a complete discussion of reasoning.*

Problem–Solution Pattern The **problem–solution pattern** used in persuasive speeches takes a variety of forms. The two most popular forms are the *problem-solution-benefits* and *problem-solution-action* patterns. In both, you begin with a detailed discussion of the problem, its seriousness, and its effect on the audience. Next, you present ways to solve or lessen the problem. Finally, you describe benefits resulting from your solution or recommend a particular course of action. Another effective form of problem–solution speeches is the **problem-cause-solution pattern**. In this form you begin with a detailed discussion of the problem including its seriousness and the current and future effects on the audience. Next you discuss the causes of the problem citing facts and evidence. Once the audience is clear on the causes of the problem, they are more likely to understand and be persuaded by your solution or solutions to the problem. To get your audience involved in the problem, causes, and solutions, use persuasive appeals that relate directly to them and their needs. → *See Chapter 13 for suggestions on using persuasive appeals.*

Ivette Ale (2006, October 17), a student at Cypress College, presented a sample problem–solution persuasive speech for the 2006 Pacific Southwest Collegiate Forensics Association Seminar. In her speech, titled "Plan B: The Morning-After Pill," Ivette discussed how some states are denying this pill to rape victims and what to do to solve this problem:

I. Problem with Plan B [**Problem**]

   A. Belief that Plan B is an abortion pill.

   B. Lack of information to the public.

   C. Politics of abortion.

   D. Misinformation about Plan B.

II. Solutions to Plan B [**Solution/Action**]

   A. Federal action.

   B. Personal action.

Ivette's speech was originally prepared for a forensics competition and won her first place in the California Community College Forensics Association state championship. → *To watch a video clip of Ivette's complete speech, along with audience Q&A, go to* **video.google.com** *and type in "2006 PSCFA Seminar—Persuasive Speech."*

Comparative Advantages Pattern The **comparative advantages pattern** is a persuasive pattern that is normally used when your audience agrees with you on the problem but may not agree on the solution. In your introduction, you need only a brief mention of the problem because the audience is already familiar with it. In the body of the speech, compare possible solutions. Usually you will want to show how one course of action or solution is superior to the others.

Lee Scott (2007, April 24), then the CEO and president of Wal-Mart Stores Inc., presented the closing keynote address titled "Health Care in America" to the 2007 World Health Care Congress. In this speech, Scott used the comparative advantages pattern to show how Wal-Mart's plan is more efficient than other plans:

I. The disconnection of the current state of health care is unacceptable. [**Current plan ineffective**]

   A. Disconnect with consumer.

   B. Disconnect with patient.

   C. Disconnect with transaction.

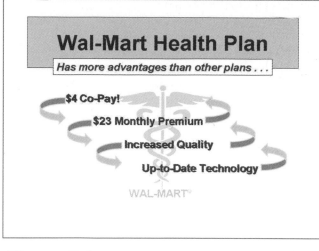

Figure 7.4

Scott might have used this slide with his persuasive talk

II. Wal-Mart's health care plan provides connection. [**Wal-Mart plan superior**]

A. Provides connection by having $4 co-payment.

B. Provides plans that have $23-a-month premiums.

C. Incorporates the most up-to-date technology.

D. Increases quality of health care for Wal-Mart employees.

→ *To read the complete speech, go to* **walmartfacts.com/media/128219083279537500.pdf**.

Criteria Satisfaction Pattern Whether you are dealing with people, products, services, or ideas, the **criteria satisfaction pattern** is a persuasive tool that works well even when audience members oppose your position. First, establish criteria (guidelines or rules) that should be followed when evaluating proposals. Don't forget to consider the values and needs of your audience when selecting and explaining your criteria. ("I'm sure we all agree that the professor we choose must be knowledgeable and fair.") Second, show how your proposal meets or exceeds the criteria. ("Not only is Professor X knowledgeable and fair, she is also a dynamic speaker.") If you can get your listeners to agree with your criteria, the chances are good that they will also agree with a proposal that satisfies it.

Using the criteria satisfaction pattern, Farah M. Walters (1993), president and CEO of University Hospitals in Cleveland and a member of the National Health Care Reform Task Force, gave a speech called "If It's Broke, Fix It: The Significance of Health Care Reform in America":

I. Any health care plan should be measured against six fundamental principles: [**Necessary criteria**]

A. Provide security for all Americans.

B. Provide choice of physician.

C. Provide continuity of care.

D. Be affordable to the individual, to business, and to the country.

E. Be comprehensive in terms of coverage.

F. Be user-friendly for both consumers and providers.

II. The health care plan designed by the National Health Care Reform Task Force meets all six of these fundamental principles. [**Plan meets criteria**]

The Motivated Sequence The **motivated sequence** was developed by communications professor Alan Monroe more than 50 years ago. It is similar to the problem–solution–action pattern and is especially effective with speeches designed to actuate an audience to support a particular policy. The motivated sequence involves five steps: attention, need, satisfaction, visualization, and action (Gronbeck et al., 1999). Let's take a brief look at each step (Hamilton, 2011).

- *Attention step.* Grab your listeners' attention (using any of the methods described in this book) by introducing the problem your speech will address.

- *Need step.* Describe the specific problem using credible, logical, and psychological appeals (discussed earlier in Chapter 4), prove that the problem is serious enough to need solving, and show how the problem relates specifically to your listeners.

- *Satisfaction step.* Satisfy the need by presenting one or more solutions to the problem. Be sure to demonstrate the workability and feasibility of the solution, as well as answer possible audience objections. Use a variety of powerful supporting materials to support your statements (see Chapter 6).

- *Visualization step.* Vividly picture the future for your audience, which should increase their emotional involvement and their willingness to follow your advice. Use either positive (how great conditions will be when your proposal is implemented), negative (how undesirable conditions will be if your proposal is not implemented), or contrast methods (begin with the negative and end with the positive).

- *Action step.* Conclude your speech by challenging your audience to take a particular action—you want a personal commitment from them. Say exactly what you want them to do and how they can do it.

Using the motivated sequence to organize a speech urging the use of mediation instead of lawyers in divorce cases could result in the following outline:

I. Over half of all marriages end in divorce [**Attention**]

II. Divorce settlements are problematic [**Need**]

    A. They are expensive and lengthy.

    B. They promote destructive competition and create emotional stress.

    C. They clog the courts.

III. Divorce by mediation solves these problems. [**Satisfaction**]

IV. Imagine saving time, money, and headaches. [**Visualization**]

V. If future divorce occurs, use mediation. [**Action**]

Active Critical Thinking

To think further about organizing an effective speech, complete the following:

- Select a topic for either an informative or a persuasive speech that you plan to give in the future.

- Using main points from the selected topic, create outlines using four different organizational patterns. Share your outlines with several classmates, asking which they think would be the most interesting approach to your topic. If they seem to have a preference, what do you think made it the favorite?

Now that we have examined the organization of your main points (Step 6 in the Basic Steps for Preparing a Speech), let's move to Step 7—developing your introduction and conclusion. First, we'll discuss how to prepare the introduction.

Organizing the Introduction of Your Speech

Using a database like InfoTrac College Edition, EBSCOhost, or CQ Researcher, run a keyword search with *oral presentations* or *public speaking* to find the most current suggestions for preparing and presenting a speech. Try out one of these suggestions in your next speech.

Many good speeches fail because their introductions are confusing and dull. Just because people show up at your speech doesn't mean they plan to listen—unless you make it impossible for them not to. For example, look at the following introductions. It's easy to tell which one is more effective, isn't it?

> "Today, I want to talk to you about a hobby of mine—using a metal detector to search for metal objects in yards, parks, and around deserted buildings."
>
> "It's three days until the end of the month. How many of you could use a little extra money right about now? I certainly could, and I've got some. In my hand is a check for $92 made out in my name. Last month about this time, I received a check for $34. Where did I get this money? No, it wasn't from the lottery. I found it! I found the money represented by these checks by using an inexpensive metal detector. Today, I'm going to tell you about this hobby of mine that pays me money instead of costing money."

An effective introduction has four basic goals:

* *Catch the audiences' attention* and focus it on your topic.

* *Motivate the audience to listen* by pointing out how your topic will benefit them.

* *Establish credibility and rapport* with your audience by creating a common bond and letting them know about your expertise and experience with the topic.

* *Present your thesis statement,* which includes clarification of your central idea and main points.

> An effective introduction should take no more than 10 to 15 percent of your total speaking time—approximately 30 to 45 seconds in a 5-minute speech; 45 to 60 seconds in a 7-minute speech.

As we discuss each introductory goal in more detail, take a look at an earlier informative speech, "Our Solar System and the Three Dwarves" by Kara Hoekstra. How well does Kara's introduction on page 157 include each of the four goals? → *See Chapter 4 for Kara's complete speech.*

Goal 1: Catch the Audience's Attention

You can use Speech Builder Express to help create an introduction to your speech. Select "Introduction" from the left-hand menu and follow the instructions. For short reminders from this chapter about introductions, click on the "Tutor" button.

We learned in the chapter on listening that listeners pay attention only to information that is important to them or of interest to them. We also learned that few listeners ever hear the first sentence or two of a speech because they are still getting settled mentally. Those are two good reasons for not beginning a speech with a statement of purpose.

It's up to you, the speaker, to spark the interest of audience members and focus their attention on your topic. Following are a variety of supporting materials you can use to capture audience attention—they are in alphabetical order for ease of use. Which one to use depends on your preference and on your audience interests. However, for any attention-getter to be successful, you need to practice it until you feel confident and it flows smoothly.

Sample Introduction

My very excellent mother just served us nine pizzas [Visual 1].
My very elegant mother just sat upon nine porcupines.
My very easy method just set up nine planets.

Now, the phrases I just stated are memory aids that help us remember the order of the planets by applying the first letter of each word to the first letter of each planet: Mercury, Venus, Earth, Mars, Jupiter, Saturn, Uranus, Neptune, and Pluto. But, what if I told you there were no more pizzas, no more porcupines, and no more planets? Now, as children we grew up knowing that there were nine planets in our solar system. However, experts have recently demoted Pluto to a dwarf planet. Now, speaking of experts, I don't happen to claim to be an expert in astronomy or anything—it just happens to have been an interest of mine since childhood. What is really interesting about this subject is that what we have known as children has recently changed. And even though Pluto has been reclassified, it is not alone.

You are about to discover the changes in our solar system, including the new definitions for a planet and a dwarf planet, the reason Pluto didn't make the cut for a planet, and the two other objects in our solar system now considered dwarf planets as well.

Analysis
Kara begins her speech with three memory phrases that could be used to remember the names and order of nine planets—good attention-getters, even for listeners who already know that the number of planets has changed. Her colorful and interesting PowerPoint visuals also add audience interest.

Kara establishes her credibility with her visual aids and by telling us that astronomy has been an interest of hers from childhood. She relates to the audience by mentioning that what she and they learned about the planets as children is now wrong.

Kara reviews the three main points to come as a transition into the body of her speech. Her computer visual listing her main points adds interest and should make it easier for the listeners to identify and recall her points.

Definitions and Explanations Although speakers don't usually think of definitions and explanation as effective ways to begin a speech, they can work well if you are careful. For example, John J. Scherer (2010), founder of the Scherer Leadership Center, began his speech with a definition:

> Many of you don't realize this—it's a little early for you—but do you know the definition of a mid-life crisis? A mid-life crisis is when you get to the top rung of your ladder only to realize that you leaned it against the wrong wall. Now I'm going to take the few minutes I have with you here to do absolutely everything I can to help you lean your ladder against the right wall (p. 351).

Demonstrations A demonstration of a procedure or skill is another method for getting the attention of your audience. Any demonstration needs to be brief yet impressive. An informational speech about types of dead-bolt locks might use the following brief demonstration as an attention-getter:

> *[Two miniature door frames are placed on a table by the speaker. One frame is labeled "A"; the other is labeled "B."]* The lock on door A is the same type of lock that 85 percent of you have on your doors. Anyone can pick this type of lock. *[The speaker then reaches into his pocket and pulls out a common bobby pin, straightens it, places it in the lock, and in less than two seconds has door A swinging open.]* However, the lock on door B has a special dead-bolt lock that no one

can pick. In fact, the only way a person could get in this door without a key would be to kick in the door frame. *[He then takes out another bobby pin and tries to open door B, with no success. He looks directly at his audience.]* Which door would you feel safer sleeping behind at night?

Fables, Sayings, Poems, and Rhymes   Opening with a piece of folklore—a fable, saying, poem, or rhyme—can also stimulate listener attention. Speaking on the importance of allowing others to succeed, CEO Allan Freeth (2010) used a **fable** (a fictitious story with animal characters, used to teach a moral lesson) to grab the attention of his audience and prepare them for his purpose:

> There is an Indian proverb about a merchant on a train with two baskets—one open, the other covered. In the open basket there are crabs from the sea shore.
>
> But the passengers cannot see what is in the covered basket. The only clue to its contents is a few feathers poking-out from the weaving, and a soft cooing sound.
>
> On enquiry, the merchant confirms the covered basket contains doves.
>
> He explains the cover is necessary because whenever they have the chance to escape to freedom, they fly away.
>
> The crabs though, he explains with a frown, ensure no one can aspire beyond the pack. Once one starts climbing out, the rest pull them back— hence no need for a lid or cover. I often feel that Kiwis—here at home at least, are the crabs with the impulse to pull everyone back into the basket (p. 290).

Instances—Brief Examples   Two or more brief examples are also effective at grabbing the attention of an audience. In a speech to the National Conference of State Legislatures, speechwriter Joan Detz (2009) used a list of brief examples to illustrate what she meant by "little speeches:"

> Welcome, everyone. Let's get started right away. I know you've had a full conference week, and I want to make sure you walk away with all the public speaking information you need . . .
>
> Today, I'm going to focus on all those "little speeches" you're asked to give. You know what I mean: giving an award . . . getting an award . . . retirement remarks . . . dedications . . . fundraisers . . . patriotic ceremonies . . . memorial tributes . . . anniversaries . . . introducing a speaker . . . welcoming a special guest . . . moderating a panel. The list goes on. In short, all those times when you're asked to "just say a few words" (p. 447).

Instances—Detailed Narratives   A detailed factual or hypothetical instance (called a narrative or illustration) is an effective way to stimulate listener interest. Remember, the key is to give enough vivid detail that your listeners can picture the event. Here's a sample narrative used by Robert K. Ross, M.D. (2003), to begin his speech "A Cry for Help":

> It was about six months ago when, in the middle of the night at about 1:30 a.m., my wife and I were awakened by a shrill screaming of our, at that time, 9-month-old infant daughter. For those of you that are parents, particularly those of you that are mothers, you know your kids have different kinds of cries and you get to kind of know what the quality of the issue is by the cry. This wasn't the kind of cry that was associated with a bottle-feeding or a diaper being wet. . . . [In vivid detail, Dr. Ross describes what happened] (p. 51).

Forest Whitaker, in his 2007 Oscar acceptance speech for Best Actor (he played Idi Amin in *The Last King of Scotland*), touched the audience with his personal narrative (Billington & Whitaker, 2007):

> When I was a kid, the only way that I saw movies was from the backseat of my family's car. At the drive-in. And, it wasn't my reality to think I would be acting in movies, so receiving this honor tonight tells me that it's possible. It is possible for a kid from East Texas, raised in South Central L.A. in Carson, who believes in his dreams, commits himself to them with his heart, to touch them, and to have them happen.
>
> Because when I first started acting, it was because of my desire to connect to everyone. To that thing inside of each of us. To that light that I believe exists in all of us. Because acting for me is about believing in that connection and it's a connection so strong, it's a connection so deep, that we feel it. And through our combined belief, we can create a new reality.

→ *To listen to Whitaker's speech, go to* **www.youtube.com** *and search for "79th Academy Awards: Forest Whitaker."*

If you do not have a factual narrative (instance) to draw on, a hypothetical instance in vivid detail can work as well—listeners picture themselves as part of your narrative and become more personally involved. Here's a sample hypothetical narrative:

> Have you ever considered winning the lottery? Imagine waking up one morning and turning on the radio just in time to hear the last four winning lotto numbers. Those are your numbers! You race to the kitchen, where you left the stubs, just in time to hear them announce the winning numbers again . . . [In vivid detail, describe the various emotions the winner might feel.]

Humor   A joke or humorous instance is a popular way to introduce a speech. Keep in mind, however, that the joke must be related to your speech topic. Imagine a speaker telling a couple of jokes. The audience is relaxed and in a lighthearted mood when the speaker suddenly says, "I now want to talk to you about the high cost of funerals." How do you think the audience will react? They will laugh, of course, because the speaker has prepared them for humor, not for a serious speech on funerals. They think this statement is another joke. If the speaker had begun with a humorous incident related to the high cost of funerals, the audience would have been more prepared for the speech topic. However, most of them would likely consider funeral humor in poor taste.

Humor is not the best choice for introducing every topic. Similarly, self-disparaging humor—where you use yourself as the brunt of a joke—can backfire, causing the audience to view you as less interesting and less competent (Hackman, 1988). Speaking at the 1988 Democratic Convention, Ann Richards used several types of humor successfully, including self-disparaging humor. → *Read about Richards, in our "Speaking to Make a Difference" feature for this chapter, and her successful use of humor, beginning on page 161.*

When kept brief and light, humor can be very effective (Detz, 2010). For example, on February 16, 2010, Cynthia Starks began her presentation on "How to Write a Speech" with humor and three instances:

> On this date—Feb. 16, 1923—archeologist Howard Carter entered the burial chamber of King Tutankhamen. There he found a solid gold coffin, Tut's intact mummy and priceless treasures.
>
> On Feb. 16, 1959, Fidel Castro took over the Cuban government 45 days after overthrowing Fulvencia Battista.

As president, George W. Bush used humor effectively in his speeches.

And America's first 9-1-1 emergency phone system went live in Haleyville, Alabama on Feb. 16, 1968.

Today, I won't be revealing priceless treasures. I promise not to overthrow anyone, or generate any 9-1-1 calls. But I do hope to reveal a few speechwriting secrets, provide a little revolutionary thinking and a sense of urgency about the speeches you ought to be giving (p. 153).

In deciding whether to use jokes or humorous instances, make sure that humor is appropriate for your topic and that you are good at using it. Although anyone can tell a humorous instance, not everyone can tell a joke. Nothing is worse at the beginning of a speech than a joke that falls flat. For most people, adding humor in a speech is much easier than telling a joke. President George W. Bush (2007) uses humor effectively in his speeches—take, for instance, his commencement address at Miami Dade College:

> It is always a pleasure to be back here to Miami, and I thank Dr. Padron for asking me. It hasn't escaped my attention that when you were look-ing for Bushes to invite, I came in fourth. Laura spoke at your North Campus commencement in 2004, my mother spoke, brother Jeb has spoken here twice. Before I stepped on the stage, I asked him for some advice. I said, "Jeb, give me some advice." He said, "Floridians hold their politicians to strict term limits: 8 years for a governor and 15 minutes for a commencement speaker." I will do my best.

→ *Read President Bush's commencement address at* http://georgewbush-whitehouse.archives.gov/news/releases/2007/04/20070428-3.html. Click on the video icon to hear the speech.

Questions Asking a rhetorical or an actual question is a good way to get listeners involved. A **rhetorical question** is designed to make the audience think—no real answer is expected. Asking your audience, "If I could prove that every penny would be spent purchasing items of clothing for the needy, would you be willing to donate from $1 to $5?" is a rhetorical question. But asking your audience, "How many of you had breakfast before coming to class this morning?" is an actual question for which a response is expected. To make sure your audience realizes that you want a show of hands, raise your own hand as you ask the question, or say, "I would like a show of hands on this question: How many of you had breakfast before coming to class this morning?" Be careful that your rhetorical question relates specifically to your topic and is interesting enough that people will listen.

Quotations A quotation or paraphrase from a well-known source can grab the interest of your audience if you read it with good vocal variety and eye contact and if the expert has something of real interest to say. Quotations are more effec-tive when the audience is familiar with the source. Steve Rogel (2003)—chairman, president, and CEO of Weyerhaeuser Company and a scouting enthusiast for more than 48 years—successfully introduced his speech "Business Ethics and the Boy Scout Code" by using expert opinion, as follows:

> Mahatma Gandhi, the great Indian leader, once said, "There are seven things that will destroy us: wealth without work; pleasure without conscience; knowledge without character; religion without sacrifice; politics without principle; science without humanity; business without ethics."
>
> While each of these topics is deserving of attention in its own right, I'm going to focus on the last of Gandhi's concerns—business without ethics—in

relation to the values embedded in the Boy Scout code. Specifically, does being a good scout help one become a good business leader? And can we apply the ethics of scouting to the business of business? (p. 403)

Reference to the Occasion Referring to the event in your introduction is essential if you are speaking at a special occasion, such as when President Obama (2010) gave the commencement address at West Point:

It is wonderful to be back at the United States Military Academy—the oldest continuously occupied military post in America—as we commission the newest officers in the United States Army (p. 320).

However, for regular classroom speeches, there is no need to mention how thrilled you are to be there for the first day of informative presentations.

Startling Facts Revealing one or more startling facts is another good way to grab listeners' attention. When your facts involve statistics, make them meaningful by relating them to your listeners' frames of reference. If you were speaking to a group of life insurance underwriters, the following startling statistics indicating a change in consumer spending might grab listener attention (Mathas, 2010):

There are strong signs that this "great recession" was an attitude-changing and behavior-changing event. In 2009, Americans' credit card spending dropped to the lowest levels in over 30 years. In 2009, the U.S. personal savings rate rose to its highest levels in 15 years (p. 36).

Speaking to Make a Difference

While she was the state treasurer of Texas and a newly announced candidate for governor (Martin, 2004), Ann Richards presented the keynote address at the 1988 Democratic National Convention in Atlanta. The text and video of her entire speech can be found at **www.americanrhetoric.com** by searching for "Ann Richards: 1988 Democratic National Convention Address."

I'm delighted to be here with you this evening, because after listening to George Bush all these years, I figured you needed to know what a real Texas accent sounds like.

Twelve years ago Barbara Jordan, another Texas woman, made the keynote address to this convention, and two women in a hundred and sixty years is about par for the course. But if you give us a chance, we can perform. After all, Ginger Rogers did everything that Fred Astaire did. She just did it backwards and in high heels.

I want to announce to this nation that in a little more than 100 days, the Reagan - Meese - Deaver - Nofziger - Poindexter - North - Weinberger - Watt - Gorsuch - Lavelle - Stockman - Haig - Bork - Noriega - George Bush [era] will be over!

You know, tonight I feel a little like I did when I played basketball in the eighth grade. I thought I looked real cute in my uniform. And then I heard a boy yell from the bleachers, "Make that basket, bird legs." And my greatest fear is that

same guy is somewhere out there in the audience tonight, and he's going to cut me down to size, because where I grew up there really wasn't much tolerance for self-importance, people who put on airs.

* * *

Now, in contrast, the greatest nation of the free world has had a leader for eight straight years that has pretended that he cannot hear our questions over the noise of the helicopters. And we know he doesn't wanna answer. But we have a lot of questions. And when we get our questions asked, or there is a leak, or an investigation, the only answer we get is, "I don't know," or "I forgot."

But you wouldn't accept that answer from your children. I wouldn't. "Don't tell me you 'don't know' or you 'forgot.'" We're not going to have the America that we want until we elect leaders who are gonna tell the truth; not most days but every day; leaders who don't forget what they don't want to remember. And for eight straight years George Bush hasn't displayed the slightest interest in anything we care about. And now that he's after a job that he can't get appointed to, he's like Columbus discovering America. He's found child care. He's found education. Poor George. He can't help it. He was born with a silver foot in his mouth.

continued

Ann Richards had long been known as a humorous and gutsy speaker in her home state, but her keynote address filled with wit and down-home values brought her to national attention. Her speech not only focused listeners on the values of the Democratic Party, it launched her race for governor of Texas (Martin, 2004).

Let's take a specific look at Richards' use of humor in this entertaining address.

- *Humor in the introduction captured audience attention.* While humor is a very popular way to introduce a speech, it must relate to the topic at hand. Richards did this by poking fun at the incumbent Republican vice president, George Bush. The laughter and applause indicated the audience's enjoyment. Richards didn't stop there; she went on to poke fun at the male-dominated structure of the Democratic Party when she commented that "two women in a hundred and sixty years is about par for the course." Research indicates that "people laugh at what surprises them or is otherwise unexpected" (Martin, 2004, p. 271). Perhaps this is why Richards' statement about Ginger Rogers—which she borrowed from a TV journalist (Rabinowitz, 1988)—was so successful.

- *Richards' humor helped Democrats see her as a political "insider"* (Martin, 2004). As a woman and a Texan, it is likely that many listening to her address viewed her basically as an "outsider." According to Martin, Richards used humor to underscore her Texas (insider) authenticity [with her Bush joke] while criticizing the outsider position of women marginalized in national party politics [with her Ginger Rogers joke] (p. 280). She cemented her insider status further when later in her speech she "framed Bush as wealthy and incapable of communicating with the working class . . . pampered and opportunistic" (p. 281).

- Finally, *Richards took a risk in using self-deprecating humor.* Although self-deprecating humor (where speakers poke fun at themselves to build rapport with the audience) can be successful, as it was in Richards' case, there is a risk that listeners will turn the humor against the speaker and perceive them as inadequate. In other words, instead of feeling a common bond with Richards because they had also experienced an "embarrassing personal incident" (Martin, p. 280), the audience might have viewed her as lacking because of her fear of being ridiculed in public.

Although Richards' keynote address is best known for its humor, keep in mind that humor alone won't make an effective speech unless you are a stand-up comic. Instead, Richards wove her humor into a well-organized and well-supported speech. Her points were clear; her introduction and conclusion were effective. When you read or watch the complete speech online, listen for her use of old sayings to help clarify her viewpoints, like "that old dog won't hunt" or "how the cow ate the cabbage." She related to the audience with "personal anecdotes, concrete examples and brief narratives" (Dow & Tonn, 1993, p. 289).

As you watch the speech online, note her use of repetition, with the words "that's wrong" repeated at the end of each of several specific examples. This generated audience involvement—especially when she ended the series with the quip "Nothing's wrong with you that you can't fix in November." Still, it was her humor that caught the attention of the convention delegates and newspaper columnists alike and raised her into the national limelight—which, after all, was perfect for a Texas gubernatorial candidate.

Questions: Do you think Richards' type of humor was appropriate for a keynote address televised around the world? Why might some listeners have found her humor offensive? After reading her entire speech, critique her conclusion and overall organization. What changes would you recommend, if any?

Remember

Attention-getters include . . .

- Demonstrations of a procedure or skill
- Fables, sayings, poems, or rhymes
- Humor
- Instances—brief examples
- Instances—detailed narratives (factual or hypothetical)
- Questions (rhetorical or actual)
- Quotations (or paraphrases)
- Reference to the occasion or event
- Startling facts

Goal 2: Motivate Your Audience to Listen

Unfortunately, just because your listeners laugh at your opening joke or pay attention to your personal instance doesn't mean they will continue to listen. They must be made to feel that there is some advantage in it for them. In other words, what will your speech do for your listeners? Will it show them how to reduce stress, lose weight, have more interesting dates, improve their health, or what? When you answer the "So what? Why should I care?" question that goes through listeners' minds, you are motivating them to listen. To determine how best to relate your topic to your audience, refer to the demographic and psychological information you discovered earlier when you analyzed your audience. ➜ *Refer to Chapter 3, Table 3.2, for a list of additional motivators.*

Depending on your topic, it is possible to combine both the attention-getting and motivation goals of your introduction. For example, the door-lock demonstrations described in the preceding section not only grabbed attention but also included a reason for listening—saving money and increasing personal safety (See page 157). Persuasive speakers commonly combine the attention and motivation steps, as Cedrick McBeth did in his classroom speech "Cell Phones: Don't Chat and Drive."

As you read the following excerpt from Cedrick's speech, think about which basic needs he is appealing to. If you had been in the audience, would you have been motivated to listen to his speech?

> On June 17, 2006, Alexander Manocchio reached for a ringing cell phone and killed Karyn Cordell and her unborn son. You see, Manocchio was driving a car at the time. Now two people are dead and Alexander's life is in a shambles, all because he answered a phone. Alexander faces two counts of vehicular homicide. How many of us in this classroom are also guilty of putting lives at risk by talking on cell phones while driving a car? I'll bet almost all of us have done it and many of us do it every day. But do we ever consider the dangers of talking on our cell phones while driving a car? As I read the statistics and studied this situation, I became convinced that cell phone use while driving has become an unacceptable risk. Today I hope to convince you that using a cell phone while driving an automobile should be illegal.
> ➜ *Refer to Chapter 12 for Cedrick's complete speech.*

Goal 3: Establish Credibility and Rapport

The third goal of an effective introduction is to establish your credibility (believability) as a speaker and develop rapport (feelings of respect and liking) with your audience, using the following:

- *Share your expertise with the audience.* If you have personal experience with your topic, this is the time to mention it ("I have taught CPR for the past five years" or "I have played racquetball since I was old enough to hold a racquet"). There's no need to wear all of your medals or bring in your trophies, but it is important to let your audience know of your expertise.

- *Mention why the topic is important to you.* If you don't have personal experience with your topic, your audience will want to know why you selected it. Did you write a paper on it in another course and discover that the subject really mattered to you? Are you interested in it because of something that happened to a family member or a friend? Unless it's too personal, sharing this kind of information with your audience will add to your credibility and help establish rapport with your audience.

- *Cite expert sources you consulted.* If your listeners are unfamiliar with your experts, you will need to establish their qualifications. The number of sources you will need in order to establish your credibility often depends on your topic. If you are discussing the advantages of joining a fraternity or sorority and have been a member of such a group for two years, you can depend largely on your own personal credibility. But if you have never been a member, your personal opinion on this topic will not carry much weight. You will need to strengthen your credibility by using outside experts.

- *Show gender and cultural sensitivity.* When audience members do not find your speech credible because of gender-inappropriate language, they will not hear your important message. In addition, culture must be a factor in establishing credibility and rapport with your audience; establish a common ground with your audience and use gender-sensitive examples. ➡ *Refer to Chapter 9 for specific gender and cultural suggestions.*

EXPRESS/CONNECT

You can use Speech Builder Express to help you create your thesis statement. Select "Thesis Statement" from the left-hand menu and follow the instructions. For short reminders from this chapter about thesis statements, click on the "Tutor" button.

Goal 4: Present Your Thesis Statement

It is amazing how many speakers fail to present a clear thesis statement. Their introduction may make the general topic they are discussing clear, but their exact purpose and the main points to be covered may not be clear until later in their speech, if then. A good **thesis statement** includes identification of the topic and a preview of the main points you plan to present.

State Purpose (if Informative) or Position (if Persuasive) Remember: Audience members are not always skilled listeners. If they have to do too much work to figure out your purpose, they will probably take a mental holiday. Unless you need to build suspense or your audience is hostile, you will want to quickly make your purpose or position as clear as possible. Jennie Hansen (2010), speaking to primary care providers about patient safety, included the following position statement:

> … as a career health care professional, I hold the view that systemic and individual change [in patient safety] has, and will be, far more productive in reducing medical errors than will pointing the finger of blame, or targeting individual providers (p. 158).

Preview Main Points Listing your main points after you state your specific purpose will improve the chances that your audience will recall them later. If you are using visual aids during your speech, this is an excellent time to present one, because audience members are more likely to remember information that they can both see and hear. ➡ *Guidelines for creating visual aids are covered in Chapter 10.*

We've already read Jennie Hansen's position statement. Now let's see how she previewed her main points:

> So, today, I'm going to focus on the positive. What can we do? Much has been done, but much more remains to be done. What can Health Care Reform do for patient safety? What can health professional schools do? What can health care consumers do? And finally, what can you do as health professionals? I can't cover it all, but my goal here today is to offer some ideas and resources you'll want to follow up on (pp. 158–159).

Optional Content for Speech Introductions

We've discussed the four basic goals of an introduction. The following are three optional elements that you may occasionally wish to include:

1. **Background Information** If you need to include some clarifying information but don't wish to spend enough time on it to make it a main point, cover it in the introduction. For example, in an informative speech about the causes, effects, and cures for anorexia, a definition of anorexia is background information that would help clarify your topic. Persuasive speeches using the comparative advantages or claim patterns of organization often need to review the seriousness of the problem as background information during the introduction of the speech. However, if you are using a problem–solution pattern to organize your main arguments, you will cover the problem in the body of the speech.

2. **Definition of Unfamiliar Terms** For some speech topics, you may need to define unfamiliar terms right at the start. For example, it would be a mistake to assume that everyone in your audience knows that *STD* stands for "sexually transmitted disease," that *MBWA* stands for "management by wandering around." In the introduction to a speech titled "U.S. Public Diplomacy," Kathy R. Fitzpatrick (2004) defined what she meant by *public diplomacy:*

   > In official government jargon, public diplomacy is a nation's efforts to understand, inform, and influence the people of other nations. Many—including myself—view it as international public relations. The goal of U.S. public diplomacy is—or at least the goal should be—to develop and sustain positive relationships between the United States and foreign publics (p. 413).

3. **Mention of Handouts** Only rarely should you distribute handouts during your speech—it's usually better to wait until the end. But do let your audience know that they are available. For example, if you had a computer visual or transparency showing contact information for organizations providing free information, many listeners would want to take notes, and the shuffle to find paper and pencil would be distracting. But if you mentioned in your introduction that you would pass out a handout listing the organizations and their phone numbers at the conclusion of your speech, audience members could relax and spend their time listening.

Using a database like InfoTrac College Edition, EBSCOhost, or ProQuest, conduct a keyword search for *thesis statement* and *position statement,* and see what advice you can find on making a clear and powerful thesis statement.

Active Critical Thinking

To think further about speech organization, complete the following:

- Select the informative or persuasive speech topic you used in the previous activity, and outline a possible introduction including the four main goals discussed above.

- Would any of the optional items be helpful for your speech topic? Why or why not?

Now that we have thoroughly examined the organization of the introduction and body of your speech, let's discuss how to create a conclusion that will leave your audience feeling satisfied and pleased.

Organizing the Conclusion of Your Speech

No speech is complete without the refocusing and closure a conclusion provides. A conclusion includes at least the following functions:

- Clue the audience that you are nearing the end of your presentation by *summarizing your central idea and main points.*

- *End with a memorable, refocusing thought* that relates back to the introduction, if possible. Persuasive speakers may refocus the audience by visualizing the future or challenging the audience to change a behavior or belief. If a question–and–answer (Q&A) session will follow your speech, provide a brief summary before the Q&A and another one after it to redirect audience attention back to the central ideas of your speech and to provide closure.

> An effective *conclusion* should take no more than 10 to 15 percent of your total speaking time—approximately 30 to 45 seconds in a 5-minute speech, 45 to 60 seconds in a 7-minute speech..

Sample Conclusion

Because of the new definitions set forth by astronomers, we now know the criteria involved in classifying planets. The main factor that sets Pluto apart from the other eight planets is that Pluto lives in a cluttered home and is forced to orbit among lots of space debris in the Kuiper Belt. And because Eris and Ceres meet the dwarf-planet criteria as well, they have been classified in the new group also. Are there any questions?

[Q&A session]

Thank you for your questions. There are no longer nine planets in our solar system *[Visual 8]*. We now have eight classical planets and three dwarf planets. So how do we go about remembering the order of the planets and dwarf planets now? *Many Very Educated Men Just Shook Up Nonsense* and *Committees Prove Everything.* The IAU debate, of what I'm assuming consisted mostly of men, changed things as we know them—and as always, committees prove everything.

So now that we know Pluto, Eris, and Ceres are officially the three dwarves, what does this mean for the future of our solar system? As new discoveries are made in the Kuiper Belt region, it's possible that other objects may be classified as dwarf planets as well. Perhaps you will be interested in keeping your eyes and ears out for new discoveries, and who knows—pretty soon we may be calling our home the Solar System and the *Seven* Dwarves.

Analysis
Kara summarizes her main points well. Because she planned a question-and-answer period immediately after her speech, a detailed initial conclusion was not necessary. However, do you think she needed to add a final statement as well?

After the Q&A, Kara brings closure by including a final summary and presents the audience with a new memory aid for remembering the planets and another one for remembering the dwarf planets.

Kara concludes with a challenge for her listeners to stay tuned for additional discoveries and uses a clever play on her title, changing "Our Solar System and the Three Dwarves" to "Our Solar System and the Seven Dwarves."

As we discuss each function of an effective conclusion in more detail, take a look at Kara's conclusion to her speech "Our Solar System and the Three Dwarves." How well does her conclusion on page 166 include the two goals?

→ *See Chapter 4 for Kara's complete speech.*

Summarize Main Ideas

In an informative speech, the goal of the summary is to restate the purpose of your talk or your main points. A summary can be general (referring to the topic of the speech) or specific (listing the main points). Your choice depends on how important it is for listeners to remember specific points. If you want them to recall your main points or remember specific details from your speech, use a visual aid during your summary.

Whether general or specific, an effective summary is the first part of a good conclusion.

In her classroom speech "Outdoor Oklahoma," a student named Christina used the following summary:

> So the next time you're looking to escape into a corner of wilderness for a moment of solitude, go to Oklahoma and check out four of nature lovers' dream spots: Quartz Mountain State Park, Lake Tenkiller, Talimena Drive, and Arbuckle Wilderness.

Refocus Audience Attention

You don't want your listeners to forget your message the minute they leave the room. Try to make your final thought so memorable that they continue to think and talk about your speech long after it's over. Any of the supporting materials used to gain attention in the introduction of your speech can also be used effectively to end your speech—especially the following:

Offer a Closing Thought Speaking to the Institute of World Affairs about "U.S. Public Diplomacy," Kathy R. Fitzpatrick (2004) refocused her audience's attention with the following quote and closing thought:

> In closing, I'd like to share with you a quote by novelist Ursula LeGuin, who said: "There have been great societies that did not use the wheel, but there have been no societies that did not tell stories."
>
> As a nation, we can have the mightiest military and the most sophisticated technology. But such strengths ultimately will not matter if we fail to capture the minds and hearts of people around the world with the enduring story of freedom and democracy.
>
> America must tell its story—and must tell it well. The security and prosperity of the citizens of the United States of America depend on it (p. 416).

Refer to the Introduction Another effective way to refocus audience attention is to refer to your introduction. The delightful and compelling speech titled "Light the Fire: Communicate with Your Child" is an excellent example of tying the introduction and conclusion together. Speaking at a parents' workshop sponsored by the Heart of America Suzuki Teachers Association, Joan E. Aitken (1993), an assistant professor at the University of Missouri-Kansas City, used the following introduction and conclusion:

> **Introduction** As I light these four candles, I want to share some things I've heard my 5-year-old child say . . .
>
> CANDLE 1: "Whoops."
> CANDLE 2: "Why do elephants put dirt on their backs?"
> CANDLE 3: "Knock, knock." ("Who's there?") "Bananas." ("Bananas who?") "Bananas are something monkeys like to eat. Ha, ha, ha, tee-he, ho."
> CANDLE 4: "Your lap is my favorite place, Mom."
>
> As I blow out these four candles, I want to share some things I've said to my son . . .
>
> CANDLE 1: "What's the matter with you?"
> CANDLE 2: "I don't know why elephants do things."
> CANDLE 3: "I don't get it. Is that joke supposed to be funny?"
> CANDLE 4: "Ow. You're getting so big. Get off me."
>
> **Conclusion** After a 30-minute speech on how to communicate with your child: In closing, I want to light these four candles again, saying other words I try to use.
>
> CANDLE 1: My child said: "Whoops." And I said: "That's okay. What do you need to do to fix it, Wade?"
> CANDLE 2: "Why do elephants put dirt on their backs?" "You ask the most interesting questions. I've noticed the elephants in the zoo do that. Do you suppose it makes them cool? Maybe it's their sunscreen. What do you think?"
> CANDLE 3: "Knock, knock." ("Who's there?") "Bananas." ("Bananas who?") "Bananas are something monkeys like to eat. Ha, ha, ha, tee-he, ho." "Darlin', I love to hear you laugh."
> CANDLE 4: "Your lap is my favorite place, Mom." "Then, come sit. You are the light of my life!" (p. 477)

Issue a Challenge In a persuasive speech titled "The Dynamics of Discovery: Creating Your Own Opportunities," Catherine B. Ahles (1993) issued this challenge: As you go forward to discover your world of possibilities, I challenge you to think about the seven questions I've posed tonight:

- Are you creating your own opportunities?
- Can you make more informed choices?
- How keenly are you paying attention?
- How daring are you?
- What are your convictions?
- How strong is your confidence?
- What is your personal philosophy? (p. 352)

Visualize the Future Because your audience may not be good at doing it themselves, in persuasive speeches you need to visualize the future for them—the future with or without your proposal. Kim, a student speaking on drunk driving, visualized a future with year-round sobriety checkpoints in this way:

> Take a moment and picture a world where we could all feel safer on our roads again. We could all go out on New Year's Eve, because, quite frankly,

those of us who do drink responsibly won't go out on this night now because we are afraid of the other people on the road. Families wouldn't have to be as fearful of going on a vacation over a long holiday weekend such as Memorial Day, Labor Day, or the Fourth of July; they wouldn't feel as threatened by the other drivers on the road. Wouldn't this safety be worth the inconvenience of stopping at sobriety checkpoints?

Don't forget to visualize the future for your audience as you conclude your persuasive speech. Look them right in the eye, use forceful and dynamic delivery, and speak with emotion and sincerity.

Look your listeners in the eye, use forceful and dynamic language, and speak with emotion and sincerity while you paint a vivid mental picture of the future. You want to encourage listeners who are almost persuaded—they just want to see how your topic relates to them one more time— without, of course, using faulty reasoning or unethical emotional appeals. ➔ *For a discussion of faulty or fallacious reasoning, see Chapter 13.*

Using Q&A

The key to successful **Q&A** sessions is to know your topic really well and to anticipate audience questions. Make a note card or two to refer to if needed, listing important sources, experts, and organizations. As you come up with possible questions, prepare one or two visual aids to use when answering them. All you may need is one or two overlays (for example, a bar graph containing new information) or a new computer visual of a chart to add to visuals that you plan to use in your speech. Of course, it's always possible that none of these questions will be asked, but if they are, your audience can't help being impressed. ➔ *See Kara's Q&A in Chapter 4.*

Here are some additional suggestions to help you with your Q&A session:

- *Repeat each question before answering it,* to make sure everyone has heard the question.

- *Rephrase any confusing or negative questions* in a clear and positive manner.

- *Think a moment before answering each question.* If you don't know the answer, say so and refer the questioner to someone in the audience who does know, or tell the person that it's a good question and that you will find the answer and let him or her know at the next meeting.

- *Watch for irrelevant or complex questions.* If you think a question is irrelevant or will take too long to answer, thank the person for the question and mention that you will talk with him or her personally about it after the session.

- *Don't argue or get angry or defensive* while answering questions. What you say during the Q&A session will affect the audience's overall judgment of your credibility and your speech.

- *Mention in your introduction that there will be a short Q&A period at the end of your speech,* and ask audience members to write out questions during the speech. After your initial conclusion, collect the questions, select three or four good ones, and answer them—ignoring the less desirable ones.

- *Stay on time.* Watch your time, and end the session with a final conclusion that refocuses audience attention and puts a pleasing closure on your speech.

As you can see, the conclusion of a speech is essential. If you see that time is running out, don't eliminate your conclusion. It is better to abbreviate your final point (or even skip it entirely) than to leave out your conclusion. Of course, if you time your speech while practicing, you won't have to worry about leaving anything out.

Active Critical Thinking

To think further about speech organization, complete the following:

- Select the informative or persuasive speech topic you used in the previous activity, outline a possible conclusion, and list at least three questions that your audience might ask during Q&A.

- Share your conclusion and questions with at least one other classmate for their suggestions.

Polishing Your Speech

Now that you have selected a topic, prepared a rough-draft outline, researched for content and supporting materials, and prepared your introduction and conclusion, it is time to give a final polish to your speech by preparing a more detailed preparation outline and adding connectors.

Polishing Using a Preparation Outline

Whereas your rough draft contained only main points and supporting information, your preparation outline also includes your introduction and conclusion. Use the following guidelines to develop your own preparation outline:

- First, add subpoints and supporting material to the main points of your rough-draft outline. Main points are normally written in complete sentences; the subpoints and supporting material may be in complete sentences, phrases, or keywords (follow your instructor's preferences). Make sure the items in each level follow the outlining tips in Figure 7.5.

- Next, write out sentence transitions to use between main points.

- Include a list of references at the end of the outline using the correct style (normally MLA or APA—check with your instructor).

- In addition to references at the end of your outline, indicate sources used within the outline by citing the author, date, and page (such as Smith, 2006, p. 29).

TIPS FOR CREATING OUTLINES

Tip 1: Use standard outline numbering

    1. First main point
       A. Subpoint or supporting material
          1. Supporting material

Tip 2: Indent for faster comprehension

Yes: A. Testing	**No**: A. Testing
1. Standard-Binet (IQ test)	1. Standard-Binet (IQ test)
2. Attention Deficit Rating Scale	2. Attention Deficit Rating Scale
3. Oppositional Defiant Scale	3. Oppositional Defiant Scale

Tip 3: Include 2 subpoints per level when possible

Yes: A. Testing	**No**: A. Testing
1. Standard-Binet (IQ test)	1. Standard-Binet (IQ test)
2. Attention Deficit Rating Scale	2. Attention Deficit Rating Scale
3. Oppositional Defiant Scale	3. Oppositional Defiant Scale
B. Treatment	B. Treatment
1. Ritalin	1. Ritalin
2. Clonidine	

Tip 4: Make items in each level parallel

Yes: "Aspirin"	**No**: "Aspirin"
• Prevents most heart attacks	• Prevention
• Makes major heart attacks minor	• Makes major heart attacks minor
• Minimizes strokes	• There will be less likelihood of death and disability from strokes
[Each starts with a verb]	[A noun, verb phrase, and sentence used]

Tip 5: Capitalize the first word each level

Yes: A. Prevents heart attacks	**No**: A. prevents heart attacks	**No**: A. Prevents Heart Attacks
B. Minimizes strokes	B. minimizes strokes	B. Minimizes Strokes

Figure 7.5

Follow These Tips When Planning Your Outline

- Identify the locations of visual aids in your speech with boldface and brackets: for example, **[Visual #1].**

- Once you are sure that your main points are complete, write the introduction and conclusion in complete sentences, partial sentences, or phrases. Normally these steps are not outlined, but you may outline them if you wish.

- Finally, check your outline for readability—read it several times out loud, looking for any problem areas. Your outline should resemble Kara's preparation outline in Figure 7.6.

Figure 7.6

Kara's Preparation Outline

Title: "Our Solar System and the Three Dwarves" by Kara Hoekstra

Topic: Our solar system has changed within the past year and now consists of eight classical planets and three dwarf planets.

Thesis: Recent changes in how we see our solar system include new definitions for *planet* and *dwarf planet*, demotion of Pluto from planet status, and discovery of two new dwarf planets.

INTRODUCTION

- **Attention-getter:** Show image (Crayon coloring) of solar system (as we knew from childhood). State the three mnemonics (randomly found on Internet) and then connect the two ideas. What if I told you there were no more *pizzas* . . . no more porcupines . . . no more planets? *[Visual 1]*

- **Audience motivation:** The solar system we learned about as children has changed, and it's possible that more changes could be made. Besides that, space is just so darn cool.

- **Establish credibility:** Astronomy has been an interest of mine since childhood, thanks to my father.

- **Preview:** Most of us have grown up knowing that our solar system consists of nine planets. However, experts have recently demoted Pluto to a dwarf planet. But even though Pluto has been reclassified, it's not alone. The new definition has included two other objects as dwarf planets as well. In our discussion of planets and dwarf planets, we'll go over
  —the criteria involved to be considered a planet and dwarf planet,
  —why Pluto didn't make the cut, and
  —the two other objects now considered dwarf planets.

[Transition] The new terms for planet and dwarf planet were voted on in August of 2006 by the International Astronomical Union. Due to some new discoveries, the IAU felt it was important to redefine the term "planet" and establish the new term "dwarf planet." NASA's website posts the definitions for each new term.

BODY

I. **NASA's new definitions**
   A. Three pieces of criteria must be met in order for an object in our solar system to be considered a planet. *[Visual 2]* (Ref #3)
      1. Orbits the sun.
      2. Nearly spherical in shape.
      3. Has cleared the neighborhood around its orbit ("swept out," so to speak).
   B. To be considered a dwarf planet, an object must meet four pieces of criteria. *[Visual 3]* (Ref #4)
      1. Orbits the sun.
      2. Nearly spherical in shape.
      3. Not a satellite (doesn't orbit another planet).
      4. Has NOT cleared the neighborhood around its orbit (major difference).

[Transition] Now that we know the definitions of a planet and dwarf planet, what exactly is it that Pluto is lacking?

II. **Why Pluto is different from the other eight**
   A. An online article in *Today's Science* (2006) tells us the big difference between Pluto and the other eight planets is that those eight have cleared out their respective orbits.
      1. Earth does not travel through bits of debris while making its yearly orbit around the sun *[Visual 4]*.
         [Illustrate the lack of debris as if the Earth was just traveling along its orbit and sweeping its path along the way, leaving a clean, debris-free orbit.]
      2. *Pluto is in the Kuiper Belt region and has much debris to cross [Visual 5]*.
   B. What the decision really all came down to is this: Pluto dwells in a cluttered home.
      1. The Kuiper Belt is composed of icy debris and asteroids.
      2. Pluto's orbit is roughly in the middle of the Kuiper Belt, causing it to travel through a cluttered field while making its journey around the sun.

Figure 7.6

Kara's Preparation Outline *(continued)*

[Transition] To recap, planets and dwarf planets have a few things in common. Both must orbit the sun. Both must be nearly spherical in shape. And in addition, dwarf planets cannot orbit another planet. But the MAJOR difference between the two is that dwarf planets have not cleared out their orbits. As a result of the new definition, IAU members officially declared two other objects as dwarf planets as well.

III. Eris and Ceres

    A. An article in *Newsweek* tells us that in April of 2006, Caltech astronomer Mike Brown confirmed the discovery of an object similar to Pluto *[Visual 6]*.

        1. Brown named the object Eris and determined that Eris is located just beyond Pluto in the Kuiper Belt.

        2. Eris orbits the sun, is round, is not a moon, and dwells in the cluttered Kuiper Belt.

        3. Eris is now considered the largest dwarf planet in our solar system.

    B. Online resource: Wikipedia tells us that Ceres, originally discovered in 1801, is the largest asteroid in the asteroid belt *[Visual 7]*.

        1. The asteroid belt is located in between the orbits of Mars and Jupiter and is filled with many irregular-shaped asteroids in orbit around the sun.

        2. Not only is Ceres different because it's the largest asteroid, it's also the only round one.

        3. Ceres orbits the sun, is round in shape, is not a moon, and dwells in the cluttered asteroid belt.

CONCLUSION

- **Initial summary:** Because of the new definitions set forth by astronomers, we now know the criteria involved in classifying planets. The main factor that sets Pluto apart from the other eight planets is that Pluto lives in a cluttered home and is forced to orbit among lots of space debris in the Kuiper Belt. And because Eris and Ceres meet the dwarf planet criteria as well, they have been classified in the new group also. Do you have any questions?

- **Question-and-Answer Session**

- **Final summary:** *[Visual 8]* There are no longer nine planets in our solar system. We now have eight classical planets and three dwarf planets. So how do we go about remembering the order of the planets and dwarf planets now?
  —Many Very Educated Men Just Shook Up Nonsense
  —Committees Prove Everything
The IAU debate, which I'm assuming consisted mostly of men, changed things as we know it—and as always, committees prove everything.

- **Refocus:** So now that we know Pluto, Eris, and Ceres are officially the three dwarves, what does this mean for the future of our solar system? As new discoveries are made in the Kuiper Belt region, it's possible that other objects meeting the four bits of criteria could be declared dwarf planets as well. Perhaps as more discoveries in the Kuiper Belt unfold, you'll keep your eyes and ears open for new dwarf planets. Pretty soon we may be calling our home the Solar System and the *Seven* Dwarves.

REFERENCES:

1. Adler, J. (2006, September 4). Of cosmic proportions. *Newsweek*, 44–50.
2. Ceres (dwarf planet). (2007, March 27). *Wikipedia*. Accessed at **en.wikipedia.org/wiki/ceres_%28dwarf_planet%29**.
3. Dwarf planets: What defines a planet? (2007, March 22). NASA. Accessed at **solarsystem.nasa.gov/planets/profile. cfm?object= dwarf&display=overview**.
4. Kuiper Belt. (2007, March 22). *NASA*. Accessed at **solarsystem.nasa.gov/planets/profile.cfm?object=kbos**.
5. Pluto: A (dwarf) planet by any other name . . . (2006, September 26). Today's Science at facts.com. Accessed at Facts On File News Services, **ezp.tccd.edu:2085**.

Page 2

Polishing by Adding Transitions and Connectors

When you **highlight main points** (making the important ideas in your speeches stand out and connect to each other), it's much easier for listeners to follow and remember your messages. Also, if listeners drift off for a moment, they have a better chance of reorienting themselves if your speeches include highlighting techniques. There are four effective ways to highlight and connect your points: transitions, signposts, internal summaries, and repetition and restatement. Let's look briefly at each of them.

Transitions A **transition** is a word, phrase, or brief sentence used to link ideas, main points, or major parts of a speech. Transitions help listeners follow the development of the speaker's ideas and keep them from getting lost. Examples of transitions are words such as *also, although, but, because,* and *however;* phrases such as *in addition, on the other hand, for example,* and *in other words;* and brief sentences like the following:

> "If you don't remember anything else from this speech, be sure to remember this."
>
> "This next point will be of special interest to all parents."
>
> "No mistake can be more costly than this last one."
>
> "Although my third point sounds complicated, in reality it's the easiest process of all."

Bill Gates, in his speech at the 2007 International Consumer Electronics Show (CES), incorporated transitions in his tag-team speech with Robbie Bach (Gates & Bach, 2007). ➤ *For a complete text of the speech, see* **www.microsoft.com** *and search for "2007 CES Speech."*

Two excerpts from the speech show use of transitions:

> "One of the first things I notice when I use Windows is how easy it is to find all my information on the PC."
>
> "Now I want to talk a little bit about gaming, and I want to start with Games for Windows."

Signposts A **signpost** is a specific type of transition (like a road sign) that clearly indicates where the speaker is going next. For example, instead of saying, "And the next step is … ," say, "The third step is … ." Instead of saying, "Another benefit that occurs when you stop smoking is … ," say, "The second benefit that occurs when you stop smoking is …" Continuing with Bill Gates' speech example (Gates & Bach, 2007), we find that he also uses signposts as he maneuvers through information. Gates, in closing the speech, stated, "Finally, if you want to grow the capacity, you don't have to think about volumes.…" This signpost signals that the end of the speech is near. Audiences appreciate knowing when the speech is close to completion.

Internal Summaries Don't wait until the conclusion of the speech to summarize. Provide occasional **internal summaries**, such as in this example:

> So far I've covered two important points to consider in choosing a day care—the location and the outside appearance of the facility. Both are fairly easy to research. The next item is just as important, but much more difficult to research.

When Robbie Bach, president of Entertainment & Devices for Microsoft, joined Gates in the previously mentioned speech, he used an internal summary to move from one point to another by saying, "So Bill talked about connected

EXPRESS CONNECT

You can use Speech Builder Express to help you create your transitions. Select "Transitions" from the left-hand menu and follow the instructions. For short reminders from this chapter about transitions, click on the "Tutor" button.

experiences, and I want to talk today and expand on that and talk about connected entertainment" (Gates & Bach, 2007).

Repetition and Restatement Use **repetition** to help your listeners remember exact words or figures. The following are examples of repetition:

> "The Federal Government spends almost $65 billion on IT each year (*Managing for Results,* 2007, p. 30). Imagine! $65 billion a year on information technology! Based on my salary, I can't even fathom how much $65 billion really is."

Use **restatement** (rewording) to make sure your listeners grasp a key concept. For example:

> Each year in the United States, 350,000 premature deaths are caused by smoking—that's equivalent to 920 fully loaded 747 jumbo jets crashing.

To polish your speech so listeners will follow and remember your ideas, try using several or all of these techniques. It's up to you as a speaker to make your speeches so interesting and easy to follow that audiences can't help listening to them and remembering them.

Active Critical Thinking

To think further about polishing your speech, complete the following:

- Using the speech you have been working on during this chapter, create a quality preparation outline. Be prepared to turn it in for instructor comments.

- Which transitions and connectors discussed above do you think will add the most polish to your speech? Give an example.

EXPRESS/CONNECT

You may have noticed the Express Connect boxes in the margins of this chapter, telling you about Speech Builder Express, which your instructor may have bundled with your text. Now that you have a good idea of what is required in the organization of a speech, you may want to use the assistance of Speech Builder Express, which will help you with outlining (including your purpose, thesis statement, organizational pattern, introductions, conclusions, and transitions) and will even help you put your references into the proper format. Once you have completed the outline, the final step of Speech Builder Express gives you the chance to review your outline, looking for errors and additions you wish to make. Although your instructor may have special requirements for your outline, this software helps you prepare the basics and gives you confidence that your speech is well organized.

Summary

Great ideas and outstanding supporting materials will be lost on the audience if your speech is not well organized. Clear and memorable presentations that flow smoothly are the result of four important steps.

First, *organize the body of the speech.* To organize your main points, you can use a chronological, spatial (or geographic), topical (or claim), causal, problem–solution, comparative advantages, criteria satisfaction, or motivated sequence pattern. Main points should be stated clearly and backed up with a variety of supporting materials designed to hold the audience's attention as well as clarify and prove your ideas.

Next, *organize the introduction.* Include an attention-getter, motivate the audience to listen, establish credibility and rapport, clearly state your purpose, and preview the main points of the speech. If your main points are brief and parallel (and are presented on a transparency or other visual aid), it will be easier for the audience to remember them. In the introduction, it may also be necessary to include background information, define unfamiliar terms, or briefly mention handouts.

Next, *organize the conclusion* of your speech. The conclusion includes a summary of the main points and refocuses audience attention so that listeners will remember your speech long after it is finished. In persuasive speeches, the refocus step may also include a visualization of the future and a challenge to action. Any type of supporting materials that can be used to get attention at the beginning of the speech can also be used to refocus attention at the end. Be sure to leave the audience satisfied, with a feeling of closure, especially after a Q&A session.

Finally, add polish to your speech by creating a more detailed preparation outline and adding quality transitions and connectors. A preparation outline allows you (and others you may ask) to see any problem areas that you would miss if you were using a written manuscript. By following the advice in this chapter, you are well on your way to giving an outstanding presentation.

Essentials of Public Speaking Online CourseMate

Use your Online Resources for *Essentials of Public Speaking* for quick access to the electronic study resources that accompany this chapter. Your Online Resources include access to InfoTrac College Edition, Personal Skill Building Activities and Collaborative Skill Building Activities, a digital glossary, sample speeches, and review quizzes.

Key Terms

causal pattern 151	highlight main points 171	Q&A 169
chronological pattern 150	inductive reasoning 152	repetition 175
claim or reason pattern 151	internal summary 174	restatement 175
comparative advantages pattern 153	motivated sequence 154	rhetorical question 160
criteria satisfaction pattern 154	problem–solution pattern 153	signpost 174
deductive reasoning 152	problem-cause-solution pattern 153	spatial (or geographic) pattern 150
		thesis statement 164
		topical pattern 149
		transition 174

Personal Skill Building

1. Brainstorm a list of topics about which you feel credible to speak. Select three of them and establish your credibility on each subject. Make sure you are able to answer these questions: What makes you credible? How are you building rapport? What makes you interested in this topic? Why did you select this topic?

2. Watch a question-and-answer session on CNN during one of the talk shows. Using the guidelines provided in this book, evaluate how well the Q&A session was handled. What techniques did the host use the most? How could the session have been more effective?

3. Take a careful look at the organizational pattern you have selected for the speech you are currently working on. Is it possible that another pattern could create more audience interest? If you aren't sure, prepare outlines using other patterns, and ask classmates or friends which one they like best.

4. After giving an informative or persuasive speech in class, offer a Q&A session in which classmates ask four to seven questions. Don't forget to include a final conclusion at the end of the Q&A.

5. Check out the following websites. You can access these sites using your Online Resources for *Essentials of Public Speaking,* Chapter 7:

- Patricia Fripp, a San Francisco-based executive speech coach, gives advice on organizing a speech in her article "Want Your Audiences to Remember What You Say? Learn the Importance of Clear Structure" at **www.fripp. com/art.clearstructure.html**.

- The article from the Advanced Public Speaking Institute explores how to use humor to spice up an otherwise dull question-and-answer session. View **public-speaking.org/public-speaking-qafunny-article.htm**.

- To practice writing a quality thesis statement, read and apply the suggestions from the following websites: "Developing a Thesis Statement" by the University of Wisconsin–Madison Writing Center (**wisc.edu/writing/ Handbook/Thesis.html**) and "Introductions and Thesis Statements" by the Hamilton Writing Center at Hamilton College (**hamilton.edu/ writing/introductions.html**).

- Look at several introductions and conclusions from current or historical speeches. Go to **americanrhetoric.com** and click on "Top 100 Speeches."

- Lenny Laskowski gives additional advice on Q&A sessions in his article "How to Handle That Dreaded Question & Answer Period" at his website **ljlseminars.com**—click on "Public Speaking Tips" and then select the specific article.

Collaborative Skill Building

1. In small groups, select a speech that is available in both written and video-taped versions from the *Essentials of Public Speaking* Online Resources. Watch the actual speech, and then have each group member individually identify the following: (1) the exact line on which the introduction ends, (2) the exact line where the conclusion begins, (3) a list of the main points, and (4) the organization pattern used.

    As a group, compare results and determine the success of the introduction, conclusion, and main points on a 5-point scale, with 1 being low and 5 high. Be prepared to share your results with other groups or the class.

2. In small groups, select a topic for an informative speech that has not yet been given in the class. Brainstorm a list of possible main points and organize them into two different patterns of organization (topical, causal, chronological, or geographical). Select the pattern that the group thinks would make the best speech, and create both an introduction and a conclusion for the speech topic. Be sure that you include all the steps/goals that are usually found in an

effective introduction and conclusion. Have one volunteer from the group prepare to give the introduction to the other group members; a second volunteer should present the conclusion. What is one strength and one weakness of the introduction and one strength and one weakness of the conclusion. How could each be changed into a strength? If time remains, repeat both presentations to the entire class or another group.

Presenting Your Speech

Test Your Knowledge CourseMate

What do you know about verbal, visual, and vocal delivery?

Some of the following statements about presenting a speech are true; others are common misconceptions that research has proven false.

Directions: If you think the statement is generally accurate, mark it T; if you think the statement is a misconception, mark it F. Then compare your answers with those at the end of Chapter 8. You can also take this quiz through your Online Resources for *Essentials of Public Speaking*, and if requested, e-mail your responses to your instructor.

_____ 1. The main reason for using visual aids is to entertain your audience.

_____ 2. If you can use words to create mental pictures in the minds of your listeners, it isn't necessary to use visual aids.

_____ 3. An audience typically waits until after you have completed the introduction to decide whether your speech will be interesting enough to listen to.

_____ 4. When you are speaking, you should either look just over your listeners' heads, or find one or two people who seem interested and talk to them.

_____ 5. Using a markerboard or chalkboard as a visual aid is good because you already know how to use it—practice is seldom necessary.

_____ 6. To make your visual aids more interesting, use several colors and several typefaces.

_____ 7. You should avoid using sexist language because some of your audience members may be turned off by it and not listen to your message.

_____ 8. If practicing your speech out loud is embarrassing or inconvenient, going over it mentally will be just as good.

_____ 9. In order to make the text easy to read, you should use all capital letters on your visuals.

_____ 10. If you have a good memory, it is better to memorize your speech than to take a chance on forgetting part of it.

8

Delivering Your Message

Nonverbal communication is important to successful speaking. Quintilian, a noted Roman rhetorician, gave his students detailed suggestions on gestures and facial expressions in *De Institutione Oratoria*. Some of his suggestions included:

- Use the head to indicate humility or haughtiness.
- Use the face to show sadness, cheerfulness, or pride.
- Strike the thigh to show indignation.
- Use the fingers to indicate specific ideas.

During ancient times there were two basic ways to communicate with an audience—by written word or directly to the audience face-to-face. Today's speakers have so many other choices all related to technology. Let's consider communicating by telephone. Even though the phone seems low tech by today's standards, companies are reinventing its use—from the telephone interview for customer satisfaction surveys to employee interviews. These money-saving approaches have one thing in common with Quintilian's advice—nonverbal communication is still important. In fact, the best phone interviews occur when interviewees use the same facial expressions, gestures, and clothing they would use if speaking face-to-face. *Why do you think speaking while smiling and gesturing—maybe even walking around—makes the speaker sound more enthusiastic, caring, and "real"?*

Learning Objectives

As you read Chapter 8,

- *Identify* the different delivery methods used in presenting a successful speech, and *select* which ones would work best for your situations.
- *Polish* your speech delivery by listing and using verbal, visual, and vocal delivery tips.
- *List* and *practice* the suggestions offered to improve your speech delivery.

WHAT DO BILL GATES, JERRY SEINFELD, AND OPRAH WINFREY HAVE IN COMMON? They are enthusiastic, interesting, powerful, persuasive, and—most important of all—believable (see the box on the page 182 for specifics). In their book *You've Got to Be Believed to Be Heard,* Decker and Denney (1993, p. 9) put it this way: Unless you make "emotional contact" with your audience to the point where they "like you, trust you, and believe you," they won't really hear what you have to say (p. 9). Therefore, although delivery isn't more important than what you have to say, *without good delivery, your audience may never hear you*. Delivery is that important!

This chapter will give you important delivery suggestions, beginning with selecting the best methods of delivery; moving on to making your speeches believable by improving your verbal, visual, and vocal deliveries; looking at the importance of immediacy behaviors to audience learning; and ending with correct rehearsal procedures. ➔ *Chapter 9 covers specific pointers on how to perfect your use of language.*

Selecting the Best Method of Delivery

Often the success of your presentation depends on which method of delivery you choose: extemporaneous speaking using brief notes or visual aids, impromptu speaking, speaking from manuscript, or speaking from memory.

Speaking from Brief Notes (Extemporaneous Speaking)

Usually you will be most effective and connect best with your audience if you speak extemporaneously. An **extemporaneous speech** is not memorized or written out word for word; it is developed from an outline and presented from brief speaking notes. In planning an extemporaneous speech, follow the Basic Steps for Preparing a Speech that we have been discussing in the preceding chapters. Each time you give an extemporaneous presentation, it will be a little different, because you have not memorized it.

To prepare speaking notes, turn your preparation outline into keyword notes and copy them onto one or two note cards. Write each quotation on separate, additional cards. Check with your instructor who may prefer that you do not use notes at all. With computer visuals, you probably won't need any additional notes, but be sure to have a hard copy with you in case of equipment failure.

Speaking from brief keyword notes allows you to speak in a conversational tone, maintain good eye contact with listeners, and alter your speech if feedback indicates that some listeners may be confused. ➔ *See more on speaking notes in Chapter 11.*

Using a database like InfoTrac College Edition, EBSCOhost, or CQ Researcher, you can find several interesting articles on extemporaneous speaking. Run a keyword or subject search for extemporaneous speaking.

Speaking from Visual Aids (Also Extemporaneous Speaking)

Many business and professional speakers use another form of extemporaneous speaking—speaking from visual aids (Smith, 2004). Like the outlined extemporaneous presentation, the visual-aid method is not memorized or written out word for word. Instead of note cards, however, speakers use their PowerPoint slides as a memory device or refer to printed copies of their slides (nine per page works well).

If you plan to use animation so that each point comes in at the click of the mouse, consider building your own bullets, which allows them to remain stationary along with the title. This helps you recall exactly how many points you planned for each slide. In contrast, PowerPoint bullets, which fly in with each point, make it difficult to remember how many points a slide has—especially if you are a bit nervous. ➔ *For specifics, see the PowerPoint Speaker's Guide under "Student Resources for Chapter 10" at the* Essentials of Public Speaking *website.*

Speaking Impromptu

An **impromptu speech** is one given without prior knowledge of the specific topic and without detailed notes or manuscript—obviously a hazardous way to give a major speech. However, anytime you are unexpectedly asked a question (in class, at a PTA meeting, or on your job), your response is an impromptu

Believable Speakers

These speakers do more than just prepare well-organized and well-supported ideas; they present their ideas in a believable manner.

Jeff J Mitchell/Getty Images

Bill Gates

In Chapter 1, Bill Gates' 2007 Harvard commencement speech was highlighted in the "Speaking to Make a Difference" box on pp. 5–6. The focus of Gates' speech was that the graduates had a great opportunity to make a difference in the world through their actions and their philanthropic giving. Gates' business credibility, giving through his foundation, his humor, and his personal anecdotes made his speech a powerful one. Since that time, Bill and his wife, Melinda, along with Warren Buffett, have continued their philanthropic message by challenging America's billionaires to pledge to give at least 50% of their wealth during their lives or at their death (Loomis, 2010). According to Loomis (p. 86), if only the *Forbes* 400 wealthiest people pledged 50% of their wealth, that could amount to over $600 billion. Gates' believability and connection with his audience may make the difference in the amount of money actually given.

Kevin Mazur/Getty Images

Jerry Seinfeld

With a degree in communication and theater from Queens College, Jerry Seinfeld began his career in comedy by appearing on the Johnny Carson and the David Letterman late-night shows. He soon developed his own popular NBC TV show, *Seinfeld,* which ran for nine years. Seinfeld even wrote a book called *Seinlanguage.* He is an effective public speaker who keeps audiences laughing at his comedic messages. What makes Seinfeld so successful? He relates to his audience by using observational humor (on-the-spot humor from observing the speaking situation and everyday life). According to fellow comedian John Kinde (2006), "The skill of observational humor puts you in the present moment. This, by itself, gives you a magical connection with your audience."

Kevin Dietsch-Pool/Getty Images

Oprah Winfrey

Oprah Winfrey became a popular talk-show host at a time when it seemed that no one could compete with Phil Donahue. One month after she arrived in Chicago, her show, *A.M. Chicago,* drew even with *Donahue,* and after three months it nosed ahead (Oprah Winfrey, 1987). Although Oprah's national TV show continued to lead the talk-show ratings, in 2010 she announced that she would be ending from her long-running show with the 2011 season. The *Washington Post* described Oprah as "the inescapable queen of talk television, radio, magazines, film and just about every other form of communication thus far invented" (Strauss, 2007). Why has Oprah been so successful? She makes it seem as if she is speaking directly to each of her listeners; she is real, and she is believable.

speech. Ideally, even though you have no time to prepare for the specific question, you will sound intelligent, authoritative, and confident because you have practiced answering questions. Wiles (2001) recommends that you set up a video camera and tape yourself answering some difficult questions asked by a friend. The more you practice, the more confident you will become.

When asked to do impromptu speaking, try the following (Stone & Bachner, 1994):

- *Appear confident* (even if you must pretend).

- *Decide on your conclusion or objective first* so that everything you say can lead up to it in an organized manner.

- *Begin with a general statement or background information* to give yourself time to think of one or more supporting reasons for your conclusion.

- *Introduce your supporting reasons with the word "because"* to give yourself time to think. For example:

  Q: Do you think speech training should be a requirement for all college students?

  A: *Because* most college students have to give presentations in upper-level courses, and *because* many college students will be getting jobs that demand speaking skills, I see speech training as an important requirement for all college students.

Another technique for answering impromptu questions is a simple *three-step method* recommended by Dr. Susan Huxman of Wichita State University: (1) Make a single point, (2) support that point, and (3) restate that point.

Question-and-answer sessions are another type of impromptu speaking. Even though you should plan for possible questions, many questions will be unexpected and require an impromptu response. Answer these questions directly and honestly. Exceptions are questions that you don't wish to answer or for which you don't have an answer (and feel it would be unacceptable to say, "I don't know"). In such cases, it may be justifiable to change the topic. Politicians are very good at changing the subject by using such comments as:

"That's an important question—almost as important as . . ."

"I was hoping someone would ask me that question, because it gives me an opportunity to talk about . . ."

"Could I come back to that question? I've been wanting to reply to the remark this gentleman made earlier. He said . . ."

"I think we need to look at the problem from a different angle . . ."

If you don't have figures and sources at your fingertips, you can use a personal, family, or humorous instance to clarify and support your point. For example, in an impromptu speech on "What types of animals make the best pets?" a student supported her point that the best pets are dogs by telling the audience about her three dogs. She told what kinds of dogs she had, gave their names, and described an instance that showed what good companions they were. The instance was both humorous and heartwarming. The audience loved her speech. ➡ *Chapter 6 gives more examples of instances.*

There's no telling when your next impromptu speaking opportunity may occur, but it could be one of the most important and successful short speeches you give. You will probably have several opportunities to give impromptu speeches in class. Try the techniques suggested here until you find a technique or a variety of techniques that work best for you.

Using a database like InfoTrac College Edition, CQ Researcher, or EBSCOhost (see their Military and Government Collection, which includes *Vital Speeches*), run a keyword search for *Republican Convention* and *Democratic Convention,* and look for the keynote addresses from the two most recent conventions in *Vital Speeches.* Read the text of a speech (watch the actual speech on **americanrhetoric.com** or YouTube), and write a brief critical review of the speech, including its organization, content, and delivery.

Speaking from a Manuscript

Although it might seem that reading your speech would be a safe way to avoid a blunder, speaking from a manuscript is much harder than speaking from notes. It's difficult to use good vocal variety and maintain direct eye contact while reading a speech. Also, unless you are free to deviate from the manuscript, you can't respond to verbal or nonverbal listener feedback; your talk will likely seem stiff and remote.

Politicians and top-level business and professional people who must give copies of their speech to the media prior to their speaking usually read from a manuscript. These public figures need to make sure that what they say cannot be misquoted or misinterpreted. This is especially true in an emergency or unexpected situation (such as the briefing of the press in Iraq after the capture of Saddam Hussein). When it is very important that they not say something unintentionally, they use a manuscript.

If you must use a manuscript, here are some tips:

- Be sure that the manuscript is double or triple spaced and in 14- or 16-point type.

- Place the manuscript pages into a stiff binder.

- Practice holding the binder high enough that you can glance down at it and then glance up and make eye contact with your listeners without having to move your head.

- Practice, practice, and practice until your pitch, rate, volume, and emphasis make you sound authoritative yet conversational and your movements seem natural.

Speaking from Memory

Speaking from memory has even more drawbacks than reading from a manuscript. First, because it takes a great deal of time and effort to memorize a speech, it won't work on occasions when there's only enough time to decide on your main points and find the necessary supporting materials. Second, speaking from memory makes it difficult to react to listener feedback. A question from a listener can make you forget the next sentence or even the rest of your speech. Or, if facial expressions indicate audience confusion, you can hardly risk deviating from your practiced speech to add another example. Also, it's difficult to make your delivery relaxed, spontaneous, and believable if you are trying to recall memorized text. Always memorizing your speech is a crutch that could easily work against you in the future.

Some speakers do feel more comfortable memorizing their opening and closing remarks, and, occasionally, the transitions between main points. Memorizing small segments such as these shouldn't cause a problem—just don't memorize the entire speech.

Active Critical Thinking

To think further about methods of delivery, complete the following:

- Which method of delivery do you use most often? What strengths and weaknesses does it have for you? Give an example of each.
- Which methods do you think work best for a classroom speech, and which should be avoided? Why?

Polishing Your Delivery: Verbal, Visual, and Vocal

Speakers like Bill Gates, Jerry Seinfeld, and Oprah Winfrey have developed believability by perfecting their verbal, visual, and vocal delivery through plenty of hard work and practice. For example, speaking of his craft, Jerry Seinfeld said, "I will spend an hour taking an eight-word sentence and making it five" (Fripp, 2007). Let's begin by looking at verbal delivery.

Verbal Delivery

Verbal delivery involves *your overall speaking style, including the words you choose and the way you construct sentences.* Fortunately, in today's world listeners expect speakers to use a fairly informal language style and reserve formal language for written reports.

- This was not the case in 1863 when *Abraham Lincoln gave the Gettysburg Address,* and may account for why his usual direct, easy-to-understand approach was not appreciated by some critics of the day (Wilson, 2005).

- Whereas Lincoln's speech was one of solemn dedication for the soldiers that had died at Gettysburg, *Martin Luther King Jr.'s "I Have a Dream" speech* was more of a rally speech where the audience expected "vivid imagery and emotionally stimulating language" (Johannesen et al., 2000, p. 259).

Your delivery style is uniquely your own, but it is good to look at these great speeches to see whether any of their verbal techniques would work for you. → *See Martin Luther King Jr.'s speech in the "Speaking to Make a Difference" in this chapter; Lincoln's Gettysburg Address is highlighted in Chapter 9, pp. 212–213.*

Although verbal delivery should be appropriate to the situation (as the differences between Lincoln's and King's styles indicate), generally oral communication is best when it is *specific* (gives details), *simple* (easy to understand), and *vivid* (paints a picture for the listener) That means that short, simple sentences are best, and it is perfectly all right to use personal pronouns such as *I, we, you,* and *us,* as well as contractions such as *I've* and *won't.* → *See Chapter 9 for details on perfecting your use of language.*

One of the most serious mistakes a speaker can make is to use extremely technical words, or *jargon,* even in a professional setting. Don't assume that your audience will be impressed or that everyone uses or understands the same technical terms that you do. To drive home this point, one professor who was training people to write government forms and regulations created a sample of the worst kind of bureaucratic communication:

> We respectfully petition, request, and entreat that due and adequate provision be made, this day and date herein under subscribed, for the satisfying of these petitioners' nutritional requirements and for the organizing of such methods of allocation and distribution as may be deemed necessary and proper to assure the reception by and for said petitioners of such quantities of cereal products as shall, in the judgment of the aforementioned petitioners, constitute a sufficient supply thereof (Hensley, 1992, p. 117).

According to the professor, it illustrates how most bureaucrats would write "Give us this day our daily bread."

People are so used to using jargon that they don't stop to think that not everyone uses the same terms. For example, how many noncollege students would understand this statement: "I registered late for my TTH* but left my add slip* in the dorm. By the time I made it to class, everyone was gone except the TA* because the class was killed*. I really needed this class to improve my GPA*." Or, how many people would understand this business person: "Please send your reschedule in SAP* format ASAP*. Our supplies schedule is moving to the right*, and the company has used up its set aside*."

Another mistake that many speakers make is using language that risks offending audience members due to gender, culture, age, or disabilities. For example, avoid using gender-specific terms (such as *he* used as a generic term to refer to both males and females), and replace them with gender-neutral alternatives (such as *humanity* instead of *mankind*). ➔ *See Chapter 9 for additional words and their suggested alternatives. Also, look again at Chapter 3 for a review of usage differences based on culture. Pay special attention to low- and high-context cultures and monochromic/polychromic cultures in determining language and examples to use.*

Putting your ideas into simple, easy-to-understand language that fits the frames of reference of your listeners and is vivid, specific, and bias-free can be hard at first. But as you work on the basics of delivery and keep in mind the principles discussed here, an effective language and speaking style should become natural for you. ➔ *Additional language tips are included in Chapter 9.*

Visual Delivery

Your **visual delivery** includes *your overall appearance, facial expressions, eye contact, posture, gestures, and even the visual aids you use*—all affect how you are perceived by the audience.

Appearance Right or wrong, audience members use your appearance as their first clue to your status and credibility (Knapp & Hall, 2002), and first impressions tend to remain strong "even in the face of subsequent contradictory cues" (Burgoon & Hoobler, 2002, pp. 263–264). Unless you are certain that some other style of dress is more appropriate for the audience and the occasion, dress on the conservative side. For women, this means a suit or dress in a classic style and a simple hairstyle and minimal jewelry (Damhorst & Fiore, 2000). For men, this means dress slacks and a sport coat or a suit and tie and dark shoes (Molloy, 1996). Dark clothes generally communicate authority, rank, and even competence (Damhorst & Reed, 1986).

Appearance is the first clue an audience has when determining a speaker's status and credibility.

Stockbyte/Jupiter Images

Facial Expressions and Eye Contact We all enjoy listening to speakers who smile appropriately, look at us while speaking, and seem to enjoy giving the speech. Therefore, your nonverbal communication as a speaker determines how the audience perceives you (Becze, 2007), and your facial expressions even affect their judgment of your credibility (Masip, Garrido, & Herrero, 2004). With speakers who appear tense,

---

*Legend: TTH (class that meets on Tuesdays and Thursdays); add slip (official form showing that a course has been added); TA (teaching assistant); killed class (class closed or dropped, usually due to low enrollment); GPA (grade point average); SAP (management/accounting/inventory software); ASAP (as soon as possible); to the right (behind schedule); set aside (emergency funds).

Speaking to Make a Difference

Martin Luther King Jr.'s "I Have a Dream" speech was ranked as the best political speech of the twentieth century by the vote of 137 top American public-address scholars (Lucas & Medhurst, 1999). This notable speech was presented by King in 1963 at the Lincoln Memorial in Washington, D.C., to an audience of over 250,000 peaceful civil rights demonstrators. The entire "I Have a Dream" speech can be found at **www.americanrhetoric.com**.

AP Photo

Let us not wallow in the valley of despair, I say to you today, my friends.

And so even though we face the difficulties of today and tomorrow, I still have a dream. It is a dream deeply rooted in the American dream.

I have a dream that one day this nation will rise up and live out the true meaning of its creed: "We hold these truths to be self-evident, that all men are created equal."

I have a dream that one day on the red hills of Georgia, the sons of former slaves and the sons of former slave owners will be able to sit down together at the table of brotherhood.

I have a dream that one day even the state of Mississippi, a state sweltering with the heat of injustice, sweltering with the heat of oppression, will be transformed into an oasis of freedom and justice.

I have a dream that my four little children will one day live in a nation where they will not be judged by the color of their skin but by the content of their character.

I have a *dream* today!

I have a dream that one day, down in Alabama, with its vicious racists, with its governor having his lips dripping with the words of "interposition" and "nullification"—one day right there in Alabama little black boys and black girls will be able to join hands with little white boys and white girls as sisters and brothers.

I have a *dream* today!

* * *

And so let freedom ring from the prodigious hilltops of New Hampshire. Let freedom ring from the mighty mountains of New York. Let freedom ring from the heightening Alleghenies of Pennsylvania.

Let freedom ring from the snow-capped Rockies of Colorado.

Let freedom ring from the curvaceous slopes of California.

But not only that.

Let freedom ring from Stone Mountain of Georgia.

Let freedom ring from Lookout Mountain of Tennessee.

Let freedom ring from every hill and molehill of Mississippi.

From every mountainside, let freedom ring. And when this happens, when we allow freedom to ring, when we let it ring from every village and every hamlet, from every state and every city, we will be able to speed up that day when *all* of God's children, black men and white men, Jews and Gentiles, Protestants and Catholics, will be able to join hands and sing in the words of the old Negro spiritual, "Free at last! Free at last! Thank God Almighty, we are free at last!"

There are many reasons why King's "I Have a Dream" speech was selected as the century's best. We will look at only one—his delivery.

- King's delivery included outstanding *vocal variety*. As you know from this chapter, an audience is more likely to listen closely to your speech and to better understand your ideas if you speak with good vocal variety (effective use of volume, pitch, emphasis, and rate). King was a master at all of these, as you can tell from listening to the video of his speech. For example, he began his "I Have a Dream" speech at 92 words per minute and ended at a much faster, more dynamic 145 words per minute (Atkins-Sayre, 2007). For most of us, vocal variety also includes a voice that is conversational, natural, and enthusiastic. King's naturally appealing speaking style made him a master of all these except possibly one. As a Baptist minister, his style would not be called conversational, which was just as well, because people weren't at the rally for a conversation—they wanted what Hansen refers to as a "pulpit

performance" (Hansen, 2003). They wanted to be inspired, motivated, and given hope—and they were.

- Second, King kept his listeners involved with his *verbal delivery*. Verbal delivery includes the language you choose and the way you construct sentences in your presentation. The best language is vivid (paints a picture for the listener), specific (gives details), and simple (easy to understand). King painted word pictures with his vivid language choices, as in this passage: "I have a dream that one day even the state of Mississippi, a state sweltering with the heat of injustice, sweltering with the heat of oppression, will be transformed into an oasis of freedom and justice." Contrasting "heat of injustice" and "heat of oppression" with "oasis of freedom" paints a clear picture for an audience hoping for justice. King was also good at using onomatopoeia (where words sound like their meanings). His repetition of the word *ring* in "let freedom ring" represented church bells that seemed to ring louder and louder, leading to his memorable finish.

continued

- Another aspect that made King's speech so effective was his *method of delivery*—he used memory, manuscript, and extemporaneous styles in this speech. Part of his material included songs, quotations, and phrases from previous speeches and sermons that were essentially memorized. For example, his concluding section on "Let freedom ring" was given in a less polished form at a 1958 commencement for Morehouse College (Papenfuse, 2007). Part of his speech was a handwritten manuscript, which he basically followed for the first 10 minutes (Hansen, p. 70); at that point his speech became more of an extemporaneous one. Neither the "I Have a Dream" sequence nor the "Let freedom ring" concluding section were in King's original written remarks. According to Hansen, "Had King not decided to leave his written text, it is doubtful that his speech at the march would be remembered at all" (p. 135). Perhaps King departed from his manuscript because of audience reactions, or it may have been due to the urging of gospel singer Mahalia Jackson, who is said to have called from the side of the stage, "Tell them about the dream, Martin! Tell them about the dream!" (McGonigal, 2005).

"I Have a Dream" was a persuasive speech urging "rededication to the black non-violent civil rights movement" and to its central values: "courage, faith, hope, freedom, justice, equality, non-violence, sacrifice, dignity, and discipline" (Johannesen et al., p. 259).

Question: If you had been in the vast crowd that day, how do you think you would have reacted to the environment, the speech, and King's delivery?

---

don't smile, and only rarely make eye contract, listeners will probably interpret their behavior in one of two ways:

1. *Observation:* The speaker is nervous.
   Reason: The speaker is not prepared, is inexperienced, or is uncertain.
   Conclusion: Listening is not worth my time.

2. *Observation:* The speaker won't look us in the eye.
   Reason: The speaker is lying, is trying to manipulate us, or doesn't respect us.
   Conclusion: Listening is not worth my time.

In either case, your audience will tune out.

When you make eye contact, hold your gaze for three to five seconds before moving on to someone else; if your eyes dart too quickly, you will appear nervous. Also be sure to look at people in all parts of the room—some speakers inadvertently favor one side or the other.

Posture, Movement, and Gestures   A relaxed yet straight *posture* makes you look confident, friendly, and energetic. Avoid slumping and hunching your shoulders or putting your weight on one hip; both postures make you look less confident, less interested, and less believable. In addition, the confidence indicated by a strong upper-body posture can be sabotaged by nervous foot tapping. Generally, an open posture (with relaxed arms and confident gestures) gives you a confident look; a closed or stiff posture (with folded arms and awkward movements) gives you a nervous appearance (Pincus, 2007). For the best posture, take a comfortable, open stance with one foot slightly ahead of the other, and lean slightly forward without locking your knees. This posture gets you ready to move in any direction, yet makes it almost impossible to sway or rock as some speakers do. Also, leaning slightly forward indicates that you have a positive feeling toward the audience.

Don't be afraid to move around occasionally. *Movement* can add interest, energy, and confidence to your presentation. Move at the beginning of an idea to add emphasis, or move as a transition between ideas. If you are using computer-generated visuals (such as PowerPoint slides), using a remote presentation mouse allows you to advance slides regardless of where in the room you are at the time. Practice using the remote until you feel confident.

Not only do effective speakers use good posture and build movement into their speeches, they also make use of *gestures*. There are four categories of gestures; three of them can be effective for speakers, and one of them should be avoided (Ekman, 1992; Morris, 1994).

Film portrayals of effective speakers, such as in the film Elizabeth, *show the speaker communicating verbally, visually, and vocally with their audiences.*

- **Emblems** are body movements and gestures that are so specific that they easily replace a word or idea. For example, if you put your finger to your lips, everyone knows to be quiet; if you ask a question and hold up your hand, the audience knows that you want them to answer with a show of hands. You may also use emblems during an example or narrative to make the meaning clear to the audience. However, don't forget that not all cultures interpret emblems the same way. George W. Bush discovered this during his inauguration when he and others made the "Hook 'em Horns" gesture as the University of Texas band marched past. Although he intended the emblem to represent the Texas Longhorn, which is the mascot at UT, the gesture means "cuckold" to people from many countries (Knapp & Hall, 2002) and "Satan" to people in other countries such as Norway (Bush Shocks Foreigners, 2005).

  → *For a discussion of emblems used around the world, see* Gestures: The Do's and Taboos of Body Language Around the World *by Axtell (1998).*

- **Illustrators** are specific movements or gestures intended to expand or clarify a word or an idea. For example, you could show the size of something with a wide gesture or point in the direction chosen by the character in your narrative. However, be sure to make your illustrating gestures appropriate for the audience; as mentioned earlier, not all gestures are perceived the same way by all cultures. As Eckert (2006) notes, "The use of sweeping hand gestures by many Greeks and Italians is considered overwhelming to those from East Asian cultures, where body movement is minimized" (p. 48). On the other hand, remember that just to look "normal," gestures must be slightly exaggerated when in front of an audience—a small pointing gesture that would be effective when talking to three or four people will probably not even be noticed if used in front of a large audience.

- **Regulators** are movements or gestures that control the flow of a conversation in small groups, like breaking off eye contact to signal that the conversation is over. In a presentation, regulators such as body positioning and eye contact are used to indicate to sections of an audience that you are speaking directly to them. For example, if you turn your body to the left and look upward, audience members on the left side of the auditorium's upper deck know that they haven't been left out.

- **Adaptors**, which are gestures and movements that signal nervousness, should be avoided when speaking. Even if you are feeling a bit anxious, you don't want your audience to notice; so when you practice in front of your friends or family, have them look for stress gestures like rubbing your ear or nose, flipping your hair, or tapping your foot.

In general, the best gestures are natural ones. If you don't worry about them, appropriate gestures will usually occur naturally. When speaking to a group of friends about an exciting event, you don't worry about when or how to gesture. In the same way, if you concentrate on getting your meaning across while speaking, your gestures will come more naturally. However, don't forget that the larger the audience, the bigger your gestures must be just to appear normal. Not only do gestures vary according to the size of the audience, but the diversity of your audience will also dictate which gestures are appropriate. According to nonverbal researchers Bowen and Montepare (2007), "nonverbal behavior and language are open to considerable misinterpretation unless the cultural context and meanings are taken into consideration" (p. 186). ➔ *Check Chapter 1 for examples of nonverbal gestures that cause cross-cultural misunderstandings.*

If possible, videotape yourself while practicing your speech, or have a friend observe you and make suggestions. Make sure that your gestures are noticeable, and look out for any distracting ones. If you notice a nervous gesture (such as rubbing your cheek), make a concentrated effort to stop it or to replace it with a more appropriate gesture. Check your awareness of which gestures stimulate or hinder listening by answering the questions in Figure 8.1. When not gesturing, rest a hand on the lectern or let your hands fall naturally at your sides. Using visual aids will keep your hands so busy that you won't have time to worry about them.

Handling Objects and Handouts The value of using *objects* to clarify points and add interest can easily be seen by watching a cooking or home-design show on television. One student, inspired by the way people on these types of programs use objects, used four jogging shoes as well as a cutaway model of the inside of a shoe to illustrate his points in a speech on selecting jogging shoes.

- *Don't use objects (or models) that are too small for the audience to see clearly*— frustrated audiences will stop listening. If needed for clarity, use a drawing or an enlarged model of the object, but when possible have the real object on hand for the audience to view after your speech is finished.

- *Do practice using objects*—when poorly handled they can distract from your speech and your credibility. For example, one student who was giving a speech about bowling dropped his bowling ball on the floor—the audience was not impressed. Another speaker brought in a kitchen knife designed to cut through anything, but when he tried to slice through an aluminum can, he failed.

Just like objects, *handouts* can either add to or distract from your speech if they are not used correctly. Consider the following:

- *Don't distribute handouts before or during the speech unless the audience needs to use them during your speech*—audience members will likely read them (or handle them if they are objects) instead of listening to you. If a handout is needed during the speech, be prepared for a loss of attention as it is distributed.

- In some professions, speakers are expected to hand out paper copies of their computer slides to audience members. If so, *reduce the size of the original visuals by 20 percent* (Rabb, 1993). Even better would be to post them online for audience viewing.

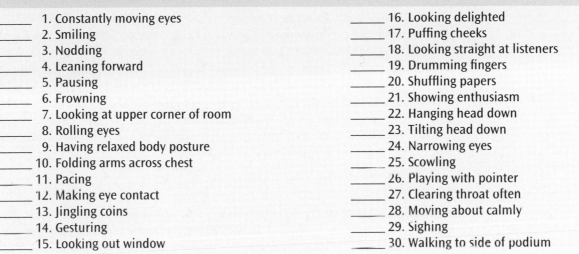

Directions: Put an *S* by those behaviors you think would stimulate listening. Put an *H* by those behaviors you think would hinder listening.* You can also complete this quiz online at the CourseMate for *Essentials of Public Speaking.*

_____ 1. Constantly moving eyes
_____ 2. Smiling
_____ 3. Nodding
_____ 4. Leaning forward
_____ 5. Pausing
_____ 6. Frowning
_____ 7. Looking at upper corner of room
_____ 8. Rolling eyes
_____ 9. Having relaxed body posture
_____ 10. Folding arms across chest
_____ 11. Pacing
_____ 12. Making eye contact
_____ 13. Jingling coins
_____ 14. Gesturing
_____ 15. Looking out window

_____ 16. Looking delighted
_____ 17. Puffing cheeks
_____ 18. Looking straight at listeners
_____ 19. Drumming fingers
_____ 20. Shuffling papers
_____ 21. Showing enthusiasm
_____ 22. Hanging head down
_____ 23. Tilting head down
_____ 24. Narrowing eyes
_____ 25. Scowling
_____ 26. Playing with pointer
_____ 27. Clearing throat often
_____ 28. Moving about calmly
_____ 29. Sighing
_____ 30. Walking to side of podium

Answers:
Behaviors 2–5, 9, 12, 14, 16, 18, 21, 23, 28, and 30 would stimulate listening. The remaining behaviors would most likely hinder listening.

*Based on an exercise in Burley-Allen, 1982, p. 113.

Figure 8.1

Nonverbal Awareness Check

Check your awareness of a speaker's nonverbal behaviors by completing the scale above.

Adapting Visual Delivery to the Media Businesses and organizations of all sizes are now using media (including closed-circuit television, teleconferencing, Web-based meeting technology, online videos, and podcasts) for advertising and for employee education and training. Because media presentations can be replayed, it's important that your visual messages make the right impression. Knowing how to adapt your presentation to media should give you a definite career boost. Carefully consider the following media tips (Blythin & Samovar, 1985; Greaney, 1997; Hamilton, 2008; Howard, 2002; Smudde, 2004):

- *Be conscious of your visual image.* Don't slump or fidget. Maintain direct eye contact with the interviewer. Gesture, lean forward a bit, and show that you have deep feelings on the subject.

- *Choose the color of your clothes carefully.* Avoid white (even as trim) and warm or hot colors such as red, pink, or orange. Avoid stripes, polka dots, or patterns, because they tend to bleed together. Solid, neutral, or cool colors are best. Slight contrasts in color are desirable, but avoid sharp contrasts or clothes made of shiny material. For example, a light blue blouse or shirt would look good with a medium-blue suit. Men can add a darker blue tie. Men and women with blond hair should wear a darker shirt or blouse to give a slight contrast. Men and women with dark complexions should select colors that are either darker or lighter than their complexions.

- *Avoid shiny jewelry* (rings, necklaces, tie clasps).

- *Wear slenderizing clothes*—the camera will make you look heavier. Dresses or suits that are fitted or belted at the waist are recommended for women; men also look slimmer in suits that are somewhat fitted at the waist. The lights are hot, so you will also want to wear cool clothes.

- *Men generally do not need makeup.* If they have a heavy beard or a shiny forehead, the producer may suggest applying some powder. Women should wear modest, everyday makeup (eyeliner is suggested).

- *Look directly into the camera* (if there is no audience) as though the camera were a person. If you have an audience, consider the camera as an audience member and include it as you scan the audience. Not looking into the camera will give the appearance that you are not making eye contact with the audience. If the lights are so bright that you are squinting, tell the floor manager so they can be adjusted.

Vocal Delivery

Not only do effective speakers work on their verbal and visual delivery, they are also very aware of their vocal delivery. **Vocal delivery** includes *how you use your tone, volume, pitch, emphasis, and rate to interest, motivate, and persuade an audience.* There is more to delivery than just your words and how you look. According to Jacobi (2000) in *How to Say It with Your Voice,* "... people are judged not by what they know or do, and not by the content of their speech, but simply *by the way they sound to others*" (p. 4). In fact, he says, "Nothing you can do for your image will give you as much bang for the buck as improving the way you sound" (p. 4).

An audience is more likely to listen closely to your speech and understand your ideas if you speak in a conversational, natural, and enthusiastic voice. **Vocal variety**, the key to a conversational voice, is achieved by varying volume, pitch, emphasis, rate, and pauses in a natural manner, as well as articulating and pronouncing words clearly.

Volume and Pitch For your first speeches, don't strive for perfect delivery. Concentrate on using enough volume and pitch changes to sound conversational and interesting.

Volume, the loudness and softness of your voice, is important in several ways. First, you need to speak loudly enough to be heard all over the room. Second, you need to vary your volume in order to make the speech interesting. Third, you need to increase and decrease your volume to emphasize certain words or phrases.

If your volume (which depends on the amount and force of the air you expel while speaking) is generally too soft, practice saying the word *stop,* emphasizing the *ah* sound while rapidly expelling as much air as possible. Say the word *stop* loudly enough that a person passing by the room could hear you. Don't yell; just speak loudly and project your voice. Practice speaking at this louder volume until it feels comfortable.

Pitch, the highness and lowness of vocal tones, is also important to vocal variety. Effective speakers use two types of pitch changes: (1) steps in pitch (changes between high, medium, and low pitch) and (2) pitch inflection (gradually rising or falling pitch). Together, these pitch changes add interest and energy to speakers' voices and communicate subtle meanings:

- *Pitch Step.* Read the sentences at the top of page 192 aloud, following the indicated step changes in pitch, and decide which one sounds best:

Using a database like InfoTrac College Edition, EBSCOhost, or CQ Researcher, run a keyword search for speaking tips. Try using *public speaking techniques* and *public speaker**.

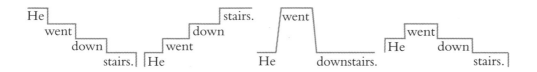

- *Pitch Inflection.* A rising pitch at the end of a sentence usually signals a question (*She stole the money* ⤴), whereas a falling pitch indicates a statement or understanding (*She stole the money* ⤵). A drawn-out rising pitch implies doubt (*Really* ⤴); a drawn-out high falling pitch implies a lightbulb understanding (*Oh, now I understand* ⤵); and a low falling pitch indicates boredom (*Sure* ⤵).

- *Upspeak.* Some speakers (especially during a question-and-answer session) use an upward pitch inflection (called **upspeak**) at the end of declarative sentences and phrases. When overused, the audience will likely perceive this as a sign of insecurity or a desire to gain approval. Say the following sentences, ending each with a downward inflection:

  Hello, my name is _____ _____ ⤵. I am a confident speaker ⤵.

  Now say the same two sentences, ending each with an upward inflection:

  Hello, my name is _____ _____ ⤴. I am a confident speaker ⤴.

Could you hear the difference? With downward inflections, the sentences sound confident; with upward inflections, they sound as if you are asking for approval. Therefore, if you want to sound more interesting and authoritative, use more pitch step and inflection, but limit your use of upspeak.

Emphasis, Rate, and Pauses Good vocal variety requires more than just effective use of volume and pitch. To make your voice as expressive as possible, you also need to develop your use of emphasis, speaking rate, and pauses.

Emphasis, stressing a word in order to give it significance, is an important ingredient of vocal variety. When you emphasize a word, (1) your pitch goes up (usually followed immediately by a downward inflection), and (2) your volume increases. For a demonstration of this point, say the sentence below five times, each time emphasizing a different word, as shown. Listen to your pitch and volume as you speak. You should be able to give five different meanings to the sentence.

Why did you fire him?

Why *did* you fire him?

Why did *you* fire him?

Why did you *fire* him?

Why did you fire *him*?

Rate, how fast or slowly you speak, is especially important in maintaining listeners' attention. Constantly speaking at the same rate can lull your listeners to sleep. Work on varying your speaking rate. Try speaking faster to show excitement or enthusiasm and to emphasize key points; speak more slowly to indicate importance, to build suspense, or to indicate boredom.

Pauses, or "live silence," and **phrases,** groups of words preceded and followed by pauses, also add to listener interest and understanding. Pauses and phrases can be short, medium, or long. If you have ever been told that you speak too fast, it probably means that you don't pause long enough or often enough for your listeners to absorb your ideas. Pauses not only make phrases easier to understand but can also add suspense and dramatic effect. Try not to fill the "live silence" of a pause with distracting vocalizations such as *ah, uh, um, OK, and uh, well uh,* or *you know.* The silence may seem awkward at first, but pauses give your listeners time to absorb your ideas. To see the power of pauses, read the sentences in Figure 8.2, pausing where indicated with a slash.

Figure 8.2

Read the sentence, pausing at each slash.

Use of Pauses (pause with each slash)	
That / outfit / looks great / on / you.	Too many pauses for effective phrasing.
That outfit looks great on you.	No pauses needed; the speaker sounds sincere.
That outfit looks great / on you.	A pause after "great" sounds like no one but you would consider wearing it.

Articulation and Pronunciation Both articulation and pronunciation are important for maximum audience understanding. Although they are often used synonymously, they are really very different.

Articulation, the production of clear and distinct speech sounds, is vital for audience understanding. Many speakers tend to run words together or leave off some word endings (for example, *Whadayamean* instead of *What do you mean, Seeya* instead of *See you,* and *goin'* instead of *going*). Practice making your articulation crisp and clear by exaggerating all the sounds as you read aloud a rhyme like "Peter Piper picked a peck of pickled peppers" or "To sit in solemn silence in a dull, dark dock."

Pronunciation, saying words according to standard usage, is not always easy. Words that a speaker pronounces incorrectly are difficult for listeners to ignore. If your speech includes several mispronounced words, the audience may begin to doubt your credibility. For example, the chancellor of a large college continually mispronounced the word *registration* when speaking to the faculty. Instead of *rej-i-stra´-shun* the chancellor always said *red-ster-a´-shun,* which made him sound uneducated. Take a look at the list of commonly mispronounced words in Figure 8.3 to see if you need to work on any of them.

Figure 8.3

Which words do you pronounce incorrectly?

Commonly Mispronounced Words		
Word	**Correct Use**	**Incorrect Use**
Arctic	Arc-tic	Ar-tic
Ask	Ask	Aks
Athlete	Ath-lete	Ath-a-lete
February	Feb´-ru-ary	Feb-yu-ary
Get	Get	Git
Height	Height	Heighth
Library	Ly-brery	Ly-berry
Mirror	Mirr-or	Mirr
Picture	Pic-ture	Pitch-er
With	With	Wit or Wid
Nuclear	Nu-kle-er	Nu-ku-lur

Immediacy Behaviors

Researchers use the term **immediacy behaviors** for the verbal, visual, and vocal behaviors that instructors use to promote a sense of closeness and personal interaction with students. Studies show that students learn significantly more, have a better attitude toward the classroom experience, and attend more regularly when instructors use these behaviors (Kelsey et al., 2004; Pogue & AhYun, 2006; Rocca, 2004)—even when the class is a Web course (Arbaugh, 2001; LaRose & Whitten, 2000). Although research on immediacy behavior has focused on teachers and students, public-speaking environments have similar characteristics.

The three speakers mentioned at the beginning of the chapter (Bill Gates, Jerry Seinfeld, and Oprah Winfrey) use immediacy behaviors. What are these behaviors?

Verbal immediacy behaviors include:

- Using humor sensitively.
- Citing personal instances and experience.
- Establishing yourself as part of the group by using *we, us,* and *our.*
- Praising individuals for their work, actions, or comments.
- Referring to people by name (especially when giving praise).
- Occasionally asking for opinions and questions.
- Conversing with the audience before and after the presentation.

Vocal immediacy behaviors include:

- Conversational tone and natural-sounding speaking voice.
- Enthusiasm showing in voice.
- Effective use of volume and emphasis.
- Natural-sounding pitch variety.
- Effective speaking rate.

Visual immediacy behaviors include:

- Making eye contact.
- Smiling at appropriate times at individuals as well as at the group as a whole.
- Keeping a relaxed posture.
- Gesturing naturally.
- Moving around rather than staying behind the lectern.

To decrease the psychological distance between you and your listeners and replace it with a feeling of closeness, make your verbal, visual, and vocal immediacy behaviors work for you.

Active Critical Thinking

To think further about delivery, complete the following:

- Which type of delivery (verbal, visual, or vocal) works best for you? Give an example.
- For the other two types of delivery, select a tip from the text that you plan to implement in your next speech, and explain why you chose them.

Testing Your Knowledge of Delivery

Directions: Answer the following questions. You can also take this quiz online through your *Essentials of Public Speaking* Online Resources and, if requested, e-mail your responses to your instructor.

___ **1.** T/F A falling pitch inflection at the end of a sentence usually indicates doubt.

___ **2.** T/F Volume is the highness and lowness of vocal tones.

___ **3.** A scientist is preparing a detailed report on acid rain, which will be given before Congress and may be broadcast on national television. Which mode of delivery is best for this kind of presentation?
   a. manuscript
   b. impromptu
   c. memorized
   d. extemporaneous

___ **4.** When you "emphasize" a word with your voice, what happens?
   a. Your volume increases.
   b. Your pitch rises.
   c. Your volume increases and your pitch rises.
   d. None of the above.

___ **5.** Which of the following is *not* an example of an immediacy behavior?
   a. Standing behind the podium or table.
   b. Referring to the group as *we, us,* and *our.*
   c. Citing personal instances or examples.
   d. Referring to people by name.

Answers
1. F; 2. F; 3. a; 4. c; 5. a

So far we have looked at methods of delivery; improving your verbal, visual, and vocal delivery; and the importance of immediacy behaviors to audience learning. Finally, we are ready to discuss the importance of rehearsing your speech.

Practicing Your Speech

There is a big difference between reading about delivering a speech effectively and actually doing it. The only way to transfer what you have read in this chapter to what you do is to practice. Remember that your goal is to sound confident and natural—just the way you do when talking to friends. If you have been visualizing yourself giving an effective speech since reading Chapter 2, you have taken an important first step toward confident delivery. If you haven't been visualizing, find the positive statements you wrote about yourself as a speaker and read them several times. As you read each one (for example, "It's easy for me to make direct eye contact with my audience while speaking"), picture yourself in front of the class, looking directly at the audience and feeling good about it.

Feeling confident while speaking is one of the benefits of practicing. The following suggestions will help you as you practice:

• At least in the beginning, you will probably want to *practice using some type of speaking notes*. However, the fewer the notes, the better! Check with your professor to see if notes are allowed during your speech.

- *Practice your speech out loud.* Thinking through it silently does not count as practice; it may help you check for problems of organization and familiarize yourself with the content, but it won't help at all with your vocal or visual delivery and will help only a little with your verbal delivery. There is no substitute for standing and using your notes and visual aids, practicing your gestures and eye contact, and speaking aloud.

- *If you feel nervous, practice alone at first.* Tape-record yourself in order to get feedback on your vocal delivery, or practice in front of a mirror—research has found this to be an effective practice method (Smith & Frymier, 2006). If possible, practice in a room similar to the one in which you will be speaking. If your practice room does not have the equipment necessary for using your visuals, simulate handling them.

- After you begin to feel comfortable with your speech, *practice in front of friends or family members.* Smith and Frymier (2006) found that students who practiced in front of four or more people made higher grades than those who practiced in front of one to three people. They also found that practicing in front of an audience (regardless of the size) was better than practicing alone. Ask your audience for specific comments on your verbal, visual, and vocal delivery. Practice making direct eye contact and using gestures. If you have a video camera, let a friend film you so that you can observe yourself. If you discover any awkward spots in your talk, decide how to alter the speech to smooth them out.

- When you practice your speech, *practice using your visual aids and any objects.* Videotape yourself if possible, or ask a friend to observe one of your final practices.

- Try to *get plenty of sleep the night before your speech.* On the day of the speech, get to class early so that you can compose yourself, check to see that your notes and visuals are in the proper order, and read through your outline one last time.

- *If you are using PowerPoint, have a backup.* For example, bring an extra CD or USB flash drive; e-mail your slideshow to yourself to access from the Internet; and print off four to six slides per page in case the computer quits working and you need them for notes.

If you are a non-native speaker and have some problems with English or have a noticable dialect, here are some additional suggestions to make sure you are clearly understood by your audience. First, use PowerPoint—making sure that your first slide includes your title and a list of your main points. Also, when you rehearse, do so using a fairly loud volume, making your articulation more pronounced and your speaking rate slower than normally used by native speakers.

Remember: No one expects perfection. If you make a mistake, correct it if necessary and go on. Then forget it. If you have practiced until you feel comfortable with your speech and have visualized yourself giving a successful speech, you should feel excited and confident. Also, although practice is important, don't try to memorize your speech. Each time you practice, the speech should sound

Dwayne Newton/PhotoEdit

Before rehearsing in front of others, practice in front of a mirror (as this speaker is doing). Once you feel comfortable, ask friends or family members to listen and give you suggestions.

a little different. If you leave something out or add something during the actual speech that you had not planned to, the speech will likely have a more spontaneous feel; plus, the audience likely won't realize it—they don't have your outline in front of them. The audience isn't looking for mistakes—they are enjoying your presentation. You should relax and enjoy it as well.

Active Critical Thinking

To think further about speech delivery, complete the following:
- When you think about delivering a speech, what stands out as your main strength? Give an example from one of your previous speeches.
- What main delivery weakness seems to occur when you speak? Explain how you plan to practice for your next speech to minimize this weakness.

Summary

Successfully delivering your message depends on several factors. First, your method of delivery can affect the success of your speech. In most cases, speaking from a manuscript or memorizing your speech should be avoided. Impromptu speaking is a good way to gain confidence in speaking. If you can add a personal or humorous instance, not only will your audience enjoy your speech, but you will feel more relaxed as well. The preferred method of delivery for most classroom speeches is extemporaneous speaking, which involves careful preparation and speaking from brief notes or visual aids.

Another important aspect of your delivery deals with your verbal, visual, and vocal codes. Effective visual delivery entails paying close attention to your appearance, facial expressions, eye contact, posture, movement, and gestures, as well as to the content and handling of your visual aids. Effective vocal delivery is achieved by varying volume, pitch, emphasis, rate, and pauses, as well as making sure your articulation is clear and your pronunciation is correct. The best speaking voice is one that sounds conversational, natural, and enthusiastic. Rarely do people achieve their best speaking voice without practice. Effective verbal delivery results from the use of vivid, specific, simple, and bias-free language. It is also important that your verbal message fit the frames of reference of your listeners. Your delivery can also be enhanced by using immediacy behaviors such as making direct eye contact, smiling, being vocally expressive, using humor, and referring to your audience as *we*. These behaviors reduce the psychological distance between speaker and audience.

The only way to transfer what you have learned from this chapter into a dynamic, believable delivery is to practice. First, visualize yourself giving a successful speech. Then practice your speech aloud using visual aids. You will soon find yourself getting compliments on the way you deliver your speeches.

Essentials of Public Speaking Online CourseMate

Use your Online Resources for *Essentials of Public Speaking* for quick access to the electronic study resources that accompany this chapter. Your Online Resources include access to InfoTrac College Edition, Personal Skill Building Activities and Collaborative Skill Building Activities, a digital glossary, sample speeches, and review quizzes.

Key Terms

adaptors 190	immediacy behaviors	regulators 189
articulation 194	195	upspeak 193
emblems 189	impromptu speech 181	verbal delivery 185
emphasis 193	pauses 193	visual delivery 186
extemporaneous speech	phrases 193	vocal delivery 192
181	pitch 192	vocal variety 192
illustrators 189	pronunciation 194	volume 192
	rate 193	

Personal Skill Building

1. To get an idea of how your voice sounds to others, leave a detailed message on your answering machine or voice-mail system. Do this regularly until your vocal variety and tone project the warmth, enthusiasm, or authority you desire (Decker & Denney, 1993).

2. Make a list of what you think makes a credible speaker, remembering the qualities that were discussed in this chapter. Also create a list of qualities that you think are not desirable in a speaker. Compare your list with those of your classmates. What qualities are common on the lists? How can you avoid or correct the qualities you find undesirable?

3. Find a person in the media whom you believe is a good speaker. Write down what you feel makes him or her a good speaker. How is the selected speaker demonstrating strong visual, vocal, and verbal delivery? Can you identify examples of these qualities? How can you adapt your speaking to include these qualities?

4. Using a database like InfoTrac College Edition, EBSCOhost, or CQ Researcher, conduct a keyword or subject-guide search for the term *gestures*. How many articles did you locate? Read at least two of the articles, and share any speaking tips that you find.

5. Check out the following websites. You can access these sites under the Student Resources for Chapter 8 at the *Essentials of Public Speaking* website.

   - Amy Slagell et al. gives advice in the article "Public Speaking Tips: General Advice for Verbal and Non-Verbal Skill Development." Find the free PDF at **www.cfsph.iastate.edu/TrainTheTrainer/pdfs/GeneralPs.pdf**.

   - Paul Lawrence Vann, a motivational speaker, offers tips on becoming a confident speaker by being well prepared and respecting the audience in his article "Why You Should Never Fear Giving Your Next Speech." Find it at **ezinearticles.com/?why-you-should-never-fear-giving-your-next-speech**.

   - This helpful website from Rice University helps you identify the best way to handle visual aids within a speech and how to recover from visual-aid mistakes: **ruf.rice.edu/~comcoach/handling.html**.

Collaborative Skill Building

1. In small groups of 4 or 6, select two one-minute segments from a speech that uses effective language style. (Use InfoTrac College Edition or EBSCOhost to find a current issue of *Vital Speeches,* or look under the "Student Resources" for Chapters 1, 4, 9, or 11 to 13 on the *Essentials of Public Speaking* website for sample student speeches.) Divide into teams, and practice reading the selections. On the appointed day, a person from each team should have a "read-down"— both students reading the same selection at the same time, each student using good visual and vocal delivery. At the end of each reading, have the group members vote on which speaker held their attention more of the time. Repeat the process until everyone has had a chance to participate in the reading. This activity is fun and shows the importance of good delivery when reading quotes during a speech.

2. In small groups of classmates, select a scene or cutting from a play, a short story, or a children's storybook (such as a Dr. Seuss book). Assign characters or parts to each person, and practice presenting the selection as a readers' theater. (In a readers' theater, participants sit on stools and speak directly to the audience, not to each other, thereby creating the action in the minds of the audience.) Be sure to make your vocal and visual cues fit the story. When the group is pleased with the delivery, present your readers' theatre to another group or to the class. Ask the audience to select two main strengths they observed in your presentation.

Quiz Answers

Answers to Unit Three Quiz on page 179: Test Your Knowledge of Verbal, Visual, and Vocal Delivery.

1. *False.* Although visual aids do add to the interest and enjoyment of the audience, that is only one of the reasons why effective speakers use them. A more important reason is to help listeners remember the main points of the message. You may be surprised to learn that average listeners remember approximately 10 percent of what they hear, but as much as 65 percent of what they hear and see.

2. *False.* Certainly your audience will listen more attentively and, therefore, remember your ideas better when you paint vivid mental pictures of scenes and events. But some well-designed visuals will make your presentation even more powerful. ➔ *See pages 206–207 for a discussion of the use of vivid words.*

3. *False.* Listeners assess visual messages (whether intentional or not) before they even hear any verbal messages. This means that preparation is critical. ➔ *Check Chapter 7 for information you need for effectively organizing your presentations. This chapter includes advice on last-minute verbal, visual, and vocal checks; Chapter 10 includes advice on designing effective visual aids.*

4. *False.* Besides being a valuable source of feedback from your audience, making eye contact with listeners throughout the audience makes them feel that you are one of them and that you care about them. When an audience feels friendly toward you, they listen more attentively and are more likely to believe what you are saying. ➔ *For information on effective delivery, see Chapter 8.*

5. *False.* Regardless of the types of visuals you use, practice is essential if you want to feel confident and give an effective speech. Markerboards and chalkboards have their uses, but for most speaking occasions, a more polished visual aid is recommended. → *See Chapter 10 for types of visual aids and tips for using them effectively.*

6. *False.* With the possibilities offered by computer software, it is tempting to fill your visuals with lots of typefaces, colors, and pieces of clip art. Although you may have created a lovely piece of art, it will not be effective as a visual if it doesn't emphasize main points and group-related data. → *Chapter 10 will give you the information needed to produce visual aids that are the envy of your classmates and colleagues.*

7. *True.* You don't want to alienate your listeners by using sexist language. → *Figure 9.1 suggests gender-neutral alternatives for some common terms.*

8. *False.* Thinking through your speech does not help you make the connection between the brain and the mouth. There is no substitute for practicing your speech aloud while using your notes and visuals. Oral practice will make you feel confident and allow you to give a speech that both you and your audience will enjoy. → *Review Chapter 2 for confidence suggestions.*

9. *False.* Although some textbooks favor using only capital letters on your visuals, and media departments in many organizations use them, research shows that words written in all caps are more difficult to read than those written in both uppercase and lowercase letters. → *See Figure 10.9 for more on the drawbacks of using all capital letters.*

10. *False.* Although memorizing your opening and closing statements is all right if it makes you feel more comfortable, memorizing the entire speech has several drawbacks. Speaking from keyword notes is preferable, because it allows you to speak in a relaxed, conversational way. → *See page 184 to learn more about the drawbacks of speaking from memory.*

9

Perfecting Language Style

FLASH **BACK**

In his *Orator,* Cicero describes three kinds of rhetorical styles—*plain*, *middle*, and *grand*. Skilled rhetoricians were advised to vary their use of styles:

- **The *plain style*,** used to prove or inform, was an "easy" style, subdued in delivery, language, and ornamentation.
- **The *middle style*,** used to gain attention or entertain, was a polished style that included humor, wit, and ornamentation of all kinds.
- **The *grand style*,** reserved for persuasive situations, was eloquent, dramatic, and fiery. However, Cicero cautioned speakers that to use only the Grand style could make them appear demented.

FLASH
FORWARD

Although we don't use the same labels—*plain, middle,* and *grand*—that Cicero used to discuss the delivery styles appropriate for informative, entertaining, and persuasive speeches, there are similarities. For example, a persuasive speech certainly has more forcefulness and dynamism, showing why the audience should agree with a particular position; an informative speech is more conversational and subdued, encouraging audience members to make up their own minds about the material presented; while an entertaining speech is more relaxed, humorous, and witty. However, just as in Cicero's day, audiences have certain expectations of speakers and would be uncomfortable or even disturbed if a speaker used an inappropriate style. *Do you think it's possible for beginning speakers to be flexible in the use of speaking styles, or should they work on a blend of styles to use in all situations? Why or why not?*

Learning Objectives

As you read Chapter 9,

- *Explain* why language choices are so important in a successful speech, and *list* the characteristics of an effective language style.
- *Identify* the important stylistic devices used by professional speakers, and *select* two that you will work to implement in your own speeches.
- *Discuss* how speaker bias (especially gender and culture bias) can show up in the language choices speakers make and what alternatives are available.

Read the following speaker comments, and select the more persuasive one (a or b):

1. a. Although there are three frequently presented arguments in favor of legalizing drugs, none of them holds up under careful scrutiny. In fact, as you will see, all three arguments are based on faulty reasoning. The first fallacious argument is . . .

    b. Let's look at three arguments in favor of drug legalization. The first argument is . . .

2. a. When legislation on sobriety checkpoints comes up for a vote in your county, think about what I've said in making your decision.

    b. When legislation on sobriety checkpoints comes up for a vote in your county, vote yes. It's time we made our roads safe again.

3. a. There are three points that I'd like to cover today about the Electoral College.

    b. There are three points I'd like to cover today that will demonstrate how hopelessly out of date and ineffective the Electoral College really is.

It wasn't difficult to choose, was it? Persuasive language generally specifies a preferred belief or action and is more forceful than informative language. Now that you have given a number of speeches and are aware of some of the strengths and weaknesses of your delivery, it is time to polish your verbal delivery and perfect your use of language style. As a speaker, your use of language can clarify your ideas, add impact and interest to your message, enhance the audience's perception of you as an ethical speaker, and add forcefulness to your main points or arguments.

Why Language Choices Are So Important

To see how changing a single word can create different emotional reactions, consider the following example:

> A boy called to his mother that he saw a "snake." Hurrying to his aid, the boy's amused mother used a broom handle to dislodge what turned out to be a sleeping garden hose.

Reread the sentences, replacing *amused* with (1) *frightened,* (2) *furious,* and then (3) *long-suffering.* How did these words affect your reaction to the anecdote? Your choice of words influences your listeners' reaction to your speech. Language choices are important for three reasons:

1. *Language can clarify your ideas and arguments* by creating vivid mental images for your audience. Even though your listeners may not have personally experienced what you are talking about, they can experience it through the mental image your words create. A good mental image creates both a picture and the accompanying feelings—such as pride, frustration, sadness, or guilt.

2. *Language can influence your audience's attitudes and behaviors.* Advertisers and politicians certainly know the power of language. They know that people who display bumper stickers, campaign buttons, and T-shirts with their logo are more likely to vote for the candidate or remain loyal to the product because, in using these items, they have already committed themselves (Larson, 2010).

3. *Language can make your ideas and arguments personally resonate with audience members.* When the language used makes people "feel" that an idea relates to them personally, they are more likely to pay attention and may even be more persuaded

4. *Language can add to audience interest and enjoyment.* You don't have to be an expert speaker to make your speeches interesting and enjoyable—just use words that are simple, specific, vivid, and forceful (as discussed in the following section).

Active Critical Thinking

To think further about the importance of language choices, complete the following:

- Take a moment to recall your previous speeches. On the basis of evaluation forms and audience comments, in what ways do you use language that is especially effective?
- Which main area do you feel could use some work? Why?

Effective Language Style

Style is the way you use language to express your ideas. Although language choices must be appropriate to the situation, generally the best language is simple, specific, vivid, and forceful.

Simple Language

Good speakers use simple language. Rarely are listeners impressed by speakers who use long, technical words or who sprinkle each sentence with jargon. In other words, there is no reason to use *precipitation* instead of *rain*. During World War II, President Franklin Delano Roosevelt reacted strongly to the wordiness of this government memo about wartime blackout procedures (O'Hayre, 1966):

> Such preparations shall be made as will completely obscure all federal buildings and non-federal buildings occupied by the federal Government during an air raid for any period of time from visibility by reason of internal or external illumination. Such obscuration may be obtained either by blackout construction or by termination of the illumination.

Roosevelt was so offended by the overblown writing that he immediately sent back this rewritten version:

> Tell them that in buildings where they have to keep the work going, to put something over the windows; and, in buildings where they can let the work stop for awhile, to turn out the lights.

Using confusing jargon or unfamiliar technical terminology rather than plain language can have serious consequences in both writing and speaking. For example:

- Between 1999 and 2001 (years of high corporate loss), companies with CEOs who used clear-language lost an average of $4.1 billion; companies with CEOs who used confusing-jargon lost an average of $26.7 billion (Big Spin = Big Losses, 2003).

- Patients with limited reading ability are in real need of plain language from doctors and nurses (in oral instructions as well as in office paperwork). Reading problems "cost the U.S. health care system $73 billion annually" and "increase the risk of hospitalization by 53 percent" (Silverman, 2003).

- The disintegration of the space shuttle *Columbia* in 2003 may have been partly due to confusing language. According to the Columbia Accident Investigation Board (CAIB), the foam that broke off the external tank, hitting the left wing, was labeled by the program managers as an "action" rather than an "in-flight anomaly," giving the incorrect impression that the loss of foam was "not a safety-of-flight issue" (CAIB, 2003, p. 137). Apparently, the seriousness of the situation was obscured by the unclear terminology used.

Specific Language

Specific words are concrete rather than abstract. **Abstract words** describe intangible concepts that are difficult to picture (such as *devotion* or *health*), whereas **concrete words** describe tangible things that listeners can picture (such as *apple* or *smile*). If your words are specific enough, the audience will most likely have a clear picture of your meaning. Which of the following is easier to picture?

My dog is mischievous.

or

My West Highland white terrier may look like an angel, but she has a mischievous heart. When she was a puppy, I left her locked in the kitchen for one hour. She peeled off the wallpaper as far up as she could reach, tugged a loose tile off the floor and ripped it to pieces, and chewed holes in the bottom three slats of the mini blinds. One hour—one puppy! How could we name her anything else but Mischief?

Using specific language is especially important when the intent of your message is to persuade. Remember: The purpose of persuasion is to *influence* choices, not to distort or confuse choices.

Avoid Ambiguous Words Instead of specific words, some speakers use **ambiguous words**—words that have vague, unclear meanings that can be understood in more than one way. When used unintentionally (such as "My children like our cat more than me"), ambiguous words can be confusing; when used deliberately to sway an audience, they are unethical.

For example, instead of presenting a clear stand on taxation, a senator might use the ambiguous phrase *responsibility in taxation and education,* hoping that it will be interpreted positively by people with differing views. When words have ambiguous meanings, listeners use their own frames of reference to interpret them. In the example just mentioned, voters who believe that teachers are underpaid might think the senator is advocating "spending tax dollars" and vote in his favor; those who think that educational spending is too high might think the senator is advocating "cutting educational spending" and also vote in his favor (Larson, 2010, p. 145). Although using specific words that make clear the intended fiscal policy could lose votes for the senator, using ambiguous words to deceive listeners into taking an action that they would not normally take is unethical.

Using a database like InfoTrac College Edition, EBSCOhost, or CQ Researcher, run a keyword search using "*plain language*" (in quotes) and note the wide range of professions complaining about the lack of plain language. You might also run a keyword search using *ambiguity, ambiguity and language,* and *strategic ambiguity* for additional articles.

Ellen DeGeneres—stand-up comedian, talk-show host, and former American Idol judge—is known for her personable and vibrant speaking style.

Avoid Euphemisms Some speakers try to remove emotional overtones from words by using euphemisms. **Euphemisms** are words or phrases with positive overtones (connotations) substituted for those with negative overtones. In some cases this might be a wise thing for a speaker to do. For example, *special* sounds more accepting than *handicapped,* and *husky* doesn't carry the negative connotation of *fat* or *obese.* Considering how upset Americans were after the explosion of the space shuttle *Challenger,* NASA's decision to refer to the crew's coffins as "crew transfer containers" reflected the agency's (perhaps misguided) attempt to diminish the horror. But when a euphemism is used to mask, mislead, or manipulate audience response, it is unethical. This was the case when the phrase "ethnic cleansing" was used to describe the genocide in Bosnia in 1995 or in Sudan in 2004.

Vivid Language

In addition to simple yet specific words, effective speakers use vivid language. For the most impact, use the active rather than the passive voice (active: "Jorge shoved John"; passive: "John was shoved by Jorge"). Vivid speakers avoid vague phrases such as "It is believed," they use a variety of interesting supporting materials, and they speak directly to their listeners as though they were having a private conversation with them. Vivid (concrete) words—especially ones that stimulate mental images in listeners' minds—are also easier to remember (Bryden & Ley, 1983; Hishitani, 1991; Richardson, 2003). For example, words like *friend, snake,* and *corpse* are high-imagery words and are easier to remember than words like *devotion, greed,* and *cost,* which are low-imagery (abstract) words.

Adding some vivid adjectives to the concrete words will enhance the imagery even further (for example, "a long, slimy snake"). Because concrete words are easier to remember, using them in your speech is likely to make your entire message more memorable.

Vivid speakers also use words to paint a mental picture in the minds of listeners. In fact, vivid language is a mental visual aid. Returning to our example of the boy and the "snake," which of the following descriptions paints a clearer picture?

> A child claimed that he saw a large snake, but when his mother found it, it was only a garden hose.

> *or*

> An eight-year-old boy called to his mother that he saw a huge green snake lurking under the porch. Hurrying to his aid, his amused mother used a broom handle to dislodge what turned out to be a sleeping garden hose.

Picture in your mind what you are describing, and you will find that it is easier to transfer this mental picture to your audience through your language.

Forceful Language

As the examples at the beginning of the chapter illustrate, the words you use in a speech can carry varying degrees of force or strength. **Forceful language** (which involves effective use of volume, emphasis, and pitch) is especially important in persuasion—it adds to the audience's confidence in the speaker (Bradac & Mulac, 1984; Gibbons et al., 1991; Sparks et al., 1998).

Let's take a closer look at the third set of speaker comments from the beginning of the chapter. Statement 3a ("There are three points that I'd like to cover today about the Electoral College") not only implies (incorrectly) that this will be an informative speech, but gives no indication of the speaker's position. However, statement 3b ("There are three points I'd like to cover today that will demonstrate how hopelessly out of date and ineffective the Electoral College really is") makes it clear that this will be a persuasive speech, indicates the speaker's position, and conveys confidence through forceful language. The persuasive process has already begun. Even in an informative speech, forceful language can give listeners confidence in you and in your evidence.

Speaking forcefully tends to be harder for women than for men. In a speech called "Taking the Stage: How Women Can Achieve a Leadership Presence," Judith Humphrey (2001), president of the Humphrey Group, gave this advice:

> If you're taking the stage, do so with bold clear language. We find in our work that many women have trouble being direct. Introductory phrases like "in my opinion," "as I see it," or "it's only a thought" downplay our ideas. There's too much apologizing and self-correction in the language women use.

1995. Reprinted courtesy of Bunny Hoest and Parade

"Let's change 'Some of the guys' to 'We the people.'"

When women do express their ideas directly, they often soften the impact. They use weak verbs: "I think," "I will attempt to," "I'm trying to," "I'm not sure." They use qualifiers: "I'd just like to review." They use past tense. For example: "What I wanted to talk about today was our priorities." (Instead of "I'd like to talk about our priorities.") They also use emotional language and the language of dependency—talking about "being concerned" or "needing that."

In contrast, I listen to the strong words of Margaret Thatcher when she told Britons about the campaign to retake the Falkland Islands: "Now we are present in strength on the Falkland Islands. Our purpose is to repossess them. We shall carry on until that purpose is accomplished."

There's no mistaking her steely resolve. Her sentences are short and to the point. She doesn't qualify, apologize, correct or undercut herself (p. 437).

Start by concentrating on one or two of these language characteristics. Tape-record a practice speech session and then listen and evaluate it. Replace vague words with specific and vivid ones, and record your speech again. Repeat the process until you are satisfied with your language choices.

Active Critical Thinking

To think further about language style, complete the following:

- Do you think that using *Post Traumatic Stress Disorder* (PTSD) to label the psychological distress that military personnel experience in war zones causes us to view it differently than if it were labeled *battle fatigue* or *shell shock*? Explain your reasons.
- Think of an euphemism used in society. Is it used to facilitate communication or to obscure it? Why?

Stylistic Devices

In addition to having actual and implied meanings, words can have a texture or "feel"—what persuasion expert Charles Larson (2010) calls the "thematic dimension" of language. This ability of words "to set a mood, a feeling, or a tone or theme" is "their most important persuasive aspect" (p. 152). If your listeners are in the right frame of mind for a particular topic, you will have a better chance of communicating your ideas and concerns to them. Stylistic language devices can help you establish a mood, both in the introduction and during your presentation.

Stylistic devices gain their entertaining and persuasive power by "departing from everyday language usage" (Cooper & Nothstine, 1992; see also Williams & Cooper, 2002). A **stylistic device** either (1) rearranges sentences in unusual ways or (2) changes "the main or ordinary meaning of a word" (p. 168). This section will cover several of the most popular stylistic devices: alliteration and assonance, antithesis, hyperbole, onomatopoeia, personification, repetition and parallelism, and simile and metaphor. Begin by practicing two or three of these devices. Then add more until you have tried them all. Select the ones that seem most valuable to you, and incorporate them into your own style.

Alliteration and Assonance

Alliteration is the repetition of consonants (usually the first or last letter in a word), such as "Each Wednesday, Willy washes his woolens." In a speech titled "Conveying the Environmental Message," Peter G. Osgood (1993) used alliteration with the *c* sound in his conclusion:

> It is a matter of culture and it is a matter of conversion. And finally, it is a matter of leadership, commitment and communication (p. 270).

In his 1961 inaugural address, President John F. Kennedy used several stylistic devices, including alliteration. How many *s* sounds do you hear in this sentence?

> So let us begin anew, remembering on both sides that civility is not a sign of weakness and sincerity is always subject to proof (Kennedy, 2000, p. 251).

Assonance is the repetition of vowel sounds, such as in "The low moans of our own soldiers . . . " (Larson, 2010, p. 140). In his 1961 inaugural address, Kennedy also used assonance several times:

> . . . for only when *our arms are* sufficient beyond doubt . . .

> . . . instruments of peace . . . *We renew* our pledge to *prevent* it from becoming . . . (p. 251).

Don't overdo alliteration and assonance, however. Be especially careful with alliteration. You don't want to sound like President Warren G. Harding, who told his audience at the Republican Convention in 1912:

> Progression is not proclamation nor palaver. It is not pretense nor play on prejudice. It is not of personal pronouns, nor perennial pronouncement. It is not the perturbation of a people passion-wrought, nor a promise proposed (Eigen & Siegel, 1993, p. 467).

Antithesis

Antithesis occurs when a sentence contains two contrasting ideas in parallel phrases. Antithesis can bring contrasts into sharper focus (Hart, 1997), which is probably why antithesis was one of President Kennedy's favorite stylistic devices. Here are three examples of antithesis from his 1961 inaugural address:

> If a free society cannot help the many who are poor, it cannot save the few who are rich (Kennedy, 2000, p. 251).
> Let us never negotiate out of fear, but let us never fear to negotiate (p. 251).
> And so, my fellow Americans, ask not what your country can do for you, ask what you can do for your country (p. 252).

Hyperbole

Hyperbole is extreme exaggeration used for emphasis ("We either vote for this bill, or we die"). In a speech titled "Power, Parity, Personal Responsibility, and Progress," William H. Harris (1993) used both hyperbole and metaphor (both in italics) to impress on his audience the importance of action:

> And the answers will require creativity and discovery. I wish you Godspeed as you create and make your discoveries, but I assure you that *if you neither create nor discover in this essential arena, all of us will reap a whirlwind of despair* . . . (p. 536).

Hyperbole can arouse emotion and stimulate thought, but it must be used carefully so that listeners do not take it at face value or view it as a lie by an unethical speaker.

Onomatopoeia

Although speakers are less likely to use **onomatopoeia**—a device using words that sound like their meanings, such as *buzz, hiss, swish, fizz,* and *ring*—these words can be quite useful in creating a feeling or mood. Martin Luther King Jr. used onomatopoeia many times for effect in his speeches. You are probably most familiar with his use of the word *ring* in his 1963 "I Have a Dream" speech. The way he pronounced the word in "Let freedom ring" created a powerful image of a church bell ringing. And as he repeated it over and over, the ringing seemed to get louder and more intense as he built up to his memorable conclusion:

> So let freedom ring from the prodigious hilltops of New Hampshire. Let freedom ring from the mighty mountains of New York. Let freedom ring from the heightening Alleghenies of Pennsylvania!
> Let freedom ring from the snow-capped Rockies of Colorado!
> Let freedom ring from the curvaceous slopes of California!
> But not only that.
> Let freedom ring from Stone Mountain of Georgia!
> Let freedom ring from Lookout Mountain of Tennessee!
> Let freedom ring from every hill and molehill of Mississippi.
> From every mountainside, let freedom ring. And when this happens . . . when we allow freedom to ring, when we let it ring from every village and every hamlet, from every state and every city, we will be able to speed up that day when all of God's children, black men and white men, Jews and Gentiles, Protestants and Catholics, will be able to join hands and sing in the words of the old Negro spiritual, "Free at last! Free at last! Thank God Almighty, we are free at last!" (King, 2000, p. 262)★ ➤ *See a discussion of King's "Dream" speech in Chapter 8, "Speakers Who Made a Difference," pp. 187–188.*

Through onomatopoeia and dynamic delivery in his "I Have a Dream" speech, Martin Luther King Jr. inspired his listeners.

AFP/Getty Images

Personification

Personification is giving human characteristics or feelings to an animal, object, or concept (as in "Mother Nature"). Used in moderation, this device is effective in clarifying ideas. For example, to clarify the importance of keeping computers in top-notch condition, you might personify the computer, as one student did:

> Your PC unit will be much more cooperative if you remember to defragment the hard drive regularly, since otherwise your computer exhausts itself rummaging through disorganized bits of files.

★Reprinted by arrangement with the Estate of Martin Luther King Jr., c/o Writer's House as agent for the proprietor, New York, NY. Copyright © 1963 Martin Luther King Jr., copyright renewed 1991 by Coretta Scott King.

Repetition and Parallelism

In King's speech, onomatopoeia wasn't the only stylistic device he used. He also used repetition and parallelism. **Repetition**—repeating a word or series of words in successive clauses or sentences (usually at the beginning)—is an effective way to keep listeners' attention. King's repetition of "Let freedom ring" was very effective. Abraham Lincoln, this chapter's featured speaker in "Speaking to Make a Difference," was also fond of using repetition and parallelism as well as many other stylistic devices in his speeches. Read about the stylistic devices he used in his famous Gettysburg Address on page 212.

Parallelism is the grouping of similarly phrased ideas. As you saw in King's speech, parallelism increases the pace and "therefore generates psychological momentum in listeners" (Hart, 1997, p. 151). In his keynote address to the 2004 Republican National Convention, California Governor Arnold Schwarzenegger (2004) used repetition and parallelism:

> My fellow immigrants, my fellow Americans, how do you know if you are a Republican? I'll tell you how.
>
> If you believe that government should be accountable to the people, not the people in the government, then you are a Republican! If you believe a person should be treated as an individual, not as a member of an interest group, then you are a Republican! If you believe your family knows how to spend your money better than the government does, then you are a Republican! If you believe our educational system should be held accountable for the progress of our children, then you are a Republican! . . .

In his address to Congress on September 20, 2001, President George W. Bush gave a stirring address, which was interrupted by applause 31 times (Wilson, 2003). In part, his success was due to the rhythm and momentum created by short, parallel sentences such as: "We will not tire. We will not falter. And we will not fail" (p. 735).

Simile and Metaphor

Similes and metaphors compare dissimilar items in order to clarify one of the items. **Similes** make direct comparisons using *like* or *as* ("Happiness is like ice cream—both can melt away if you aren't careful"). **Metaphors** are implied comparisons and do not use *like* or *as;* instead, they speak of one item as though it were another ("Happiness is an ice cream cone"). Similes and metaphors create vivid images that improve listeners' understanding and retention of your speech. They can also be very persuasive—they can set a positive or negative tone that influences audience attitudes.

→ *Similes and metaphors are similar to figurative comparisons, discussed in Chapter 6.*

In his conclusion, J. Peter Grace (1993) used the following simile to finalize the tone in a speech titled "Burning Money: The Waste of Your Tax Dollars":

> Now there's a lot of talk coming out of Washington these days about reducing the deficit and, at the same time, increasing government spending. Well, let me tell you, that's like trying to lose weight on a diet of french fries and Big Macs (p. 566).

John F. Kennedy's 1961 inaugural address also includes several examples of metaphor (in italics):

> . . . to assist free men and free governments in casting off the *chains* of poverty (Kennedy, 2000, p. 251) . . . And if a *beachhead* of cooperation may push back the *jungle* of suspicion . . . (p. 252).

Remember

Stylistic devices include . . .

- *Alliteration*—repetition of consonants (usually the first or last letter in a word).
- *Antithesis*—two parallel but contrasting ideas contained in one sentence.
- *Assonance*—repetition of vowel sounds.
- *Hyperbole*—deliberate exaggeration.
- *Metaphor*—implied comparison between two items without using *like* or *as*.
- *Onomatopoeia*—use of words that sound like their meanings.
- *Parallelism*—similarly phrased ideas presented in succession.
- *Personification*—assigning human characteristics or feelings to animals, objects, or concepts.
- *Repetition*—a word or series of words repeated in successive clauses or sentences.
- *Simile*—direct comparison between two items using the words *like* or *as*.

Speaking to Make a Difference

Abraham Lincoln is a household name and needs little introduction. As the sixteenth U.S. president, he played a pivotal role in the abolition of slavery and oversaw the Union victory in the American Civil War. Moreover, he is remembered for particularly memorable speeches, such as the Gettysburg Address. Following the bloody battle of Gettysburg during the Civil War, a judge asked that some land be set aside for a national cemetery in which to bury the casualties from the Union. Edward Everett was the main speaker for the dedication ceremony and spoke for two hours; President Lincoln was invited almost as an afterthought to "formally set apart these grounds to their sacred use by a few appropriate remarks" (White, 2005, p. 229) and spoke less than three minutes. Yet how many people remember Everett's name, let alone have read the complete text of his speech? The Gettysburg Address can be found at **www.americanrhetoric.com** by searching for "Abraham Lincoln Gettysburg Address."

Library of Congress

Four score and seven years ago our fathers brought forth on this continent a new nation, conceived in liberty and dedicated to the proposition that all men are created equal.

Now we are engaged in a great civil war, testing whether that nation or any nation so conceived and so dedicated can long endure. We are met on a great battlefield of that war. We have come to dedicate a portion of that field as a final resting place for those who here gave their lives that that nation might live. It is altogether fitting and proper that we should do this.

But, in a larger sense, we cannot dedicate, we cannot consecrate, we cannot hallow this ground. The brave men, living and dead, who struggled here have consecrated it far above our poor power to add or detract. The world will little note nor long remember what we say here, but it can never forget what they did here. It is for us, the living, rather, to be dedicated here to the unfinished work, which they who fought here have thus far so nobly advanced. It is rather for us to be here, dedicated to the great task remaining before us—that from these honored dead we take increased devotion to that cause for which they gave the last full measure of devotion—that we here highly resolve that these dead shall not have died in vain, that this nation under God shall have a new birth of freedom, and that government of the people, by the people, for the people shall not perish from the earth.

History tells us that Lincoln's "few appropriate words" were exactly that: few and highly appropriate. Even the primary speaker, Everett, later informed Lincoln that "I should be glad . . . that I came as near the central idea of the occasion, in two hours, as you did in two minutes" (Everett, 1863). Lincoln's famous Gettysburg Address met with mixed reactions when it was written, but his poignant speech has withstood the critical eye of time and become "one of the most famous compositions in the American language" (Wilson, 2005, p. 69).

Let's explore some of the things that make this speech effective:

- *Antithesis.* A good example of antithesis in the Gettysburg Address comes from the line " . . . or long remember what we say here, but it can never forget what they did here," in which Lincoln uses the opposite ideas of remembering and forgetting to add emphasis to the fact that the place upon which his audience stood was to be a burial ground for soldiers. Other antithetical statements in the Address include lines referencing life/death and preserving the old/celebrating the new (Ryan, 1995, pp. 85–86).

- *Parallelism and the Power of Three (Tricolon).* These two stylistic devices (parallelism and tricolon) were some of Lincoln's favorites—used in more than just the Gettysburg Address—and were often woven together in his speeches (Ryan, p. 85). The famous phrase " . . . government of the people, by the people, for the people . . . " illustrates how well Lincoln used parallelism. He used a tricolon—"three parallel phrases, each consisting of three words, with 'people'

repeated three times" (Ryan, p. 86)—to create a powerful introduction to a powerful closing statement.

- *Repetition.* What is striking about the Gettysburg Address is not that Lincoln used stylistic devices; it is the prowess with which he combined them in such a short speech. In order to drive home the importance of the occasion and to transition into a discussion of the bigger picture (White, p. 247), Lincoln used repetition with parallelism and a tricolon. "But, in a larger sense, we cannot dedicate, we cannot consecrate, we cannot hallow this ground."

Lincoln's use of antithesis, parallelism, tricolon, and repetition are just a few of the stylistic devices that made the Gettysburg Address go down in history as one of the greatest American speeches. When the historians of Lincoln's time wrote, "We have a President without brains" (Wilson, 2005, p. 68), one has to wonder which of today's underappreciated speakers will be lauded in a hundred years.

Questions: How effective are stylistic devices in forming a relationship with the audience? Which stylistic devices do you feel are the strongest? Why?

Test Your Knowledge Quiz

CourseMate

Testing Your Knowledge of Stylistic Devices

Directions: Here are excerpts from eight speeches. Identify the stylistic device(s) in each excerpt. You can also take this quiz through your *Essentials of Public Speaking Online Resources* and, if requested, e-mail your responses to your instructor.

_____ 1. "The mother of all wars." —Saddam Hussein's prediction of the 1991 Gulf War

_____ 2. " . . . and that government of the people, by the people, for the people shall not perish from the earth." —Abraham Lincoln (1983)

_____ 3. "America is not like a blanket—one piece of unbroken cloth, the same color, the same texture, the same size. America is more like a quilt—many patches, many pieces, many sizes, and woven and held together by a common thread." —Jesse Jackson (2000, p. 274)

_____ 4. "Attitude, not aptitude, determines altitude." —Richard L. Weaver II (1993)

_____ 5. "Fellow citizens, we observe today not a victory of party, but a celebration of freedom . . . ." —John F. Kennedy (2000, p. 250)

_____ 6. "But, in a larger sense, we cannot dedicate, we cannot consecrate, we cannot hallow this ground." —Abraham Lincoln (1983)

_____ **7.** "Ours is a nation that has shed the blood of war and cried the tears of depression." —George Bush (1992)

_____ **8.** "Tax money flows into Washington, irrigating the bureaucratic gardens." —James P. Pinkerton (2000)

Answers
1. Hyperbole
2. Repetition and parallelism
3. Simile
4. Alliteration
5. Antithesis
6. Repetition and parallelism
7. Personification
8. Metaphor

Active Critical Thinking

To think further about stylistic devices, complete the following:

- Which stylistic devices do you think will be the most effective with your classroom audience? Why?
- Using an outline for a speech you have given or one you plan to give, select two or three stylistic devices and write them out in complete sentences. Be prepared to share them with a classmate; see if he or she can identify the devices used.

Biased Language

The only message that counts is the one that gets received. In other words, what you meant to say is less important than what the audience thought you said. Not only can your use of language enhance the effectiveness of your speech, it can also have negative effects if you aren't careful. Language can indicate speaker bias and create listener bias. Gender and culture are the two most common areas of biased language used by speakers.

Gender Bias

Avoid using *he* as a generic term to refer to both males and females. Although you may mean both male and female when you use generic terms, *he* conjures up male images in the minds of many audience members (Hamilton, 1988). A study of college students conducted in 1993 found that both male and female students tended to use masculine pronouns when referring to a person who is a judge, an engineer, or a lawyer, and to use feminine pronouns for nurses, librarians, and teachers (Ivy et al., 1993). According to Diana K. Ivy and Phil Backlund (2008), when speakers use generic masculine words such as *he, mankind, sportsman,* and *workmanship,* or feminine terms such as *stewardess, waitress,* and *actress,* they are helping to maintain sex-biased perceptions. → *See Figure 9.1 for lists of some common gender-specific terms and suggested alternatives.*

Culture Bias

Because listeners supply the meanings of words on the basis of their own frames of reference, you must choose your language carefully. The more diverse your

Biased Words and Phrases	Gender-Neutral Alternatives
Anchorman	Anchor, Newscaster
Actress	Actor
Chairman	Chair, Chairperson, Coordinator
Fellow classmates	Classmates
Fireman	Firefighter
Lady, Girl, Gal, or Doll	Woman
Mailman or Postman	Mail carrier, Postal worker
Mankind	Humankind, Humanity, People
Man-Made	Artificial, Synthetic, Manufactured
Policeman or Policewoman	Police officer
Signing your John Hancock	Signing your name
Stewardess or Steward	Flight attendant

Figure 9.1

Alternatives to Gender-Specific Terms

Source: Diana K. Ivy and Phil Backlund. *Exploring GenderSpeak: Personal Effectiveness in Gender Communication.* New York: McGraw-Hill, 2004. By permission of authors.

audience, the more likely it is that their frames of reference will differ from yours. By the year 2025 in the United States, it is expected that non–Hispanic whites will drop to 60 percent of the population, while both the Hispanic and Asian populations will double (Wellner, 2003). The most effective speakers are sensitive to the diverse backgrounds of their listeners and make their language as free of culture bias as possible. ➡ *For more on gender and speaking, see Chapter 3; for more on frames of reference, see Chapter 1; for more on analyzing audience differences, see Chapter 4.*

Active Critical Thinking

To think further about bias and language, complete the following:

- Give an example of gender or culture bias that was applied to you (or someone you know). How did it affect you (or the person in your example), and how did it affect the communication in general?
- Conversations often involve *marking*, which means that a person's gender, cultural background, or other characteristics are mentioned even when the descriptor is irrelevant (e.g., "woman doctor"). Do you consider marking to be a sign of bias or just a tool in effective communication? Why?

Sample Student Speech: "Endometriosis" By Rebecca Decamp

The following persuasive speech, "Endometriosis," deals with the dangerous affects of endometriosis and was given by Rebecca DeCamp to her speech class and as a persuasive contest selection at the 2009 Phi Rho Pi National Tournament. The speech was to be memorized and last no more than 10 minutes. As you read this speech and watch it on the *Essentials of Public Speaking* website under "Student Resources for Chapter 9," notice Rebecca's language style. Was her use of language simple, specific, vivid, and forceful? Did she use any stylistic devices? What specific changes would you recommend to make this speech more persuasive?

Sample Persuasive Speech

ENDOMETRIOSIS

by Rebecca DeCamp

At the age of 26, Laurie Calcaterra was ready to start a family, but after a few years of trying, she was unable to conceive. Laurie started having pelvic pain that the doctors couldn't figure out. She started missing work around her periods since she couldn't walk. Finally, one day, she was in so much pain her husband rushed her to the emergency room. After an ultrasound, the doctors discovered that she had a large cyst on her right ovary. Taken directly to surgery, they found that Laurie has late stages of endometriosis.

Nearly 5.5 million women in the United States are affected by endometriosis according to the *Contra Costa Times of Walnut Creek California* on February 20, 2009. That is twice the amount of patients with Alzheimer's and seven times as many as those with Parkinson's. To help us understand the affects of endometriosis, let's look at what endometriosis is, then the new cause of endometriosis, and finally what the government, industry and even we can do to solve this problem.

Let's begin with a look at what endometriosis is. Endometriosis is a crippling disease with three ineffective cures. The definition of endometriosis in the July 21, 2009, *Irish Times* is a condition in which cells from the lining of the womb travel to other parts of the body, and often adhere to the ovaries, fallopian tubes and abdominal cavity. These patches respond to the hormones of the menstrual cycle and each month they thicken, build up with blood and then break down. But, unlike the lining of the womb, they have nowhere to go and can cause damage, like inflammation, internal scarring and adhesions. The most common symptoms include increasing levels of pain before and during periods, unusually long and heavy periods, painful urination, inability to have sex, and in most cases infertility.

To some, these symptoms can sound like normal period pain or "cramps." Let me assure you that women with endometriosis are in pain well beyond the normal limits. During their periods, women with endometriosis usually don't move around much. The increasing levels of pain manifest into days that they are unable to walk. If it isn't the pain that has these women stay home, then it is the heavy bleeding that keeps them close to a bathroom. In many cases they change a tampon or pad every thirty minutes as opposed to every 4 to 6 hours. Endometriosis can cause pain depending on where the adhesions are located. There may be only a little on a sensitive internal organ that can cause severe pain, but there can also be internal scarring that attaches the organs together, sometimes causing the uterus to completely flip over.

So, how do we cure such terrible affects of this disease? Certainly there must be some good medical research going on to prevent a disease of this magnitude. But there isn't a cure. Women with endometriosis are given only three options. First, they can start taking continuous birth control, which prevents a period at all. However, this causes many side effects and doesn't help when a couple is trying to conceive. The second option, which is for later stages of endometriosis, offers a shot doctors can administer that is called Lupron, which shuts down estrogen production and causes your body to go into early menopause. Lupron has a whole other set of side effects, like early osteoporosis. And the third option is having a hysterectomy, which is the complete removal of a woman's uterus and ovaries. Surprisingly, after a hysterectomy, some women still suffer from the pain of adhesions not removed in the abdominal cavity.

Now that we've seen what endometriosis is, how it affects women and what cures are available, I want to talk about a new dominant cause of endometriosis that appears to contribute to endometriosis—dioxins and feminine hygiene products. According to the *EPA,*

Sample Persuasive Speech *(continued)*

on September 22, 2009, dioxins are an accidental by-product of a multitude of industrial processes in which chlorine is present—such as chemical and plastics manufacturing, pesticide and herbicide production, and pulp and paper bleaching.

This may seem like something that wouldn't affect anyone that doesn't live directly by a plant that produces these products, but there is something that women use once a month that is. According to the *U.S. Food and Drug Administration* on January 27, 2009, tampons and sanitary pads made of rayon or bleached cotton contain low levels of dioxins.

These levels are tested in parts per trillion, so the risk was originally thought of as low. The *National Institutes of Health* has been researching health risks to women, including counts of endometriosis from the presence of dioxins. They found that dioxins build up in the body over time in a process of bioaccumulation and they concentrate in fatty tissues. If the National Institutes of Health know about this, why are these dioxins still allowed in our most sensitive products, you may be wondering.

Companies haven't changed because of the money being made on these products. *Proctor & Gamble* reported that the *Tampax* brand is one of their half-billion-dollar brands in their 2008 year-end report. "Let's do the math," says the November 10, 2008, *Gazette from Montreal:* "If a woman used four tampons and four pads per day, five days a month for about 35 years, that adds up to 16,800 tampons and pads . . . " Now, for a woman with endometriosis, changing every half hour for even 12 hours results in 24 tampons and pads for five days for 35 years . . . this adds up to 50,400 tampons and pads. Companies like *Kimberly-Clark,* producer of *Kotex*, who report in their annual financials that they net 8.3 billion, *Playtex Products Inc.,* and *McNeil-Personal Products Company* who produce *O.B.* tampons also report in the millions. You see why the big companies are not willing to change—we really are talking about millions and billions of dollars these companies are making on feminine products.

Now that we have talked about what dioxins are, where they come from, and why big companies aren't doing anything to change from what they are currently producing, I want to talk about solutions on a government, industry and personal level. Solutions require immediate action on the part of our government, the companies that make tampons, and from each of us. As stated in our very own Constitution, our government is here to "establish justice, insure domestic tranquility, provide for the common defense, promote the general welfare, and secure the blessings of liberty to ourselves and our posterity."

The research is out there; it is just not being enforced. There is legislation, introduced in Congress back in January 2003, about health risks to women from tampons. But rules don't make one bit of difference if they are not enforced. The USFDA was put in place to make sure those ingredients, purposefully in a product or not, are safe for use. The *National Center for Toxicological Research* has a goal to "Strengthen and improve scientific and human capital management and expand training and outreach to retain and train scientific experts critical to address FDA's scientific needs," as reported on their website last updated on July 10th, 2009.

If the legislation and government enforcement were effective, the companies would have to follow suit. Go to any of the companies' websites that I mentioned before and you will see on all of them a section about Toxic Shock Syndrome, a disease that is related to the absorbency of a tampon and the length of time you leave a tampon inside your body, but not anywhere will you see anything about dioxins. These companies should have an organic option and start putting information on their web pages about the dangers of dioxins.

As for the rest of us, our action should be in education. As a whole, women's periods are still a "hush-hush" subject. We all should be talking about it. Not just mother to daughter, but single father to daughter as well. There are some alternative products out there. Neither are

Sample Persuasive Speech *(continued)*

these organic products advertised nor are they readily available, but we can all start asking for them at our local grocery stores. Products like Seventh Generation and Natracare are two producers of organic non-chlorine bleached tampons. They are usually found in upscale supermarkets like Whole Foods and Market Street and are more expensive than their dioxin-carrying counterparts. But if we all start asking for them, those big companies may find that they have to change to the new market trends and accommodate us. The more we talk about it in public the more women and young girls will know about the seriousness of not talking and not knowing. We could have a huge impact.

Today, we have discussed what endometriosis is, the new dominant cause—dioxins, and what solutions there are. Women are creatures of habit—the products that your mother first bought you, you will buy your growing daughter when the time comes. I believe that the only way to change our current path is thru research and education. Laurie Calcaterra, my sister, is currently on her first round of Lupron. Every day is a new experience for her. Between the mood swings, bone pain and night sweats, she is learning how to make her way through this ordeal. Let's all be a part of the solution so that cases like Laurie's become a thing of the past.

References:

1. Beaudin, M. (2008, November 10). Time of the month revisited; 'Women look at the DivaCup like it fell from outer space,' but reusable feminine hygiene products earn good reviews—and converts—among a group of local women. *The Gazette (Montreal)*. Retrieved from **http://thegazette.canwest.com**.
2. DeVito, M. J., & Schecter, A. (2009, January 27). Exposure assessment to dioxins from the use of tampons and diapers. *Environmental Health Perspectives*, 1(1), 23–28. Retrieved from **http://www .endometriosisassn.org**.
3. *The Irish Times*. (2009, July 21). East meets west for treatment of endometriosis.
4. Proctor & Gamble year-end financial report (unaudited). (2008, December 22). Retrieved from **http://www.pg.com/investors/annualreport2008/financials**.
5. U.S. EPA. (2009, September 22). Risk characterization of dioxin and related compounds—Draft Dioxin Reassessment. Washington D.C., Bureau of National Affairs. Retrieved from **http://www .endometriosisassn.org/pdfs/Endo-and-Dioxins.pdf**.
6. *U.S. Food* and *Drug Administration Report*. (2009, January 17). Tampons, asbestos, dioxin & toxic shock syndrome. Retrieved from **http://www.endometriosisassn.org/pdfs/Endo-and-Dioxins.pdf**.
7. Yadegaran, J. (2009, February 20). Endometriosis a painful, puzzling reproductive disease. *Contra Costa Times* (Walnut Creek, California). Retrieved from **http://www.contracostatimes.com**.

Summary

Although effective organization, content, and delivery are essential for a successful speech, perfecting your language style adds the polish that makes your speech shine. The most effective language is simple, specific, vivid, and forceful. Language creates mental images in the minds of your listeners, influences audience attitudes and behaviors, and adds interest and enjoyment to your speeches. Professional speakers use a variety of stylistic devices: alliteration and assonance, simile and metaphor, onomatopoeia, repetition and parallelism, antithesis, hyperbole, and personification. These devices are especially important in persuasive speaking, because words can set a mood, develop a feeling, or generate a theme. If listeners are in the right frame of mind for a particular topic, you will have a better chance of communicating your ideas and concerns to them. Of course, you must keep your speech free of gender and culture bias.

Essentials of Public Speaking Online CourseMate

Use your Online Resources for *Essentials of Public Speaking* for quick access to the electronic study resources that accompany this chapter. Your Online Resources include access to InfoTrac College Edition, Personal Skill Building Activities and Collaborative Skill Building Activities, a digital glossary, sample speeches, and review quizzes.

Key Terms

abstract words 205	metaphors 211
alliteration 209	middle style 202
ambiguous words 205	onomatopoeia 210
antithesis 209	parallelism 211
assonance 209	personification 210
concrete words 205	plain style 202
euphemisms 206	repetition 211
forceful language 207	similes 211
grand style 202	style 204
hyperbole 209	stylistic device 208

Personal Skill Building

1. Try to develop three stylistic devices for use within your speech. After you have developed these, see if your classmates can identify which stylistic devices you are using.

2. Examine local and national headlines in the news. Are the papers using the most specific language possible? See if you can find examples in which the reader could find more than one meaning in a headline. Share these headlines in class to evoke discussion on the importance of specific language.

3. Compare and contrast speakers who use informative language with speakers who use forceful language. What makes the two language styles so obvious? Do you think it would be possible to be persuasive while using informative language? Make a list of words more likely to be used in an informative speech, and contrast it with another list of words you might expect to hear in a persuasive speech.

4. Use a database like InfoTrac College Edition, EBSCOhost, or ProQuest to conduct keyword searches to find two examples of the following: "*stylistic devices*" (in quotes), *speak★ style* (which will locate speaking style, speaker style, speaker's style, etc.), *metaphor in language, metaphor and language,* and any other stylistic devices that interest you.

5. Check out the following websites. (You can access these sites using your Online Resources for *Essentials of Public Speaking,* Chapter 9).

- Read the article "How to Achieve Better Impressions in Computer-Mediated Communication" by Yuliang Liu and Dean Ginther from the Department of Psychology and Special Education at Texas A&M Commerce. The article can be found on ERIC by searching the name of the article or the authors.

- This website gives an excellent resource for further explaining stylistic devices and how they are best used with rhetoric: **www.ego4u.com/en/cram-up/writing/style**.

- Read the article "The Power of Persuasive Language," and study the reasons why correct language is so vital to the success of a speech. Go to **ezinearticles.com** and search for "The Power of Persuasive Language."

- The History Channel at **history.com** features many famous speakers. To listen to the language used by these speakers, click "Great Speeches," then click on the "Videos" link on the left. Another excellent site for reading speeches and listening to great speakers is **americanrhetoric. com**. Browse the site or go to the "Top 100 Speeches" link. Most of the speeches featured in "Speaking to Make a Difference" in each chapter come from **americanrhetoric.com**.

Collaborative Skill Building

1. In groups of three or four select a well-known public figure with a distinctive speaking style. Separate the speaker's visual and vocal techniques from his or her verbal language techniques. Try to determine what stylistic devices this person uses. Share your discoveries with another group or the entire class.

2. In small groups of three to five, go to **YouTube** and listen to Taylor Mali, a slam poet, read "Totally like whatever, you know?" Google *slam poetry* and locate two good samples of the genre that present an argument and support the argument with ideas and language use. Select the poem the group likes best and do the following:

   (1) Analyze the language used in the poem for stylist devices and how well these devices work;

   (2) practice reading the poem, making the language come alive;

   (3) select a group member to perform the poem for other groups or the class; and

   (4) follow the presentation with a discussion of the language used. *Activity adapted from Carmack (2009).*

3. In small groups of four, work together to make sure that each member's persuasive speech includes a minimum of two stylistic devices—three or four would be better. Once these devices have been added, each member should practice verbally delivering these stylistic devices to the group until they are clear and smooth.

4. Read the following passage from a speech about health care by James S. Todd (1993), executive vice president of the American Medical Association. In small groups, determine how many different stylistic devices you can find. Compare answers with another group.

There is no quick fix. It is essential we do it right, and that will not be easy.

All any of us can do is watch—and wait—and sometimes worry.

If there is one message I have today, it is this: The physicians of America are worried.

Don't get me wrong. We're not worried that change is coming. That we welcome. What worries us is the strong possibility that real change won't occur at all.

We're worried that politics and miscalculation will conspire to keep the administration from achieving the kind of meaningful reform the president promised during his campaign.

We're worried that the Clinton plan may be too enormous to comprehend, too complex to explain, too expensive to defend . . . Senator Phil Gramm says managed competition is like a five-legged animal. It might work, but we sure don't see any running around in nature . . .

We're worried that the administration's package of health care benefits could turn into a high-priced Christmas tree, one that's so loaded with ornaments the cost will be prohibitive (p. 523).

10

Preparing Effective Visual Aids

FLASH **BACK**

Although ancient orators weren't aware of our current research on picture memory, they did know the importance of vividness. They knew that audiences were more likely to pay attention to and be persuaded by visual images painted by the speaker. In his *Rhetoric* (Book III, Chapters 10–11), Aristotle describes the importance of words and graphic metaphors that should "set the scene before our eyes." He defines *graphic* as "making your hearers see things" (Aristotle [translated by W. R. Roberts], 1971, pp. 663–664).

FLASH **FORWARD**

Creating visual images with language is just as important today as it was in ancient times even if you plan to use visual aids. When you use storytelling or present a detailed factual or hypo-thetical narrative, follow the advice of Walter Fisher in his **Narrative Paradigm** (Fisher, 1987). According to Fisher, a good narrative must have both probability and fidelity. Your narrative has *probability* if it is clear and your characters behave as real people; it has *fidelity* if your story "rings true" to your audience because it is culturally and historically accurate. *What well-known speakers, politicians, or educators have you heard that tell stories with probability and fidelity?*

Learning Objectives

As you read Chapter 10,

- *Explain* the benefits that the use of visual aids plays in a successful speech and the types of visual aids most often used.
- *Identify* several guidelines and tips to use in planning your visual aids.
- *List* the basic design principles to use with computer-generated slides and *discuss* why each is so important to a polished and professional visual presentation.
- *Identify* several guidelines and tips to use in designing effective text and graphic slides
- *List* and *discuss* ways to customize your computer slides; *discuss* guidelines for effectively using various types of visual aids during a presentation.

IMAGINE THAT YOU GO INTO A PHARMACY LOOKING FOR BREATH MINTS AND SEE two brands available. One brand's mints are small, oval, and brown and have no scent. They are in a plain, white plastic container with the brand name printed in a nondescript font. The price for these mints is very reasonable. The other brand's mints, which cost three times as much, look homemade and smell like peppermint. The mints are wrapped in a paper that crinkles when you touch it and packaged in an attractive tin with the brand name printed in a nostalgic typeface. Which would you purchase? According to Claudia Kotchka, Procter & Gamble's vice president for design innovation and strategy (from 2001–2008), not only would you be more likely to choose the mint with the interesting, visual packaging, you would be willing to pay up to 400 percent more for it (Reingold, 2005)!

Kotchka knew that the visual aspects of a product make a difference in customer satisfaction. In fact, she worked to get her P&G designers to "listen with their eyes" (Reingold, ¶12) so that the products they design do more than meet a need, they also "infuse delight into customers' lives" (Reingold, ¶4). For speakers, interesting and powerful visual aids make comprehension of facts and ideas easier to grasp and easier to remember. The can also affect listener attitudes and leave them with an overall feeling of enjoyment. Unfortunately, many speakers (including instructors) either don't use visual aids or use ones that are overcrowded and difficult to read. Let's look more closely at the many benefits of using visual aids as a part of your presentations.

Benefits of Using Visual Aids

Winston Churchill and Martin Luther King Jr. were both great speakers who were riveting without the help of visual aids. They were speakers who could create pictures in the minds of their audiences through vivid words, narratives, analogies, and other supporting materials. Such techniques are very important, but for most of us, we still need visual aids—especially in speeches containing complex, technical information. Today's speakers who know the power of visual aids are reluctant to give presentations without them because of the following powerful benefits.

Visual Aids Speed Comprehension and Add Interest

The saying "a picture is worth a thousand words" is usually true. A single visual aid can save you many words and, therefore, time. A look at right brain/left brain theory explains why visuals speed listener comprehension. While the left hemisphere of the brain specializes in analytical processing, the right hemisphere specializes in simultaneous processing of information and pays little attention to details (Bryden & Ley, 1983; Russell, 1979). Speakers who use no visual aids or only charts and statistics are asking the listeners' left brains to do all the work. After a while, even a good left-brain thinker suffers from information overload, begins to make mistakes in reasoning, and loses interest. In computer terminology, "the system shuts down." The right brain, however, can quickly grasp complex ideas presented in graphic form (Thompson & Paivio, 1994).

To illustrate this point, look at the statistical data on advertising expenditures in Table 10.1. In six seconds, can you tell which advertising

Table 10.1 Statistical Data in Table Form Can Often Be Difficult to Grasp

Advertising Expenditures in Millions (247,472 represents $247,472,000,000)		
Medium	2000	2004	2008
Broadcast TV	$44,802	$46,264	$43,734
Direct mail	44,591	52,191	59,622
Magazines	12,370	12,247	12,960
Newspapers	49,050	46,614	35,788
Radio	19,295	19,581	17,535
Yellow pages	13,228	14,002	13,844
Total	**247,472**	**263,766**	**270,767**

Source: U.S. Bureau of the Census. *Statistical Abstract of the United States, 2010.* Washington, D.C.: GPO, Table 1243, p. 767.

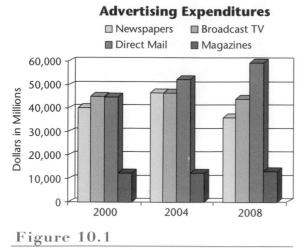

Advertising Expenditures

Figure 10.1

Statistical Data in Graph Form on Advertising Expenditures (Easier to Grasp)

expenditure is now the number one business expenditure? Probably not. Now look at the data presented in the form of a graph in Figure 10.1. At a glance, you can tell that although direct mail was even with broadcast TV in 2000, by 2008 it had moved to the highest expenditure. Therefore, when you need to include complicated data in a speech, comprehension will be quicker and more complete if you present the data in visual form.

Visual Aids Improve Audience Memory and Recall of Content

Ralph Nichols, the father of research on listening, maintains that a few days after a verbal presentation, listeners have forgotten most of what they heard. He theorizes that even good listeners remember no more than 25 percent—and probably much less (Wolff et al., 1983). In fact, as shown in Figure 10.2, 10 percent recall is what you can expect from listeners when no visual aids are used (Zayas-Baya, 1977–1978). But recall improves dramatically when speakers use high-quality visual aids (Huang & Pashler, 2007). Research by the University of Minnesota and 3M Corporation found that speeches using visual aids improved immediate recall by 8.5 percent and improved delayed recall (after three days) by 10.1 percent (Vogel et al., 1986, 1990). Hamilton (1999) found that audience recall of an informative presentation was 18 percent better when visual aids were used than when they were not.

When pictures and color are added to visuals, audience memory of content is improved even more:

- **Visual aids that include a picture or image produce better recall**. Visual pictures and images are easier to remember than printed words or spoken words (Perecman, 1983). Therefore, visual aids are more likely to stimulate recall when they include pictures and images—especially when you follow these four guidelines:

1. *Use pictures and images with some explanatory words* (written words should be brief; spoken words can be longer). Summarizing research in instructional media, E. P. Zayas-Baya presents statistics showing that when verbal and visual information are presented together, they are more effective than either verbal or visual information alone (see Figure 10.2). Richard Mayer, in his book *Multimedia Learning* (2009), calls this the **coherence principle** and says that people learn better when pictures and words are used together.

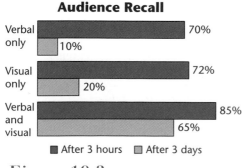

Audience Recall

Figure 10.2

Audience Recall Rates Are Greater When Speakers Use Visual Aids

2. *Place your pictures and images immediately next to the words they represent.* Not only should verbal and visual information be presented together, but according to Mayer (2009) and his **contiguity principle**, audiences learn better when pictures are placed side by side with their explanatory words.

3. *Make sure your pictures and images serve as memory anchors.* Selecting a picture just so you can have a picture will likely hamper audience recall. However, if you choose the picture carefully, it will summon up a main point or concept to your listeners well after the presentation is over—in other words, the picture serves as an "anchor" (Thompson & Paivio, 1994; Alesandrini, 1982).

4. *Select pictures and images that are as vivid as possible.* A picture of your dog looking cute would be a normal picture; a picture of your dog eating cake while wearing a party hat would be a vivid picture. Vivid pictures and vivid mental images are coded in both the left and right hemispheres of the brain, making them easier to store and retrieve (Perecman, 1983; Soto & Humphreys, 2007). You can also improve the memory of spoken words by making them vivid so they stimulate mental images in the listener's minds (Hishitani, 1991).

- **Color visual aids produce the best recall.** Not only is audience recall better when visual aids are used, but it is best when color visuals are used. For example, the Bureau of Advertising found that recall of ad content is 55% to 78% greater for color ads than for black-and-white ads (Johnson, 1990, p. 7). Hamilton (1999) found that high-quality color visuals used in informative speeches produced better recall than did poor-quality color visuals and definitely better than did black-and-white visuals (regardless of their quality). Although we remember content presented in color better than we do black-and-white content, not all color is remembered equally well. For example, people remember the color *yellow* better than they do any other color and remember the color green less than they do any other color (Bynum et al., 2006).

Visual Aids Decrease Presentation Time

One researcher estimates that the average supervisor spends as much as 40 percent of the workweek in meetings and conferences (Tortoriello et al., 1978). Because people can comprehend information faster and more completely when visual aids accompany the verbal explanation, meetings take less time if visuals are used. The study by the University of Minnesota and 3M Corporation mentioned previously found that the use of visuals could reduce the length of the average business meeting by 28 percent (Vogel et al., 1990).

Visual Aids Improve Speaker Credibility

If you are in a situation where your credibility is low or unknown to others, visuals are especially important. One study found that low-credibility speakers who use visual aids can overcome an audience's view of them as untrustworthy and nonauthoritative, and can elicit the same level of audience retention as high-credibility speakers (Seiler, 1971). The study conducted by the University of Minnesota and 3M Corporation also found that an "average" presenter who uses visuals can be as effective as an "expert" presenter who uses no visuals (Vogel et al., 1990). The minute the audience sees the first visual aid, they are surprised; by the second, they decide that the speaker is obviously prepared and settle back to enjoy the speech.

Types of Visual Aids

Although the options for visual aids are limited only by your imagination and the speaking situation, we will look at the following types that are typically the most often used by speakers: the easiest-to-use visuals—objects, models, and handouts; flip charts and posters; markerboards and chalkboards; audiovisual aids; and, finally, the most-used visuals—computer-generated slides.

- **Objects, Models, and Handouts**—*Objects* can be effective visual aids as long as they are large enough to be seen yet small enough to display easily. To keep from distracting audience members, wait until your presentation is completed before passing objects around the audience for a closer view. If an object is too small, too large, or too dangerous to be used as a visual aid, you might use a *model* instead. For example, a model car, a model office layout, or a model of an atom would all be effective visual aids. *Handouts* can be both a help (they limit the audience's need to take notes) and a distraction (the audience may read the handout instead of listening to you). So unless you need the audience to do something with the material while you are speaking (like answer a survey or mark a checklist), it's better to give handouts at the conclusion of your speech. But don't forget to tell your audience in the introduction to your speech that a handout will be provided. → *For specifics on handling objects and handouts, see Guidelines at the end of the chapter.*

Notice how the speaker is standing close to the easel to keep from blocking the audience's view.

Jacobs Stock Photography/BananaStock/Jupiter Images

- **Flip Charts and Posters**—Flip charts and posters tend to set an informal mood, are simple to prepare, and can add a feeling of spontaneity to your presentation if you write on them as you speak. On the other hand, flip charts and posters are awkward to transport and store and can be used only with small groups (fewer than thirty people). → *For specifics on handling flip charts and posters, see Guidelines at the end of the chapter.*

- **Markerboards and Chalkboards**—Markerboards are usually preferable to chalkboards, because the glossy white of the markerboard is more attractive and there is no messy chalk residue. Also, small markerboards can be placed on an easel and moved closer to the audience for a more personal feel. However, both markerboards and chalkboards have several drawbacks, which include making speakers look less prepared and less professional than is the case with other types of visuals and requiring the speaker's back to be turned toward the audience while writing on the board. ➡ *For specifics on handling markerboards and chalkboards, see Guidelines at the end of the chapter.*

- **Audiovisual Aids**—If used with care, audiovisual aids can add interest to any speaking situation. For example, in a speech about skateboarding, you could show one or two brief cuts (filmed on your iPhone or Flip Camera or from a DVD) of a skateboarder performing various moves, a YouTube video clip, or podcast. To emphasize something special, use slow motion or pause, or replay a segment. Refer to the databases at your library, which provide access to video clips, audiotapes, podcasts, and more to enhance your presentation. PowerPoint allows you to insert video (such as MPEG or AVI) into your computer presentation. ➡ *For specifics on handling audiovisual aids, see Guidelines at the end of the chapter.*

- **Computer-Generated Slides**—The most popular visual aid in the business world today is the **computer-generated slide**. Computer-generated visuals (most often called slides) can be divided into two kinds: text and graphic. **Text slides** consist mainly of words with an occasional picture, drawing, or piece of clip art (See Visuals A–F in the color insert). **Graphic slides** use organizational charts, flow charts, diagrams and schematic drawings, maps, pictures, and/or graphs to present information with just enough words to clarify the visual (see Visuals G–J in the color insert). **Graphs** depict numerical data in visual form. *Line graphs* show changes in relationships over time, *bar graphs* compare countable data at a specific moment in time; *pie charts* and *stacked bar graphs* show parts of the whole or percentages; and *pictographs* replace bars with graphic symbols or icons.

Steve Jobs, our "Speaking to Make a Difference" speaker for this chapter, did a great job using computer-generated slides (both text and graphic) in his presentation introducing the iPhone at the 2007 Macworld Expo. Affordable computer hardware and software make it possible to produce professional, sophisticated electronic and multimedia shows with color, animation, sound, photos, and video clips. One of the most popular software programs for designing visual aids is Microsoft's PowerPoint. Many of the slides in this chapter were produced with PowerPoint. Of course, not all computer-generated slides "aid" the speaker. As a matter of fact, too many slides or slides without transitions can make a speech very difficult to follow (Rockler-Gladen, 2007). ➡ *For specifics on handling computer-generated slides, see Guidelines at the end of the chapter.*

Use a database like InfoTrac College Edition, EBSCOhost, or CQ Researcher to run a keyword search using *multimedia presentations*. Read several articles, looking for valuable advice for use in your own presentations. Share what you find with a classmate.

Active Critical Thinking

To think further about types of visual aids, complete the following:

- Which of the above types of visual aids have you used in your past speeches; which were the most successful and which were the least successful? Why?
- Speaking as an audience member, which types of visual aids are more likely to keep attention and improve memory of speech content?

Planning Your Visual Aids

Now that you understand the benefits of using visuals aids and are familiar with the most popular types, you are ready to look at other factors to be considered in planning the visual aids for your next presentation. Because most speakers today use computer-generated slides projected onto a screen, our major emphasis will concentrate on computer slides, even though you will notice that many of the guidelines in this chapter apply to other types of visual aids as well. Let's look at several important items to consider when planning your visual aids.

Begin with Your Audience in Mind

Just as analyzing the situational, demographic, and psychological aspects of your audience is critical in planning a speech, so is considering your audience prior to planning your visual aids. Not only do good visuals facilitate comprehension and memory of your ideas, they can also create audience involvement and interest and help audience members see the logic and persuasiveness of your arguments. For example, Cliff Atkinson (2007), a speaker who consults for *Fortune* 500 companies, created a PowerPoint presentation that helped win a $253-million-dollar verdict against the Vioxx Company in 2005. His PowerPoint visuals helped to convince the jury to vote against Vioxx. Atkinson understood his audience and what would motivate their understanding and comprehension of the argument. Atkinson stated, "All good design involves seeing things from the point of view of the user of the design. Preparing a good talk is design. And it is critical to see things from the point of view of the listener or viewer" (p. 2). In other words, design your visuals to fit not only you as the speaker, but the audience as well. → *For specifics on audience analysis, see Chapter 4. Also, see basic design principles as well as specific design tips for using text and graphic slides later in this chapter.*

Consider the Benefits of Using Color

Although many speakers go overboard by using too many colors in their slides, when used correctly color has many benefits for the planner:

- *Color visuals are more persuasive than black-and-white* (Vogel et al., 1986, 1990).

- *Color visuals produce better recall and sales.* As mentioned earlier, one benefit of using color in visual aids and advertisements is that color produces better recall. The Bureau of Advertising also found that sales from color ads are 50 to 80 percent greater than sales from noncolor ads (Johnson, 1990).

- *Colors add spatial dimensions.* Cool colors (such as green and blue) are more passive and stationary. Dark colors appear farther away, while light colors appear nearer. Warm colors (such as orange and red) are more active and seem to jump forward from a neutral background such as gray (Marcus, 1982).

- *Colors produce an emotional response.* Cool colors generally have a calming effect; warm colors generally have a stimulating, invigorating, and sometimes anger-producing effect (Gardano, 1986). → *For specifics on how to use color, see the end of this chapter.*

Sample Text Visuals

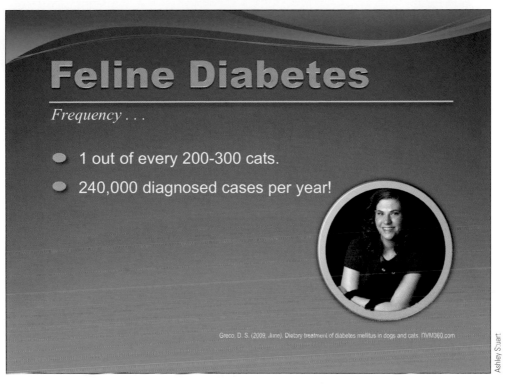

Visual A

Design template, photo, and Kristen ITC typeface add color and interest.

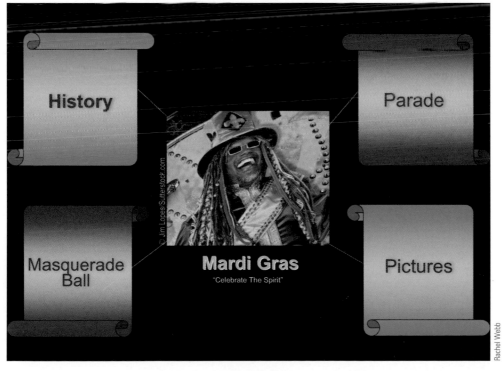

Visual B

Colorful poster and scrolls are used to introduce topics to be covered in this speech on Mardi Gras.

Visual C

The blue and red color theme is carried throughout.

Visual D

Note the use of subtitles and arrows to locate sections of a Greek theater.

Visual E

Flying text, produced from PowerPoint Word Art, is used as an alternative to bullets.

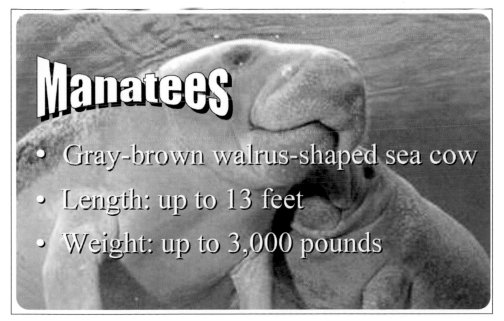

Visual F

A personal photo of manatees at Sea World is used as background; note the shadow boundary around the text.

Sample Graphic Visuals

© Alexander Orlov/Shutterstock.com

Cassandra Garcia

Visual G

A colorful photo is used as an opening slide.

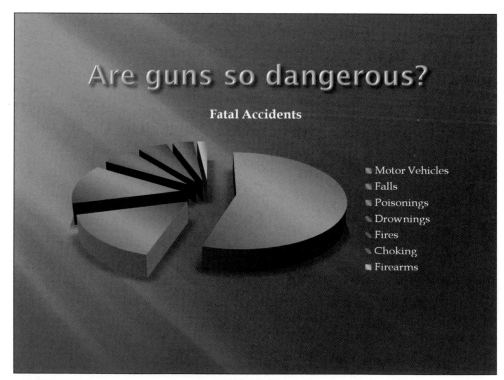

Visual H

Produced on PowerPoint 2010's chart feature.

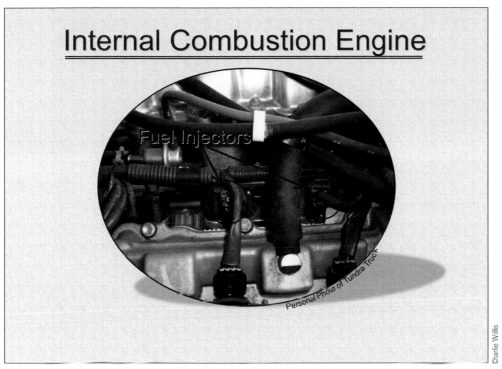

Visual I

The photo of the engine is clarified by reference circles and arrows.

Visual J

Bar graph prepared using PowerPoint Insert Table feature.

Visual Aids to Revise

Visual Ka

Name five weaknesses with this visual on the Westin Resort.

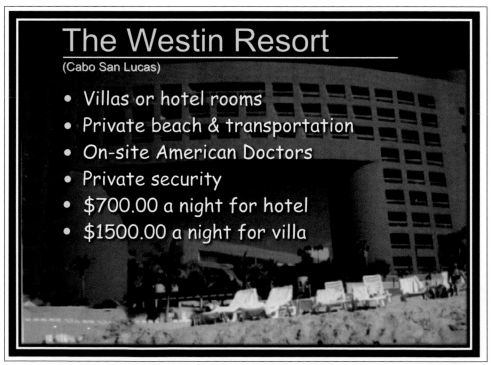

Visual Kb

Why is this version of Visual Ka improved? What additional changes would make it even better?

Visual La

Name five weaknesses with this visual on Bearded Dragons.

Visual Lb

What specific changes make this visual improved over Visual La? What additional changes would you recommend?

Gene Therapy

Disease	Incidence	Nature of Illness
Kidney disease	500,000	Kidney failure
Down syndrome	250,000	Mental retardation
Sickle-cell anemia	100,000	Impaired circulation
Cystic fibrosis	30,000	Respiratory infections
Hemophilia	20,000	Uncontrolled bleeding
Phenylketonuria (PKU)	<10,000	Mental deficiency
Retinoblastoma	10,000	Cancer of the eye
Artherosclerosis	6.7 million	Vascular disease
Cancer	5 million	Uncontrolled cell growth
Alzheimer's disease	2–4 million	Mental degeneration
Schizophrenia	1.5 million	Psychotic disorder
Diabetes	20 million	Pancreatic disorder
Multiple sclerosis	250,000	Loss of myelin

Source: International Biotechnology Association.

Visual M

Using the information in Chapter 10, what are the strengths and weaknesses of this visual?
What would you do to make it even better?

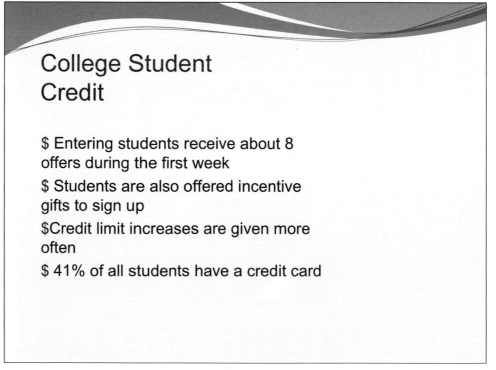

College Student Credit

$ Entering students receive about 8 offers during the first week

$ Students are also offered incentive gifts to sign up

$Credit limit increases are given more often

$ 41% of all students have a credit card

Visual N

Using the information in Chapter 10, what are the strengths and weaknesses of this visual?
What would you do to make it even better?

Determine the Types and Number of Visuals to Use

The majority of visuals used by speakers are text slides. You will find them very helpful during the introduction of your speech as you present your main points and during the conclusion when you summarize your ideas. Graphic slides such as bar graphs and pie charts add interest and show the meaning of and relationship between numbers; they are usually used to support one or more of your main points. When possible, use both text and graphic slides to add interest and variety.

Creating visuals is so enjoyable that some speakers use too many. Visual overload can be just as deadly to audience attention as verbal overload; therefore, limit the number of visuals/slides you use. To decide how many to prepare, use the following formula:

$$\underline{\text{Length of speech}} + 1 = \textbf{Suggested maximum number of visuals/slides}$$
$$2$$

For example, for a 6-minute speech, use a maximum of four visuals (6 divided by 2 plus 1); for a 10-minute speech, a maximum of six (10 divided by 2 plus 1). If you decide that your situation or topic needs more visuals/slides, use caution—some situations may warrant more visuals, but most do not. To avoid problems, remember that "less is more," and follow the design tips offered later in this chapter.

Make PowerPoint Your Ally

The first case of **PowerPoint poisoning** seems to have been diagnosed on August 16, 2000. That day, in his Dilbert cartoon strip, Scott Adams coined the term for the malady, described as *a text-induced coma that listeners experience when there are too many PowerPoint slides or the slides are too long, have too many bullets, or are too confusing.* (There have been many cartoons since then that have described other aspects of the problem.)

Business people who watch more than 100 PowerPoint presentations per year were surveyed to find out what annoys them the most (Paradi, 2009). The top five most annoying items are listed for you on page 230. Do you agree with this list? What would you add? Do you disagree with any of the items in this list?

EXPRESS CONNECT

You can use Speech Builder Express to help you organize your visual aids. Select "Visual Aids" from the left-hand menu and follow the Instructions. For short reminders from this text about transitions, click on the "Tutor" button.

AS YOU CAN CLEARLY SEE IN SLIDE 397...

GAAAAH!

"POWERPOINT" POISONING.

www.dilbert.com   scottadams@aol.com

© 2000 United Feature Syndicate, Inc.

DILBERT: Copyright 2000. Scott Adams/Dist. by United Feature Syndicate, Inc.

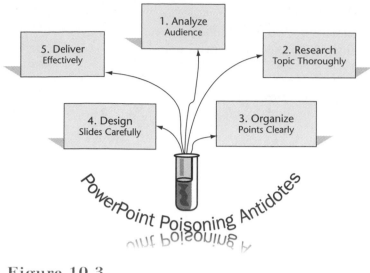

Figure 10.3

Use These PowerPoint Antidotes To Avoid "Poisoning" Your Audience.

1. Speakers who read from their slides (69.2 percent).

2. Text too small to read (48.2 percent).

3. Complete sentences used instead of phrases or bullet points (48.0 percent).

4. Color choices that make slides difficult to read (33.0 percent).

5. Charts too complex to understand (27.9 percent).

Computer-generated slides can either aid your presentation or they can be so irritating that they work against your efforts to communicate. To make sure that PowerPoint becomes your ally, carefully consider the five items in Figure 10.3. By considering your audience, researching, organizing, designing, and delivering carefully, you will have applied an antidote to any type of PowerPoint poison. By making PowerPoint your ally, you will enhance rather than diminish communication. ➤ *For more specifics, see Guidelines for Using Your Visual Aids Effectively at the end of this chapter.*

Active Critical Thinking

To think further about planning your visual aids, complete the following:

- Think about the visual aids, especially the PowerPoint slides, that you have seen used by a professor or have used yourself. What was a main weakness, and which planning category probably caused it?
- What "fix" to the weakness would you recommend? Why?

Using Basic Design Principles

The templates that come with the PowerPoint software are often more concentrated on a "look" or "style" than they are on clarity and audience readability (Stoner, 2007), which means that the burden of effective slide design falls on the speaker. Therefore, it is important for you to know what works, what doesn't, and why slide design is so important. In *The Non-Designer's Design Book,* Robin Williams (2008, p. 13) discusses four **basic design principles**—guidelines for constructing all well-designed slides whether text or graphic:

- **Contrast**—Elements such as size, color, line thickness, and font choice should not be merely similar; instead, they should show contrast by being noticeably different. When contrast is visually attractive, it grabs the listener's attention.

- **Repetition**—Every element on a slide should repeat at least once, if possible, to add to its organization and unity. For example, if a title is steel blue, that color should repeat in the photo or clipart or in the color of the bullets; a line in one part of the slide could also be repeated in another location.

- **Alignment**—Every element should have a visual connection with another element on the slide; placement of elements should not be arbitrary. For example, the bullets and title could align on the left side, the underline and photo could align on the right. Alignment creates a clean, sophisticated look.

- **Proximity**—To reduce clutter and give a structured feel, place items relating to each other close together so that they become one visual unit. Even double spacing may be too far apart—it can make items look like separate units instead of part of a group.

Analyzing Figure 10.4 Let's illustrate how these four design principles can make a difference in the quality of a visual aid by applying them to the slide in Figure 10.4.

What do you see that is effective? The speaker has chosen an easily readable font, Arial, that seems appropriate for the topic. The font is large enough for easy audience viewing (the title is in 36 point and the main ideas in 32 point), and no unnecessary words have been used. There is plenty of empty space—called **white space**—around the top, bottom, left, and right sides of the text, which gives a clean, professional look. Also, an underline separates the title from the main points, which helps the audience grasp the organization of the slide. This visual, then, is basically good.

But it's bland, isn't it? Nothing attracts the eye. This slide does not follow the four basic design principles presented by Williams.

Redesigning Figure 10.4 Let's look at specific problem areas and redesign the slide, following the design principles:

1. *First of all, there isn't enough* **contrast**. The font size of the main points and the title are too similar. The bullets (squares in front of the main points) do repeat, but they are too light to be noticed. One way to improve the slide would be to considerably increase the font size of the title, because it is short (a single word)—our redesigned slide uses 60 point for the title. Putting the title in boldface would also help contrast it in size with the main points. Note that the addition of color adds interest and power as well. With the main points divided into five points and reorganized so each begins with a red letter that spells the word *HEART,* we have added an acronym that adds interest and contrast.

2. *There isn't enough* **repetition**. Although the bullets repeat, nothing else does. Even a boldfaced title would need to be repeated somewhere; perhaps the bullets could be filled in, the underline could be made bold, or a photo could be added with a

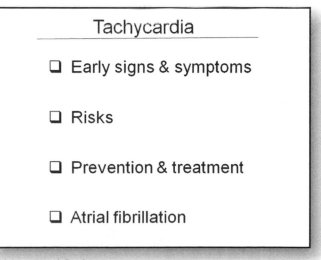

Figure 10.4

How Would You Improve This Slide?

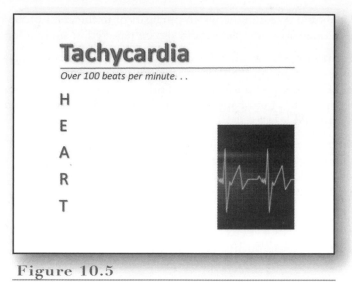

Figure 10.5

One Approach to Redesigning Figure 10.4

bold element. In the redesigned slide, notice how the color of the title repeats with the photo and first letter of each line—these beginning letters which spell "heart" have taken the place of bullets. You could spell *heart* in red and repeat the red color in the subtitle. Repetition is subtle, but very professional looking.

3. ***Alignment*** *is incomplete.* Although the main points align with each other, they don't line up with anything else on the page. According to Williams, "Every item should have a visual connection with something else on the page" (p. 27). Right now, neither the title nor the underline have a connection. One improvement would be to have the title and underline span the visual from left to right. In the redesigned slide, the bullets (or, in this case, the blue letters) are left aligned with the title and the underline and the graphic is right aligned with the underline. Note that the addition of a graphic adds warmth and visual interest and repeats in color with the title.

Used Cars	(817) 555-1212
Connor Blake	
6195 Del Lane Mansfield, TX	

Figure 10.6

How Would You Improve This Business Card?

4. ***Proximity*** *is weak.* The main points are double spaced and appear as if there are five separate items on the page rather than a group. In the redesigned slide, closer proximity between the main points makes them a visual unit and increases reading ease.

Active Critical Thinking

To think further about basic design principles, complete the following:

- Consider the business card in Figure 10.6; it has problems with all four design principles.
- Explain the changes you would recommend, and print out a revised business card to share with your classmates. Then compare your card with the one located on the *Essentials of Public Speaking* website, Chapter 10, or provided by your instructor.

Speaking to Make a Difference

Steve Jobs is best known as the CEO of Apple, which he cofounded in 1976. Through the years, Apple has been a consistent innovator in the electronics industry with its Apple and Macintosh computers, the OS X operating system, its consumer-friendly software, and more recently its iPod, iTunes, and iPhone (Steve Jobs, 2007). But Jobs has also made a difference as a speaker. Since 1997, his keynote presentation at the annual Macworld Expo has been a trademark of the show.

The text below is from the introduction to Jobs' 2007 presentation, made to an enthusiastic audience that laughed and clapped and enjoyed themselves. Visit **Google.com** and look for **Introducing the new iPhone PART 1** to watch the beginning of Job's speech.

AF Photo/Paul Sakuma

This is a day I've been looking forward to for two and a half years. Every once in a while a revolutionary product comes along that changes everything. One is very fortunate if you get to work on just one of these in your career. Apple has been very fortunate that it's been able to introduce a few of these into the world. In 1984 we introduced the Macintosh. It didn't just change Apple, it changed the whole industry. In 2001 we introduced the first iPod, and it didn't just change the way we all listened to music, it changed the entire music industry.

Well today, we're introducing *three* revolutionary products of this class. The first one is a widescreen iPod with touch controls. The second is a revolutionary mobile phone. And the third is a breakthrough Internet communications device. So, three things: a wide screen iPod with touch controls; a revolutionary mobile phone; and a breakthrough Internet communications device. An iPod, a phone,

an Internet communicator. An iPod, a phone . . . are you getting it? These are *not* three separate devices! This is one device.

And we are calling it iPhone! Today, Apple is going to reinvent the phone. And here it is [shows humorous visual]. No, actually, here it is. But we are going to leave it there for now.

Before we get into it, let me talk about a category of things. The most advanced phones are called smartphones, so they say. They typically combine a phone plus some e-mail capability plus . . . the Internet—the baby Internet—in one device. And they all have plastic, little keyboards on them. The problem is they're not so smart, and they're not so easy to use. If you kind of make a business school 101 graph of a smart axis and an easy-to-use axis, regular cell phones are kind of right there [shows graph]. They're not so smart and not so easy to use. Cell phones are at the bottom. But smartphones are definitely a little smarter, but they are actually harder to use—really complicated. Just for the basic stuff people have a really hard time figuring out how to use them.

But we don't want to make either one of these things. What we want to do is to make a leap-frog product that is way smarter than any mobile device has ever been and super easy to use. This is what iPhone is—we are going to reinvent the phone with a revolutionary new interface.

Let's look at a few of the visually appealing things Jobs did in his presentation to make it so outstanding:

- *Use of blank space.* At several points during Jobs' presentation, the audience is treated to blank or single-image shots on the projector. "A blank screen from time to time also makes images stronger when they do appear" (Reynolds, 2005). Jobs is especially adept at using subtle, nearly blank slides to bring listeners back to what he is saying. Where our excerpt picks up, the screen shows only the Apple logo in the center, lit from behind. It's simple and focuses the attention back on Jobs. Using this technique, when he gets to the "we introduced the Macintosh" line, the audience watches the perfectly timed appearance of an old Macintosh computer, to remind them what it looked like.

- *Humor with slides.* Just reading the transcript doesn't give the impression that the line "And here it is . . ." would be anything but a segue into a slide of the iPhone. However, Jobs "seems to catch the audience by surprise" (Some Comments . . . , 2007), and they laugh as he reveals a slide of a fake iPhone: a regular iPod with a

rotary phone dial where the controls should be. This was especially effective and humorous because he had just spent time building up to and creating wild excitement for the new product (Gallo, 2007). "Jobs has fun, and it shows" says Carmine Gallo, author of *The Presentation Secrets of Steve Jobs* (2010, p. 208).

- *One theme per slide.* Generally speaking, Jobs keeps his slides simple. For example, when he is discussing the "three revolutionary products," he does not show all three on the same slide; he separates them into three separate slides (Gallo, 2007). This is part of Jobs' aesthetic of simplicity that allows his slides to flow smoothly (Reynolds, 2007).

- *Textually sparse.* As we've discussed before, using too many words on a slide can cause your audience to lose interest in what you are saying. In Jobs' presentations, he generally does not use "slides with bullet points and mind-numbing data." Instead, "an image is all he needs" to punctuate his words and keep his audience interested (Gallo, 2007). In other words, Jobs is adept at "getting the maximum impact with a minimum of graphic elements" (Reynolds, 2005).

continued

Not only was Steve Jobs' Macworld 2007 speech introducing the iPhone well organized, well practiced, colorful, and interesting, but it also incorporated various visual aids in a clever and effective way. He could have given his audience slides bogged down with text and technical specs. Instead, with each point punctuated by images and live demonstrations, Jobs made his presentation as exciting as the eagerly anticipated new product he was introducing.

Questions: After watching parts of Jobs' actual presentation (or his 2010 presentation at Macworld), what specific guidelines, tips, and basic design principles do you think he followed? Did you see any that he failed to use? Why is Jobs considered to be a successful speaker?

Designing Your Visual Aids

Steve Jobs is famous for the clever slides that accompany his presentations, but in many classrooms and business meetings PowerPoint poisoning is the usual rather than the exception. In an article in the *Wall Street Journal,* G. Jaffe said that the Pentagon is waging war on PowerPoint, which has been called a "growing electronic menace" (2000, p. A1). Many presentations are too long (100 slides or more), too confusing, too wordy, and cluttered with showy effects (fancy backdrops, distracting slide transitions, spinning pie charts, and "booming tanks"). Tad Simons, past editor-in-chief of *Presentations* magazine, puts it this way: "That's the reason there are so many awful PowerPoint presentations in the world—because people without a lick of design sense are out there creating their own slides, inflicting their ineptness on unsuspecting audiences everywhere" (Bajaj, 2004). But you don't need to be one of those inept people. You already know what plans you need to make before beginning to design your slides and other visual aids. If you carefully follow the five tips detailed in this section for designing visual aids, you will be ready to perfect your PowerPoint presentation by customizing the commercial materials you have used from PowerPoint files or from other resources. ➔ *See "Using PowerPoint to Customize Your Slides," which appears later in this chapter.*

TIP #1: Use the Correct Font Size

One of the most common mistakes that even experienced speakers make in preparing visuals is using text that is too small for easy audience viewing. For posters, flip charts, chalkboards, and markerboards, use these guidelines:

Correct Font Sizes	
for Posters, Flip Charts, Chalkboards, & Markerboards	
Titles	3 inches high
Subtitles	2 to 2 1/2 inches high
Text	1 1/2 inches high

Although these size recommendations may seem too large at first, they will ensure that even the people in the back row can see your message clearly.

For projected computer slides, font size is measured in points, not inches. (A point is about 1/72 of an inch.) Your audience will be able to see your slides if you use a font that is no smaller than the following point sizes:

Correct Point Sizes **For Computer-Generated Slides***	
Titles	30–36 points
Subtitles	24 points
Text	18 points (if no subtitle, use 24 points)

***Note:** These are minimum sizes—go larger when possible.

Using smaller point sizes than those listed here (except for a credit line under your photos, which can be as small as 12 point) may result in a frustrated audience. Test out your slides in a room the approximate size of the one you will use for your speech—you may be surprised at how much larger your titles and text could be.

TIP #2: Select Fonts with Care

For projected computer slides, you will need to select one or two **fonts** (often called typefaces). Fonts are divided into two types: sans serif and serif. A **sans serif font** (a geometric-looking typeface) is recommended for titles or emphasis. Sans serif fonts include Arial, Futura, Tahoma, and Optima. A **serif font** (with small lines, or finishing strokes, that extend from letter stems) is especially good for text and small labels on charts. Serif fonts include Times New Roman, Palatino, Bodoni, and Century.

As you can see from the list of fonts and the images they convey, fonts affect the readability of your slides and will either reinforce or distract from the tone of your speech For example, if your topic is serious, you wouldn't want to use Bodoni Black, which is a playful font. Sometimes the font you choose depends as much on your audience as on the topic. For example, if you were speaking to a group of skeptical parents about the educational values of a day-care facility, a Times New Roman font would give your slides an official, confidence-inspiring look. If you were emphasizing the personal, loving attention that the day-care facility gives to each child, Century would be a good choice because it conveys a friendly tone.

Selecting a Font by Image or Tone	
Arial	Professional
Bodoni	Trendy
Bodoni Black	**Playful**
Century	Friendly
Verdana	Young
Futura	Modern
Garamond	*Sophisticated*
Times New Roman	Official
Tahoma	**Urban**

Sometimes the only way to be sure that your slides are sending the message you desire is to see them projected on a screen; once they are enlarged, the tone is more obvious. Have a friend or classmate critique the font to make sure they can read and understand your message. Use special care in combining fonts. As mentioned previously, sans serif fonts are usually used for titles, and serif fonts for text. Generally, *use no more than two different fonts per slide, and use the same fonts for all the slides in a speech*—consistency projects professionalism. Even though instructions in some PowerPoint handbooks recommend that you use a different font on every slide, consistency is usually a good idea.

TIP #3: Follow Design Tips for Text Slides

The tips for text slides are summarized in Figure 10.7 (revised from Holcombe & Stein, 1996). Before reading further, look at the figure and identify which tips listed in the slide are actually misused in it. Then continue reading the text and see

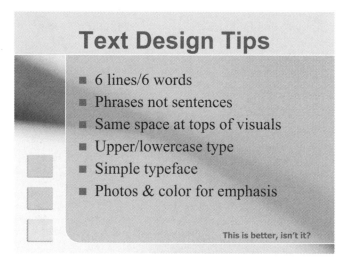

Figure 10.7

Effective Slides Can Be Read in Six Seconds or Less. Can You Read This Slide in Six Seconds?

Text Design Tips

- 6 lines/6 words
- Phrases not sentences
- Same space at tops of visuals
- Upper/lowercase type
- Simple typeface
- Photos & color for emphasis

This is better, isn't it?

Figure 10.8

Which Computer Slide Would You Rather Have an Instructor Use in Class—This One or the One in Figure 10.7?

if you were correct. Remember, *if it takes too long or too much effort to read a slide (more than six seconds, for example), the audience is forced into a reading mode rather than a listening mode.* Recall from Chapter 3 that research confirmed that your audience cannot listen and read at the same time. Design tips for text visuals include:

- **Limit slides to six lines of text and six words per line.** The "Rule of Six" basically says that you should include no more information on a slide than a listener can grasp in approximately 6 seconds or less. Six seconds of material is approximately 6 lines with no more than six words per line (approximately 40 characters across). The Rule of Six doesn't mean six bullets with wraparound text—it means 6 total lines. However, if you are using lists of single words, then eight lines could work. Using motion to bring in each point with its supporting material and then having it disappear when the next point comes in is one way to keep visible text to a minimum. Just remember that you don't want to read off the slide, so the fewer words on the slide the better. In that way, keywords serve as a reminder for the speaker and, along with a photo or image, serve as an aid to audience memory.

- **Use phrases rather than sentences.** Sentences take too long to read (as in Figure 10.7), but short phrases allow for quick comprehension (as in Figure 10.8). Which slide would you rather have an instructor use in a lecture? If your audience needs more information than you can place on your slide, put it in a handout to give them at the end of the speech, or use drop-down boxes that disappear when the next item is clicked.

- **Leave the same space at the top of each slide.** Many speakers incorrectly center the content on each slide—that is, they leave an equal amount of white space above and below the text. This means that some slides have only a few lines in the middle, whereas others are filled with text. As a result, each time a computer slide is projected onto the screen, the audience has to search for the title. Your presentation will look more professional and be easier to comprehend if the text begins at the same depth on each slide, about 1 1/2 inches from the top is optimal; for posters and flip charts, 3 inches.

- **Use upper- and lowercase letters.** ONE OF THE EASIEST WAYS TO ENSURE AUDIENCE COMPREHENSION OF YOUR SLIDES IS TO USE UPPERCASE AND LOWERCASE LETTERS RATHER THAN ALL CAPITALS. See how your reading slowed down with all caps? If you need a larger title, use a larger font size instead of using all caps. Research has shown that text in all caps is more difficult to read and comprehend. To see why this is true, try a brief experiment using Figure 10.9. The word *official* has been divided into upper and lower parts.

  Hold your hand over the top part and ask at least four people to read the bottom part. Now hold your hand over the bottom part and ask four other people to read the top part. Which part were more people able to read correctly more quickly? The reason the top part was easier to read is that *word recognition comes mainly from the upper half of lowercase letters.* But when a word is put in all caps, it becomes a shapeless box that cannot be instantly recognized (Baskette et al., 1992).

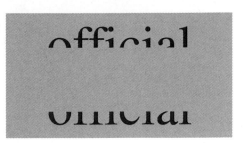

Figure 10.9

Word-Recognition Experiment

Word recognition comes mainly from the upper half of lowercase letters, which is why all caps are difficult to read.

Source: Adams, Faux, & Rieber, 1998

- **Use simple fonts.** Many of the fonts available for use on personal computers are completely inappropriate and basically illegible except when used just for special emphasis—see the title in Figure 10.7 for example. Simple fonts are always easier to read than script or fancy ones. Begin with the fonts suggested earlier in the chapter; they have stood the test of time and are known to work for slides.

- **Use photos/clip art, a large font, or color for emphasis.** One of the basic design principles we discussed earlier is contrast. Photos, clip art, larger type, and color all add contrast and emphasis. The largest and boldest type will always be read first unless you have also used color. If you want to direct your audience's attention to a portion of a complicated diagram, color is the way to do it. Even on a color visual, a bright, contrasting color will focus your audience's attention. ➡ *We discuss the use of color near the end of this chapter.*

TIP #4: Follow Design Tips for Graphic Slides

In order for graphic slides to trigger the right brain and allow for rapid comprehension of complicated data, design the visuals carefully. In addition to the basic design principles of contrast, repetition, alignment, and proximity discussed earlier, the following additional tips apply specifically to graphic slides (revised from Holcombe & Stein, 1996):

- **Limit data to what is absolutely necessary**—Figure 10.10 illustrates the importance of using only the data needed to support your points. If your speech deals only with sales, the data lines for earnings and dividends (as well as the distracting grid lines) are not necessary and actually obscure the seriousness of the sales decline. However, you could prepare an additional slide showing the data lines for earnings and dividends to use while answering questions at the end of your speech. When you use more than one data line, be sure to label each one. ➡ *See Chapter 7, pp. 169–170, for Q&A suggestions.*

Figure 10.10

Limiting Data,
Background Lines, and
Datapoints

*Limit data, background lines,
and datapoints to what is
needed to support your verbal
points.*

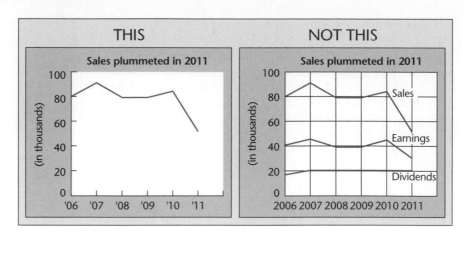

Figure 10.11

Grouping Data

*Group distracting data under
a general heading.*

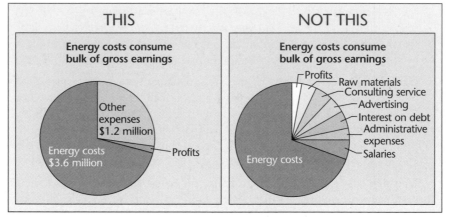

- **Keep background lines and data points to a minimum**—In most
  cases, grid lines and data points (such those in Figure 10.10) should be
  eliminated. They are distracting, take too much time to interpret, and are
  not usually necessary for understanding. Use them only if you know that
  your audience (say, a group of engineering students) expects grid lines and
  data points, but include only essential data points and make the grid lines
  lighter than the data lines.

- **Group data when possible**—Even after you have limited the data to
  only what is necessary, see if there are any small categories of data that you
  can group into one larger category. Figure 10.11 illustrates this tip. When
  seven small categories of costs were grouped under the general heading
  of "Other expenses," the pie chart became much easier to grasp. If necessary, you could follow this pie chart with a visual that lists the contents of
  "Other expenses."

- **Make bars wider than spaces between them**—When the white space
  between the bars in a bar graph is wider than the bars, as in the graph in
  Figure 10.12 on page 239, the "trapped" white space visually pushes the
  bars apart, making them seem unrelated (Williams, 2008). Therefore, for
  easier comparison, make the bars a little wider than the spaces between
  them, whether the bars are horizontal or vertical.

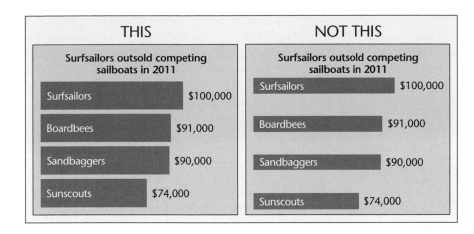

Figure 10.12

Limiting White Space
For viewing ease, make the space between bars narrower than the bars.

- **Always use headings**—Whether your graphic slide is a chart, graph, map, or picture, always use a title or heading for clarity. For example, it might seem obvious to you that your drawing shows the correct position to begin water skiing, but without a title or heading, it wouldn't be immediately clear to everyone in your audience.

TIP #5: Use Color With Extra Care

Using color in your visuals is so much fun that it's easy to go overboard. In fact, too many colors or the wrong colors can definitely create PowerPoint poison for your listeners and is just as distracting as a cluttered pie chart or too many words. Selecting effective color combinations is difficult; but if used correctly, color can highlight, organize, and add interest to your speech content (Baird et al., 1987; Conway, 1988; Johnson, 1995; Pastoor, 1990; Vogel et al., 1990):

- *Use the same color scheme for all visuals in any one speech.* Don't be tempted to use a different color background for each visual or for each title. Consistency projects professionalism and organization.

- *Know the difference between hue and saturation.* **Hue** is an actual color—each color on the color wheel is a different hue. **Saturation** is the amount of color used in the selected hue (fully saturated colors are vivid; low-saturated colors show more gray and appear paler).

- *Use different hues for unrelated items; use a single hue with different saturation levels for related items.*

- *For graphs and charts, use fully saturated hues to make them easier to read.* Also, research has found that blue, cyan (greenish blue), and red are the favored colors for highlighting important items on graphs and charts.

- *For backgrounds and texts, select hues low in saturation.* Adults aged 20 to 56 were asked to select text and background color preferences from over 800 color combinations shown on video monitors. Low-saturated colors were preferred in almost all cases.

- *Contrast text and figures with the background.* For legibility, dark backgrounds require light letters, bullets, and figures; light backgrounds should have the opposite. When light colors (such as pastels) are used for figures, bullets, or letters against a light background, they should have a darker color outline or shadow. For example, blue letters on a dark blue or black background will be almost impossible to read; white or yellow letters on a dark back-ground will be easy to read. Contrast can also be created by varying the saturation of color (such as placing a fully saturated figure on a partially saturated background). *The contrast between lightness and darkness is the most important factor of visibility.*

* *Avoid using colors that can look the same at a distance,* such as red and brown; red-orange and orange; and yellow and yellow-green. On the other hand, most basic colors (such as black, white, red, yellow, blue, green, purple, and pink) are easy to distinguish as long as they are not used in the above problem combinations.

* *Limit the number of colors you use.* Using more than four colors usually makes visuals look cluttered and slows down audience comprehension.

* *Avoid placing opposites on the color wheel directly next to each other.* Color opposites such as blue and orange or red and green appear to vibrate when placed side by side, so pick colors for bar graphs and pie charts carefully. Also, be especially careful about using red and green, because some people have red-green color blindness and may not even realize it.

* Finally, *to be sure that your color choices are effective, project them onto a screen and check them.* The wrong color combinations can make your visuals difficult to read. Also, be aware that the colors you see on your computer monitor may not be the exact colors that the audience sees projected on the screen—video projectors vary in the set of color chips they use and even in the way they are adjusted.

Active Critical Thinking

To think further about designing computer slides, complete the following:
* Select one of the slides included in this chapter and redesign it following the design tips in this section.
* Explain why you made the changes you did. Print off a copy of the completed slide to share with your classmates.

Using PowerPoint to Customize Your Visuals

When using computer-generated slides, nothing is worse than having the audience sigh with boredom and think, "Oh, I've seen those photos or that clip art before." When you use the design templates that come with software programs, you run that risk. This will never happen to you if you customize your visuals. **Customizing** means that you take a basic idea or template and change and adapt it so it follows the design principles and tips presented earlier, relates to your specific audience, and becomes your own.

To customize your slides, follow these simple steps:

1. *Type your speech outline into the Speech Template (or AutoContent Wizard or PowerPoint design template).* The Speech Template will open to Outline view. To view your outline in slide form, click on the *"Slide Sorter View"* button (bottom left of screen). **Note:** Any changes you make to individual slides will update the outline; also, any changes you make to the outline

will update your slides. → *If you haven't used the Speech Template yet, go back to Chapter 2 and reread the section on "Trait Anxiety and Technology." The Speech Template can be found under "Student Resources for Chapter 2" at the* Essentials of Public Speaking *website.*

2. *Get ready to customize* (don't skip these steps).

   • *Turn on the ruler and guides from the View menu if they are not already visible.* Drag the vertical guide (dashed line) to where you want your left margin. **Note:** Although the guides will not print or show during your presentation, they are a great help with alignment. Titles and text are left aligned in the speech template. To change alignment, click on the text; when a text box appears, click on the edge of the highlighted box and use the up, down, left, or right arrow keys to move the text box.

   • *Turn off the "Snap to Grid" feature* by clicking the "Draw" button in the Drawing toolbar, choosing "Snap," and then choosing "Snap to Grid." This allows you to position text, lines, or images more accurately using the arrow keys on the right side of your keyboard.

3. *Open the PowerPoint Speaker's Guide and download or print a copy to use while creating and customizing your visuals.* The guide includes both basic and advanced suggestions (for both PowerPoint 2003 and 2007). "Basic Suggestions" includes how to customize text, lines, bullets, backgrounds, design, clip art, and color. "Advanced Suggestions" includes customizing titles with boxes; customizing clip art, scanned images, and video; adding animation, transitions, and sound; building custom bullets; and adding recorded narration. → *The PowerPoint Speaker's Guide can be found on the CourseMate for the* Essentials of Public Speaking.

4. *Begin customizing titles, text, bullets, clip art, color, sound, movement, and so forth.* Even if you decide to use one of PowerPoint's design templates instead of the Speech Template (choose "Format/Apply Design," and select a template), you should always customize it to fit your specific presentation and audience. And for the best results, follow the text and graphic slide-design suggestions in this chapter. **Note:** If you are worried about being nervous during your presentation, *definitely build your own custom bullets* (see instructions under the "Advanced Suggestions" of the Speaker's Guide). Building your own bullets that remain stationary with the title instead of flying in with each main point allows you to know exactly how many points are located on each slide—a definite confidence builder.

5. *Save your presentation to a disk, CD, or USB flash or thumb drive, and test it by trying it on a different computer.* **Note:** PowerPoint 2003, 2007, and 2010 have a feature under "File/Package" for CD that lets you save your entire presentation to a CD or flash drive—much better than previous versions. It includes a new Viewer that allows your presentation (created in PowerPoint 2000 or later) to run on any computer operating Windows 98 Second Edition or later, even when PowerPoint is not installed on the computer. The Viewer is available free on Microsoft's website at **www. microsoft.com**; type "PowerPoint 2010 Viewer" in the search box or look for it on Google. For a backup, you might wish to also send a copy of your presentation to your e-mail so it can be accessed through the Internet if you need it.

Guidelines For Using Your Visual Aids Effectively

There is more to great visuals than planning and designing them—you have to use them effectively. The following includes a brief overview of the basics:

Objects, Models, and Handouts: If you use them, follow these tips:

- *When using objects and models, size is critical.* Unless the audience can clearly see the object or model, don't use it. Instead, take a picture of the object and show an enlarged view on a slide or go to **Google.com/images** or **Google.com/videos** for models and pictures of objects to use.

- *Handouts usually cause more problems than benefits.* Unless the audience needs to use the handout during your speech (such as answering questions to indicate the risk of having a heart attack), it is best to wait until the end of the speech to offer handouts to audience members.

Flip Charts and Posters: If you decide to use them, follow these tips:

- When using flip charts, *leave a blank page between each page you plan to write on or use water-based markers*—permanent markers tend to bleed through newsprint. *Flip charts normally include only one idea per page.* When you have finished one idea, simply flip the page to the next idea. The final page should include all your key ideas to refresh the listeners' memory during your summary.

- When several key ideas are included on a poster, *cover each idea with a strip of paper* that can easily be removed as you reach that idea in your talk, or give a brief overview of all the items on the poster and then go back and discuss each one in detail. When finished with a poster, cover it with a blank poster or reverse the poster to its blank side.

- Posters and flip charts can also be used to *call attention to single words or phrases* (technical words, new or seldom-used words, or foreign words or phrases).

Markerboards and Chalkboards: When using marker and chalkboards, follow these tips:

- *Make sure that your letters are large enough to be read easily*—generally, a capital letter should be 3 inches high and basic text at least 1 1/2 inches high. Make sure that colors are bold and avoid pastels.

- *Practice is vital.* Learning to speak and draw at the same time can be difficult. Also, unless you practice ahead of time, your work might not come out as you expected. Information may either be too small to see or so large that you run out of space; you might draw your sketch in the wrong proportions; or you might forget the spelling of a key word.

Computer-Generated Visuals: When using computer-generated visuals, follow these tips:

- *Remember that the main point of using visuals is to aid listener understanding.* Using too many slides, too much text, or too many colors, typefaces, or sounds distracts from your message. Everything must work together to simplify meaning and direct audience attention. ➔ *See Using Basic Design Principles and Designing Your Visual Aids on pp. 230–240.*

- *Use sounds sparingly, if at all.* The first time we hear a sound (applause, for example) it's unique; each additional time we hear it, it's a distraction.

- *Select images carefully and choose the best format for them.* For clip art, many people use GIF (graphics interchange format) as their image file format, but

GIF uses a much larger file than JPEG or PNG. For more advanced clip art and especially logos, the PNG (portable network graphics—pronounced "ping") format may be a better option. To change text or pictures into a different image format on a PC, open Accessories, choose Paint, paste the information/image, adjust it if needed, and click "Save As" to save it as a JPEG or PNG.

- *Make sure that the audience can see you when the lights are turned off.* Select a room with appropriate lighting over the speaker stand. If the listeners are likely to take notes, a room with soft lights on a dimmer switch can light both the audience and the speaker. New data projectors are often so bright that overhead lights can remain on.

- *Make sure the visuals can be seen by all.* For a small group (probably not more than eight), your computer presentation slides can be viewed directly on the computer screen. For larger groups, you will need to project the images onto a larger screen using an all-contained video or data projector.

- *Try using a cordless mouse or remote* such as Logitech's Cordless Presenter so you can advance slides and control volume from anywhere in the room.

- *Speak in a conversational manner, and don't read from your visuals.* According to the **personalization principle** (Mayer, 2001), audiences learn better when speakers use a conversational style instead of a formal one.

- *Before clicking to the next slide, give the oral transition to the next idea;* then change slides (Zelazny, 2000). This keeps the audience from reading the slide before you are ready.

- *Come prepared with a backup plan in case of equipment failure.* For example, bring a printed copy of your PowerPoint slides to use as notes, have a second copy of your CD on a USB flash or thumb drive, and/or e-mail your PowerPoint to yourself so it can be accessed through the Internet. It's also a good idea to bring a handout of the most important slides (print 2–9 slides per page) to give to the audience in case of equipment failure.

- *Look at your computer screen and your audience,* but do not turn away from the audience to look at the projection screen behind you unless you need to point to something—then, use a laser pointer.

Audiovisual Aids: If you decide to add video and/or sound to your presentation, follow these tips:

- Make sure the video or audio is cued to the right location. Normally the sound should be turned off when showing video, so you can talk as you would with other visuals.

- Make sure you include a copy of the actual audio or video file in the folder with your PowerPoint presentation. Test it out on a different computer to make sure all is working.

- Keep the audio or video clips short; 15–30 seconds is plenty. If there is sound, test it ahead of time for correct volume.

- PowerPoint allows you to insert video (such as MPEG or AVI) into a computer presentation; choose "Insert/Movies" and "Sounds/Movie" from File, or "Movie" from Clip Organizer. ➔ *For specifics, see the PowerPoint Speaker's Guide (Advanced Suggestions) under "Student Resources for Chapter 10" at the* Essentials of Public Speaking *website.*

Summary

The benefits of using visual aids in speeches cannot be overemphasized. Visual aids have so much power because they (1) speed listener comprehension, (2) improve audience memory, (3) decrease the time needed to present a message, and (4) add to speaker credibility. In short, speakers should consider visual aids as essential.

Computer-generated slides are the most commonly used types of visual aids today—you will certainly want to practice designing and using a variety of slides until you are comfortable with them.

When designing your text and graphic slides, remember to select your fonts with care and to use a large enough font size for everyone in the audience to read with ease. Also keep in mind the four basic design principles—contrast, repetition, alignment, and proximity—as well as the specific design principles for text and graphic slides. Have fun with color, but use it with caution.

Essentials of Public Speaking Online ⫸CourseMate

Use your Online Resources for *Essentials of Public Speaking* for quick access to the electronic study resources that accompany this chapter. Your Online Resources feature the *PowerPoint Speaker's Guide: Basic and Advanced Suggestions,* the visuals featured in the color insert in this chapter, access to InfoTrac College Edition, Personal Skill Building activities, Collaborative Skill Building activities, a digital glossary, sample speeches, and review quizzes.

Key Terms

basic design principles 230	customizing computer slides 240	personalization principle 243
coherence principle 224	fonts 235	PowerPoint poisoning 229
computer-generated slides 227	graphic slides/visuals 227	sans serif font 235
computer slides/visuals 227	graphs 227	saturation 239
contiguity principle 224	hue 239	serif font 235
	Narrative Paradigm 222	text slides/visuals 227
		white space 231

Personal Skill Building

1. What do we mean when we say, "Quality visual aids anchor your audience to the concept you are presenting?" Share your interpretation with a classmate.

2. Select a manuscript of a speech on a topic that you can speak about with enthusiasm. For speech ideas, look in *Vital Speeches* (in your college library or via InfoTrac College Edition) or check out one of the videotaped speeches on the *Essentials of Public Speaking* website. Prepare two slides that the speaker could have used with the speech.

3. On the basis of this chapter, prepare a list of the 5 most important do's and don'ts for designing computer slides. Compare your list with those of one or two classmates and justify your choices.

4. Practice the design rules covered in this chapter by redesigning one or more of the computer slides in the color-insert section. Print copies of your redesigned slides to share with a classmate.

5. Check out the following websites. You can access these sites using your On-line Resources for *Essentials of Public Speaking,* Chapter 10.

   - Go to Microsoft's website and download the Viewer described on p. 241, Type "PowerPoint 2007 Viewer" in the search box (or "PowerPoint 2010 Viewer"). You'll also find PowerPoint templates, photos, clip art, and animations on **microsoft.com**.

   - Check out the winning slide designs at **Slideshare.net** (see http://www.slideshare.net/contest/worlds-best-presentation-contest-2009). Be sure to notice the winners use of white space.

   - For valuable technical articles and critiques of presentation equipment, see **presentations.com**, from the publishers of *Presentations* magazine, and **zdnet.com**. For free downloads, see the following sites:

     —**Animationfactory.com** for animated clip art.

     —**Webplaces.com/html/sounds.htm** for sound clips.

     —**Freesound.org** (requires registration) or **soundbible.com** for sound clips.

     — **Adobe.com/downloads** to download the free Flash Player and Shockwave Player.

Collaborative Skill Building

1. As a class, select three computer slides from this chapter that need revision. Then, in small groups of three to six, redesign the three visuals implementing the guidelines from the chapter. Print off your final versions to show on a document camera if your classroom has one, show them as handouts, or bring a USB flash drive to show your slides using a data projector. Taking one problem computer slide at a time, have each group present their redesigned versions. Class members can vote for the best redesigned slide, or ask three people from the community or the department to serve as judges. When the best slides have been selected, summarize specific reasons why each winning slide was chosen.

2. In small groups of four or six, select a speech from Vital Speeches of the Day (see an online copy or the Military and Government Collection in EBSCOhost) or a student speech from the Student Resources at the *Essentials of Public Speaking* website. Prepare at least four computer slides that the speaker could have used with his or her speech. Make sure that your slides are professional and follow the guidelines in the text. Be prepared to share your slides with other groups or the class.

3. In small groups complete the following:

   • Go back to the Active Critical Thinking box on page 246 and have each group member complete the assignment.

   • Share each other's revised business cards and select the best one or two out of your group.

   • Working together, add to and revise these cards until they represent the best from your group. Make sure that your revisions followed the guidelines for effective visuals contained in the chapter.

   • Check the *Essentials of Public Speaking* website (CourseMate) for Chapter 10 and find the revised card for Figure 10.6. Compare your business card revisions with the sample card and discuss which card is the best and why.

   • Be prepared to share your cards(s) with the class or another group explaining what makes your card(s) so effective.

Types of Speeches

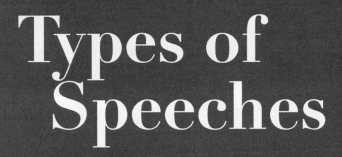

What do you know about preparing different types of speeches?

The following questionnaire is designed to call attention to common misconceptions you may have about speech preparation.

Directions: If you think the statement is generally accurate, mark it T; if you think the statement is a myth, mark it F. Then compare your answers with the explanations at the end of Chapter 11. You can also take this quiz through your Online Resources for *Essentials of Public Speaking,* and if requested, e-mail your responses to your instructor.

_____ **1.** A speech of introduction needs to be fairly long, otherwise, the speaker may feel slighted.

_____ **2.** Electronic computer visuals are usually more persuasive if they are in color.

_____ **3.** After a question-and-answer session, it is very important to present a final, memorable conclusion in order to reestablish control and leave the audience with a feeling of closure.

_____ **4.** Simply mentioning the source of the evidence used makes a speech more persuasive.

_____ **5.** It's unethical to use special knowledge of your listeners' needs and wants in order to change their way of thinking.

_____ **6.** Good logic will persuade almost anyone.

_____ **7.** You can greatly increase low credibility by using professional-looking visual aids.

_____ **8.** It is a good idea to avoid using humor in informative speeches unless you are a professional entertainer or are very experienced in public speaking.

_____ **9.** The basic procedure for beginning an informative speech is as follows: You walk to the front, pause for a second, state your topic and purpose, and then present your attention-getter.

_____ **10.** When you give the source of your evidence, it is normally more persuasive to mention the source before presenting the evidence.

11

Informative Speaking

FLASH BACK

Quintilian and Cicero believed that regular and careful speechwriting would improve speaker eloquence and carry over into extemporaneous situations. For example, Cicero (*De Oratore*, Book I, Section XXXIII) indicates that the careful language in a written introduction will cause the speech that follows (even when extemporaneous) to "proceed in unchanging style." He compares this process to a boat moving at full speed: even when the crew stops rowing, the boat continues moving in the same direction.

FLASH FORWARD

There are at least two ways to look at Cicero's advice on writing out a speech using careful and eloquent language. On the one hand, today's audiences expect delivery to be extemporaneous—interesting, enthusiastic, and conversational. Beginning speakers who write out a speech tend to read it or memorize it—causing a loss of enthusiasm and conversational quality. Therefore, writing out a speech may have disadvantages. On the other hand, educators fear that students who spend hours sending text messages by phone or communicating on Twitter or some other social media will speak in short sentences without any eloquent language—so writing out a speech might have advantages. *Based on your experience, what do you think about Cicero's advice—does it still apply in today's technology-based society?*

Learning Objectives

As you read Chapter 11,

- *Define* an informative presentation, and *discuss* how it differs from a persuasive speech and the two types of informative speeches.
- *List* and *describe* the tools to aid understanding and memory.
- *Identify* the steps and strategies used in preparing an informative speech.

BECAUSE SHARING INFORMATION IS SOMETHING WE DO ALMOST EVERY DAY, IT MAY seem strange to have a complete chapter on informative speaking. In a way, this reasoning is correct, because each of the previous 10 chapters covered specifics you will need to remember and apply to make your informative speech an outstanding success.

Ch. 1: Communicate effectively and ethically.

Ch. 2: Build speaker confidence.

Ch. 3: Thwart audience listening problems.

Ch. 4: Analyze the expected audience.

Ch. 5: Choose, outline, and research your topic.

Ch. 6: Select a variety of supporting materials.

Ch. 7: Follow appropriate format.

Ch. 8: Deliver the message confidently.

Ch. 9: Polish language style.

Ch. 10: Design quality visual aids.

Each of these chapters provides information to help you prepare and present an effective informative speech that your audience will understand and remember. Let's take a specific look at informative speaking.

Informative Speaking: Overview

When planning an informative speech, it is important to know the difference between an informative and a persuasive speech and the different types of informative presentations available.

What Is an Informative Speech

An informative speech promotes understanding of an idea, conveys a body of related facts, or demonstrates how to do or make something. In other words, if your speech increases awareness by introducing the latest information about a topic or body of related facts; deepens your listeners' knowledge of a complicated term, concept, or process, or aids in your listeners' mastery of a skill, it is informative. Informative speeches are not meant to influence choices or opinions— that is the purpose of persuasive speeches—but they may be indirectly persuasive. For example, a listener may volunteer to help at the local food bank after hearing an informative speech about various community organizations, even though the speaker's intention was not to recruit help. *One of the primary differences between informative and persuasive speeches is the speaker's goal:* The informative speaker's goal is to deepen understanding, to instruct, to teach; but the persuasive speaker's goal is to gain agreement, to sell a product, or to encourage an action.

Effective informative speakers do the following (Lehman & DuFrene, 2008, pp. 82–84):

- Present information in a truthful, fair, and objective manner.
- Avoid exaggerated, embellished, or distorted facts.
- Design visual aids to represent facts and relationships without distortion.
- Express ideas and concepts in a clear and easy-to-understand manner.
- Use tact, allowing the audience to retain feelings of self-worth.

There are many ways to categorize informative speeches, but basically all informative speeches can be divided into two broad categories: demonstration speeches and informational speeches. Although informational speeches are the most common, you will likely find opportunities to give demonstration speeches as well. The following sections include tips on how to give both the informational and the demonstration speeches and a sample student speech of each to illustrate the typical organization differences.

A demonstration speech promotes understanding by showing how to do or make something. This speaker is showing how to make origami.

© Jacksonville Journal Courier/The Image Works

Demonstration Speeches

In a **demonstration speech**, the speaker shows how to do or make something while explaining each step to the listeners so clearly that later they can remember the process and achieve the same results themselves. For instance, a demonstration speech about flower arranging might include a visual aid listing the do's and don'ts of making beautiful flower arrangements, but the main focus would be the demonstration of each step, resulting in one or more completed arrangements. You would bring flowers, vases, water, and preservatives—all the supplies that you would need to explain and show each step in the creation of a lovely arrangement. Or if you gave a demonstration speech about how to prepare delicious nonalcoholic drinks for special occasions, you would bring all the ingredients and prepare the drinks in front of the audience, explaining each step. You might have volunteers try their hand at squeezing lemons or blending ingredients. Handing out copies of the recipes *after* your concluding remarks should insure that your listeners leave with a feeling of satisfaction. Figure 11.1 later in this chapter includes sample topics for demonstration speeches.

Be aware that a demonstration speech usually takes more time than an informational speech—especially when audience participation is involved. To make sure that you won't run out of time, do a dress rehearsal and add one minute to the time it took. Figure 11.2 later in this chapter includes sample topics appropriate for demonstration speeches. Although the basic steps for planning a speech are also discussed later in this chapter, the following items especially important for demonstration speeches are given here:

- **Visual aids** (such as graphics, charts, pictures, objects, models, and videos) to clarify the development of a skill. ➔ *See Chapter 10 for specifics on preparing and using visual aids.*

- **Effective supporting materials** (such as explanations, examples, illustrations, comparisons, and expert opinion) to add interest, clarification, and proof. ➔ *See Chapter 6 for specifics on types of supporting materials.*

- **The organizational format** (topical, spatial/geographic, chronological, or causal) that will best meet the needs of the audience and your topic. ➔ *See Chapter 7 for specifics on informative organizational formats.*

Sample Demonstration Speech: "Origami for Storytelling" by Cassandra Ferrell

The following demonstration speech, "Origami for Storytelling," was presented by Cassandra Ferrell in her public speaking class. Cassandra's assignment was to prepare a 4- to 6-minute informative speech (either informational or a demonstration) on a topic of her choosing; either PowerPoint slides or actual objects were required. Cassandra decided to demonstrate her skill at Japanese origami (folding paper to form various objects) and show how to use origami to tell a story to entertain a fussy child. The speech on the next page was transcribed from the video of her speech. As you read this speech, think about changes you would make if you were speaking about the

Sample Demonstration Speech

ORIGAMI FOR STORYTELLING
by Cassandra Ferrell

Introduction:

Hurry, hurry, hurry. Step right up, ladies and gentlemen. I'm going to show you something amazing today. In my hand you may see an ordinary sheet of paper—but it's not! No, my friends, this is a mystical, magical storytelling machine.

As a parent of two small children, I often feel like I am in a circus, trying to keep them entertained. For example, when you are waiting to be seated at a restaurant or when you are waiting in the doctor's office, I utilize the art of paper folding to try to keep their attention if only for a moment. I will share my technique with you today. I'm going to give you a brief history of paper folding, which is also known as origami; I'm going to show you a few items that you might have made that you didn't know were origami; and then I'm going to show you how to create a few things utilizing a single sheet of paper and use them to tell a story.

First Main Point:

Even though the art of origami is an ancient art form, you might have used it in your everyday life and not known it. The origin of origami is a matter of debate. However, the website **www.origami.as** speculates that it was derived in China right after the invention of paper and then migrated to Japan in the late sixteenth century. A form of origami also made its way to the Arab world. Now the Muslim religion forbids the creation of representational figures, so they used origami techniques to create geometric figures, which they utilized as visual aids in the study of mathematics. Even American children today use origami and they don't even realize it. For example, how many of you have created a letter for portability [*shows a handmade envelope*], or how many of you remember fortune-tellers [*shows a paper fortune-teller that fits over four fingers*]? Also paper frogs [*shows a simple paper frog held between a thumb and two forefingers*]; even something as simple as this [*holds up a folded paper triangle*] that's utilized in playing a tabletop version of football is a form of origami.

Second Main Point:

Now that I've given you a brief history, let me show you how to make a few things. The first thing we are going to make is a hat. What you will do

Introduction:

Cassandra begins her speech as a circus ringmaster calling in the passerby to see the "mystical, magical story-telling machine" as she waves a piece of paper in the air. She then establishes her credibility and previews the main points she plans to include in her speech.

Q: What do you think of Cassandra's method of getting attention and did she motivate you to want to listen? Why or why not?

First Main Point:

In her first main point, Cassandra gives the probable origin of origami and shows four examples of paper objects used by American children that are unknowingly examples of origami.

Q: Do you think showing examples of objects used during childhood might help gain the interest of audience members? Why or why not?

Second Main Point:

In Cassandra's second main point, she shows her audience how to make three simple paper

Sample Demonstration Speech *(continued)*

is take a sheet of paper, fold it in half, and pull the corners of your paper toward you until they meet in the center—just like that [*holds up paper with corners folded*]. Now you will take the bottom edge and pull it up until you meet the corners you pulled down [*shows paper*]. You will do one side and flip it over and do the other side. And now you have a very wearable hat [*completed hat is shown*].

From this hat you can easily make a cup. Now to do this, all you need to do is to tuck in the corners and take your hat and pull from the center. [*When she pulls, the corners come undone and she says, "Oh, no." She quickly makes another one.*] Pull it a little easier than that. Pull from the center until you have created a diamond shape—just like that [*shows diamond shape*]. Now you want to pull one of your bottom points of the diamond until it meets the top point of the diamond—which will look like this [*shows folded paper*]. Turn it over and do the same on the other side. And now you have a very usable cup [*shows cup*].

Now from here, we're going to create a boat. Again, we will pull from the middle—just like that. This time we're going to take the top edges of the diamond and pull them out. And now you have a boat.

Third Main Point: Now that I've shown you how to make a hat, a cup, and a boat, I'm going to show you how to turn them into a story. Once upon a time, there was a little boy who wanted to go outside and play on a hot summer's day. Now his mother made him wear a hat for protection [*shows paper hat*]. Now this little boy played hard and became thirsty. So he went inside to get himself a drink of water [*folds the hat into a cup*]. Once he got his cup he looked at it—because, you see, he was an imaginative little boy—and he saw a boat [*shows cup folded into a boat*]. He wanted to be a captain on a pirate's ship. So he created his boat and set sail on the Seven Seas. All of a sudden, he came into a violent storm and the storm rocked the boat [*shows boat rocking on the waves*]. It tore off the front half [*rips off the front end of the paper boat*]; then it tore off the back end of the boat [*rips off the back end of the boat*]; and it even tore off part of the sail [*tears off the top point of the boat*]. And when his mother went outside to look for him, all she was able to find was a little boy's T-shirt [*opens the paper object to show a T-shirt shape*].

objects--a hat, cup, and boat. Each object builds from the previous object almost making the process seem like "magic."

When she makes a mistake with the cup, she laughs and says, "Oh no" which the audience enjoys almost as though they were children watching. It also shows that perfection is not needed in order to enjoy origami.

Although many demonstration speakers have problems speaking and demonstrating at the same time, Cassandra did not.

Q: What did you think about Cassandra's instructions? Were they simple yet specific enough to follow? Why or why not?

Third Main Point:

For her third main point, Cassandra shows how to turn the objects made earlier into a fun story that would keep any child's interest.

She ends with a surprise for the audience—she turns the boat into yet another paper object (a t-shirt).

Q: What do you think of Cassandra's main points— were they appropriate for a demonstration speech? Rate the effectiveness of her main points on a scale of 1 (low) to 5 (high). Explain the reason for your rating.

Sample Demonstration Speech *(continued)*

Conclusion: In conclusion, even just a simple sheet of paper will spark the imagination of a child. By showing you a brief history of paper making; by showing you a few items you can make; and giving you a story you can utilize with your newfound knowledge, I hope that I can give any parent a little peace of mind—even when they are waiting for a haircut. Thank you and happy folding.

Conclusion:

Cassandra ended with a summary and a final thought that was mainly related to parents.

Q: What else could she have used in her conclusion to leave even non-parents thinking about her topic?

same topic. ➜ *To watch and analyze a video clip of Cassandra's speech, look under "Student Resources for Chapter 11" through your Online Resources for* Essentials of Public Speaking.

Informational Speeches

An **informational speech** increases awareness by introducing the latest information about a topic or body of related facts, or presents information promoting understanding of a complicated idea, term, or concept. It does not aid in mastery of a skill. The focus of an informational speech is on content and ideas, not on how to do or make something. For example, in an informational speech about flower arranging, you could talk about the aesthetic value of flowers, flower selection, and flower placement while using visual aids (one listing main points, one showing an effective arrangement, and one showing a poor arrangement), and conclude by showing an actual flower arrangement. Most informational speeches (such as the sample student speech later in this chapter) cover topics that are not appropriate for demonstration speeches (for example, youth fads, stress prevention, or vacation suggestions). Figures 11.2 and 11.3 later in this chapter include sample topics appropriate for informational speeches.

Sample Informational Speech: "Bacterial Meningitis" by Emily Wilson

Emily Wilson presented the following informative speech, "Bacterial Meningitis," in her speech class. Emily's assignment was to prepare a 4- to 6-minute informative speech about a topic of her choosing. Because she had a friend stricken by this disease, Emily decided to inform her classmates on the dangers of meningitis. Visual aids were required; minimal notes were allowed. The following is Emily's preparation outline. Although Emily used visual aids in her speech, they are not included in the outline below. What visuals would you suggest? As you read this speech, think about changes you would make if you were speaking about the same topic. Pay special attention to her introduction and conclusion. Did she include all the necessary steps? ➜ *To watch and analyze a video clip of Emily Wilson's speech with visual aids, look under "Student Resources for Chapter 11" through your Online Resources for* Essentials of Public Speaking.

Sample Informational Speech

BACTERIAL MENINGITIS
by Emily Wilson

Title: "Bacterial Meningitis" by Emily Wilson
Exact Purpose: After listening to my presentation, the audience will become aware of the danger surrounding meningitis by understanding what it is and how it can hurt us.

Introduction:

I. **Attention-getter:** How many of you have heard or been affected by meningitis? How many of you know someone that has experienced the effects of meningitis? [Visual #1]

II. **Qualifications:** I personally have not been affected by meningitis, but I do have a friend who has suffered from this silent killer. She has recovered from her experience but still has minor neurological problems.

III. **Motivation:** According to the National Meningitis Association, there are an estimated 3,000 cases annually of bacterial meningitis in the U.S., and out of those 3,000 cases about 330 people will die. Teens are more likely to die than younger or older people—so it really relates to us.

IV. **Thesis:** Today we are going to look at what bacterial meningitis is, how you get it, and what happens when you are infected. These three main points will help you to understand the significant danger of meningitis. [Visual #2]

Body I. What is bacterial meningitis?
  A. Bacterial meningitis is a serious and dangerous infection of the meninges.
    1. The infection travels up the spinal cord into the brain.
    2. Once in the brain, bacterial meningitis causes swelling in the normal meninges made up of the dura mater, the arachnoid, and the pia mater. [Visual #3].
  B. According to the article "Bacterial Meningitis: Disease/Disorder Overview" from the Health and Wellness Resource Center, there are two leading strands of bacterial meningitis. [Ref. #1]
    1. Meningococcal
    2. Pneumococcal

Introduction:

Emily's introduction includes all the important steps usually included in an informative speech. Her use of statistics was a good way to motivate the audience to listen to this topic that relates to them personally.

Q: If Emily had used the statistics as an attention getter, would it have made her introduction even stronger? Why or why not?

Main Point:

Emily had pages and pages information on her topic but finally narrowed it down to three important main points: What is bacterial meningitis; How do you get it; and what can you expect if you are infected.

Q: Looking at her outline, do you think she chose the best main points of interest and value to her audience? What other main point might she have included?

Sample Informational Speech *(continued)*

Transition: Next, let's look at how we contract a meningitis infection such as the meningococcal strand.

II. How do we get bacterial meningitis, or where does it strike?
  A. Bacterial meningitis is actually found naturally in the body. [Visual #4]
    1. The bacteria are in everyone's body.
    2. Bacterial meningitis is only triggered when your body experiences a drastic change.
  B. Bacterial meningitis can be spread unless you are careful.
    1. Bacterial meningitis is spread by coughing, kissing, sharing food. [Ref. #2]
    2. It is spread through ear, throat, and sinus infections.
    3. Blood infected by bacterial meningitis spreads to the brain.

Transition: Now that we understand how bacterial meningitis is contracted, let's look at what happens when we are infected.

III. What happens when we get it?
  A. Death or severe brain damage occurs to many people.
    1. Bacterial meningitis causes swelling in the meninges.
    2. Swelling causes the brain to put extreme pressure against the skull.
  B. Amputations are common.
    1. Amy Purdy was a college student when she contracted bacterial meningitis and had to have both of her legs amputated at the knee.
      a. This tragedy struck her overnight.
      b. Within 24 hours she went from being a healthy college student with two perfectly good legs, to an ICU resident with two amputated legs and massive internal damage.
    2. Amy surprised everyone. She not only survived, but she continued skiing, as you can see in this picture of Amy. [Visual #5]

Supporting Materials:

One strength of Emily's speech is that she uses a variety of supporting materials to clarify as well as add interest and proof to her main points.

Q: How many different supporting materials can you list that Emily used? Evaluate their general quality on a scale of 1 (fair) to 5 (excellent).

Transitions:

Emily's transitions into her second and third main points are brief yet specific. Putting them into her outline shows their importance.

Q: Do you see any places where an internal summary, a repetition, or a restatement would add clarity to her message? Be specific.

Visual Aids:

Emily used five PowerPoint slides in her speech--all were text slides with visual anchors except for one graphic slide showing the layers of the meninges.

Q: What additional graphic slide do you think would have made an effective visual aid?

Sample Informational Speech *(continued)*

C. Neurological damage may last a lifetime.
   1. Almost all survivors have neurological damage.
   2. According to the National Meningitis Association, 20% of cases usually suffer from extreme damage of the kidneys, brain, and liver.
   3. Less-serious neurological damage results in such things as loss of hearing and slow response capabilities.

Conclusion   I. Although you may think to yourself that this harmful infection will not strike you, no one is impervious to this quick, silent killer.

II. It is important to remember that it is a serious bacterial infection that can be caught from someone coughing on you and could potentially kill you within the next 24 hours.

III. Now that you are aware of bacterial meningitis, I hope that you will be able to use this new knowledge to your future benefit.

References   1. *Bacterial meningitis: Disease/disorder overview.* (2008, November). Retrieved from the Health and Wellness Resource Center database.

2. Centers for Disease Control. (2009, August 6). *Meningitis: Transmission*. Retrieved from http://www.cdc.gov/meningitis/about/transmission.html.

Conclusion:

Emily reminds her audience how easy it is to contact bacterial meningitis and how fast it can potentially kill them.

Q: Do you think her final thought was effective or too strong? Why or why not?

References:

Emily cited her sources during her presentation which is necessary to show that you have credibility and have researched your topic.

Q: In this situation, were two sources enough? Why or why not?

Remember

A demonstration speech . . .

- Promotes a skill—making or doing.
- Shows how to accomplish a task step by step.

An informational speech . . .

- Promotes understanding—knowing.
- Focuses on content and ideas; may discuss how something is made but will not actually make it.

Active Critical Thinking

To think further about types of informative speeches, complete the following:
- What are two main differences or characteristics between demonstration and informational speeches?
- List two good possible speech topics for each type of informative speech. Share your list with a classmate and see if they agree with you.

Tools to Aid Understanding and Memory

In addition to using a variety of supporting materials (discussed in Chapter 6) and the last-minute guidelines for outlines, speaking notes, using visual aids, and speech rehearsal summarized later in this chapter, informative speakers have several tools to aid audience understanding and improve their memory of speech content. Which tools will work best in your speech depends on your audience and the speech topic. For example, does your audience already know something about your topic, or will it be new to them? Is your topic fairly simple to understand, or does it involve a complicated term, concept, or process? Will the idea or concept covered in your topic be easy for your "lay" audience to believe intuitively, or are they likely to be skeptical (Rowan, 1995)? Each of the following approaches can be used for either demonstration or informational speeches.

Definition

If your audience is unfamiliar with your topic, the use of one or more definitions will likely be needed. According to *Webster's New World Dictionary*, a **definition** is "a statement of what a thing is; being definite, explicit, and clear." Usually, a definition by itself is not enough to make a concept or term totally clear. Definitions are often followed by one or more of the following: a comparison or contrast, one or two examples, the *etymology* of the word (the origin or root meaning), a *synonym* (word with a similar meaning), an *antonym* (word with an opposite meaning), or a list of *essential features* (features that are always present if the definition is correct). → *See Chapter 6 for a review of comparisons and other supporting materials.*

Description

Another tool to aid listener understanding of an informative speech is **description**: painting a vivid, detailed picture of the topic using concrete words and figures of speech. Vivid, concrete words that paint a clear mental picture for the audience (such as the description of a West Highland white terrier on page 205 or the description used to clarify the meaning of a billion on page 128) not only aid understanding, but they also maintain audience attention and interest. Descriptions are even more compelling when they include figures of speech, such as similes (that compare items using the word *like* or *as*—"your eyes work like a camera"), metaphors (that are implied comparisons and do not use *like* or *as*—"the pupil of the eye is the camera aperture"), and onomatopoeia (words that sound like their meaning, such as *buzz* or *ring*). → *See Chapter 9 for a review of similes, metaphors, onomatopoeia, and other figures of speech.*

Explanation

When a topic or concept is complex, is likely to be difficult to believe, or needs a process clarified, one or more explanations (which may include definitions and descriptions) are needed. An explanation is a statement about the relationship between certain items and often answers the questions *how, what,* and *why.* Good explanations are enhanced by quality visual aids, use of clear connecting words (like *because* and *for example*), and comparing old knowledge with new knowledge (Kosslyn & Rosenberg, 2006; Rowan, 1995). With complex topics, it's best to start with the "big picture" and then show how the parts or processes work and interrelate (Mayer & Andersen, 1992; Rowan, 1990, 1995). When you present a topic that listeners may find difficult to believe, it is best to first discuss the "lay" theory or belief and why it seems plausible, discuss why it is inaccurate, and then present the more acceptable concept or theory (Brown, 1992; Rowan, 1991).

→ *See Chapter 6 for more on explanations.*

Narration

Using narratives is an excellent way to improve understanding and grab audience interest (Ballard, 2003; Fisher, 1987; Robinson, 2000). A **narration** is a story about real or imagined things, people, or events told with detail and enthusiasm. Narrations are used in business to enliven "speeches, sales pitches, training sessions, and presentations on otherwise dry or technical topics" (Quinones, 1999). In fact, Quinones reports that executives pay as much as $4,000 for an "executive storytelling" seminar (p. 4).

According to Fisher (1987), an outstanding narration or story has two important qualities: *probability* (the story is easy to follow and makes sense) and *fidelity* (the story rings true to the audience). Fisher considers former President Ronald Reagan a master storyteller and suggests that this ability helped earn him the title "The Great Communicator," even though his speeches often contained factual errors (pp. 145–157).

If you aren't experienced in using narrations, try telling personal-experience stories from your own life. Many famous people use self-narratives in their speeches. Oprah Winfrey's address at the Wellesley College commencement (1997), where she comically relates her experience of learning to be herself instead of trying to imitate Barbara Walters, serves as an effective example of using a personal-life narrative in a speech:

> I remember going on the air many times and not reading my copy ahead of time. I was on the air one night and ran across the word "Barbados." That may be *Barbados* to you but it was "Barb-a-does" to me that night, and telling the story as an anchorwoman about a vote in absentia in California, I thought it was located near San Francisco. This is when I broke out of my Barbara shell, because I am sitting there, crossing my legs, trying to talk like Barbara, be like Barbara, and I was reading a story about someone with a "blaze" attitude which, if I had gone to Wellesley, I would have known it was *blasé*, and I started to laugh at myself on the air and broke through my Barbara shell and had decided on that day that laughing was OK, even though Barbara hadn't at that time. It was through my series of mistakes that I learned I could be a better Oprah than I could be a better Barbara. I allowed Barbara to be the mentor for me, as she always has been, and I decided then to try to pursue the idea of being myself and I am just thrilled that I get paid so much every day for just being myself, but it was a lesson long in coming, recognizing that I had the instinct; that inner voice that told me that you need to try to find a way to answer to your own truth was the voice I needed to be still and listen to.

Seven years earlier, Barbara Bush (the "Speaking to Make a Difference" speaker for this chapter) also gave a commencement address to Wellesley graduates. She used narratives as a way to relate to her audience and as a type of evidence to support her ideas. As you read her address in "Speaking to Make a Difference," see if you think her stories had fidelity from a student's viewpoint.

Be sure to pick stories that will relate to your audience with fidelity and probability, and don't forget to practice, practice, and practice. → *For more on narratives, see "Personalize your speeches with narratives" in Chapter 3 and "Instances" in Chapter 6.*

The "Stickiness Factor"

In our high-tech world where people have little patience for messages that aren't "current, relevant, and immediate—and delivered on a screen" (Weaver, 2007, p. 353), it is very difficult to make our messages "stick" in the minds of our listeners. In *The Tipping Point,* Malcolm Gladwell (2002) defines the "**stickiness factor**" as that part of a message that "makes an impact. You can't get it out of your head. It sticks in your memory" (p. 25). It's like a song or commercial that you keep singing over and over until you are sure it's driving you crazy. Wouldn't it be nice if you could get your ideas to stick in the minds of your listeners like that? Not only do speakers want their listeners to *understand* what they have to say (as discussed earlier in this chapter), but speakers also want listeners to *remember* what they have to say.

In Chapter 3 we discussed the importance of listeners transferring information from their short-term to their long-term memories and gave 10 suggestions on how speakers could help listeners in this transfer process. See how many of these "stickiness" suggestions you remember (see Figure 11.1). These are all proven memory techniques supported by research psychologists. → *For more specifics and sources, refer to the section in Chapter 3 called "Incorporate Cues to Aid Memory."*

Figure 11.1

"Stickiness" suggestions

"STICKINESS" TIPS
Tip 1: Grab attention with very first words
Tip 2: Use acronyms and other mnemonic devices
Tip 3: Repeat information like commercials do
Tip 4: Reflect with audience on situation/problem
Tip 5: Get audience involved in answering questions
Tip 6: Use emotional examples
Tip 7: Relate new information to what is known
Tip 9: Compare ideas to audience experiences
Tip 10: Encourage audience to share what they learned with others

Active Critical Thinking

To think further about tools to aid understanding and memory, complete the following:

Gladwell says it takes hearing a commercial six times before we remember it (2002, p. 92). How can you apply this information to your speech? Think of at least two possible ways.

Speaking to Make a Difference

Although she doesn't have a degree—in fact, she dropped out of college her sophomore year to marry George Bush—Barbara Bush's 1990 commencement address to Wellesley College in Massachusetts was voted as one of the top 100 political speeches of the twentieth century. The following is an excerpt from that speech. Full text, audio, and video can be found by going to **www.americanrhetoric.com** and searching for "Barbara Bush Commencement Address at Wellesley College."

Cynthia Johnson/Time Life Pictures/Getty Images

Wellesley, you see, is not just a place but an idea—an experiment in excellence in which diversity is not just tolerated, but is embraced. The essence of this spirit was captured in a moving speech about tolerance given last year by a student body president of one of your sister colleges.

She related the story by Robert Fulghum about a young pastor, finding himself in charge of some very energetic children, hits upon the game called "Giants, Wizards, and Dwarfs." "You have to decide now," the pastor instructed the children, "which you are—a giant, a wizard, or a dwarf?" At that, a small girl tugging at his pants leg asked, "But where do the mermaids stand?" And the pastor tells her there are no mermaids. And she says, "Oh yes there are—there are. I am a mermaid."

Now this little girl knew what she was, and she was not about to give up on either her identity, or the game. She intended to take her place wherever mermaids fit into the scheme of things. "Where do the mermaids stand? All of those who are different, those who do not fit the boxes and the pigeonholes?" "Answer that question," wrote Fulghum, "And you can build a school, a nation, or a whole world." As that very wise young woman said, "Diversity, like anything worth having, requires effort—effort to learn about and respect difference, to be compassionate with one another, to cherish our own identity, and to accept unconditionally the same in others."

You should all be very proud that this is the Wellesley spirit. Now I know your first choice today was Alice Walker—guess how I know!—known for *The Color Purple.* Instead you got me—known for the color of my hair. Alice Walker's book has a special resonance here. At Wellesley, each class is known by a special color. For four years the Class of '90 has worn the color purple. Today you meet on Severance Green to say goodbye to all of that, to begin a new and a very personal journey, to search for your own true colors . . . And as you set off from Wellesley, I hope that many of you will consider making three very special choices.

The first is to believe in something larger than yourself, to get involved in some of the big ideas of our time. I chose literacy because I honestly believe that if more people could read, write, and comprehend, we would be that much closer to solving so many of the problems that plague our nation and our society.

And early on I made another choice, which I hope you'll make as well. Whether you are talking about education, career, or service, you're talking about life—and life really must have joy. It's supposed to be fun.

One of the reasons I made the most important decision of my life, to marry George Bush, is because he made me laugh. It's true, sometimes we've laughed through our tears, but that shared laughter has been one of our strongest bonds. Find the joy in life, because as Ferris Bueller said on his day off, "Life moves pretty fast; and if you don't stop and look around once in a while, you're gonna miss it."

(I'm not going to tell George you clapped more for Ferris than you clapped for George.)

The third choice that must not be missed is to cherish your human connections: your relationships with family and friends . . . At the end of your life, you will never regret not having passed one more test, winning one more verdict, or not closing one more deal. You will regret time not spent with a husband, a child, a friend, or a parent . . . If you have children, they must come first. You must read to your children, and you must hug your children, and you must love your children. Your success as a *family,* our success as a society, depends not on what happens in the White House, but on what happens inside your house.

For 50 years, it was said that the winner of Wellesley's annual hoop race would be the first to get married. Now they say the winner will be the first to become a CEO. . . . Both of those stereotypes show too little tolerance for those who want to know where the mermaids stand. . . . So I want to offer a new legend: the winner of the hoop race will be the first to realize her dream—not society's dreams—her own personal dream.

And . . . who knows? Somewhere out in this audience may even be someone who will one day follow in my footsteps, and preside over the White House as the President's spouse—and I wish *him* well. . . .

When it was announced that Barbara Bush would be the commencement speaker, a petition from 150 of the 600 graduating seniors from the all-female college complained that "Wellesley teaches that we will be rewarded on the basis of our own merit, not on that of a spouse. To honor Barbara Bush . . . contravenes what we have been taught over the last four years at Wellesley" (Butterfield, 1990a, p. B6). Mrs. Bush declined to make a comment prior to the presentation, but very cleverly invited Raisa Gorbachev, previous university professor and wife of President Mikhail S. Gorbachev of the Soviet Union, to join her on the podium. Wellesley was obviously honored when Gorbachev accepted, and the graduating seniors were pleased (Butterfield, 1990b).

So what else made this speech so effective?

- *Audience Analysis.* Barbara Bush definitely analyzed her audience and began quiet repairs even before the scheduled address. Two months prior to her address, approximately one-fourth of the graduating students were vocally unhappy with her invitation to speak. Yet by the time of the commencement, most of them were mollified that Mrs. Gorbachev (a woman they considered "qualified" because she had had her own career) would also be speaking at the commencement (*Wellesley Students Hail Raisa Gorbachev*, 1990).

continued

- *Supporting Materials.* Mrs. Bush selected supporting materials that directly related to her audience. For example, she began with a narrative from "a student body president of one of your sister colleges," which highlighted the importance of tolerance. She also used a quote from a popular movie, *Ferris Bueller's Day Off.* Another example occurred near the end of the speech when she said, "Who knows? Somewhere out in this audience may even be someone who will one day follow in my footsteps, and preside over the White House as the President's spouse," then paused dramatically before finishing with, "and I wish him well." The audience "roared with laughter and gave Mrs. Bush a ringing ovation" (Butterfield, 1990b, p. A1).

- *Strong Arguments.* In a gentle way, Mrs. Bush refuted the arguments presented by the protesting graduates. While challenging them to make three important choices in life (serving others, enjoying life, and cherishing human connections), she made the point that a career is not necessarily the most important goal in life. By referring to the traditional Wellesley hoop race, Mrs. Bush pointed out that "Both of these stereotypes show too little tolerance . . . So I want to offer a new legend: the winner of the hoop race will be the first to realize her dream." According to Schweizer and Hall (2007), "She deftly argued that by imposing narrow definitions of the 'proper' roles of women, her protesters had undermined their own argument."

Not only did the audience reaction declare Barbara Bush's address a success, but "rave reviews on the nation's front pages and television shows confirmed her victory" (Robinson, 1990, p. A25). It is rare that a commencement address creates this much controversy and receives this much public attention. The graduates from the Wellesley College class of 1990 are likely to remember their commencement speaker long after they have retired from their careers.

Questions: Not only was Barbara Bush included as one of the 100 top speakers of the twentieth century on **americanrhetoric .com**, but she was also included in Schweizer and Hall's book, *Landmark Speeches of the American Conservative Movement.* Why do you think her speech was honored by both the website and the authors?

Steps in Preparing an Informative Speech

The Basic Steps for Preparing a Speech are listed in the Quick Start Guide at the beginning of the text. We will review these steps as they relate specifically to preparing an informative speech. As you read this material, see if your informational or demonstration speech needs any additional work, or perhaps a bit of polishing.

Analyze Your Potential Audience

The best informative speeches are designed for a specific audience. Analyzing their situational, demographic, and psychological characteristics will help you figure out what your audience probably knows about the topic and how to make it interesting to them. In addition, analyzing their attitudes toward your topic will also help you tailor your speech to the audience. As you begin preparing an informative speech, ask yourself the following questions:

- What *situational characteristics* of my audience could affect the success of my speech? For example, how much do they know about the topic? What are their general opinions of me? Will anyone be speaking before me? Is the room equipped for the type of speech that I plan to give?

- On the basis of the *demographic characteristics* of audience members (for example, age, marital status, children, major group memberships, hobbies), how can I make my topic interesting and beneficial to them?

- What *attitudes, beliefs, or values* relevant to my topic do audience members already have? How can I use these psychological factors to communicate my ideas better?

Apply a splint	Dribble a basketball	Make gift bows
Apply clown makeup	Edit your photos on your	Mat and frame pictures
Bid on eBay	computer	Pack a travel bag efficiently
Change a cloth diaper	Fold a flag	Swing a golf club
Clean and store silver	Give CPR to an adult/	Take your blood pressure
items	child	Teach your dog a trick
Decorate holiday cakes	Insert a video into a slide	Use a digital camera
Do origami (Japanese paper	Keep score bowling	Use a metal detector
folding)	Make artificial flowers using	correctly
Do rope tricks	tissue paper	Use the Heimlich maneuver

- Is my *audience likely to be friendly, neutral, uninterested, or hostile*? What types of visual aids will impress this audience? What types of attention-getters will interest them (for example, personal instance, startling statement, or quote)? ➜ *For more information on audience analysis, see Chapter 4.*

Determine Your Topic, Exact Purpose, and Main Points

Because your goal in this course is to learn how to give effective speeches, don't worry about finding the "perfect" topic. As long as it fits the requirements of the assignment, is something that you know about and are interested in, and is of value to your audience, the topic should be fine. Check Figure 11.2 for sample demonstration topics and Figures 11.3 and 11.4 for sample informational topics.

Once you have selected your topic, narrow it to fit the time limits and decide on your exact purpose. It is better to thoroughly illustrate and support a few points than it is to try to "say it all." Write your exact purpose in one clear and simple sentence beginning with "After hearing my speech, the audience will . . ." As shown in Figure 11.5 later in this chapter, Chung-Yan stated his exact purpose as follows: "After listening to my speech, the audience will be aware of the three different ways of Chinese fortune-telling—palm reading, face reading, and fortune-telling sticks."

After stating your exact purpose, select three to five main points. If you are familiar with your topic, you probably already have a good idea of what main points to include. If not, take five minutes to brainstorm a list of possible points. Then combine and eliminate some of them until you arrive at three to five possible ones (you may change your mind after researching the topic).

Prepare a Rough-Draft Outline of Main Points and Desired Information

Unless you want to spend more time than necessary, don't overlook this important step. Basically, a rough-draft outline should include a list of possible main points and supporting information. Don't wait until after you do your research to make the rough-draft outline; if you do it first, it will save you research time. ➜ *See Chapter 5 for suggestions on making a rough-draft outline.*

Research Your Topic, Looking for Quality Supporting Materials

Of course, the whole point of researching your topic is to make sure you know what you are talking about, to add to your personal credibility, and to find a variety of supporting materials that will add interest, clarity, and proof to your informative topic. You can find supporting evidence for your speech by looking at printed materials, computer databases, and the Internet; conducting personal interviews;

Business
Casual dress in the
   workplace
Credit cards and the teen
   market
E-mail abuse
Culture in the workplace
Internships
Job-seeking on the Internet
Pros/cons of Internet use
Male/female management styles
Sales techniques that work
Blogs—are they safe?

Family
Dealing with Alzheimer's
The blended family
Wills and living trusts
Teen pregnancy
Adoption-law changes

Food/Beverages
Ethnic foods
Low-calorie cooking
Mad cow disease
Shopping on a budget
Vegetarianism/Veganism

Health
Acai Berry Diet
Diabetes on the rise
Eating disorders
Government health care
Indoor air pollution
Lowering cholesterol
Cord blood banks

Nursing shortage
Sleep disorders
Bottled water—necessary?

Holiday
A vacation spot
Gifts everyone will love
Holiday depression
Holiday safety tips

Miscellaneous
A famous person
Review of a favorite book
Topic related to your job
Topic related to your major

Multicultural
Diversity training at work
Ethnic traditions
Global warming
Global water shortages
Muslims in America
The "Ugly" Americans
U.S.-Mexico relations

National
Alternative fuels
Homeland security
Post Traumatic Stress
   Disorder
Preventing terrorism
Recent court decisions
Restructuring Social
   Security
Space-program future
Veterans who can't find
   jobs

Personal
Building lasting marriages
Dealing with stress
Dressing on a budget
Effective resumes
Memory techniques
Study techniques
Volunteering

Pets/Animals
Best pets for children
One-bite rule for dogs
Pets on airplanes

Social Issues
AIDS update
ADA—what we should know
Assisted suicide
Charity scams
Fetal-tissue research
New immigrants
Sexual abuse and clergy

Sports/Hobbies
Reflective clothing and
   joggers
Reforming college sports
Soccer fans
Tennis tips
Tips on watching football

Technology
Building a Web page
Copyright and the Internet
Electric and hybrid cars
Message-board ethics
Viruses and hackers

Figure 11.3

Sample Informational Speech Topics (General Categories).

and recalling personal experiences. As you do your research, look for both verbal and visual supporting materials. I strongly suggest that in addition to printed sources, you use the electronic databases available through your college and city libraries. Here are some suggestions. → *For other research suggestions, see Chapter 5.*

- *For current news topics:* Use CQ Researcher (which includes detailed articles ranging from 15 to 20 pages) or EBSCOhost, which is especially good for current business topics (also see Business Source Complete).

- *For health, medical, and sports topics:* Student Resource Center–College edition by Gale is especially good; also, use the following databases in EBSCOhost: Consumer Health Complete, Health Source: Consumer Edition, Health Source: Nursing/Academic Edition, or MEDLINE.

How	What	Why
How does the eye see colors?	What is evolution?	Why is abstract art more difficult than portraiture to understand?
How does radar work?	What is the difference between stocks and bonds?	Why is perception subjective rather than objective?
How does podcasting work?	What is the structure of the federal court system?	Why do natural foods contain dangerous toxins?
How do digital cameras work?	What is the greenhouse effect?	Why do people yawn?
How does blogging work?	What is Plato's cave analogy?	Why is irradiated food healthy (or dangerous)?
How does human vision work?	What are the tenets of Islam?	
How do men get breast cancer?	What are the tenets of Christianity?	
How do DNA molecules pass on genetic information?	What is the trickle-down theory?	
	What does "Manifest Destiny" mean?	

Figure 11.4

Sample Informational Speech Topics—How, What, and Why (adapted from Rowan, 1995).

- *For issues with controversy* (remember that informative speeches can only present information—not try to convince or persuade): Opposing Viewpoints Research Center as well as Issues and Controversies include articles on both sides of controversial issues.

- *For videos and podcasts:* Look at the Media Library in the Science Resource Center or the media tab in EBSCOhost.

It is the speaker's task to (1) provide the maximum amount of information, (2) do it in a short amount of time, and (3) make sure the information is clear, interesting, and believable. The only way to do this is to use quality supporting materials that you have found while researching. Make sure that you plan to use at least two different supports for each main point—more is usually better. For example, to support your first point, you might begin with a definition or explanation, add a detailed factual instance, and conclude with a direct quotation or a visual aid. Your second main point might begin with two or three brief instances, followed by a hypothetical instance, and so on. If you can't identify your supports, you are probably using explanation—an often-overused type of support. Limit your use of statistics and explanation, and increase your use of instances, comparisons, and expert opinions, as well as fables, sayings, poems, and rhymes. → *See Chapter 6 for specifics on types and examples of supporting materials.*

Determine How Best to Organize Main Points

Of the four organizational patterns typically used in informative speeches—topical, chronological, spatial/geographic, and causal—speakers tend to use the topical pattern most often, as Chung-Yan did in the speech on Chinese fortune-telling. However, the topical pattern is not necessarily the best for every speech. For one thing, because it is used so often, it is less likely to attract interest. Unusual topics and less-used patterns of organization are more likely to attract interest; therefore, try the chronological, spatial/geographic, or causal pattern instead. → *See Chapter 7 for a detailed discussion of the four organizational patterns for informative speeches.*

Plan Your Introduction and Conclusion

Never begin your speech with a statement of purpose. Always begin with an attention-getter. Also, never end your speech with only a summary of your purpose; instead, after the summary, end with a final memorable attention-getter that will leave your audience thinking about your speech. → *Chapter 7 discusses the basic elements in speech introductions and conclusions.*

Test Your Knowledge Quiz

Testing Your Knowledge of Organizational Patterns

Directions: Here are six mini-outlines, each with a title and main points. Identify how the main points of each outline are organized, by selecting (a) topical, (b) chronological, (c) spatial or geographic, or (d) causal. Write the letter in the blank. You can also take this quiz online at the *Essentials of Public Speaking* website and, if requested, e-mail your responses to your instructor.

_____ 1. "History of the Arabian Horse"
    I. Origin of the breed.
    II. Impact on the desert Bedouins.
    III. Introduction to Europe and North America.
    IV. Modern Arabian horse

_____ 2. "Traffic Woes"
    I. Traffic accidents have increased.
    II. The chief reason for these accidents is the increased speed limit.

_____ 3. "Preparing an Elegant Mincemeat-Pear Tart"
    I. Prepare the pastry.
    II. Prepare the streusel topping.
    III. Bake crust 20 minutes at 350 degrees.
    IV. Arrange mincemeat and pears into partially baked crust.
    V. Add streusel topping and bake 15 to 20 minutes at 425 degrees.

_____ 4. "Lyme Disease"
    I. Symptoms elusive.
    II. Diagnosis difficult.
    III. Treatment varied.

_____ 5. "Who Was Involved in Building the U.S. Space Station?"
    I. The Goddard Space Flight Center in Greenbelt, Maryland.
    II. The Lewis Research Center in Cleveland, Ohio.
    III. The Marshall Space Flight Center in Huntsville, Alabama.
    IV. The Johnson Space Flight Center in Houston, Texas.

_____ 6. "Do You Fit Your Birth-Order Mold?"
    I. "Brilliant" firstborns.
    II. "Forgotten" middle children.
    III. "Get-away-with-murder" lastborns.

Answers
1. (a) chronological pattern   2. (d) causal pattern   3. (b) chronological pattern
4. (a) topical pattern   5. (c) spatial/geographic pattern   6. (a) topical pattern

If you decide to use humor, it is generally best to avoid self-disparaging humor (where you make yourself the brunt of a joke)—it has a negative effect on an audience (Martin, 2004). Read about the self-disparaging humor used by Ann Richards in "Speaking Who Made a Difference," Chapter 7. Normally, it is much better to direct humor at your occupation or profession instead; research indicates that this does not harm your image (Gruner, 1985).

Make a Preparation Outline, Apply Critical thinking, and Plan Speaking Notes

To add polish to your speech and make sure it flows smoothly, you will need to expand your rough-draft outline into a more detailed preparation outline, apply critical thinking to your speech, and prepare speaking notes if you wish to use them while speaking.

Polish with a Preparation Outline

Here are some final suggestions to add polish to your presentation:

- Avoid writing out your speech word for word as though it were a paper; this key mistake is more of a handicap than a help. It is difficult to read from a manuscript without sounding monotone and without looking more at the paper than the audience. No one wants to listen to someone reading to them—instead they are looking for an enthusiastic, conversational speaker with great gestures and facial expressions. Although most speakers discover that brief notes are more helpful, some speakers do write out the introduction and conclusion to make sure they begin and end exactly as intended. If you try this approach, make sure you don't sound like you are reading. Formalize your rough outline into either a phrase or complete-sentence outline instead of writing it in manuscript form. (See a sample preparation outline in Figure 11.5.) Make sure all quotations and statistics are complete. Read or talk through the speech. If you find that a section is awkward, adjust it and go through the speech again. You may decide to add another example or remove one. You may even decide to do some more research. Whatever you do, don't memorize the speech—an extemporaneous speech should be a little different each time it's given.

- Use the critical thinking form in Figure 11.6 for a final check to make sure your main points as well as your supporting materials have clarity, are significant, and are accurate.

- Check your outline carefully, looking for any unintentional plagiarism. Plagiarism occurs anytime we use the words or ideas of another person without giving them credit (whether the content is paraphrased or word for word, whether the person is living or dead, whether the information is in print or on the Internet). As we discussed in Chapter 1, plagiarism not only ruins your credibility as a speaker, but it can ruin your academic career as well. To make sure you are not unintentionally plagiarizing, check the following, all of which are examples of plagiarism:
    - Main points taken directly from another speech or article with no source given.
    - Content taken word for word from another speech or an article with no source given.
    - Information taken from Wikipedia with no source given. (Although Wikipedia is a free encyclopedia—which means you don't have to pay to use it—this does not mean it is free to use information without citing it. Also, Wikipedia is generally not an acceptable source for academic writing and research.)
    - Information or ideas taken word for word from any online site or blog with no source given.
    - Speeches (written and posted to the Internet by someone else) used by you, either verbatim or in part, with no sources given.

Figure 11.5

Chung-Yan Mung's
Preparation Outline

SAMPLE PREPARATION OUTLINE: "CHINESE FORTUNE-TELLING"

by Chung-Yan Mung

The following informative preparation outline was presented by Chung-Yan Mung for his speech, "Chinese Fortune Telling." Chung-Yan's assignment was to prepare a 4- to 6-minute informative speech about a topic of his choosing. Because he has roots in Hong Kong and experience with fortune-telling, he decided to inform his classmates about three different ways the Chinese tell fortunes. Visual aids were required and no notes were allowed for this speech. To watch and analyze a video clip of Chung-Yan's speech, look at the CourseMate for *Essentials of Public Speaking*.

Title: "Chinese Fortune-Telling" by Chung-Yan Mung

Exact Purpose: After listening to my speech, the audience will be aware of the three different ways of Chinese fortune-telling—palm reading, face reading, and fortune-telling sticks.

INTRODUCTION

I. Do you want to know what your future will be?

II. In general, people want to know the future, because knowledge of the future means control of the future.

III. As I am from Hong Kong, I have experienced the mysterious but unique practice of fortune-telling in the traditional Chinese culture.

IV. So today, I am going to talk about three different kinds of Chinese fortune-telling: palm reading, face reading, and fortune-telling sticks.

BODY

I. One kind of Chinese-fortune telling is palm reading.

    A. Palm reading, also termed as palmistry, is the process of foretelling a person's future by the imprints and marks on the palm.

        1. Palmistry is based upon the interpretation of the general characteristics of a person's hands.

        2. Palmistry focuses on the study of lines, their patterns, and other formations and marks that appear on the palms and fingers.

    B. Palmistry is divided into two subfields: the palm itself and the fingers.

        1. The three principal lines on your palm are heart, head, and life lines; if lines are deep, clear, and have no interruptions, it is a sign of a smooth and successful life.

        2. Fingers are also important in palm reading: length of the index and ring fingers each indicates different beliefs.

Transition So now that you have understood the basic ideas of palm reading, let us go on to a second kind of Chinese fortune-telling: face reading.

II. The Chinese believe that the face can also be used to predict the future and fortune of an individual.

    A. Face reading is the Chinese art of predicting a person's future and fortunes by analyzing the different elements of his or her face.

   1. The major facial features used in developing the fortune are the nose, mouth, forehead, eyebrows, and eyes.

   2. The face shapes show the basic constitution and attributes.

  B. Balance and proportion are important in face reading, as in paintings.

Transition Last but not least, the Chinese also use fortune-telling joss sticks.

  III. The oldest known method of fortune-telling in the world is the use of fortune-telling sticks.

   A. They are for giving an indication of the possibilities of the future, instead of telling exactly what will happen.

   B. This method, which is part of religious practice, takes place in a temple.

    1. A believer selects numbered sticks from a bamboo case containing 78 sticks.

    2. Believers burn joss sticks, then kneel before the main altar.

CONCLUSION

  I. In conclusion, when people know more and more about Chinese fortune-telling, they begin to understand that these methods are quite scientific and, to a certain extent, accurate.

  II. So, I hope what you have learned today about palmistry, face reading, and joss sticks will give you an appreciation for Chinese culture and fortune-telling practices.

WORKS CITED:

Bright, M. Chinese face reading for health diagnosis and self knowledge. The Wholistic Research Company. **www.wholisticresearch.com/info/artshow. php3?artid=96** (accessed October 18, 2005).

British-born Chinese website. Fortune telling. **www.britishbornchinese.org.uk/ pages/culture/customs/fortunetelling.html** (accessed October 17, 2005).

Find Your Fate website. What is palmistry? **www.findyourfate.com/palmistry/ palmistry.htm** (accessed October 16, 2005).

Hong Kong Tourism Board. Sik Sik Yuen Wong Tai Sin Temple. **www.discoverhongkong. com/eng/touring/popular/ta_popu_wong.jhtml** (accessed October 18, 2005).

King-Man, S. C. Fortune telling. Chinese University of Hong Kong. **www.se.cuhk. edu.hk/~palm/chinese/fortune** (accessed May 2005).

Polish by Thinking Critically About Your Speech Once you have completed your preparation outline but before you present your speech, it is important to subject your topic, outline, and supporting materials to a thoughtful assessment to make sure that they have clarity, accuracy, depth, and significance (Elder & Paul, 2003b). As a speaker, you have the potential of impacting a large number of people, and, therefore, have the responsibility of questioning what you present in your informative and persuasive speeches. Questioning is a form of **critical thinking**, which is defined as "skilled and active interpretation and evaluation of observations, communications, information and argumentation" (Fisher & Scriven, 1997, p. 20). Because not all evidence and not all sources are reliable, it is up to you to question everything and decide what to include in each speech you make.

When you engage in reflective thinking, you are challenging your interpretation of facts, challenging your evidence, and challenging your logic (Facione & Facione, 2007). This isn't easy to do. Many people "consider their personal beliefs sufficient justification for their opinions and view any challenge as a personal attack" (Elder & Paul, 2003a, p. 24). Yet critical thinking requires that speakers look at the ideas, supports, arguments, and sources in their preparation outlines and challenge them. As well as questioning the beliefs of others, you also need to challenge your own beliefs before presenting them to your audience. To get you started evaluating your presentation outline, use the questions provided in Figure 11.6.

When you have answered the Critical Thinking Questions in Figure 11.6, make any necessary deletions or additions to your preparation outline. If you decide to use speaking notes, you are now ready to prepare them.

Polish by Planning Speaking Notes (if allowed by the assignment) Brief key words or phrases designed for use during the actual speech and written on note cards or paper are called **speaking notes**. Don't be tempted to speak

Figure 11.6

Critical Thinking Questions

Critical Thinking Questions

Directions: Answer these questions as they apply to your speech topic, outline, supports, and sources.

1. The main purpose for selecting my speech topic was . . .
2. The key question in my mind when I chose this topic was . . .
3. The most important information (facts, experiences, data) in this speech is . . .
4. The main inferences/conclusions I plan to present in this speech are . . .
5. The key concept/idea(s) that must be clear to my listeners in order for them to understand my speech is/are . . .
6. The main assumption(s) I am taking for granted that might be questioned is/are . . .
7. If my audience takes my facts or position seriously, the implications or consequences that are likely to follow include . . .
8. If my audience ignores or fails to take my facts or position seriously, the implications or consequences that are likely to follow include . . .
9. Besides my personal point of view toward this topic, which is . . . , another point of view I might consider is . . .
10. The conclusions/assumptions my listeners will likely draw from the supporting materials (comparisons, statistics, quotations, narratives, etc.) included in my outline are . . .
11. The conclusions/assumptions my audience will likely draw from my introduction and/or conclusion are . . .
12. Questions my listeners are likely to ask about my speech are . . .

*Adapted from pages 5 and 10 of Elder, L. & Paul, R., (2003b). *The Miniature Guide to Critical Thinking: Concepts and Tools.* Dillon Beach, CA: The Foundation for Critical Thinking.

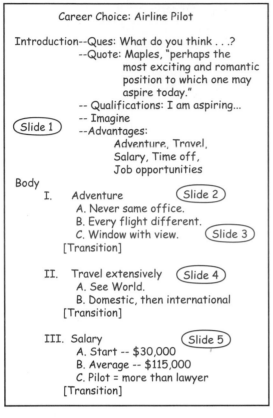

Career Choice: Airline Pilot

Introduction--Ques: What do you think . . .?
            --Quote: Maples, "perhaps the
                    most exciting and romantic
                    position to which one may
                    aspire today."
            -- Qualifications: I am aspiring...
            -- Imagine
(Slide 1)   --Advantages:
                    Adventure, Travel,
                    Salary, Time off,
                    Job opportunities
Body
    I.   Adventure   (Slide 2)
          A. Never same office.
          B. Every flight different.
          C. Window with view.   (Slide 3)
          [Transition]

    II.   Travel extensively   (Slide 4)
          A. See World.
          B. Domestic, then international
          [Transition]

    III. Salary   (Slide 5)
          A. Start -- $30,000
          B. Average -- $115,000
          C. Pilot = more than lawyer
          [Transition]

Figure 11.7

Sample of a Student's Speaking Notes on a 4-by-6-Inch
Note Card.

from your preparation outline. Beginning speakers often want to use a manuscript with complete sentences while speaking because they think it will make them feel more secure—however, because it is difficult to read from a manuscript, beginning speakers usually appear either insecure or unprepared. Experienced speakers will tell you that *complete sentences are usually no help while speaking,* whether in a manuscript or speaking notes. Your eyes can't grasp more than three or four words at a time. As a result, speakers whose notes are written in complete sentences (or even long phrases) usually either (1) end up reading the notes word for word (which means they can't make eye contact with the audience and have a stilted speaking style) or (2) they forget the notes and try to "wing it" and leave out much of the interesting detail they intended to include.

Effective speaking notes are brief, include key words or phrases, use color and underlining so that important words will stand out, and include action notes (such as pause *and* louder*) in the margins.* Your speaking notes may be in outline form if you wish, but it's not necessary. Many speakers prefer to use note cards (one 4-by-6-inch card is usually enough), because they are easy to hold and to see, especially when reading a quotation. Some speakers prefer a single sheet of paper so they can see the entire speech at one time. However, using a sheet of paper has disadvantages. If you place your notes on a lectern, chances are the lectern will not be tall enough for easy reading. If you decide to hold your notes, a sheet of paper is large enough to be distracting, and it may shake, making you look nervous. If you use transparencies, you can jot notes on the cardboard frames and won't need to use cards or other types of notes. In fact, after you rehearse your speech a few times with computer visuals or transparencies, you will probably discover that you really don't need any notes at all. ➤ *See Figure 11.7 for a student's speaking notes.*

Prepare Visual Aids

Look at your preparation outline and rough out some possible visuals. One might be a text visual with a title, photo or clip art, and a list of the main points in your speech; and you could use it again in your conclusion. Another might include a graph of some statistics or a picture that illustrates a point. ➤ *Chapter 10 includes information for preparing all types of visual aids.*

Here are some final suggestions to add polish to your visual aids:

• Make sure that your visuals don't distract from your speech and that your delivery complements your visuals (such as relaxed body posture, gestures, and eye contact).

• Make sure that it takes no more than three to six seconds to comprehend your PowerPoint slides (otherwise your audience will read instead of listening to you).

- Check your text slides to make sure your titles are one line only, and use a font no smaller than 30 points in size; avoid use of all caps; include no more than six lines of text; use phrases, not sentences; and make effective use of color, contrast, repetition, alignment, and proximity.

- Check your graphic slides to make sure you have limited and grouped data, included titles on all slides, minimized the use of grid lines, used bars a little wider than the space between them, and made effective use of color, contrast, repetition, alignment, and proximity.

- Conduct a technological rehearsal as described in the next section.

Practice Your Speech Both Physically and Technologically

As you know, mentally thinking through your speech will not have the same result as practicing it aloud. A successful speech practice involves (1) standing up and using your speaking notes and visual aids in an environment similar to the one in which you will speak, and (2) conducting a technological practice to test your PowerPoint slides and any equipment to be used. ➙ *Chapters 8 and 9 include advice on effective delivery.*

Here are some final suggestions for effective speech practice:

- Practice giving your speech in front of friends or family members. If possible, have someone make a video for you to watch. If all else fails, practice in front of a mirror.

- If you have notes, make sure they are barely visible and that you are maintaining good eye contact with your audience.

- Check that your delivery is loud enough, is conversational (not read), and that you sound enthusiastic (with varied pitch, volume, rate, and emphasis).

- Check your attention getter to make sure it flows smoothly and you feel comfortable using it—if not, revise it.

- Listen to see if your language is simple, brief, and vivid, yet specific—if not, keep practicing.

- Make sure your transitions allow main points to flow smoothly from one to the next—if not, reword them.

- Listen to see if your ideas are clear and easy to understand (ask your friends or family).

- Finally, if time allows, listen to see if you are using verbal immediacy behaviors (such as personal examples; references to *we, us,* and *our;* and references to individuals by name).

Here are some final suggestions for an effective technological rehearsal:

- Test your presentation by trying your disk, CD, or USB flash or thumb drive on a different computer. If you are using Microsoft, not all computers have Windows 7 or PowerPoint 2010; until both are in common use, it is a good idea to save your slides to the previous version (go to "Save As," and in the window called "Same As Type," scroll down to "PowerPoint 97–2007" and save). **Note:** The PowerPoint feature under "File/Package for CD" lets you save your entire presentation to a CD. It includes a new

Use a database like InfoTrac College Edition, EBSCOhost, or CQ Researcher to search for *speechwriting, speech writing, public speaking, oral presentation*,* and *technical presentation**. Look for articles written by professionals in your major on preparing and presenting effective speeches. Look for speaking suggestions that you can use.

Viewer that allows any presentation (created in PowerPoint 2000 or later) to run on any computer operating Windows 98 Second Edition or later, even when PowerPoint is not installed on the computer. The Viewer is available free on Microsoft's website (**www.microsoft.com**).

- If you are using Microsoft, use Ctrl + F7 to see the slides on your laptop screen at the same time the audience sees them on the wall screen. Once PowerPoint has loaded, open your slides to a full-screen presentation by clicking F5. Better yet, save your presentation as a PowerPoint show (.PPS)—go to File/Save As, select "PowerPoint Show," and click "Save." Now a simple double click on your presentation icon will immediately show a full-screen view of your opening slide without any indication that PowerPoint is running—much more professional!

- Make sure that there is adequate lighting so the audience can see your facial expressions as well as the screen, and so you can see any notes. If not, bring a pencil flashlight or small lamp to clip on the stand.

- Use a remote control if possible—it frees you from the keyboard and gives you speaker control.

- Move back and forth between slides by pressing the number of the slide and then the Enter key. For example, if you are on slide 6 when someone asks a question about slide 3, simply press 3 and Enter to switch to slide 3.

- Print a paper copy of your slides by selecting "Handouts" from the Print menu (four to six slides per page) and "Frame Slides." Number your slides for easy reference in case you need to move back and forth between slides.

- For important presentations, have a backup form of the slides in case of equipment or power failure. It is also a good idea to e-mail your presentation to yourself so it can be accessed through the Internet if needed (Hamilton, 2011, pp. 366–367).

This chapter has presented a look at what's involved in preparing and presenting an informative speech. The next chapter will apply the Basic Steps for Preparing a Speech to persuasive speeches.

Summary

There are two basic types of informative speeches—demonstration and informational. In a demonstration speech, the visuals become the focus of the speech because you are showing how to make or do something; in an informational speech, slides complement and clarify your ideas.

When preparing an informative speech, follow these 10 steps: (1) analyze your audience; (2) determine your topic, exact purpose, and main points; (3) rough out an outline of main points and supporting information; (4) research the topic to find supporting materials; (5) select the best supporting material for each main point; (6) determine how to organize your main points; (7) develop the introduction and conclusion; (8) expand the rough outline into a preparation outline and prepare your speaking notes; (9) prepare your visual aids; and (10) practice your speech both physically and technologically. Until you are an experienced speaker, try to use these steps in the order suggested. You are now ready to present an outstanding informative presentation.

Essentials of Public Speaking Online CourseMate

Use your Online Resources for *Essentials of Public Speaking* for quick access to the electronic study resources that accompany this chapter. Your Online Resources feature the Test Your Knowledge quizzes on pages 247 and 265, a video of Chung-Yan's speech on page 267, the Informative-Demonstration Speech Evaluation on page 276, access to InfoTrac College Edition, Personal Skill Building activities, Collaborative Skill Building activities, a digital glossary, sample speeches, and review quizzes.

Key Terms

critical thinking 268	description 257	speaking notes 269
definition 257	informational speech	stickiness factor 259
demonstration speech	253	
250	narration 258	

Personal Skill Building

1. Prepare a 3- to 4-minute demonstration speech. Follow the guidelines in this chapter for preparing your speech. Determine what visuals to use and how to prepare them with maximum effectiveness.

2. Prepare a 4- to 7-minute informational speech to be followed by up to 2 minutes of questions from the audience and a 1-minute (or less) final summary. Unless your instructor indicates otherwise, prepare a minimum of two transparencies or computer slides; other types of visuals may be used as well. Follow the guidelines in this chapter for preparing your speech.

3. Listen to and read popular speeches (such as the "Speaking to Make a Difference" example for this chapter). Find an example of each of the tools that aid an informative speech—definition, description, explanation, and narration— in a video of one of these speeches by going to your Online Resources for *Essentials of Public Speaking*. Share your findings with your classmates.

4. Select a subject in your major or minor field of study that is either unknown to most people or misunderstood due to its complexity. Interview class members to determine problems, research the topic, and prepare three of the following: a definition, a description, an explanation, or a narration. Exchange your paragraphs with a class member; include comments and suggestions. If time permits, present your presentation to the class for evaluation.

5. Check out the following websites. You can access these sites under the Student Resources for Chapter 11 at the *Essentials of Public Speaking* Online Resources.

   - The University of Hawaii's Speech Department has an excellent website providing 10 steps for preparing a speech and provides sample speeches you can examine. Go to this site: **www.hawaii.edu/mauispeech/html/ preparing_speeches.html**.

- Search "Public Speaking" through EBSCOhost or CQ Researcher databases and then click on an interesting article. How will your approach to speaking change based on this view of public speaking?

- Read the article "Key Words in Instruction: Audience Analysis" by Daniel Callison and Annette Lamb. Search "Audience Analysis" through EBSCOhost and then click on the article above.

Collaborative Skill Building

1. In groups of three to five, prepare three visual aids Chung-Yan could have used in his speech "Chinese Fortune-Telling" or Emily Wilson could have used in her speech "Bacterial Meningitis." Use PowerPoint and include color, clip art, transitions, and even sound. Each group should present its slides to the class and then turn in a copy to the instructor for evaluation.

2. In groups of four or five, use the Informative/Demonstration Speech Evaluation in Figure 11.8 and evaluate Emily Wilson's speech. What grade do you think the speech deserves? See if you can agree as a group for each of the 20 evaluation items. Compare your group's total points for Emily's speech with that of other group evaluations. If you like, you can watch Emily's speech and complete your evaluation on the CourseMate for *Essentials of Public Speaking*.

Quiz Answers

Answers to the Unit Four Quiz on page 247: Test Your Knowledge of Different Types of Speeches.

1. *False.* A good speech of introduction focuses attention on the featured speaker, not on the person giving the introduction. Therefore, speeches of introduction are brief—seldom longer than five minutes.

2. *True.* Although much more research needs to be done, it does appear that color (when used correctly) is more persuasive. A study by the University of Minnesota and 3M Corporation found that color transparencies were more persuasive than black-and-white ones; the Bureau of Advertising found that readers are 80 percent more likely to read a color ad than a black-and-white one and 55 to 78 percent more likely to purchase an item shown in a color ad (Johnson, 1990; Vogel et al., 1986, 1990). ➤ *See Chapter 10 for more information on color visuals.*

3. *True.* Speakers often make the mistake of letting the Q&A period get out of control or run on too long. When this happens, audience members may forget how positive they felt about your speech. To direct the audience back to your speech topic, thank them for their participation, respond to the last question, and then sum up your topic with a final, memorable conclusion. ➤ *See Chapter 8 for more suggestions on how to handle Q&A—question and answers.*

4. *False.* Although you should always cite the source of evidence, research indicates that mentioning only the source, not the qualifications of the source, makes the evidence less persuasive than citing no source at all (Bostrom & Tucker, 1969; Ostermeier, 1967). ➤ *See Chapter 13 for additional information.*

5. *False.* Although manipulation is unethical, analyzing your audience members so that you know their needs and wants is simply good research. How else are you going to make sure that your message fits their frames of reference so that they will give you a fair hearing? ➡ *Audience analysis is discussed in Chapter 4.*

6. *False.* Research has found that few people are persuaded by logic alone. In fact, most people can't even distinguish illogical arguments from logical ones. An argument is logical only if your audience views it as such, and people will view an argument as logical if they can relate to it personally. For example, listeners might be uninterested in giving money to clean up the environment until they realize that the local lake is so polluted that their beloved water sports will be banned unless the county receives enough money to have the lake cleaned before summer.

7. *True.* Professional-looking visual aids impress an audience. Because you have obviously worked hard on them, they enhance your credibility. ➡ *Credibility is discussed in Chapter 13.*

8. *False.* There is a big difference between using humor and telling jokes. Few speakers are able to tell jokes effectively. They forget the punch line or leave out a pertinent detail, making the punch line meaningless. However, most speakers can add humor to their speeches with well-placed examples or unexpected facial or vocal expressions. As long as it is appropriate to your topic, humor has a place in informative speeches. ➡ *See Chapter 8 for more information on humor.*

9. *False.* The correct procedure is to walk to the front, pause, and immediately begin with an attention-getter ("Last week my favorite uncle was playing basketball with his two teenage sons when . . .") before stating your purpose.

10. *False.* Unless the source is a famous, well-liked person, it is more persuasive to cite the source after presenting the evidence. Research indicates that it is better to let the audience absorb the evidence before judging it by its source ➡ *See Chapter 13 for more information about presenting evidence.*

Informative/Demonstration Speech Evaluation

Name: _____ Topic: _____ Date:_____

Grades: Outline: _____ Presentation:_____ Other:_____

Ratings: 1 (Missing), 2 (Poor), 3 (Fair), 4 (Good), 5 (Excellent)

Did INTRODUCTION: Comments:

  1. Begin with attention-getter?   1 2 3 4 5

  2. Motivate audience to listen?   1 2 3 4 5

  3. Establish credibility?   1 2 3 4 5

  4. Make purpose clear?   1 2 3 4 5

  5. Preview main points?   1 2 3 4 5

Were MAIN IDEAS:

  6. Easy to identify and follow?   1 2 3 4 5

  7. Arranged in an effective pattern?   1 2 3 4 5

  8. Characterized by smooth transitions?   1 2 3 4 5

Was SUPPORTING MATERIAL:

  9. Well documented during the speech?   1 2 3 4 5

10. Adequate in verbal supports? [Use +, √, –.]   1 2 3 4 5

    ___ *Statistics?*   ___ *Rhymes, sayings, poems, demonstrations?*

    ___ *Comparisons?*   ___ *Short instances (examples)?*

    ___ *Expert opinions?*   ___ *Detailed instances (illustrations)?*

    ___ *Explanations/definitions?*   ___*Other:*

11. Adequate in visual supports? [Use +, √, –.]   1 2 3 4 5

    ___ *Interesting?*   ___ *Professional?*

    ___ *Easy to see?*   ___ *Handled well?*

Did CONCLUSION:

12. Summarize topic and main ideas?   1 2 3 4 5

13. Close in a memorable way and use effective Q&A (if appropriate)?   1 2 3 4 5

Was DELIVERY characterized by:

14. Natural, conversational quality?   1 2 3 4 5

15. Direct eye contact?   1 2 3 4 5

16. Minimal (or no) use of notes?   1 2 3 4 5

17. Freedom from distracting mannerisms? [Check]   1 2 3 4 5

    ___ *"Uh"/ "Um"/ "And uh"/ "You know"/ "Well"/ "OK"?*

    ___ *Plays with pencil, clothes, hair, or pointer?*

    ___ *Nervous laugh or cough?*

    ___ *Slouches, taps feet, paces, or sways?*

    ___ *Other?*

18. Effective vocal delivery (volume, pitch, rate, and emphasis)?   1 2 3 4 5

Was PRESENTATION AS WHOLE:

19. Suited to assignment and time limit?   1 2 3 4 5

20. Accompanied by quality outline (and other items)?   1 2 3 4 5

                                                         Total: _____

Figure 11.8

Informative/Demonstration Speech Evaluation Form

12

Persuasive Speaking: Individual or Team

The Greek general Pericles was known for the power of his oratory. Some of the most impressive monuments of ancient Greece owe their existence to his political persuasion. First, he convinced the Delian Defense League to transfer its war treasury to Athens where it would be kept safe. Then he convinced the Athenians that this money should be used not for war but for peaceful purposes—to rebuild the Acropolis (previously destroyed by the Persians) and to build beautiful marble structures designed to last for generations, such as the Parthenon and the Great Temple of Athena.

The *Speaking to Make a Difference* feature that appears in each chapter highlights 14 speakers that used their speaking skills to make a difference in the United States: from Bill Gates, who urged graduates to donate their time and money to solve major problems around the world; to Harry Markopolos, who did his best to warn people of the Madoff Ponzi scheme; to Martin Luther King Jr , who sought to make all people have equal rights; to President Barack Obama, who gave a moving eulogy at Fort Hood after a shooter wounded and killed several at a military graduation. *What speakers—especially motivational or persuasive speakers—can you think of who have used their speaking abilities to make a difference in your community, your country, or the world?*

Learning Objectives

As you read Chapter 12,

- *Define* the term *persuasion*; *explain* how a persuasive speech differs from an informative one, what makes a good argument, and what appeals make a persuasive speech persuasive.
- *Identify* the different types of persuasive speeches and when each is the most effective.
- *List* and *discuss* the main steps involved in preparing a persuasive speech.
- *Pinpoint* several characteristics of successful team presentations.

THINK OF HOW OFTEN WE USE PERSUASION IN OUR DAILY CONVERSATIONS AT SCHOOL, at work, and with friends and family. For example, we may:

- Convince a professor that our reasons for turning in a paper late are justified.

- Persuade our boss that ordering supplies from a different company would save money.

- Argue with our friends that going to a movie would be more fun than going to a hockey game.

- Appeal to our family about the plight of children in northern Uganda so that they will donate money to help.

In other words, we are all familiar with persuasion. That familiarity and your speaking experiences have prepared you for one of the most interesting yet complex types of speaking: persuasive speaking. We will cover persuasive speaking in two chapters: This chapter will introduce persuasion, the basic types of persuasive speeches, how to pick topics for each type, and the basic steps needed for preparing a successful persuasive speech, whether an individual speech or a team presentation. The next chapter will take a more detailed look at how to be truly persuasive by using *ethos* (ethical appeal), *pathos* (emotional appeal), and *logos* (logical appeal). Both chapters include sample persuasive speeches for you to use as guides in creating your own speeches. Keep in mind that persuasion is complex and will require serious involvement from you—but the end result of being able to persuade or sell your ideas to others is well worth the effort!

Persuasive Speaking: An Overview

When planning a persuasive speech, it is important to understand what persuasion really is, how it differs from informing, how to plan an effective argument, and what appeals to use in making your speech really persuasive.

What Is a Persuasive Speech?

Persuasion occurs when you ethically but intentionally organize your communication to influence the attitudes, behaviors, and choices of a specific audience. This definition includes three important aspects: (1) persuasion is intentional; (2) persuasion involves ethical influence, not control; and (3) persuasion requires careful audience analysis. Let's look at each of these points in more detail.

Successful Persuasive Speakers *Intend* to Persuade Their Listeners Persuasive speakers take a definite stand and, through various kinds of persuasive appeals, urge their listeners to hold a particular belief or take a certain action. The ineffective persuasive speaker, in contrast, presents information and options, hoping that the audience will be persuaded, but fails to specify which options are best and avoids taking a definite stand. Which of the following two approaches do you think would be more persuasive?

Approach 1
We've discussed some of the possible solutions to the crisis in our educational system. I hope you will consider them carefully in deciding how best to solve our educational dilemma.

Approach 2

We've looked at a variety of crisis. However, there's only one that has a record of success in every district where it has been tried. There's only one that appears to please students, parents, teachers, and taxpayers alike. There's only one that deserves our support, and that plan is . . .

The first approach does not indicate which option is best or which solution the speaker advocates. Considering the many different frames of reference in your audience, you cannot assume that listeners will automatically reach the conclusion that you believe is best. On the other hand, the second approach leaves no doubt as to which plan the speaker advocates. This explicit approach decreases the chances of misunderstanding and increases the probability of persuasion. After reviewing the research on the topic, O'Keefe (1990, 1997) concludes: "The overwhelmingly predominant finding is that messages that include explicit conclusions or recommendations are more persuasive than messages without such elements" (1990, p. 160). → *For more on arguments and audience expectations, see Chapter 13.*

Successful Persuasive Speakers Use *Influence*, not Control or Manipulation The second important aspect of persuasion is that it is meant to *influence*, not control or manipulate. Taking a stand does not mean that you want to force your listeners to do what you want—there is no coercion in persuasion. Brembeck & Howell (1976) were among the first communication specialists to clarify the differences between *informing, persuading,* and *coercing* (see Figure 12.1). To *inform* is to increase the number of options available (the more listeners know, the more choices they have). To *persuade* is to limit the options that are perceived as acceptable. The only way to know what your audience perceives as acceptable is by researching their attitudes, beliefs, values, and needs. To *coerce* is to eliminate or exclude options (coercion is not persuasion). → *See Chapter 4 for specifics about audience analysis.*

Bill Meadows, president of the Wilderness Society, intends to persuade as he urges listeners to save Arctic wildlife from oil drilling.

Figure 12.1

Difference between Informing, Persuading, and Coercing

Inform – Persuade – Coerce	
To Inform	**Increases the number of options available to listeners:** • The more information, the more options. • Listeners invited to use the information as they see fit.
To Persuade	**Limits the number of options listeners perceive as acceptable:** • Ethical logos, pathos, and ethos presented to show why certain options not acceptable. • The best option(s) are made clear and explicitly recommended and supported.
To Coerce	**Removes options and choices from listeners:** • Threats, manipulation, and/or force used by speaker. • Unethical logos, pathos, and ethos may be used as well.

Successful Persuasive Speakers *Analyze Their Audiences* **Carefully** All speeches require audience analysis for success; however, persuasion requires even more diligence on the part of the speaker. In order to frame your message so your audience will more likely agree with your arguments and/or solutions, you must know their psychological information—their values, beliefs, attitudes, and needs. For example, as we discussed in Chapter 4, because values are difficult to change, it is good for persuasive speakers to show how their arguments and solutions fit into one or more of the audience's values.

If your audience comes from more than one culture or a culture different than your own, you will need to be even more careful in analyzing your audience prior to the speech. For example, individualistic/low-context/M-time cultures like the United States or Canada are perfectly happy when the persuasive speaker makes an explicit recommendation as to the best position or action needed to solve a particular problem. However, as we discussed in Chapter 3, collectivistic/high-context/P-time cultures such as Japan or Mexico prefer "speeches that build on audience history and take a cautious, back-door approach to points; content that is indirect, implicit, and filled with personal stories and analogies; conclusions that are obvious without being stated; and speakers who are aware of social face-saving and allow listeners to determine meaning" (Chapter 3, p. 54). ➤ *For more on cultural differences, see Chapter 3; see Chapter 4 for more on audience analysis.*

How Do Persuasive and Informative Speeches Differ?

Many speakers think that the main difference between informative and persuasive speaking occurs in the conclusion of their speech. But it takes more than a concluding sentence or two to persuade most people. Persuasion begins with your introductory comments and continues through your concluding remarks.

In addition to the intent, influence, and audience analysis of the speaker, mentioned above, persuasive speeches differ from informative speeches in four ways: supporting materials, delivery, language style, and organizational patterns (see Figure 12.2):

Persuasive Versus Informative Speeches		
	Persuasive	**Informative**
Supporting Materials	Mainly for proof and credibility.	Mainly for clarity and interest.
Delivery	Dynamic, forceful, persuasive.	Conversational, enthusiastic, friendly
Language Style	Forceful, direct; stylistic devices that add persuasive power.	Simple, vivid; stylistic devices that clarify and keep attention.
Organizational Patterns	• Claim/Reasons • Problem–Solution • Problem–Cause–Solution • Criteria Satisfaction • Comparative Advantages • Motivated Sequence	• Topical • Chronological • Geographical • Causal

Figure 12.2

How Do Persuasive and Informative Speeches Differ?

- **Supporting Materials** All speeches need a variety of supporting materials to maintain audience interest and to prove the accuracy of the information. However, persuasive speeches must also prove that the recommended position or action is the most desirable. Therefore, it is critical for persuasive speakers to present supporting materials that prove their position (such as expert opinion, statistics, and factual instances or narratives). For example, suppose your speech is about corporate social responsibility and you are trying to get your audience to take a particular action. If you present one or two narratives about employees who lost their savings and their homes because of the Madoff Ponzi scandal, chances are that the emotion in the narratives will arouse audience social consciousness, causing the audience to respond to your challenge (adapted from Green, 2006, pp. 164–165).

- **Delivery** Although delivery is important in all speeches, it is even more important in persuasive speeches because it affects how an audience judges the speaker's credibility—which, in turn, affects the speaker's persuasiveness. For example, trustworthiness, a factor in credibility, is affected by eye contact, speaking rate, vocal quality, and vocal variety. If you recall in Chapter 9, the FlashBack presented Cicero's description of the proper style for an informative speech as the *Plain Style* that is more subdued in delivery, language, and ornamentation. However, he described the proper style for a persuasive speech as the *Grand Style,* which is more eloquent, dramatic, and fiery. Cicero's advice is still followed by today's successful speakers. While a credible delivery is important to both informative and persuasive speakers, informative speakers generally use a more relaxed delivery that makes them look confident and friendly, while persuasive speakers are more likely to use movement and strong gestures to emphasize the importance of their speech position. In general, persuasive delivery needs to be more forceful and direct than informative delivery.
  → *For more on vocal delivery, see Chapter 8. For more on credibility and delivery, see Chapter 13.*

- **Language style** The way you use words to express ideas—your language style—is a key factor in the success or failure of both informative and persuasive speeches. Informative speakers use language that is simple yet vivid and use stylistic devices designed to clarify and keep attention. On the other hand, persuasive speakers use language that is more forceful and direct and select stylistic devices that add persuasive power by setting the proper tone or mood for persuasion. Persuasive speakers are more likely to let emotion show in their choice of words and to use emotional appeals, or pathos, to convince listeners that their arguments and solutions are worth adopting. Language style also includes how you use *transitional statements* between your main points. For example, transitions are used in an informative speech to smoothly connect topics; but in a persuasive speech, transitions are used to link arguments in a way that helps convince the audience that your opinion and suggested actions are the correct ones. → *See Chapter 8 for a review of delivery and Chapter 9 for a review of language style.*

- **Organizational Patterns** Informative organizational patterns (such as topical, chronological, geographical, and causal) are intended to present information *without biasing* audience opinions. In contrast, persuasive organizational patterns (such as the claim/reasons, problem-solution or problem-cause-solution, criteria satisfaction, comparative advantages, and motivated sequence patterns) are intended to influence audience opinions. Effective persuasive speakers use organization to help make their speeches more persuasive. John F. Kennedy is featured in this chapter in the "Speaking to Make a Difference" feature. Compare JFK's organization in his inaugural address with the informative patterns discussed in Chapter 7. For other samples, look for speeches in InfoTrac College Edition or other databases and in the *Vital Speeches* journal. It is also interesting to look on YouTube for both persuasive and informative speeches—you will see examples of what to do and what not to do. ➤ *See Chapter 7 for specifics on organizational patterns.*

What is an Effective Argument?

An effective **argument** occurs when you present sufficient evidence and reasoning to support a claim made in your persuasive speech. According to the Toulmin Model of an Argument (Toulmin, 1979; see also Verlinden, 2005), an argument has three basic components:

1. The **Claim**, which is a position statement; it is a conclusion you hope your audience will reach.

2. The **Evidence**, which supports the claim with materials such as examples, statistics, and expert opinions.

3. The **Warrant**, which justifies the evidence and shows how it supports the claim.

Making a position statement is only the beginning of an argument—to be effective it must be supported with evidence and then justified with a warrant that shows how the evidence is connected to the claim. Most warrants also need **Backing**, which Toulmin says verifies the date and expertise of the evidence. For an example, let's use Cedrick's speech, *Cell Phones: Don't Chat and Drive,* shown later in this chapter:

1. *Claim*—"Using a cell phone increases the likelihood that you will be involved in an accident."

2a. *Evidence*—"In 2001, cell phone use was a factor in 1,032 accidents and eight fatalities in Texas alone."

2b. *Evidence*—"Regardless of the age or the driving experience of the driver, the risk of being in a collision when using a cell phone is four times higher than when not talking on the phone."

3. *Warrant*—"The 2001 statistics were reported by Susan Dunn in a 2004 article in *USA Today*."

Do you think the warrant would be stronger if Cedrick had added *backing* and given the expertise of Susan Dunn and discussed how the statistics had been compiled? His second piece of evidence is compelling but wasn't directly attributed to a source—it is missing the warrant.

Whether you are a speaker planning arguments to use in your speech or an audience member listening to a speaker's arguments, keep in mind that quality arguments need more than just a claim—they also need quality evidence and a warrant that justifies the evidence and ties it directly to the claim. ➤ *See the different types of claims (position statements) that are presented later in this chapter.*

What Appeals Make a Speech Really Persuasive?

In his *Rhetoric* [translated by Roberts, 1954], Aristotle advised speakers that there were three **means of persuasion** and that all three of them, if used correctly, must relate to the audience. These means or appeals still used today include:

- *ethos* (which refers to the ethics or character of the speaker—an audience believes in and is persuaded more by the "good man");

- *pathos* (which refers to the emotional needs of the audience—an audience that feels that an argument relates to or solves one of their psychological needs is more likely to be persuaded); and

- *logos* (which refers to the logical proof used to support arguments—an audience that is convinced that an argument or solution is reasonable is more likely to be persuaded by it).

A single appeal—just ethics or emotion or logic—may work with some audience members. However, if you want your speech to be really persuasive, use all three appeals. → *Because these appeals are so important, most of the next chapter (Chapter 13) is devoted to discussing how to use them effectively yet ethically.*

Active Critical Thinking

To think further about persuasive speaking, complete the following:

- Select a topic you think will make a good persuasive speech; it could be the topic you plan to use in your own upcoming persuasive speaking situation.

- Select an argument that could be made in the speech and list the claim, one piece of evidence, and a warrant for the argument. Be prepared to share your answers with a classmate and get their feedback.

Types of Persuasive Speeches

The basic types of persuasive speeches are the speech to convince, the speech to actuate, and the speech to stimulate or intensify social cohesion. Each differs in the degree of audience reaction sought: The **speech to convince** seeks intellectual agreement from listeners, the **speech to actuate** asks listeners for both intellectual agreement and action of some type, while the **speech to intensify social cohesion** works with audience members who are already in intellectual agreement and have taken some action but are in need of additional enthusiasm, encouragement, and motivation (Johannesen et al., 2000).

The Speech to Convince

In a speech to convince, you want your audience to agree with your way of thinking. You aren't asking listeners to *do* anything. For example, in a speech about latchkey children, a student named Maria tried to convince her audience that latchkey children are causing many problems for society and that four relatively simple solutions could alleviate these problems, benefiting both the children and society. Maria didn't ask her audience to write to Congress, vote for a particular bill, or donate money. She just wanted to convince her audience that 10 million latchkey children represent a serious—but solvable—problem for society. The speech to convince is also a good choice when listeners disagree with your position and you know that it is unlikely that you can move them to action in a single speech.

The Speech to Actuate

In a speech to actuate, you want your audience to go one step past agreement and take a particular action. First, you must convince listeners of the merits of your ideas; then you want to move them to action. Most speakers try to persuade the audience *to do something* that they haven't been doing (such as write a letter to their local representative, volunteer their time, or buy a particular product). In addition to doing something they haven't been doing, there are three other types of action you might ask for. You can urge the audience members to:

- Continue doing something (continue eating balanced meals).
- Stop doing something (stop waiting until the last minute to study for exams).
- Never start doing something (never start smoking cigarettes).

Depending on your topic and your audience, you may want to include more than one request for action. For example, in a speech about alcohol, you might encourage audience members who drink to use a designated driver, urge drinkers who have used designated drivers to continue to do so, and recommend that those who don't drink never start.

The Speech to Stimulate or Intensify Social Cohesion

In a speech to stimulate or intensify social cohesion, you want your audience to go past agreement and action (because they already have both of these) and get to a higher level of enthusiasm and motivation. In other words, you are trying to get your audience to become more enthusiastic, more motivated, or more productive.

Figure 12.3

Three Types of Persuasive Speeches— How Do They Differ?

Types of Persuasive Speeches	
Speech to Convince	**Seeks only intellectual agreement.** • Does not ask for action. • Especially good for listeners who disagree with your position.
Speech to Actuate	**Seeks both intellectual agreement and action. Audience asked to . . .** • do something new or different • continue doing something; • stop doing something; • avoid (never begin) doing something.
Speech to Intensify Social Cohesion	**Seeks a higher level of enthusiasm and motivation from listeners.** • Requires vivid emotional appeals and dynamic delivery. • Used when listeners already in intellectual agreement and have taken some action but have lost enthusiasm due to cost, time, or difficulty.

Speaking to Make a Difference

Giving an inaugural address that sets just the right tone for the presidency is always important for a new president, but in 1961 John F. Kennedy faced a particular challenge. He had won the election, but only by a very slight majority. Voters were concerned about his age (at 43 he was the youngest man ever elected president) and questioned if he had the experience to keep the country safe from Communism. Some voters also had doubts about having a Roman Catholic president for the first time (John Kennedy, 2007). On the day of his inauguration, Kennedy met the challenge and delivered one of the most acclaimed speeches in our country's history. "Every literate American recalls the essence of the words John Kennedy spoke on the steps of the U.S. Capitol that cold morning of January 20, 1961" (Renehan Jr., 2004). Below is the last part of the address. The full transcript, audio, and video of the address can be found by visiting **www.americanrhetoric.com** and searching for "John F. Kennedy's Inaugural Address."

AP Photo

We dare not forget today that we are the heirs of that first revolution. Let the word go forth from this time and place, to friend and foe alike, that the torch has been passed to a new generation of Americans—born in this century, tempered by war, disciplined by a hard and bitter peace, proud of our ancient heritage, and unwilling to witness or permit the slow undoing of those human rights to which this nation has always been committed, and to which we are committed today at home and around the world.

Let every nation know, whether it wishes us well or ill, that we shall pay any price, bear any burden, meet any hardship, support any friend, oppose any foe, to assure the survival and the success of liberty.

This much we pledge—and more.

* * *

To those people in the huts and villages of half the globe struggling to break the bonds of mass misery, we pledge our best efforts to help them help themselves, for whatever period is required—not because the Communists may be doing it, not because we seek their votes, but because it is right. If a free society cannot help the many who are poor, it cannot save the few who are rich.

* * *

But neither can two great and powerful groups of nations take comfort from our present course—both sides overburdened by the cost of modern weapons, both rightly alarmed by the steady spread of the deadly atom, yet both racing to alter that uncertain balance of terror that stays the hand of mankind's final war.

So let us begin anew—remembering on both sides that civility is not a sign of weakness, and sincerity is always subject to proof. Let us never negotiate out of fear, but let us never fear to negotiate.

* * *

In your hands, my fellow citizens, more than mine, will rest the final success or failure of our course. Since this country was founded, each generation of Americans has been summoned to give testimony to its national loyalty. The graves of young Americans who answered the call to service surround the globe.

Now the trumpet summons us again—not as a call to bear arms, though arms we need—not as a call to battle, though embattled we are—but a call to bear the burden of a long twilight struggle, year in and year out, "rejoicing in hope; patient in tribulation," a struggle against the common enemies of man: tyranny, poverty, disease, and war itself.

Can we forge against these enemies a grand and global alliance, North and South, East and West, that can assure a more fruitful life for all mankind? Will you join in that historic effort?

In the long history of the world, only a few generations have been granted the role of defending freedom in its hour of maximum danger. I do not shrink from this responsibility—I welcome it. I do not believe that any of us would exchange places with any other people or any other generation. The energy, the faith, the devotion which we bring to this endeavor will light our country and all who serve it. And the glow from that fire can truly light the world.

And so, my fellow Americans, ask not what your country can do for you—ask what you can do for your country.

My fellow citizens of the world, ask not what America will do for you, but what together we can do for the freedom of man.

Finally, whether you are citizens of America or citizens of the world, ask of us here the same high standards of strength and sacrifice which we ask of you. With a good conscience our only sure reward, with history the final judge of our deeds, let us go forth to lead the land we love, asking His blessing and His help, but knowing that here on earth God's work must truly be our own.

Persuasive speeches are used to convince, actuate, and create social cohesion. Elements of all three types are in Kennedy's inaugural address, but this is primarily a speech to intensify social cohesion. His speech does not necessarily try to persuade Americans to new action, but rather to "urge reenergized commitment to central social values and goals" (Johannesen et al., p. 249).

Let's examine how John F. Kennedy made use of various public speaking techniques to win over the audience in his 1961 inaugural address.

- **Social cohesion** Kennedy's presidential inaugural address is a great example of a speech designed to increase social cohesion, because it paid "tribute to the values of the group," a necessity for a socially cohesive speech (Johannesen et al., 246). Beginning with the line ". . . that the torch has been passed to a new generation of Americans . . .," Kennedy continued to refer back to the social cohesion he desired in his audience.

continued

- **Audience analysis** Kennedy had to know his audience and know how they would react to his words. Especially for a newly elected president, this step is key to establishing credibility. "An inaugural address by an American president typically reflects some now-traditional expectations and characteristics" (Johannesen et al., p. 249). A good example of how Kennedy played to his audience comes in the line ". . . a struggle against the common enemies of man: tyranny, poverty, disease, and war itself." Here, Kennedy mentioned several things to which an audience as broad as his could relate and unite against. Clearly, he did understand his audience, for those who heard it were moved, Ernest Hemingway among them, who said of Kennedy: "It is a good thing to have a brave man as our President in times as tough as these for our country and the world" (Renehan Jr., 2004).

- **Stylistic devices** Among the stylistic devices used in Kennedy's inaugural speech are metaphor, parallelism, and antithesis (Johannesen et al., p. 250). Metaphor can be found in other parts of the address, such as in the lines ". . . to assist free men in casting off the chains of poverty . . ." and "And

if a beachhead of cooperation may push back the jungle of suspicion. . . ." Kennedy's often-overlooked line "Let us never negotiate out of fear; but let us never fear to negotiate" exemplifies parallelism, as does his most famous line, ". . . Ask not what your country can do for you—ask what you can do for your country." Antithesis is used in the lines above and in "If a free society cannot help the many who are poor, it cannot save the few who are rich."

John F. Kennedy will long be remembered, not for his untimely death, but for the power and meaning of the words he spoke while he lived (Renehan Jr., 2004). Listening to Kennedy, one hears the forcefulness and power in his voice; reading the text of his inaugural address, one feels his credibility and power through the choice of words and stylistic devices that resonated with so many Americans. That collective American memory, in addition to the mentioned devices, points to Kennedy as undeniably one of the greatest persuasive speakers of the twentieth century.

Questions: Can you find other passages in Kennedy's inaugural address that illustrate the stylistic devices mentioned? What else made this speech so effective?

You are attempting to get them to recommit to the cause. This type of speech is needed when your listeners have lost some of their enthusiasm, perhaps because the effort took longer than they expected, was more difficult than they imagined, or cost more than anticipated.

According to Johannesen et al. (2000), speeches that intensify social cohesion include the following: sermons; eulogies; speeches of dedication, commemoration, commencement, keynote, welcome, farewell, award, nomination, or acceptance; inaugural addresses; and even rallies and demonstrations (pp. 342–343). Although it might be important to remind listeners of the values that caused them to believe the way they do and behave the way they have, the real focus is on vivid emotional appeals and forceful, dynamic delivery.

Which type of persuasive speech you pick will depend on the assignment, your preferences, and the topic. For example, the "cultural bias of standardized tests," "the breakdown of the family," and "the necessity of teen curfews" are topics that are better suited to speeches to convince than to actuate. On the other hand, the "need for volunteers in the community" and "health problems resulting from recycled cabin air in commercial airliners" are topics that lend themselves to audience action. For the first topic, you might urge listeners to spend at least one hour a week as a volunteer. For the second, you might recommend that listeners write to commercial airlines and the Federal Aviation Administration. Speeches to intensify social action could include a rally speech on the Iraq War given to the College Democrats or the chancellor's appreciation-dinner address to the 300 biggest campaign donors on "meeting the new giving goal."

Active Critical Thinking

To think further about persuasive speaking, complete the following:

- Use the topic you selected in the earlier critical thinking activity, or select a new topic that you think will make a good persuasive speech.
- Explain which type of persuasive speech you think will work best for this topic and why.
- Which two persuasive appeals do you think will be the most important for this topic?

Explain why you made the choices you did.

Sample Persuasive Speech: "Drinking and Driving" by Lorna McElaney

The following persuasive speech, "Drinking and Driving," was presented by Lorna McElaney to her public speaking class, where she was voted best speaker. This sample speech was transcribed from her videotape and then re-taped being given by Peter Boyd, because Lorna was not available. The assignment specified a 4- to 7-minute persuasive speech using visual aids. Lorna chose a speech to actuate, in which she tried to persuade the audience to sign a petition and join a "Lights On for Life" campaign. Lorna's speech will be referred to throughout the chapter to illustrate how she went about preparing the speech. As you read her speech, think about the changes you would make if you were speaking about the same subject.

➜ *To watch and analyze a video clip of Lorna's speech, look under "Student Resources for Chapter 12" through your Online Resources for* Essentials of Public Speaking.

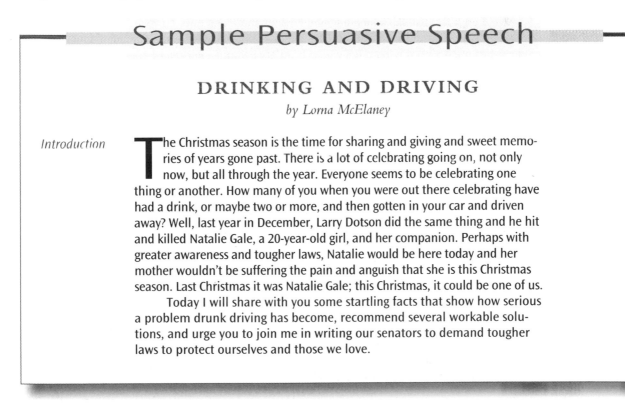

Sample Persuasive Speech

DRINKING AND DRIVING

by Lorna McElaney

Introduction

The Christmas season is the time for sharing and giving and sweet memories of years gone past. There is a lot of celebrating going on, not only now, but all through the year. Everyone seems to be celebrating one thing or another. How many of you when you were out there celebrating have had a drink, or maybe two or more, and then gotten in your car and driven away? Well, last year in December, Larry Dotson did the same thing and he hit and killed Natalie Gale, a 20-year-old girl, and her companion. Perhaps with greater awareness and tougher laws, Natalie would be here today and her mother wouldn't be suffering the pain and anguish that she is this Christmas season. Last Christmas it was Natalie Gale; this Christmas, it could be one of us.

Today I will share with you some startling facts that show how serious a problem drunk driving has become, recommend several workable solutions, and urge you to join me in writing our senators to demand tougher laws to protect ourselves and those we love.

Sample Persuasive Speech *(continued)*

Body

Step 1: Problem

According to the National Highway Safety Department [*Visual 1*], two out of five people in their lifetime will be in an auto, alcohol-related accident. That means three or four of you in this classroom will be in an auto accident involving alcohol. Mothers Against Drunk Driving, in their *Summary of Statistics,* reports that over 17,000 people in the United States were killed in auto/alcohol-related accidents last year. Now that's a lot, although some of you might not think it's a lot compared to our total population. But if it's your brother or your sister or a friend or an acquaintance, that's one too many.

Alcohol-Related Facts

- 2 of 5 people in accident
- 17,400 killed in U.S. last year
- 1,800 killed in Texas last year
- Only 20–30% conviction rate

Visual 1

According to an article in the *Dallas Morning News,* last year we had 1,800 alcohol-related deaths in Texas—1,800 senseless deaths. You know we Texans boast about our number one Cowboys, and our great state, and we are number one in a lot of things. Well, now we are number one in alcohol-related deaths. I don't want to be known for that—do you?

Only 20 to 30 percent of arrests lead to conviction. This sends a clear message to people—you are not going to get caught, or if you do get caught drinking and driving, you are going to get a slap on your hand, maybe a fine, a night in jail, and that's it!

Last year at this time, Officer Alan Chick was killed by a repeat offender. He was doing his job; he was helping a motorist on the side of the road. And this drunk came along and hit him and killed him. A repeat offender with eight prior convictions! The Chick family won't have new Christmas memories this year. His wife Lisa and two young children will have to rely on past memories. As this example and these statistics show, drunk driving is a serious problem in Texas.

Step 2: Solution

What should be done? There are many things that can be done. According to MADD, Mothers Against Drunk Driving, we need to have more sobriety checkpoints. You hear about them at holiday time—at Christmas, July Fourth, Memorial Day—but that's not enough. We need them the year round so people will know that they can be stopped any time, not just during the holiday time. Maybe they will think twice before they get behind the wheel.

We also need legislation to lower the legal alcohol level. Right now in Texas, before you are considered legally drunk, your blood alcohol level must be .10 or higher. MADD is appealing to the legislature to lower that level to .08. The Insurance Institute of Highway Safety says that when a person's alcohol level is at .05, the probability of a crash begins to increase significantly. People are driving around in lethal weapons—their cars. They can't handle .10. It's obvious with all the deaths that we have.

We also need stronger penalties for drunk driving. As reported by the *Dallas Morning News,* Texas has the most lenient DWI penalties in

Sample Persuasive Speech *(continued)*

the nation. Our laws must change. For example, Ohio has implemented stricter laws for DWI offenders. First-time offenders can now have their license revoked at the scene, or a new license plate is put on their vehicle identifying them as a person who has been pulled over for drinking and driving. Second-time offenders can have their cars impounded. So we see there are things that can be done to lessen the DWI problem.

Step 3: Action

Action must be taken now. And we must all take part in that action. December is National Drinking and Driving Awareness Month. On December 16 the National Highway Safety and Traffic Administration is calling for "Lights On for Life" day. Please join in this promotion in remembrance of those killed in alcohol- and drug-related traffic accidents and to show our government representatives that we want change.

Visual 2

You can also make a difference by writing your senators. I have a letter here today that I have written to Senator Kay Bailey Hutchison, urging her to take the legal actions I have discussed in this speech. If you agree with me, at the end of my presentation, come up and sign this letter. *[Shows letter]*

Conclusion   We must demand more sobriety checkpoints, a lower legal alcohol level, and tougher penalties for drunk driving. If we don't, we can look forward to more senseless deaths this Christmas. And next Christmas, like Natalie's mother and Officer Chick's family, it could be us with nothing but memories of someone dear. The time for action is now. Let's stop these senseless deaths [*Visual 2*]. Let's get these drunks off the road before they kill someone we love. I'm going to leave you with a sobering excerpt from a poem called "Prom Night" that was anonymously sent in to a local radio station.

> I went to a party, Mom;
> I remembered what you said.
> You told me not to drink, Mom,
> So I drank soda instead.

> I felt really proud inside, Mom,
> The way you said I would.
> I didn't drink and drive, Mom,
> Even though others said I should.

> I know I did the right thing, Mom;
> I know you are always right.
> The party is finally ending, Mom,
> And everyone drives out of sight.

Sample Persuasive Speech *(continued)*

As I got into my car, Mom,
I knew I'd get home in one piece
Because of the way you raised me, Mom,
So responsible and sweet.

I started to drive away, Mom;
But as I pulled out onto the road,
The other car didn't see me, Mom,
And hit me like a load.

As I lay on the pavement, Mom,
I hear the policeman say,
"The other guy is drunk," Mom,
And now I'm the one who'll pay.

This is the end, Mom.
I wish I could look you in the eye
To say these final words, Mom,
"I love you and good-bye."

Preparing Your Persuasive Speech

As discussed earlier, the general steps for preparing a speech are similar for informative and persuasive speeches. However, the first and second steps are usually reversed for persuasive speeches, because persuasive speakers begin with a topic they feel passionate about and adapt that topic as needed to fit a particular audience. A common mistake made by students is that they write an informative speech and add a "tag" line at the end asking for support. For example, a student presents an informative speech on drinking and driving, and then her final statement is, "So I hope that you will not drink and drive after listening to my speech." Keep in mind that persuasion begins in the introduction and continues to the end. Just asking your audience to do something in the last sentence of your speech does not make it a persuasive speech. ➜ *For information about preparation steps common to all speeches, refer to Chapter 7.*

Determine Your Topic, Position Statement, and Type of Speech

Although successful persuasive speakers carefully analyze their audiences, they seldom select a topic with a particular audience in mind as is done in informative speaking—they usually select a topic because they feel strongly about it. Getting your audience to reevaluate their beliefs is what persuasion is all about. However, because they often speak to more than one audience on the same topic, persuasive speakers' arguments, supporting materials, and persuasive appeals may change depending on the audience's beliefs, attitudes, and values.

To select your topic, position statement, and type of persuasive speech, consider the following guidelines.

Selecting Your Topic If you have been keeping a list of possible speech topics on note cards, you probably know exactly which topic you want to speak about. However, if you haven't decided on a topic, consider these suggestions:

- *Select a topic that fits the assignment.* Your assignment may specify a type of persuasive speech, an organizational pattern, or a time limit.

- *Select a controversial topic.* A controversial topic is one that has at least two conflicting views. The controversy may be over whether a problem exists or what to do about it. For example, everyone may agree that teenage pregnancy is a serious problem but may disagree about how to solve it.

   For speeches to convince, the topic must be controversial. For example, the topic "Everyone should exercise for their health" is not controversial. On the other hand, the following topics would be controversial for most audiences: "Parents should encourage their children to participate in pee-wee football;" "Irradiated vegetables are unhealthy;" "Sex education should be taught at home, not at school." Even experts disagree about these topics.

   For speeches to actuate, controversial topics are preferable but not always necessary. For example, although the need for exercise could not be used as a topic for a speech to convince, you could use it in a speech to actuate. Just because your listeners know that exercise is healthy doesn't mean that they exercise. Therefore, you might wish to persuade your audience to put aside their many excuses and make a commitment to exercise regularly.

- *Select a topic you feel strongly about.* Persuasion includes more than just logic; it also involves feelings. You will be more confident giving a speech about a topic that arouses strong feelings in you. Are there controversial issues in society or politics, the workplace, education or college life, sports or the media, health, or personal topics about which you have definite opinions? What changes (if any) in thinking or action would you recommend to your classmates in relation to these issues? Make a list of possible topics. Then check Figure 12.4 for additional ideas. If you feel strongly about any of these topics or if they cause you to think of additional topics, add them to your list. Now, select from this list of possible topics the ones that would be the most appropriate for your assigned speech.

Lorna, whose sample-speech preparation outline on drinking and driving appears in Figure 12.8, felt so strongly about the problems involved with drunk driving that no other topic seemed appropriate for her persuasive speech. Because of her friends' experiences with drunk drivers and the fact that her two children would be driving soon, Lorna was genuinely concerned about the high number of accidents involving drunk drivers.

- *Select a topic that you already know a lot about (if possible).* Use this criterion to narrow your list. The topics about which you have the strongest feelings are probably the ones you know the most about, either from reading or from personal experience. If you aren't sure which of two issues to select for your speech, you may want to delay your decision until you have written a position statement for each topic. You might also want to poll your audience before making the final decision.

Business Issues

Casual dress affects work
Companies should hire more disabled workers
Emotions don't belong at work
Banning forensic accounting
Homelessness should be a priority
More company training programs are needed
Workplace ethics need an overhaul

Family Issues

Playing too many video games
Condom distribution in schools
Everyone should have a will
Parents must exercise more control
Sex education should not be taught in school
Sleep deprivation causes low grades

Food Issues

Alcohol—no advertising at sports events
Drinking age should be lowered
Healthy people eat low-carb foods
Overseas vegetables need government controls

Health Issues

Indoor air pollution
Irradiated vegetables are dangerous
Lower your cholesterol now
MyPyramid Plan is the best plan
Nursing shortage is caused by low pay
Popular diets cause obesity
Regular exercise is needed

Multicultural Issues

America is responsible for rebuilding Iraq
Ethnic traditions should be celebrated
Global warming is the fault of humans
Muslims in America deserve fair treatment
U.S.–Mexico relations need serious improvement

Personal Issues

ADHD can be cured
Depression requires intervention
STDs can be avoided by abstinence
Stress is alleviated by exercise and diet
Taking vitamin supplements is dangerous
Volunteerism is a college student's responsibility

Pet/Animal Issues

Animal research is a necessary evil
People who have pets are healthier
Retirement centers should allow pets

Political Issues

Farm subsidies must be stopped
Homeland Security should receive more funding
Mandatory drug testing violates personal rights
Military service should be required of all citizens
NAFTA is producing as expected
National healthcare policy is needed in America

Social Security needs restructuring
State polling devices need modernizing
Terrorism is a real threat to citizens
Women should be allowed in combat areas

Social Issues

Assisted suicide is an individual right
Clergy charged with sexual abuse should resign
Legalizing fetal tissue research
Gay marriage is a state's choice
Illegal immigrants should not be citizens
Racial quotas are still necessary
Stricter penalties are needed for DWI offenses
Teen pregnancy

Sports/Hobby Issues

College sports need reforming
Hobbies are good for your health
Sports salary cap should be implemented
Violence at sports events shows moral decline

Technology Issues

Cell phones should be banned from class
Computer hackers deserve stricter punishment
Hybrid cars lower need for foreign oil
Internet regulation will decrease pornography
Virus-checker software is worth the cost

Figure 12.4

Sample Persuasive Speech Topics

Deciding on Your Position Statement A **position statement**, similar to the exact purpose of an informative speech, is a simple sentence that states the speaker's position on the topic. As discussed earlier, the Toulmin model calls this a *claim* and says it is a conclusion you hope your audience will reach. A single word, such as *abortion,* is not enough because it does not specify the speaker's position.

A statement such as "Abortion should be illegal in all cases except those in which the woman's life is in danger" makes the speaker's exact position clear.

In his *Rhetoric,* Aristotle divides persuasive issues into four types:

- *Being* (fact)—Does evidence of harm exist?

- *Quality* (value)—Does the problem violate basic societal goals or values?

- *Procedure* (policy)—Is action or change required?

- *Quantity* (scope)—Is the problem great enough to make it a social issue?

Today, most persuasive writers combine policy and scope and categorize position statements or claims as statements of fact, value, or policy:

- *Statement of fact*—indicates that the speaker will present evidence to persuade the listeners that a debatable point is or is not true. (In contrast, an informative speech is about a topic that is accepted as true.) Sample statements of fact include "Irradiated vegetables are unhealthy," "Nuclear power plants are a safe energy source," and "Lee Harvey Oswald was part of a conspiracy."

- *Statement of value*—indicates that the speaker will present arguments and evidence to persuade listeners that an idea, object, or person is or is not good (or ethical or wise or beautiful). In other words, the speaker will offer evidence in support of a judgment. Sample statements of value include "The U.S. space program is a wise use of taxpayers' money," "The death penalty is a civilized and moral form of punishment," and "It is immoral to use animals in medical research." Because values are core to individuals, it is important to note that it is not easy to persuade people to change values—a partial change may be all you can expect.

- *Statement of policy*—indicates that the speaker will use both facts and value judgments to recommend a certain policy or solution. Sample statements of policy include "Cigarette advertising should be banned from all sports events," "Drugs should be legalized," and "Homeowners should no longer bag their grass clippings."

Unless your assignment specifies the type of position statement to use, brainstorm two or three possible statements of fact, value, and policy for your topic. Looking at the ways in which you could approach your topic will help you narrow it. You may need to do some initial research on your topic before you feel confident making a position statement.

> *Although Lorna knew that she wanted to speak against drunk drivers, her position statement could have been any of the following claims:*
>
> 1. **Statements of fact:** *"Stiff DWI penalties deter drunk driving" or "Drivers with blood alcohol levels higher than .08 are incapable of making safe driving decisions."*
>
> 2. **Statements of value:** *"Setting the blood alcohol level at .10 is irresponsible" or "The DWI laws of other states are more responsible than the DWI laws in Texas."*
>
> 3. **Statements of policy:** *"The state of Texas must implement tougher penalties for drunk driving" or "Texas citizens should demand that local and state representatives take stronger measures against drunk drivers."*

It is important to know whether you are using a claim or position statement of fact, value, or policy, because each type of position statement requires different kinds of supporting materials (see "Prepare a Rough-Draft Outline of Main Points and Needed Information" on page 296) and different types of persuasive appeals. This means that your research will be somewhat different for each. ➜ *Types of persuasive appeals are covered in Chapter 13.*

Deciding on the Type of Speech If you haven't already decided whether you want to convince or actuate your audience, now is the time to make that decision. Do you want your audience to simply agree with your position, or do you want them to actually do something? The organization of your speech will be somewhat different depending on your goal.

> *Lorna decided that she wanted her audience to take some responsibility for getting tougher DWI laws, so she chose a speech to actuate. In her research, she looked for specific ways in which her listeners could lobby state and national representatives to vote for tougher DWI laws.*

Once you have decided on your topic, position statement, and type of persuasive speech, you are ready to analyze your specific audience's attitudes toward your position.

Analyze Audience Attitudes Toward Your Position

Because this persuasive speech will be given to the same audience that heard your earlier informative speech (your classmates), you already know a great deal about them. If you don't already know your audience, you will need to conduct a detailed analysis like the one you conducted before preparing your informative speech. Review the situational, demographic, and psychological information you gathered and update it if necessary. Then take a look at the following questions that relate to the ethical and emotional appeals you choose to use in your speech:

- Will my classmates' current opinions of me add to my credibility (ethical appeal) or take away from it? What can I do to increase my credibility?
  ➜ *Establishing credibility is covered in Chapter 13.*

  > *Lorna felt that her credibility with her classmates was good. She was a few years older than most of them, and they often came to her for advice. They seemed to view her as open minded and trustworthy. To make sure she appeared competent on her topic, she knew that she would need to cite several respected sources on drinking and driving. She also planned to interview the director of the local MADD (Mothers Against Drunk Drivers) organization.*
  >
  > *Her one problem was dynamism, an important element of credibility. She was naturally a soft-spoken person and felt embarrassed about showing emotion in front of an audience. But she was determined to be more forceful and personal in her delivery and began practicing in front of a mirror; she even videotaped herself several times.*

- What are my classmates' beliefs and values about my topic? How can I use these beliefs and values to communicate my arguments better?

  > *Although Lorna knew that several of the students in her class drank heavily at parties, she had heard them mention the importance of having a designated driver and felt that they believed that driving after drinking was irresponsible. On the basis of speeches her classmates had given in class, she also knew that they valued family security and self-respect—two values that are threatened by drunk driving.*

- What basic needs (physiological, safety, social, self-esteem, or self-actualization) do most of my classmates have that will make the need for my topic obvious?

Lorna decided that safety, social, and self-esteem needs (emotional appeals) were the audience needs that related best to the topic of drinking and driving. Her classmates wanted their friends and family members to avoid accidents (safety need), yet enjoyed the companionship and sense of belonging that social gatherings bring (social need) and would feel a sense of pride knowing that they had taken steps to ensure their own safety as well as that of their friends and loved ones (self-esteem need).

Once you have reviewed and updated your audience-analysis notes, you are ready to assess audience reactions to your position statement. In planning your persuasive arguments, you will want to conduct an audience **attitude poll** (see Figure 12.5) designed to (1) find points on which you and your audience agree (common ground) and (2) learn audience objections to your position. Although an attitude poll is not always appropriate or possible outside the classroom, in the classroom it is an excellent learning tool. The information you collect will help you select the types of arguments and evidence to use in your speech. For example, should you look at both sides of the issue by discussing some objections to your position? (Of course, you will refute these objections by showing why your position is the better choice.) Or should you ignore possible audience objections and present only arguments that support your position? → *Chapter 13 will answer these questions and many others to help you determine the best arguments and evidence to use in your speech.*

The attitude poll should include your topic, position statement, and the response categories "Strongly disagree," "Disagree," "Undecided," "Agree," and "Strongly agree." Each potential audience member will read your position statement and check the response category that most closely represents his or her attitude toward it. The more specific your position statement, the more certain you can be that the audience responses are accurate. Therefore, it's a good idea to include a brief explanation in the form of a "because" statement along with your position statement. Also, make sure that your position is completely clear. For example, your audience may agree that stricter laws are needed to deter drug use but may disagree with you on the meaning of *stricter*.

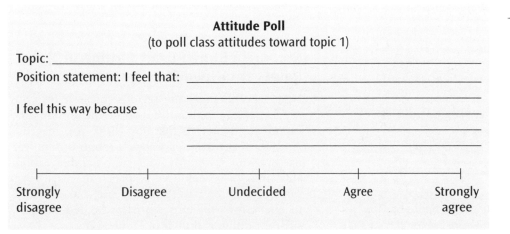

Figure 12.5

Sample Attitude Poll (enlarge on copier for use in class)

Lorna made her position statement very precise by including a "because" statement and describing some of the solutions she had in mind:

Topic: *Drinking and driving*

Position statement: *I feel that we should demand that our government take stronger measures against drunk drivers (more sobriety checkpoints, loss of driver's license for a specified time, a longer jail sentence, and so on).*

I feel this way because *so many needless deaths occur from drunk driving and because Texas has the most lenient DWI penalties in the nation.*

Here are the results of Lorna's attitude poll:

		✓✓✓✓✓	
✓	✓✓	✓✓✓✓✓✓	✓✓
Strongly disagree	*Disagree*	*Undecided*	*Agree*	*Strongly agree*

Listeners are more likely to be persuaded by your ideas if they consider you credible. Although there are many ways to establish credibility, an important one is to focus on points of *common ground*. Listeners are more likely to be persuaded by speakers whom they view as similar to them in some way (McCroskey & Teven, 1999; McGuire, 1985; O'Keefe, 1990; Perloff, 2003). The more you know about your audience, the easier it is to find points of agreement such as opinions about related issues, problems you have in common, and values you hold dear.

To learn why people disagree with your position, you may wish to leave a space at the bottom of your attitude poll where people can briefly describe their objections. By anticipating likely objections, you can plan ways to refute them during the speech.

When polls are not appropriate, you can interview the person in charge and one or two other members of the audience. Or you can merely anticipate likely objections on the basis of the beliefs, attitudes, and values you know the audience holds.

Prepare a Rough-Draft Outline of Main Points and Needed Information

Before conducting any serious research on your topic, make a rough outline of the main points and supporting materials that you think you may use. As with informative speeches, a rough outline can narrow your search for information and save valuable time. Also, seeing your speech in visual form can stimulate creative thinking and make it easier to check for problems. Lorna's roughed-out persuasive outline is shown in Figure 12.6.

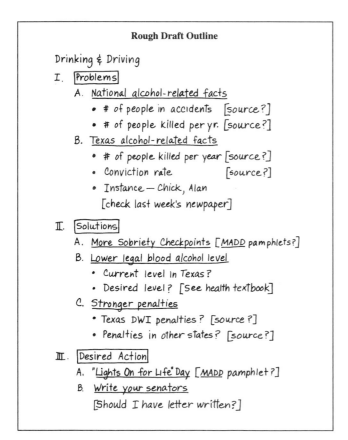

Rough Draft Outline

Drinking & Driving
I. Problems
    A. National alcohol-related facts
       • # of people in accidents [source?]
       • # of people killed per yr. [source?]
    B. Texas alcohol-related facts
       • # of people killed per year [source?]
       • Conviction rate   [source?]
       • Instance — Chick, Alan
         [check last week's newpaper]
II. Solutions
    A. More Sobriety Checkpoints [MADD pamphlets?]
    B. Lower legal blood alcohol level
       • Current level in Texas?
       • Desired level? [See health textbook]
    C. Stronger penalties
       • Texas DWI penalties? [source?]
       • Penalties in other states? [source?]
III. Desired Action
    A. "Lights On for Life" Day [MADD pamphlet?]
    B. Write your senators
       [Should I have letter written?]

Figure 12.6

Lorna's Rough-Draft Outline for Her Persuasive Speech, "Drinking and Driving"

Research Your Topic

Careful research is the key to a successful persuasive speech. Although you will want to include personal experiences to support your arguments, persuasive speeches are supported largely by outside sources such as printed materials, computer databases, and interviews with experts. As you locate these sources, look through them for (1) arguments for and against your position, (2) answers to possible objections from the audience, and (3) benefits of your position.

Research Arguments For and Against Your Position You should research both sides of your position for several reasons. First, it is the ethical thing to do—you can assure your audience that you have done careful research. Second, researching both sides ensures that you are using the "best" arguments in your speech. And finally, researching both sides adds to the list of likely objections you discovered during the audience-analysis step. This is especially valuable when you can't poll your audience. → *For additional help on research, see Chapter 5.*

Research Answers to Major Audience Objections Even though you can't answer all objections in your speech, you should be ready for any questions during the Q&A session after the speech. Once you know the basic objections to your position, you can research ways to refute them. Some objections may be based on faulty reasoning—if so, bring it to your audience's attention. Some objections may be based on false or misleading information, so you will need to research for the correct information. And some objections may be valid ones that you can't disprove with reasoning or facts. When this is the case, admit it to your audience. Most audiences are impressed by this type of admission; it shows that you are an ethical speaker who has carefully researched the topic. Of course, you will want to show that the benefits of your position (or plan) far outweigh this single objection. In your research, try to find a quotation from a noted expert, explaining why the objection does not weaken your position.

Comparing the benefits of your position to any disadvantages is one way to refute objections. For example, you might say, "Although my proposal has one disadvantage, it is an insignificant one compared to the many advantages." Another way to refute objections is to compare the benefits of your proposal with those of a rival proposal. Assuming that both proposals could solve the problem, the more persuasive would be the one with the greater number of advantages or the more important advantages.

Research Additional Benefits If you can show that your position not only solves the problem under discussion but also provides additional, unexpected benefits, you will be even more persuasive. To increase your chances of persuasion, present these additional benefits during the conclusion. For example, Maria concluded her speech about latchkey children (mentioned earlier in the chapter) by summarizing the problem and reviewing how her solutions would be an effective remedy. She further added to her persuasiveness by presenting a transparency listing six additional benefits of her solutions (such as increased self-esteem and improved social skills of the children).

Select the Best Supporting Materials

Persuasive speakers use logic, evidence, emotional appeals, and their own credibility to connect with audience members and persuade them. Although it is good to use a variety of supporting materials to clarify points and maintain audience interest, *persuasive speeches should primarily use materials that prove* (such as expert opinion, statistics, brief and detailed factual instances, and literal comparisons). In addition, ethically sound materials are especially important in persuasive speaking, because you are asking your listeners to trust you and change their opinions. Double-check your arguments, evidence, and reasoning to make sure your speech is ethical. Remember to cite your sources during your speech.

Determine How Best to Organize Your Main Points

In this step, you will first consider three important aspects about your topic and, second, use these aspects in choosing one of the many available persuasive patterns.

Important Aspects to Consider Which organizational pattern you choose depends on (1) whether you are giving a speech to convince, to actuate, or to intensify social cohesion; (2) whether your position statement is written as a statement of fact, value, or policy; and (3) your personal preferences and/or assignment requirements. Let's look at each in more detail:

1. *Consider your speech type*—to convince or actuate. Recall that a speech to convince seeks to obtain intellectual agreement from listeners, whereas a speech to actuate seeks both agreement and action. If you plan to give a speech to convince, you can choose any of the organizational patterns except problem–solution–action and cause–result–action, because they call for action. You would choose one of those two for the speech to actuate (the problem–solution–action pattern is the most popular).

2. *Determine your position statement*—fact, value, or policy. For statements of fact, the claim and the causal patterns (cause–effect–solution and cause–result–action) are especially effective. For statements of value, choose a claim or criteria satisfaction pattern. For a statement of policy, the problem–solution–benefits, problem–solution–action, and comparative advantages patterns are recommended.

3. *Follow assignment requirements* and *consider personal preferences*. If the class assignment specifies which pattern to use, make sure your speech type and position statement are compatible. Your preferences should also play a role in what pattern you select.

Choosing the Best Persuasive Pattern You can choose from a variety of patterns to organize the body of a persuasive speech. The patterns discussed previously include the claim, causal, problem–solution, comparative advantages, and criteria satisfaction patterns. ➔ *See the Quick Start Guide and Chapter 7 for a discussion of these organizational patterns.*

In addition to the persuasive patterns already discussed, there is one other popular method of organizing a persuasive speech—called the motivated sequence. Developed by communications professor Alan Monroe more than 50 years ago, it is similar to the problem–solution–action pattern and is especially effective with speeches to actuate using a statement of policy (Gronbeck et al., 1994). The motivated sequence includes the introduction and conclusion as well as your main points. It has five steps: attention, need, satisfaction, visualization, and action. Let's take a brief look at each step.

1. *Attention step.* Grab your listeners' attention (using any of the methods described earlier) and build a desire in them to continue listening.

2. *Need step.* Direct the audience's attention to a specific problem. Describe the problem using credible, logical, and emotional appeals, and show how the problem affects your listeners. → *See Chapter 13 for details on persuasive appeals.*

3. *Satisfaction step.* Satisfy the need described in the previous step by presenting a solution. The following framework is suggested: "(a) briefly state what you propose to do, (b) explain it clearly, (c) show how it remedies the problem, (d) demonstrate its workability, and (e) answer objections" (Gronbeck et al., p. 209). In demonstrating the feasibility of the solution as well as answering objections of audience members, be sure to use supporting materials that will add proof to your statements. → *See Chapter 6 for examples of supporting materials.*

4. *Visualization step.* Vividly picture the future for your audience, using the positive, the negative, or the contrast method. With the *positive method,* you picture the improved future the audience can expect when your solution is implemented. With the *negative method,* you picture the undesirable conditions that will continue to exist or will develop if your solution is not adopted. The *contrast method* begins with the negative and ends with the positive. The purpose of visualization is to "intensify audience desire or willingness to act—to motivate your listeners to believe, to feel, or to act in a certain way" (Gronbeck et al., p. 211).

5. *Action step.* Conclude your speech by challenging your audience to take a particular action—you want a personal commitment from them. Say exactly what you want them to do and how they can do it. → *See Chapter 7 for suggestions on how to issue a challenge in your conclusion.*

Remember

For speeches to convince . . .

- When stating your position as a *statement of fact,* use the claim or cause–effect–solution pattern.
- With a *statement of value,* use the claim or criteria satisfaction pattern.
- With a *statement of policy,* use the problem–solution benefits or comparative advantages pattern.

For speeches to actuate . . .

- With a *statement of fact,* use the claim or cause–result–action pattern.
- With a *statement of value,* use the claim or criteria satisfaction pattern.
- With a *statement of policy,* use the problem–solution–action or comparative advantages pattern.

For speeches to intensify social cohesion . . .

- With *statements of fact, value, or policy,* try using the claim, problem–solution, or comparative advantages pattern.

Check your knowledge of the basic persuasive organization patterns by taking the following quiz. If you have problems with any of the patterns, review that pattern in Chapter 7.

Testing Your Knowledge of Persuasive Patterns

Directions: Here are six mini outlines, each with a title and main points. Identify the organizational pattern of the main points as (a) claim, (b) causal, (c) problem–solution, (d) comparative advantages, or (e) criteria satisfaction. Write the letter of your choice in the appropriate blank. You can also take the quiz under "Student Resources for Chapter 12" in CourseMate (the *Essentials of Public speaking* website) and, if requested, e-mail your responses to your instructor.

_____ **1.** "Stem Cell Research"

    I. Stem cell research could provide needed pancreatic cells for those with diabetes.

    II. Stem cell research could give further hope for those with Parkinson's disease.

    III. Stem cell research could continue work to help those with spinal cord injuries.

    IV. Stem cell research must be supported by citizens and governments around the world.

_____ **2.** "Making Divorce Sensible"

    I. When divorce is settled in court, it's expensive and lengthy, promotes destructive competition, and clogs the court system.

    II. Divorce settled by mediation solves these problems.

    III. In addition to solving basic divorce problems, mediation has an important benefit: It allows both parties time to stabilize personally.

_____ **3.** "Overweight Americans"

    I. Losing weight by dieting has very few advantages.

    II. Losing weight by lowering fat intake has several important advantages.

_____ **4.** "Becoming a Blood Donor"

    I. Blood donors are crucial to alleviating America's blood shortage.

    II. Blood donors are essential if new medical treatments (such as heart and bone-marrow transplants) are to continue.

    III. Blood donors are of paramount importance in disasters such as 9-11.

_____ **5.** "Helping the Homeless" (Fitzgerald, 1994)

    I. Any workable solution for helping the homeless must meet the following guidelines:

        A. Respect the rights and dignity of the homeless.

        B. Require that the homeless work for shelter and food.

        C. Offer drug- and alcohol-abuse prevention programs.

        D. Offer hope.

    II. Our community's attempt to help the homeless by giving them money and housing violates all of the above guidelines.

_____ **6.** "Good Mothers"

    I. Many single mothers with children must put them in day care during work hours.

II. In several recent cases, the court has taken custody from single mothers who placed their children in day care rather than caring for them at home.

III. Such decisions are irresponsible and must be reversed.

Answers

1. (a) claim pattern; 2. (c) problem–solution–benefits pattern; 3. (d) comparative advantages pattern; 4. (a) claim pattern; 5. (e) criteria satisfaction pattern; 6. (b) cause–effect–action pattern.

Plan the Introduction and Conclusion

An effective persuasive introduction includes (1) an attention-getter, (2) a motivation to listen, (3) evidence of your credibility, and (4) a preview of your purpose and main points. Also, for some of the organizational patterns (such as comparative advantages), you need to mention the background of the problem briefly in the introduction.

An effective conclusion includes (1) a summary of your arguments, position, or recommendations, and (2) a memorable ending (including visualizing the future and a challenge or appeal for action). Don't assume that your audience knows exactly what to do—specify the exact position or action that you want them to take. You will also be more persuasive if your listeners perceive that they are capable of performing the action you are requesting of them (Beck & Lund, 1981). When listeners feel that the problem you have described is serious ("In six months all the landfills in the state will be filled to capacity, and we will have no place to put our garbage") but they are not capable of solving it ("Even if I do purchase fewer packaged items, one family isn't going to make enough difference"), they are likely to reject your message and even do the opposite of what you recommend (Witte, 1992a). Make it as easy as possible for your listeners to comply with your request. For example, if you ask them to contact their senators, provide a handout with each senator's name, address, and phone number. Or, as Lorna did, have a letter already written and ask audience members to sign it. A copy of Lorna's letter (which everyone in her class signed) is shown in Figure 12.7.

Senator Kay Bailey Hutchison
703 Hart-Senate Office Building
Washington, D.C.

Dear Ms. Hutchison,

As you are well aware, here in the state of Texas we have a serious problem with drinking and driving. Texas is now number one in the nation with the highest incidence of alcohol-related deaths. People who drink and drive in this state know that their chances of being pulled over for a DWI are slim. If they are stopped and arrested, their punishment is a night in jail or a fine—in other words, a slap on the hand. In order to bring senseless deaths and injury to a halt, we must change our laws. Penalties for first-time and repeat offenders must be stricter to deter people from drinking and driving.

Ohio has implemented stronger penalties for first-time and repeat offenders. For example, first-time offenders can now have their license revoked at the scene or a new license plate put on their vehicle identifying them as persons who have been pulled over for drinking and driving. Second-time offenders can have their cars impounded. Texas and all states in the nation need similar laws.

This is a very serious issue that everyone needs to be aware of—it affects us not only during holidays but all year long. We hope to see more-aggressive and immediate action taken before one more death or injury occurs. We are asking you to use your influence to save lives in Texas and the nation.

Sincerely,

Figure 12.7

Letter Lorna Asked Her Classmates to Sign in the Conclusion of Her Persuasive Speech

Make Preparation Outlines and Speaking Notes

Expanding your rough-draft outline into a preparation outline will allow you to check the organization of your speech. See Figure 12.8 for Lorna's preparation outline. Which tool you choose depends on your personal preferences. As you know from your informative speech, the preparation outline is more formally structured and should include transitions to link your arguments, a list of references

Figure 12.8

Lorna's Persuasive Preparation Outline

Lorna's Preparation Outline

Title: "Drinking and Driving" by Lorna McElaney
Position Statement: Texas citizens should demand that government representatives take stronger measures against drunk drivers. (Speech to actuate/statement of policy)

INTRODUCTION
- **Attention-getter:** Christmas celebration. *Question:* How many of you when you are out celebrating have had a drink, or maybe two or more, and gotten into your car and driven away? *Example:* Larry Dotson and Natalie Gale.
- **Credibility:** [Presented in student introduction]
- **Audience motivation:** Last Christmas it was Natalie Gale and her friend; this Christmas, it could be one of us.
- **Purpose/Preview:** Today I will share with you some startling facts and hopefully persuade you to join me in writing our senators to demand tougher laws to protect ourselves and those we love.

BODY
I. **The number of auto/alcohol-related accidents indicates a serious problem. [Visual 1]**
   A. Nationally, 2 of 5 involved in auto/alcohol accidents.
   B. Nationally, 17,000 killed in auto/alcohol accidents.
   C. In Texas, 1,800 killed in auto/alcohol accidents.
      1. Texas #1 state in alcohol-related deaths.
      2. Only 20–30 percent of arrests lead to conviction.
      3. Example of Officer Chick.

[Transition] What should be done? There are a lot of things that can be done.

II. **There are several workable solutions to the DWI problem.**
   A. Year-round sobriety checkpoints.
   B. Legal blood alcohol level lowered from .10 to .08.
   C. Stronger penalties for drunk driving.
      1. Texas's lenient DWI laws.
      2. Ohio's stricter DWI laws.

[Transition] Action must be taken now. And we must all take part in that action.

III. **Action must be taken now.**
   A. "Lights On for Life" promotion on December 16.
      1. In remembrance of those killed by drunk drivers.
      2. To show government representatives we want change.
   B. Letter to Senator Kay Bailey Hutchison. [Visual 2]

CONCLUSION
- **Summary:** We must demand more sobriety checkpoints, a lower blood alcohol level, and tougher penalties for drunk driving.
- **Visualize:** If we don't, more senseless deaths. **[Visual 3]**
- **Challenge:** The time for action is now. Let's get these drunks off the road before they kill someone we love.
- **Refocus:** I'm going to leave you with a sobering excerpt from a poem called "Prom Night" that was anonymously sent to a local radio station.

REFERENCES:
1. Barlow, Y. 1994. Texas alcohol road deaths drop but state has highest proportion of such fatalities, study shows. *Dallas Morning News.* December 3, 1994. Sec. NEWS.
2. Ford, J. Drunken driver gets life in death of FW officer: Widow gives emotional testimony. *Dallas Morning News.* Sec. NEWS.
3. Mothers Against Drunk Driving. 1994. A 1994 summary of statistics: The impaired driving problem. Irving, TX: MADD (Mothers Against Drunk Driving).
4. Mothers Against Drunk Driving. 1993. *Maddvocate: A Magazine for Victims and Their Advocates* 6 (Fall).
5. Mothers Against Drunk Driving. 1994. *20 X 2000: Five-year plan to reduce impaired driving.* Dallas, TX: MADD (Mothers Against Drunk Driving).
6. National 3D Prevention Month Coalition. May 1994. *Lights on for life handbook.* Washington, D.C.: National Highway Traffic Safety Administration.
7. North, Kim. 1994. Sobering message: Woman whose daughter was victim of holiday DWI driver stresses perils. *Dallas Morning News.* December 12, 1994. Sec. NEWS.
8. "Prom Night." 1994. An anonymous poem read on Sunny 95 FM radio station. Dallas, TX.

(with their page numbers), and brackets to indicate where you want to use visuals and identify types of supporting materials.

Remember that expanding the body (main arguments) of your speech into a preparation outline will improve your flexibility as a speaker far more than writing out your speech word for word. With an outline, you will also be able to evaluate your organization and supporting materials at a glance—something you can't do with a manuscript.

Your speaking notes are one of the last things to prepare. For most people, "the fewer words the better" is a good guide. If you have too many words in your speaking notes, you may be tempted to read them—a sure way to decrease your dynamic delivery. Speaking notes can be on a single page, on note cards, or in mind-map form. If you had any problems with the speaking notes you used for your informative speech, try to correct those difficulties in this speech. → *For more on speaking notes, see Chapter 7.*

Prepare Visual Aids and Rehearse Your Speech

You probably know exactly what visual aids you want to use. If not, sketch out some possible slides as you read through your outline. For example, you could make a text slide of an important definition or a list of your main arguments, or you could make a graphic slide of some important statistics. Take a look at the suggestions for rehearsing your speech listed in Chapter 8, pp. 196–198. The only difference between this advice and advice for a persuasive speech is that delivery may be even more important to the persuasive speaker, because delivery affects credibility and credibility affects persuasion. Practice your speech on your feet, using your slides and speaking with a strong, enthusiastic voice. Always practice in front of friends or family members if possible. Research covered in Chapter 8 shows that students who practice in front of other people make better grades—the more people in the audience, the higher the grade (Smith & Frymier, 2006).

Active Critical Thinking

To think further about persuasive speaking, complete the following:

- Use one of the topics you selected in the critical thinking activity on pages 283 or 287 or select a new topic that you think will make a good persuasive speech or that you plan to use in your next speech.
- Write a position statement for the speech, using either a statement of fact, value, or policy; explain why you selected this approach.
- Select a persuasive organization pattern from Chapter 7 and list your main points to follow this pattern.
- List at least two possible audience objections toward your position statement and main points and suggest how you could answer these objections in the speech. Cite one quality source that you could use to support your answer to at least one objection.

Once you have completed the steps in preparing a persuasive speech, don't forget the importance of evaluation.

Evaluating Speeches—Yours and Others

One of the surest ways to make sure you understand the steps in preparing a persuasive speech is to evaluate other speakers as well as yourself; even a video of yourself practicing your speech will help you see your strengths and weaknesses. Use the Persuasive-Speech Evaluation Form in Figure 12.9 at the end of this chapter to help you prepare for your own persuasive speeches, evaluate your speeches after you've given them, and evaluate your classmates' speeches. ➤ *You can access this form online under "Student Resources for Chapter 12" at the* Essentials of Public Speaking *Online Resources.*

Sample Student Speech Analysis: "Cell Phones: Don't Chat and Drive" by Cedrick McBeth

The following persuasive speech, "Cell Phones: Don't Chat and Drive," was adapted from a speech given by Cedrick McBeth to his public speaking class. Cedrick's assignment was to prepare a 4- to 7-minute persuasive speech on a topic of his choosing. Visual aids were optional and notes were allowed—Cedrick did not use either. The following speech was transcribed from the video of his speech. As you read Cedrick's speech, identify its type: Is it a speech to convince, actuate, stimulate or intensify social cohesion? How persuasive did you think his speech was? Did he need visual aids? If so, what would you suggest? If you were evaluating this speech using the evaluation form in Figure 12.9, how many total points would you give him? ➤ *To watch a video clip of Cedrick's speech, look under "Student Resources for Chapter 12" in CourseMate (the* Essentials of Public speaking *website).*

Sample Persuasive Speech

CELL PHONES: DON'T CHAT AND DRIVE

by Cedrick McBeth

On June 17, 2006, Alexander Manocchio reached for a ringing cell phone and killed Karyn Cordell and her unborn son. You see, Manocchio was driving a car at the time. Now two people are dead and Alexander's life is in a shambles, all because he answered a phone. Alexander faces two counts of vehicular homicide. How many of us in this classroom are also guilty of putting lives at risk by talking on cell phones while driving a car? I'll bet almost all of us have done it and many of us do it every day. But do we ever consider the dangers of talking on our cell phones while driving a car? As I read the statistics and studied this situation, I became convinced that cell phone use while driving has become an unacceptable risk. Today I hope to convince you that using a cell phone while driving an automobile should be illegal.

Step 1: Problem

Let's begin by establishing that using a cell phone while you're driving has become a serious and growing problem. Overall, cell phone usage has increased tremendously in the last 12 to 14 years. According to the Cellular Telecommunications & Internet Association, as of August 2004, 168 million people used cell phones, compared to only 4.3 million in 1990. That's a 390 percent increase.

Not surprisingly, according to Vermont Legislative Research Shop, this jump in cell phone use has been accompanied by a jump in traffic accidents linked to cell phone use. According to a 2004 article in *USA Today* by Susan Dunn, in Texas alone during 2001, cell phone usage was considered a contributing factor in 1,032 accidents and resulted in eight fatalities.

Regardless of the age or the driving experience of the driver, the risk of being in a collision when using a cell phone is four times higher than when not talking on the phone.

Not only does cell phone usage increase the likelihood of an accident, but it also increases the likelihood of fatalities. An independent study done in 2002 by the Harvard Center for Risk Analysis found that driving while using a cell phone increases the risk to 6.4 fatalities per million drivers annually. The study also found that the chance that a driver using a cell phone would kill a pedestrian or other motorists was 1.5 per one million people. Extrapolating from these figures, with 210 million licensed drivers in the U.S., this amounts to roughly 1,660 fatalities per year stemming from cell phone–related accidents.

So, I'm sure you'll agree that we have a problem. But how does using a cell phone while driving create accidents? Whether we realize

Analysis

Cedrick begins his speech with a factual instance of a situation that has serious consequences: Reaching to answer a ringing cell phone (something most drivers have done) results in two deaths. He reinforces the seriousness of his topic by reminding the audience that talking on a cell phone while driving is something that most people do every day.

Cedrick appeals to safety needs in his attempt to motivate his classmates to get involved. He clearly states his position.

Q1: How would you evaluate his introduction—what are its strengths and weaknesses?

In the body of his speech, Cedrick makes sure his audience realizes exactly how serious the problem is by using statistics.

Q2: How do you rate the sources for his statistics such as the Cellular Telecommunications & Internet Association and the Harvard Center for Risk Analysis?

His use of sources should also help establish his trustworthiness and competency as a speaker.

Q3: How do you rate his credibility?

Although Cedrick concentrates on statistics in his speech, he also uses a variety of other supporting materials.

Q4: How many can you find, and of what quality are they?

Audience analysis indicated that Cedrick's classmates already agreed with the general problem, so he presented only one side of his topic.

Q5: Do you think he made the right decision?

Just in case his listeners feel like they are good-enough drivers to avoid an accident while using a cell phone, he tries to make his statistics as personal as possible.

Q6: How well does he accomplish this?

Sample Persuasive Speech *(continued)*

it or not—and no matter how experienced we are as drivers—we are distracted from paying attention to the road when we use a cell phone while driving. Think about it: When you access your phone or dial a number, you lose eye contact with the road. Even if you use a hands-free phone, your mental attention is split between your conversation and ever-changing road conditions. Being absorbed in a conversation affects your ability to concentrate on driving, and this can jeopardize your safety and that of pedestrians and people in other cars.

Step 2: Solution

Now, let's consider a solution. In order to eliminate this problem, I recommend that we petition our congressional and state representatives to enact policies that prohibit the use of cell phones while driving a car. Drivers would be required to pull over to a safe place before making a call, and the policy would apply to drivers of all ages. The public would be informed of the policy via mainstream news sources. If this sort of policy were enacted, fewer people would use cell phones while they were driving, they would be less distracted, and the result would be a decrease in the overall number of accidents and fatalities per year.

In conclusion, I've shown you today how the increased use of cell phones over the past several years has led to increasing use of cell phones while driving, which in turn has led to an increase in car accidents and fatalities. I've also explained how cell phones distract drivers both physically (such as when they look for their phones and dial them) and mentally (such as when their conversation distracts them from their driving). And, finally, I've recommended that we ask the government to enact a policy that would greatly reduce the use of cell phones while driving and thus reduce driver distractions and the accidents they cause.

I began this speech by telling you of Alexander Manocchio, a cell phone user who killed a pregnant woman. I'd like to end by quoting a woman who lost her 2-year-old daughter because a man felt he could safely drive a car while talking on his cell phone:

My name is Patricia Peña. On November 2, 1999, my 2-year-old daughter Morgan and I were on our way home when our car was broadsided by another vehicle. Police reports proved that the crash was caused by a driver who was paying more attention to his cell phone than to the road and, as a result, ran a stop sign at 40 miles per hour. Morgan was rushed to the hospital, where she clung to life for the next 16 hours. But she never regained consciousness and was pronounced dead at 4:58 a.m. on November 3.

This is just one of many such accidents that have increased with the use of cell phones by drivers. I just pray this never happens to you or someone you love.

Cedrick appeals to logic when he explains that "when you access your phone or dial a number, you lose eye contact with the road." For audience members who are thinking that they are different because they have a hands-free phone, Cedrick assures them that that they are still at risk—their attention is still split between the road and the phone conversation.
Q7: Do you think this use of logic is effective?

Once the problem is clear and fully supported, Cedrick moves to his solution, which is general and encourages his listeners to take certain steps, without urging them to sign a petition or make a call.
Q8: Do you think he made the right decision? Why or why not?

In his conclusion, Cedrick gives a detailed summary of the areas he included in his speech: 1) increase in cell phone use while driving has caused an increase in accidents and fatalities; 2) cell phones are both a physical and mental distraction; and 3) cell phone use while driving should be illegal.

After the summary, Cedrick ties his conclusion back to the introduction by referring to the opening instance of Alexander Manocchio, whose cell phone use led to the death of a pregnant woman and her unborn child. He ends with an appeal to safety needs and uses an emotional appeal by quoting a mother who lost her young daughter in an accident caused when a car ran a stop sign because the driver was talking on his cell phone.
Q9: How would you rate Cedrick's conclusion—is there anything else you think he should add?

Active Critical Thinking

To think further about evaluating speakers, complete one or more of the following:

- Practice evaluating by using the form in Figure 12.9 to critique Cedrick's speech. To critique his delivery, watch his video *located under* "Student Resources for Chapter 12" at the *Essentials of Public Speaking* CourseMate. Total your points and compare answers with a classmate and verify your evaluation with your instructor.

- In addition to completing the evaluation form in Figure 12.9, answer questions Q1-Q9 written in boldface in the analysis section to the right of Cedrick's speech. Be specific but brief.

- Video your next speech (or use a video of a previous speech) and critique it using the form in Figure 12.9. Which part of your speech surprised you because it was better than you expected; which part of your speech needs the most work and what do you plan to do to improve?

Team Presentations

How do you feel about working in teams or giving team presentations enthusiastic or full of dread? People who can work effectively in teams are more likely to succeed in today's rapidly changing job market (McNerney, 2006) and to be valued by nonprofit organizations as well. Consider these examples of team presentations:

- You are part of a newcomer orientation team for your dorm. Each team member is responsible for briefing new students on a particular aspect of college life.

- For your final class project, you and three other students decide to give a team presentation on a controversial topic. Each of you will focus on a different aspect of the topic, and then your team will open the floor to audience questions and comments.

- A complex rezoning issue is up for vote in your community. To help inform the public and answer questions, the city council has asked you and four other community members with special knowledge and differing views to present a panel discussion for broadcast on the local cable channel.

- College administrators have announced an across-the-board budget cut for next year. Because a portion of the budget cut must come from student activities, the student council has appointed you and six other students to a problem-solving team. Your assignment is to decide which student activities should be cut and to present your decisions to a joint meeting of administrators and student-council representatives.

- A Burger Bar wants to move into your quiet neighborhood, and the community must unite in persuasive voices at town-hall meetings to keep this from happening.

The above are good examples of the many opportunities today for working in teams and for giving team presentations. A **team** is normally composed of three to seven members who actively work together toward a particular goal (solving a problem, gathering information, or planning an informative or persuasive presentation).

Five is considered the most productive size for a team, because it is large enough to supply needed information and to share the workload yet small enough to give each member a chance for maximum participation.

A **team presentation** (whether informative or persuasive) involves the collaborative organization and presentation of material by team members to an audience, often using one of various public-discussion formats: forum, symposium, panel, or some combination of the three. Team presentations have the obvious *advantages* of shared responsibility, more expertise during the presentation and Q&A session, and an impressive appearance. However, they also have *disadvantages:* Team presentations are difficult to coordinate to fit everyone's schedule, require more time to develop than an individual speech, and call for effective leadership and member cooperation to minimize squabbles and misunderstandings.

Effective Team Presentations

Successful team presentations have three characteristics (Leech, 1992):

- Well-organized, well-supported, smooth-flowing content.
- Creative, professional, and well-used visual aids.
- Smooth, polished, and dynamic team performance.

Content Team presentations should follow the basic steps discussed in Chapter 11 and this chapter. In the initial organization stage, you might benefit from having all members write their ideas on Post-it notes—one idea per note (Epson America, 2003). Use a wall or tabletop to organize the notes, moving them around until a basic outline is formed.

Later, each presenter can prepare a brief outline of the main points in his or her part of the presentation and tape the list to the wall for ease of viewing by other members. While you read each outline, imagine that you are an audience member. Is each presentation completely clear? Are the main points obvious? Would you doubt any of the main points? What additional information or slides would ease those doubts? Does each member's presentation flow smoothly into the next, or do transitions need work? Finding and correcting problems early in the planning process is very important. Otherwise, you may be forced to make last-minute changes requiring new slides Then, instead of a relaxed dry run of the entire presentation, you'll have a tense, frantic session.

Visual Aids Although objects and posters are sometimes used by teams, usually computer slides are the visual aid of choice. All slides used should be consistent in appearance throughout the presentation. Use the same logo

Successful team presentations require practice, revision, and more practice.

Gary Conner/PhotoEdit

(if you have one), colors, background or template, fonts and type sizes, as well as clip art and graphics. If one member has poorly prepared slides, the overall team impact is diminished. Unless all team members are aware of and agree on what makes a quality slide, it's a good idea to have all final slides prepared by one group member or by the graphic arts department in your organization. Prepare all slides early enough that they will be available for practice and so that any needed corrections can be made. → *Review Chapter 10 for specific suggestions on preparing effective computer slides and other visual aids.*

Team members should practice using their slides in front of at least one other team member, who can offer suggestions if needed. Awkward handling of slides can ruin the effect of a well-organized presentation. Be sure to time individual and the total team presentation. One way to estimate the length of the team presentation by the number of slides you plan to use. Most people spend at least 1 minute on each slide, so 20 slides mean at least a 20-minute presentation. Cut the number if necessary, because it is important to stay within prearranged time limits.

Performance A polished and dynamic team performance requires practice, revision, and more practice. Each member should practice alone or with a partner, and then the team should have one or more dry runs of the entire presentation. Videotape the practice sessions, if possible.

One team member needs to be the coordinator/leader —preferably a member with past team experience, speaking experience, and leadership abilities. Marjorie Brody (2003) recommends that the team leader should be a "subject matter expert." The leader also needs to be a person who can be objective in critiquing and directing the presenters. During the actual presentation, the coordinator presents the introduction and conclusion, introduces members, provides transitions if members fail to do so, and directs the question-and-answer session. If you decide to have a Q&A session, plan ahead how you will handle it. Anticipate possible questions and determine who has the most expertise to answer questions about specific topic areas. → *See Chapter 7 for specific suggestions on using Q&A.*

If your team presentation will be videotaped, taped for closed-circuit viewing; or to appear on a teleconference, television talk show, or news interview, you will need to adapt your presentation by making strategic verbal, visual, and vocal changes. → *Be sure to follow the suggestions in Chapter 8 for adapting your presentation to the media.*

Team Presentation Formats

Team presentation formats include the symposium, panel, forum, or any combination of the three. Any of the formats can be used to share information, instruct others, problem solve, or promote an idea or cause.

Symposium In a **symposium**, each team member presents a formal 2- to 10-minute speech on one aspect of the symposium's topic. The purpose may be to inform and instruct or even to persuade. Probably the oldest recorded symposium (described by Plato) took place in Athens around 415 B.C. and consisted of seven participants presenting formal speeches on their views of the nature and definition of love (Jones, 1970).

Panel In a **panel**, discussion team members informally discuss a problem or topic of interest in front of an audience. Although no formal speeches are presented, team members contribute freely and equally because they are organized, well prepared, and have a specific purpose. The team coordinator guides members through an organized procedure agreed on ahead of time. It is not unusual to find panelists disagreeing with, correcting, or interrupting each other, which is very enjoyable for the audience.

Forum When open audience participation with the team is planned, it is referred to as a **forum**. The term is derived from ancient Rome, where a forum referred to a public square where political and legal business was conducted. The traditional New England town meeting is a modern-day forum.

Problem Solving for Team Presentations

Successful teams use the following basic problem-solving procedure, based on John Dewey's (1991) well-known reflective thinking process, as a general tool to help them make decisions—whether in a private planning session (e.g., trying to decide on content for a team presentation) or when presenting a panel discussion in front of an audience.

Step 1: Identify the Problem First, the team must agree that a problem exists and define the nature of the problem in a specific, factual, and descriptive manner. Ask questions such as: When did the problem first arise? Who is affected? What are the implications? When must the problem be solved? Once the problem seems clear, test that understanding by stating the problem as a question and writing it down for all to see. Continue discussion until all team members are satisfied with the wording.

Because Step 1 is so time consuming, team members often choose to complete this step ahead of the public discussion. In that case, the coordinator briefly recaps the previous discussion and reads the team's exact definition of the problem to the audience. Then the team begins its discussion with Step 2.

Step 2: Analyze the Problem Begin analyzing the problem by listing the topics and information the team needs to discuss. Next, narrow down the list to a manageable length, and discuss what is known about each item. (Here, members share their research and personal knowledge.) Be sure to look at all sides of the problem, and include opinions and objections you think your audience is likely to have. Informative panels use the analysis step to educate audience members; persuasive panels use the analysis step to investigate fallacious reasoning and introduce persuasive evidence. ➤ *See the information on fallacious reasoning in Chapter 13.*

Step 3: Establish Criteria Criteria are guidelines, boundaries, standards, or rules against which the team agrees to evaluate or judge proposed solutions to the problem. For example, possible criteria to use in deciding which student activities to cut from the college budget might read as follows:

Any decision we reach about student activities must:

- Be agreeable to a majority of team members.
- Inconvenience the smallest number of students.
- Give preference to low-budget yet high-learning activities.
- Be decided within two weeks.

The team now makes a list of any criteria they think a solution should meet. They then assess the importance of each criterion, eliminating the least important until only three to five remain. Next, the criteria should be divided into two categories: "must have" (required) and "wants" (desired). Rank the "wants" from most to least desired. Keep the "must have" category to a minimum, and check to see that each one is absolutely necessary and not just a high-level "want." These "must have" and "want" criteria will be used later in Step 5.

Establishing the criteria is a *key step* in the basic problem-solving procedure—it speeds up team decisions and improves the quality of those decisions. In fact, once Step 3 is completed, the most difficult part of the process is over.

Step 4: List Possible Solutions Within the team's time and budget limitations, list as many solutions as you can. It is tempting to list and evaluate (Step 5) at the same time. However, evaluations should be postponed until Step 5 to keep the formation of your list speedy and creative. At this time, don't worry about the quality of your alternatives or whether they meet the criteria; quantity, not quality, should be the goal in this step.

In panel discussions, to speed up this step, each member should bring a list of possible solutions. Then, one at a time, each member suggests a single solution, which the coordinator writes on the board for all to see. The process continues until all solutions are included. Review the completed list to make sure no important ideas were omitted. Don't forget to include "doing nothing" as an alternative—it serves as a basis of comparison to the other proposed solutions.

Step 5: Evaluate Solutions If the team did a good job of establishing criteria, Step 5 will be amazingly simple. As you move through this step, be sure to depersonalize the discussion by separating the person from the solution he or she proposed.

- First, eliminate solutions that do not meet all the "must have" criteria agreed upon in Step 3.

- Next, discuss each remaining solution's strengths and weaknesses (refer to research presented in Step 2 when necessary).

- Determine how well each solution meets each "want" criterion by assigning a point value to each—usually from 1 (low) to 5 (high).

- Determine which suggested solution has the most points and meets the most important criteria. The answer should be obvious, but if not, additional discussion (and even criteria) may be needed in order for a consensus decision to be reached. More than one solution may be desired in some cases.

Step 6: Discuss How to Implement Solutions The final stage is to decide how the agreed-upon solution(s) should be put into practice. In deciding how to implement what the team has endorsed, consider who will be responsible for overseeing implementation, when it will begin, how long it will take, and what resources are needed. This step may be omitted to save time in the panel discussion.

Sometimes in discussing implementation, a team will find that a solution that seemed excellent on paper is in fact not feasible. For example, if a school board decided to implement uniforms to solve theft of clothing then discovered that parents refused to comply, the members would need to rethink this decision. In such cases, the team must return to Step 5 to select another alternative.

Don't forget that after each presentation, team members should evaluate each other and the presentation as a whole to determine strengths and weaknesses. If at all possible, videotape your presentations to more clearly assess the team's verbal, visual, and vocal communication.

Active Critical Thinking

To think further about team presentations, complete the following:

- Think of a team presentation you participated in for this or another class.
- Explain the success or lack of success of this team. Which characteristic of a successful team was most responsible for the success or lack of success of your team? Give an example to illustrate your answer. Be prepared to share this example with the class if asked.

Summary

Persuasion is communication intended to influence choice. Although persuasion is intentional, it should not coerce. Persuasive speeches differ from informative speeches in four aspects: supporting materials, language style, delivery, and organizational patterns. There are three basic types of persuasive speeches: (1) the speech to convince, in which you want audience agreement; (2) the speech to actuate, in which you want both audience agreement and audience action; and (3) the speech to intensify social cohesion, where you strive to convince the audience to commit to higher levels of enthusiasm, motivation, or productivity.

Effective persuasive speeches are carefully organized and supported. The Basic Steps for Preparing a Speech will help you prepare your introduction, body, and conclusion. The introduction includes getting listener attention, motivating the audience to listen, establishing speaker credibility, and stating your position and main arguments.

The body of your persuasive speech may follow any of these organizational patterns: claim, causal (cause–effect–solution or cause–result–action), problem–solution (problem–solution–benefit or problem–solution–action), comparative advantages, or criteria satisfaction. The pattern you choose depends on your goal (to convince, to actuate, or to intensify social cohesion) and the type of position statement (fact, value, or policy) you are using.

As with informative speeches, the conclusion begins with a summary and ends with refocusing attention in a memorable way. In addition, the persuasive conclusion normally includes two more items: visualizing the future for the audience and issuing a challenge or appeal for action.

Team presentations involve the collaborative presentation of material by several people. Effective team presentations are characterized by well-organized content, professional visual aids, and dynamic team performance, and may take the format of a symposium, panel, or forum. Successful teams use basic problem-solving procedures when planning their presentations and during participation in panel discussions. Whether you are speaking by yourself or as part of a team, the information covered in this chapter and in this text can help you give interesting, professional presentations.

Essentials of Public Speaking Online ⊿CourseMate

Use your Online Resources for *Essentials of Public Speaking* for quick access to the electronic study resources that accompany this chapter, including a video of Lorna's speech seen on pages 287–290. the Test Your Knowledge quiz on page 300, the Persuasive-Speech Evaluation Form on page 315, InfoTrac College Edition, Personal Skill Building activities, Collaborative Skill Building activities, Active Critical Thinking boxes, a digital glossary, sample speeches, and review quizzes.

Key Terms

arguments 282	means or appeals of	speech to convince 283
attitude poll 295	persuasion 283	speech to intensify
backing 282	panel 309	social cohesion 283
claim 282	persuasion 278	symposium 309
emotional appeal 278	position statement	team 307
evidence 282	292	team presentation 308
forum 310	speech to actuate 283	warrant 282

Personal Skill Building

1. Read Cedrick McBeth's persuasive speech on pages 305–306. Identify whether it is a speech to convince, to actuate, or to intensify social cohesion, and what type of position statement Cedrick appears to be using—fact, value, or policy. Next, evaluate the quality of Cedrick's introduction and conclusion. What changes if any would you recommend? Compare your answers with those of a classmate.

2. Prepare a 7- to 10-minute speech to actuate using a position statement of policy following the preparation steps covered in this chapter. Prepare an attitude poll to determine how your audience feels about your topic (enlarge Figure 12.5 on a copier or prepare your own poll). Unless you make your position statement and why you feel the way you do completely clear, the audience responses my be inaccurate. If your instructor doesn't reserve a special day for you and your classmates to poll each other, pass your poll around immediately before class begins several day prior to your scheduled speech. If you find that several students disagree with your position, try to determine why they disagree.

3. For the persuasive speech that you will be giving in class, conduct a critical thinking evaluation by answering the Critical Thinking Questions in Figure 11.6 on p. 269. Be prepared to turn this evaluation in to your instructor.

4. After each persuasive speech given in class, one member of the class should volunteer or be assigned by the instructor to present a 1- to 2-minute impromptu rebuttal or supporting speech. This is a fun way to practice impromptu speaking.

5. Prepare a 1-minute speech of introduction to give prior to a classmate's persuasive speech. Make sure each speaker in the class has someone to introduce him or her. (Follow the guidelines for speeches of introduction in Chapter 14, "Special Occasion Speaking.")

CourseMate

6. Check out the following websites and online activities. (You can access these sites through your Online Resources for *Essentials of Public Speaking*.)
The ability to compose and articulate a message to persuade to move an audience is an art. Use these speeches on YouTube to critique persuasive speeches:

   - Listen for differences in informative and persuasive language. Watch Daniel Sauble's persuasive speech on stem cell research on YouTube by searching for "Daniel Sauble stem cell research." Compare Daniel's speech to Maria Kiehnle's informative speech (search for "Informative speech by Maria Kiehnle"). Pay particular attention to the differences in language usage—Daniel selects words that ignite emotion, while Maria uses speech that is descriptive.

   - To learn more about the Toulmin Model of Argument, check out The Toulmin Project Home Page created by Soukup and Titsworth at the University of Nebraska at Lincoln: **www.unl.edu/speech/comm109/Toulmin/index.htm**.

   - Identify patterns of organization. In a speech on commercial television programming (search YouTube for "persuasive speech McCafferty"), a student speaker uses distinct organization of three main points and a slide presentation to highlight specifics of each point. Also notice how she verbally cites her sources in support of the thesis of the speech.

   - Listen to various uses of narratives. In the speech "Smoking Kills," which you can find on YouTube by searching for "Smoking kills persuasive speech," the student tells a personal story from his own life. Search YouTube for "persuasive speech," and you will have numerous examples.

Collaborative Skill Building

1. In small groups of four or five, look through the August 2010 issue of *Vital Speeches* for a persuasive/motivational speech that the groups like. The speeches in this issue were given at 2010 commencement exercises at various colleges in the United States. Once everyone has read the speech, analyze it by answering the following questions and ranking each on a scale of 1 (low) to 5 (high): (1) Which type of persuasive organization was used, and how effective do you think it was? (2) Was the position statement fact, value, or policy? (3) Identify at least four different types of supporting materials used and the success of each; and (4) Critique the language style used by the speaker. Share your findings with those of another group or the class, making sure you mention any tips you gained from this speech and speaker.

2. In small groups, write fact, value, and policy position statements for each of the following persuasive issues: (1) airline safety; (b) volunteerism; (c) computer hacker; (d) care for the homeless. When finished, compare your statements with those of other groups. Decide which statement is best and why.

Persuasive-Speech Evaluation Form

Name: _____ Topic: _____ Date: _____
Grades: Outline: _____ Presentation: _____ Other: _____

Ratings: 1 (Missing), 2 (Poor), 3 (Fair), 4 (Good), 5 (Excellent)

Did **INTRODUCTION**:   1 2 3 4 5   Comments:
     1. Begin with attention-getter?   1 2 3 4 5
     2. Motivate audience to listen?   1 2 3 4 5
     3. Establish credibility?   1 2 3 4 5
     4. Make thesis/position clear?

Were **MAIN IDEAS**:   1 2 3 4 5
     5. Easy to identify and follow?   1 2 3 4 5
     6. Arranged in effective pattern?   1 2 3 4 5
     7. Characterized by good transitions?

Was **SUPPORTING MATERIAL**:   1 2 3 4 5
     8. Well documented during speech?   1 2 3 4 5
     9. Adequate in verbal supports? (Use +, ✓, –)
       ___ *Statistics?*   ___ *Expert opinions?*
       ___ *Comparisons?*   ___ *Fables/sayings/poems/rhymes?*
       ___ *Instances?*   ___ *Explanations?*

Did **SPEAKER PERSUASIVELY**:   1 2 3 4 5
     10. Use evidence and logic?   1 2 3 4 5
     11. Establish credibility?   1 2 3 4 5
     12. Relate to psychological needs of listeners?

Did **CONCLUSION**:   1 2 3 4 5
     13. Summarize topic and main ideas?   1 2 3 4 5
     14. Visualize future; ask for audience acceptance?   1 2 3 4 5
     15. Close in a memorable way?

Was **DELIVERY** characterized by: 1 2 3 4 5
     16. Dynamic, yet conversational quality?   1 2 3 4 5
     17. Confidence (in posture, gestures, and eye contact)?
     18. Freedom from distracting mannerisms? (Check)   1 2 3 4 5
       ___ *"Uh"/ "Um"/ "And uh"/ "You know"/ "Well"/ "OK"?*
       ___ *Plays with pencil, clothes, hair, or pointer?*
       ___ *Nervous laugh or cough?*
       ___ *Slouches, taps feet, paces, or sways?*
       ___ *Over-reliance on notes?*
       ___ *Other?*
     19. Effective vocal delivery (volume, pitch, rate, and emphasis)?   1 2 3 4 5
     20. Effective language use and at least one stylistic device?   1 2 3 4 5
     21. **Extra Credit**: Adequate in visual supports? (Use +, ✓, –)   1 2 3 4 5
       ___ *Interesting?*   ___ *Professional? opinions?*
       ___ *Easy to see?*   ___ *Handled well?*

                             Total: _____

Figure 12.9

Persuasive-Speech Evaluation Form

13

Persuasive Methods and Theories

Reasoning by analogy and reasoning by metaphor have been successful persuasive tools since ancient Greek times. Aristotle believed the use of metaphors indicated a speaker's intelligence, as he said in his *Poetics:* "…The greatest thing by far is to be a master of metaphor. It is the one thing that cannot be learnt from others, and it is also a sign of genius, since a good metaphor implies an intuitive perception of the similarity in dissimilars" (Aristotle [translated by Ingram Bywater], 1974, sec. 1459.5).

In Chapter 9 on language, we discussed the metaphor—"an implied comparison between two items without using *like* or *as*"—as a stylistic device still used by successful speakers in today's society. In fact, persuasive expert Charles Larsen (2010) calls the metaphor "the most powerful, more persuasive" of the figures of speech (p. 132). Good metaphors "have universal and cross cultural themes" (p. 133) so are familiar to most audiences. Comparing the outstanding student in a group of newly graduated students with one of the few, early growing plants that break through the ground in the early spring is an example of an easily understood metaphor. *Do you think you would enjoy and understand professors more if they used metaphors? Why?*

Learning Objectives

As you read Chapter 13,

- *Explain* the role that *Logos* (evidence and logic) plays in a persuasive speech; the various methods of presenting evidence; when to present one or both sides of your position; and avoiding fallacious reasoning.

- *Explain* the role that *Ethos* (speaker credibility) plays in a persuasive speech; the basic elements of credibility; and the unethical use of credibility.

- *Explain* the role that *Pathos* (psychological needs) plays in a persuasive speech; fear appeals; and the unethical use of emotional appeals.

- *Discuss* ways to use persuasive theory when speaking persuasively.

ONE OF THE MOST ENJOYABLE YET CHALLENGING SPEECHES IS THE PERSUASIVE SPEECH. Persuasive speaking is enjoyable because you speak on issues that you feel strongly about, and you get a chance to present your information and influence others. At the same time, politicians can testify to how difficult it is to persuade people; many of them have experienced a **boomerang effect**, which means that fewer people agreed with them at the end of their speech than agreed at the beginning of it.

Therefore, regardless of what type of persuasive speech you are giving (a speech to convince, to actuate, or to intensify social cohesion) or whether you are dealing with a proposition of fact, value, or policy, *there are at least three basic appeals that must be established and addressed in your speech if you wish to be truly persuasive*:

1. Logos: The evidence and logic of your message.
2. Ethos: Your credibility and expertise.
3. Pathos: The psychological needs of your audience.

Although all three basic appeals play a role in persuasion, different speaking situations call for a different level of importance for each. This chapter will look in detail at these three persuasive appeals and discuss what to do to make them work for you. We will also discuss unethical types of persuasive appeals that you should avoid when you are the speaker, and recognize and resist when you are the listener.

Using a database like Info-Trac College Edition, EBSCOhost, or CQ Researcher, run a subject-guidesearch on *Aristotle*. Read the following articles: "Ethical Decision Making in Public Relations: What Would Aristotle Say?" by Martinson and "Aristotle's Advice for Business Success" by Laabs.

Logos: Using Evidence and Logic Skillfully

Of the three persuasive appeals, the effectiveness of evidence and logic is the most ambiguous. Although we like to think of ourselves as logical thinkers and we expect speakers to use logic and evidence in their speeches, we are often swayed more by other factors, as we will see in this chapter. Nevertheless, when listeners are persuaded, they tend to attribute the persuasion to the superior logic and evidence used by the speaker.

Evidence and Logic Defined

Evidence supports the logical arguments of a speech and includes factual instances, expert and personal opinions, and statistics. **Logic**—from the Greek *logos*, or reason—has been defined as "the study of orderly thinking, the sequence and connection of thoughts and ideas as they relate to one another" (Bell, 1990, p. 262). In other words, logic connects the pieces of evidence in a manner that creates a meaningful and persuasive argument. Don't forget to challenge your own beliefs and evidence as you are preparing your speech. Apply the Critical Thinking Questions in Figure 11.6 (page 269) to your persuasive outline, concentrating on your evidence and logic. → *See Chapter 6 for additional types of supporting material that can serve as evidence.*

Evidence and Logic as Persuasive Tools

Researchers are finding that using evidence and logic as tools to persuade may not be as effective as was previously thought and that certain ways of using evidence may actually hinder persuasion. Note the following research findings (for a summary, see Reinard, 1988; Reynolds & Reynolds, 2002):

Purestock/Getty Images

Successful persuasive speakers use evidence and logic skillfully, establish their credibility in a personal manner, and appeal to listeners' psychological needs.

- Listeners have difficulty distinguishing between logical and illogical evidence and between high quality and low quality (Bettinghaus & Cody, 1997; Dresser, 1963; McCroskey, 1967). Apparently, even though listeners think logic and evidence are important, they often cannot identify either in speeches.

- Logical-sounding words and phrases (such as *therefore, as a result, it is only logical that*, and *it is possible to conclude*) have surprising power to convince listeners that a presentation is logical. In general, when these words are used, a speech is judged to be more logical, regardless of its actual content (Bettinghaus & Cody, 1997). This finding indicates how unethical speakers who use logical-sounding words are able to fool their listeners.

- In order for the evidence to persuade them, listeners must be aware and accept that the evidence exists (Reynolds & Reynolds, 2002). Therefore, speakers and advertisers are more persuasive who make it clear that what they are presenting is truly evidence (O'Keefe, 1998; Pfau & Louden, 1994).

- Low-ability listeners who are not personally involved with the topic will tend to be persuaded when a large amount of evidence is presented—even if the evidence is of poor quality (Petty & Cacioppo, 1984, 1996).

- Listeners already in favor of the speaker's proposal, or who believe the speaker to be credible, tend to rate the speech as being high in evidence even if no actual evidence is presented (Cathcart, 1955; Dresser, 1963). In most cases, the listeners' view of the speaker's credibility and attitude toward the topic are more important persuasive factors than the evidence presented.

- Speakers whose credibility has not been established can use evidence effectively to increase their credibility and thereby increase their persuasiveness (McCroskey, 1970; Olson & Cal, 1984). O'Keefe (1998) found consistent confirmation that citing evidence in a speech improves the credibility of most speakers.

- There is a "significant persuasive advantage for messages providing information source citations" (O'Keefe, 1998, p. 67). However, when evidence is used, mentioning only the source of the evidence without explaining who this "expert" is does not make the presentation more persuasive. In fact, unless the source's qualifications are mentioned by the speaker, citing an unfamiliar source makes the presentation less persuasive (Bostrom & Tucker, 1969; Ostermeier, 1967).

- Normally, it is more effective to cite the source and his or her qualifications after the evidence has been presented. Speakers should cite the source before the evidence only when they know that their listeners consider that source to be highly credible (Cohen, 1964; Reynolds & Burgoon, 1983).

- Speakers who support their assertions by citing firsthand experiences (self-reference speakers) are considered more trustworthy and more persuasive than speakers who refer only to high-prestige sources (Ginossar & Trope, 1980; Koballa, 1989; Reinard, 1988).

- Speakers appear credible who provide sufficient information in a citation for the audience to find the source (if they so desire) (Inch et al., 2006, p. 145).

- Personal examples and experiences tend to be more persuasive than statistical or numerical data (Kazoleas, 1993), especially for listeners who disagree with the speaker (Slater & Rouner, 1996). Personal examples and experiences have a longer-lasting persuasive effect than those from secondhand sources (Ostermeier, 1967; Papageogis, 1963). Statistical evidence may be more persuasive for audience members who already support the speaker (Slater & Rouner, 1996). In most cases, speakers should include both narrative and statistical evidence (Allen et al., 2000).

- Research has indicated that audiences are more easily persuaded when the arguments presented are novel or new (Morley, 1987; Morley & Walker, 1987). Listeners who disagree with your topic won't be persuaded by the same arguments and evidence that failed to persuade them in the first place. However, new arguments and evidence, or even old arguments presented in a novel or unusual way, may be successful.

Methods of Presenting Evidence

There are four principal ways of presenting evidence, and a summary of the research in the preceding section indicates some important differences among the four methods (see Figure 13.1):

- Method 1—*assertion + evidence + source:* "We need to paint our workroom walls a bright color [*assertion*] because this normally increases productivity by 20 percent [*evidence*], according to Kenneth Johnson [*source*]."

- Method 2—*assertion + evidence.* "We need to paint our workroom walls a bright color [*assertion*] because this normally increases productivity by 20 percent [*evidence*]." Note that the evidence is not linked to a source or documented in any way.

- Method 3—*assertion + evidence + source + qualifications of source:* "We need to paint our work-room walls a bright color [*assertion*] because this normally increases productivity by 20 percent [*evidence*], according to Kenneth Johnson [*source*], research director for Business Color Inc. [*qualification of source*]."

- Method 4—*assertion + firsthand experience:* "We need to paint our work-room walls a bright color [*assertion*]. Twice I have been in departments that painted their work areas bright colors, and both times productivity increased approximately 20 percent [*firsthand experience*]."

As Figure 13.1 shows, Method 1 is generally the least persuasive of the four methods. As discussed earlier, citing a source without giving the source's qualifications is even less persuasive than presenting evidence with no source at all. The most persuasive type of evidence is firsthand experience.

Best Methods When You Are Unknown to Your Audience When speaking to an audience who does not know you well (such as your classmates at the beginning of the term), Methods 3 and 4 are the best for presenting evidence.

Figure 13.1

Persuasiveness of
Evidence Presented in
Four Different Methods

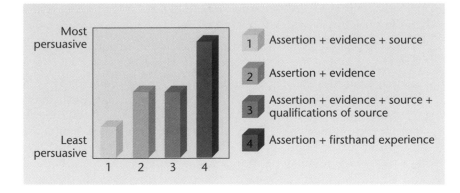

There are several reasons for using Method 3 (assertion + evidence + source + qualifications of source) for audiences that do not know you:

- You can enhance your credibility by citing sources they consider prestigious.

- These listeners will expect you to include documented evidence in your speech. To appear credible (and to improve your persuasiveness), you must meet their expectations.

- Documented evidence can counteract opposing arguments your audience is likely to hear later.

- Communication researcher James McCroskey (1970) found that audiences are less affected by the opposing view of a second speaker if the first speaker's message contains documented evidence. For example, consider two speeches about year-round schooling—one against that cites authoritative sources and one in favor that cites no authoritative sources. If we hear the "con" speech first and are persuaded, when we hear the "pro" speech we are likely to realize that this speaker's sources are inadequate and to retain our "con" opinion. But if we hear the "pro" speech first and are persuaded, the chances are that when we hear the "con" speech we will realize that the "pro" speaker's sources were weak and will side with the "con" speaker.

Method 4 (assertion + firsthand experience) can also be effective when you are unknown to your audience. It is especially effective if the person introducing you presents you as an authority. Would you be more persuaded if you heard about the effects of drugs from a speaker who quoted from a book on the subject or from an ex-addict or relative of a drug addict? However, Method 4 should be used only if you have considerable firsthand experience and know more about the topic than do most of your listeners. Even so, you should come prepared with more than just personal experience.

If you make an objective and complete search for relevant evidence (both for and against your idea) as part of your speech preparation, when someone asks for additional evidence, you will be prepared.

Best Methods When You Are Known to Your Audience When speaking to an audience who knows you well (such as a club or work group that you have belonged to for some time), Method 2 (assertion + evidence without sources) and Method 4 (assertion + firsthand experience) are effective. Method 2 is especially appropriate when your speaking time is limited. Because your audience knows you (assuming that your credibility and expertise are good), they will view extensive documentation as a waste of time. Also, you don't need to cite sources when your

Using a database like InfoTrac College Edition, EBSCOhost, or CQ Researcher, run a keyword search on *persuasion*. Look through the articles and count the number of professions interested in persuasion. Find at least one article on courtroom persuasion.

audience is made up of colleagues who are somewhat familiar with your topic. Even when the speech is about a new concept or product, your audience will normally have enough general knowledge of the field to determine whether your evidence and conclusions are reasonable.

If you are uncertain about whether you should cite your sources, a compromise might be to name your sources (prestigious sources only) on your visuals. For example, at the bottom of a visual showing the results of a national survey of business trends, you could print simply "Dun and Bradstreet, December, 2008."

Whether to Present One or Both Sides of Your Position

Should you present only arguments that support your position, or should you introduce and refute opposing arguments (counterarguments) as well? Research indicates these general guidelines (Allen, 1991, 1998; Hovland et al., 1967; Kamins & Marks, 1987).

Present only your side of the argument when:

- Your listeners agree with your proposal and have a well-developed belief system (in other words, they are not new to the opinion). Presenting negative arguments they have not thought of, even if you refute them well, may create doubt and sabotage your attempt at persuasion. These listeners are more interested in a pep rally-type presentation.

- Your listeners know nothing about your topic (too many arguments cause confusion).

- You want them to take an immediate action (such as donating money at the door as they leave).

- There is little chance that they will hear the other side from another speaker or the news media.

Present both sides of the argument when:

- Your listeners are fairly knowledgeable about your topic.

- They agree but are fairly new to the opinion and have undeveloped belief systems.

- They disagree with your proposal.

- You are not asking for immediate action.

- There is a good chance that they will hear the other side from another speaker or the news media.

Knowledgeable listeners, especially those who disagree with you, will be suspicious of you if you present only one side. Just as presenting documented evidence in your speech can help listeners resist later opposing arguments, presenting both sides also serves to "inoculate" listeners. Researchers have found that in one-sided presentations, listeners generally expect "to receive the most important arguments at the beginning of the message," but in two-sided presentations, listeners generally expect "to receive the most important arguments at the end of a message" (Igou & Bless, 2007, p. 261). This is important to remember, because audiences that have their expectations met are more likely to experience attitude change.

The Inoculation Theory   According to William McGuire's (1985) **inoculation theory**, "inoculating" a listener against opposing ideas is similar to inoculating a person against a disease. The person who has never heard the other side on a topic will be susceptible to those arguments, just as a person who has lived in a germ-free environment is susceptible to catching a disease. Immunity can be produced by giving a shot containing a weakened form of the disease or, in the case of a speech, by presenting a "brief look" at opposing arguments along with facts and logic disproving them. This "inoculation" helps listeners remain resistant to counterarguments. When they hear opposing arguments, they can say: "Oh, yes, I knew that. However, it's not important (or true), because research shows that …"

Presenting both sides also seems to make listeners resistant to arguments that the speaker did not cover (An & Pfau, 2004; Papageogis & McGuire, 1961; Pfau, 1997; Szabo & Pfau, 2002). Inoculating listeners even helps them build their own counterarguments. When hearing a new argument, they are likely to say, "Based on what I know, this argument couldn't be true because…" Listeners who are highly involved and have critical thinking skills are the best at building these counterarguments (Gass & Seiter, 1999).

The Safest Course: Both Sides   Once you poll your classmates, you will have a better idea of whether you should include both sides or only one side of your issue. However, on the basis of the inoculation theory (and because polling is usually not possible), the safest course is to present both sides (Allen, 1991). Whether your listeners agree or disagree with you, they will usually be in a position to hear opposing arguments. Also, presenting both sides shows that you have thoroughly researched the issue—a sure boost to your credibility (Hass & Linder, 1972).

Presenting both sides does not mean giving the opposition equal time. Presenting the "other side" means mentioning one or two objections to your plan and then either (1) showing how each objection is based on inaccurate information or faulty reasoning, or (2) if an objection is accurate, showing how it is minor compared to the many advantages of your proposal. For example, in a speech about the importance of drinking bottled water, you might admit that cost is a disadvantage but that the small increase in the family budget is minimal compared to the decreased risk to the family's health.

Logical Reasoning

Successful persuasive speakers typically use one of four patterns of reasoning to organize evidence into logical, persuasive arguments: deductive, inductive, analogical, or causal.

Deductive and Inductive Reasoning   For your argument to be considered logical, its assumptions (premises) must support its conclusion. Use of deductive and inductive reasoning patterns are two ways to make sure your premises support your conclusions (Kahane & Cavender, 2002). As discussed in Chapter 7, *deductive reasoning* presents the conclusion first and then proceeds to specific supporting cases; *inductive reasoning* starts with the specific cases before presenting the general conclusion.

For example, suppose you want to argue that your company should provide affordable child care for employees. If use deductive reasoning, you will state your general conclusion first ("To improve employee satisfaction, Bag It Inc. should provide child care for the children of its employees") and then support it with specific cases ("Companies A, B, and C have recently begun providing child care, and each has experienced improved employee satisfaction"). If you use inductive reasoning, you will present the supporting cases first ("Companies A, B, and C have recently begun providing child care, and each has experienced improved employee satisfaction") and finish with your conclusion ("By providing day care, Bag It Inc. could increase employee satisfaction also").

The best method depends on your audience. Listeners who are hostile to your conclusion may simply stop listening if you use the deductive pattern. So, even though your evidence might have stimulated them to rethink their positions, you have already lost them. The inductive approach is better when a significant number of audience members are likely to oppose your conclusion—especially if you can catch their interest with powerful stories and vivid personal instances. On the other hand, when most audience members are likely to agree with your conclusion, they will be drawn in by deductive reasoning because they will be interested in hearing your choice of supporting evidence.

Analogical and Causal Reasoning   Reasoning by comparison, called analogical reasoning, is used to *explain* and *clarify*. Causal reasoning (especially cause-effect reasoning) is used to prove.

Analogical reasoning occurs when you compare a familiar example with an unfamiliar one. For example, suppose you wanted to urge adoption of a state income tax. Using analogical reasoning, you would show several important similarities between your state and State A and then suggest that because State A has benefited from a state income tax, your state would also benefit from one. Reasoning from analogy cannot serve as absolute proof (because the two items being compared are not identical), but it can be a powerful way to persuade your audience of the merits of your argument. You can use either literal or figurative comparisons in analogical reasoning. Comparing a jogger wearing cheap jogging shoes to a jogger wearing shoeboxes tied to his feet is an example of a *figurative analogy* (Whately, 1997). Showing similarities between occasional joggers and professional runners and then telling listeners that, like professional runners, the occasional joggers should wear only a special type of shoe is an example of a *literal analogy*.

Causal reasoning occurs when you imply a causal link between two items (for example, fatty foods cause high cholesterol levels in humans). According to persuasion expert Charles Larson (2010), cause-effect reasoning (the most common type of causal reasoning) is used "to identify events, trends, or facts that have resulted in certain effects" (p. 214). Because causal reasoning is used to prove, you must make sure that what you are claiming as a cause-effect relationship isn't just a chance association. Ask yourself these questions (Herrick, 1995):

- *Do the events occur together consistently?* (For example, Melissa always sneezes violently when a dog comes near her.)

- *Does the cause consistently precede the effect?* (A dog is nearby every time Melissa sneezes violently.)

- *Is the cause sufficient to produce the effect by itself?* (Dogs cause excessive sneezing in many people who are allergic to them.)

- *Is it possible that a third factor is the cause of the events?* (Melissa has taken allergy tests, and she's allergic only to dogs.)

If you can answer yes to the first three questions and no to the final one, you can be fairly confident that your cause-effect relationship is real.

Fallacious Reasoning

Unfortunately, not all reasoning is logical reasoning; some speakers, knowingly or unknowingly, use types of **fallacious** (false or faulty) **reasoning** (Larson, 2010; Shapiro, 2007). Seven of the most typical types of fallacious reasoning are discussed in this section for two reasons: (1) so that you can avoid using them, and (2) so that, if in your research you find fallacious objections to your position (or plan), you can recognize them and effectively rebut them in your speech.

Ad Hominem *Ad hominem* is a Latin phrase meaning "to (or against) the person." Speakers using the **ad hominem** fallacy are attempting to divert attention from a weak argument by attacking the person who questions it (for example, "Who are you to question the high cost of my plan? You can't even balance your own checkbook."). The idea is that if the critic can be discredited, chances are that his or her criticism will be discredited too. There is nothing wrong with questioning a person's credibility if it is relevant to the issue at hand. But the *ad hominem* fallacy is much more than a credibility check—it is an unwarranted personal attack (often involving name-calling) designed to distract the audience from a discussion of the issues (Shapiro, 2007, p. 77).

Ad Populum The **ad populum** (Latin for "to the people") fallacy is another way to distract attention from an investigation of the issues. However, instead of attacking another person's credibility, the speaker argues, "How could this idea possibly be wrong when public opinion says it's right?" In other words, why waste time with evidence when "everyone" agrees on the point (for example, "You've asked whether some German shepherds are vicious, but everyone knows that they are the best and most loyal dogs in the world.").

Appeal to Ignorance (Ad Ignoratiam) Speakers who appeal to ignorance (**ad ignoratiam**) are saying that because no one can prove that a claim is false, it must be true. The purpose of this appeal is to put the opposition on the defensive and convince the audience that the burden of proof is now on them ("You can't prove that UFOs don't exist, can you? No one has ever been able to disprove the existence of UFOs. Therefore, it's obvious that they do exist."). When the opposition is unable (or unwilling) to disprove the claim, the claim is obviously true, says the speaker. However, arguing that "because something has not been disproved, it has been proved" (Herrick, 1995, p. 227) is fallacious reasoning.

Begging the Question **Begging the question** is a type of circular reasoning; it "asserts that something is because it is" (Bell, 1990, pp. 278–279). A Sony Corporation ad illustrates this type of reasoning. In speaking about the Trinitron XBR television, the ad states: "The best statement we can make about this television is that it's the best television we've ever made" (Bell, p. 279). This is a "catchy" ad—but it contains no evidence. In begging-the-question arguments, the audience is supposed to assume that the question (considered debatable by most people) has already been answered and no longer requires supporting evidence.

Hasty Generalization The **hasty generalization** fallacy (which is more common with inductive reasoning) occurs when a conclusion is based on too few examples or on isolated examples. This kind of conclusion is based on a sample that is too small to be representative of the population it comes from. The following is an example of a hasty generalization:

- A survey of students in one inner-city school found that 20 percent carried weapons.
- Last month in our own city, there were two incidents involving handguns.
- We need to install gun detection equipment in every school in the state.

Post Hoc The Latin phrase *post hoc* means "after the fact." The **post hoc** fallacy (which is more common with deductive reasoning) occurs when the speaker claims a causal relationship simply because one event followed another event. But just because Event B followed Event A doesn't prove that A caused B. The following is an example of *post hoc* reasoning:

- People are drinking more carbonated drinks than they did 30 years ago.

- Incidents of cancer have increased in the past 20 years.

- Therefore, carbonated drinks cause cancer.

Slippery Slope The **slippery slope** fallacy occurs when a speaker asserts that taking a particular step will lead to a serious and undesirable consequence (for example, listening to rock music will lead to drug use among teenagers) and does not provide adequate evidence to support the assertion. The term *slippery slope* implies that if you take one step, you will inevitably slip all the way down the slope and land in an even worse situation.

Now that you are aware of fallacious reasoning, take another look at your persuasive outline and make sure that, in your desire to influence, you haven't knowingly or unknowingly attempted to fool your audience (Shapiro, 2007, calls this "conning" your audience) by using one of these types of faulty reasoning. When your audience has limited knowledge of your topic, it requires special effort not to take advantage of them.

Remember

Fallacious reasoning includes . . .

- *Ad hominem*—attacking the person rather than the argument.
- *Ad populum*—arguing that because "everyone" knows an idea is right, it can't be wrong.
- *Ad ignoratiam*—arguing that because no one can prove that an idea is false, it must be true.
- *Begging the question*—asserting that something is because it is.
- *Hasty generalization*—basing a general conclusion on too few examples or on isolated examples.
- *Post hoc*—claiming a causal relationship simply because one event followed another event.
- *Slippery slope*—asserting that taking a particular step will automatically lead to a dangerous consequence.

Active Critical Thinking

To think further about logos, complete the following:

- Select a sample persuasive speech from this chapter or Chapter 12; or locate a persuasive speech from **americanrhetoric.com** or *Vital Speeches*.
- Identify two uses of logos and evaluate the effectiveness of each.
- Identify any use of fallacious reasoning. Be prepared to share your answers with a classmate and get their feedback.

Ethos: Establishing Credibility

Another important factor in persuasion is your own credibility, or **ethos**, as a speaker. A credible speaker is someone with ethical proof, someone whom listeners perceive as believable—in short, someone in whom they can place their confidence. Aristotle, in his *Rhetoric*, urges speakers to make sure they are perceived to be of good sense, goodwill, and good moral character. Today's research still supports the importance of credibility—in fact, the greater your credibility, the more persuasive you are (O'Keefe, 1990). Consider, for example, candidates running for political office or students competing for your vote for student body president. Or how about an instructor who recommends that you sign up for an additional course that's not part of your degree plan? In all these cases, the credibility of the persuader would likely play a role in your decision.

Credibility as a Persuasive Tool

Researchers are finding that a speaker's credibility depends on such factors as the situation, the listeners' involvement with the topic, and the listeners' similarity to the speaker. Here are examples of research findings (for a summary, see *Persuasion: Theory and Research,* by O'Keefe, 1990):

- Listeners who have very low *involvement* with the topic tend to be more persuaded by the expertise of the speaker than by the quality of arguments or evidence. However, listeners who are *very involved* with the topic are more persuaded by high-quality arguments than by the credibility of the speaker (Bhattacherjee & Sanford, 2006; Petty & Cacioppo, 1986; Ratneshwar & Chaiken, 1991; Tesser & Shaffer, 1990). One explanation for this finding is that involved listeners are more likely to evaluate the arguments presented by the speaker, but uninvolved listeners are more likely to be influenced by their impressions of the speaker (Eagly & Chaiken, 1993; Reardon, 1991). This finding is based on research following the Elaboration Likelihood Model of Petty and Cacioppo (1984, 1996). ➜ *For an explanation of the Elaboration Likelihood Model of Persuasion, see page 336.*

- When a persuasive message is sent by audio, video, e-mail, or the Internet, the level of listener persuasion varies depending on the channel used. ➜ *See "Using Persuasion and Technology" on page 335 for more details.*

- *Perceived similarity* between audience members and the speaker may enhance persuasion by increasing the perceived trustworthiness or competence of the speaker (O'Keefe, 1990, pp. 148–151). For example, when audience members perceive attitudinal similarities between themselves and a speaker (even when these similarities aren't specifically related to the topic of the speech), they like the speaker better and rate his or her trustworthiness higher (Applbaum & Anatol, 1972; Berscheid, 1985; McCroskey & Teven, 1999). For example, suppose you like pets and discover from the speaker's attention-getter that he or she has two pets. Would this similarity of attitude increase your liking of the speaker—even if the speaker's topic happened to be recycling? Research indicates that this is likely. However, although listeners *like* speakers better when they discover similarities (even when unrelated to the topic), they judge speakers as more *competent* only when perceived similarities are relevant to the topic (O'Keefe, 1990).

Basic Elements of Credibility

A speaker's credibility results from four basic elements: trustworthiness, competency, dynamism, and objectivity (Smith 1973; Whitehead, 1968). As you read this section, remember that in order for credibility to aid your persuasiveness, *being* credible isn't enough—you must also *appear* credible in the eyes of your audience.

Trustworthiness Most listeners determine the credibility of speakers by observing all four basic elements and "averaging" them. But in fact, trustworthiness (honesty, fairness, and integrity) is the most important of the four basic elements of credibility. When speakers appear untrustworthy, their credibility is questioned regardless of the other three elements (Smith, 1973, p. 309).

Several factors affect whether listeners perceive speakers as untrustworthy. For example, speakers who avoid eye contact, shift their eyes rapidly from place to place, or always look over the listeners' heads appear to be ashamed or to have something to hide, and thus are perceived as untrustworthy. Speakers who don't articulate, who speak in a breathy or nasal voice, or who speak either in a monotone or too rapidly also are perceived as less trustworthy (Addington, 1971). In addition to having an effective verbal delivery style, you can improve your perceived trustworthiness by presenting both sides of an argument and by appearing friendly and likeable (Chaiken, 1986). This includes relaxed delivery, smiling, direct eye contact, and using immediacy behaviors. Hosman (2002) also found that using active instead of passive sentence structure improves the speaker's believability.

➡ *Immediacy behaviors are discussed in Chapter 8.*

Competency The second basic element of credibility is *competency*. Listeners are more likely to judge a speaker as credible if they perceive him or her as competent (knowledgeable, experienced, expert) on the topic. However, speakers who use **nonfluencies**—inaccurate articulation, vocalized pauses (like *ah* or *uh*), and unnecessary repetition of words—are often judged as low on competence (McCroskey & Mehrley, 1969; McCroskey & Young, 1981). In addition to avoiding nonfluencies, you appear more competent by citing personal instances related to the topic, citing prestigious sources, speaking in a confident manner, using high-quality visual aids, and wearing more-traditional, high-status clothing (Behling & Wil liams, 1991).

Dynamism Another basic element of credibility is **dynamism**. A dynamic speaker is forceful and enthusiastic and uses good vocal variety. Have you noticed that you can often tell who is in charge simply from the forcefulness of his or her delivery? If you avoid direct eye contact, are soft-spoken, use very little vocal emphasis, and appear hesitant, you give the impression that you are uncertain about what you are saying (not competent) or that you are trying to deceive your listeners (untrustworthy).

To be effective, a dynamic speaker must sustain a conversational tone. Researchers have found that speakers using low or moderate levels of dynamism are perceived as conversational and judged as credible.

Financial speaker Suze Orman is known for her personable and dynamic style.

However, speakers who overdramatize are perceived as less conversational and more unnatural and phony, and are judged as less credible (Pearce & Conklin, 1971).

Objectivity The fourth element of speaker credibility is *objectivity*. An objective speaker is open-minded and fair and appears to view evidence and arguments in an unbiased manner. You can appear objective by avoiding false reasoning and by discussing both sides of your proposal (of course, you must show why your arguments are best).

If the listeners don't know you, or if they perceive you as having low credibility, review the options listed in the following Remember box and select several of these to use in your next persuasive speech.

Remember

Improve your credibility by . . .

- Having a highly credible expert on the topic (or someone of higher rank) introduce you and establish you as a competent and trustworthy speaker.
- Supporting your assertions with up-to-date, carefully documented evidence and sources considered credible to your listeners.
- Identifying your views with those of a respected person or institution.
- Presenting both sides of an issue to show your willingness to be fair and honest.
- Presenting your ideas in a smooth, forceful, and self-assured manner, while maintaining good eye contact.
- Establishing a common ground with your listeners by identifying beliefs, memberships, or problems you share.
- Recognizing (in content and delivery) the formal status and knowledge of your listeners.

Unethical Use of Credibility

Unfortunately, some speakers give the appearance of credibility in order to hide the fact that their evidence is incomplete or even misleading. The stereotype of the used-car salesperson who gives every outward appearance of being honest in order to get the customer to buy a "lemon" illustrates this point. Unethical speakers who are forceful and dynamic, make direct eye contact, and give every appearance of sincerity may be able to temporarily persuade an audience to agree with their ideas or buy their products. However, when listeners eventually realize that these speakers have based their arguments on inadequate or faulty evidence, they are no longer fooled.

Active Critical Thinking

To think further about ethos, use the same persuasive speech you selected in the previous activity and complete the following:

- Identify at least three ways in which the speaker established credibility, and evaluate the effectiveness of each.
- Identify any unethical use of credibility. Be prepared to share your answers with a classmate and get their feedback.

Pathos: Appealing to Listeners' Psychological Needs

Even though you include logic and evidence in your presentations and are perceived to be a credible speaker, you will not be successful at persuasion unless you also adapt your arguments to the psychological needs of your listeners (Harris, 1993). In Chapter 4 we defined a *need* as "a state in which an unsatisfied condition exists." Striving to satisfy our needs is a great motivator for all people. Because needs are based on values, beliefs, and attitudes, they arouse emotions. A certain amount of emotional appeal, or *pathos*, is needed in a persuasive speech. This doesn't necessarily mean that you want audience members to become teary eyed. It means that you want them to feel that your topic relates to them personally—that they have a stake in the outcome of your speech. Mary Fisher, our "Speaking to Make a Difference" speaker for this chapter, is an excellent example of a speaker who used both credibility and emotional appeal to full effect in presenting a difficult topic to an initially unreceptive audience. She turned a noisy convention hall into a place of silence and received a standing ovation.

Personalizing Your Persuasive Argument

Why don't more people participate in blood drives or do volunteer work or vote in elections? Because we don't feel any emotional stake in them. We expect other people to take care of these good works. We say, "I'm too busy working, studying, or raising a family" or "My vote won't make any difference." The challenge of the persuasive speaker is to make us realize that the issue does relate to us.

Logic and evidence are not enough to convince listeners. For example, you have probably had an argument when you knew that you were right, yet when you presented all the facts, the other person's response was, "I don't care. I don't believe it." As persuasive speakers, we need to remember that it isn't evidence unless audience members think it's evidence. But if we can get our listeners to relate personally to our evidence—to decide that the topic is important to their needs—they are likely to consider our evidence logical and reasonable. Therefore, narratives serve as a connection between logic and emotion (Dillard & Nabi, 2006; Green, 2006). ➡ *See Chapter 3 (pp. 62–63) for a review of how listeners avoid being persuaded.*

The following example illustrates the importance of relating your message to listeners' personal needs:

> An excellent vice president decided to retire early, much to the disbelief of his coworkers. All kinds of inducements (such as a substantial salary increase, more office help, and a new car) were offered to convince him to stay with the company. When inducements didn't work, his colleagues pointed out how much he was needed. Nothing was successful. On his last day with the company, he was having lunch in the executive dining room with the president and two other executives. The president began to discuss a completely new and risky project the company was contemplating. Almost in jest, the president suggested that the vice president stay and head the new project. He accepted. None of the other appeals had related to his personal need for achievement. The challenge presented by the new project was something he could not resist (Hamilton, 2011, p. 385).

Speaking to Make a Difference

Mary Fisher was not the sort of person you would expect to admit that she was HIV positive: the daughter of a wealthy fundraiser, mother of two, a successful professional, and a former assistant to the president of the United States (McGee, 2003). Yet she stood before the 1992 Republican National Convention in Houston and declared that she was there "to lift the shroud of silence which has been draped over the issue of HIV and AIDS. I have come tonight to bring our silence to an end." Although she has given many speeches since, it was "A Whisper of AIDS" that first thrust her into the AIDS limelight and brought her national attention. Following are excerpts from that speech. Full text, audio, and video can be found by going to **www.americanrhetoric.com** and searching for "Mary Fisher."

BOB DAEMMRICH/AFP/Getty Images

In the context of an election year, I ask you here in this great hall, or listening in the quiet of your home, to recognize that the AIDS virus is not a political creature. It does not care whether you are Democrat or Republican; it does not ask whether you are black or white, male or female, gay or straight, young or old.

Tonight, I represent an AIDS community whose members have been reluctantly drafted from every segment of American society. Though I am white and a mother, I am one with a black infant struggling with tubes in a Philadelphia hospital. Though I am female and contracted this disease in marriage and enjoy the warm support of my family, I am one with the lonely gay man sheltering a flickering candle from the cold wind of his family's rejection.

This is not a distant threat; it is a present danger. The rate of infection is increasing fastest among women and children. Largely unknown a decade ago, AIDS is the third leading killer of young-adult Americans today—but it won't be third for long. Because, unlike other diseases, this one travels.... And we have helped it along. We have killed each other—with our ignorance, our prejudice, and our silence.

* * *

We may take refuge in our stereotypes, but we cannot hide there long, because HIV asks only one thing of those it attacks. Are you human? And this is the right question. Are you human? Because people with HIV have not entered some alien state of being. They are human....

My call to the nation is a plea for awareness. If you believe you are safe, you are in danger. Because I was not hemophiliac, I was not at risk. Because I was

not gay, I was not at risk. Because I did not inject drugs, I was not at risk.... If you do not see this killer stalking your children, look again. There is no family or community, no race or religion, no place left in America that is safe. Until we genuinely embrace this message, we are a nation at risk.

* * *

Someday our children will be grown. My son Max, now four, will take the measure of his mother. My son Zachary, now two, will sort through his memories. I may not be here to hear their judgments, but I know already what I hope they are. I want my children to know that their mother was not a victim. She was a messenger. I do not want them to think, as I once did, that courage is the absence of fear. I want them to know that courage is the strength to act wisely when most we are afraid. I want them to have the courage to step forward when called by their nation or their Party and give leadership, no matter what the personal cost.

I ask no more of you than I ask of myself or of my children. To the millions of you who are grieving, who are frightened, who have suffered the ravages of AIDS firsthand: Have courage, and you will find support. To the millions who are strong, I issue the plea: Set aside prejudice and politics to make room for compassion and sound policy.

To my children, I make this pledge: I will not give in, Zachary, because I draw my courage from you. Your silly giggle gives me hope; your gentle prayers give me strength; and you, my child, give me the reason to say to America, "You are at risk." And I will not rest, Max, until I have done all I can to make your world safe. I will seek a place where intimacy is not the prelude to suffering. I will not hurry to leave you, my children, but when I go, I pray that you will not suffer shame on my account.

To all within the sound of my voice, I appeal: Learn with me the lessons of history and of grace, so my children will not be afraid to say the word *AIDS* when I am gone. Then, their children and yours may not need to whisper it at all.

God bless the children, and God bless us all.

Mary Fisher had two main goals for this speech: to bring AIDS from a seldom-used taboo word to an acknowledged and recognized problem, and to change people's attitudes toward all people with AIDS. Her 10-minute speech, which was strikingly different from the "notably anti-gay and religiously conservative tone of the rest of the convention" (McGee, 2003, pp. 192–193), occurred in the middle of the afternoon when most delegates paid little attention to speakers. So her audience was both hostile to her message and uninterested—not a desirable situation. Yet, in just a few minutes, Fisher produced "a dramatic, concrete, and immediate effect on the crowd" (p. 192). Although "many of the delegates at first seemed not

to be listening … By the middle of her speech almost everyone was staring up at the podium, quiet and with grave expressions" (Kelly, 1992).

Let's examine two reasons why this persuasive speech was able to capture undivided audience attention in such unfriendly circumstances:

- *Credibility.* As discussed in this chapter, establishing credibility with the audience is an essential part of successful persuasive speaking. Fisher exhibited several basic elements of credibility. As seen in the video on **americanrhetoric.com**, she creates as much eye contact as is possible in such a venue, staring at the

continued

camera and panning across the audience. She speaks eloquently, using proper articulation, no vocalized pauses, and active sentence structure, as in this poignant passage: "Tonight, HIV marches resolutely toward AIDS in more than a million American homes, littering its pathway with the bodies of the young—young men, young women, young parents, and young children." Fisher also exhibited strong, persuasive vocal qualities when she said, "HIV asks only one thing of those it attacks. Are you human? And this is the right question. Are you human? Because people with HIV have not entered some alien state of being. They are human." Fisher creates trustworthiness, competency, and dynamism as she speaks—credibility she needs to captivate the audience.

- *Emotional appeal.* Another element in Fisher's speech that grabbed attention and began the persuasive process was her use of emotional appeal. "By presenting herself as an example of the point she was trying to make, Fisher sought a greater national sensitivity to the plight of AIDS victims" (Johannesen et al., p. 168). Her topic, which was already sensitive, became even more so when she told the audience

that their safety was on the line as well: "The lesson history teaches is this: If you believe you are safe, you are at risk." Here she appealed to a basic need (see "Using Maslow's Hierarchy of Needs" in this chapter). She used her own story as a point upon which to draw emotional attention from the audience. The most obvious use of this was in the last few paragraphs (Johannesen et al., p. 168), in which she spoke directly to her sons. The camera panned to the audience, and some of those filmed were in tears. She finished to a standing ovation.

Mary Fisher has, in the years since her moving speech, become a worldwide advocate for AIDS awareness. She is now active on the leadership council of the Global Coalition on Women and AIDS, her own Clinical AIDS Research and Education Fund (CARE), and on the speaking circuit (Mary Fisher, 2006). Most recently, she became Special Representative for the Joint United Nations Programme on HIV/AIDS.

Question: In addition to credibility and emotional appeal, what other persuasive appeals or speaking techniques did Fisher use to create a powerful persuasive speech?

Getting Your Audience Involved

Another way for the audience to see the connection between your position and their needs is to get them involved during your presentation. In his book *Presentations That Change Minds* (2006), Josh Gordon suggests: "Audience involvement means your audience is actively comparing what you are sharing with what they already know, evaluating it, raising concerns, and participating in a dialogue" (p. 4). Check Figure 13.2 for suggestions on how to create audience involvement based on Gordon's suggestions (pp. 4–12). Of course, to get your audience involved, you have to research them ahead of time and really know them. Two last-minute techniques that also work include: (1) arriving early and chatting with people as they come in; and (2) asking a few questions during the speech with audience giving applause or a show of hands for the answers.

Using Maslow's Hierarchy of Needs

Discovering your listeners' basic needs and motives is an essential part of audience analysis. As far back as 1954, psychologist Abraham Maslow presented his hierarchy of needs as one way to identify audience needs: physiological, safety, social, esteem, and self-actualization. As discussed earlier, the lower-level needs must generally be satisfied before the next level becomes important. For example, rarely will you persuade an

Figure 13.2

How to Get Your
Audience Involved

Audience Involvement	
Relevancy of Topic	Get your audience excited from the beginning by showing how your topic relates to a need or interest of theirs.
Fun With the Unexpected	Surprise your audience with the unexpected, like asking them to identity lines from famous songs or company logos.
Commonalities	Share something that you and your audience have in common.
Passion for Topic	Audiences respond to speakers who show their passion for the topic—let it show in your voice.
Graphics and Charts	Use charts for more than facts—show comparisons/contrasts of features or competitors and ask your audience if the chart agrees with their experiences.

audience that is concerned mainly with safety needs by appealing to higher-level needs such as esteem or self-actualization (see Figure 13.3). At the same time, needs that have already been satisfied are no longer persuasive. → *See Chapter 4 for more on Maslow's hierarchy of needs.*

To use the hierarchy of needs to figure out how you can be most persuasive, first decide which needs your topic addresses. Next, using the list in Figure 13.4, select the relevant motivational appeals for those needs. Last, develop your persuasive

Figure 13.3

Relating Listeners'
Needs for Safety to a
Successful Persuasive
Approach

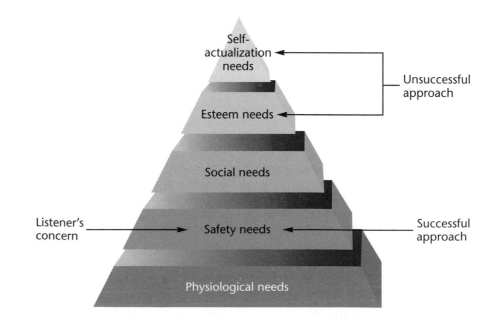

Physiological Needs

Bodily comfort (food, shelter, clothing, air, and water)
Physical enjoyment and activity
Sufficient rest and sleep
Sexual attractiveness

Safety Needs

Freedom from fear and the unknown
Freedom from fear of punishment
Freedom from fear of death
Need for conformity
Desire for law and order
Protection from injury or poor health
Financial and job security

Freedom from censorship and restraint

Social Needs

Need to give and receive love
Companionship and friendship
Dating, marriage, and family ties
Feeling of belonging
Loyalty
Respect for the Deity
Need to give and receive sympathy
Helping the needy

Esteem Needs

Feeling of pride
Recognition from self and others
Status, prestige, and reputation

Sense of achievement
Sense of value and worth
Happiness with appearance
Freedom from guilt
Need for power and control

Self-Actualization Needs

Developing one's potential
Being responsible for own decisions
Need for creative outlets
Need to expand knowledge
Reaching worthwhile goals
Being the best person possible
Need to be challenged

Figure 13.4

Motivational Appeals for Each of Maslow's Need Categories

argument around the selected motivational appeals. The following persuasive statements illustrate motivational appeals to various basic needs:

* Exercise regularly for a sexier, slimmer you. [*physiological need of sexual attractiveness*]

* It may seem like graduation is a long way off, but anything worth having is worth waiting and working for. [*esteem need of sense of achievement*]

* Unless we take a leadership role in this international crisis, America will lose its standing among nations. [*esteem needs of status, prestige, and reputation*]

* Aren't you tired of being afraid to take a car trip with your family during the holidays because of the drunks out on the roads? [*safety need of protection from injury*]

* Let your children know how you feel about them. Send them to school each day with a nourishing, hot breakfast. [*social need to give and receive love*]

When using emotional appeal, keep in mind that listeners appear to be "more motivated by the thought of losing something than by the thought of gaining something" (Dillard & Pfau, 2002, p. 520). Therefore, when messages are framed to stress potential losses that may occur if a certain action is not taken, persuasion is enhanced. Loss framing is especially effective in situations involving risk and uncertainty (De Dreu & McCusker, 1997; Tversky & Kahneman, 1981).

Fear Appeals

Appeals designed to arouse negative emotions are called **fear appeals**. Fear appeals cause listeners to feel threatened or afraid, in contrast to positive emotional appeals, which cause listeners to feel emotions such as pride or sympathy. Notice that the motivational appeals listed in Figure 13.4 contain both positive and fear appeals.

Although arousing fear in listeners is not easy (Boster & Mongeau, 1984), research indicates that when it is done successfully, a high level of fear is more likely to result in persuasion than a medium or low level of fear (Sutton & Eiser, 1984). To make your fear appeals successful, research suggests that you do three things in your argument (Maddux & Rogers, 1983; Rogers, 1975):

1. Show that there will be significant consequences if change does not occur.
2. Show how likely the consequences are.
3. Indicate what action(s) the audience can take to halt or minimize the consequences.

For example, if you were giving a speech about the importance of exercising regularly, you would (1) describe personal consequences of not exercising regularly (such as weight gain, heart disease, cancer, and lack of energy); (2) show the audience how likely it is that they will gain weight, lose energy, or get heart disease or cancer if they don't exercise regularly; and (3) explain simple, inexpensive actions they can take to prevent these consequences. Without Step 3, listeners are likely to feel that nothing they can do will prevent the problem, and as a result they will avoid being persuaded. In fact, when listeners perceive the likelihood of the threat to be high but the effectiveness of the solution to be low, *they may actually do the opposite of what you are recommending*—this is the boomerang effect discussed at the beginning of the chapter (Eagly & Chaiken, 1993; Witte, 1992a, 1992b).

Unethical Use of Emotional Appeals

Emotional appeals are a necessary part of a persuasive speech, but when they are used in place of evidence or are deliberately misused, they are unethical. Here are two unethical psychological appeals that you should avoid using in your persuasive speeches.

Fabrication of Similarities As you have learned, establishing similarities with your audience can increase your credibility and persuasiveness. However, some persuasive speakers fabricate or greatly exaggerate similarities with their audiences. For example, a speaker who has played golf only a few times in his life may try to win over his golfing audience by referring to himself as a "golf fanatic."

Exaggeration Speakers who use exaggeration typically overestimate "the costs, problems, or negative consequences of a new proposal" (Herrick, 1995, p. 230). Rather than giving specifics, they use emotionally loaded terms to draw a response from the audience. For example, the statement "We've received hundreds of phone calls in violent opposition to Senator Johnson's proposal" could get an audience upset enough to forget to look for specific evidence. Exactly how many phone calls? Is this more or less than the usual number of phone calls received? What exactly is "violent" opposition?

Active Critical Thinking

To think further about pathos, use the same persuasive speech you selected in the previous activity and complete the following:

- Identify at least three motivational appeals used in the speech and the category of needs each appeal related to; evaluate the effectiveness of each appeal.
- Were any fear appeals used? If so, how effective were they?

Using Persuasion and Technology

Do people react differently to persuasive messages that are sent electronically? It's impossible to answer with certainty, because the research is undeveloped in this area. What we do know is that people tend to react differently to different communication channels (Booth-Butterfield & Gutowski, 1993):

- When persuasive messages are conveyed by *audio or video*, an audience is persuaded more by the communicator's credibility than by evidence.

- When persuasive messages are conveyed in *traditional print media* (such as memo, report, and magazine), an audience is more persuaded by the data and the quality of the evidence than by the communicator's credibility.

Why the difference? Perhaps time is a factor. Print messages can be reread and the evidence can be evaluated more carefully, whereas audio and video messages are usually listened to or viewed only once (Chaiken & Eagly, 1983).

Which type of appeal—evidence or credibility—is more persuasive when *electronic media* carry the message? Preliminary research indicates that we are persuaded more by the communicator's credibility than by the evidence—similar to our reaction to the audio and video channels. Further, when a persuasive message is presented with an emotional appeal and fits in with our value system, a type of "instant ethos" occurs (Gurak, 1997). It causes us to trust the message even when we do not know the author. Research on victims of fraud (especially Internet fraud) found that most of them gave little attention to the substance of the message once they believed the sender was honest (Priester & Petty, 1995). According to R. B. Cialdini (2009) in his book *Influence: Science and Practice*, several irresistible "click-whir" responses lead to instant ethos:

- *Reciprocation*—If you give me something, I feel obligated to reciprocate.

- *Commitment and consistency*—Once I have purchased a product or committed myself to an action, I tend to defend that decision consistently (even if the decision was a poor one).

- *Social proof*—If other people are doing it or believe it, I am more likely to want to do it or believe it.

- *Likeability*—If I like you (usually because we are alike in one or more ways), I am more likely to be influenced by you.

- *Authority*—I tend to be influenced by people I perceive to have authority.

- *Scarcity*—When I perceive an item to be scarce, I value it more.

How many of these techniques do you recognize from messages and ads that you have received in the mail and over the Internet? Obviously, persuasion is a powerful tool. If speakers have an ethical responsibility, persuasive speakers have an even greater responsibility.

Active Critical Thinking

To think further about persuasion and technology, complete the following:

- Select a television commercial and identify which of the "click-whir" responses the ad was designed to stimulate.
- Evaluate the effectiveness and honesty of the commercial. Be specific.

Using Persuasive Theory When Speaking

There are many theories about persuasion. Some, such as the inoculation theory, have already been discussed in this chapter, and others, such as the Elaboration Likelihood Model, have been briefly mentioned. Table 13.1 (p. 337) summarizes some of the more important persuasive theories. Take a look at each of these theories.

Although all these theories contain important information and advice for persuasive speakers, the last two offer the most practical, easy-to-use advice for the beginning speaker. Both theories will be discussed further.

Elaboration Likelihood Model of Persuasion

According to developers Richard Petty and John Cacioppo (1986), the **Elaboration Likelihood Model (ELM)** of persuasion indicates which of two routes for processing arguments audience members will likely use. If they are motivated (involved and interested in your topic) and have the ability to process information, they are more likely to use the *central route*, characterized by careful critical thinking and consideration of arguments and evidence. However, if audience members are not motivated (have less involvement or interest in the topic) and/or are unable to process information, they are more likely to use the *peripheral route*—taking a shortcut to decision making that involves less critical thinking and evaluation of arguments and is based more on senses and cues that aren't directly related to the topic (such as a speaker's credibility or attractiveness).

So, what does the ELM of persuasion suggest to speakers? If audience analysis indicates that your audience is likely to use the central route to processing, you can expect them to question all that they hear and take an active role in generating their own arguments (Booth-Butterfield & Welbourne, 2002). Therefore, you need to present well-supported logic and evidence and even present both sides of the issue, while still showing how your position is the better one. It's interesting to note that when highly motivated listeners using the central route are persuaded, their attitudes are "more resistant to counter-persuasion, persistent over time, and predictive of future behavior" (Booth-Butterfield & Welbourne, p. 157).

On the other hand, if you have audience members who will likely process arguments using the peripheral route, the ELM suggests that they are less interested in logic and evidence and more influenced by catchy visuals, narratives, personal experiences, use of immediacy behaviors, and organization using rhymes or acronyms. Because most audiences include both types of processors, speakers will usually want to relate to both types of audience members. ➜ *See Chapter 4 for suggestions on handling the uninterested audience.*

Social Judgment Theory

First proposed by psychologists Muzafer Sherif and Carl Hovland (1961) and expanded by Sherif, Sherif, and Nebergall (1965), the **social judgment theory** explains how people evaluate messages based on internal anchors (past experiences). According to this theory, the more ego involved we are with a social issue or topic, the more likely our judgments will be influenced by an internal anchor. Furthermore, according to Sherif and Hovland, "The individual's stand on a social issue is conceived as a range or latitude of acceptance" (pp. 128–129). In other words, on an issue, each listener will view some messages or positions as acceptable

Table 13.1 Important Theories Concerning Persuasion

Information-Integration Theory

Basic approach

The way people accumulate and organize information (about a situation, event, person, or object) can result in attitude change (Littlejohn & Foss, 2008, pp. 75–77). Attitudes are affected by the valence and weight of information received. *Valence* refers to whether the information supports (+ valence) or refutes (– valence) previous beliefs; *weight* refers to how much credibility is assigned to the information.

Respected theorist

Martin Fishbein (Fishbein & Ajzen, 1975). Your intention to change behavior is determined by your attitude toward the behavior *times* the strength (weight) of that attitude *plus* your beliefs about what others think you should do *times* the strength of these other opinions.

Consistency Theories

Basic approach

Because people prefer consistency and balance and feel threatened by inconsistency, attitude change can occur when information creates inconsistency (Littlejohn & Foss, pp. 78–80).

Respected theorist

Leon Festinger (1957), *theory of cognitive dissonance.* Dissonance creates stress and tension in people, which cause them to (1) seek to reduce the dissonance and (2) avoid other dissonance-creating situations.

Respected theorist

Milton Rokeach (1969, 1973), *theory of attitudes, beliefs, values. Attitudes* are feelings of like or dislike; *beliefs* are the reasons we hold the attitudes we do, and *values* are deep-seated principles that direct behaviors. Persuasion may occur when the speaker shows how certain behaviors are consistent with audience values or when a particular value is shown to be less (or more) important now than in the past.

Elaboration Likelihood Model

Basic approach

Elaboration likelihood involves the probability that listeners will evaluate arguments critically (Littlejohn & Foss, pp. 73–75).

Respected theorists

Richard Petty and John Cacioppo (1986). When evaluating arguments, people either use the *central route* (elaborate carefully and critically) or the *peripheral route* (decide quickly using little critical thinking). For motivated and able people, elaboration leads to attitudes that are resistant to change.

Social Judgment Theory

Basic approach

People use internal anchors (past experience) as reference points when making judgments about messages (Littlejohn & Foss, pp. 71–73). Anchors are more likely to influence the judgments of those who are *ego involved* with the topic.

Respected theorists

Muzafer Sherif (Sherif & Hovland, 1961; Sherif et al., 1965). A person's ego involvement determines messages that are acceptable (*latitude of acceptance*), totally unacceptable (*latitude of rejection*), or merely tolerable (*latitude of noncommitment*). The larger a person's latitude of rejection, the more difficult he or she is to persuade. Attitude change results when people perceive that an argument fits within their latitude of acceptance. When an argument falls in their latitude of rejection, a *boomerang effect* may occur—the original attitude may be strengthened rather than changed.

(*latitude of acceptance*), some as unacceptable (*latitude of rejection*), and others as merely tolerable (*latitude of noncommitment*). Social judgment theory proposes that the larger a person's latitude of rejection, the more difficult he or she is to persuade.

Obviously, as with the ELM of persuasion, audience analysis is crucial if persuasion is to occur. The audience poll mentioned in Chapter 12 (Figure 12.5) is one way to determine your audience's views: "Strongly agree" and "Agree" could represent the latitude of acceptance; "Strongly disagree" and "Disagree" could represent the latitude of rejection; and "Undecided" could represent the latitude of noncommitment.

So, what does social judgment theory suggest to persuasive speakers? First, attitude change results when people perceive that an argument fits within their latitude of acceptance. It may be up to you to point out that your position does fit in their latitude of acceptance and remind them how important your position is to them and those they love. Second, the larger a person's latitude of rejection, the more difficult he or she is to persuade (especially if the person is ego involved with the topic). In fact, when an argument falls in his or her latitude of rejection, a boomerang effect may occur—the original attitude may be strengthened rather than changed. Therefore, persuasion is more likely if you advocate a change that is only a small step outside the latitude of acceptance or within the latitude of noncommitment; asking for a complete change in opinion will likely fail. Presenting quality evidence, establishing your credibility, and showing how you and the audience have common ground will also aid in persuasion. If time allows, plan a series or campaign of persuasive appeals—attitudes can change over time (Gass & Seiter, 1999).

Both theories—the Elaboration Likelihood Model and the social judgment theory—offer additional information for the persuasive speaker that should be used along with the information already covered in this chapter and the previous chapter on persuasion.

Active Critical Thinking

To think further about persuasive theory, complete the following using the topic you plan to use in your own persuasive speaking situation to come:

- *Relate* the speech topic and main arguments to the Social Judgment Theory or the Elaboration Likelihood Model. What does the theory you picked say about the speech and its persuasiveness?
- *Be prepared* to share your answers with a classmate and get their feedback.

Sample Persuasive Speech: "Together, We Can Stop Cyber-Bullying" by Adam Parrish

The following persuasive speech, "Together, We Can Stop Cyber-Bullying," was given by Adam Parrish. Adam's persuasive speech is a speech to actuate that uses the Problem-Cause-Solution pattern of organization. Do you think this was the best pattern for this topic? What would you have done differently? → *To watch and analyze a video clip of Adam's speech, look under "Student Resources for Chapter 13" on your Online Resources for* Essentials of Public Speaking.

Sample Persuasive Speech

TOGETHER, WE CAN STOP CYBER-BULLYING

by Adam Parrish

"I'll miss just being around her." "I didn't want to believe it." "It's such a sad thing." These quotes are from the friends and family of 15-year-old Phoebe Prince, who, on January 14, 2010, committed suicide by hanging herself. Why did this senseless act occur? The answer is simple… Phoebe Prince was bullied to death.

Many of us know someone who has been bullied in school. Perhaps they were teased in the parking lot or in the locker room. In the past, bullying occurred primarily in school. However, with the advent of new communication technologies such as cell phones, text messaging, instant messaging, blogs, and social networking sites, bullies can now follow and terrorize their victims anywhere, even into their own bedrooms. Using electronic communications to tease, harass, threaten, and intimidate another person is called cyber-bullying.

As a tutor and mentor to young students, I have witnessed cyber-bullying first hand, and by examining current research, I believe I understand the problem, it causes, and how we can help end cyber-bullying. What I know for sure is that cyber-bullying is a devastating form of abuse that must be confronted on national, local, and personal levels.

Today, we will examine the widespread and harmful nature of cyber-bulling, uncover how and why it persists, and pinpoint some simple solutions we must begin to enact in order to thwart cyber-bullies and comfort their victims. Let's begin by tackling the problem head on

Many of us have read rude, insensitive, or nasty statements posted about us or someone we care about on social networking sites like MySpace and Facebook. Well, whether or not those comments were actually intended to hurt another person's feelings, if they did hurt their feelings, then they are perfect examples of cyber-bullying.

Cyber-bullying is a pervasive and dangerous behavior. It takes place all over the world and through a wide array of electronic media. According to Keith and Martin's article in the winter 2005 edition of *Reclaiming Children and Youth*, 57 percent of American middle-school students had experienced instances of cyber-bullying ranging from hurtful comments to threats of physical violence. Quing Li's article published in the journal *Computers in Human Behavior*, noted that cyber-bullying is not gender biased. According to Li, females are just as likely as males to engage in cyber-bullying, although women are 10 percent more likely to be victimized.

While the number of students who are targets of cyber-bullies decreases as students age, data from the *Youth Internet Safety Survey* indicates that the instances of American high school students being cyber-bullied had increased nearly 50 percent from 2000 to 2005. The problem does not exist in the United States alone.

Sample Persuasive Speech *(continued)*

Li noted that internet and cell-phone technologies have been used by bullies to harass, torment, and threaten young people in North America, Europe, and Asia. However, some of the most horrific attacks happen right here at home.

According to Keith and Martin, a particularly disturbing incident occurred in Dallas, Texas, where an overweight student with multiple sclerosis was targeted on a school's social networking page. One message read, "I guess I'll have to wait until you kill yourself which I hope is not long from now, or I'll have to wait until your disease kills you." Clearly, the cyber-bullying is a worldwide and perverse phenomenon. What is most disturbing about cyber-bullying is its effects upon victims, bystanders, and perhaps even upon bullies themselves.

Cyber-bullying can lead to physical and psychological injuries upon its victims. According to a 2007 article in the *Journal of Adolescent Health,* Ybarra and colleagues noted that 36 percent of the victims of cyber-bullies, are also harassed by their attackers in school. For example, the Dallas student with MS had eggs thrown at her car and a bottle of acid thrown at her house.

Ybarra et al. reported that victims of cyber-bullying experience such severe emotional distress that they often exhibit behavioral problems such as poor grades, skipping school, and receiving detentions and suspensions. Furthermore, smith et al. suggested that even a few instances of cyber-bullying can have these long-lasting negative effects.

What is even more alarming is that, according to Ybarra and colleagues, victims of cyber-bullying are significantly more likely to carry weapons to school as a result of feeling threatened. Obviously, this could lead to violent outcomes for bullies, victims, and even bystanders.

Now that we have heard about the nature, scope, and effects of cyber-bullying, let's see if we can discover its causes. Let's think back to a time when we may have seen a friend or loved one being harassed online. Did we report the bully to the network administrator or other authorities? Did we console the victim? I know I didn't. If you are like me, we may unknowingly be enabling future instances of cyber-bullying.

Cyber-bullying occurs because of the anonymity offered to bullies by cell phone and internet technologies, as well as the failure of victims and bystanders to report incidents of cyber-bullying. You see, unlike schoolyard bullies, cyber-bullies can attack their victims anonymously.

Ybarra and colleagues discovered that 13 percent of cyber-bullying victims did not know who was tormenting them. This devastating statistics is important because, as Keith and Martin noted, traditional bullying takes place face-to-face and often ends when students leave school. However, today, students are subjected to nonstop bullying, even when they are alone in their own homes.

Perhaps the anonymous nature of cyber-attacks partially explains why Li found that nearly 76 percent of victims of cyber-bullying and 75 percent of bystanders never reported instances of bullying to adults. Victims and bystanders who do not report attacks from cyber-bullies can unintentionally enable bullies.

Sample Persuasive Speech *(continued)*

According to De Nies, Donaldson, and Netter of *ABCNews.com* (2010) several of Phoebe Prince's classmates were aware that she was being harassed but did not inform the school's administration. Li suggested that victims and bystanders often do not believe that adults will actually intervene to stop cyber-bullying. However, *ABCNews.com* reports that 41 states have laws against bullying in schools and 23 of those states target cyber-bullying specifically.

Now that we know that victims of cyber-bullies desperately need the help of witnesses and bystanders to report their attacks, we should arm ourselves with the information necessary to provide that assistance. Think about the next time you see a friend or loved one being tormented or harassed online. What would you be willing to do to help?

Cyber-bullying must be confronted on national, local, and personal levels. There should be a comprehensive national law confronting cyber-bullying in schools. Certain statutes currently in state laws should be amalgamated to create the strongest protections for victims and the most effective punishments for bullies as possible.

According to Limber and Small's article titled, *State Laws and Policies to Address Bullying in Schools*, Georgia law requires faculty and staff to be trained on the nature of bullying and what actions to take if they see students being bullied.

Furthermore, Connecticut law *requires* school employees to report bullying as part their hiring contract. Washington takes this a step further, by protecting employees from any legal action if a reported bully is proven to be innocent. When it comes to protecting victims, West Virginia law demands that schools must ensure that a bullied student does not receive additional abuse at the hands of his or her bully.

Legislating punishment for bullies is difficult. As Limber and Small noted, zero-tolerance polices often perpetuate violence because at-risk youth, i.e., bullies, are removed from all of the benefits of school, which might help make them less abusive. A comprehensive anti cyber-bullying law should incorporate the best aspects of these state laws and find a way to punish bullies that is both punitive and has the ability to rehabilitate abusers. However, for national laws to be effective, local communities need to be supportive.

Local communities must organize and mobilize to attack the problem of cyber-bullying. According to Greene's 2006 article published in the *Journal of Social* Issues, communities need to support bullying prevention programs by conducting a school-based bullying survey for individual school districts. We can't know how to best protect victims in our community without knowing how they are affected by the problem. It is critical to know this information as Greene noted, only three percent of teachers in the United States, perceive bullying to be a problem in their schools.

Local school districts should create a Coordinating Committee made up of "administrators, teachers, students, parents, school staff, and community partners" to gather bullying data and rally support to confront the problem. Even if your local school district is unable or unwilling to mobilize

Sample Persuasive Speech *(continued)*

behind this dire cause, there are some important actions you can take personally to safeguard those you love against cyber-bullying.

There are several warning signs that might indicate a friend or loved one is a victim of a cyber-bully. If you see a friend or loved one exhibiting these signs, the decision to get involved can be the difference between life and death.

According to Keith and Martin's article, *Cyber-Bullying: Creating a Culture of Respect in a Cyber World*, victims of cyber-bullies often use electronic communication more frequently than do people who are not being bullied. Victims of cyber-bullies have mood swings and difficulty sleeping, they seem depressed and/or become anxious, victims can also become withdrawn from social activities and fall behind in scholastic responsibilities. If you witness your friends or family members exhibiting these symptoms there are several ways you can help.

According to Raskauskas and Stoltz's 2007 article in *Developmental Psychology*, witnesses of cyber-bullying should inform victims to take the attacks seriously, especially if the bullies threaten violence. You should tell victims to report their attacks to police or other authorities, to block harmful messages by blocking email accounts and cell phone numbers, to save copies of attacks and provide them to authorities.

If you personally know the bully and feel safe confronting him or her, do so! As Raskaukas and Stoltznoted, bullies will often back down when confronted by peers.By being a good friend and by giving good advice, you can help a victim report his or her attacks from cyber-bullies and take a major step toward eliminating this horrendous problem So, you see, we are not helpless to stop the cyber-bulling problem as long as we make the choice NOT to ignore it.

To conclude, *Cyber*-bullying is a devastating form of abuse that must be reported to authorities. Cyber-bullying is a worldwide problem perpetuated by the silence of both victims and bystanders. By paying attention to certain warning signs, we can empower ourselves to console victims and report their abusers.

Today, I'm imploring you to do your part to help stop cyber-bullying. I know that you agree that stopping cyber-bullying must be a priority. First, although other states have cyber-bullying laws in place, ours does not. So I'm asking you to sign this petition that I will forward to our district's State Legislators. We need to make our voices heard that we want specific laws passed to stop this horrific and to punish those caught doing it.

Second, I'm also asking you to be vigilant in noticing signs of cyber-bullying and then taking action. Look for signs that your friend, brother, sister, cousin, boyfriend, girlfriend, or loved one might be a victim of cyber-bullying and then get involved to help stop it! Phoebe Prince showed the warning signs, and she did not deserve to die so senselessly. None of us would ever want to say, "I'll miss just being around her." "I didn't want to believe it." "It's such a sad thing." about our own friends or family members. We must work to ensure that victims are supported and bullies are confronted nationally, locally, and personally.

Sample Persuasive Speech *(continued)*

I know that if we stand together and refuse to be silent, we can and will stop cyber-bullying.

References

Greene, M. B. (2006). Bullying in schools: A plea for measure of human rights. *Journal of Social Issues, 62*(1), 63–79.

Keith, S., & Martin, M. (2005). Cyber-bullying: Creating a culture of respect in the cyber world. *Reclaiming Children and Youth, 13* (4) 224–228.

Li, Q. (2007). *New bottle of old wine: A research of cyberbullying in schools. Computers in Human Behavior, 23,* 1777–1791.

Limber, S. P., & Small, M. A. (2003). State laws and policies to address bullying in schools. *School Psychology Review, 32*(3), 445–455.

DeNies, Y., Donaldson, S., & Netter, S. (2010, January 28). Mean Girls: Cyberbullying blamed for teen suicides. Retrieved from http://abcnews.go.com/GMA/Parenting/girls-teen-suicide-calls-attention-cyberbullying/story?id=9685026

Raskauskas, J., & Stoltz, A. D. (2007). Involvement in traditional and electronic bullying among adolescents. *Developmental Psychology, 43*(3), 564–575.

Smith, P. K., Mahdavi, J., Carvalho, M., Fisher, S. Russel, S., & Tippett, N. (2008). Cyberbullying: It's nature and impact in seconday school pupils. *Journal of Child Psychology and Psychiatry, 49*(4), 374–385.

Ybarra, M. L., Diener-West, M., & Leaf, P. J. (2007). Examining the overlap in internet harassment and school bullying: Implications for school intervention. *Journal of Adolescent Health, 41,* S42–S50.

Ybarra, M. L., Mitchell, K. J., Wolak, J., & Finkelhor, D. (2006). Examining characteristics and associated distress related to internet harassment: Findings from the second Youth Internet Safety Survey. *Pediatrics, 118,* 1169–1177.

Summary

This chapter covered three of the basic appeals or factors that lead to persuasion: (1) the evidence and logic of the message, (2) the credibility of the persuader, and (3) the psychological needs of the listeners. Although some people may think that the message's logic and evidence are far more important than other factors, research does not support this notion. In fact, appeals to psychological needs are frequently required to convince an audience of the truth and importance of evidence. Successful persuasive speakers consider all three basic appeals when preparing their speeches.

When you present the source of your evidence, give the qualifications of the source. In most cases, presenting the source by itself is less persuasive. Make sure your speeches do not contain the types of fallacious reasoning discussed in this chapter: *ad hominem, ad populum, ad ignoratiam,* begging the question, hasty generalization, post hoc, and slippery slope. In addition, you may be able to refute objections to your position by pointing out fallacious reasoning.

When planning how to improve your credibility as a speaker, keep in mind the four elements of credibility: trustworthiness, competency, dynamism, and objectivity. Remember that persuasion requires more than evidence and credibility—equally important is an emotional appeal to your audience's needs. When planning how to appeal to the psychological needs of your audience, select motivational appeals based on the analysis of your audience's attitudes, beliefs, and values.

Finally, as you plan your persuasive arguments, consider the persuasive theories in Table 13.1. Pay special attention to the Elaboration Likelihood Model of persuasion and the social judgment theory, which give insight on how audience members will likely process and make judgments about your persuasive arguments.

Essentials of Public Speaking Online CourseMate

Use your Online Resources for *Essentials of Public Speaking* for quick access to the electronic study resources that accompany this chapter, including a video of Adam's speech on pages 339–343, access to InfoTrac College Edition, Personal Skill Building activities, Collaborative Skill Building activities, Active Critical Thinking boxes, a digital glossary, sample speeches, and review quizzes.

Key Terms

ad hominem 324	dynamism 327	inoculation theory 321
ad ignoratiam 324	Elaboration Likelihood	logic 317
ad populum 324	Model 336	nonfluencies 327
analogical reasoning	ethos 326	*post hoc 325*
323	evidence 317	reasoning 323
begging the question	fallacious reasoning 323	slippery slope 325
324	fear appeals 333	social judgment theory
boomerang effect 317	hasty generalization	336
causal reasoning 323	324	

Personal Skill Building

1. You may use fallacious reasoning without thinking about the impact. Have a fellow classmate examine your speech for use of fallacious reasoning. Remember the importance of proof and evidence. Are there places within the speech where fallacious reasoning is used instead of proof? If so, revise your speech accordingly.

2. Retake the PRCA-24 (Personal Report of Communication Apprehension) without looking at the answers you gave at the beginning of the course. You can find a self-scoring PRCA-24 on your Online Resources for *Essentials of Public Speaking*. To send your scores to your instructor and yourself, insert the proper e-mail addresses when requested. Compare these scores with your

previous scores. Write a brief comparison of the scores and discuss what these scores say about you as a speaker. Show the comparison to your instructor. The lower your totals, the more confident you have become.

3. Read the Sample Student Speech in this chapter, "Untreated Depression in America" by Sean Stewart, or watch it on the *Essentials of Public Speaking* CourseMate. You will note that Sean did not use visual aids in his presentation. Decide on computer visuals that would add to Sean's speech and prepare at least two of them.

4. For the persuasive speech you began preparing in Chapter 12, plan specific appeals to logic, credibility, and audience needs that will enhance your persuasiveness. Which of the methods for presenting evidence do you think will work best with your audience? Do you think deductive, inductive, analogical, or causal patterns of reasoning will be most effective?

5. To enhance your persuasiveness by improving your delivery, practice visualizing your positive statements about how effective a speaker you are. Remember that for maximum effect when using positive imagery, you must do more than just read your statements. You need to say each positive statement out loud, see yourself standing in front of the class performing your speech with ease, and feel confident while visualizing your success.

6. Using a database like InfoTrac College Edition, EBSCOhost, or ProQuest, locate a recent article on persuasion from a psychology or speech communication journal. Prepare a 2- to 3-minute review of it to present to the class (clear the article with your instructor).

7. Check out the following websites. You can access these sites under the Chapter 13 Online Resources for *Essentials of Public Speaking*.

   • What logical fallacies are being used by you, or, better yet, on you? Go to **nizkor.org/features/fallacies**. On this webpage, Dr. Labossiere examines the most common logical fallacies and gives examples that help the reader better understand the fallacies.

   • The following article from presentation-pointers.com offers many valuable tips for the public speaker. Read the article "7 Aspects of a Dynamic Presentation" by Lenny Laskowski, an international professional speaker. Go to **presentation-pointers.com**, click on Author List, Lenny Laskowski, then the article title.

   • Read the article "Motivation—Applying Maslow's Hierarchy of Needs Theory" by Robert Tanner, a highly practiced training, development, and organizational consultant. Go to **ezinearticles.com** and search "Hierarchy of Needs Theory" to find the article.

   • Listen to President Richard Nixon's resignation address given August 8, 1978, at **americanrhetoric.com** (search for "Richard Nixon Resignation Speech"). Do you think this speech raised Nixon's credibility in the eyes of the American public?

   • Go to **archives.gov** to check out several interesting propaganda posters from World War II and the history behind them. Click on the link "Online Exhibits," then browse to the link to the exhibit, "Powers of Persuasion: Posters from World War II." Select a poster and determine the persuasive appeals used in it. Do you see any fear appeals?

CourseMate

Collaborative Skill Building

1. It is easy to fall for fallacious reasoning. Two areas most reliant on fallacious reasoning are advertising and election campaigns. In small groups, analyze either an ad or an election campaign and identify at least three examples of fallacious reasoning used. Plan to present your results to another group or the class.

2. In small groups, select four motivational appeals from Figure 13.4. Find a current radio or television commercial that illustrates each appeal. Plan a presentation to share your examples with your instructor, a classmate, or the entire class.

3. In small groups, read and listen to the sample persuasive speech by Adam Parrish (pages 339–343) and identify the exact line numbers where each part of the introduction, body, and conclusion begin and end*; evaluate the introduction, body, and conclusion on a five-point scale with "5" representing an excellent rating and "1" representing a poor rating or critique the speech using the persuasive evaluation form in Figure 12.9. Compare your results with another group.

    *a) The attention getter, audience motivation, speaker qualifications, and thesis/position statement which are all parts of the speech's introduction;
    b) The problem, cause, and solution which are parts of the speech's body;
    c) The final summary and call to action which are parts of the speech's conclusion.

14

Special Occasion Speaking

FLASH BACK

The first chapter mentioned that Aristotle in his *Rhetoric*, divided speaking into three categories: **forensic** (speaking in court), **deliberative** (political or legislative speaking), and **epideictic** (ceremonial speaking). Although there are many types of ceremonial or special occasion speeches that deal with praise (or blame) of a person, object, place, or ideal, Aristotle felt that the best ones relate to the audience and build on what the audience admires or hates the most about character, virtue, achievements, or contributions. In his *De Oratore*, Cicero adds that audiences are especially impressed if the person being praised received no profit or reward and if their deed was a benefit to the community or to humankind in general.

FLASH FORWARD

People who can give great special occasion speeches are admired today just as they were in Aristotle's time. And just as in ancient times, the key to giving a great ceremonial speech is audience analysis. Whether you are giving a toast at a wedding or anniversary, presenting an award, introducing a guest speaker, or giving praise or blame to a place or ideal, it is not only the subject of the speech but the audience you must please. In addition, there is another key for successful ceremonial speeches that may differ from ancient times—the length of the speech— today's speakers are expected to be brief. In fact, Joan Detz, speechwriter and author of *Can You Say a Few Words* (2006), recommends that 3-minutes is a good length for most ceremonial speeches. *Why do you think that today's audience is less tolerant of a "long" speech than an audience in Aristotle's time?*

Learning Objectives

As you read Chapter 14,

- *Define* the term *special occasion speech*.
- *Explain* how a special occasion speech differs from an informative or persuasive speech.
- *Identify* the different types of special occasion speeches and pinpoint what is needed to make each the most effective.

YOUR PUBLIC-SPEAKING EXPERIENCE WILL INCLUDE INFORMATIVE AND PERSUASIVE PRESENTATIONS. Often, however, you will be in situations that invite a somewhat different approach to public communication. Significant events in people's lives call for public recognition. From birth announcements to eulogies, the rituals of life involve the ritual of speech making. Consider the following situations and the role a public presentation would play:

- You have just received an award and are asked to "say a few words."

- Your best friend is getting married. At the reception, you are responsible for proposing a toast to the newlyweds.

- A local civic organization invites you to give a speech at their annual fundraising banquet.

- Your college roommate has just been elected class president. The campaign manager asks if you would be willing to introduce your friend, who will then make her victory speech.

- Your favorite uncle has just died. The family asks you to deliver a memorial speech at the funeral.

- Your campus is dedicating a statue to military personnel who gave their lives in defending their country and you are asked to make the dedication.

These examples represent just a few of the many special occasions where public speaking is expected.

Special Occasion Speaking: An Overview

Special occasion speeches—or ceremonial speeches—differ from informative and persuasive speeches. Unlike informative presentations, ceremonial addresses do not offer large doses of new knowledge or present detailed instructions. Unlike persuasive presentations, special occasion speeches do not generally deal with controversial issues or attempt to change the way audiences think or act although they do tend to stimulate and motive feelings. In general, ceremonial presentations avoid controversy and reaffirm the audience's beliefs. Figure 14.1 outlines the key characteristics of informative, persuasive, and special occasion speaking.

Organization of Special Occasion Speeches

Special occasion addresses, like informative and persuasive speeches, are organized with an introduction, a body, and a conclusion. Let's look at the **introduction** first. No matter whether you start your speech with a compelling story, a memorable

Figure 14.1

Objectives of Informative, Persuasive, and Special Occasion Speaking

	Informative	Persuasive	Special Occasion
Goal	Share knowledge: instruct, demonstrate	Influence belief or action: gain compliance, alter behavior	Entertain reinforce strengthen bonds among audience members
Sample Topic	To explain the process of public speaking	To convince listeners that they should take a course in public speaking	To congratulate students in a public speaking class after their first speech

quote, or a startling fact, you should include something in your introduction that evokes the common values or feelings that have brought your audience together. For example, Congresswoman Barbara Jordan, who delivered the keynote address at the 1976 Democratic National Convention, began her talk by pointing out how the participants were continuing a 144-year-old tradition. Also, as the first African American woman ever to deliver the address, she acknowledged the party's role in making this part of the American dream come true for her. After referring to the history of Democratic nominating conventions, she said, "And our meeting this week is a continuation of that tradition…but tonight here I am. And I feel that notwithstanding the past, my presence here is one additional bit of evidence that the American Dream need not forever be deferred" (Jordan, 1992). Sixteen years later, as the keynote speaker for the 1992 Democratic National Convention, Jordan referred to her 1976 presentation and reminded the audience that they had won the presidency that year—so why not win this year as well? (Jordan, 2010).

Depending on your audience and the occasion, you may need to establish your credibility in the introduction as well. This is especially important if you are unknown to the audience or if your expertise on the topic is unknown. And, in most special occasion speeches, you should clearly state the purpose of your remarks and preview your main points—although in some speeches to commemorate, it may be more appropriate to state the purpose only. For example, in a brief toast, tribute, or eulogy, no preview is necessary.

In the **body** of a special occasion speech, you will want to concentrate especially on making your main points clear and on supporting them with a variety of entertaining and even inspiring materials. ➡ *Review Chapter 6 for a summary of the various types of supporting materials.*

The **conclusion** of special occasion speeches refocuses audience interest not simply on the presentation but on who the listeners are and what they stand for. The speech gives audience members an opportunity to strengthen their sense of identity and purpose. This is especially true in the eulogy. Note how President Obama in the conclusion of his Fort Hood eulogy drew audience members together and reinforced American values. After reminding listeners that the following day was Veterans Day, he stated:

> This generation of soldiers, sailors, airmen, Marines and Coast Guardsmen
> have volunteered in a time of certain danger. They are part of the finest
> fighting force that the world has ever known. They have served tour after
> tour of duty in distant, different and difficult places. They have stood watch
> in blinding deserts and on snowy mountains. They have extended the
> opportunity of self-government to peoples that have suffered tyranny and
> war. They are man and woman; white, black, and brown; of all faiths and
> stations - all Americans, serving together to protect our people, while giving
> others half a world away the chance to lead a better life.

➡ *For more on Obama's Fort Hood eulogy, see this chapter's* Speaking to Make a Difference *feature on pages 359–360.*

Because visual aids can capture audience attention rapidly and effectively, they can be especially useful in special occasion speeches. During his final State of the Union address, Ronald Reagan (1986) complained about the unnecessary complexity of congressional regulations. Instead of just talking about wasteful paperwork, Reagan placed near the podium the bound volumes of the several-thousand-page-long federal budget, which weighed in at more than 20 pounds. That gesture demonstrated more clearly than any words just how much paperwork Congress was generating.

Although PowerPoint slides are normally not an option for short presentations, you can use visual aids to your advantage during a special occasion speech. If you are introducing a well-known writer, you might display a stack of his books to show how productive his career has been. If you are presenting an award, you could show a chart that lists the criteria for the award and then match the recipient's accomplishments to the criteria. In addition to props, Joan Detz (2009) also recommends using letters, music, posters, and photographs. Keep alert to the opportunities for incorporating visual aids into special occasion speeches, especially when you want to offer audience members a concrete reminder of what they should recall from the speech.

Purposes of Special Occasion Speaking

Special occasion speaking was already well established in Greece by the fifth century B.C. In the fourth century B.C., Aristotle recognized ceremonial speeches as a class of oratory known as *epideictic* (sometimes called *epidictic*), which he defined as speeches of praise or blame (Aristotle, 1924). These speeches would reinforce the values of the community by praising virtue and condemning vice.

Today, the opportunities for ceremonial speeches abound. These presentations perform an important function because they are designed to strengthen the listeners' commitment to values they hold dear. Thus, a speaker at a special occasion serves as far more than a mere ornament. Although there are many types of special occasion speeches, the following are the most common: speeches of introduction, presentations of awards, acceptance speeches, commemorative speeches (including tributes, toasts, and eulogies), and after-dinner speeches (including speeches given at graduations, conventions, meetings, and luncheons).

Active Critical Thinking

To think further about special occasion speaking, complete the following:

- List several special occasion speeches you have heard over the last year— your list may include a toast at a wedding, an introduction to a speaker, a eulogy, or an after dinner speech. Identify where each speech occurred.
- Select the best speaker from your list and discuss at least two skills that made the speaker successful. Be prepared to share your list with other students or the class.

Speeches of Introduction

The **speech of introduction** is one of the most common types of ceremonial oratory. The introductory speech simply prepares the audience for the featured speaker(s). Although speeches of introduction tend to be short, often five minutes or less, they must accomplish a lot. An effective speech of introduction should do the following (adapted from Marshall, 2010):

- Tell the listeners enough about the featured speaker that they will understand the person's qualifications and why he or she was selected to speak.
- Encourage the audience to listen by telling them "what's in it for them."
- Generate interest in the upcoming presentation by sharing a positive impression or story about the speaker or telling how you first met the speaker.
- Welcome the featured speaker to the stage by giving the title of the presentation and repeating his or her name.

Introductory speeches might seem simple: You just get up and tell the audience who will speak and what the topic will be. However, there is much more to a good speech of introduction. The introduction of a speaker prepares the audience to listen to that person. By giving listeners a basic idea of what to expect, you enable them to adapt better to the speaker and topic. An introduction also allows you to express appreciation to the speaker. If you are introducing a speaker, you might note why the topic is particularly relevant to some recent events in the community. This official recognition becomes especially important when you are representing the group that sponsored the speaker's appearance. When a speaker is being introduced, that person's reputation and credibility temporarily lie in the hands of whoever gives the introduction (Campbell & Huxman, 2008, p. 237).

To avoid the embarrassment of presenting inaccurate information, verify all facts about the speaker you will introduce. Whenever possible, get biographical information directly from the speaker. This is the only way you can be certain that your information is accurate. Of course, if the person is well known, you may be able to find additional information in *Who's Who,* the *Dictionary of American Biography,* or other biographical references. You may also want to interview some of the speaker's friends or professional associates—a good source for personal anecdotes that will help reveal the speaker as an individual. Remember, however, to review your introduction with the featured speaker to ensure accuracy and reduce the risk of saying something inappropriate (Campbell & Huxman, 2008, p. 237). Imagine revealing information you thought was interesting, only to have the speaker become angry or embarrassed that you included some facts that were not supposed to be discussed publicly.

Remember that speeches of introduction are short. Ordinarily, such a speech should last only a small fraction of the time scheduled for the featured speech. Exactly how long should your introductory speech be? Rarely does an introductory speech last more than a few minutes. For example, if you are going to introduce a classmate who is delivering a seven-minute speech, your introduction should take no more than one to two minutes.

Because speeches of introduction are so common and their use is so specific, speakers can fall into the trap of using platitudes. Any speech genre that is well established invites the use of stock phrases that can instantly make a presentation seem trite. At best, such remarks will tell the audience that your presentation lacks originality. A speech of introduction filled with platitudes also sends a clear message that you did not gather specific information about the speaker. Figure 14.2 lists some stock phrases to avoid when making a speech of introduction (adapted from Joan Detz, 2000 and 2002).

Also, before your speech, make absolutely sure you know how to pronounce the speaker's name. Even a slight mispronunciation can be embarrassing for you and disconcerting to the speaker. One of the worst instances of garbling a speaker's name happened at a banquet honoring the renowned Russian poet Yevgeny Yevtushenko. The introducer didn't make just a little slip. He mangled the Russian's name so grievously that the poet himself yelled out the correct pronunciation. The introduction ended with the unnerved introducer saying: "I present…" He paused, looked at his notes, gave a puzzled frown, totally mispronounced Yevtushenko's name again, and sat down. Before they applauded, most of the audience shouted in unison the correct pronunciation. The lesson is, whatever it takes, make sure you pronounce the speaker's name correctly.

Correctness extends to the title a speaker wants you to use. This point is very important, because social roles and especially gender roles are changing rapidly. For example, don't assume that just because a speaker holds a PhD she wants to be called "Dr." Some women prefer to be called "Ms.," others prefer their professional

Figure 14.2

Stock Phrases to
Avoid in Introductory
Speeches

1. *"Here is someone who needs no introduction...."* If so, then you never should have begun your speech. The audience will probably think, "Needs no introduction? Then sit down and keep quiet."

2. *"We are truly honored to have with us today...."* This comment is too vague to have value. You would do better to explain briefly why the speaker's presence is an honor.

3. *"Without further ado...."* You have just trivialized your own remarks, treating them as "flurry, confusion, upset, excitement, hubbub, noise, turmoil." The preface "without further" labels your speech inconsequential.

4. *"It is indeed a high privilege...."* This is another empty phrase that should be replaced with specifics.

5. *"On this most memorable occasion...."* You cannot judge now how memorable this event will be in the future. I have heard this phrase used to describe many decidedly forgettable events. I would list them, but I can't recall what they were.

6. *"We have none other then...."* This comment is at best redundant. It sounds as if you weren't sure whether the speaker was an impostor, and you just wanted to make sure the audience recognized him or her.

titles, and still others avoid all titles. Many political and religious offices carry with them titles that are part of professional etiquette. For example, judges have the title "The Honorable" before their name. Government officials have other titles appropriate to their offices (such as "Supervisor" and "Congresswoman"). The proper form of address is a combination of professional etiquette and the individual's preference. Instead of relying on generalizations about what "that sort" of speaker might prefer, confirm the appropriate form of address with the speaker directly.

Exactly what should your speech of introduction include? Your speech should do the following:

- State who you are if the audience does not know already.

- Highlight the speaker's name. In most cases, you should mention the speaker's name early in your speech and again as the last thing you say so that the audience will remember it.

- Recognize the reason for the occasion. Why is this speaker here now?

- Express appreciation to the speaker.

- Include only biographical information relevant to the occasion and preapproved by the speaker.

- Whenever appropriate, add some specific, personal material that humanizes the speaker—after clearing this with him or her.

- Mention the topic of the speaker's talk.

A speech of introduction should focus audience attention on the featured speaker, not on you. Some speeches of introduction include so much explanation of the occasion that the audience learns little about the actual speaker. Also, be careful to avoid upstaging the speaker by making frequent references to yourself, your accomplishments, or your qualifications to give the introduction. Briefly mention who you are, then place the featured speech at the center of your presentation. Resist the temptation

In speeches of introduction...

- Don't speak for too long.
- Don't mispronounce the featured speaker's name.
- Don't give inaccurate or unwanted biographical information about the featured speaker.
- Don't upstage the featured speaker.
- Don't evaluate the upcoming speech instead of letting the audience decide for itself.

to evaluate the speech, because the listeners can make an informed judgment only after they have listened to the speaker. For example, don't say, "Marie's speech will be the finest presentation you'll ever hear on Haiku poetry." Specific analyses and evaluations mean little to an audience that has not yet heard what it should be appraising.

Active Critical Thinking

To think further about speeches of introduction, complete the following:
- Plan a speech of introduction to give before a classmate's final speech.
- How will this speech differ in length and content from a typical informative speech?

Award Presentations

Another common ceremonial speech is the presentation of an award. This type of speech should emphasize the worthiness of the person receiving the award and explain the award's significance. An **award presentation** should include at least the following components (Sternberg, 1984):

- The name of the award and the reason it is being given.
- The name of the winner and his or her reason for winning.
- The reason you are glad to present the award.

The content of your presentation "should be so specific that it couldn't possibly be said about anyone else" (Detz, 2000, p. 78). The more your remarks identify the recipient as unique, the more the audience will recognize the award as a personal distinction for the winner. Compare the impact of these fictitious presentations:

> Award A: Now we come to the Outstanding Freshman award. And the winner is Elvira Earp. Congratulations, Elvira.

> Award B: The award of Outstanding Freshman recognizes scholastic achievement and public service. This year's winner isn't content with a perfect 4.0 grade point average. She sets aside time from her busy schedule to work with children who have cerebral palsy. On weekends, you can find her teaching adult literacy classes at the public library. I am happy to present this award to a model for my own children: Elvira Earp.

If you had won the award, which presentation would make you feel more acknowledged?

In addition to being specific, effective awards should also provide generous praise, be personal with a "real life" story, be sincere, and be inspirational (Deetz, 2000, p. 79).

Active Critical Thinking

To think further about award presentations, complete the following:

- Prepare an award presentation to give to one of your classmates for something they have done this semester or a speech they have given.
- Write out the award presentation following the guidelines above and prepare to give it in class if asked.

Acceptance Speeches

An **acceptance speech** demands more from the recipient of an award than a simple "thank you." A properly crafted acceptance concisely expresses gratitude and dignifies the occasion by recognizing the significance of the award.

Your acceptance speech should show your goodwill toward the audience, the presenter, and the sponsor of the award. The speech should do the following, although not necessarily in this order (Reager, et. al, 1960, p. 155):

- *Thank the donor and presenter.*

- *Demonstrate modesty while avoiding hackneyed phrases that ring false.* Don't say, "I really don't deserve this," because it insults the donors by implying that they made the wrong choice. You could, for example, show humility by pointing to how you will try to live up to the high standards of the award.

- *Thank others who may have contributed to your success.* If you have ever watched the Academy Awards on television, you'll recall that almost every acceptance speech includes a list of people the winner wishes to thank. Make sure you acknowledge those who contributed to your success, but only those who contributed directly. Giving more than a handful of thank-yous begins to sound like the recital of a grocery list—and holds about the same amount of interest for the audience.

- *Regardless of the gift or award, express your pleasure at receiving it.* I have seen some award recipients actually mock the presenter by ridiculing a gift they were given. Such behavior is rude and ungracious. Even if you think the award itself is hideous or cheap, someone has exerted effort and thought in trying to find something appropriate.

- *Express appreciation in your conclusion.* Reiterating your gratitude shows that you acknowledge the award as a favor and appreciate it.

By following these simple guidelines, you will generate an acceptance speech that is fitting and polite. Your acceptance speech should also demonstrate your understanding of the award's deeper significance. If you received the Outstanding Freshman award mentioned earlier, for example, your acceptance would call attention to its connection with the ideals of scholastic excellence and community service. Also, thinking ahead about structuring your acceptance speech in this way will help you avoid blurting out the first thought that comes to your mind in the excitement of the moment. For example, in 1984, Sally Field received the Oscar for Best Actress for her performance in *Places in the Heart*. Her acceptance speech consisted of an outburst of tears and the inane pronouncement, "You like me! You really, really like me!"

By contrast, Elie Wiesel's 1986 Nobel Peace Prize acceptance speech epitomizes an appropriate response to the situation (Andrews and Zarefsky, 1992). He begins by demonstrating modesty: "It is with a profound sense of humility that I accept the honor you have chosen to bestow upon me. I know: your choice transcends me." Wiesel recognizes that the award acknowledges not simply his efforts in raising public consciousness about the Holocaust but those of others who have suffered: "This honor belongs to all the survivors and their children, and through us, to the Jewish people with whose destiny I have always identified." He concludes with a brief but eloquent acknowledgment of the award and its sponsors: "Thank you, Chairman Aarvik. Thank you, members of the Nobel Committee. Thank you, people of Norway, for declaring on this singular occasion that our survival has a meaning for mankind."

Active Critical Thinking

To think further about acceptance speeches, complete the following:
- Take the award presentation that you wrote in the above activity.
- Now, write an acceptance speech the person might give upon receiving the award. Explain why you included each item in the speech and why you think it is appropriate. Be prepared to deliver your acceptance speech to your class or to a small group of classmates.

Commemorative Speeches

Commemorative speeches are another type of special occasion address. These speeches formally recognize and honor a person, organization, or occasion. A **commemorative speech** can occur in a variety of circumstances, from celebrating a coworker's retirement, to congratulating a friend for winning the lottery, to remembering a person who has just died. There are three basic types of commemorative speeches: tributes, toasts, and eulogies.

Tributes

An effective **tribute** renews the kinship between speaker and audience while recognizing the occasion. Norman Schwarzkopf's going-home speech to the troops serving in the Gulf War on March 8, 1991, provides a good example of a tribute. Schwarzkopf begins by emphasizing his closeness with the troops. Because all of them are soldiers, he praises that fact and adds "inside" references to military units in jargon that other soldiers will understand: "It's a great day to be a soldier! Big Red One, First Team, Old Ironsides, Spear Head, Hell on Wheels platoon, Jay Hawk patrol, today you're going home." His use of these terms establishes him as one of the group—in this case, military personnel. Here we see one characteristic of tributes: recognizing or creating the identity of the audience.

Schwarzkopf proceeds to summarize the events that made the occasion memorable. This exemplifies a second quality of tributes—commending the audience's shared history or revered heroes: "Valiant charges by courageous men over 250 kilometers of enemy territory. Along with a force of over 1,500 tanks, almost 250 attack helicopters, over 48,500 pieces of military equipment, moving around, behind, and into the enemy and totally breaking his back and defeating him in 100 hours." Another example of evoking a revered hero occurred in Martin Luther King Jr.'s "I Have a Dream" speech. He refers to Abraham Lincoln, the president known for his role in bringing slavery to an end, as a "great American, in whose symbolic shadow we stand today" at the Lincoln Memorial in Washington, D.C. ➜ *For more on King's I Have a Dream speech, see the* Speaking to Make a Difference *feature in Chapter 8.*

Tributes, therefore, generally honor an individual, organization, or occasion while commending the audience's shared history or revered heroes. However, some forms of tributes, such as the toast and eulogy, call for special consideration.

Toasts

An abbreviated type of commemorative speech is the **toast**, a very brief set of remarks traditionally delivered while audience members hold aloft glasses of wine or champagne. Although toasts have evolved into symbolic gestures that might include water or no beverage at all, one element has been preserved: the speech. We hear short toasts in many contexts. The traditional Jewish toast consists of a simple "L'chaim!" translated, "To life!" Löwenbrau beer used to begin their commercials with the toast "Here's to good friends." When a special occasion calls for a toast, however, the remarks must be more specific.

Because toasts originated with everyone holding a glass aloft, they were brief. That custom remains unchanged—a toast rarely lasts more than a minute or two. Because of their brevity, toasts may be memorized. The speaker has very little time, and a toast is almost always on behalf of someone or something specific. As a result, the toast itself should focus on one specific quality or theme that emphasizes the reason for the occasion. According to Kevin McDonald in his book *Cheers!* (2004), "The most moving toasts are often personal accounts punctuated by well-chosen quotes" (p. xi). ➜ *For effective quotes, refer to McDonald's book,* Cheers! *or Google "quotations" for online lists of quotations and books of quotations such as* Bartlett's Familiar Quotations.

However, gratuitous comments such as "Here's to the happy couple" given at a wedding fail to capitalize on the potentially dramatic effect of toasts (McDonald, 2004). The guests have paused to hear inspiring words, not clichés. Similarly, comments that run counter to the desired mood spell disaster. You might have heard wedding toasts in the spirit of "Here's to Bubba and Bertha. Hope this marriage turns out better than Bubba's last one. Lots of luck."

This speaker is checking for gestures and facial expressions as he prepares for a wedding toast.

Eugene Choi/iStockphoto.com

Sample Student Speech: "My Grandfather, John Flanagan Sr." by Tara Flanagan

The following commemorative speech of tribute, "My Grandfather, John Flanagan Sr.," was given by Colorado State University student Tara Flanagan in a public speaking class. Tara's assignment was to give a three- to five-minute tribute about a person she admired. As you read this speech, see how well Tara followed the guidelines for presenting an effective special occasion speech. ➜ *To watch and analyze a video clip of Tara's speech, look under "Student Resources for Chapter 14" through your Online Resources for* Essentials of Public Speaking.

Sample Speech of Tribute

MY GRANDFATHER, JOHN FLANAGAN SR.

by Tara Flanagan

As I wiped the streams that flowed down my face, I saw out of the corner of my eye a group of homeless men enter the room. My sadness turned to anger as I watched these uninvited guests interrupt *my grandfather's* funeral. They were like unwanted ants invading a family picnic. After our pastor concluded his eulogy, I went to the back of the room to ask them to leave. "Excuse me," I said, "but this is my grandfather's funeral, and only invited guests are allowed inside." And one of the men looked at me, and he said, "You must be Tara. Your grandfather carried a picture of you in his wallet." Much to my surprise, these homeless men were friends of my grandfather. My grandfather was never a good judge of people. He was just better at not judging them at all. As I walked around the room, I saw many people that neither my family nor I recognized, but each one of them had a story on how my grandfather had touched them with his love and kindness. My grandfather was a loving, brave man with an amazing sense of humor, and these virtues never shone brighter for me than they did on the day of his funeral.

From the funeral home, our entourage headed to the cemetery to place my grandfather in his final resting place. It was a hot July day, and the sun was just pounding down on our car. We were following the white hearse when all of the sudden it stopped, and this terrible, white smoke began billowing out of the hood. It laid there like a huge, immovable beached whale. My father began laughing as the cars piled up behind us, and he said, "I bet your grandfather had something to do with this." My grandfather had an amazing sense of humor. This incident reminded us of the many jokes he told and pulled on our family. Making his own hearse break down on the day of his funeral to give us all a good laugh wasn't beyond him.

I remembered a time when my grandfather cheered me up when I was younger. I was visiting my father for the summer, and I was incredibly homesick. I missed my mom and my sister very badly. He spent the entire afternoon telling me silly knock-knock jokes and doing random things just to make me laugh. And I remember feeling so much better. My homesickness melted away. My grandfather always had a way of making our family laugh and feel better, and the day of his funeral was no exception.

When we finally got the white whale back on the road, we drove into the lush cemetery. There were flowers blossoming and a gentle stream that ran through the middle. It was like a scene out of the Garden of Eden. There to greet us were several gentlemen dressed in their Marine best. They carried with them large guns and gave my grandfather his twenty-one-gun salute. After the service I spoke with them, and they told me of my grandfather's bravery while he served in World War II. One of the men had actually served with my grandfather. He told me a story about how my grandfather had saved his live, and they ended up being the only two men out of the entire platoon to survive. At the end of the war they even saw the famous raising of the flag at Iwo Jima.

Living, laughing, loving life: My grandfather was an amazing man who taught me so much about humor, courage, and compassion. Even though his funeral was the saddest day of my life, I was uplifted by all the lives that he had touched. I hope that someday I can learn to love people more than I judge them, just like he did.

Eulogies

Another type of commemorative speech is the **eulogy**, which offers tribute to someone who has died (the word *eulogy* comes from the Greek for "good words"). The tradition of eulogizing probably extends to nearly the beginning of human speech. Pericles' funeral oration in 431 B.C. for those who had perished in the Peloponnesian War was the first fully recorded eulogy delivered as a public speech (Thucydides, 1972). It exemplifies the basic format eulogies still follow. Your audience will expect a eulogy to do the following:

- Recognize the death.
- Temper the audience's grief by explaining how the deceased "lives on."
- Redefine the audience's relationship to the deceased.
- Reassure the audience that life will continue.
- Sometimes advise the audience on how the death should affect their own lives (Foss, 1983; Jamieson & Campbell, 1982).

Perhaps more than other types of ceremonial speeches, the eulogy must "reknit the community," because members have suffered a loss. In his eulogy for the astronauts who perished aboard the space shuttle *Challenger,* Ronald Reagan stressed that the tragedy had brought all Americans together in spite of their differences. Speaking of his wife and himself, Reagan said, "We know we share this pain with all of the people of our country. This is truly a national loss" (Mister, 1986).

A brief examination of United Nations Ambassador Adlai Stevenson's 1965 eulogy for Winston Churchill shows what a eulogy can accomplish (Ryan, 1992).

Component of Eulogy	Fulfillment in Stevenson's Speech
Recognize the death.	Sir Winston Churchill is dead. The voice that led nations, raised armies, inspired victories and blew fresh courage into the hearts of men is silenced.
Show how the deceased lives on.	Churchill, the historian, felt the continuity of past and present, the contribution which mighty men and great events make to future experience; history's "flickering flame" lights up the past and sends its gleams into the future.
Redefine the relationship to the deceased.	One rather feels a sense of thankfulness and of encouragement that throughout so long a life, such a full measure of power, virtuosity, mastery and zest played over our human scene.
Offer reassurance.	Contemplating this completed career, we feel a sense of enlargement and exhilaration.… Churchill's life uplifts our hearts and fills us with fresh revelation of the scale and reach of human achievement.

Eulogies offer praise for the deceased, but the compliments must be sincere and proportionate to the actual accomplishments. Even a grief-stricken audience can recognize overly lavish praise. Claiming that the deceased was "faultless" or "perfect" rings false because everyone has shortcomings. Concentrate on the person's strengths while remaining realistic. Because a eulogist usually knows the deceased personally, some specific anecdotes that illustrate the character of the departed are especially appropriate. According to Jerry Weissman, author of *Presenting to Win* (2006), an anecdote is "a *very* short story, usually one with a human interest angle" (p. 88). Ronald Reagan is an example of a speaker who used anecdotes well.

According to Weissman, "He was always ready with a brief tale about the brave soldier, the benevolent nurse, or the dignified grandfather as a way of illustrating his themes. Invariably, the tale would coax an empathic nod or a smile of recognition from his audience" (p. 88).

A poorly wrought eulogy can be interpreted as disrespectful or simply ridiculous. For example, in an episode of *Star Trek: The Next Generation,* Lieutenant Commander Data offers an overly general eulogy for a brilliant scientist who has just died: "To know him was to love him. And to love him was to know him. Those who knew him, loved him. Those who did not know him, loved him from afar." In contrast, an effective eulogy will be specific to the deceased and geared to the audience. Stevenson's moving tribute to Winston Churchill was full of quotes from Churchill and personal remembrances of the great leader's habits and mannerisms. Adapting his comments to the dignitaries of many nations who were in attendance, Stevenson emphasized Churchill's roles in founding the United Nations and his belief that "humanity, its freedom, its survival, towered above pettier interests—national rivalries, old enmities, the bitter disputes of race and creed" (Stevenson, p. 246).

Speaking to Make a Difference

On November 11, 2009, President Barack Obama presented a eulogy for the thirteen people killed at the Fort Hood military complex in Texas by a rampaging gunman. Excerpts from the speech are included below. For the complete speech, see **americanrhetoric.com**.

Charles Ommanney/Getty Images

We come together filled with sorrow for the thirteen Americans that we have lost; with gratitude for the lives that they led; and with a determination to honor them through the work we carry on.

This is a time of war. And yet these Americans did not die on a foreign field of battle. They were killed here, on American soil, in the heart of this great American community. It is this fact that makes the tragedy even more painful and even more incomprehensible

For those families who have lost a loved one, no words can fill the void that has been left. We knew these men and women as soldiers and caregivers. You knew them as mothers and fathers sons and daughters; sisters and brothers.

But here is what you must also know: your loved ones endure through the life of our nation. Their memory will be honored in the places they lived and by the people they touched. Their life's work is our security, and the freedom that we too often take for granted. Every evening that the sun sets on a tranquil town; every dawn that a flag is unfurled; every moment that an American enjoys life, liberty and the pursuit of happiness - that is their legacy.

Neither this country - nor the values that we were founded upon - could exist without men and women like these thirteen Americans. And that is why we must pay tribute to their stories.

* * *

[At this point in Obama's eulogy, he told a brief story about each of the men and women slain.]

These men and women came from all parts of the country. Some had long careers in the military. Some had signed up to serve in the shadow of 9/11. Some had known intense combat in Iraq and Afghanistan, and some cared for those who did. Their lives speak to the strength, the dignity and the decency of those who serve, and that is how they will be remembered.

That same spirit is embodied in the community here at Fort Hood, and in the many wounded who are still recovering. In those terrible minutes during the attack, soldiers made makeshift tourniquets out of their clothes. They braved gunfire to reach the wounded, and ferried them to safety in the backs of cars and a pick-up truck.

One young soldier, Amber Bahr, was so intent on helping others that she did not realize for some time that she, herself, had been shot in the back. Two police officers - Mark Todd and Kim Munley - saved countless lives by risking their own. One medic - Francisco de la Serna - treated both Officer Munley and the gunman who shot her.

It may be hard to comprehend the twisted logic that led to this tragedy. But this much we do know - no faith justifies these murderous and craven acts; no just and loving God looks upon them with favor. And for what he has done, we know that the killer will be met with justice - in this world, and the next.

* * *

We are a nation that endures because of the courage of those who defend it. We saw that valor in those who braved bullets here at Fort Hood, just as surely as we see it in those who signed up knowing that they would serve in harm's way.

We are a nation of laws whose commitment to justice is so enduring that we would treat a gunman and give him due process, just as surely as we will see that he pays for his crimes.

We are a nation that guarantees the freedom to worship as one chooses. And instead of claiming God for our side, we remember Lincoln's words, and always pray to be on the side of God.

continued

We are a nation that is dedicated to the proposition that all men and women are created equal. We live that truth within our military, and see it in the varied backgrounds of those we lay to rest today. We defend that truth at home and abroad, and we know that Americans will always be found on the side of liberty and equality. That is who we are as a people.

Tomorrow is Veterans Day. It is a chance to pause, and to pay tribute - for students to learn of the struggles that preceded them; for families to honor the service of parents and grandparents; for citizens to reflect upon the sacrifices that have been made in pursuit of a more perfect union.

* * *

We need not look to the past for greatness, because it is before our very eyes.

* * *

Here, at Fort Hood, we pay tribute to thirteen men and women who were not able to escape the horror of war, even in the comfort of home. Later today, at Fort Lewis, one community will gather to remember so many in one Stryker Brigade who have fallen in Afghanistan.

Long after they are laid to rest - when the fighting has finished, and our nation has endured; when today's servicemen and women are veterans, and their children have grown - it will be said of this generation that they believed under the most trying of tests; that they persevered not just when it was easy, but when it was hard; and that they paid the price and bore the burden to secure this nation, and stood up for the values that live in the hearts of all free peoples.

So we say good-bye to those who now belong to eternity. We press ahead in pursuit of the peace that guided their service. May God bless the memory of those we lost. And may God bless the United States of America.

Obama's received great acclaim for his eulogy, given in front of 15 thousand military personnel and families as well as the millions listening by radio, television, and the Internet. Let's look at a few specifics as to why the speech was so successful.

- **Appropriate length.** Obama's eulogy lasted slightly less than 15 minutes and was a "small masterpiece" according to John Dickerson (2009), who said, "The president had great material and he knew not to get in its way" (1). A good special occasion speech is normally brief; Obama's was.

- **Personal stories.** Obama's speeches generally include one or more inspirational stories. According to Joan Detz, speaker and author of *Can You Say a Few Words* (2006), audiences like stories and specifics. In this eulogy, Obama gives brief, specific stories about each of the thirteen men and women killed by the gunman. The stories, as the one offered for the first serviceman honored, give tribute to each person and make them seem real to those listening:

    Chief Warrant Officer Michael Cahill had served in the National Guard and worked as a physician's assistant for decades. A husband and father of three, he was so committed to his patients that on the day he died, he was back at work just weeks after having a heart attack.

- **Appropriate format.** Based on the information presented in this chapter, Obama followed the expected format for a good eulogy. He recognized the deaths, tempered the audience's grief, redefined America's relationship to the deceased, and reassured those listening that life and the cause they died for will continue. He applauded their greatness when he said, "We need not look to the past for greatness, because it is before our very eyes." And he assured their cause when he concluded with,

    "Long after they are laid to rest ... it will be said of this generation that they believed under the most trying of tests; that they persevered not just when it was easy, but when it was hard; and that they paid the price and bore the burden to secure this nation, and stood up for the values that live in the hearts of all free peoples."

Questions: In the Fort Hood Eulogy, Obama also used effective delivery and stylistic devices. Read or listen to the entire speech at **AmericaRhetoric.com** and find at least two stylistic devices (listed in Chapter 9) Obama used in his speech. Explain why they were effective.

Active Critical Thinking

To think further about commemorative speeches, complete the following:

- Find at least three quotations that would be appropriate for a wedding or anniversary toast. Cite the source for each quotation and explain how you would use each quote for the best effect.

- Assume that you are asked to give a tribute that honors a person, an organization, or an occasion. Pick the audience and decide on three values or beliefs you could use in your tribute that would relate to your audience. Select one value or belief and show how you could incorporate it into your speech for the best effect. Relate your answer specifically to the information in this chapter.

After-Dinner Speeches

The final type of ceremonial speech—the **after-dinner speech**—is far less serious than the eulogy. This type of speech gets its name from the fact that it is often delivered as the conclusion to a meeting that includes a meal. The name now signifies any speech that is light, entertaining, and often inspirational in tone. Occasions for after-dinner speeches abound, and they form a part of special events such as political rallies, graduation exercises, conventions, and bar and bat mitzvahs. It would not be exaggerating to observe, "The after-dinner speech is one of the great rituals of American public speaking and public life" (Osborn, et al., 2009, p. 454). After-dinner speaking has become so established that it is an oratorical event at many interscholastic and intercollegiate speech contests.

Because after-dinner speeches are generally meant to be entertaining, they should avoid controversy and overly technical explanations while still reinforcing a central theme. Also, even when an after-dinner speech is humorous, there is no need to keep audience members laughing constantly. If you are asked to deliver this kind of speech, you should not feel obligated to put together a comedy monologue or an uninterrupted series of jokes. Forced humor such as this can end up detracting from your speech. Furthermore, people differ significantly in their ability to be humorous (Wanzer, et. al., 1995), and different audiences will consider different things funny.

Be especially careful to avoid any comments that might have a chance of offending. Be aware that what you consider mild swearing could be interpreted by others as obscene, marking you as crude and inconsiderate. Ethnic, racist, sexist, and homophobic jokes are always unacceptable. The same goes for jokes that ridicule people who are mentally or physically challenged.

Ideally, you should gear your choice of humor to the background and interests of your audience. This type of humor creates a sense of identification between speaker and audience. Such a feeling of collegiality helps bond the speaker and the audience, letting the listeners know that the speaker is "one of us." Barbara Bush effectively established identification with her audience during her 1990 commencement address at Wellesley College. Recognizing that the graduating seniors at the women's college wanted to embark on careers traditionally closed to women, she quipped: "Who knows? Somewhere out in this audience may even be someone who will one day follow in my footsteps, and preside over the White House as the president's spouse. I wish him well" (Bush, 1994)! At its most powerful, humor can show that the speaker and the audience share similar motivations and reactions. ➜ *For more on Barbara Bush's after-dinner commencement address, see the* Speaking to Make a Difference *feature in Chapter 11.*

In general, the after-dinner speech will mark a specific event, so it's a good idea to reaffirm the occasion and the reason your audience has chosen to get together. You will find that vivid narratives, instances, and jokes are especially effective in bringing ideas and events to life. You can use several related items to maintain audience interest and enjoyment, or you can focus the entire speech on a single extended story or illustration. Either way, the speech should carry a lesson that applies to the specific audience.

A final work of advice: In many cases as an after-dinner speaker you will have to compete with distractions such as courses being served, glasses being filled, plates being cleared, and servers moving around the room. Make sure you speak with sufficient volume and clear enunciation to overcome these sounds. Also remember that the attention span of your audience will be low after a heavy meal, so you should include plenty of attention-getting material throughout the speech. ➜ *For types of supporting materials that have attention-getting potential, see Chapter 6.*

For digestible after-dinner speeches...

* Do use narratives and examples.
* Do use humor specific to the situation.
* Do keep the tone entertaining and light.
* Do focus your remarks on a central theme relevant to the occasion.
* Don't have complex or controversial content.
* Don't use overworked jokes, especially "A funny thing happened on the way to this speech..."
* Don't force humor; present only what you can deliver comfortably and skillfully.
* Don't ever use humor that can be considered racist, sexist, or otherwise offensive.

Active Critical Thinking

To think further about after-dinner speeches, complete the following:

* The June issue of *Vital Speeches* in 2009 is full of commencement speeches—a type of after-dinner speech. Read several of these speeches and select one that you especially like.
* Write a several paragraph evaluation of the chosen commencement speech giving at least four specific reasons why it was effective. Relate your evaluation to this chapter. What one suggestion would you offer to make the speech even better?

Summary

Special occasion speeches reinforce the shared identity and values of an audience. Regardless of the type of special occasion speech, its objective is to strengthen the bonds that unite the listeners.

There are several types of special occasion speeches. A speech of introduction focuses attention on a subsequent speaker and prepares the audience to listen to that person. Speeches of introduction are brief and highlight the featured speaker, not the person giving the introduction.

Speeches that are presentations of awards should include not only the name of the recipient but the reason that person deserves the honor. In speeches of acceptance, the recipient demonstrates humility and expresses appreciation to the sponsor of the award and to anyone who contributed to the winner's achievement.

Commemorative speeches are tributes to a person, event, or cause. Toasts are abbreviated tributes traditionally delivered at festive occasions such as weddings. Eulogies are tributes to someone who has died. When giving a eulogy, the speaker should acknowledge the death, redefine the relationship to the deceased, comfort the audience, and show what lasting contribution the deceased has made.

After-dinner speeches are light, entertaining presentations that generally include humor. When using humor, tailor the humorous remarks to the audience and the occasion. The more specific the jokes and anecdotes, the better the speaker and the audience will identify with each other.

Essentials of Public Speaking **Online** CourseMate

Use your Online Resources for *Essentials of Public Speaking* for quick access to the electronic study resources that accompany this chapter, which include access to InfoTrac College Edition, Personal Skill Building activities, Collaborative Skill Building activities, Active Critical Thinking boxes, and any InfoTrac College Edition activities, a digital glossary, sample speeches, and review quizzes.

Key Terms

acceptance speech 354	commemorative speech 355	special occasion speeches 348
after-dinner speech 361	conclusion 349	speech of introduction 350
award presentation 353	body 349 eulogy 358	toast 356
	introduction 348	tribute 355

Personal Skill Building

1. If you are using InfoTrac College Edition, locate a recent article giving pointers on special occasion speeches (especially commemorative and after-dinner speeches). Prepare a one- to two-minute review to share with the class.

2. Prepare a one-minute speech of introduction to give prior to a classmate's informative, persuasive, or after-dinner speech. Follow the guidelines for successful speeches of introduction included in this chapter.

3. Write a two- to three-minute tribute to give that honors a real or fictitious person, an organization, or an occasion. Be sure to follow the suggestions given in the text. Be prepared to deliver your toast and/or tribute to your class or to a small group of classmates.

4. Pretend you have just received an important award presented to you by the chairperson of your department. Prepare a two-minute acceptance speech to give to the class.

5. Check out the following websites: (You can access these sites using your Online Resources for *Essentials of Public Speaking,* Chapter 14.)

 CourseMate

   • Go to TED talks at **www.ted.com/talks** and find examples of outstanding special occasion speeches. To find ceremonial speeches, change the **Show by length** to 3 or 6 minutes.

   • Listen to J. K. Rowling's commencement address at Harvard University: the Fringe Benefits of Failure at **http://www.ted.com/talks/jk_rowling_the_fringe_benefits_of_failure.html**.

   • Listen to a moving eulogy from Oprah Winfrey on the death of Rosa Parks at **www.americanrhetoric.com/speeches/oprahwinfreyonrosaparks.htm**.

- For a humorous welcome for a corporate luncheon in Australia by Jean Kittson (a well-known Australian comedienne), go to **www.youtube. com/watch?v=c5J0pwi_Tkg**.

- Ben Stiller gives a humorous award presentation for Best Achievement in Makeup at the 2010 Oscars. Go to **www.youtube.com/ watch?v=A87InzywZOY**.

Collaborative Skill Building

1. Divide the class into groups. Recalling special occasion speeches you have observed in the past, make a list of annoying behaviors that speaker's should avoid. Find a movie or television show that illustrates an annoying special occasion speech. Prepare a group presentation of your list of behaviors and illustrating sample movie/television show to present to the class or to share with another group.

2. In small groups of four to six, divide into subgroups of two. Each pair will plan to give an introduction to each other's final classroom speech—exchange the necessary information about the speech topic as well as personal information. Use the text for ideas of what information you should gather about each other. Keep the introductions to a minute. Once the introductions are planned, practice the speeches in front of the full group asking for two things they really like about the speech and two suggestions to make it even better. At a later meeting, if time allows, present the speech a second time looking for at least one final suggestion. The speeches of introduction should be given prior to each student's final classroom speech and will probably be graded by your instructor.

References

2010–2011 Criteria: Criteria for accrediting engineering programs. (2009). Accreditation Board for Engineering and Technology (ABET, Inc.) at http://www.abet.org/Linked%20Documents-UPDATE/Criteria%20and%20PP/T001%2010-11%20TAC%20Criteria%2011-3-09.pdf.

About, 2010. (2010). National Oceanic and Atmospheric Administration (NOAA). Retrieved from http://www.externalaffairs.noaa.gov/speakers.html.

Adams, J. M., Faux, D. D., & Rieber, L. J. (1988). *Printing technology* (3rd ed.). Albany, NY: Delmar.

Addington, D. W. (1971).The effects of vocal variations on ratings of source credibility. *Speech Monographs, 38,* 242–247.

Ahles, C. B. (1993, March 15). The dynamics of discovery: Creating your own opportunities. *Vital Speeches, 59,* 350–353.

Aitken, J. E. (1993, May 15). Light the fire: Communicate with your child. *Vital Speeches, 59,* 473–477.

Ale, I. (2006, October 17). Persuasive Speech. 2006 PSCFA Seminar, youtube.com. Accessed July 26, 2007, at video.google.com/videosearch?q=persuasive+speech.

Alesandrini, K. L. (1982). Image eliciting strategies and meaningful learning. *Journal of Mental Imagery, 6,* 125–140.

Allen, M. (1991, Fall). Meta-analysis comparing the persuasiveness of one-sided and two-sided messages. *Western Journal of Speech Communication, 55,* 390–404.

Allen, M. (1998). Comparing the persuasive effectiveness of one-and two-sided messages. In M. Allen & R. W. Preiss (Eds.), *Persuasion: Advances through meta-analysis* (pp. 87–98). Cresskill, NJ: Hampton.

Allen, M., & Preiss, R. W. (1997). Comparing the persuasiveness of narrative and statistical evidence using meta-analysis. *Communication Research Reports, 14,* 125–131.

Allen, M., Berkowitz, S., Hunt, S. & Louden, A. (1999). Education on critical thinking. *Communication Education, 48,* 18–30.

Allen, M., Bruflat, R., Fucilla, R., Kramer, M., McKellips, S., Ryan, D. J., & Spiegelhoff, M. (2000).Testing the persuasiveness of evidence: Combining narrative and statistical forms. *Communication Research Reports, 17,* 331–336.

Allen, M., Hunter, J. E., & Donohue, W. A. (1989). Meta-analysis of self-report data on the effectiveness of public speaking anxiety treatment techniques. *Communication Education, 38,* 54–76.

American Program Bureau. (2009). *Harry Markopolos: Whistleblower.* Retrieved from http://www.apbspeakrs.com/speaker/harry.markolopos.

An, C., & Pfau, M. (2004). The efficacy of inoculation in televised political debates. *Journal of Communication, 54,* 421–436.

Anderson, K. (1999). Stories travel further and faster than facts. *Broadcast Engineering, 41*(9), 88.

Applbaum, R. L., & Anatol, K. W. (1972). The factor structure of source credibility as a function of the speaking situation. *Speech Monographs, 39,* 216–222.

April 2009 Web Server Survey. (2009, April 8). *Netcraft.com.* Retrieved from http://news.netcraft.com/archives/web_server_survey.html.

Arbaugh, J. B. (2001). How instructor immediacy behaviors affect student satisfaction and learning in Web-based courses. *Business Communication Quarterly, 64*(4), 42–54.

Archer, D., & Akert, R. M. (1977). Words and everything else: Verbal and nonverbal cues in social interpretation. *Journal of Personality and Social Psychology, 35,* 443–449.

Argyle, M. (1973). The syntaxes of bodily communication. *International Journal of Psycholinguistics, 2,* 78.

Aristotle. (1924). Rhetoric. W. R. Roberts (Trans.). In W. D. Ross (Ed.), *The works of Aristotle* (Vol. II). Oxford: Clarendon.

Aristotle. (1954). Rhetoric. W. R. Roberts (Trans.). New York: Modern Library.

Aristotle. (1971). *Works of Aristotle.* W. R. Roberts (Trans.). Vol. II. London: Oxford University Press.

Aristotle. (1974). *Poetics.* I. Bywater (Trans.). London: Oxford University Press.

Atkinson, C. (2007). PowerPoint usability: Q&A with Don Norman. In *Sociable Media.* Retrieved August 8, 2007, from www.sociablemedia.com/articles_norman.htm.

Atkins-Sayre, W. (2007, October 9). Delivery. *University of Southern Mississippi Speaking Center.* Accessed at www.usm.edu/speakingcenter/handout/delivery.pdf.

August 2006 Web Server Survey. (2006, August 1). Netcraft.com. Accessed August 12, 2006 from news.netcraft.com/archives/2006/08/01/august_2006_web_server/html.

Axtell, R. E. (1998). *Gestures: The do's and taboos of body language around the world.* New York: Wiley.

Ayres, J. (1988). Coping with speech anxiety: The power of positive thinking. *Communication Education, 37,* 289–295.

Ayres, J. (1991). Using visual aids to reduce speech anxiety. *Communication Research Reports, 8,* 73–79.

Ayres, J., & Ayres, T. A. (2003). Using images to enhance the impact of visualization. *Communication Reports, 16*(1), 47–55.

Ayres, J., & Hopf, T. S. (1985). Visualization: A means of reducing speech anxiety. *Communication Education, 34,* 318–323.

Ayres, J., & Hopf, T. S. (1989). Visualization: Is it more than extra attention? *Communication Education, 38,* 1–5.

Ayres, J., & Hopf, T. S. (1990, January).The long-term effect of visualization in the classroom: A brief research report. *Communication Education, 39,* 75–78.

Ayres, J., Heuett, B., & Sonandre, D. A. (1998). Testing a refinement in an intervention for communication apprehension. *Communication Reports, 11*(1), 73–85.

Ayres, J., Hopf, T. S., & Ayres, D. M. (1994). An examination of whether imaging ability enhances the effectiveness of an interview designed to reduce speech anxiety. *Communication Education, 43,* 252–258.

Ayres, J., Hopf, T. S., & Ayres, D. M. (1997). Visualization and performance visualization: Applications, evidence, and speculation. In J. Daly, J. C. McCroskey, J. Ayres, T. S. Hopf, and D. M. Ayres (Eds.), *Avoiding communication: Shyness, reticence, and communication apprehension* (2nd ed.) (pp. 401–422). Cresskill, NJ: Hampton.

Baird, R. N., Turnbull, A. T., & McDonald, D. (1987). *The graphics of communication* (5th ed.). New York: Holt, Rinehart & Winston.

Bajaj, G. (2004, March 26). An interview with Tad Simons. Presentations.com. Accessed January 11, 2008 from www.indezine.com/products/powerpoint/personality/tadsimons.html.

Ballard, B. (2003, June). Six ways to grab your audience right from the start. *Harvard Management Communication Letter*, 3–5.

Balz, D. (1997, September 7). Farewell to the "people's princess." Washington Post Foreign Service. Accessed July 10, 2007 from www.washingtonpost.com/wp-srv/inatl/longterm/diana/stories/funeral0906.htm.

Baram, M. (2007, April 11). CBS News fires producer, revamps procedures after plagiarism incident. ABC News. Accessed June 4, 2007, from abcnews.go.com/print?id=3031455.

Barker, J. (2006). Meta-Search Engines. UC Berkeley. Accessed August, 13, 2006 from www.lib.berkeley.edu/teachinglib/guides/internet/metasearch.html.

Barker, L. L., & Watson, K. H. (2000). *Listen up: How to improve relationships, reduce stress, and be more productive by using the power of listening*. New York: St. Martins.

Bartlett, T. (2006, April 3). Ohio U. says 37 former graduate students committed plagiarism and could face a range of penalties. *The Chronicle of Higher Education*. Accessed at chronicle.com.

Baskette, F. K., Sissors, J. Z., & Brooks, B. S. (1992). *The art of editing* (5th ed.). New York: Macmillan.

Bateman, T. S., & Snell, S. A. (2009). *Management*. Boston: McGraw-Hill.

Beatty, M. J. (1984). Physiological assessment. In J. A. Daly and J. C. McCroskey (Eds.), *Avoiding communication shyness, reticence and communication apprehension* (pp. 95–106). Beverly Hills, CA: Sage.

Beatty, M. J. (1988). Situational and predispositional correlates of public speaking anxiety. *Communication Education*, 37, 28–39.

Beatty, M. J., & McCroskey, J. C. (1998). Interpersonal communication as temperamental expression: A communibiological paradigm. In J. C. McCroskey, J. A. Daly, M. M. Martin, & M. J. Beatty (Eds.), *Communication and Personality: Trait perspectives* (pp. 41–67). Cresskill, NJ: Hampton Press, Inc.

Beatty, M. J., Balfantz, G. L., & Kuwabara, A. Y. (1989). Trait-like qualities of selected variables assumed to be transient causes of performance state anxiety. *Communication Education*, 38, 277–289.

Beck, K. H., & Lund, A. L. (1981). The effects of health seriousness and personal efficacy upon intentions and behavior. *Journal of Applied Social Psychology*, 11, 401–415.

Becze, E. (2007, April). Nonverbal communication can say a lot about you. *ONS Connect*, 22(4), 30.

Bedard, P. (2004, October 10). Big John goes for some GOP threads. *U.S. News & World Report*, 137(12), 6.

Behling, D. U., & Williams, E. A. (1991). Influence of dress on perceptions of intelligence and expectations of scholastic achievement. *Clothing and Textiles Research Journal*, 9(4), 1–7.

Behnke, R. R., & Sawyer, C. R. (1999). Milestones of anticipatory public speaking anxiety. *Communication Education*, 48(1), 165–172.

Bell, K. (1990). *Developing arguments: Strategies for reaching audiences*. Belmont, CA: Wadsworth.

Bem, S. L. (1981a). *Bem sex-role inventory: Professional manual*. Palo Alto, CA: Consulting Psychologists Press.

Bem, S. L. (1981b). Gender schema theory: A cognitive account of sex typing. *Psychological Review*, 88, 354–364.

Benoit, W. L., & Brinson, S. L. (1999). Queen Elizabeth's image repair discourse: Insensitive royal or compassionate queen? *Public Relations Review*, 25(2), 145–151.

Berkman, R. (2000, January 21). Searching for the right search engine. *Chronicle of Higher Education*, B6.

Berscheid, E. (1985). Interpersonal attraction. In G. Lindzey & E. Aronson (Eds.), *Handbook of social psychology* (3rd ed., Vol. 2, pp. 413–484). New York: Random House.

Bettinghaus, E. P., & Cody, M. J. (1997). *Persuasive communication* (5th ed.). New York: Holt, Rinehart & Winston.

Bhattacherjee, A., & Sanford, C. (2006, December). Influence processes for information technology acceptance: An elaboration likelihood model. *MIS Quarterly*, 30(4), 805–825.

Big spin = big losses. (2003, May). *Research*, 22.

Billington, A., & Whitaker, F. (2007, February 26). Post-Oscar: Forest Whitaker's brilliant acceptance speech. Firstshowing.net. Accessed July 23, 2007 at www.firstshowing.net/2007/02/26/forest-whitakers-acceptance-speech/.

Bippus, A. M., & Daly, J. A. (1999). What do people think causes stage fright? Naive attributions about the reasons for public speaking anxiety. *Communication Education*, 48, 63–72.

Blythin, E., & Samovar, L. A. (1985). *Communicating effectively on television*. Belmont, CA: Wadsworth.

Booth-Butterfield, M., & Booth-Butterfield, S. (1992). *Communication apprehension and avoidance in the classroom*. Edina, MN: Burgess.

Booth-Butterfield, S., & Gutowski, C. (1993, Winter). Message modality and source credibility can interact to affect argument processing. *Communication Quarterly*, 41, 77–79.

Booth-Butterfield, S., & Welbourne, J. (2002). The elaboration likelihood model: Its impact on persuasion theory and research. In J. P. Dillard & M. Pfau (Eds.), *The persuasion handbook: Developments in theory and practice* (pp. 155–173). Thousand Oaks, CA: Sage.

Borisoff, D., & Merrill, L. (1991). Gender issues and listening. In D. Borisoff & M. Purdy (Eds.), *Listening in everyday life: A personal and professional approach*, pp. 59–85. New York: University Press of America.

Boster, F. J., & Mongeau, P. (1984). Fear-arousing persuasive messages. In R.N. Bostrom (Ed.), *Communication yearbook* (pp. 330–375). Beverly Hills, CA: Sage.

Bostrom, R. N. (1988). *Communicating in public: Speaking and listening*. Santa Rosa, CA: Burges.

Bostrom, R. N., & Tucker, R. K. (1969, March). Evidence, personality, and attitude change. *Speech Monographs*, 36, 22–27.

Bourhis, J., & Allen, M. (1992). Meta-analysis of the relationship between communication apprehension and cognitive performance. *Communication Education*, 41, 68–76.

Bowen, E., & Montepare, O. M. (2007, April). Nonverbal behavior in a global context dialogue questions and responses [Electronic version]. *Journal of Nonverbal Behavior*, 31, 185–187.

Bradac, J. J., & Mulac, A. (1984). A molecular view of powerful and powerless speech styles: Attributional consequences of specific language features and communication intentions. *Communication Monographs*, 51, 307–319.

Brannon, K. (2010, April 12). Spanking can make children more aggressive later: Study. *PHYSORG.com*. Retrieved from http://www.physorg.com/news190321386.html.

Brash, P. W. (1992, November 15). Beyond giving a speech. *Vital Speeches*, 59, 83–84.

Brembeck, W. L., & Howell, W. S. (1976). *Persuasion: A means of social control*. Englewood Cliffs, NJ: Prentice Hall.

Brewer, G. (2001, March). Snakes top list of Americans' fears. Gallup News Service. Accessed June 23, 2004 at www.gallup.com/poll/1891/snakes-top-list-americans-fears.aspx.

Bristow, L. R. (1994, March 15). Protecting youth from the tobacco industry. *Vital Speeches*, 60, 333–336.

Brody, M. (2003). Team presentations: A winning combination. 3M Meeting Network. Accessed December 27, 2004, at 4hoteliers.com/4hots_fshw.php?mwi=931.

Brown, D. E. (1992). Using examples and analogies to remediate misconceptions in physics: Factors influencing conceptual change. *Journal of Research in Science Teaching*, 29, 17–34.

Brown, R. E. (2010). The convergence of public relations and public diplomacy: A digital drama. *Vital Speeches, 76(7), 297–298.*

Brownell, J. (2006). *Listening: Attitudes, principles, and skills* (3rd ed.). Boston: Allyn & Bacon.

Brownell, J. (2009). *Listening: Attitudes, principles, and skills* (4th ed.). Boston: Allyn & Bacon.

Brownell, J. (2010). The skills of listening-centered communication. In A. D. Wolvin (Ed.), *Listening and human communication in the 21st century* (pp. 141–157). Malden, MA: Wiley-Blackwell.

Bryden, M. P., & Ley, R. G. (1983). Right hemispheric involvement in imagery and affect. In E. Perecman (Ed.), *Cognitive processing in the right hemisphere* (pp. 116–117). New York: Academic.

Burgoon, J. K., & Hoobler, G. D. (2002). Nonverbal signals. In M. L. Knapp and J. A. Daly (Eds.), *Handbook of interpersonal communication* (3rd ed.) (pp. 240–299). Thousand Oaks, CA: Sage.

Burgoon, J. K., & Hoobler, G. D. (2002). Nonverbal signals. In M. L. Knapp and J. A. Daly (Eds.), *Handbook of Interpersonal Communication* (3rd ed.) (pp. 240–299), Thousand Oaks, CA: Sage.

Burley-Allen, M. (1982). *Listening: The forgotten skill*. New York: Wiley.

Bush, B. (1994). Commencement address at Wellesley College. In V. L. DeFrancisco and M. D. Jensen (Eds.), *Women's voices in our time: Statements by American leaders*. Prospect Heights, IL: Waveland.

Bush, G. H. W. (1992). Transcript of President Bush's radio address on his defeat at the polls. *The New York Times*, A26.

Bush, G. W. (2007, April 28). President Bush delivers commencement address at Miami Dade College. Whitehouse.gov. Accessed July 26, 2007, at www.whitehouse.gov/news/releases/2007/04/20070428-3.html.

Buss, A. H. (1980). *Self-consciousness and social anxiety*. San Francisco: Freeman.

Butterfield, F. (1990a, May 4). At Wellesley, a furor over Barbara Bush. *The New York Times*, A1, B6. Accessed at ProQuest Historical Newspapers *New York Times* (1851–2004) database.

Butterfield, F. (1990b, June 2). Family first, Mrs. Bush tells friend and foe at Wellesley. *The New York Times*, A1, A5. Accessed at ProQuest Historical Newspapers *New York Times* (1851–2004) database.

Bynum, C., Epps, H., & Kaya, N. (2006, December). Color memory of university students: Influence of color experience and color characteristic. *College Student Journal*, 40(4), 824–831.

CAIB: *Columbia* Accident Investigation Board, (2003, August). Report Volume 1. Washington, DC: Government Printing Office.

Campbell, K. K., & Huxman, S. S. (2008). *The rhetorical act* (4th ed.). Boston: Wadsworth Cengage Learning.

Carmack, H. J. (2009, January). Slam this: Understanding language choice and delivery in argument using slam poetry. *Communication Teacher, 23(1)*, pp. 19–22.

Carroll, D. (2009). United Airlines Song Background (detailed version). *Dave Carroll Music.com*. Retrieved from http://www.davecarrollmusic.com/story/united-breaks-guitars/

Carroll, J. (2007, June 4). Americans remain negative on state of nation's moral values. *The Gallup Poll Daily Briefing* magazine. Accessed June 9, 2007, from gallup.com.

Carr-Ruffino, N. (1985). *The promotable woman: Becoming a successful manager* (3rd ed.). Belmont, CA: Wadsworth.

Cathcart, S. (1955, August). An experimental study of the relative effectiveness of four methods of presenting evidence. *Speech Monographs*, 22, 227–233.

Chaiken, S. (1986). Physical appearance and social influence. In C. P. Herman, M. P. Zanna, & E. T. Higgins (Eds.), *Physical appearance, stigma, and social behavior: The Ontario symposium* (Vol. 3, pp. 143–177). Hillsdale, NJ: Erlbaum.

Chaiken, S., & Eagly, A. (1983). Communication modality as a determinant of persuasion: The role of communicator salience. *Journal of Personality and Social Psychology*, 45, 241–256.

Chao, E. L. (2007). Remarks. In Asian American Government Executives Network. Retrieved July 14, 2007, from Department of Labor website: www.dol.gov/_sec/media/speeches/20070712_agen.htm.

Christie, C. (2010, May). A new course, long overdue: Budget speech to the legislature of New Jersey. *Vital Speeches, 76(5)*, 222–229.

Cialdini, R. B. (1993). *Influence: The psychology of persuasion*. New York: Quill.

Cicero. (1959). *De Oratore*. E. W. Sutton (Trans.). Cambridge, MA: Harvard University Press.

Clanton, J. (1989, April 1). Plutonium 238: NASA's fuel of choice. *Vital Speeches*, 55, 375.

Coe, W. C., & Scharcoff, J. A. (1985, April). An empirical evaluation of the neurolinguistic programming model. *International Journal of Clinical and Experimental Hypnosis*, 33, 310–318.

Cohen, A. R. (1964). *Attitude change and social interaction*. New York: Basic.

Cohen, R. (1991). *Negotiating across cultures: Communication obstacles in international diplomacy*. Washington, DC: U.S. Institute of Peace.

Conditt, C. M. (2000). Culture and biology in human communication: Toward a multi-causal model. *Communication Education*, 49(1), 7–24.

Conley, T. M. (1990). *Rhetoric in the European tradition*. New York: Longman.

Conway, A. (1988). The interaction of color code type and information type on the perception and interpretation of visual displays. *Dissertation Abstracts International*, 48, 2123–2124.

Cooper, M. D., & Nothstine, W. L. (1992). *Power persuasion: Moving an ancient art into the media age.* Greenwood, IN: Educational Video Group.

Cowan, N. (2001). The magical number 4 in short-term memory: A reconsideration of mental storage capacity. *Behavioral and Brain Sciences*, 24, 87–114.

Crawford, A. F. (2003). *Barbara Jordan: Breaking the barriers.* Houston: Halcyon Press.

Crook, C. W., & Booth, R. (1997, January). Building rapport in electronic mail using accommodation theory. *Advanced Management Journal*, 62(1), 4–13.

Daly, J. A., & Friedrich, G. W. (1981). The development of communication apprehension: A retrospective analysis of contributory correlates. *Communication Quarterly*, 29, 243–255.

Daly, J. A., Vangelisti, A. L., & Weber, D. J. (1995). Speech anxiety affects how people prepare speeches: A protocol analysis of the preparation process of speakers. *Communication Education*, 62, 383–397.

Daly, J. A., Vangelisti, A. L., Neel, H. L., & Cavanaugh, P. D. (1989). Pre-performance concerns associated with public speaking anxiety. *Communication Quarterly*, 37, 39–53.

Damhorst, M., & Fiore, A. M. (2000). Women's job interview dress: How the personnel interviewers see it. In M. L. Damhorst, A. Miller, & S. O. Michelman (Eds.), *The meaning of dress* (pp. 92–97). New York: Fairchild.

Damhorst, M., & Reed, J. A. P. (1980). *Effects of clothing color on assessment of characteristics of job applicants.* Paper presented at the 71st annual meeting of the American Home Economics Association.

Damhorst, M., & Reed, J. A. P. (1986). Clothing, color value and facial expression: Effect on evaluations of female job applicants. *Social Behavior and Personality*, 14(1), 89–98.

Dance, A. (2007, July 6). Women no chattier than men. *Star–Telegram*, 8A.

Darling, A. L., & Dannels, D. P. (2003). Practicing engineers talk about the importance of talk: A report on the role of oral communication in the workplace. *Communication Education*, 52, 1–16.

Dauch, R. E. (2004, June 15). Detroit—in the cross hairs: The American auto industry. *Vital Speeches*, 70, 537–541.

De Dreu, C. K., & McCusker, C. (1997). Gain–loss frames and cooperation in two-person social dilemmas: Transformational analysis. *Journal of Personality and Social Psychology*, 72, 1093–1106.

Decker, B., & Denney, J. (1993), *You've got to be believed to be heard.* New York: St. Martin's.

Denman, M. (2005, Winter). How to create memorable lectures. *Speaking of Teaching*, 14(1), 1–5. Retrieved June 3, 2007 from http://ctl.stanford.edu/newsletter/memorable_lectures.pdf.

dePaola, T. (1985). What are little boys made of? *Mother goose.* New York: Putnam, 1985.

Detz, J. (2000). *It's not what you say, it's how you say it.* New York: St. Martin's.

Detz, J. (2002). *How to write and give a speech (2nd ed.).* New York: St. Martin's Press.

Detz,, J. (2006). *Can You Say a Few Words?* (2nd rev. ed.). New York: St. Martin's Press.

Detz, J. (2007, December). 12 tips to improve your next presentation. *Vital Speeches*, 73 (12), 540–542.

Detz, J. (2009, October). A thorough speech on brief speech-making: Mastering the three-minute speech. *Vital Speeches, 56(10)*, pp. 447–450.

Dewey, J. (1991). *How we think* (reprint of 1910 ed.). Buffalo: Prometheus.

Dickerson, J. (2009, January 17). The storyteller. *Slate.com.* Retrieved from http://www.slate.com/id/2208776/pagenum/2.

Dickerson, J. (2009, November 10). What he said: President Obama's small masterpiece of a speech at Fort Hood. *Slate.com.* Retrieved from http://www.slate.com/id/2235277.

Dillard, J. P., & Nabi, R. L. (2006, August). The persuasive influence of emotion in cancer prevention and detection messages. *Journal of Communication*, 56, 123–139.

Dillard, J. P., & Pfau, M. (2002). *The persuasion handbook: Developments in theory and practice.* Thousand Oaks, CA: Sage.

Dolliver, M. (2010, March 8). How people react to male vs. female voiceovers. *Adweek.com.* Accessed July 12, 2010, at http://www.adweek.com/aw/content_display/news/agency/e3ie0341f942810261f54e20d17078f7923.

Dow, B. J., & Tonn, M. B. (1993). 'Feminine style' and political judgments in the rhetoric of Ann Richards. *Quarterly Journal of Speech*, 79, 286–302.

Drake, A. (2005). Evaluating information found on the World Wide Web. Tarrant County College Library Workshop handout, Fort Worth, Texas.

Dresser, W. R. (1963, August). Effects of "satisfactory" and "unsatisfactory" evidence in a speech of advocacy. *Speech Monographs*, 30, 302–306.

Duff, D. C., Levine, T. R., Beatty, M. J., Woolbright, J. & Park, H. S. (2007). Testing public anxiety treatments against a credible placebo control. *Communication Education, 56(1)*, 72–88.

Dulek, R. E., Fielden, J. S., & and Hill, J. S. (1991, January/February). International communication: An executive primer. *Business Horizons*, 22.

Eagly, A. H., & Chaiken, S. (1993). *The psychology of attitudes.* Fort Worth, TX: Harcourt Brace Jovanovich.

Eckert, S. (2006). *Intercultural communication.* Mason, OH: South-Western.

Egodigwe, L. (2003). Here come the suits: Raising the style standard in the office. *Black Enterprise*, 33(8), 59.

Eigen, L. D., & Siegel, J. P. (1993). *The Macmillan dictionary of political quotations.* New York: Macmillan.

Ekman, P. (1992). Are there basic emotions? *Psychological Review*, 99(3), 550–554.

Elder, L., & Paul, R. (2003a). Why the analysis of thinking is important. In *A miniature guide for students and faculty to the foundations of analytic thinking: How to take thinking apart and what to look for when you do: The elements of thinking and the standards they must meet* (pp. 1–3) [Brochure]. Dillon Beach, CA: Foundation for Critical Thinking.

Elder, L., & Paul, R. (2003b). *The miniature guide to critical thinking: Concepts and tools.* Dillon Beach, CA: Foundation for Critical Thinking.

Ellard, G. (2007, March 27). I know it when I see it: Moral judgments and business ethics. *Vital Speeches*, 73(5), 193–196.

Ellis, A. (2004). *Rational emotive behavior therapy: It works for me—it can work for you.* Amherst, New York: Prometheus Books.

Elsea, J. E. (1985). Strategies for effective presentations. *Personnel Journal*, 64, 31–33.

Emmert, P., Emmert, V., & Brandt, J. (1993). An analysis of male-female differences on the listening practices feedback report. *Journal of the International Listening Association*, special issue, 43–55.

Epson America (2003). Rules for team presentations, basics: Delivery. Epson Presenters Online. Accessed February 10, 2003, at www.presentersonline.com/basics/delivery/rulesforteam.shtml.

Evans, D. L., Beakley, G. C., Crouch, P. E., & Yamaguchi, G. T. (1993). Attributes of engineering graduates and their impact on curriculum design. *Journal of Engineering Education*, 82, 203–211.

Everett, E. (1863, November 20). Letter from Edward Everett to Abraham Lincoln. The Abraham Lincoln Papers at the Library of Congress. Accessed February 8, 2008 at memory.loc.gov/cgi-bin/query/r?ammem/mal:@field(docid+@lit(d2813300)).

Facione, P. A., & Facione, N. C. (2007, March/April). Talking critical thinking. *Change*, 39–44.

February 2004 web server survey. (2004). Accessed February 3, 2004 at news.netcraft.com/archives/web_server_survey.html.

Festinger, L. (1957). *A theory of cognitive dissonance.* Stanford, CA: Stanford University Press.

Fishbein, M., & Ajzen, I. (1975). *Belief, attitude, intention and behavior: An introduction to theory and research.* Reading, MA: -Addison-Wesley.

Fisher, A. & Scriven, M. (1997). *Critical thinking: Its definition and assessment.* Point Reyes, CA: Edgepress.

Fisher, W. R. (1987). *Human communication as narration: Toward a philosophy of reason, value, and action.* Columbia: University of South Carolina Press.

Fisher, W. R. (1987). *Human communication as narration: Toward a philosophy of reason, value, and action.* Columbia, SC: University of South Carolina Press.

Fitzpatrick, K. R. (2004, April 15). U.S. public diplomacy: Telling America's story. *Vital Speeches*, 70(13), 412–416.

Flink, H. (2007). Tell it like it is: Essential communication skills for engineers. *Industrial Engineer*, 39(3), 44–48.

Foss, K. A. (1983). John Lennon and the advisory function of eulogies. *Central States speech Journal, 34*, 187–194.

Freeth, A. (2010, July). Big enough to succeed: A fierce argument for big business. *Vital Speeches, 76(7)*, 290–293.

Friedman, R. A., & Currall, S. C. (2003). Conflict escalation: Dispute exacerbating elements of e-mail communication. *Human Relations, 56(11)*, 1325–1347.

Fripp, P. (2007). Speak to be remembered and repeated. Fripp.com. Accessed October 6, 2007 at www.fripp.com/beremembered.html.

Gallo, C. (2006, May 22). Terminate your public speaking fears. *Business Week Online*. Accessed from EBSCO Publishing.

Gallo, C. (2007, July 6). Steve Jobs' Greatest Presentation. *Business Week Online*. Accessed at: www.businessweek.com/smallbiz/content/jul2007/sb2007076_474371.htm?chan=search.

Gallo, C. (2010). *The presentation secrets of Steve Jobs: How to be insanely great in front of any audience.* New York: McGraw-Hill.

Gandy, D. (2007, July). The secret to becoming very wealthy. *Vital Speeches*, 73(7), 305–306.

Gardano, A. C. (1986, May). Cultural influence on emotional response to color: A research study comparing Hispanics and non-Hispanics. *American Journal of Art Therapy*, 24, 119–124.

Gass, R. H., & Seiter, J. S. (1999). *Persuasion, social influence, and compliance gaining.* Boston: Allyn & Bacon.

Gass, R. H., & Seiter, J. S. (2007). Persuasion, social influence, and compliance gaining (3rd ed.). Boston: Allyn & Bacon.

Gates, B., & Bach, R. (2007, January 7). Transcript of keynote remarks by Bill Gates, chairman, and Robbie Bach, president, entertainment & devices division. In *Press-Pass Information for Journalists*. Accessed July 23, 2007, at www.microsoft.com/presspass/exec/billg/speeches/2007/01-07ces.mspx.

Geddes, D. (1992). Sex roles in management: The impact of varying power of speech style on union members' perception of satisfaction and effectiveness. *Journal of Psychology Interdisciplinary and Applied*, 126, 589–608.

Gibbons, P., Busch, J., & Bradac, J. J. (1991). Powerful versus powerless language: Consequences for persuasion, impression formation, and cognitive response. *Journal of Language and Social Psychology* 10, 115–133.

Gibson, J. (2006, December). The breakfast of champions: Teaching audience analysis using cereal boxes. *TSJC Online* (Online journal of the Texas Speech Communication Association). Accessed July 14, 2007 from www.etsca.com/tscjonline/1206-cereal/.

Ginossar, Z., & Trope, Y. (1980). The effects of base-rates and individuating information on judgments about another person. *Journal of Experimental Social Psychology*, 16, 228–242.

Gioia, D. (1992). Pinto fires and personal ethics: A script analysis of missed opportunities. *Journal of Business Ethics*, 11 (5–6), 379–389.

Giuliano, C. P. (2004, Summer). What made Ronald Reagan "the great communicator." *The Public Relations Strategist*, 46–47.

Gladwell, M. (2002). *The tipping point: How little things can make a big difference.* New York: Little, Brown & Co.

Goodall, J. (2003, November 15). Dangers to the environment: The challenge lies in all of us. *Vital Speeches*, 70, 71–78.

Goodwin, L. V. (2007, April 18). Public speaking—One key strategy to overcome fear. Ezinearticles.com. Accessed from ezinearticles.com/?expert-la_velle_goodwin.

Gordon, J. (2006) *Presentations that change minds: Strategies to persuade, convince, and get results.* New York: McGraw-Hill.

Goss, B. (1982). Listening as information processing. *Communication Quarterly*, 30, 306.

Gov.ca.gov (2005). Governor Schwarzenegger embarks on trade mission to China. Accessed Nov. 13, 2005 at gov.ca.gov/index.php?/press-release/1215/.

Grace, J. P. (1993, July 1). Burning money: The waste of your tax dollars. *Vital Speeches*, 59, 566.

Greaney, T. M. (1997). Five keys to a successful media interview. *Communication World*, 14 (5), 35–38.

Green, M. C. (2006, August). Narratives and cancer communication. *Journal of Communication*, 56, 163–183.

Greenleaf, C. T. (1998). *Attention to detail: A gentleman's guide to professional appearance and conduct.* New York: Mass Market Press.

Griffin, E. (1994). *A first look at communication theory.* New York: McGraw-Hill.

Gronbeck, B. E., German, K., Ehninger, D., & Monroe, A. H. (1999). *Principles of speech communication: Brief* (13 ed.). Reading, MA: Addison-Wesley.

Gronbeck, B. E., McKerrow, R. E., Ehninger, D., & Monroe, A. H. (1994). *Principles and types of speech communication* (12th ed.). New York: HarperCollins College.

Gruner, C. R. (1985). Advice to the beginning speaker on using humor: What research tells us. *Communication Education, 34,* 142–147.

Guerrero, L., Jones, S., & Boburka, R. (2006). Sex differences in emotional communication. In K. Dindia & D. J. Canary (Eds.), *Sex differences and similarities in communication* (pp. 242–261). Mahweh, NJ: Erlbaum.

Guffey, M. E. (2010). Business communication: Process and product (6th ed.). Boston: Wadsworth Cengage Learning.

Gurak, L. J. (1997). *Persuasion and privacy in cyberspace: The online protests over Lotus Marketplace and the Clipper Chip.* New Haven, CT: Yale University Press.

Hackman, M. Z. (1988, Winter). The reactions to the use of self-disparaging humor by informative public speakers. *Southern Speech Communication Journal, 53,* 175–183.

hairybeast. (2007, April 11). Katie Couric and incidental plagiarism. Accessed June 4, 2007 from hairybeast.wordpress.com/2007/04/11/katie-couric-and-incedental-plagiarism/.

Hall, E. T. (1976). *Beyond culture.* Garden City, NY: Doubleday.

Hall, E. T. (1992). *The hidden dimension* (reprint ed.). Gloucester, MA: Peter Smith, 1992.

Hall, E. T., & Hall, M. R. (1990). *Understanding cultural differences: Germans, French and Americans.* Yarmouth, ME: Intercultural Press.

Hall, J. L., Householder, B. J., & Greene, K. L. (2002). The theory of reasoned action. In J. P. Dillard and M. Pfau (Eds.), *The persuasion handbook: Developments in theory and practice* (pp. 259–286). Thousand Oaks, CA: Sage.

Hamilton, C. (1999). The effect of quality and color visual aids on immediate recall, attitude toward speaker, and attitude toward speech. Unpublished dissertation, University of North Texas, Denton, TX.

Hamilton, C. (2008). *Communicating for Results* (8th ed.). Belmont, CA: Thomson Wadsworth.

Hamilton, C. (2011). *Communicating for Results* (9th ed.). Boston, MA: Wadsworth Cengage Learning.

Hamilton, D. (2000, March). Prepare and practice. *Officepro, 14.*

Hamilton, L. C. (1988). Using masculine generics: Does generic "he" increase male bias in the user's imagery? *Sex Roles, 19,* 785–799.

Hankin, J. N. (2002, June 1). Make a difference, have no regrets. *Vital Speeches, 68,* 506–508.

Hankin, J. N. (2003, December 1). Two-year colleges: Changes and trends in faculty, students, and missions. *Vital Speeches, 70*(4), 121–128.

Hansen, D. D. (2003). *The dream: Martin Luther King Jr. and the speech that inspired a nation.* New York: Ecco.

Hansen, M. V., & Allen, R. G. (2002). *The one minute millionaire: The enlightened way to wealth.* New York: Harmony Books.

Harris, T. E. (1993). *Applied organizational communication: Perspectives, principles, and pragmatics.* Hillsdale, NJ: Erlbaum.

Harris, W. H. (1993, June 15). Power, parity, personal responsibility, and progress: The agenda for African Americans in the 1990s. *Vital Speeches, 59,* 536.

Hart, R. P. (1997). *Modern rhetorical criticism* (2nd ed.). Boston: Allyn & Bacon.

Haseley, K. A. (2004, February 1). Dealing with public anger: New approaches to an old problem. *Vital Speeches, 70,* 242–244.

Hass, R. G., & Linder, D. E. (1972). Counterargument availability and the effects of message structure on persuasion. *Journal of Personality and Social Psychology, 23,* 227.

Hauser, M. H., & Hughes, M. A. (1988). Defining the cognitive process of listening: A dream or reality? *Journal of the International Listening Association, 2,* 75–88.

Heath, D. (1991). *Fulfilling lives: Paths to maturity and success.* San Francisco: Jossey-Bass.

Heider, F. (1958). *The psychology of interpersonal relations.* New York: Wiley.

Hensley, C. W. (1992, December 1). What you share is what you get: Tips for effective communication. *Vital Speeches, 59,* 117.

Herrick, J. A. (1995). *Argumentation: Understanding and shaping arguments.* Scottsdale, AZ: Gorsuch Scarisbrick.

Hishitani, S. (1991). Vividness of image and retrieval time. *Perception and Motor Skills, 73,* 115–123.

Hofstede, G. & Hofstede, G. J. (2005). *Cultures and organizations: Software of the mind,* revised and expanded 2nd ed. New York: McGraw-Hill (pp. 78–79).

Hofstede, G. (2001). *Culture's consequences: Comparing values, behaviors, institutions, and organizations across nations* (2nd ed.). Thousand Oaks, CA: Sage.

Holcombe, M. W., & Stein, J. K. (1996). *Presentations for decision makers* (3rd ed.). New York: Van Nostrand Reinhold.

Holm, J. H. (1981). *Business and professional communication.* Boston: American Press.

Holschuh, J. P., & Nist, S. L. (2007). *Effective college learning.* -Boston: Pearson Education.

Hosman, L. H. (2002). Language and persuasion. In J. P. Dillard & M. Pfau (Eds.), *The persuasion handbook: Developments in theory and practice* (pp. 233–258). Thousand Oaks, CA: Sage.

House, A., & Dallinger, J. M. (1998). Androgyny and rhetorical sensitivity: The connection of gender and communicator style. *Communication Reports, 11,* 11–20.

Houston, J. (1997). *The possible human: A course in enhancing your physical, mental, and creative abilities* (reprint ed.). Los Angeles: Tarcher.

Hovell, B., & Barrett, K. (2009, February 4). Madoff whistle-blower slams SEC. *ABC News.* Retrieved from http://abcnews.go.com/Politics/story?id=6802350&page=1.

Hovland, C. I., Lumsdaine, A. A., & Sheffield, F. D. (1967). The effects of presenting "one-side" vs. "both sides" in changing opinions on a controversial subject. In R. L. Rosnow & E. J. Robinson (Eds.), *Experiments in persuasion* (pp. 201–225). New York: Academic.

Howard, C. M. (2002). Polishing your spokesperson skills for news media interviews. *Public Relations Quarterly, 47*(4), 18–20.

Hsu, C. (2004, Fall). Sources of differences in communication apprehension between Chinese in Taiwan and Americans. *Communication Quarterly, 52,* 370–390.

Huang, L., & Pashler, H. (2007). A Boolean map theory of visual attention. *Psychological Review, 114*(3), 599–631.

Humphrey, J. (2001, May 1). Taking the stage: How women can achieve a leadership presence. *Vital Speeches, 67*, 437.

Igou, E. R., & Bless, H. (2007, September). Conversational expectations as a basis for order effects in persuasion. *Journal of Language and Social Psychology, 26*(3), 260–273.

Imhof, M. (1998). What makes a good listener? Listening behavior in instructional settings. *International Journal of Listening, 12*, 81–105.

Inch, E. S., Warnick, B., & Endres, D. (2006). Evidence: The foundation for arguments. In *Critical thinking and communication: The use of reason in argument* (5th ed., pp. 129–161). Boston: Allyn and Bacon. (Original work published 1989.)

Isaac, A. R., & Marks, D. F. (1994, November). Individual differences in mental imagery experience: Developmental changes and specialization. *British Journal of Psychology, 85*, 479–497.

Ivie, Tonya. (2007). Personal conversation with author.

Ivy, D. K., & Backlund, P. (2004). *Exploring GenderSpeak: Personal effectiveness in gender communication* (3rd. ed). New York: McGraw-Hill.

Ivy, D. K., Bullis-Moore, L., Norvell, K., Backlund, P., & Javidi, M. (1993). *The lawyer, the babysitter, and the student: Non-sexist language usage and instruction.* Paper presented at the annual meeting of the Western States Communication Association, Albuquerque, NM.

Ivy, D. L., & Backlund, P. (2008). *Gender speak: Personal effectiveness in gender communication* (4th ed.). Boston: Pearson Allyn Bacon.

Jackson, C. V. (2009, July 9). Passenger uses YouTube to get United's attention. *Chicago Sun-Times.com.* Retrieved from http://www.suntimes.com/technology/1658990,CST-NWSunited09. Article.

Jackson, J. L. (2000). The rainbow coalition. In R. L. Johannesen, R. R. Allen, W. A. Linkugel, and F. J. Bryan, *Contemporary American Speeches* (9th ed., pp. 271–279). Dubuque, IA: Kendall/Hunt.

Jacobi, J. (2000). *How to say it with your voice* (Pap/Com ed.). New York: Prentice Hall.

Jaffe, G. (2000, April 26). What's your point, Lieutenant? Just cut to the pie charts—the Pentagon declares war on electronic slide shows that make briefings a pain. *The Wall Street Journal*, p. A1.

Jamieson, K. H., & Campabell. K. K. (1982). Rhetorical hybrids: Fusions of generic elements. *Quarterly Journal of Speech, 68*, 146–157.

Janusik, L., & Wolvin, A. (2007). *24 hours in a day: A communication time study update.* Paper presented at the annual meeting of the National Communication Association, Chicago, IL.

Javed, N. (1993). *Naming for power.* New York: Linkbridge.

Job Outlook 2010. (2009, November). How employers view candidates (p. 21–24). *National Association of Colleges and Employees.* Retrieved from http://www.naceweb.org

Johannesen, R. L, Allen, R. R., Linkugel, W. A., & Bryan, F. J. (2000). *Contemporary American Speeches* (9th ed.). Dubuque, IA: Kendall/Hunt.

John Kennedy. Whitehouse.gov. Accessed on October 14, 2007 at www.whitehouse.gov/history/presidents/jk35.html.

Johnson, D. D. (1995). Color adaptation for color deficient learners. *Visual Arts Research, 21*, 26–41.

Johnson, V. (1990, February). Picture perfect presentations. *Toastmaster*, 7.

Jones, J. M. (2007, December 4). Effects of year's scandals evident in honesty and ethics ratings. The Gallup Poll Tuesday Briefing Online. Accessed January 3, 2008 from gallup.com.

Jones, J. M. (2010, May 17). Americans' outlook for U.S. morality remains bleak. *The Gallup Poll Daily Briefing* magazine. Accessed July 12, 2010, from gallup.com at http://www.gallup.com/poll/128042/Americans-Outlook-Morality-Remains-Bleak.aspx.

Jones, W. T. (1970). *The classical mind: A history of Western philosophy* (2nd ed.). New York: Harcourt Brace Jovanovich.

Jordan, B. C. (1992). Democratic convention keynote address. In H. R. Ryan (Ed.), *Contemporary American Public Discourse* (3rd ed., p. 274). Prospect Heights, IL: Waveland.

Jordan, B. C. (2010). Change: From What to What? In P. A. Lawler (Ed.), *American political rhetoric* (pp. 279–280). Lanham, MD: Rowman & Littlefield.

Jowett, G. S., & O'Donnell, V. (2006). *Propaganda and Persuasion* (4th ed.). Thousand Oaks, CA: Sage.

July 2010 Web Server Survey. (2010, July 16). *Netcraft.com.* Retrieved July 29, 2010 from http://news.netcraft.com/archives/2010/07/16/july-2010-web-server-survey-16.html.

Kahane, H., & Cavender, N. (2002). *Logic and contemporary rhetoric: The use of reason in everyday life* (9th ed.). Belmont, CA: Wadsworth.

Kamins, M. A., & Marks, L. J. (1987). Advertising puffery: The impact of using two-sided claims on product attitude and purchase intention. *Journal of Advertising, 16*, 6–15.

Kazoleas, D. C. (1993, Winter). A comparison of the persuasive effectiveness of qualitative versus quantitative evidence: A test of explanatory hypotheses. *Communication Quarterly, 41*, 40–50.

Kelly, L., & Keaten, J. A. (2000). Treating communication anxiety: Implications of the communibiological paradigm. *Communication Education, 49*, 45–57.

Kelly, Michael (1992). AIDS speech brings hush to crowd. *The New York Times* online, August 20, 1992. query.nytimes.com/gst/fullpage .html?res=9e0cefdf153df933a1575bc0a964958260&sec=&spon=.

Kelsey, D. M., Kearney, P., Plax, T. G., Allen, T. H., & Ritter, K. J. (2004). College students' attributions of teacher misbehaviors. *Communication Education, 53*(1), 40–55.

Kennedy, J. F. (2000). Inaugural address: John F. Kennedy. In R. L. Johannesen, R. R. Allen, W. A. Linkugel, & F. J. Bryan (Eds.), *Contemporary American speeches* (9th ed., pp. 249–252). Dubuque, IA: Kendall/Hunt.

Kiehnle, M. (2007, February 10.). Informative speech by Maria Kiehnle. Youtube.com. Accessed July 26, 2007, at www.youtube.com/watch?v=koe4ta00vzc&v2.

Kiel, P. (2008, December 18). The world's largest hedge fund is a fraud. *ProPublica.com.* Retrieved from http://www.propublifa.org/article/the-worlds-largest-hedge-fund-is-a-fraud-1219.

Kinde, J. (2006). Why spontaneous humor is powerful. John Kinde's HumorPower.com. Accessed October 6, 2007 at humorpower.com/art-whysponthumor.html.

King, M. L., Jr. (2000). I have a dream. In R. L. Johannesen, R. R. Allen, W. A. Linkugel, & F. J. Bryan (Eds.), *Contemporary American speeches* (9th ed., pp. 258–262). Dubuque, IA: Kendall/Hunt.

Knapp, M. L., & Hall, J. A. (2002). *Nonverbal communication in business interaction* (5th ed). Belmont, CA: Wadsworth.

Koballa, T. R., Jr. (1989). Persuading teachers to reexamine the innovative elementary science programs of yesterday: The effect of anecdotal versus data-summary communications. *Journal of Research in Science Teaching*, 23, 437–449.

Kosslyn, S. M., & Rosenberg, R. S. (2006). *Psychology in context* (3rd ed.). Boston: Allyn and Bacon.

Kosslyn, S. M., & Rosenberg, R. S. (2009). *Psychology in context* (4th ed.). Boston: Allyn & Bacon.

Kosslyn, S. M., Pascula-Leone, A., Felician, O., Camposano, S., Keenan, J. P., Thompson, W. L., Ganis, G., Sukel, K. E., & Alpert, N. M. (1999). The role of area 17 in visual imagery: Convergent evidence from PET and rTMS. *Science*, 284, 167–170.

Lamb, C. W., Hair, J. F., & McDaniel, C. (2004). *Marketing*. Mason, OH: South-Western.

Lamm, R. D. (1993, July 1). New world of medical ethics. *Vital Speeches*, 59, 549–550.

LaRose, R., & Whitten, P. (2000). Re-thinking instructional immediacy for Web courses: A social cognitive exploration. *Communication Education*, 49(4), 320–338.

Larson, C. U. (2006). *Persuasion: Reception and responsibility* (11th ed.). Belmont, CA: Wadsworth.

Larson, C. U. (2010). *Persuasion: Reception and responsibility* (12th ed.). Boston: Wadsworth Cengage Learning.

Leaper, N. (1999). How communicators lead at the best global companies. *Communication World*, 16, 33–36.

Leech, T. (1992). *How to prepare, stage, and deliver winning presentations* (2nd ed.). New York: AMACOM.

Lefton, R. E., Buzzotta, V. R., Sherberg, M. (1991). *Effective motivation through performance appraisal: Dimensional appraisal strategies* (new ed.). New York: Psychologica Association, Inc.

Lehman, C. M, & DuFrene, D. D. (2005). *Business communication* (14th ed.). Mason, OH: South-Western.

Lehman, C. M, & DuFrene, D. D. (2008). *Business Communication* (15th ed.). Mason, OH: South-Western.

Lincoln, A. (1983). Gettysburg address. In P. B. Kunhardt, Jr., *A new birth of freedom* (p. 240). Boston: Little, Brown.

Lipsman, A. (2009, May 12). Twitter.com quadruples to 17 million U.S. visitors in last two months. *ComScore.com*. Retrieved from http://blog.comscore.com/2009/05/twitter_traffic_quadruples.html.

Littlejohn, S. W., & Foss, K. A. (2008). *Theories of human communication* (9th ed). Belmont, CA: Thomson Wadsworth.

Loomis, C. J. (2010, July 5). The $600 billion challenge. *Fortune*, 162(1), 82–92.

Lucas, S., & Medhurst, M. (1999, December 15). 'I have a dream' leads top 100 speeches of the century. University of Wisconsin news release. Accessed at www.news.wisc.edu/releases/3504.html.

Lundeen, S. W. (1993). Metacognitive listening. In A. D. Wolvin and C. G. Coakley (Eds.). *Perspective on listening*. Norwood, NJ: Ablex.

Ma, J. (2009). Change can be good: Don't be scared to do something different. *Vital Speeches, 75(6)*, 256–257.

Maddux, J. E., & Rogers, R. W. (1983). Protection motivation and self-efficacy: A revised theory of fear appeals and attitude change. *Journal of Experimental Social Psychology*, 19, 469–479.

Maltz, M. (1960). *Psycho-cybernetics*. New York: Prentice Hall.

Managing for Results, pdf. (2007). In *The budget for fiscal year 2007* (27–37). United States Government. Accessed November 28, 2007 from origin.www.gpoaccess.gov/usbudget/fy07/pdf/budget/ results/pdf (to access, go to www.gpoaccess.gov/usbudget/fy07 and click on "Browse the FY07 budget" and then on "Managing For Results" (228K.pdf)).

Maney, K. (1999, May 12). Armed with PowerPoint, speakers make pests of themselves. *USA Today*, p. 3B.

Manzo, K. K. (2004, June 16). N.C. School Board chairman resigns over plagiarism. *Education Week*, 23(40), 4.

Marcus, A. (1982). Color: A tool for computer graphics communication. In D. Greenberg, A. Schmidt, and V. Garter (Eds.), *The computer image: Application of computer graphics*. Reading, MA: Addison-Wesley.

Markopolos, H. (2005, November 27). The world's largest hedge fund is a fraud. Retrieved from http://online.wsj.com/documents/Madoff_SECdocs_20081217.pdf.

Markopolos, H. (2010). *No one would listen: A true financial thriller*. Hoboken, NJ: Wiley.

Marks, D. F. (1999). Consciousness, mental imagery and action. *British Journal of Psychology*, 90, 567–585.

Marshall, L. B. (2010, April 15). What to say when introducing a speaker (Episode 87). The Public speaker Quick and dirty tips.com. Accessed from http://publicspeaker.quickanddirtytips.com/What-To-Say-When-Introducing-Speaker.aspx.

Martin, D. M. (2004). Balancing on the political high wire: The role of humor in the rhetoric of Ann Richards. *Southern Communication Journal*, 69(4), 273–288.

Mary Fisher named UNAIDS Special Representative (2006). UN News Centre online. May 18, 2003. www.un.org/apps/news/story.asp?newsid=18528&cr=hiv/aids&cr1=.

Masip, J., Garrido, E., & Herrero, C. (2004). Facial appearance and impression of credibility: The effects of facial babyishness and age on person perception. *International Journal of Psychology*, 39(4), 272–289.

Maslow, A. H. (1954). *Motivation and personality*. New York: Harper & Brothers.

Maslow, A. H. (1973). A theory of human motivation. In R. J. Lowry (Ed.), *Dominance, self-esteem, self-actualization: Germinal papers of A. H. Maslow* (pp. 153–173). Monterey, CA: Brooks/Cole.

Mason, S. (2007). Gender gap in technology. *Vital Speeches*, 73(4), 159–163.

Mathas, T. (2010, January). Leaving Las Vegas: Why we must help Americans stop gambling on their financial futures. *Vital speeches, 76(1),* 36–39.

Mayer, R. E. (2001). *Multimedia learning*. New York: Cambridge University Press.

Mayer, R. E., & Anderson, R. B. (1992). The instructive animation: Helping students build connections between words and pictures in multimedia learning. *Journal of Educational Psychology*, 76, 1089–1105.

Maysonave, S. (1999). *Casual power: How to power up your nonverbal communication and dress down for success*. Austin, TX: Bright Books.

Mayer, R. E. (2009). *Multimedia learning* (2nd ed.). New York: Cambridge University Press.

Mazer, J. P., Murphy, R. E., & Simonds, C. H. (2007). I'll see you on "Facebook": The effects of computer-mediated teacher self-disclosure on student motivation, affective learning, and classroom climate. *Communication Education*, 56(1), 1–17.

McCroskey, J. C. (1967). The effects of evidence in persuasive communication. *Western Speech*, 3, 189–199.

McCroskey, J. C. (1970, August). The effects of evidence as an inhibitor of counter-persuasion. *Speech Monographs*, 37, 188–194.

McCroskey, J. C. (1972). The implementation of a large-scale program of systematic desensitization for communication apprehension. *Speech Teacher*, 21, 255–264.

McCroskey, J. C. (1982). Oral communication apprehension: A reconceptualization. In M. Burgoon (Ed.), *Communication yearbook 6*. Beverly Hills, CA: Sage.

McCroskey, J. C., & Beatty, M. J. (2000). The communibiological perspective: Implications for communication instruction. *Communication Education*, 49, 1–6.

McCroskey, J. C., & Mehrley, R. S. (1969). The effects of disorganization and nonfluency on attitude change and source credibility. *Speech Monograph*, 36, 13–21.

McCroskey, J. C., & Teven, J. (1999). Goodwill: A reexamination of the construct and its measurement. *Communication Monographs*, 66, 90–103.

McCroskey, J. C., & Young, T. J. (1981). Ethos and credibility: The construct and its measurement after three decades. *Central States Speech Journal*, 32, 24–34.

McCroskey, J. C., Fayer, J. M., & Richmond, V. P. (1985). Don't speak to me in English: Communication apprehension in Puerto Rico. *Communication Quarterly*, 33(3), 185–192.

McDonald, K. P. (2004). *Cheers! 1,024 toasts and sentiments for every occasion*. New York: Black Dog & Leventhal Publishers.

McGarvey, R. (1990, January/February). Rehearsing for success: Tap the power of the mind through visualization. *Executive Female*, 35.

McGee, Jennifer (2003). A pilgrim's progress: Metaphor in the rhetoric of Mary Fisher. *Women's Studies in Communication*, 26(2), 191–213. ProQuest database.

McGonigal, M. J. (2005, September 1). Dreaming Mahalia. *Emusic* magazine. Accessed October 16, 2007 at www.emusic.com/features/spotlight/290_200509.html.

McGuire, W. J. (1985). Attitudes and attitude change. In G. Lindzey and E. Aronson (Eds.), *Handbook of social psychology*, Vol. 2 (3rd ed., pp. 287–288). New York: Random House.

McLean, J. (2009, October 19). State of the blogosphere 2009 introduction. *Technorati.com*. Retrieved from http://technorati.com/blogging/article/state-of-the-blogosphere-2009-introduction.

McNerney, J. (2006, March). Secrets of high-performing executive teams: Fundamentals of leadership. *Vital Speeches*, 72(11), 349–352.

Meichenbaum, D. (1985). *Stress inoculation training*. New York: Pergamon.

Meyer, J. (2000). Humor as a double-edged sword: Four functions of humor in communication. *Communication Theory*, 10(3), 310–331.

Miller, G. A. (1956). The magical number seven, plus or minus two: Some limits on our capacity for processing information. *Psychological Review*, 63, 81–97.

Minnich, J. (2006, October 16). "I have a dream" top American speech of 20th century. *Rotary News*, 16.

Mister, S. M. (1986). Reagan's challenger tribute: Combining generic constraints and situational demands. *Central States speech Journal*, 37, 158–165.

Molloy, J. T. (1988). *New dress for success*. New York: Warner.

Molloy, J. T. (1996). *The new woman's dress for success book*. New York: Warner.

Morley, D. D. (1987, June). Subjective message constructs: A theory of persuasion. *Communication Monographs*, 54, 183–203.

Morley, D. D., & Walker, K. B. (1987). The role of importance, novelty, and plausibility in producing belief change. *Communication Monographs*, 54, 436–442.

Morris, D. (1994). *Body talk: The meaning of human gestures*. New York: Crown.

Mossberg, W. S. (2005, April 5). Product reviews: Vertical search sites promising. *Tucson Citizen*. Retrieved from http://www.tucsoncitizen.com/news/business/040605d1_vertical.

Motley, M. (1995). *Overcoming your fear of public speaking: A proven method*. New York: McGraw-Hill.

Mullane, M. (2007). *Riding rockets: The outrageous tales of a space shuttle astronaut*. New York: Scribner.

Munter, M. (1993, May/June). Cross-cultural communication for managers. *Business Horizons*, 36, 69.

Murrell, T. (2005). Public speaking tips: Lessons from former U.S. President Ronald Reagan. Ezinearticles.com. Accessed at ezinearticles.com/?public-speaking-tips:-lessons-from-former-us-president-ronald-reagan&id=42061.

Nelson, M. C. (2004, March 15). On the path: Business's unfinished journey to diversity. *Vital Speeches*, 70, 336–339.

Nevid, J. S. (2006). In pursuit of the "perfect lecture." *APS Observer*, 19(2). Accessed July 3, 2007 from www.psychologicalscience.org/observer/archive/index.cfm?issue=140.

New York Times. (1980, July 15). As reported in *Current biography yearbook*, 1987, p. 259.

Nichols, M. (1996). *The lost art of listening: How learning to listen can improve relationships*. New York: Guilford.

Nickerson, R. S. (1980). Short-term memory for complex meaningful visual configurations: Demonstration of capacity. *Canadian Journal of Psychology*, 19, 155–160.

Noonan, P. (1998). *On speaking well: How to give a speech with style, substance, and clarity*. New York: Regan Books.

Nooyi, I. (2010, June). Short-term demands vs. long-term responsibilities: One corporate CEO's search for balance. *Vital Speeches*, 76(6), 246–250.

O'Hayre, J. (1966). *Gobbledygook has gotta go*. U.S. Department of the Interior, Bureau of Land Management. Washington, DC: Government Printing Office.

O'Keefe, D. J. (1990). *Persuasion: Theory and research*. Newbury Park, CA: Sage.

O'Keefe, D. J. (1997, Summer). Standpoint explicitness and persuasive effect: A meta-analytic review of the effects of varying conclusion articulation in persuasive messages. *Argumentation and Advocacy*, 54–60.

O'Keefe, D. J. (1998). Justification explicitness and persuasive effects: A meta-analysis review of the effects of varying support articulation in persuasive messages. *Argumentation and Advocacy*, 35, 61–75.

Obama, B. (2007, February 10). Full text of Senator Barack Obama's announcement for President. On Obama '08. Retrieved July 23, 2007, from www.barackobama.com/2007/02/10/ remarks _of_senator_barack_obam_11.php.

Obama, B. (2010). We see your sense of duty. *Vital Speeches, 76(7)*, 320–324.

Online.wsj.com. (2009, February 4). Text of Markopolos Testimony. Retrieved from http://online.wsj.com/public/ resources/documents/MarkopolosTestimony20090203.pdf.

Oprah Winfrey. (1987). *Current Biography Yearbook*, 610–614.

Osborn, M., Osborn, S., & Osborn, R. (2009). *Public speaking* (8th.ed.). Boston: Allyn & Bacon, Pearson Education.

Osgood, P. G. (1993, February 15). Conveying the environmental message: Getting green is better than seeing red. *Vital Speeches*, 59, 269–271.

Ostermeier, T. H. (1967, June). Effects of type and frequency of reference upon perceived source credibility and attitude change. *Speech Monograph*, 34, 137–144.

Painter, K. (2007, May 14). Paging Dr. Blog . . . *USA Today*, 7.

Paivio, A. (1971). *Imagery and verbal processes*. New York: Holt, Rinehart & Winston.

Papageogis, D. (1963). Bartlett effect and the persistence of induced opinion. *Journal of Abnormal and Social Psychology*, 67, 61–67.

Papageogis, D., & McGuire, W. (1961). The generality of immunity to persuasion produced by pre-exposure to weakened counterarguments. *Journal of Abnormal and Social Psychology*, 62, 475–481.

Papenfuse, E. C. (2007, February 28). Commencement address to the graduating class of Morgan State College, June 2, 1958. Maryland State Archives. Accessed October 16, 2007 at www.msa.md.gov/msa/speccol/sc5600/sc5604/html/king_memorial.html.

Paradi, D. (2005). What annoys audiences about PowerPoint presentations? Thinkoutsidetheslide.com. Accessed June 23, 2006, at http://thinkoutsidetheslide.com/pptresults2005.htm.

Paradi, D. (2009). Results from the 2009 annoying PowerPoint survey. Accessed from http://www.thinkoutsidetheslide.com/ articles/annoying_powerpoint_survey.htm.

Park, H. S., Livine, T. R., Westerman, C. Y., Orfenen, T., & Foregger, S. (2007). The effects of argument quality and involvement type on attitude formation and attitude changes: A test of dual-process and social judgment predictions. *Human Communication Research*, 33, 81–102.

Pastoor, S. (1990). Legibility and subjective preference for color combination in text. *Human Factors*, 32, 157–171.

Pastor resigns after admitting plagiarism. (2004, June 15). *Christian Century*, 121(12), 16.

Pearce, W. B., & Conklin, F. (1971). Nonverbal vocalic communication and perceptions of a speaker. *Speech Monographs*, 38, 241.

Perecman, E. (Ed.). (1983). *Cognitive processing in the right hemisphere*. New York: Academic.

Perloff, R. M. (2003). *The dynamics of persuasion: Communication and attitudes in the 21st century* (2nd ed.). Mahwah, NJ: Erlbaum.

Perloff, R. M. (2010). The dynamics of persuasion: Communication and attitudes in the 21st century (4th ed.). New York: Routledge.

Petty, R. E., & Cacioppo, J. T. (1984). The effects of involvement on response to argument quantity and quality: Central and peripheral routes to persuasion. *Journal of Personality and Social Psychology*, 46, 69–81.

Petty, R. E., & Cacioppo, J. T. (1986). *Communication and persuasion: Central and peripheral routes to attitude change*. New York: Springer-Verlag.

Petty, R. E., & Cacioppo, J. T. (1996). *Attitudes and persuasion: Classic and contemporary approaches*. Boulder, CO: Westview.

Pfau, M. (1997). Inoculation model of resistance to influence. In G. A. Barnett & G. J. Boster (Eds.), *Progress in communication sciences: Advances in persuasion* (Vol. 13, 133–171). Norwood, NJ: Ablex.

Pfau, M., & Louden, A. (1994). Effectiveness of adwatch formats in defeating political attack ads. *Communication Research*, 21, 325–341.

Phillips, G. M. (1977). Rhetoritherapy versus the medical model: Dealing with reticence. *Communication Education*, 26, 34–43.

Phillips, G. M. (1991). *Communication incompetencies: A theory of training oral performance behavior*. Carbondale: Southern Illinois University Press.

Philpott, J. S. (1983). The relative contribution to meaning of verbal and nonverbal channels of communication: A meta-analysis. Unpublished Master's thesis, University of Nebraska.

Pincus, A. (2007, July 18). The presentation imperfect. *Business Week Online*. Accessed at Academic Search Elite.

Pinel, J. P. J. (2006). *Biopsychology* (6th ed). Boston: Allyn & Bacon.

Pinkerton, J. P. (2000). The new paradigm. In R. L. Johannesen, R. R. Allen, W. A. Linkugel, and F. J. Bryan, *Contemporary American Speeches* (9th ed., p. 327). Dubuque, IA: Kendall/Hunt.

Pletcher, B. (2000). Plan of reaction: Finding calm from stress lies just a deep breath away. *Fort Worth Star-Telegram*, January 10, 11.

Pocock, R. (2010). The power of compound interest: Making an investment in yourself. *Vital Speeches, 76(8)*, 359–360.

Pogue, L. L., & AhYun, K. (2006, July). The effect of teacher nonverbal immediacy and credibility on student motivation and affective learning. *Communication Education*, 55(3), 331–344.

Porter, K. (2003). *The mental athlete: Inner training for peak performance in all sports*. Champaign, IL: Human Kinetics.

Porter, K., & Foster, J. (1986). *The mental athlete: Inner training for peak performance*. New York: Ballantine.

Priester, J. R., & Petty, R. E. (1995). Source attributions and persuasion: Perceived honesty as a determinant of message scrutiny. *Personality and Social Psychology Bulletin*, 21(6), 637.

Putnam, L. P., & Heinen, S. (1976, Summer). Women in management: The fallacy of the trait approach. *MSU Business Topics*, 47–53.

Quinones, E. (1999, August 1). Companies learn the value of storytelling. *The New York Times*, 4.

Quintilian. (1856). *Quintilian's institutes of oratory; or, Education of an orator*. J. S. Watson (Trans.). London: H. G. Bohn.

Rabb, M. Y. (1993). *The presentation design book: Tips, techniques and advice for creating effective, attractive slides, overheads, multimedia presentations, screen shows and more* (2nd ed.). Chapel Hill, NC: Ventana.

Rabinowitz, D. (1988, August 17). It's tough keeping your wit about you. *The Wall Street Journal*, 1. Accessed at ProQuest-database.

Raines, C. (2002). Generations at work: Managing millennials. Generationsatwork.com. Accessed July 11, 2007, from www.generationsatwork.com/articles/millenials.htm.

Randall, K. (2005). No average student: Community college students not your typical undergrads, says college of education survey. Accessed July 11, 2007 from www.utexas.edu/features/2005/college/index.html.

Ratneshwar, S., & Chaiken, S. (1991). Comprehension's role in persuasion: The case of its moderating effect on the persuasive impact of source cues. *Journal of Consumer Research*, 18, 52–62.

Reagan, R. (1986, January 28). Address to the nation. *Weekly compilation of presidential documents, 22(5)*, 104.

Reager, R. C., Crawford, N. P., & Stevens, E. L. (1960). *You can talk well*. New Brunswick, NJ: Rutgers University Press.

Reardon, K. (1991). *Persuasion in practice*. Newbury Park, CA: Sage.

Reinard, J. C. (1988, Fall). The empirical study of evidence: The status after fifty years of research. *Human Communication Research*, 15, 3–59.

Reinfeld, H. (2007, January 1). Public speaking—now that is scary. *Las Vegas Business Press*, 24(1), 6.

Reingold, J. (2005, June). The interpreter. *FastCompany*, 95, 59–61. Accessed June 28, 2006, from ProQuest database.

Renehan, E. J., Jr. (2004). JFK wrote his own 'ask not' speech. *San Francisco Chronicle* online. October 24, 2004. www.sfgate.com/cgi-bin/article.cgi?f=/c/a/2004/10/24/rvgkl99jm61.dtl.

Reynolds, G. (2005). Gates, Jobs, and the Zen aesthetic. Presentation Zen. Accessed at presentationzen.blogs.com/presentationzen/2005/11/the_zen_estheti.html.

Reynolds, G. (2007). Learning from Bill Gates and Steve Jobs. Presentation Zen. Accessed at www.presentationzen.com/presentationzen/2007/09/steve-bill-redu.html

Reynolds, R. A., & Burgoon, M. (1983). Belief processing, reasoning and evidence. *Communication Yearbook*, 7, 83–104.

Reynolds, R. A., & Reynolds, J. L. (2002). Evidence. In J. P. Dillard and M. Pfau (Eds.), *The persuasion handbook: Developments in theory and practice* (pp. 427–444). Thousand Oaks, CA: Sage.

Richardson, A. (1952). *Mental imagery*. New York: Springer.

Richardson, H. L. (1999). Women lead in style. *Transportation & Distribution*, 40(4), 78–82.

Richardson, J. T. (2003). Dual coding versus relational processing in memory for concrete and abstract words. *European Journal of Cognitive Psychology*, 15(4), 481–509.

Richmond, V. P., & McCroskey, J. C. (1998). *Communication: Apprehension, avoidance, and effectiveness* (5th ed.). Scottsdale, AZ: Gorsuch Scarisbrick.

Richmond, V. P., & Roach, D. (1992). Willingness to communicate and employee success in U.S. organizations. *Journal of Applied Communication Research*, 20, 95–115.

Roberts, J. L. (2007, April 10). Couric's contretemps. *Newsweek* magazine. Accessed June 4, 2007 from www.msnbc.msn.com/id/18046837/site/newsweek/page/0/.

Robertson, A. K. (1994). *Listen for success: A guide to effective listening*. Burr Ridge, IL: Irwin Professional Publishing.

Robinson, G. J. (2000). *Did I ever tell you the one about the time: How to develop and deliver a speech using stories that get your message across*. New York: McGraw-Hill.

Robinson, J. (1990, June 3). For Barbara Bush: Undisputed stardom; triumph at Wellesley will be a tough act to follow. *The Boston Globe*, 25.

Robinson, T. E. (1997). Communication apprehension and the basic public speaking course: A national survey of in-class treatment techniques. *Communication Education*, 46, 188–197.

Rocca, K. A. (2004). College student attendance: Impact of instructor immediacy and verbal aggression. *Communication Education*, 53(2), 185–195.

Rockler-Gladen, N. (2007, July 29). PowerPoint for public speaking: How to use PowerPoint slides in a speech or presentation. On Suite101 Enter Curious. Retrieved from collegeuniversity.suite101.com/article.cfm/powerpoint_for_public_speaking.

Rodin, J. (2009, June). Discoveries are important in every sector. *Vital speeches, 75(6)*, 261–264.

Rogel, S. (2003, April 15). Business ethics and the Boy Scout code. *Vital Speeches*, 69, 403–406.

Rogers, R. W. (1975). A protection motivation theory of fear appeals and attitude change. *Journal of Psychology*, 91, 93–114.

Rokeach, M. (1969). *Beliefs, attitudes, and values: A theory of organization and change*. San Francisco: Jossey-Bass.

Rokeach, M. (1973). *The nature of human values*. New York: Free Press.

Rokeach, M. (2000). *Understanding human values* (new printing). New York: Free Press.

Ronald Reagan. (2004). Whitehouse.gov. Accessed October 8, 2007, at www.whitehouse.gov/history/presidents/rr40.html.

Ross, L. D. (1977). The intuitive psychologist and his shortcomings: Distortions in the attribution process. In L. Berkowitz (Ed.), *Advances in experimental social psychology*, Vol. 10 (pp. 173–220). New York: Academic.

Ross, R. K. (2003, November 1). A cry for help: Healthcare: Does anybody care about unequal treatment? *Vital Speeches*, 70, 51–53.

Rowan, K. E. (1990). The speech to explain difficult ideas. *Speech Communication Teacher*, 4, 2–3.

Rowan, K. E. (1991). When simple language fails: Presenting difficult science to the public. *Journal of Technical Writing and Communication*, 21, 369–382.

Rowan, K. E. (1995, July). A new pedagogy for explanatory public speaking: Why arrangement should not substitute for invention. *Communication Education*, 44, 236–250.

Russell, P. (1979). *The brain book*. New York: Dutton.

Ryan, H. R. (1995). *U.S. presidents as orators: A bio-critical sourcebook*. Westport, CT: Greenwood Press.

Saad, L. (2006, May 25). Morality ratings the worst in five years: Americans becoming more pessimistic about morals. Gallup News Service. Accessed May 28, 2006, at poll.gallup.com/content/default.aspx?ci=22942. Must be member to access.

Saad, L. (2009, Dec. 9). Honesty and ethics poll finds congress' image tarnished. *The Gallup Poll Tuesday Briefing Online*, galluppoll.com. Accessed July 10, 2010, at http://www.gallup.com/poll/124625/Honesty-Ethics-Poll-Finds-Congress-Image-Tarnished.aspx.

Samovar, L. A., & Porter, R. E. (2004). *Communication between cultures* (5th ed.). Belmont, CA: Wadsworth.

Sandberg, J. (2006, November 14). Tips for PowerPoint: Go easy on the text; please spare us. *The Wall Street Journal*, B1.

Saunders, F. (2000). Web wonders. *Discover*, 21(6), 31–32.

Scanlon, P. M., & Neumann, D. R. (2002). Internet plagiarism among college students. *Journal of College Student Development*, 43(3), 374–385.

Schab, F. R., & Crowder, R. G. (1989). Accuracy of temporal coding: Auditory-visual comparisons. *Memory and Cognition*, 17, 384–397.

Scherer, J. (2010, August). Go for Tov: Learning to "come home to yourself." *Vital Speeches, 76(8)*, pp. 351–354.

Schwarzenegger, A. (2004, August 31). Text of Arnold Schwarzenegger's speech. boston.com. Accessed at www.boston.com/news/politics/conventions/articles/2004/08/31/text_of_arnold_schwarzeneggers_speech.

Schwarzenegger, A. (2007, February). Difficult choices to make. *Vital Speeches*, 73(2), 66–69.

Schwarzenegger.com. (2001). The education of an American. At www.schwarzenegger.com/en/life/hiswords/words_en_sac_perspectives.asp?sec=life&subsec=hiswords.

Schweizer, P., & Hall, W. C. (2007). *Landmark speeches on the American conservative movement*. College Station, TX: Texas A&M University Press.

Scott, L. (2007, April 24). Closing keynote address: Health care in America 2007. World Health Care Congress. Retrieved July 26, 2007, from Wal-Mart Web site: walmartfacts.com/media/ 128219083279537500.pdf.

Seidenberg, I. (2009). Customer satisfaction is the most important thing: The future of the telecommunications industry. *Vital Speeches, 75(6)*, 270–274.

Seiler, W. J. (1971, Winter). The conjunctive influence of source credibility and the use of visual materials on communication effectiveness. *Southern Speech Communication Journal*, 37, 174–185.

Shapiro, I. D. (2007, January). Fallacies of logic: Argumentation cons. *A Review of General Semantics*, 64(1), 75–86.

Sharp, H., Jr., & McClung, T. (1966). Effects of organization on the speaker's ethos. *Speech Monographs*, 33, 182–183.

Sheikh, A. A. (Ed.) (1983). *Imagery: Current theory, research, and application*. New York: Wiley.

Sherif, M., & Hovland, C. I. (1961). *Social judgment*. New Haven, CT: Yale University Press.

Sherif, M., Sherif, C., & Nebergall, R. (1965). *Attitude and attitude change: The social judgment–involvement approach*. Philadelphia: Saunders.

Shrader, R. W. (2010, February 4). Buying the future Facing up to threats and envisioning a different future. *Vital Speeches, xx (xx)*, 156–158.

Silverman, J. (2003, September 1). Improve health literacy by using plain language. *Internal Medicine News*, 36(17), 68.

Simons, T. (2004, January 7). Bullets may be dangerous, but don't blame PowerPoint. *Presentations* magazine. Accessed

December 27, 2004, at www.allbusiness.com/services/business-services-advertising/4248555-1.html.

Slater, M. D., & Rouner, D. (1996). Value-affirmative and value-protective processing of alcohol education messages that include statistical evidence or anecdotes. *Communication Research*, 23, 210–235.

Smiley, T. (2007, July). Make a Contribution. *Vital Speeches*, 73(7), 307–309.

Smith, P. B., & Bond, M. H. (1994). *Social psychology across cultures: Analysis and perspective*. Boston: Allyn & Bacon.

Smith, R. G. (1973). Source credibility context effects. *Speech Monographs*, 40, 303–309.

Smith, R. V. (2004). *The elements of great speechmaking: Adding drama and intrigue*. Lanham, MD: University Press of America.

Smith, T. E., & Frymier, A. B. (2006). Get 'real': Does practicing speeches before an audience improve performances? *Communication Quarterly*, 54(1), 111–125.

Smudde, P. M. (2004). The five p's for media interviews: Fundamentals for newbies, veterans and everyone in between. *Public Relations Quarterly*, 49(2), 29–35.

Some comments about the iphone unveiling presentation (2007, January 16). The Closet Entrepreneur. Accessed at: theclosetentrepreneur.com/some-comments-about-the-iphone-unveiling-presentation.

Soto, D., & Humphreys, G. W. (2007, June). Automatic guidance of visual attention from verbal working memory. *Journal of Experimental Psychology: Human Perception and Performance*, 33(3), 730–737.

Sparks, J. R., Areni, C. S., & Cox, K. C. (1998). An investigation of the effects of language style and communication modality on persuasion. *Communication Monographs*, 65, 108–125.

St. John, S. (1995, September). Get your act together. *Presentations* magazine, 9, 26–33.

Starks, C. (2010, April). How to write a speech. *Vital Speeches, 76(4)*, pp. 153–156.Mathas, T. (2010, January). Leaving Las Vegas: Why we must help Americans stop gambling on their financial futures. *Vital Speeches, 76(1)*, pp. 36–39.

Steil, L. K., Barker, L. L., & and Watson, K.W. (1983). *Effective listening: Key to your success*. Reading, MA: Addison-Wesley.

Steil, L. K., Summerfield, J., & De Mare, G. (1984). *Listening: It can change your life*. New York: Wiley.

Stephan, K. M., Fink, G. R., Passingham, R. E., Silbersweig, D., Ceballos-Baumann, A. O., Frith, R. D., & Frackowiak, R. S. J. (1995). Functional anatomy of the mental representation of upper extremity movements in healthy subjects. *Journal of Neurophysiology*, 73, 373–385.

Sternberg, P. (1984). *Speak up! A guide to public speaking*. New York: Julian Messner.

Steve Jobs: CEO, Apple. (2007). Apple.com. Accessed at www.apple.com/pr/bios/jobs.html.

Stevenson, A. E. (1992). Eulogy on Sir Winston Churchill. In H. R. Ryan (Ed.), *Contemporary American Public Discourse* (3rd ed., pp. 245–248). Prospect Heights, IL: Waveland.

Stibbe, M. (2007, May). Strategic business blogging. *Directors*, 60(10). 24.

Stone, J., & Bachner, J. (1994). *Speaking up: A book for every woman who wants to speak effectively*. New York: Carroll & Graft.

Stoner, M. R. (2007, July). PowerPoint in a new key. *Communication Education*, 56(3), 354–381.

Strauss, V. (2007, April 3). Coup that is Oprah has Howard gushing. Washingtonpost.com. Accessed August 13, 2007, at www.washingtonpost.com/wp-dyn/content/article/2007/04/02/ar2007040201495.html.

Sullivan, M. P. (2004, May 1). How Boomer generational DNA will change healthcare: Creating more satisfied patients. *Vital Speeches*, 70, 443–445.

Sussman, M. (2009, October 19). Who are the bloggers? *Technorati.com*. Retrieved from http://technorati.com/blogging/article/day-1-who-are-the-bloggers1.

Sutton, S. R., & Eiser, J. R. (1984). The effect of fear-arousing communications on cigarette smoking: An expectancy-value approach. *Journal of Behavioral Medicine*, 7, 13–33.

Szabo, E. A., & Pfau, M. (2002). Nuances in inoculation: Theory and applications. In J. P. Dillard & M. Pfau (Eds.), *The persuasion handbook: Developments in theory and practice* (pp. 233–258). Thousand Oaks, CA: Sage.

Tannen, D. (1995). The power of talk: Who gets heard and why. *Harvard Business Review*, 73(5), 138–149.

Taylor, J. (2004). A second coming of age. *American Demographics*, 26(5), 36–38.

Tennyson, R. D., & Cocchiarella, M. J. (1986). An empirically based instructional design theory for teaching concepts. *Review of Educational Psychology*, 56, 40–71.

Tenoper, C., & King, D. W. (2004). Communication patterns of engineers. Hoboken, NJ: Wiley-Interscience.

Tesser, A., & Shaffer, D. R. (1990). Attitudes and attitude change. *Annual Review of Psychology*, 41, 479–523.

Thayer, J. (2001, April 15). The purpose of life: Where have all the heroes gone? *Vital Speeches*, 67(13), 404–408.

The Man Who Knew. (2009, June 14). *CBS 60 Minutes*. Retrieved from http://www.cbsnews.com/video/watch/?id=5088137n.

Thompson, K., Leintz, P., Nevers, B., & Witkowski, S. (2010). The integrative listening model: An approach to teaching and learning listening. In A. D. Wolvin (Ed.), *Listening and human communication in the 21st century* (pp. 141–157). Malden, MA: Wiley-Blackwell.

Thompson, L. A., Driscoll, D., & Markson, L. (1998). Memory for visual-spoken language in children and adults. *Journal of Nonverbal Behavior*, 22, 167–187.

Thompson, V. A., & Paivio, A. (1994). Memory for pictures and sounds: Independence of auditory and visual codes. *Canadian Journal of Experimental Psychology*, 48(3), 380–395.

Thucydides. (1972). *History of the Peloponnesian war* (Intro.). R. Warner and M. I. Finley (Trans.). New York: Penguin.

Tice, L. E. (1980). *Investment in excellence* (cassette series, tape no. 1). Seattle: The Pacific Institute.

Tice, L. E., & Quick, J. (1997). *Personal coaching for results*. Nashville, TN: Thomas Nelson.

Tice, L. E., & Steinberg, A. (1989). *A better world, a better you: The proven Lou Tice "Investment in excellence" program*. Englewood Cliffs, NJ: Prentice Hall Direct.

Ting-Toomey, S. (2000). Managing intercultural conflicts effectively. In L. A. Samovar & R. E. Porter (Eds.), *Intercultural communication: A reader* (9th ed.), 388–400. Belmont, CA: -Wadsworth.

Ting-Toomey, S., & Chung, L. C. (2004). *Understanding intercultural communication*. Cary, NC: Oxford University Press.

Titsworth, B. S. (2004). Students' notetaking: The effects of teacher immediacy and clarity. *Communication Education*, 53, 305–320.

Todd, J. S. (1993, June 15). Health care at the brink. *Vital Speeches*, 59(17), 522–524.

Tortoriello, T. R., Blatt, S. J., & DeWine, S. (1978). *Communication in the organization: An applied approach*. New York: McGraw-Hill.

Toulmin, S. (1974). The Uses of Argument. New York: Cambridge UP.

Tracy, L. (2005, March 1). Taming hostile audiences: Persuading those who would rather jeer than cheer. *Vital Speeches*, 71(10), 306–312.

Trevino, L. K., & Nelson, K. A. (2004). *Managing business ethics* (3rd ed.). Hoboken, NJ: Wiley.

Triandis, H. C. (1995). *Individualism and collectivism*. Boulder, CO: Westview.

Tversky, A., & Kahneman, D. (1981). The framing of decisions and the psychology of choice. *Science*, 211, 453–458.

U.S. Bureau of the Census. (2003). *Statistical abstract of the United States*. Washington, DC: GPO, p. 794.

Veninga, R. L. (2006, July 1). Star Throwing 101. *Vital Speeches*, 72(18/19), 544–545.

Verlinden, J. (2005). *Critical thinking and everyday argument*. Belmont, CA: Thomson Wadsworth.

Vest, D., Long, M., & Anderson, T. (1996). Electrical engineers' perceptions of communication training and their recommendation for curricular change: Results of a national survey. *IEEE Transactions of Professional Communication*, 12, 343–370.

Voelker, D. (2007, May). History and technology: Blogging for students. *Perspectives*, 45(5), 28–29.

Vogel, D. R., Dickson, G. W., & Lehman, J. A. (1986). *Persuasion and the role of visual presentation support. The UM/3M study* (in-house publication, pp. 1–20). St. Paul, MN: 3M Corporation.

Vogel, D. R., Dickson, G. W., & Lehman, J. A. (1990, July 27). Persuasion and the role of visual presentation support: The UM/3M study. In M. Antonoff (Ed.), *Presentations that persuade. Personal Computing*, 14.

Wall Street Journal. (2007, May 22). Allstate Life Insurance Company full-page advertisement. *The Wall Street Journal*, A16.

Walters, F. M. (1993, September 1). If it's broke, fix it: The significance of health care reform in America. *Vital Speeches*, 59, 687–691.

Walters, L. (1993). *Secrets of successful speakers*. New York: McGraw-Hill.

Walton, D. (1998). *Ad hominem arguments*. Tuscaloosa: University of Alabama Press.

Wanzer, M., Booth-Butterfield, M., & Booth-Butterfield, S. (1994). The funny people: A source-orientation to the communication of humor. *Communication Quarterly*, 43, 142–154.

Warnick, B., & Inch, E. S. (1994). *Critical thinking and communication: The use of reason in argument* (2nd ed.). New York: Macmillan.

Wasley, P. (2006, June 2). Review confirms plagiarism by Ohio U. graduate students and recommends professors' dismissals. *The Chronicle of Higher Education*. Accessed at chronicle.com.

Watson, K. W., Barker, L. L., & Weaver, J. B., III. (1995). The listening styles profile (LS-16): Development and validation of an instrument to assess four listening styles. *International Journal of Listening*, 9, 1–13.

Weaver, R. L., II. (2003, July 15). What you don't get out of a college education: Personal success skills necessary to exceed in school and in life. *Vital Speeches*, 69(19), 604–608.

Weaver, R. L., II. (2007, August). Sticky ideas. *Vital Speeches of the Day*, 73(8), 353–356.

Webster, Richard (2006). *Creative visualization for beginners*, pp.1–2. St. Paul, MN: Llewellyn Publications.

Weissman, J. (2006). Presenting to win: The art of telling your story (Updated version). Upper Saddle River, NJ: Prentice Hall.

Wellesley students hail Raisa Gorbachev. (1990, May 20). *The New York Times*, A26. Accessed from ProQuest Historical Newspapers *New York Times* (1851–2004) database.

Wellner, A. S. (2003). The next 25 years. *American Demographics*, 25(3), 24–27.

Whately, B. P. (1997). Perceptions of rebuttal analogy: Politeness and implications for persuasion. *Argumentation and Advocacy*, 33, 16–19.

Whitbeck, C. (2007). Sixth grade graduation commencement. Official web site of the Douglas School Principal. Accessed September 22, 2007 at mail.ab.mec.edu/~cwhitbeck.

White, Jr., R. C. (2005). *The eloquent president: A portrait of Lincoln through his words*. New York: Random House.

Whitehead, J. R. (1968). Factors of source credibility. *Quarterly Journal of Speech*, 54, 61–63.

Whitworth, J. M. (2003, October 15). We must not forget: Looking back at 9/11. *Vital Speeches*, 70, 25–28.

Wiesel, E. (1992). Acceptance of the Nobel Peace Prize. In J. R. Andrews & D. Zarefsky (Eds.), Contemporary American voices (pp. 419–420). White Plains, NY: Longman.

Wiles, C. (2001). Impromptu speaking: The secret is to prepare for spontaneity. *Harvard Management Communication Letter*, 4(12), 7–9.

Williams, M. R., & Cooper, M. D. (2002). *Power Persuasion: Moving an ancient art into the media age* (3rd ed.). Greenwood, ID: Alistair Press.

Williams, R. (2008). *The Non-designer's design book: Design and typographic principles for the visual novice* (2nd ed.). Berkeley: Peachpit.

Wilson, A. B. (2003, September 15). In defense of rhetoric: Exercising leadership. *Vital Speeches*, 69, 734–736.

Wilson, D. L. (2005, July 4). They said he was a lousy speaker: His style could be too plain for the taste of his time, but much that Lincoln said speaks powerfully to us. *Time*, 166(1), 68–69.

Winfrey, O. (1997). Oprah Winfrey's commencement address at Wellesley College May 30, 1997. On Oprah Winfrey's commencement address. Retrieved September 9, 2007, at www.wellesley.edu/publicaffairs/commencement/1997/winfrey.html.

Winstein, K. J., & Golden, D. (2007, April 27). MIT admissions dean lied on resume in 1979, quits. *The Wall Street Journal*, B1.

Wise, R., Chollet, F., Hadar, U., Friston, L., Hoffner, E., & Frackowiak, R. (1991). Distribution of cortical neural networks involved in word comprehension and word retrieval. *Brain*, 114, 1803–1817.

Witt, P. L., & Wheeless, L. R. (2001, October). An experimental study of teachers' verbal and nonverbal immediacy and students' affective and cognitive learning. *Communication Education*, 50(4), 327–342.

Witt, P. L., Brown, K. C., Roberts, J. B., Weisel, J., Sawyer, C. R., & Behnke, R. R. (2006). Somatic anxiety patterns before, during, and after giving a public speech. *Southern Communication Journal*, 71(1), 87–100.

Witte, K. (1992a, December). Putting the fear back into fear appeals: The extended parallel process model. *Communication Monographs*, 59, 329–349.

Witte, K. (1992b). The role of threat and efficacy in AIDS prevention. *International Quarterly of Community Health Education*, 12, 225–249.

Wolff, F. I., Marsnik, N. C., Tracey, W. W., & Nichols, R. G. (1983). *Perceptive listening*. New York: Holt, Rinehart & Winston.

Wolvin, A., & Coakley, C. G. (1996). *Listening* (5th ed.). Dubuque, IA: Brown & Benchmark.

Wood, J. (2007). *Gendered lives* (7th ed). Belmont, CA: Wadsworth.

Wood, J. (2011). *Gendered lives* (9th ed). Belmont, CA: Wadsworth.

Wooldridge, E. T., III. (2004, December). Order a PowerPoint stand-down. *Proceedings of the United States Naval Institute*, 130, 85.

World News Network. (2009, February 4). SEC Hearing Harry Markopolos Testifies. Retrieved from http://wn.com/SEC_Hearing_Harry_Markopolos_Testifies.

www.defense.gov. (2007, September 14). Operation Iraqi Freedom (OIF) U.S. Casualty Status. Accessed September 14, 2007, at www.defenselink.mil/news/casualty.pdf.

Younis, S. (2006). Biography. Chrisreevehomepage.com. Accessed October 1, 2007 at www.chrisreevehomepage.com/biography.html.

Zagacki, K. S., Edwards, R., & Honeycutt, J. M. (1992, Winter). The role of mental imagery and emotion in imagined interaction. *Communication Quarterly*, 40, 56–68.

Zarefsky, D. (1980). Lyndon Johnson redefines 'equal opportunity': The beginnings of affirmative action. *Central States Speech Journal*, 31, 85–94.

Zayas-Baya, E. P. (1977–1978). Instructional media in the total language picture. *International Journal of Instructional Media*, 5, 145–150.

Zelazny, G. (2000). Say it with presentations: *How to design and deliver successful business presentations*. New York: McGraw-Hill.

Zhang, Y., Butler, J., & Pryor, B. (1996). Comparison of apprehension about communication in China and the United States. *Perceptual and Motor Skills*, 82, 1168–1170.

Glossary

abstract word Describes intangible concepts that are generally difficult to picture (such as *devotion* or *health*).

acceptance speech A special occasional speech where the recipient of an award expresses gratitude for the award and dignifies the occasion by recognizing the award's significance.

acronym A word formed from the first letter of each word of a compound term; for example, TIPS (Tell, Identify, Participate, and Schedule).

adaptors Gestures and movements that signal nervousness, such as rubbing the ear or nose, flipping hair, or tapping a foot.

ad hominem A type of fallacious reasoning that tries to divert attention from the real issue by attacking the person who presents the argument.

ad ignoratiam A type of fallacious reasoning that appeals to ignorance: because a particular belief cannot be disproved, therefore it must be true.

ad populum A type of fallacious reasoning that appeals to popular opinion as support for an argument.

after-dinner speech A special occasion speech that is light, entertaining, and often inspirational in tone.

alliteration The repetition of consonants (usually the first or last letter in a word).

alternative search engine Uses nonstandard means of sorting or ranking the Web pages it finds in a search.

ambiguous word A word with a general, vague, and unclear meaning.

analogical reasoning Reasoning by comparing a familiar example with an unfamiliar one; used to explain and clarify.

androgynous Comes from the Greek words for *male* and *female,* and denotes the integration of both masculine and feminine characteristics.

antithesis A stylistic device in which two parallel but contrasting ideas are contained in a single sentence.

argument An effective **argument** occurs when you present sufficient evidence and reasoning to support a claim made in your persuasive speech. There are three parts to a good argument: claim, evidence, and warrant.

articulation The clear and distinct production of speech sounds.

assonance The repetition of vowel sounds.

attitude A feeling of approval or disapproval of a person, group, idea, or event.

attitude poll A poll of potential audience members undertaken prior to writing a speech, to gauge their level of agreement or disagreement toward the speech topic and the position statement.

attribution theory Describes how people process information and use it to explain the behavior of others and themselves.

audience type Classification of an audience based on whether they are (1) friendly, (2) neutral or impartial, (3) uninterested or indifferent, or (4) hostile.

auditory channel A communication channel preferred by those who learn by listening; these people are more likely to use auditory words such as *talked, sounded, heard,* and *said.*

award presentation A special occasional speech that emphasizes the worthiness of the person receiving the award and explains the award's significance.

backing Part of the Toulmin Model of an Argument where the expertise and date of the source is cited.

basic design principles Guidelines used to construct the elements of all well-designed visuals. Principles include contrast, repetition, alignment, and proximity.

begging the question A type of fallacious reasoning that asserts that something is simply because it is.

belief The mental acceptance that something is true even if it can't be proved.

body (of speech) The main part of a speech that requires effective organization and supporting materials; organization that is appropriate for an informative, persuasive, or special occasional speech; and supporting materials that clarify, add interest, and persuade as needed.

Boolean operator A joining word such as *and, or,* or *not* that is used to specify the relationship between search words.

boomerang effect When fewer people agree with the speaker at the end of the speech than before it began.

blog A weblog, or personal journal, located on the Internet.

brainstorming Spontaneously listing ideas.

causal pattern A way of arranging the main topics of a speech so the main points have a cause–effect or effect–cause relationship.

causal reasoning Reasoning that implies a causal link between two items; used to prove.

chronological pattern A way of arranging the main topics of a speech on the basis of time—either in a step-by-step order or by dates.

claim Part of the Toulmin Model of an Argument where the claim or position statement is the conclusion you hope your audience will reach.

claim pattern A way of arranging the main topics of a persuasive speech so the main points are the reasons (or claims) for believing a particular fact, holding a particular value, or advocating a particular plan. Also called reason pattern.

code of ethics A written set of standards that you should strive for when speaking, to make sure you include ethical and honest information in your speeches, show respect for others, and never mislead your audience.

cognitive dissonance A feeling of discomfort when evidence is presented that is contrary to what we believe.

cognitive restructuring of self-talk A method for managing trait anxiety that involves (1) identifying irrational self-talk that produces speaker anxiety, (2) developing alternative coping statements to replace these irrational thoughts, and (3) practicing using the coping statements in stressful situations (such as group discussions or speaking situations).

coherence principle People learn better when pictures and words are used together.

collectivistic Used to describe a culture that values group membership, group obligations, and group goals more than individual needs. These cultures are relationship-oriented and value empathy, listening, and group friendships.

commemorative speech Special occasional speeches like the toast or tribute that formally recognize and honor a person, organization, or occasion.

communibiology Theory that communication apprehension is a genetically caused behavior that is inborn.

communication A process in which people share thoughts, ideas, and feelings in understandable ways.

communication skills The ability to speak, write, listen and decode messages well.

comparative advantages pattern A way of organizing a persuasive speech when the audience already agrees with the problem but may not agree on the solution. This pattern concentrates on the advantages of one course of action over another.

comparison A type of supporting material that clarifies something unfamiliar by comparing (and/or contrasting) it with something familiar.

comprehend stage The second stage of listening where the listener understands what the speaking is saying.

computer-generated slides The most popular type of visual aid where slides are created by software programs such as PowerPoint for use on the computer.

conclusion (of speech) The final step of a speech that summarizes the main points covered and ends in a memorable way. Persuasive speeches also visualize the future for the audience showing how good or how bad things can be if the audience does or does not follow the speaker's advice.

concrete words Describes tangible things that listeners can picture easily (such as *red apple* or *cheerful smile*).

contiguity principle Audiences learn better when pictures are placed side by side with their explanatory words.

credibility The quality of a speaker that inspires the feeling that he or she is believable, ethical, and a person in whom listeners can place their confidence.

criteria satisfaction pattern A way of arranging the main topics of a persuasive speech in which criteria are presented for evaluating possible plans or solutions, followed by a plan to meet or exceed the established criteria.

critical thinking Skilled and active interpretation and evaluation of observations, communications, information, and argumentation.

culture bias When speakers are not sensitive to the diverse backgrounds of their listeners and use language that shows a culture preference.

customizing To take a basic idea or PowerPoint template and adapt it so it becomes one's own.

decoding The process listeners go through in interpreting a sender's meaning.

deductive reasoning Presenting the position or general conclusion first and then providing the supporting evidence.

definition A statement of what a thing is.

deliberative speaking One of Aristotle's three categories of speaking; political or legislative speaking.

DEME A theory of conflict escalation called the dispute-exacerbating model of e-mail or DEME which says that e-mail is likely to be interpreted as more aggressive than intended.

demographic information Information about audience characteristics, such as age, gender, marital status, education, economic status, occupation, college major, political beliefs, religion, cultural background, and group identification.

demonstration Using objects or people to explain or clarify an idea.

demonstration speech A type of informative speech that shows how to do or make something.

description A vivid, detailed picture of a topic that uses concrete words and figures of speech such as similes, metaphors, and onomatopoeia.

distortion Misrepresenting or twisting facts, or stating that something is true when it is only partially true or not true at all.

dynamism A speaking style characterized by forcefulness, enthusiasm, and good vocal variety.

Elaboration Likelihood Model A theory of persuasion that indicates which of two routes for processing arguments (central or peripheral) audience members will likely use.

emblems Body movements and gestures that are so specific that they easily replace a word or idea; for example, if you put your finger to your lips, everyone knows to be quiet.

emoticon A sequence of keyboard symbols, such as :) for *happy*, used to add meaning and emotion to e-mail messages.

emotional appeal (*pathos*) An argument that appeals to the psychological needs of the listener.

emphasis Stressing a word with the voice in order to give the word significance.

encoding The process of deciding how best to organize and convey a message to a specific audience or person.

environment The time, place, and physical and social surroundings in which a speech occurs.

epideictic speaking One of Aristotle's three categories of speaking; ceremonial speaking.

ethical speaker One who researches information carefully and completely, presents only truthful information, and gives credit for all ideas and words that are not original.

ethos the credibility of the speaker; also one of the means of persuasion.

euphemism An abstract word or phrase with positive overtones substituted for a specific word with negative overtones (such as *ethnic cleansing* in place of *murder*).

eulogy A special occasion speech giving tribute to someone who has died.

evaluate stage The fourth stage of listening, in which listeners think about, evaluate, and judge the speaker and the message.

evidence Factual statements and opinions originating from a source other than the speaker, which support the logical arguments of a speech. Also part of the Toulmin Model of an Augument where the evidence supports the claim.

exact purpose A clear, simple sentence that specifies exactly what the audience should gain from an informational or demonstration speech. For example, "After hearing my speech, the audience will . . ."

exaggeration Overstating or presenting something as greater or more important than it is.

example A type of instance that is brief and gives basic facts only.

expert opinion Supporting material that refers to the ideas of another person who is an expert on the topic of the speech.

explanation Supporting material that defines or gives more information about a term or topic, gives instructions on how to do something, or describes how something works or the relationship between certain items.

extemporaneous speech A speech that is not memorized or written out word for word, but is developed and presented from brief notes or visual aids.

external noise Distractions in the environment, such as people talking or dim lighting, that interfere with communication.

external stimulus A person or object external to the listener that triggers an idea in the listener.

fables, sayings, poems, & rhymes Types of supporting materials that add interest and clarify with fictitious stories, pithy expressions, imaginative words and sounds.

fallacious reasoning False or faulty reasoning.

fear appeal A persuasive appeal that causes listeners to feel threatened or afraid.

feedback An audience's verbal, visual, and vocal responses to a speaker's message.

figurative comparison Supporting material that shows similarities or differences between two or more items from different classes or categories (such as comparing an individual to a snowflake).

fonts Typefaces that are divided into two types: sans serif and serif.

forceful language Involves the effective use of volume, emphasis, and pitch.

forensic speaking One of Aristotle's three categories of speaking; speaking in court.

forum A type of team presentation that includes open audience participation.

frame of reference A person's experience and background as they influence the way that person perceives events and messages.

framing Fitting your message to audience needs.

friendly audience An audience that has heard you speak before, has heard positive things about you, or is simply sold on your topic or position.

gender bias When speakers are not sensitive to gender differences of their listeners and use language that shows a gender preference.

geographic pattern See **spatial pattern**.

grand style Reserved for persuasive situation; is eloquent, dramatic, and fiery.

graph A visual representation of numeric data. Examples include line graphs, bar graphs, stacked bar graphs, pie charts, and pictographs.

graphic slide A visual aid consisting mainly of graphic elements with just enough words to clarify the visual. Examples include organizational charts and flow charts, diagrams and schematic drawings, maps, pictures, and graphs.

hasty generalization A type of fallacious reasoning that occurs when a conclusion is based on too few examples or on isolated examples.

heterogeneous Used to describe members of a group who differ in various ways, including interests, fields of study, work experience, and age.

hierarchical index A system, used by some search engines, in which Web sites are organized into categories.

high context Use to describe a culture that expects messages to be brief, indirect, and implicit. In such a culture, the listener takes responsibility for determining a speaker's meaning.

highlight main points To make the important ideas in a speech stand out so it is easier for listeners to follow and remember them.

homogeneous Used to describe members of a group who have a fair amount in common, including their beliefs and interests.

hostile audience An audience predisposed to dislike you, your topic, or both.

hue Any color on the color wheel.

hyperbole An exaggerated or distorted statement deliberately used to draw attention to a situation or problem.

hypothetical illustration An instance or narrative that is made up, but could happen; a statement that begins with words such as "Suppose . . . ," "Imagine . . . ," or "What would you do if . . . ?".

illustration Detailed, vivid picture or narrative.

illustrators Specific movements or gestures intended to expand or clarify a word or idea.

immediacy behavior Any verbal, visual, or vocal behavior that a speaker uses to promote a sense of closeness and personal interaction with the audience.

impartial audience See **neutral audience**.

impromptu speech A speech given without prior preparation and without notes or manuscript.

indifferent audience See **uninterested audience**.

individualistic Used to describe a culture that values the individual and individual rights more highly than group identity or group rights. These cultures are problem-oriented and value autonomy, assertiveness, and competition.

inductive reasoning Presenting specific evidence first before building up to a general conclusion.

informational speech A type of informative speech that promotes understanding/knowing; focuses on content and ideas; may discuss how something is made, but will not actually make it.

informative speech A speech that increases awareness by introducing the latest information about a topic or body of related facts; deepens listeners' knowledge of a complicated term, concept, or process; or aids in listeners' mastery of a skill. Includes two types: demonstration and informational.

inoculation theory States that inoculating a listener against opposing ideas is similar to inoculating a person against a disease.

instance Supporting material involving an example or illustration that is used to clarify, add interest, and (in some cases) prove a point.

instrumental value A guide for conduct in fulfilling a terminal value.

internal noise Conditions within listeners, such as headaches or lack of knowledge about a topic, that interfere with communication.

internal stimulus A thought generated by the listener that triggers additional thought or action.

internal summary Summaries between points to clarify areas just covered.

interpret stage The third stage of listening, in which listeners supply meaning to the messages that they have seen, heard, or felt.

introduction (of speech) The first part of a speech were the speaker grabs audience attention, motivates them to listen, establishes credibility, and presents the purpose with a preview of main points.

keyword search Locates websites that match a specific word or phrase entered by the user.

kinesthetic channel A communication channel preferred by those who learn by touching; these people are more likely to use "touch" words such as *touch, grasp, feel,* and *run*.

listener The receiver of a spoken message.

listening filters Different frames of reference causing audience members to subconsciously filter or decode what they hear speakers say in a way that may distort or change the speaker's meaning. The three main filters are culture, gender, and technology.

listening orientations The different ways in which people listen, which may be biological. There are four "listening orientations" or styles: people, action, content, and time. Women tend to show a preference for the people orientation, while men show a preference for the content orientation.

literal comparison Supporting material that shows similarities or differences between two or more items in the same class or category (such as comparing two species of saltwater fish).

logic The sequence of thoughts and ideas that connects the various pieces of evidence to create a meaningful and persuasive argument.

logos Using evidence and logic effectively; also one of the means of persuasion.

low context Used to describe a culture that expects messages to be clearly spelled out, directly and explicitly. In such a culture, it is the speaker's responsibility to make sure the meaning is provided by the words and that the message is well-organized and structured.

McCroskey's PRCA-24 Personal Report of Communication Apprehension questionnaire, which is used to determine your level of situational anxiety.

means of persuasion Three appeals that make a speech really persuasive: ethos, logos, and pathos.

memory stage The stage of listening where listeners decide what parts of the speech to retain and then attempt to store them in memory.

metaphor An implied comparison that speaks of one item as though it were something else, without using *like* or *as*.

metasearch engine A search engine that searches other search engines.

middle style Used to gain attention or entertain; a polished style that includes humor, wit, and ornamentation of all kinds.

mind map A visual aid for the mind that starts in the center of a paper with the major idea and works outward in all directions, producing a growing and organized structure composed of key words and key images.

monochromic Also known as an M-time culture, this group views time as a scarce resource which must be controlled with scheduling and appointments.

motivated sequence A method of organizing a persuasive speech that involves five steps: attention, need, satisfaction, visualization, and action.

motivation Providing a personal benefit that ensures continued audience listening.

narration A story about real or imagined things, people, or events told with detail and enthusiasm.

need Some sort of unsatisfied condition.

neutral audience An audience that considers itself objective, rational, and open to new information. Also called an *impartial audience*.

nonfluencies Speech mannerisms, such as inaccurate articulation, vocalized pauses (like *ah* or *uh*), or unnecessary repetition of words, that interrupt the flow of a speech and make the speaker appear less competent on the topic.

onomatopoeia A word that sounds like its meaning, such as *buzz, hiss,* or *fizz*.

panel A type of team presentation in which team members informally discuss a problem or topic of interest in front of an audience.

parable A fable that illustrates a moral or religious principle.

parallel points Points that include similar phrasing and sentence structure as well as the same voice (active or passive).

parallelism The grouping of similarly phrased ideas.

paraphrase Putting another person's statements into different words.

pathos An emotional argument that appeals to the psychological needs of the listener; also one of the means of persuasion.

pause A short, medium, or long silence between words; sometimes referred to as *live silence*.

personalization principle The belief that audiences learn better when speakers use a conversational style instead of a formal one.

personification Giving human characteristics or feelings to an animal, object, or concept.

persuasion Communication that is intended to influence choice.

persuasive speech A speech that seeks to influence beliefs, choices, or opinions.

phrase A group of words preceded and followed by a pause.

pitch The highness and lowness of vocal tones.

plagiarism Using the ideas of others, whether paraphrased or word for word, without giving them credit.

plain style Used to prove or inform; an "easy" style, subdued in delivery, language, and ornamentation.

polychromic Also known as a P-time culture, this group does not recognize the concept of "saving time." These cultures value harmonious relationships, so their use of time must be flexible in order to fulfill their obligations to others.

position statement In a persuasive speech, a simple sentence that states exactly how the speaker feels about the issue covered in the speech.

positive imagery A technique in which the mind is used to create a positive, vivid, and detailed mental image of accomplishment. Also called visualization.

post hoc A type of fallacious reasoning that occurs when the speaker claims a causal relationship between two events simply because one event followed the other.

PowerPoint poisoning A term coined by Scott Adams in his Dilbert cartoon strip, which refers to a text-induced coma that listeners experience when there are too many PowerPoint slides or the slides are too long, have too many bullets, or are too confusing.

PRCA-24 See McCroskey's PRCA-24.

preparation outline A detailed outline of a speech that is prepared after research is completed. In addition to main points and supporting information, it should include an introduction and a conclusion, transitions, and references.

problem-cause-solution pattern A way of arranging the main topics of a persuasive speech by first stating a problem, identifying the cause(s), and finally proposing solutions.

problem–solution pattern A way of arranging the main topics of a persuasive speech by first stating a problem and then proposing solutions.

pronunciation Speaking words with all the sounds and accents that are in general usage in a population.

Q & A Question and answer period that follows a speech.

rate The speed at which one speaks.

receive stage The first stage in listening where the listener attends to (or ignores) one or more stimuli from the multitude of stimuli available.

regulators Movements or gestures that control the flow of a conversation in small groups, like breaking off eye contact to signal that the conversation is over.

relaxation with deep breathing A method for managing anxiety that utilizes deep muscle relaxation and deep breathing while visualizing yourself giving a successful presentation.

repetition A stylistic device in which words or series of words are repeated in successive clauses or sentences (usually at the beginning of the clause or sentence).

respond stage The fifth stage of listening, in which listeners give feedback verbally and nonverbally.

restatement Rewording of a key concept to make sure listeners grasp it.

rhetoric The art of persuasive public speaking.

rhetorical question A question designed to make the audience think—no real answer is expected.

rough-draft outline A brief outline (or list) of the main points of a speech and possible supporting information, which is prepared before research is begun.

sans serif font A geometric-looking, easy-to-read typeface. Examples include Helvetica, Arial, and Optima.

saturation The amount of color in a hue.

search engine A tool (such as Yahoo!, AltaVista, HotBot, or Excite) that searches the Internet and retrieves requested information.

self talk The way you think and talk about yourself, in a positive or negative way.

serif font A typeface with small lines or finishing strokes that extend from letter stems. Examples include Times New Roman, Palatino, Bodoni, and Century Schoolbook.

signpost A specific type of transition (like a road sign) that clearly indicates where the speaker is going next.

simile A comparison that uses the word *like* or *as*.

situational anxiety A type of anxiety caused by factors present in a specific situation (for example, speaking before a new audience or being graded or critiqued while speaking).

situational information Information about the audience size, members' general expectations about the topic, and the inclusion of other speakers at an event.

skills training A process for managing anxiety that involves identifying reasonable speaking goals, determining the behaviors or skills needed to achieve each goal, and developing procedures for judging the success of each goal.

slippery slope A type of fallacious reasoning that occurs when a speaker asserts that taking a particular step will lead to a serious and undesirable consequence.

social judgment theory A theory of persuasion that explains how people evaluate messages based on internal anchors (past experiences)—the more ego involved people are with a social issue or topic, the more likely their judgments will be influenced by an internal anchor.

social network A social media site such as Facebook, MySpace, Blogspot, or Twitter.

spatial pattern A way of arranging the main topics of an informational or demonstration speech according to location in space, such as front to back, left to right, first floor to third floor, or north to east to south to west. Also called a *geographic pattern*.

speaker The sender of a spoken message.

speakers' bureau An organization within a company that is composed of employees who have expertise in some aspect of the company and are willing to share it with interested groups looking for a guest speaker.

speaking notes Brief key words or phrases, written on note cards or paper, that guide the speaker through the speech.

speech of introduction One of the most common types of ceremonial speeches where the speaker prepares the audience for the featured speaker(s) to come.

special occasion speech A speech that gives a sense of distinction to important events, such as funerals and award ceremonies.

speech to actuate A type of persuasive speech that asks listeners for both intellectual agreement and action of some type.

speech to convince A type of persuasive speech that seeks intellectual agreement from listeners.

speech to intensify social cohesion A type of persuasive speech that works with audience members who are already in intellectual agreement and have taken action, but are in need of additional enthusiasm, encouragement, and motivation.

standard search engine Uses computer "robots" to search the Web, index the pages found, and determine the relevance of the pages by mathematical calculation.

statistics Supporting material involving numbers that show relationships between items.

stickiness factor Malcolm Gladwell (2002) defines the "stickiness factor" as that part of a message that "makes an impact. You can't get it out of your head. It sticks in your memory" (p. 25).

stimulus A trigger that directs the audience's attention to your topic.

style The way a speaker uses language to express ideas.

stylistic device Any departure from everyday language usage, such as rearranging sentences in unusual ways or altering the ordinary meaning of a word, in order to establish a mood or feeling. Examples include alliteration and assonance, antithesis, simile and metaphor, onomatopoeia, repetition and parallelism, hyperbole, and personification.

subject search A search that locates websites that fit a subject in a directory of general topics.

supporting materials Any type of verbal or visual information used to clarify, prove, or add interest to the ideas presented in a speech.

symposium A type of team presentation in which each team member presents a formal 2- to 10-minute speech on one aspect of the symposium's topic.

team Three to seven people who actively work together toward a particular goal (solving a problem, gathering information, or planning an informative or persuasive presentation).

team presentation Involves the collaborative organization and presentation of material by team members to an audience.

terminal value An ideal state of being.

text visual A visual aid that includes mainly printed words with one or two pieces of Clip Art, drawings, or pictures.

theory of reasoned action Describes how people rationally calculate the costs and benefits of engaging in a particular action and think carefully about how others will view the behavior under consideration.

thesis statement In the introduction of a speech, a statement that clarifies the specific purpose of the speech and previews the main points.

toast A brief set of congratulatory remarks traditionally delivered while audience members hold aloft glasses of wine or champagne.

topical pattern A way of arranging the main topics of an informative speech in which each main point is one of several aspects of the topic.

trait anxiety The internal anxiety an individual brings to the speaking situation (for example, feelings of inadequacy when in a group or fear of looking like a fool in front of others).

transition A word, phrase, or brief sentence used to link ideas, main points, or major parts of a speech.

tribute A special occasional speech that recognizes the occasion and renews the kinship between speaker and audience.

uninterested audience Listeners with a short attention span, who wish they were someplace else. Also called an *indifferent audience*.

upspeak An upward pitch inflection that is often used at the end of declarative sentences and phrases, which gives the impression that the speaker is asking for verification or approval.

value A deep-seated principle that serves as a personal guideline for behavior.

verbal code The form in which messages are carried by spoken and written words.

verbal delivery Your overall speaking style, including the words you choose and the way you construct sentences.

vertical search engine A search engine that searches a smaller but more specific part of the Web—such as job openings or professional people that live in a specific location.

visual channel A communication channel preferred by those who learn by seeing; these people are more likely to use visual words such as *looked, looks like, visualize, see,* and *clear.*

visual code The form in which messages are carried by nonverbal means, such as personal appearance and visual aids.

visual delivery Includes your overall appearance, facial expressions, eye contact, posture, gestures, and even the visual aids you use when speaking.

vocal code The form in which messages are carried by spoken means, such as tone of voice and emphasis.

vocal delivery How you use your tone, volume, pitch, emphasis, and rate to interest, motivate, and persuade an audience.

vocal variety Achieved by varying volume, pitch, emphasis, rate, and pauses in a natural manner, as well as articulating and pronouncing words clearly.

volume The loudness and softness of the voice. It can be increased by adding to the amount and force of the air expelled while speaking.

warrant Part of the Toulmin Model of an Argument where evidence is given that supports the claim or position statement.

white space Space that contains no text or graphics.

wildcard Using an asterisk at the end of a word to search for all forms of the word. for example, *legisl** will search for *legislature, legislation, legislator,* and so on.

Index

ABET. *See* Accreditation Board for Engineering and Technology
Abstract words, 205
Acceptance, latitude of, 336–338
Acceptance speeches, 354–355
Accountants, ethics of, 15
Accreditation Board for Engineering and Technology (ABET), 8
Acronyms, 65
Action step, of motivated sequence, 155, 298–299
Actuate, speech to, 283, 284, 298, 313
Adams, Scott, 229
Adapters, 190
Ad hominem, 324, 343
Ad ignoratiam, 324, 343
Ad populum, 324, 343
Adrenaline, 28
Advertising
 audience analysis and, 97
 ethics in, 15
 fallacious reasoning and, 346
Aesop, 123
African American Web Connection, 77
After-dinner speeches, 361–362
Age
 as demographic information, 75
 language and, 186
 listening and, 49
Ahles, Catherine B., 168
Aids for, informative speeches visual, 270–271
Aitken, Joan E., 167–169
Ale, Ivette, 153
Alignment, 231, 232
Alliteration, 209
Allstate Insurance, 12
Alternative search engines, 115
Ambiguous words, 205
americanrhetoric.com, 45–46, 58, 161, 177, 187, 212, 220
Analogical reasoning, 316, 323
Androgynous, 55
Anecdotes
 in eulogies, 358
 Gates and, 6
 humor with, 57
Antithesis, 209
 in "Gettysburg Address," 213
Anxiety, 27–46. *See also* Situational anxiety; Trait anxiety
 balloons and, 4
 in China, 28
 cognitive restructuring for, 42
 communication courses for, 42

deep breathing for, 41–42
eye contact and, 45
PRCA-24 and, 29, 44
in Puerto Rico, 28
relaxation for, 41–42
self-talk for, 42
skills training for, 42
technology for, 42–43
in U.S., 28
visual aids for, 42–43
Appearance. *See* Personal appearance
Apprehension. *See* Trait anxiety
Arab countries, culture in, 12
Arguments
 persuasion and, 319
 in persuasive speeches, 282
 research for, 297
Aristotle, 2, 27, 222, 283, 293, 316, 350
Armed Forces Communications and Electronics Association, 74
Articulation, 194
Asian Americans, 77
Assertion, 319–320
"Assessing the Madoff Ponzi Scheme and Regulatory Failures" (Markopolos), 105–106
Assonance, 209
Atkinson, Cliff, 228
Attention-getters, 74, 156, 346
 for after-dinner speeches, 361
 for informative speeches, 264
 in introduction, 162
 for persuasive speeches, 301
Attention span, of listeners, 361
Attention step, of motivated sequence, 155, 298–299
Attic orators, 27
Attitude polls, 295–296
Attitudes, 80–81, 337
 audience analysis and, 95
 as frame of reference, 11
 for informative speeches, 261
 language and, 203
 needs and, 329
 persuasive speeches and, 279
 questions for, 91
Attribution theory, 50
Audience. *See also* Listeners
 heterogeneous, 73
 homogeneous, 73
 types of, 85–86
Audience analysis, 72–100, 274
 demographic information and, 75–78
 information collection for, 90–93

for informative speeches, 261–262
for persuasive speeches, 280, 294–296
psychological information and, 79–83
receptivity of, 85–86
situational information and, 73–75
using, 93–95
Audiovisual aids, 227, 243
Auditory channel, 56
Authority, 335
AVI, 243
Award presentations, 353–354

Baach Robinson & Lewis Law Firm, 127
Bach, Robbie, 174–175
Background information, in introduction, 165
Background lines, in graphic slides, 238
Backing, 282
Backlund, Phil, 214
Backup, for PowerPoint, 197, 272
Balloons, anxiety and, 4
Bankers, ethics of, 15
Bar graphs, 227
Bartlett's Familiar Quotations, 113, 122
Basic design principles, for visual aids, 230–232
Basketball players, 33
Begging the question, 324
Behaviors
 attitudes and, 81
 feedback and, 64–65
 immediacy, 195
 language and, 203
 visual, 64–65
Being, 293
Beliefs, 80, 337
 attitudes and, 81
 audience analysis and, 95
 for informative speeches, 261
 persuasive speeches and, 279
 questions for, 91
Bell Helicopter Textron, 8
Benefits, 3–8
Biases
 with culture, 214–215
 gender, 214
 Internet and, 118
 with language, 214–215
 listening and, 49
 persuasive speeches and, 281–282
Bill and Melinda Gates Foundation, 4, 5

385